Current Copyright Law

Other books by Michael Henry include:

Media Industry Documentation – Butterworths 1998

Media Industry Transactions – Butterworths 1998

Entertainment Law Volume 15 Encyclopaedia of Forms and Precedents
Fifth Edition Reissue – Butterworths 1998

Publishing and Multimedia Law – Butterworths 1994

Practical Lending and Security Precedents (Security Over Intellectual Property Section)
FT Law & Tax 1992

International Agency and Distribution Agreements (UK Section)
Butterworths US 1990

Entertainment Law Volume 15 of the Encyclopaedia of Forms and Precedents
Butterworths 1989

The Film Industry – A Legal and Commercial Analysis
Longman 1986

Jacques the Fatalist (Translation)
Denis Diderot – Penguin Classics 1986

All royalties from this book will be applied by Actionaid towards the relief of famine and poverty in the developing countries.

Giving
People
Choices

ACTIONAID

Current Copyright Law

Michael Henry
Partner, Henry Hepworth, Solicitors

Butterworths
London, Edinburgh, Dublin
1998

United Kingdom	Butterworths a Division of Reed Elsevier (UK) Ltd, Halsbury House, 35 Chancery Lane, LONDON WC2A 1EL and 4 Hill Street, EDINBURGH EH2 3JZ
Australia	Butterworths, SYDNEY, ADELAIDE, BRISBANE, CANBERRA, MELBOURNE, and PERTH
Canada	Butterworths Canada Ltd, TORONTO and VANCOUVER
Ireland	Butterworth (Ireland) Ltd, DUBLIN
Malaysia	Malayan Law Journal Sdn Bhd, KUALA LUMPUR
New Zealand	Butterworths of New Zealand Ltd, WELLINGTON and AUCKLAND
Singapore	Butterworths Asia, SINGAPORE
South Africa	Butterworths Publishers (Pty) Ltd, DURBAN
USA	Lexis Law Publishing, CHARLOTTESVILLE, Virginia

A CIP Catalogue record for this book is available from the British Library.

ISBN 0 406 89620 8

Typeset by York House Typographic Ltd
Printed by Redwood Books Ltd, Trowbridge, Wilts

Visit us at our website: http://www.butterworths.co.uk

Preface

The implementation of European Community Directives 92/100, 93/83 and 96/9 has brought about the greatest upheaval in United Kingdom copyright legislation since the enactment of the Copyright Act 1911. It has also for the first time effected the amendment of the principal copyright law by means of secondary legislation – in the shape of the Duration of Copyright and Rights in Performances Regulations 1995, the Copyright and Related Rights Regulations 1996 and the Copyright and Rights in Databases Regulations 1997.

These three statutory instruments present intellectual property law practitioners with a particular problem; not only do they amend, substitute and insert provisions in the Copyright, Designs and Patents Act 1988 but they also introduce a number of specific regulations which are not directly linked to any particular section of the principal Act. In order to advise on or consider copyright law, four separate legislative instruments need to be referred to – a rather cumbersome and unsatisfactory process which involves a correspondingly high risk of error.

The primary objective of this work is to provide a single updated and 'contextualised' version of the Copyright, Designs and Patents Act 1988, containing the full text of the Regulations included within the Act in the appropriate context. The full updated contextualised text of the Act appears in Part 2. The Regulations themselves appear in Part 3, which also contains a table of destinations indicating which part of the Act the various Regulations appear in. It is hoped that practitioners will find this volume easier to refer to than the other available alternatives.

The second objective of this work is to provide a short statement of copyright law as it stands after the implementation of the 1995, 1996 and 1997 Regulations. This appears in Part 1 of the book which, it is hoped may be of assistance both to practitioners and academics who are familiar with the old law and want to take a closer look at the manner of implementation of the new provisions relating to duration, rental rights, cable re-transmission and databases as well as to persons approaching the field for the first time.

Because, as we are constantly reminded, the copyright industries are global industries, it is necessary to view United Kingdom law in an international perspective, and the text of Part 1 therefore provides short summaries of some relevant provisions of European Community law and the other laws of other countries, such as the United States of America, Japan and China.

I am indebted to Mary Vitoria QC for taking the time to vet some of the more complex provisions of the summary of United Kingdom law and for making many helpful suggestions. Any errors or omissions which remain are however entirely my own. I would like to acknowledge the assistance of Amanda Eveleigh and Gillian Thomas. I am deeply grateful for the support and encouragement I have received from members of Butterworths' Specialist Publications Group whose skills and professionalism are unrivalled in legal publishing.

Michael Henry
Henry Hepworth
5 John Street
London
WC1N 2HH

31 December 1997

v

Contents

PART 2 COPYRIGHT, DESIGNS AND PATENTS ACT 1988 75

(For arrangement of sections see list at pp 77–87.)

PART 3 REGULATIONS AND DIRECTIVES 289

PART 1
Current copyright law

A: Qualification for copyright and database right protection in the United Kingdom: Authorship and first ownership of copyright and database right

1. Classification of works protected by copyright and database right

Under the Copyright, Designs and Patents Act 1988 copyright is capable of subsisting in nine types of work, which are divided into three categories, as follows:

original literary, dramatic, musical or artistic works[1];
sound recordings, films, broadcasts or cable programmes[2]; and
the typographical arrangement of published editions[3].

The Copyright and Related Rights Regulations 1996 introduce specific provisions in relation to satellite broadcasts[4], and introduce a new cable retransmission right[5], publication right[6], and rental right[7] but do not otherwise alter the above three categories.

The Copyright and Rights in Databases Regulations 1997 introduce a new database right with effect from 1 January 1998 in relation to databases[8].

1 Copyright, Designs and Patents Act 1988, s 1(1)(a).
2 Ibid, s 1(1)(b).
3 Ibid, s 1(1)(c).
4 See ibid, S 6A as substituted by the Copyright and Related Rights Regulations 1996.
5 See section 4 post.
6 See section 5 post
7 See section 7 post.
8 Copyright and Rights in Databases Regulations 1997, reg 13.

2. Literary, dramatic, musical and artistic works and databases

A literary work is any work, other than a dramatic or musical work, which is written, spoken or sung, and includes a table or compilation (other than a database)[1], a computer program and preparatory design material for a computer program[2]. A 'database' is a collection of independent works, data or other materials which are arranged in a systematic or methodical way and are individually accessible by electronic or other means[3]. 'Dramatic work' includes a work of dance or mime[4]. A musical work is a work which consists of music, exclusive of any words or action intended to be sung, spoken or performed with the music[5].

Copyright does not subsist in a literary, dramatic or musical work unless and until it is recorded, in writing or otherwise[6]. In order to qualify for copyright protection, no aesthetic merit is necessary for a literary work or dramatic work[7], or certain types of artistic work[8]. A work must be original in that its creation must involve a sufficient degree of skill and labour and originate from the author[9]. A literary work consisting of a database is original only if the database constitutes the author's own intellectual creation by reason of the selection or arrangement of its content.[10] A database satisfying the originality criterion will be protected as a copyright work without prejudice to the subsistence of the database right in such work[11]. Copyright is capable of subsisting in a diverse range of literary materials, including railway guides[12] and compilations[13].

Case law has not previously recognised the contribution of a person telling their memoirs to a ghost writer as giving that person the necessary status of author[14]. Under the 1988 Act, however, an original literary work which is spoken and recorded in writing or otherwise will be protected by copyright.

3

An artistic work means a graphic work[15], photograph[15], sculpture[15] or collage, irrespective of artistic quality or a work of architecture being a building[15] or a model for a building or work of artistic craftsmanship[15].

A property right or 'database right' subsists in a database which is not an original work if there has been a substantial investment in obtaining, verifying or presenting the contents of the database[16] provided that the database right will only subsist if at the 'material time'[17] namely the time the database was made (or if the making of the database extended over a period, a substantial part of that period) its maker (or if it was made jointly one of its makers) was[18]:

an individual who was habitually resident within the European Economic Area ('EEA') or was a national of an EEA State[19]; or
a body incorporated under the law of an EEA State[20] which at the material time had its central administration or principal place of business within the EEA State[21] or had links on an on-going basis between its operations and the economy of an EEA State as well as having its registered office within the EEA[22]; or
a partnership or other unincorporated body formed under the law of an EEA State[23] which at the material time had its central administration or principal place of business within the EEA[24].

So far as concerns the eligibility of a database for protection by the database right, it is immaterial whether or not the database or any of its contents is a copyright work[25]. The requirement for the maker of a database to be a natural or legal person resident or situate in an EEA State in order for the database to be eligible for protection by the database right has been relaxed in the case of the United Kingdom Sovereign State (but not, it would appear, in the case of other EEA States) in that a database made by or under the direction or control of the House of Commons or the House of Lords is eligible as of right for protection by the database right[26].

1 Copyright, Designs and Patents Act 1988, s 3(1) as amended by the Copyright and Rights in Databases Regulations 1997.
2 Copyright, Designs and Patents Act 1988, s 3(1) as substituted by the Copyright (Computer Programs) Regulations 1992.
3 Copyright, Designs and Patents Act 1988, s 3A as substituted by the Copyright and Rights in Databases Regulations 1997.
4 Copyright, Designs and Patents Act 1988, s 3(1).
5 Ibid, s 3(1).
6 Ibid, s 3(2).
7 *University of London Press Ltd v University Tutorial Press Ltd* [1916] 2 Ch 601.
8 See *George Hensher Ltd v Restawile Upholstery (Lancs) Ltd* [1976] AC 64, [1973] 2 All ER 420, HL.
9 *Dicks v Yates* (1881) 18 ChD 76, CA; *Chilton v Progress Printing and Publishing Co* [1895] 2 Ch 29, CA; *Libraco Ltd v Shaw Walker Ltd* (1913) 30 TLR 22; *MacMillan & Co Ltd v Cooper* (1923) 93 LJPC 113, PC; *Sinanide v La Maison Kosmeo* (1928) 139 LT 365, CA.
10 Copyright and Rights in Databases Regulations 1997, reg 3A(2).
11 Ibid, reg 13(2). See also section 14 post.
12 *H Blacklock & Co Ltd v C Arthur Pearson Ltd* [1915] 2 Ch 376.
13 *MacMillan v Suresh Chunder Deb* (1890) ILR 17 Calc 951; *Kelly v Morris* (1866) LR 1 Eq 697; *British Columbia Jockey Club v Standen* [1983] 2 IPR 58, [1985] 8 CPR 3d 383 (Can).
14 *Donaghue v Allied Newspapers Ltd* [1938] Ch 106, [1937] 3 All ER 503. See also *Kenrick & Co v Lawrence & Co* (1890) 25 QBD 99; *Tate v Thomas* [1921] 1 Ch 503. But *Heptulla v Orient Longman* [1989] FSR 59 suggests that if a person is closely involved in creation of the work he may be joint author even though the actual words are not his.
15 Copyright, Designs and Patents Act 1988, s 4(1). See *Creation Records Ltd v News Group Newspapers Ltd*, (1997) Times, 29 April; *Breville Europe plc v Thorn EMI Domestic Appliances Ltd* 1995 FSR 77 [sculpture]; *George Hensher Ltd v Restawile Upholstery (Lancs) Ltd* 1976 AC 64 and *Shelley Films Ltd v Rex Features Ltd* [1994] EMLR 134.
16 Copyright and Rights in Databases Regulations 1997, reg 13(1).
17 Ibid, reg 18(4)(b).
18 Ibid, reg 18(1).
19 Ibid, reg 18(1)(a).
20 Ibid, reg 18(1)(b).
21 Ibid, reg 18(2)(a).
22 Ibid, reg 18(2)(b).
23 Ibid, reg 18(1)(c).
24 Ibid, reg 18(2)(a).
25 Ibid, reg 13(2). See also Section 14 post.
26 Ibid, reg 18(3) and Regulation 14(4).

3. Sound recordings, films and broadcasts

Current copyright legislation defines a sound recording as a recording of sounds, from which the sounds may be reproduced, or a recording of the whole or any part of a literary, dramatic or musical work, from which sounds reproducing the work or part may be produced, regardless of the medium on which the recording is made or the method by which the sounds are reproduced or produced[1]. A film under current copyright legislation means a recording on any medium from which a moving image may by any means be produced[2] and, as from 1 December 1996, the soundtrack accompanying a film is to be treated as part of the film[3]. Copyright does not subsist in a sound recording or film which is or to the extent that it is a copy taken from a previous sound recording or film[4]. The Copyright, Designs and Patents Act 1988 previously applied separate copyright protection to the visual and audio elements of films but the Duration of Copyright and Rights in Performances Regulations 1995 recombine the soundtrack copyright with the film copyright.

A broadcast means a transmission by wireless telegraphy of visual images, sounds or other information which is capable of being lawfully received by members of the public or is transmitted for presentation to members of the public[5]. 'Wireless telegraphy' means the sending of electro-magnetic energy over paths not provided by a material substance constructed or arranged for that purpose but does not include the transmission of microwave energy between terrestrial fixed points[6]. The place from which a broadcast is made is the place where, under the control and responsibility of the person making the broadcast, the programme carrying signals is introduced into an uninterrupted chain of communication[7].

The 1988 Act defines 'cable programme' as any item included in a cable programme service and 'cable programme service' means a service which consists wholly or mainly of sending visual images, sounds or other information by means of a telecommunications system, otherwise than by wireless telegraphy, for reception at two or more places (whether for simultaneous reception or at different times in response to requests by different users) or for presentation to members of the public[8]. The Act provides for a number of exceptions to this definition of cable programmes[9].

1 Ibid, s 5A(1) as substituted by the Duration of Copyright and Rights in Performances Regulations 1995.
2 Ibid, s 5B(1) as substituted.
3 Ibid, s 5B(2) as substituted.
4 Ibid, s 5A(2), s 5B(4) as substituted.
5 Ibid, s 6(1).
6 Copyright, Designs and Patents Act 1988, s 178.
7 Ibid, s 6(4) as substituted by the Copyright and Related Rights Regulations 1996.
8 Copyright, Designs and Patents Act 1988, s 7(1).
9 Ibid, s 7(2)

4. Cable retransmission right

The Copyright and Related Rights Regulations 1996 introduce a cable retransmission right[1]. The owner of copyright in a literary, dramatic, musical or artistic work, sound recording or film may grant or refuse authorisation for cable retransmission of a broadcast from another EEA member state in which the work is included[2]. Cable retransmission is defined as the reception and immediate retransmission by way of a cable programme service of a broadcast[3].

The cable retransmission right can only be exercised against a cable operator through a licensing body. Where a copyright owner has not transferred management of their cable retransmission right to a licensing body, the licensing body which manages rights of the same category is deemed to manage the right[4]. Where more than one licensing body manages rights of that category, the copyright owner may choose which of them is deemed to be mandated to manage the right[5]. Any right in relation to cable retransmission must be claimed within three years of the date of the cable retransmission[6].

1 Copyright, Designs and Patents Act 1988, s 144(A) as substituted by the Copyright and Related Rights Regulations 1996, reg 7.
2 Ibid, s 144(A)(1) as substituted.
3 Ibid, s 144(A)(7) as substituted.
4 Ibid, s 144(A)(3) as substituted.

5 Ibid, s 144(A)(3) as substituted.
6 Ibid, s 144(A)(5) as substituted.

5. Published editions and publication right

Under the 1988 Act and previous legislation copyright subsists in the typographical arrangement of a published edition of a literary, dramatic or musical work quite separately and
distinctly from the work which is arranged on the printed page. 'Published edition' means a
published edition of the whole or any part of one or more literary, dramatic or musical
works[1].

The Copyright and Related Rights Regulations 1996 introduce a new property right
equivalent to copyright – publication right[2]. Where a person publishes for the first time a
previously unpublished literary, dramatic, musical or artistic work or film after the expiry of
copyright protection in that work, the 1996 Regulations provide that person is to enjoy an
exclusive publication right.

The substantive provisions of the 1988 Act relating to copyright – the rights of the copyright
owners, permitted acts, dealings with rights, remedies for infringement and copyright licensing
– apply in relation to the new publication right[3].

Publication for the purposes of the 1996 Regulations includes any communication to the
public, in particular the issue of copies to the public, making the work available by means of an
electronic retrieval system, the rental or lending of copies of the work to the public, the
performance exhibition or showing of the work in public, or broadcasting the work or including
it in a cable programme service[4].

The new publication right is infringed by any person who carries out any of these acts
without the consent of the right holder[5]. The publication right expires at the end of the period
of 25 years from the end of the calendar year in which the work was first published[6]. A work
qualifies for protection by the new publication right if it is first published in the European
Economic Area and the publisher of the work is, at the time of first publication, a national of
an EEA State[7].

1 Copyright, Designs and Patents Act 1988, s 8(1).
2 Copyright and Related Rights Regulations 1996, reg 16.
3 Although the new publication right is expressed to be 'equivalent' to copyright not all of the provisions of the
   Copyright, Designs and Patents Act 1988 apply to publication right. See reg 17 of the 1996 Regulations for the
   exceptions. No moral rights are acquired.
4 Copyright and Related Rights Regulations 1996, reg 16(2).
5 Ibid, reg 17(1).
6 Ibid, reg 16(6).
7 Ibid, reg 16(4). Neither the Regulations nor the relevant article of the Directive (93/98 Art 4) make any reference to
   the 'publisher' of the work being a legal person and it is unclear whether it is intended to refer to natural persons only
   or to both legal and natural persons.

6. Qualification for protection by copyright and database right

Copyright subsists in a work if the requirements as to its author[1] or the country in which the
work was first published or, in the case of a broadcast or cable programme, the country from
which the broadcast was made or cable programme was sent, are met[2]. A work qualifies for
copyright protection if at the 'material time' the author was a British citizen, a British
Dependent Territories citizen, a British National (Overseas), a British Overseas citizen, a
British subject or a British protected person within the meaning of the British Nationality Act
1981[3]; or an individual domiciled or resident in the United Kingdom or another country to
which the relevant provisions of the Act extend; or a body corporate incorporated under the law
of a part of the United Kingdom or another country to which the Act extends[4] or to which it
applies.[5]

For the purpose of determining copyright protection the 'material time' in the case of a
literary, dramatic, musical or artistic work is, where the work is unpublished, the time the work
was made, or, if the making of the work extended over a period, the substantial part of that
period, or, where the work is published, the time the work was first published, or, if the author
had died before that time, immediately before his or her death[6]. In respect of other types of
copyright work the 'material time' is, for a sound recording, film or broadcast, when it was
made; and for a cable programme, when it was included in a cable programme service[7].

A literary, dramatic, musical or artistic work, sound recording or film will qualify for copyright protection if first published in the United Kingdom or another country to which the relevant provisions of the 1988 Act extend[8] or apply[9]. A broadcast or cable programme will qualify for copyright protection if made or sent respectively from a place in the United Kingdom or another country to which the relevant provisions of the 1988 Act extend[10] or apply[11].

In order for a database to be eligible for protection by the database right the maker of the database is required to be a national of or resident in, or if a corporate entity conducting business and having its principal place of business situate within, the European Economic Area[12].

1 As to authorship see section 48 post.
2 Copyright, Designs and Patents Act 1988, s 153(1).
3 31 Halsbury's Statutes (4th Edn) Nationality and Immigration.
4 Copyright, Designs and Patents Act 1988, s 154(1). See also Laddie Prescott and Vitoria *The Modern Law of Copyright and Designs* (2nd edn, 1995) para 4.20.
5 Ibid, s 159(1).
6 Ibid, s 154(4).
7 Ibid, s 154(5).
8 Ibid, s 155(1).
9 Ibid, s 159(1) See also Laddie Prescott and Vitoria Vol 2, pp 442–448.
10 Ibid, s 156(1).
11 Ibid, s 159(1).
12 See section 2 ante and the Copyright and Rights in Databases Regulations 1997, reg 18.

7. Acts restricted by copyright (including rental and lending right) and acts infringing the database right

Copyright is a property right giving the owner of the right the exclusive right to:

copy the work;
issue copies to the public;
rent or lend the work to the public;
perform, show or play the work in public;
broadcast the work or include it in a cable programme service; and
make adaptation of the work or do any of the above in relation to an adaptation[1].

If a person does any of these acts without the consent of the copyright owner, then that person is committing a primary infringement of copyright[2].

The copying of a work is an act restricted by the copyright in every description of copyright work[3]. Copying in relation to a literary, dramatic, musical or artistic work means reproducing the work in any material form including storing the work by electronic means[4]; in relation to an artistic work copying includes the making of a copy in three dimensions of a two dimensional work and the making of a copy in two dimensions of a three dimensional work[5]; and in relation to a film, television broadcast or cable programme, includes making a photograph of the whole or any substantial part of any image forming part of the film, broadcast or cable programme[6]. Copying in relation to any description of work includes the making of copies which are transient or are incidental to some other use of the work[7].

Issuing copies to the public is also an act restricted by the copyright in every description of copyright work[8]. Issuing copies of a work to the public means the act of putting into circulation in the European Economic Area (EEA) copies not previously put into circulation in the EEA by or with the consent of the copyright owner or putting into circulation outside the EEA copies not previously put into circulation in the EEA or elsewhere[9]. It does not include any subsequent distribution, sale, hiring or loan of copies previously put into circulation or any subsequent importation of such copies into the United Kingdom or another EEA State[10]. The European Economic Area is the area created by the agreement (EEA Agreement) signed at Oporto on 2 May 1992 as adjusted by the Protocol signed at Brussels on 17 March 1993[11]. An EEA state means any state which is a party to the EEA Agreement[12].

The rental or lending of copies of a work to the public is an act restricted by the copyright in a literary, dramatic or musical work, an artistic work (other than a work of architecture in the form of a building or model for a building) or work of applied art, or a film or sound recording[13]. 'Rental' means making a copy of the work available for use, on terms that it will or may be returned, for direct or indirect economic or commercial advantage[14]. 'Lending' means making a copy of the work available for use, on terms that it will or may be returned, otherwise than for direct or indirect economic or commercial advantage, through an establishment which is accessible to the public[15]. The expressions 'rental' and 'lending' do not include making available for the purpose of public performance, playing or showing in public, broadcasting or inclusion in a cable programme service, making available for the purpose of exhibition in public, or making available for on-the-spot reference use[16].

The performance of a literary, dramatic or musical work[17] is an act restricted by copyright, as is the playing or showing in public of a sound recording, film, broadcast or cable programme[18]. Inclusion of a literary, dramatic, musical or artistic work, a sound recording or film, or a broadcast or cable programme[19] in a cable programme service is also a restricted act. The making of an adaptation of a work is an act restricted by the copyright in a literary, dramatic or musical work[20].

In relation to a literary work (other than a computer program or a database) or a dramatic work 'adaptation' means a translation, a version of the dramatic work in which it is converted into a non-dramatic work or a non-dramatic work in which it is converted into a dramatic work, a version of the work in which the story or action is conveyed wholly or mainly by means of pictures in a form suitable for reproduction in a book, or in a newspaper, magazine or similar periodical[21]. In relation to a computer program, 'adaptation' means an arrangement or altered version of the program or a translation of it,[22] in relation to a database it means an arrangement or altered version of the database or a translation of it[23] and in relation to a musical work it means an arrangement or transcription of the work[24].

A person infringes the database right in a database if without the consent of the owner of the database right they extract or re-utilise all or a substantial part of the contents of the database[25]. The repeated and systematic extraction or re-utilisation of insubstantial parts of the contents of a database may amount to the extraction or re-utilisation of a substantial part of those contents[26]. No act done before 1 January 1998 or after 1 January 1998 in pursuance of an agreement made before such date shall be regarded as an infringement of the database right in a database[27].

1 Copyright, Designs and Patents Act 1988, s 16(1) as substituted by the Duration of Copyright and Rights in Performances Regulations 1995. See section 73 post regarding acts of secondary infringement of copyright.
2 Copyright, Designs and Patents Act 1988, s 16(2).
3 Ibid, s 17(1).
4 Ibid, s 17(2).
5 Ibid, s 17(3).
6 Ibid, s 17(4).
7 Ibid, s 17(6).
8 Ibid, s 18 as substituted by the Copyright and Related Rights Regulations 1996, reg 9.
9 Ibid, s 18(2) as substituted.
10 Duration of Copyright and Rights in Performances Regulations 1995, reg 2 and the Copyright and Related Rights Regulations 1996, reg 2.
11 Copyright, Designs and Patents Act 1988, s 18(3).
12 Duration of Copyright and Rights in Performances Regulations 1995, reg 2 and the Copyright and Related Rights Regulations 1996, reg 2.
13 Copyright, Designs and Patents Act 1988, s 18A(1) as substituted by the Copyright and Related Rights Regulations 1996, s 10, 11. See also section 34 post and sections 62 and 64 post in relation to equitable remuneration.
14 Ibid, s 18A(2) as substituted.
15 Ibid, s 18A(2) as substituted.
16 Ibid, s 18A(3) as substituted.
17 Copyright, Designs and Patents Act 1988, s 19(1).
18 Ibid, s 19(3).
19 Ibid, s 20.
20 Ibid, s 21(1).
21 Ibid, s 21(3)(a)
22 Ibid, s 21(3) as substituted by the Copyright (Computer Programs) Regulations 1992.
23 Ibid, s 21(3)(ac) as substituted by the Copyright and Rights in Databases Regulations 1997, reg 7.
24 Ibid, s 21(3)(b).
25 Copyright and Rights in Databases Regulations 1997, reg 16(1).
26 Ibid, reg 16(2).
27 Ibid, reg 28(2).

8. Authorship, first ownership and joint ownership of copyright and the database right

The word 'author', when used in relation to a work, means the person who creates it[1]. In the case of a sound recording the author is the producer and in the case of a film the joint authors are the producer and the principal director[2]. The 'producer' of a film or sound recording is the person by whom the arrangements necessary for the making of the film or sound recording were undertaken[3]. The 'author' of a broadcast is the person making the broadcast[4] or, in the case of a broadcast which relays another broadcast by reception and immediate transmission, the person making that other broadcast[5]. In the case of a cable programme, the author is the person providing the cable programme service in which the programme is included[6]. The 'author' of the typographical arrangement of a published edition is the publisher[7]. Where a literary, dramatic, musical or artistic work is computer-generated, the 'author' is the person by whom the arrangements necessary for the creation of the work are undertaken[8].

Generally the first owner of copyright in a work is its author. The exception to this is where a literary, dramatic, musical or artistic work or a film is made by an employee in the course of their employment. In this case the employer is the first owner of any copyright in the work subject to any agreement to the contrary[9].

Where a work is produced by the collaboration of two or more authors in which the contribution of each author is not distinct, it is a work of joint authorship, for which the period of copyright protection is calculated by reference to the date of death of the survivor of the joint authors[10]. A film is treated as a work of joint authorship unless the producer and principal director are the same person[11].

The question of who was the author of an existing work is to be determined in accordance with the provisions of the Copyright, Designs and Patents Act 1988 for purposes relating to moral rights[12] and for all other purposes in accordance with the law in force at the time the work was made[13].

Where copyright is vested in joint owners, the rights are generally held by them as tenants in common in equal or other shares[14]. It should be noted that the provisions of the Copyright Designs and Patents Act 1988 deal with the legal ownership of copyright and they may not necessarily apply to the equitable ownership of copyright.

The maker of a database is the first owner of the database right in it[15]. The person who takes the initiative in obtaining, verifying or presenting the contents of a database and assumes the risk of investing in such obtaining, verifying or presenting shall be regarded as the maker of the database and as having made it[16]. Where a database is made by an employee in the course of their employment their employer shall be regarded as the maker of the database subject to any agreement to the contrary[17]. A database is made jointly if two or more persons acting together in collaboration take the initiative in obtaining, verifying or presenting the contents of the database and assume the risk in such processes[18]. References to the maker of a database in relation to a database which is made jointly are construed as references to all makers of the database[19]. Where a database is made by Her Majesty or by an officer or servant of the Crown in the course of their duties Her Majesty shall be regarded as the maker of the database[20]. Where a database is made by or under the direction or control of the House of Commons or the House of Lords the House under whose direction or control the database is made is regarded as the maker of the database[21]. If any database is made under the direction or control of both the House of Commons and the House of Lords they are regarded as joint makers of the database[22].

---

1 Copyright, Designs and Patents Act 1988, s 9(1) as substituted by the Copyright and Related Rights Regulations 1996.
2 Ibid, s 9(2)(aa)(ab) as substituted applies to films made on or after 1 July 1994.
3 Ibid, s 178.
4 Ibid, s 6(3).
5 Ibid, s 9(2)(b).
6 Ibid, s 9(2)(c).
7 Ie generated by computer in circumstances such that there is no human author of the work: ibid, s 9(2)(d).
8 Ibid, s 9(3).
9 Ibid, s 11(2) as amended by the Copyright and Related Rights Regulations 1996, reg 18(3) which include films made on or after 1 July 1994. The section previously extended only to literary, dramatic, musical or artistic works.

10 See the Copyright, Designs and Patents Act 1988, ss 10(1), 12(8)(a) as substituted by the Duration of Copyright and Rights in Performances Regulations 1955, SI 1995/3297, reg 5(1).
11 Ibid, s 11(1A)
12 See sections 45 to 58 post.
13 Copyright, Designs and Patents Act 1988, Sch, para 10.
14 See *Lauri v Renad* [1892] 3 Ch 402; *Redwood Music Ltd v B Feldman & Co Ltd* [1979] RPC 385, CA; *Marzials v Gibbons* (1874) LR 9 Ch 518.
15 Copyright and Rights in Databases Regulations 1997, reg 15.
16 Ibid, reg 14(1).
17 Ibid, reg 14(2).
18 Ibid, reg 14(5).
19 Ibid, reg 14(6).
20 Ibid, reg 14(3).
21 Ibid, reg 14(4)(a).
22 Ibid, reg 14(4)(b).

B: Country of origin of non-British works and duration of copyright and database right in the United Kingdom following implementation of EC Directives 92/100, 93/83, 93/98 and 96/9

9. Country of origin of non-British works created on or after 1 January 1996 generally

Qualification for copyright protection arises either by virtue of authorship or through first publication of the relevant work in a country to which the 1988 Act extends[1]. In the case of works of foreign origin the 1988 Act is applied by the making of Orders in Council which have the effect of granting reciprocal protection to works originating in foreign countries which apply copyright protection to United Kingdom works. Protection is accorded to foreign works where their author is a national or resident of any state in relation to which an order has been made, and where the work is first published in such a state.

In order to determine the duration of the period of copyright protection which is to be applied to foreign works the Duration of Copyright and Rights in Performances Regulations 1995 introduced into the 1988 Act a new concept and definition – that of the 'country of origin' of literary, musical or artistic works, films, sound recordings, broadcasts and cable programmes.

The purpose of the concept is to distinguish between works originating in an EEA State[2] or created by EEA nationals or EEA resident corporations which qualify for a longer term of protection and works originating outside the EEA or created by non EEA resident nationals or corporations which qualify for a shorter term of protection.[3]

1 See section 6 ante
2 See section 8 ante.
3 It will be noted that the country of origin concept is not used for determining the duration of the database right. This right only applies in relation to databases whose maker was an EEA national or EEA resident individual corporation or unincorporated association. See section 2 ante.

10. Country of origin of sound recordings, broadcasts and cable programmes created on or after 1 January 1996

In the case of sound recordings the country of origin of the work is determined by the identity of the author, and if the author is not a national of an EEA state[1], the country of which the author is a national. The author of a sound recording is the person by whom the arrangements for the making of the sound recording were undertaken. The duration of protection is calculated from 'release' of the sound recording – meaning the date the sound recording is first published, played in public, broadcast or included in a cable programme service[2].

The duration of copyright in a broadcast or cable programme is similarly calculated by reference to the identity of the 'author' being in the case of a broadcast the person making the broadcast, and in the case of a cable programme the person providing the cable programme service in which it was included. The duration of the period of copyright protection for a broadcast or cable programme service is 50 years from the end of the calendar year in which the broadcast was made or the programme was included in a cable programme service[3].

1 See section 7 ante.
2 Copyright, Designs and Patents Act 1988, s 13(A)(3) as substituted by the Duration of Copyright and Rights in Performances Regulations 1995, reg 6(1).

3 Ibid, s 14(2) as substituted by the Duration of Copyright and Rights in Performances Regulations 1995, reg 7(1).

11. Country of origin of published literary works (including databases) and dramatic, musical and artistic works and films created on or after 1 January 1996

In the case of literary, dramatic, musical, artistic works and films, the 'country of origin' is determined by the country of first publication. First publication includes simultaneous publication – ie publication in a second state within 30 days of the very first publication[1]. Where a work is first published in a Berne Convention country and is not published elsewhere, the Berne Convention country will be the 'country of origin' of the work[2]. If the work is first published in two or more countries only one of which is a Berne Convention country, then the Berne Convention country will be the 'country of origin'[3].

If the work is first published simultaneously in two or more countries of which two or more are Berne Convention countries then, if any one of those countries is an EEA state, that state will be the 'country of origin' and if two or more of those countries are EEA states the country of origin will be that state which grants the shorter or shortest period of copyright protection[4].

Databases which satisfy the originality criterion[5] will be protected by copyright for the same term as other literary works. Subject to satisfying the nationality criterion for databases[6] (which is different from the '*country of origin*' concept applicable to copyright works) they will also be protected by the database right for the period prescribed by the 1997 Regulations[7]. If a database is not eligible for copyright protection it may still be eligible for database right protection[8].

1 Copyright, Designs and Patents Act 1988, s 15(A)(b)(d) as substituted by the Duration of Copyright and Rights in Performances Regulations 1995, reg 8(1).
2 Ibid, s 15(A)(2) as substituted.
3 Ibid, s 15(A)(3) as substituted.
4 Ibid, s 15(A)(4) as substituted.
5 Copyright, Designs and Patents Act 1998, s 3A as substituted by the Copyright and Rights in Databases Regulations 1997. See also section 2 ante.
6 Copyright and Rights in Databases Regulations 1997, reg 18. See also section 2 ante.
7 Copyright and Rights in Databases Regulations 1997, reg 17. See also section 14 post.
8 See section 2 ante.

12. Country of origin of unpublished literary, dramatic, musical and artistic works and films created on or after 1 January 1996, and works published in non-Berne convention countries

If a work is unpublished or is first published in a non-Berne Convention country and is not simultaneously published in a Berne Convention country, then three possibilities apply in relation to the country of origin:

(a) If the work is a film and the maker has its headquarters or is domiciled or resident in a Berne Convention country, that country will be the country of origin[1]. It will be noted that the regulations refer to the 'maker' not the 'author' which may be interpreted as a reference to the producer alone, not the producer and the principal director of the film. The provisions of section 13B(7) of the 1998 Act as substituted by reg 8(1) of the 1995 Regulations however refer to the country of origin of a film and make reference to the 'author' of the film as well as to the concept of joint authorship. This may indicate that the reference to 'maker' in section 15(A)(5)(a) was intended to refer to the 'author' of the film which would comprise the producer and/or the principal director and not the producer alone.

The definition of 'publication'[2] requires the issue of copies to the public and does not include showing or playing a film in public. Unless copies of videograms of a film are released to the public the film may be unpublished. Consequently the identity of a film's 'author' may be important for the purposes of calculating the duration of copyright protection. Where the author of a film or other copyright work is not a national of an EEA

State, and the work is not published simultaneously in an EEA State the extended period of copyright protection provided by the 1995 Regulations will not apply.

(b) The second possibility applies to works of architecture constructed in a Berne Convention country, or artistic works incorporated in buildings or other structures situate in Berne Convention countries. The country of origin is the country in which the work of architecture or building or other structure is situate[3].

(c) The third possibility extends to include any other unpublished works as well as works first published in a non-Berne Convention country. In these cases the country of origin will be the country of which the author is a national[4]. Presumably, the nationality of the author may be determined either when the work was created or on first publication of the work and may not necessarily remain the same. The 1995 Regulations do not specify how they are to be applied if the nationality of an author changes from a Berne Convention country to a non-Berne Convention country between creation and first publication of the work.

1 Copyright, Designs and Patents Act 1988, s 15(A)(5)(a) as substituted by the Duration of Copyright and Rights in Performances Regulations 1995, reg 8(1).
2 Ibid, s 175.
3 Ibid, s 15(A)(5)(b) as substituted by the Duration of Copyright and Rights in Performances Regulations 1995, reg 8(1).
4 Ibid, s 15(A)(5)(c) as substituted.

13. Duration of copyright in existing works (British and foreign) protected on 1 January 1996 generally

The Duration of Copyright and Rights in Performances Regulations 1995 apply to:

copyright works made on or after 1 January 1996[1];
non-copyright works which first qualify for copyright protection after commencement of the 1995 Regulations[2];
existing copyright works[3];
existing works in which the copyright expired but is revived by the Regulations[4];

The Duration of Copyright and Rights in Performances Regulations 1995 make extensive amendment to the provisions in the 1988 Act which deal with duration of copyright and copyright works[5]. However the transitional provisions of the 1988 Act remain in force[6]. These transitional provisions specifically apply procedures[7] for the purpose of calculating the duration of copyright in literary, dramatic, musical and artistic works (published or unpublished), films and sound recordings[8].

The Duration of Copyright and Rights in Performances Regulations 1995 do not repeal the transitional provisions in Schedule 1, paragraph 12 of the 1988 Act and expressly provide[9] that copyright in existing copyright works which are protected on 31 December 1995 will continue to subsist until the date it would have expired under the 1988 Act, if such date is later than the date it would expire under the Regulations.

In circumstances where an existing copyright work is protected by the 1988 Act for a term which is longer than that provided in the country of origin of the work, the complex transitional provisions of the 1988 Act will therefore be relevant[10]. These provisions will continue to be relevant in the case of unpublished works. For those works the period of copyright protection is calculated from the date of first publication even if the author died 50 years before such time.

In cases where a foreign copyright work is made on or after 1 January 1996 or copyright in a work expired before 31 December 1995 but was protected on 1 July 1995 in another EEA State, the duration of copyright protection under the 1988 Act as amended by the Duration of Copyright and Rights in Performances Regulations 1995 and the Copyright and Related Rights Regulations 1996 will be no longer than the period for which the work was protected in the country of origin[11].

For the purpose of determining the duration of copyright protection following the implementation of the Duration of Copyright and Rights in Performances Regulations 1995 and the Copyright and Related Rights Regulations 1996 in many cases it will be necessary only to refer to the 1988 Act as amended by the Duration of Copyright and Rights in Performances Regulations 1995 and the Copyright and Related Rights Regulations 1996. Because the regulations expressly preserve the 1988 Act provisions for existing copyright works, it is likely that the former provisions will continue to be relevant for some time to come in relation to works which were unpublished on commencement of the 1988 Act[12] and these provisions are therefore set out in full later in this work[13].

1 Duration of Copyright and Rights in Performances Regulations 1995, reg 16(a).
2 Ibid, reg 16(b). The regulations came into force on 1 January 1996.
3 Ibid, reg 16(c) ie works in which copyright subsisted as at 31 December 1995, reg 14. Pursuant to reg 36(1) the ownership of extended copyright in films made on or after 1 July 1994 vests in the producer and principal director. See section 8 ante.
4 Ibid, reg 16(d). See section 20 post.
5 Principally ss 12, 13, and 14 which are completely revised by the Duration of Copyright and Rights in Performances Regulations 1995 and the Copyright and Related Rights Regulations 1996.
6 Copyright, Designs and Patents Act 1988, Sch 1.
7 Ibid, Sch 1, para 12.
8 Copyright, Designs and Patents Act 1988 as amended the Duration of Copyright and Rights in Performances Regulations 1995 and the Copyright and Related Rights Regulations 1996.
9 The Duration of Copyright and Rights in Performances Regulations 1995, reg 15(1).
10 Copyright, Designs and Patents Act 1988, Sch 1, para 12(4). For a summary see section 23 post.
11 Copyright, Designs and Patents Act 1988 as amended by the Duration of Copyright and Rights in Performances Regulations 1995, s 12(6), 13A(4), 13B(7) and 14(3).
12 1 August 1989.
13 See sections 23 to 29 post.

14. Duration of copyright in published literary, dramatic, musical and artistic works and photographs under the 1988 Act as amended by the 1995 and 1996 Regulations and duration of database right in databases under the 1998 Act as amended by the 1997 Regulations

Copyright in a literary, dramatic, musical or artistic work previously expired 50 years from the end of the calendar year in which the author died. From 1 January 1996 the period of protection was increased to expire 70 years from the end of the calendar year in which the author dies[1].

If a work is of unknown authorship, copyright expires 70 years from the end of the calendar year in which it was made or, if during that period the work is 'made available' to the public, 70 years from the end of the calendar year in which it is first so made available[2]. If the identity of the author becomes known before copyright expires then the work is protected for 70 years from the end of the calendar year in which the author dies[3].

'Making available' to the public includes performance in public, broadcast or inclusion in a cable programme service of a literary, dramatic or musical work or, in the case of an artistic work, exhibition in public, a film including the work being shown in public or inclusion in a broadcast or cable programme service. No account is taken where a work is made available to the public by an unauthorised act[4].

Where a work is of joint authorship, the reference to the death of the author is construed as the death of the last author to die, or, if the identity of one or more of the authors is known and the identity of one or more authors is not, the death of the last of the authors whose identity is known[5].

Where the country of origin[6] of the work is not an EEA state and the author of the work is not a national of an EEA state or, in the case of joint authorship, none of the authors is a national of an EEA state, the duration of copyright is that to which the work is entitled in the country of origin, provided that the period does not exceed the life plus 70 year period which would apply under general principles[7].

If the work is computer-generated, copyright expires at the end of the period of 50 years from the end of the calender year in which the work was made[8].

The duration of copyright in photographs is determined by the 1988 Act as amended by the Duration of Copyright and Rights in Performances Regulations 1995[9] and the provisions of the amended act apply retrospectively to all published photographs whether they were made before 1 June 1957 or on or after that date. Because, in some circumstances, the period of protection under the 1988 Act is capable of being longer than that provided by the Duration of Copyright and Rights in Performances Regulations 1995 (principally in relation to unpublished works including photographs)[10] the former provisions of the 1988 Act[11] will continue to apply.

The copyright in databases created on or before 27 March 1996 is preserved for the remainder of the relevant copyright term if such databases were copyright works immediately before 1 January 1998[12]. This provision effectively preserves copyright protection for databases which were protected as compilations before 1 January 1998 but would not subsequently be eligible for protection as literary works in view of the non-satisfaction of the originality criterion[13]. The provsion does not preclude dual copyright and database right protection for databases created on or after 1 January 1998 which satisfy the originality criterion.

The database right in a database expires at the end of the period of fifteen years from the end of the calendar year in which the making of the database was completed[14]. Where a database is made available to the public before the end of such period the database right shall expire fifteen years from the end of the calendar year in which the database was first made available[15]. Any substantial change to the contents of a database including a substantial change resulting from the accumulation of successive additions, deletions or alterations which would result in the database being considered to be a substantial new investment qualifies the database which results from that investment for its own term of protection[16]. Where the making of the database was completed on or after 1 January 1983 and on 1 January 1998 the database right begins to subsist in the database it will continue to subsist for a period of 15 years commencing on 1 January 1998[17].

1 Copyright, Designs and Patents Act 1988, s 12(1) as substituted by the Duration of Copyright and Rights in Performances Regulations 1995.
2 Ibid, s 12 (3). A number of presumptions operate to counter this potential for a perpetual copyright. See s 57(1) and s 104(4).
3 Ibid, s 12(4).
4 Ibid, s 12(5).
5 Ibid, s 12(8)(a).
6 See ibid, s 15A as substituted for the definition of 'country of origin'.
7 Ibid, s 12(6), (8)(c) as substituted by the Duration of Copyright and Rights in Performances Regulations 1995. 'EEA state' means a state which is a contracting party to the Agreement on the European Economic Area signed at Oporto on 2 May 1992, as adjusted by the Protocol signed at Brussels on 17 March 1993: Copyright, Designs and Patents Act 1988, s 172A as inserted by the Duration of Copyright and Rights in Performances Regulations 1995, reg 11.
8 Ibid, s 12 (7).
9 Copyright and Related Rights Regulations 1996, reg 19.
10 Ibid, Sch 1 para 12(4). See sections 16 and 29 post.
11 See sections 23 to 29 post.
12 Copyright and Rights in Databases Regulations 1997, reg 29.
13 See section 2 ante.
14 Copyright and Rights in Databases Regulations 1997, reg 17(1).
15 Ibid, reg 17(2).
16 Ibid, reg 17(3).
17 Ibid, reg 30.

15. Artistic work exploited by industrial process

Special copyright provisions apply where an artistic work has been exploited by or with the licence of the copyright owner, by making via an industrial process articles[1] falling to be treated[2] as copies of the work, and marketing[3] such articles in the United Kingdom or elsewhere[4].

After the end of the period of 25 years from the end of the calendar year in which such articles are first marketed, the work may be copied by making articles of any description, and anything may be done in relation to articles so made, without infringing copyright in the work[5]. The Secretary of State may by order make provision as to the circumstances in which articles are to be regarded as made by an industrial process, and exempting articles of a primarily literary or artistic character[6].

1 'Articles' does not include films: Copyright, Designs and Patents Act 1988, s 52 (6) (a).
2 For the purposes of the Copyright, Designs and Patents Act 1998, Pt 1, ss 1–179.
3 'Marketing' means being sold or let for hire or offered or exposed for sale or hire: ibid, s 52 (6) (b).
4 Ibid, s 52 (1).
5 Ibid, s 52 (2). Where only part of an artistic work is exploited, ibid, s 52 (2) applies only in relation to that part: ibid, s 52 (3). Where the corresponding provisions of the Copyright Act 1956 (ie ibid s 10 as amended) applied in relation to an artistic work at any time before 1 August 1989, the Copyright, Designs and Patents Act 1988, s 52 (2) applies

with the substitution for the period of 25 years mentioned there of the relevant period of 15 years as defined in the
Copyright Act 1956, s 10 (3): Copyright, Designs and Patents Act 1988, s 170, Sch 1, para 20 (1). Apart from this,
ibid s 52 applies only where articles are marketed after: ibid Sch 1, para 20 (2).
6 Ibid, s 52 (4).

16. Duration of copyright in unpublished literary, dramatic, musical and artistic works and photographs under the 1988 Act as amended by the 1995 and 1996 Regulations

For unpublished literary, dramatic, musical and artistic works (including photographs) the
term of protection is the longer of:

the life of the author (or last surviving author) plus 70 years[1]; and
the period ending at the end of the year 50 years after the commencement of the 1988 Act (ie
31 December 2039)[2]

provided that if the country of origin of the work is not an EEA state and the author of the work
is not a national of an EEA state the duration of copyright protection is that to which the work
is entitled in its country of origin provided it does not exceed the above period[3].

The duration of copyright in unpublished photographs merits special comment. Before the
amendment of the 1988 Act by the Duration of Copyright and Rights in Performances
Regulations 1995 the duration of copyright in unpublished photographs was determined by the
transitional provisions of the 1988 Act[4] which preserved the provisions of the Copyright Act
1911 and the Copyright Act 1956. These Acts provided different terms of protection for
photographs depending whether they were taken on or after 1 June 1957 or before that date.
These provisions have been superseded by the 1995 Regulations in all cases except where the
period of protection previously provided by the 1988 Act is longer than that provided by the
1995 Regulations.

The pre-June 1957 photograph regime may effectively be disregarded. The period of
protection for photographs taken before this time was 50 years from the end of the year in
which the photograph was taken. Even if the author of a photograph died in the year the
photograph was taken, the period of protection now provided in every case exceeds the period
provided under previous legislation[5].

The regime applying from June 1957 is, however, still relevant, in that the previous
legislation is capable of providing a longer period of protection than that provided by the 1995
Regulations. If the author of a photograph taken in June 1957 died in the same year, the
copyright in the photograph under the 1988 Act, as amended by the Regulations, would expire
on 31 December 2027. If, however, the photograph was unpublished as at the commencement
of the 1988 Act, the copyright in it would expire on 31 December 2039[6].

Where a work is of unknown authorship the term of protection is the longer of:

(a) 70 years from the end of the calendar year in which it was made[7], or
(b) if the work is made available to the public during the period specified in (a) 70 years from
      the end of the calendar year in which it is first made available[8]; or
(c) if the work is not made available to the public during the period specified in (a) the period
      ending at the end of the year 50 years after commencement of the 1988 Act (ie 31
      December 2039)[9]

provided that if the country of origin of the work is not an EEA state and the author of the work
is not an national of an EEA state the duration of copyright protection is that to which the work
is entitled in its country of origin provided it does not exceed the above period.

In the case of a previously unpublished literary, dramatic, musical or artistic work which is
published for the first time after the expiry of copyright protection in that work, the 1996
Regulations confer a new publication right[10].

1 Copyright, Designs and Patents Act 1988, s 12(2) as substituted by the Duration of Copyright and Rights in
  Performances Regulations 1995, reg 5(1).
2 Ibid, Sch 1, para 12(4).
3 Ibid, Sch 12(6) as substituted by the Duration of Copyright and Rights in Performances Regulations 1995,
  reg 5(1).

4 Copyright, Designs and Patents Act 1988, Sch 1, para 12.
5 See section 29 post.
6 See section 29 post.
7 Copyright, Designs and Patents Act 1988, s 12(3)(a) as substituted by the Duration of Copyright and Rights in Performances Regulations 1995, reg 5(1).
8 Ibid, s 12(3)(b).
9 Copyright, Designs and Patents Act 1988, Sch 1, para 12(3)(b).
10 See section 5 ante.

17. Duration of copyright in sound recordings and films under the 1988 Act as amended by the 1995 and 1996 Regulations

Copyright in a sound recording expires 50 years from the end of the calendar year in which it is made or if during that period the work is released, 50 years from the end of the calendar year in which it is released[1]. A sound recording is released when it is first published, played in public, broadcast or included in a cable programme service[2].

The revisions to the 1988 Act apply to existing works[3] and in the case of existing films the changes are significant. Copyright in a film expires 70 years from the end of the calendar year in which the death occurs of the last to die of the following persons:

(a)   the principal director;
(b)   the author of the screenplay;
(c)   the author of the dialogue; or
(d)   the composer of the music specially created for and used in the film[4].

Where the country of origin[5] of a film is not an EEA state and none of the persons listed above is a national of an EEA state, the duration of copyright is that to which the film is entitled in the country of origin provided the period does not exceed the life plus 70 year period which would apply under general principles[6].

If the identity of one or more of the above persons is not known, copyright expires 70 years from the end of the calendar year in which the last of those whose identity is known dies[7]. If the identity of all of those persons is unknown, copyright expires 70 years from the end of the calendar year in which the film was made or, if during that period the film is made available to the public, 70 years from the end of the calender year in which it is first so made available[8]. Making available to the public includes showing in public, or being broadcast or included in a cable programme service[9].

If the identity of any of these persons becomes known before the expiry of this period, then general principles apply[10]. If there is no person falling within the categories of paragraphs (a) to (d) above, then copyright expires at the end of the period of 50 years from the end of the calendar year in which the film was made.

Before the implementation of the 1995 Regulations, the soundtrack of a film (which had prior to the 1988 Act been treated as an integral part of it by the provisions of the Copyright Act 1956 relating to cinematograph films)[11] was, pursuant to the Copyright, Designs and Patents Act 1988, considered a separate sound recording, and the film was protected as a series of silent moving images[12]. The 1995 Regulations provide that the owner of copyright in a film has corresponding rights in the soundtrack when it accompanies the film (but not necessarily otherwise)[13].

The Duration of Copyright and Rights in Performances Regulations 1995 specifically provide that references to copyright in a film in relation to which copyright does not subsist as such (namely pre-June 1957 films) are references to any copyright in the film as an original dramatic work or to copyright in photographs forming part of a film, as the case may be[14].

1 Copyright, Designs and Patents Act 1988, s 13A(2) as substituted by the Duration of Copyright and Rights in Performances Regulations 1995, reg 6 (1).
2 Ibid, s 12A(3).
3 Ibid, reg 14, ie works in which copyright subsisted as at 31 December 1995. See section 13 ante, note 3 and section 8 ante, note 9.
4 Ibid, s 13B(2) as substituted by the Duration of Copyright and Rights in Performances Regulations 1995, reg 6(1).
5 See ibid, s 15A as substituted for the definition of 'country of origin'.

6 See section 14 ante, note 7.
7 Ibid, s 13B(3) as substituted.
8 Ibid, s 13B(4) as substituted.
9 Ibid, s 13B(6) as substituted.
10 Ibid, s 13B(5) as substituted.
11 Copyright Act 1956, s 13.
12 Copyright, Designs and Patents Act 1988, s 5.
13 Duration of Copyright and Rights in Performances Regulations, reg 26.
14 Ibid, reg 13 see also section 25 post.

18. Duration of copyright in broadcasts and cable programme services and published editions under the 1988 Act as amended by the 1995 and 1996 Regulations

Copyright in a broadcast or cable programme expires 50 years from the end of the calendar year in which the broadcast was made or the programme was included in a cable programme service[1]. No separate copyright arises in respect of a repeat broadcast or cable programme[2].

Where the author of a sound recording, film, broadcast or cable programme is a non-EEA national the duration of copyright under the 1988 Act as amended by the Duration of Copyright and Rights in Performances Regulations 1995 and the Copyright and Related Rights Regulations 1996 will be no longer than the period for which the work was protected in the country of origin[3].

The copyright in a typographical arrangement of a published edition expires at the end of the period of 25 years from the calendar year in which the edition was first published[4].

1 Copyright, Designs and Patents Act 1988, s 14 (2) as substituted by the Duration of Copyright and Rights in Performances Regulations 1995, reg 7 (1).
2 Ibid, s 14(5) as substituted.
3 Ibid, reg 13A(4), 13B(7), 13B(8), 14(3) as substituted.
4 Ibid, s 15. See also section 5 ante.

19. Extension of copyright

One of the principal effects of the Duration of Copyright and Rights in Performances Regulations 1995 and the Copyright and Related Rights Regulations 1996 was to extend the term of protection applicable to literary, dramatic, musical or artistic works from a period equal to the life of the author plus 50 years to the life of the author plus 70 years. The term of protection for films is also extended by a period which is capable of being determined on a case by case basis only. The extended term of protection applies to copyright works made after commencement of the 1995 Regulations and to those works in which copyright subsisted as at 31 December 1995[1].

The owner of the extended copyright in a work is the person who was the owner of the copyright immediately before 1 January 1996[2]. If the person is entitled to copyright for a period which is less than the full extended copyright term, then the extended copyright is part of the reversionary interest expectant on the termination of that period[3]. Any copyright licence or term or condition of an agreement relating to the exploitation of a copyright work which subsisted immediately before 1 January 1996 and was not to expire before the end of the then full copyright period, will continue to have effect during the extended copyright period[4].

1 Duration of Copyright and Rights in Performances Regulations 1995, reg 14.
2 Ibid, reg 18(1).
3 Ibid, reg 18(2).
4 Ibid, reg 21(1). Provision is identical where a copyright licence or term or condition was imposed by order of the Copyright Tribunal.

20. Revived copyright generally

Where the author of a literary, dramatic, musical or artistic work died more than 50 years but less than 70 years before the Duration of Copyright and Rights in Performances Regulations

1995 came into effect, the copyright in their work, will have lapsed but is revived by the Regulations provided the work was as at 1 July 1995 protected in an EEA member state.

The relevant time-period for literary, dramatic, musical and artistic works is from 1 January 1925 to 31 December 1944, and the copyrights of any author dying between those dates will have been revived, subject to the author or the work satisfying the requirements for copyright protection[1], and subject to certain provisions relating to unpublished works, and works published in non Berne convention countries[2].

The relevant period for films and photographs is more difficult to establish since previously the duration of their protection was calculated not by reference to the lifespan of persons connected with the film[3] but by reference to the date the film or photograph was exposed or taken[4] or the date on which it was published or registered (as a film)[5].

The owner of the revived copyright is the person who was the owner of the copyright in the work immediately before the copyright expired[6]. If the former copyright owner had died before 1 January 1996 or in the case of a legal person had ceased to exist before that date, the revived copyright, in the case of a film vests in the film's principal director or his or her personal representatives and in other copyright works vests in personal representatives[7] of the author of the work. Where revived copyright vests in personal representatives, it is held by them for the benefit of the person who would have been entitled to the copyright if it had been vested in the principal director or author immediately before their death and had devolved as part of their estate[8].

It will be remembered that the 1988 Act changed provisions relating to the ownership of copyright in photographs taken after its commencement[9] (which belonged previously to the person who owned the material on which the photograph was taken, and belongs now to the person who created the photograph) and the duration of their protection (previously calculated with reference to the date they were made or first published and now calculated with reference to the life of the author)[10].

The 1988 Act did not change the ownership of copyright in photographs made before its commencement, nor do the 1995 and 1996 Regulations effect changes of ownership so far as concerns existing copyright or extended copyright[11]. Where revived copyright in photographs is concerned, the position is quite different, and the ownership in the revived term of copyright vests in the author or the author's personal representatives not the previous owner[12].

1 See section 6 ante. For restored copyright in the USA see section 105 post.
2 See section 12 ante.
3 See section 17 ante.
4 See section 26 post.
5 See section 29 post
6 Duration of Copyright and Rights in Performance Regulations 1995, reg 19(1).
7 Ibid, reg 19(2).
8 Ibid, reg 19(3).
9 ie taken on or after 1 August 1989.
10 See section 29 post.
11 Duration of Copyright and Rights in Performances Regulations 1995, reg 18.
12 Ibid, reg 19(2)(b).

21. Infringement of revived copyright

Where copyright in a work has been revived, exploitation of the work while it was in the public domain is not regarded as infringing revived copyright in a work[1]. It is not an infringement of revived copyright to do anything in relation to a work after 1 January 1996 pursuant to arrangements made before 1 January 1995, nor is it an infringement to issue to the public copies of the work where the copies were made before 1 July 1995[2].

Revived copyright in a work is not infringed by including a copy or adaptation of that work in a literary, dramatic, musical or artistic work or film provided the copy or adaptation was made before 1 July 1995 or was made pursuant to arrangements made before that date[3]. It is not an infringement of revived copyright to do anything after 1 January 1996 which is a restricted act in relation to a work if the name and address of the person entitled to authorise the act cannot be ascertained by reasonable enquiry[4].

In the case of a work in which revived copyright subsists, any act restricted by copyright shall be treated as licensed by the copyright owner subject to the payment of a reasonable royalty[5] provided that the person intending to carry out such act or acts gives reasonable notice of their intention to the copyright owner, stating when they intend to begin to do the act or acts[6]. Once notice is given, the acts are treated as licensed and the amount of royalty may be determined later[7]. If agreement cannot be reached the amount of royalties is to be determined by the Copyright Tribunal[8]. One implication of this new provision is that it is therefore not possible to obtain an exclusive licence in respect of revived copyright[9].

1 The Duration of Copyright and Rights in Performances Regulations 1995, reg 23(1).
2 Ibid, reg 23(2).
3 Ibid, reg 23(3).
4 Ibid, reg 23(4).
5 Ibid, reg 24(1).
6 Ibid, reg 24(2).
7 Ibid – note however that this regulation does not apply if or to the extent that the licence to do the acts could be granted by a licensing body or if the royalties are payable under Sch 6 of the 1988 Act to the Hospital for Sick Children, Great Ormond Street, London.
8 Ibid, reg 25. Also see section 76 post.
9 See section 33 post.

22. Termination of grants of copyright in the United Kingdom and former British dominions

There are no statutory provisions which provide for the reversion or recapture of rights in works by their authors[1] if these works have been first assigned after 1 June 1957.

The Copyright Act 1911, which came into force on 1 July 1912, extended the period of copyright protection in the United Kingdom and British Dominions. Before this time the period of copyright protection for a literary work under the Copyright Act 1842 (Talfourd's Act) and the Dramatic Copyright Act 1833 was the longer of 42 years from publication or the life of the author plus 7 years. In 1911 it was decided to extend this term to a period equalling the life of the author plus 50 years. It was decided, however, that the author (and not his/her publisher or assignee) should benefit from the extension of the term of copyright. For this reason a provision was introduced into the 1911 Act giving the author or the author's estate the right to recapture rights assigned by the author before 1 July 1912[2]. The recapture right was exercisable by written notice given not more than 1 year nor less than 6 months before the rights would have expired (ie the later of 42 years from first publication or 7 years from the author's death). Recapture by the author permitted the author's assignee to exercise on a non-exclusive basis the rights previously assigned to the assignee subject to the observance of certain conditions.

The proviso to the Copyright Act 1911, s 5(2) created a total reversion of all rights first assigned by an author between 16 December 1911 and 1 June 1957 which is effective automatically 25 years from the date of death of the author. This provision was abolished by the Copyright Act 1956 and does not apply to works first assigned after 1 June 1957[3]. The effect of the proviso is preserved, however, for works assigned before that time, and the provision continues to be of relevance.

1 As to authorship see section 8 ante.
2 Copyright Act 1911, s 24 (repealed).
3 Copyright Act 1956, s 50 (2), Sch 9 (repealed).

C: Duration of copyright in the United Kingdom under former provisions

23. Relevance of former copyright provisions

The statutory provisions in force prior to the Duration of Copyright and Rights in Performances Regulations 1995 and the Copyright and Related Rights Regulations 1996 will continue to be relevant for some considerable time, as the Regulations specifically preserve former provisions relating to the duration of copyright[1].

Generally the effect of the Duration of Copyright and Rights in Performance Regulations 1995 and the Copyright and Related Rights Regulations 1996 is to extend the term of copyright for literary, dramatic, musical and artistic works and films. Their application in respect of works created on or after 1 January 1996 is clear[2].

In the case of certain categories of existing works (eg photographs, unpublished books) made before 1 January 1996, the date on which copyright ceases to subsist under the former provisions[3] is later than that provided for under the Regulations. The former statutory provisions will therefore need to be referred to where appropriate and are summarised below.

1 Duration of Copyright and Rights in Performances Regulations 1995, reg 15(1).
2 See sections 9 to 19 ante.
3 Copyright, Designs and Patents Act 1988 (before the amendments effected by the 1995 Regulations and the 1996 Regulations); Copyright Act 1956.

24. Former 1988 Act provisions relating to copyright in sound recordings

The 1988 Act provided that copyright in sound recordings, including soundtracks accompanying films, made between 1 July 1912 and 31 May 1957 subsisted for a period of 50 years from the end of the calendar year in which the recording was made[1].

The 1988 Act provided that copyright subsisting[2] in a published sound recording or film soundtrack made on or after 1 June 1957 but before 1 August 1989 continued until the end of the period of 50 years from the end of the calendar year in which the recording is first published[3].

The 1988 Act provided that copyright in a sound recording[4] or film soundtrack made on or after 1 August 1989 expired at the end of the period of 50 years from the end of the calendar year in which it has made, or, if it was released before the end of that period, 50 years from the end of the calendar year of release[5].

If a post-May 1957 sound recording or film soundtrack was not published, then the period of copyright protection provided by the 1988 Act expired 50 years from the end of 1989 (ie on 31 December 2039) or, if the sound recording or film soundtrack was published within 50 years from the end of 1989, the period of copyright protection would have expired 50 years from the end of the calendar year in which the sound recording or film soundtrack was published[6].

1 See the Copyright Act 1911, s 19 (1); Copyright Act 1956, s 50 (1), Sch 7, para 11; Copyright, Designs and Patents Act 1988 s 170, Sch, 1, para 12 (2) (d).
2 Ie by virtue of the Copyright Act 1956, s 12 (2).
3 See ibid, s 12 (3); Copyright, Designs and Patents Act 1988, Sch 1, para 12 (2) (d).

4 'Sound recording' means a recording of sounds, from which the sounds may be reproduced, or a recording of the whole or any part of a literary, dramatic or musical work, from which sounds reproducing the work or part may be produced, in either case regardless of the medium on which the recording is made or the method by which the sounds are reproduced or produced: Copyright, Designs and Patents Act 1988, s 5 (1). However, copyright does not subsist in a sound recording which is, or to the extent that it is, a copy taken from a previous sound recording: ibid, s 5 (2).
5 Ibid, s 13 (1).
6 Ibid, Sch 1, para 12 (5).

25. Former provisions relating to copyright in cinematograph films under the Copyright Act 1911

Cinematograph films made between 1 July 1912 and 31 May 1957 were the subject of three separate and overlapping types of copyright protection.

As a dramatic work

'Dramatic work' included any piece for recitation, choreographic work or entertainment in dumb show, a scenic arrangement or acting form of which was fixed in writing or otherwise and any cinematograph production where the arrangement or acting form or the combination of incidents represented gave the work an original character[1]. The 1911 Act did not contain any provision for determining the authorship of cinematograph films which were treated as dramatic works. It was, however, generally assumed that the author of a cinematograph film was the person who directed it. The term of copyright protection for films protected as dramatic works under the 1911 Act was, in general, the life of the author and the period of 50 years after his death[2].

As a series of photographs

'Photograph' included photo-lithograph and any work produced by any process analogous to photography[3]. Under the 1911 Act the term for which copyright subsisted in photographs was 50 years from the making of the original negative from which the photograph was directly or indirectly derived, and the person who was the owner of such negative at the time when such negative was made was deemed to be the author of the work[4].

As a sound recording

Since neither the dramatic copyright in the moving pictures of a cinematograph film nor the photograph copyright in the individual frames covered the sounds accompanying the moving pictures, a third level of copyright protection was available under the 1911 Act. Under that Act, copyright subsisted in records, perforated rolls and other contrivances by means of which sounds might be mechanically reproduced in like manner as if such contrivances were musical works, and the term of copyright was 50 years from the making of the original plate from which the contrivance was directly or indirectly derived, and the person who was the owner of such original plate at the time when such plate was made was deemed to be the author of the work[5].

1 Copyright Act 1911, s 35 (1).
2 Ibid, s 3.
3 Ibid, s 35 (1).
4 Ibid, s 21.
5 Ibid, s 19 (1).

26. Former provisions relating to copyright in cinematograph films under the Copyright Act 1956

With regard to cinematograph films made on or after 1 June 1957 and before 1 August 1989, the Copyright Act 1956 provided a definition of 'cinematograph film' which departed significantly from the definition and protection accorded by the 1911 Act. Pursuant to the 1956

Act a cinematograph film could not be protected as a dramatic work or as a photograph[1]. The expression 'cinematograph film' did, however, for the purposes of the 1956 Act include the soundtrack contained in the film[2].

The period of protection expired 50 years from the end of the calendar year of registration of the film or first publication[3]. 'Publication' was defined as the sale, letting on hire, or offer for sale or hire, of copies of the film to the public[4]. For a post-May 1957 film which was unpublished and is unregistered, the period of copyright protection created by the 1956 Act was technically eternal[5].

1 See the Copyright Act 1956, s 48 (1).
2 Ibid, s 13 (9).
3 See ibid, s 13 (3) as amended by the Films Act 1985, s 7 (2).
4 Copyright Act 1956, s 13 (10).
5 However, see now section 28 post.

27. Former 1988 Act provisions relating to pre-June 1957 films and sound recordings

Where a film made before 1 June 1957 was an original dramatic work within the meaning of the Copyright Act 1911, the copyright provisions of the Copyright, Designs and Patents Act 1988 applied to it as if it was an original dramatic work within the meaning of the 1988 Act[1]; the copyright protection period was, therefore, 50 years from the end of the calendar year in which the author died[2]. The same protection period applied to such films under the Copyright Act 1956[3]; the 1988 Act therefore made no change.

Pre-June 1957 films which qualified for copyright protection as photographs[4] were protected by the 1988 Act in the same way as photographs not forming part of a film[5]. On a strict reading, this would have appeared to increase the period of copyright protection for such films to the life of the photographer (not the author/owner as provided in the 1911 Act) plus 50 years[6].

With regard to the third type of copyright protection accorded to pre-June 1957 films (ie that of the soundtrack), copyright in sound recordings made before 1 June 1957 continued to subsist until the date on which it would have expired under the Copyright Act 1956[7], namely, for a period of 50 years from the end of the calendar year in which the recording was made[8].

1 Copyright, Designs and Patents Act 1988 s 170, Sch 1, para 7(2).
2 Ibid, s 12 (1).
3 See the Copyright Act 1956, ss 2 (3), 50 (1), Sch 7, para 15.
4 See section 25 ante.
5 Copyright, Designs and Patents Act 1988, Sch 1, para 7 (3).
6 See ibid, ss 4 (1) (a) (photograph is 'artistic work'), 9 (1) (author of work is the person who 'creates' it), 12 (1) (copyright period). This appeared inconsistent with the provisions of ibid Sch 1 para 12 (2) (c), which dealt with pre-1957 photographs, and also differed from the position under the Copyright Act 1956 where the 'author' of a photograph is the owner of the material on which it is taken (see ibid, s 48 (1) (not reproduced in the 1988 Act)). It is unlikely that much would have turned on this point, as the period of protection for 'photograph-protected' pre-1957 films would be the same as for 'dramatic work-protected' pre-1957 films, ie the life of the author plus 50 years.
  It is possible that the intention of the Copyright, Designs and Patents Act 1988, Sch 1, para 7, (3) may have been to refer to the 1988 copyright provisions as applied by para 12 of that Schedule. Alternatively, the sub-paragraph may be interpreted as meaning that the new copyright provisions have effect as they have effect in relation to photographs not forming part of a film made before 1 June 1957. The inconsistency has been in part remedied through the application of the 1995 Regulations which provide that both films and photographs are protected for the life of the author plus 70 years. The 'author' of the film as a dramatic work may be a different person from the 'author' of the series of photographs (see section 25 ante).
7 Copyright, Designs and Patents Act 1988, Sch 1, para 12 (2) (d). (Ibid, Sch 1, para 8 (1) does not apply in the case of pre-1957 sound tracks.)
8 Copyright Act 1956, Sch 7, para 11.

28. Former 1988 Act provisions in relation to films made on or after 1 June 1957 and before 1 August 1989

The sound track of a film to which the Copyright Act 1956 applied (ie a film made on or after 1 June 1957 but before 1 August 1989) was to be treated for the purpose of the Copyright,

Designs and Patents Act 1988 not as part of the film but as a sound recording[1]. This provision had retrospective effect but was controlled by the relevant transitional provisions in the 1988 Act which provided that copyright subsisted in a sound recording only if it subsisted in the film immediately before 1 August 1989, and continued until copyright in the film expired[2].

It will be noted that the Duration of Copyright and Rights in Performances Regulations 1995 re-combined the soundtrack copyright with the film copyright in all existing films with effect from 1 December 1996[3]. The author and first owner of copyright in the film were, under the 1988 Act, to be treated as having been author and first owner of the copyright in the sound recording[4]. Anything done before 1 August 1989 in relation to the copyright in the film was to have effect in relation to the sound recording as in relation to the film[5] where the sound recording accompanies the film (but not necessarily otherwise).

In respect of published films and registered films[6], copyright continues to subsist until the date on which it would have expired under the 1956 Act[7]. With regard to unpublished films and unregistered films, the 1988 Act amends the period of copyright protection created by the 1956 Act[8], replacing it by a period of 50 years from the end of 1989 or, if the film is published before the end of that period, a period of 50 years from the end of the calendar year in which the film is published[9].

1 Copyright, Designs and Patents Act 1988, Sch 1, para 8 (1). In other words, the 1988 Act 'unwinds' the Copyright Act 1956, s 13 (9) (which provided that a cinematograph film included the sound track associated with it) and divides the 1956 cinematograph film into one 1988 Act 'film' and one separate associated 1988 Act 'sound recording'.
2 Copyright, Designs and Patents Act 1988, Sch 1, para 8(2)(a).
3 See section 3.
4 Ibid, Sch 1, para 8 (2) (b).
5 Ibid, Sch 1, para 8 (2) (c).
6 Ie films falling within the Copyright Act 1956, s 13 (3) (a).
7 Copyright, Designs and Patents Act 1988, Sch 1, para 12 (2) (e).
8 Ie by the Copyright Act 1956, s 13 (3) (b) as amended.
9 Copyright, Designs and Patents Act 1988, Sch 1, para 12 (5).

29. Former 1988 Act provisions relating to films and photographs made on or after 1 August 1989 and before 1 January 1996

The subsistence of copyright in films made on or after 1 August 1989 and before 1 January 1996 was determined by the Copyright, Designs and Patents Act 1988, s 5. 'Film' is defined as a recording on any medium from which a moving image may by any means be produced[1], but no copyright existed in a film which was, or to the extent that it was, a copy taken from a previous film[2]. The definition of 'film' was wide enough to include audio-visual recordings made on video tape. It would seem that the method of protection given to a film depended on the medium chosen for its production. An audio-visual production made on video tape would qualify for protection both as a film or a sound recording (which was defined as a recording of sounds from which the sounds may be reproduced and was not limited to audio only recordings[3].

Where, however, an audio visual production was made using 35 mm film and separate sound recording which were then combined onto an optical negative with a three stripe magnetic track, the silent moving images would appear to have been protected as a film and the accompanying sounds would appear to have been given separate protection as a sound recording. The period of copyright protection in either case was 50 years from the end of the calendar year in which the recording or film is made[4], or, if it was released before the end of that period, 50 years from the end of the calendar year of release[5].

The position with regard to photographs is that while no specific provision relating to the duration of copyright protection in photographs was included in the 1988 Act, two provisions of the Copyright Act 1956 were not reproduced: that defining the author of a photograph as the person who at the time the photograph is taken is the owner of the material on which it is taken[6]; and that providing a specific term of copyright protection for photographs of 50 years from the end of the calendar year of publication[7].

The effect of these combined deletions would appear to have been as follows. First, the author of a post-July 1989 photograph was the person who 'created' the photograph[8] which remains the case after the coming into effect of the Duration of Copyright and Rights in

Performances Regulations 1995 and the Copyright and Related Rights Regulations 1996. Second, since no specific term of copyright protection was provided for photographs, they were protected as other artistic works and the copyright period was therefore the life of the author plus 50 years[9]. As specific transitional provisions dealt with pre-1957 and post-1957 unpublished photographs[10] as well as published photographs[11] it appears that the revised term of copyright protection applied only to photographs taken on or after 1 August 1989.

The transitional provisions of the 1988 Act relating to photographs may briefly be described as follows. For published photographs the period of protection depended on when they were made. If they were made before 1 June 1957 the period of protection was 50 years from the end of the year in which they were taken[12]. If they were made on or after 1 June 1957 the period of protection was 50 years from the end of the year of first publication[13]. For unpublished photographs of known authorship or unknown authorship taken on or after 1 June 1957 the position was as specified for certain other artistic works and literary, dramatic and musical works[14]. These provisions have now been superseded by the 1995 Regulations and are as stated above[15] except where the period of protection previously provided by legislation was longer than that provided by the Regulation.

1 Copyright, Designs and Patents Act 1988, s 5 (1).
2 Ibid, s 5 (2).
3 Ibid, s 5 (1).
4 Ibid, s 13 (1) (a).
5 Ibid, s 13 (1) (b). A sound recording or film is 'released' when it is first published, broadcast or included in a cable programme service, or, in the case of a film or sound track, the film is first shown in public; but in determining whether a work has been released no account is to be taken of any unauthorised act: ibid, s 13 (2).
6 Copyright Act 1956, s 48 (1) (definition of 'photograph').
7 Ibid, s 3 (4) proviso (b).
8 Copyright, Designs and Patents Act 1988, s 9 (1).
9 Ibid, s 12 (1).
10 See ibid Sch 1, para 12 (2) (c), (4) (c).
11 See ibid Sch 1, para 12 (2) (c).
12 Copyright Act 1956, Sch 7, para 2 and the Copyright, Designs and Patents Act 1988, Sch 1, para 12(2)(e).
13 Copyright Act 1956, s 3(4) (b).
14 Copyright, Designs and Patents Act 1988, Sch 1, para 12(4).
15 See sections 13 to 19 ante, and in particular section 16.

D: Transfers of copyright database right and rental right and mortgages of copyright and database right

30. Transfer of copyright and database right generally

Rights of copyright and database right may be transferred under English law by way of testamentary disposition, operation of law, assignment or licence. Provisions governing dealings with copyright and copyright works also apply in relation to the database right and databases[1].

1 The Copyright and Rights in Databases Regulations 1997, reg 23.

31. Transfer by testamentary disposition

On the death of an author who has left a will, copyright in the work passes automatically to the executors of the author's estate and then to the stated beneficiary. The ownership of the manuscript of the work itself can be assigned or bequeathed separately from the copyright as can an author's moral rights. If a manuscript of a work is the subject of a bequest (whether specific or general) it is construed as carrying with it the copyright in the work, subject to a contrary intention being expressed[1].

Where an author dies without leaving a will, the title to the author's copyrights devolves automatically to the President of the Family division and vests in the administrators of the estate once letters of administration have been obtained[2]. When a grant of administration has been obtained, the administrators are bound to sell all assets of the estate which they hold on trust for the beneficiaries but are entitled to exercise a power of appropriation[3].

1 See the Copyright, Designs and Patents Act 1988, s 93.
2 See the Administration of Estates Act 1925, ss 9, 55 (1) (xv) as substituted by the Administration of Justice Act 1970, s 1 (6), Sch 2, para 5 (17 Halsbury's Statutes (4th Edn) 'Executors'). See also *Redwood Music Ltd v B Feldman & Co Ltd* 1979 RPC 1 [where a person domiciled abroad dies leaving a will, title to his personal property in the UK vests in executors from the date of death and grant of probate in the UK only necessary to prove title].
3 See generally the Administration of Estates Act 1925, s 41 as amended, and 17 Halsbury's Laws (4th Edn), para 1359 et seq.

32. Transfer by operation of law

On the bankruptcy of an individual all copyrights vest in the trustee in bankruptcy[1] who may not sell or licence the work otherwise than on the terms on which the bankrupt could have done so[2]. On the liquidation of a company its assets, including rights of copyright, may be vested by the court in the liquidator[3].

In the absence of express provisions terminating an agreement between an author and (say) a publisher on the liquidation of the publisher, the author has no right to receive any payment out of sums derived by the liquidation from the disposal of the copyright and is reduced to the position of an unsecured creditor. This should be contrasted to the position between an author and an individual publisher who becomes bankrupt, where the trustee in bankruptcy is bound to make the payments to which the author would have been entitled.

On the dissolution of a company, all rights of copyright owned by it, together with any other assets, will vest in the Crown as bona vacantia[4].

1 Insolvency Act 1986, s 306 (1) (4 Halsbury's Statutes (4th Edn) 'Bankruptcy and Insolvency').
2 See generally 3(2) Halsbury's Laws (4th Edn), para 383.
3 Insolvency Act 1986, s 145 (1).
4 Companies Act 1985, s 654 (1) (8 Halsbury's Statutes (4th Edn) 'Companies').

33. Transfer by assignment or licence

Copyright and database right can also be transferred by an assignment or licence. As a general rule an assignment of copyright will be an outright transfer and must be in writing and signed by or on behalf of the assignor[1]. A licence is a permission to use rights but subject to the performance of certain conditions. Only an exclusive licence needs to be in writing and signed by the licensor[2]. A licence granted by a copyright owner or database right owner is binding on every successor in title to his or her interest in the copyright, except a purchaser in good faith for valuable consideration and without notice (actual or constructive) of the licence or a person deriving title from such a purchaser[3].

Both assignments and licences may be limited to one or more but not all of the things the copyright owner or database right owner has the exclusive right to do and to part but not all of the period for which the copyright or database right is to subsist[4].

The most significant differences between an assignment and a licence are:

(a) an assignment transfers a property right, whereas under a licence, which is a contractual right, no property rights are transferred;

(b) after assignment of the copyright or database right in a work, the assignor normally has no more rights in it and cannot terminate the assignment whereas a licensor may be able to terminate the licence if the licensee fails to perform its obligations;

(c) an assignee has the right to sue to protect the copyright or database right in the work. A licensee cannot sue unless the licensee is an exclusive licensee pursuant to a written licence in which event the licensee may commence proceedings but must once the action is under way join in the copyright or database right owner as a party if they have concurrent rights[5];

(d) on insolvency the rights of a licensee will usually revert to the copyright or database right owner whereas the assignee keeps the rights.

Mortgages of copyright in whose favour a power of sale has arisen have the right to transfer the copyright free from the mortgagor's equity of redemption, subject to the terms of the mortgage of copyright[6]. A contract relating to copyright and made by a person suffering from a mental disorder is valid if the other party acted in good faith and was not aware of the mental disorder[7]. An assignment of copyright by a minor is voidable when it is made in pursuance of a contract which is not for the benefit of the minor[8]. An assignment which is made pursuant to a contract which is in restraint of trade, or which is grossly unfair or oppressive, may be set aside[9].

1 Copyright, Designs and Patents Act 1988, s 90 (3).
2 Ibid, s 92(1).
3 Ibid, s 90(4).
4 Ibid, s 90(2).
5 Ibid, s 102.
6 *Re Jude's Musical Compositions* [1907] 1 Ch 651, CA.
7 See generally 30 Halsbury's Laws (4th Edn) paras 1005, 1006.
8 See *Chaplin v Leslie Frewin (Publishers) Ltd* [1966] Ch 71, [1965] 3 All ER 764, CA.
9 *A Schroeder Music Publishing Co Ltd v Macauley* [1974] 3 All ER 616, [1974] 1 WLR 1308, HL. See also *O'Sullivan v Management Agency and Music Ltd* 1985 QB 428; 1985 3 All ER 351 (restraint of trade and undue influence); *Elton John v James*, 1991 FSR 397 (undue influence); *Clifford Davis v WEA Records* [1975] 1 All ER 237, 1975 1 WLR 61 (contract oppressive and unfair because of parties' unequal bargaining power); *Zang Tumb Tuum Records Ltd v Johnson* 1993 EMLR 61, CA (restraint of trade); *Silvertone Records Ltd v Mountfield* 1993 EMLR 152 [restraint of trade]. Cf. *Panayiotou v Sony Music Entertainment UK Ltd* 1994 EMLR 229 (court refused to set contract aside on grounds of restraint of trade; considered restraint clauses were not, in light of commercial reality of the situation, one-sided and unfair).

34. Transfer of rental right

Where an agreement relating to film production is concluded between an author and a film producer, the author is presumed, unless the agreement provides to the contrary, to have transferred any rental right in the film to the film producer, even though the transfer may not be in writing[1]. This new provision applies in relation to agreements concluded before 1 January 1996 but does not apply to authors of the screenplay, the dialogue or music written specifically for the film[2].

Where the author has transferred the rental right, the author retains the right to equitable remuneration for the rental in respect of any film or sound recording made after 1 April 1997[3]. This right to equitable remuneration cannot be assigned other than to a collecting society and any agreement purporting to exclude or restrict the right is void[4]. The amount payable by way of equitable remuneration is agreed between the parties or, in default of an agreement, is determined by reference to the Copyright Tribunal[5].

1 Copyright, Designs and Patents Act 1988, s 93A as amended by the Copyright and Related Rights Regulations 1996. See also section 7 ante and in relation to performances sections 62 to 64 post.
2 Ibid, s 93(A) (3) as amended.
3 Ibid, s 93(B) as amended.
4 Ibid, s 93(B)(5) as amended.
5 Ibid, s 93(C) as amended.

35. Mortgages of copyright and database right

A mortgage of copyright or database right may be effected by means of an assignment of the copyright or database right with a proviso for re-assignment on redemption. An assignment of copyright or database right by way of mortgage will generally not provide sufficient security by itself, and mortgage documents will normally also include provisions dealing with intangible rights (such as things in action, rights of action, know-how etc) film materials (such as original film materials, sound recordings, script etc) and other materials. Depending on the extent of the security to be created by a mortgage, the arrangements in relation to physical materials may constitute either an assignment of the entire right, title and interest of the mortgagor in such materials or merely a charge.

A charge is a species of mortgage which is not part of a legal estate but which gives the chargee certain rights over property as security for a loan[1]. A mortgage is a conveyance of some interest in land and other property 'as security for the payment of the debt or the discharge of some other obligation for which it is given'[2]. A chargee or equitable mortgagee has no legal interest and is unable to take possession or receive rents or profits of the charged property without an order of the court[3].

The fundamental difference between a mortgage and a charge and the respective rights of mortgagee and chargee are not always clearly appreciated by lenders or their legal advisors. Unless the mortgage document contains a charge (as opposed to an assignment) in relation to physical materials provisions which relate to powers of sale[4], appointment of receiver[5], restriction on the exercise of power of sale[6] and consolidation[7] are incapable of being applied and inappropriate.

In circumstances where the mortgage document relates to property which is the subject of existing distribution or licensing agreements, the assignment should be expressed to be subject to and with the benefit of such agreements. Mortgages, charges and other security arrangements are required to be registered at Companies House[8].

1 *London County and Westminster Bank Ltd v Tomkins* [1918] 1 KV 515.
2 *Santley v Wild* [1899] 2 CH 474.
3 *Finck v Tranter* [1905] 1 KV 427.
4 Law of Property Act 1925, s 101 (1) (i).
5 Ibid, s 101 (1) (iii).
6 Ibid, s 103.
7 Ibid, s 93.
8 Companies Act 1985, s 395.

E: Permitted acts in relation to copyright and database right

36. Permitted acts in relation to copyright and database right generally

The Copyright, Designs and Patents Act 1988 specifies a number of acts which may be carried out in relation to copyright works and databases and do not infringe the copyright of the work or the database right in the database.

37. Research or private study

The use of a work for research or private study, for criticism or review or reporting of current events is permitted, provided it is fair dealing[1]. Although a positive decision was made not to define 'fair dealing' in the Act, regard must be paid to the amount and importance of the part of the work which has been taken, the purpose for which the fair dealing is carried out (what might be permissible for use in private study would not be permissible for commercial use), as well as whether the alleged fair dealing is competing with or rivalling the copyright work, and any intention of the part of the person making the fair dealing to obtain unfair commercial advantage. Case law under both the Copyright Act 1956 and the Copyright, Designs and Patents Act 1988 suggests factors to be taken into account in determining if use of the materials is fair dealing, but each case will depend on its own facts[2].

Copying by a person other than a researcher or student is not fair dealing if the person doing the copying knows or has reason to believe that it will result in copies of substantially the same material being provided to more than one person at substantially the same time and for substantially the same purpose or if it is carried out by a librarian contrary to acts permitted by a librarian[3].

The database right in a database which has been made available to the public in any manner is not infringed by fair dealing with a substantial part of its contents if:

(a)   that part is extracted from the database by a peson who is apart from this paragraph a lawful user of the database; and

(b)   it is extracted for the purpose of illustration for teaching or research and not for any commercial purpose; and

(c)   the source is indicated.

---

1 Copyright Designs and Patents Act 1988, ss 29–30. For examples, see eg *Hubbard v Vosper* 1972 2 QB 84, 1972 1 All ER 1023, 1972 2 WLR 389 (use of extracts from cult's literature to criticise cult's philosophy could be fair dealing even though literature not published to world at large); *Sillitoe v McGraw-Hill Book Co (UK) Ltd* 1983 FSR (use of substantial extracts from copyright works in commercially produced study notes was not fair dealing for the purpose of private study); *British Broadcasting Corporation v British Satellite Broadcasting Ltd*, 1991 3 All ER (use of World Cup match highlights in sports news programme was fair dealing for purpose of reporting current events); *Time Warner Entertainments Company LP v Channel Four Television Corporation plc* 1994 EMLR 1, CA (use of clips from film totalling 12 minutes in 30 minute programme capable of being fair dealing). See *Hubbard v Vosper* (1972) 2 QB 84; *Time Warner Entertainments Company LP v Channel Four Television Corporation plc* [1994] EMLR 1.
2 Ibid, s 29, (3).
3 Copyright and Rights in Databases Regulations 1997, reg 20(1).

38. Computer programs

It is not fair dealing to convert a computer program expressed in a low level language to a version expressed in a higher level language or incidentally in the course of so converting the program to copy it unless the user is decompiling the program in accordance with the Act[1].

1 Copyright, Designs and Patents Act 1988, s 29 (4).

39. Reporting current events

The use of work other than a photograph for the purpose of criticism or review or for the purpose of reporting current events does not infringe copyright so long as it is accompanied by a sufficient acknowledgement although no acknowledgement is required in connection with the reporting of current events by means of a sound recording, film, broadcast or cable programme[1]. It would also seem that use of the item must be current.[2]

1 Ibid, s 30 (2)
2 *BBC v British Satellite Broadcasting Limited* [1991] 3 WLR 174.

40. Incidental inclusion

Copyright in a work is not infringed by its incidental inclusion in an artistic work, sound recording, film, broadcast or cable programme[1] or by the issue of copies to the public or the playing, showing, broadcasting or inclusion in a cable programme service of anything which did not constitute an infringement of copyright by virtue of such incidental inclusion[2]. A musical work, words spoken or sung with music, or any part of a sound recording, broadcast or cable programme which includes a musical work or such works, is not to be regarded as incidentally included in another work if it is deliberately included[3]. For this reason caution is necessary. The question of whether any material is capable of incidental inclusion in a film or sound recording which has been edited also needs to be given further consideration.

The inclusion in a photograph, film, broadcast or cable programme service of a building, or of a sculpture or model for a building or a work of artistic craftsmanship, if permanently situated in a public place or in premises open to the public, is not an infringement of the copyright in such a work[4].

1 Copyright, Designs and Patents Act 1988, s 31 (1).
2 Ibid, s 31 (2)
3 Ibid, s 31 (3)
4 Copyright, Designs and Patents Act 1988, s 62.

41. Unascertainability of author's identity

Copyright is not infringed in a literary, dramatic, musical or artistic work where it is not possible by reasonable enquiry to ascertain the identity of the author and it is reasonable to assume that copyright has expired[1]. Case law under both the Copyright Act 1956 and the Copyright, Designs and Patents Act 1988 suggests factors to be taken into account in determining if use of the material is fair dealing, but each case will depend on its own facts.

1 Copyright, Designs and Patents Act 1988, s 57(1). See also section 42 post for an analogous new permitted act in relation to films.

42. Other permitted acts

The Copyright, Designs and Patents Act 1988 provides several exceptions to copyright infringement by educational establishments. These cover things done for purposes of instruction or examination[1]; anthologies for educational use[2]; performing, playing or showing work in the course of activities of educational establishment[3]; recording by educational establishment of broadcast and cable programmes[4]; and reprographic copying by educational establishments of passages from unpublished works[5].

Other acts permitted by the 1988 Act include incidental inclusion of works in films or sound recordings[6] dealing with works of unknown authorship where it is reasonable to assume the author died more than 70 years before[7], use of notes or recordings of spoken words[8], public reading or recitation[9], things done for the purposes of instruction or examination[10], anthologies for educational use[11], reprographic copying, public performance and recording by educational establishments[12], the making of copies of certain works by libraries and archives[13], recordings of folksongs[14], transfer or works in electronic form[15], playing of sound recordings for the purposes of a club[16], recording for supervision of broadcasts[17], recording for purposes of time-shifting[18], free public showing or playing[19], reception and retransmission of broadcasts[20], provision of sub-titled copies[21], recording for archival purposes[22] and public administration[23].

The Duration of Copyright and Rights in Performances Regulations 1995 introduced a new permitted act in relation to films[24] which extends to their accompanying soundtracks where these are exploited with the films[25]. Copyright in a film is not infringed by an act done at a time when, or in pursuance of arrangements made at a time when:

(a)   it is not possible by reasonable enquiry to ascertain the identity of any of the persons by reference to whose life the period of copyright protection of the film is ascertained; and

(b)   it is reasonable to assume that copyright has expired or that the last to die of those persons died 70 years or more before the beginning of the calendar year in which the act is done or the arrangements are made.

The provisions in paragraph (b) above[26] do not apply in relation to any film in which Crown copyright subsists or certain films whose copyright originally vested in an international organisation[27].

The Copyright and Rights in Databases Regulations 1997 introduced an analogous permitted act in relation to the new database right[28]. The database right is not infringed by the extraction or re-utilisation of a substantial part of the contents of the database at a time when, or in pursuance of arrangements made at a time when it is not possible by reasonable enquiry to ascertain the identity of the maker (or each of the makers where the database is alleged to have been made jointly[29]) and it is reasonable to assume that the database right has expired. The 1997 Regulations also provide a number of exceptions to the database right in relation to Parliamentary and judicial proceedings, Royal Commissions and statutory inquiries, material open to public inspection or on official register, material communicated by the Crown in the course of public business, public records, and acts done under statutory authority[30].

1   Copyright, Designs and Patents Act 1988, s 32.
2   Ibid, s 33.
3   Ibid, s 34.
4   Ibid, s 35.
5   Ibid, s 36.
6   Copyright, Designs and Patents Act 1988, s 31.
7   Ibid, s 57(1).
8   Ibid, s 58.
9   Ibid, s 59.
10   Ibid, s 32.
11   Ibid, s 33.
12   Sections 34, 35 and 36.
13   Ibid, ss 38, 39, 40, 41, 42 and 43.
14   Ibid, s 61.
15   Ibid, s 56.
16   Ibid, s 67.
17   Ibid, s 69.
18   Ibid, s 70.
19   Ibid, s 72.
20   Ibid, s 73.
21   Ibid, s 74.
22   Ibid, s 75.
23   Ibid, ss 45, 46, 47, 48, 49 and 50.
24   Ibid, s 66A as inserted by the Duration of Copyright and Rights in Performances Regulations 1995, reg 6(2).

25 Ibid, s 5B(2) as substituted by the Duration of Copyright and Rights in Performances Regulation 1995, reg 9(1).
26 Ibid, s 66A(1)(b)(ii).
27 Ibid, s 66A(2).
28 Copyright and Rights in Databases Regulation 1997, reg 21(1).
29 Ibid, reg 21(2).
30 Ibid, reg 20(2) and Sch 1.

F: Infringement of copyright and database right and remedies

43. Infringement of copyright and database right

The copyright of a work is infringed if any person does, in the United Kingdom, any of the acts which are restricted by copyright[1] or authorises another to do so without the permission of the copyright owner, or other authorised person. The restricted acts may be infringed if they are carried out in relation to the work as a whole or to any substantial part of it and either directly or indirectly[2]. Such infringement is referred to as primary infringement.

The Copyright, Designs and Patents Act 1988 also provides for another category of infringement of copyright known as secondary infringement. In contrast to acts of primary infringement where knowledge is not a prerequisite to liability for infringement, secondary infringement requires that the person carrying out the unauthorised act either knew or had reason to believe that they were dealing with infringed copies of a work[3]. The acts of secondary infringement are:

(a) importing an infringing copy otherwise than for private or domestic use[4];
(b) possessing or dealing with an infringing copy[5];
(c) providing means for making infringing copies[6];
(d) transmitting infringing work by means of a telecommunication system[7];
(e) permitting use of premises for infringing performance[8]; and
(f) provision of apparatus for infringing performance[9].

A person infringes the database right in a database if without the consent of the owner of the database right they extract or re-utilise all or a substantial part of the contents of the database[10]. The repeated and systematic extraction or re-utilisation of insubstantial parts of the contents of a database may amount to the extraction or re-utilisation of a substantial part of those contents[11]. No act done before 1 January 1998 or after 1 January 1998 in pursuance of an agreement made before commencement shall be regarded as an infringement of the database right in a database[12].

1 See section 7 ante.
2 Copyright, Designs and Patents Act 1988, ss 22–7.
3 Ibid. See also *LA Gear Inc v Hi-Tech Sports plc* 1992 FSR 121 *Hutchison Personal Communications Ltd v Hook Advertising Ltd* 1996 FSR 546.
4 Ibid, s 22.
5 Ibid, s 23.
6 Ibid, s 24(1).
7 Ibid, s 24(2).
8 Ibid, s 25.
9 Ibid, s 26.
10 Copyright and Rights in Databases Regulations 1997, reg 16(1).
11 Ibid, reg 16(2).
12 Ibid, reg 28(2).

44. Right to bring proceedings for infringement of copyright and database right

The owner of copyright has the right to bring proceedings in respect of infringement in order to prevent the performance of any of the restricted acts specified by statute[1].

Where a licensee is entitled to exercise the rights granted under the licence to the exclusion of all other persons, including the copyright or database right owner, the exclusive licensee has the right to commence proceedings in the licensee's own name for infringement of copyright or database right if the licence is in writing[2]. The licensee is required to join the copyright or database right owner as a party to any proceedings brought by the exclusive licensee, (whether as a plaintiff or defendant), other than interlocutory injunction proceedings[3]. It should be noted that the owner is under no obligation either to defend or pursue any claim where the owner is so joined. Any award by way of damages for infringement may be apportioned by the court between the copyright or database right owner and the exclusive licensee in such manner as the court sees fit[4].

1 Copyright, Designs and Patents Act 1988, s 16. As to the acts which constitute an infringement of copyright see ibid, ss 17–27.
2 See ibid, s 92.
3 See ibid, s 102 (1), (3).
4 See ibid, s 102 (4) (c).

45. Remedies for infringement of copyright or database right

In an action for infringement of copyright (including rental right) or database right the reliefs available to the copyright owner are the same as for any other property right. These include an injunction, damages, an order for delivery up, an order for accounts to be rendered and an order for disposal and additional statutory damages. The plaintiff is not, however, entitled to damages if at the time of the infringement the defendant did not know and had no reason to believe that copyright or database right subsisted in the work or database to which the action relates[1].

As well as civil liability, the Copyright, Designs and Patents Act 1988 provides for criminal liability in respect of copyright but not database right[2] where a person without the licence of the copyright owner:

makes for sale or hire; or
imports into the United Kingdom otherwise than for his or her private and domestic use; or
possesses in the course of a business with a view to committing any act infringing the copyright; or
in the course of a business sells or lets for hire or offers or exposes for sale or hire or exhibits in public or distributes
an article which is and which he or she knows or has reason to believe is an infringing copy of a copyright work[3].

Similarly, a person commits an offence who makes an article specifically designed or adapted for making copies of a particular copyright work or has such an article in his or her possession knowing or having reason to believe that it is to be used to make infringing copies for sale or hire or for use in the course of a business[4]. A person convicted of any such offence is liable to a fine or prison sentence or both, a prison sentence ranging from six months to two years depending on the nature of the offence[5].

1 Copyright, Designs and Patents Act 1988, s 97.
2 It will be noted, however, that certain databases may be eligible for copyright protection and the copyright criminal liability provisions would appear to be applicable to such databases. See section 2 ante, section 11 ante (notes 5 to 8 and accompanying text) and section 14 ante (notes 12 to 17 and accompanying text).
3 Ibid, s 107(1).
4 Ibid, s 107(2).
5 Ibid, s 107(4)(5).

G: Moral rights in copyright works

46. Moral rights generally

Four types of moral right are provided under the Copyright, Designs and Patents Act 1988:

(a)   the right to be identified as the author or director of a work[1];
(b)   the right to object to derogatory treatment of a work[2];
(c)   the right not to suffer false attribution of a work[3]; and
(d)   the right to privacy in respect of certain films and photographs[4].

1 See section 47 post.
2 See section 50 post.
3 See section 52 post.
4 See section 53 post.

47. The right to be identified as author of a work

The author of a copyright literary, dramatic, musical or artistic work and the director of a copyright film have the right to be identified as the author or director of the work[1]. The right applies only to copyright works which qualify for protection under the Act[2]. The rights do not extend to the creator of sound recordings, broadcasts, cable programmes or typographical arrangements of published editions. The right of an author of a literary, dramatic or musical work to be identified extends to any adaptation made from the work[3].

The author of a literary work other than words intending to be sung or spoken with music or the author of a dramatic work has the right to be identified whenever the work is published commercially[4], performed in public, broadcast, included in a cable programme service or copies of a film or sound recording including the work are issued to the public. The author of a musical work or a literary work consisting of words intended to be sung or spoken with music has the right to be identified wherever the work is published commercially, copies of a sound recording of the work are issued to the public, or a film of which the soundtrack includes the work is shown in public or copies of such a film are issued to the public. This right to be identified as the author of the work includes the adaptation of the work in any of the above situations.

The author of an artistic work has a right to be identified whenever the work is published commercially[4] or exhibited in public, or a visual image of it is broadcast or included in a cable programme service[5], whenever a film including a visual image of the work is shown in public or copies of such a film are issued to the public[6], or, in the case of a work of architecture in the form of a building or a model for a building, a sculpture or a work of artistic craftsmanship, whenever copies of graphic work representing it, or of a photograph of it, are issued to the public[7]. The director of a film has the right to be identified whenever the film is shown in public, broadcast or included in a cable programme service or copies of the film are issued to the public[8].

The right of an author or director, in the case of commercial publication[9] or issue to the public of copies of a film or sound recording, is to be identified in or on each copy or, if that is not appropriate, in some other manner likely to bring the identity of the author or director to

35

the notice of the person acquiring a copy[10]. Otherwise, the right is to be identified in a manner likely to bring the identity of the author or director to the attention of the person seeing or hearing the performance, exhibition, showing, broadcast or cable programme in question[11]. The identification must in each case be clear and reasonably prominent[12]. If the author or director, in asserting the right to be identified, specifies a pseudonym or initials or some other particular form of identification, that form must be used; otherwise any reasonable form of identification may be used[13].

1 Copyright, Designs and Patents Act 1988, s 77 (1).
2 Ie under ibid, ss 154–156 and s 159. It would therefore appear that qualification of the author is not a prerequisite to the author's enjoying moral rights.
3 Ibid, s 77 (2).
4 For the meaning of 'commercial publication' and related expressions see ibid, s 175 (2).
5 Ibid, s 77 (4) (a).
6 Ibid, s 77 (4) (b).
7 Ibid, s 77 (4) (c).
8 Ibid, s 77 (6).
9 See note 4 supra.
10 Copyright, Designs and Patents Act 1988, s 77 (7) (a).
11 Ibid, s 77 (7) (c).
12 Ibid, s 77 (7).
13 Ibid, s 77 (8).

48. Assertion of right to be identified

The right to be identified is not infringed unless it has been asserted in accordance with the provisions of the 1988 Act[1]. The right may be asserted in the following ways:

(a) on an assignment of copyright in the work, by including a statement that the author or director asserts the right to be identified[2];
(b) by an instrument in writing signed by the author or director[3];
(c) in the case of the public exhibition of an artistic work, by securing that the author is identified on the original, or on a copy made by the author, or on a frame or mount or other thing to which it is attached when the author or first owner parts with possession of the original or copy, or by including in a licence a statement signed by or on behalf of the person granting the licence that the author asserts the right to be identified[4].

The persons bound by an assertion of right are, in the case of an assertion made in an assignment, the assignee and anyone claiming notice through them whether or not they have notice[5], or, in the case of an assertion made by an instrument in writing not being part of the assignment, anyone to whose notice the assertion is brought[6]. In the case of an artistic work where the right is asserted by affixing the name to the original or copy, anyone into whose hands the original or copy comes (with or without the identification) is bound by it[7], and in the case where the assertion is made in a licence in respect of the artistic work, the licensee and anyone into whose hands a copy of the artistic work made in pursuant of the licence comes will be bound[8]. Assertion cannot be retrospective.

1 Copyright, Designs and Patents Act 1988, s 78 (1).
2 Ibid, s 78 (2) (a).
3 Ibid, s 78 (2) (b).
4 Ibid, s 78 (3).
5 Ibid, s 78 (4) (a).
6 Ibid, s 78 (4) (b).
7 Ibid, s 78 (4) (c).
8 Ibid, s 78 (4) (d).

49. Exceptions to the right to be identified

The right to be identified as author or director does not apply to or in relation to the following:

(a) computer programs[1];
(b) typeface designs[2];
(c) computer-generated works[3];
(d) anything done by or with the copyright owner's authority where copyright in the work originally vested in the author's employer as being a work produced in the course of employment[4];
(e) anything done by or with the copyright owner's authority where copyright in the work originally vested in the director's employer as being the person treated as author of the film[5];
(f) any work made for the purpose of reporting current events[6];
(g) the publication in a newspaper, magazine or similar periodical, or in an encyclopaedia, dictionary, yearbook or other collective work of reference, of a literary, dramatic, musical or artistic work made for the purposes of such publication or made available with the author's consent for the purposes of such publication[7];
(h) a work in which Crown or Parliamentary copyright subsists, or a work in which copyright originally vested in an international organisation unless the author or director has previously been identified as such in or on published copies of the work[8].

Further, the right is not infringed by any act which would not infringe copyright in the work by virtue of certain statutory provisions[9].

1 Copyright, Designs and Patents Act 1988, s 79 (2) (a).
2 Ibid, s 79 (2) (b).
3 Ibid, s 79 (2) (c).
4 Ibid, s 79 (3) (a).
5 Ibid, s 79 (3) (b).
6 Ibid, s 79 (5).
7 Ibid, s 79 (6).
8 Ibid, s 79 (7).
9 Ibid, s 79 (4). The statutory provisions are: s 30 (fair dealing), s 31 (incidental inclusion), s 32 (3) (exam questions), s 45 (Parliamentary and judicial proceedings), s 46 (1) or (2) (Royal Commissions and statutory inquiries), s 51 (design documents and models), s 52 (design exploitation), s 57 (anonymous or pseudonymous works).

50. The right to object to derogatory treatment of a work

The author of a copyright literary, dramatic, musical or artistic work and the director of a copyright film have the right not to have the work subjected to derogatory treatment[1]. 'Treatment' of a work means any addition to, deletion from, alteration to or adaptation of the work, other than a translation of a literary or dramatic work or an arrangement or transcription of a musical work which involves no more than a change of key or register[2]. A treatment of a work is derogatory if it amounts to distortion or mutilation of the work or is otherwise prejudicial to the honour or reputation of the author or director[3]. It would seem that in assessing whether an author's or director's honour or reputation has been prejudiced by another's treatment of their work the courts will apply an objective test of reasonableness[4].

In the case of a literary, dramatic or musical work, the right is infringed by a person who publishes commercially, performs in public, broadcasts or includes in a cable programme service a derogatory treatment of the work, or issues to the public copies of a film or sound recording of, or including, a derogatory treatment of the work[5]. In the case of an artistic work, the right is infringed by a person who publishes commercially or exhibits in public a derogatory treatment of the work, or broadcasts or includes in a cable programme service a visual image of a derogatory treatment of the work, or shows in public a film including a visual image of a derogatory treatment of the work or issues copies of such a film to the public[6]. In the case of a film the right is infringed by a person who shows in public, broadcasts or includes in a cable programme service or issues to the public copies of a derogatory treatment of the film[7]. Thus this right may be infringed even where copyright has been assigned if a work is substantially altered and the author has not waived his or her right to object to derogatory treatment of the work.

The right to object to derogatory treatment is also infringed by a person who possesses in the course of business, or sells or lets for hire, or exposes or offers for sale or hire, or in the course of business exhibits in public or distributes, or distributes otherwise than in the course of business so as to affect prejudicially the honour or reputation of the author or director, an article which that person knows or has reason to believe is an infringing article[8].

1 Copyright, Designs and Patents Act 1988, s 80 (1)
2 Ibid, s 80 (2) (a). See *Morrison Leahy Music Ltd v Lightbond Ltd* 1993 EMLR 144 (arguable that a compilation album consisting of short excerpts from songs altered character of original compositions and was therefore derogatory treatment).
3 Ibid, s 80 (2) (b).
4 *The Trustees of the Natural History Museum* (1996) 3 EIPR D81.
5 Ibid, s 80 (3).
6 Ibid, s 80 (4) (a), (b).
7 Ibid, s 80 (6) as amended by the Duration of Copyright and Rights in Performances Regulations 1995/3297, reg 9 (2). The sound track of a film is treated as part of the film when accompanying the film but is otherwise treated as a sound recording: see the Copyright, Designs and Patents Act 1988, s 5B (2) as substituted by the Duration of Copyright and Rights in Performances Regulations 1995, reg 9 (1).
8 See the Copyright, Designs and Patents Act 1988, s 83.

51. Exceptions to the right to object to derogatory treatment

The right to object to a derogatory treatment of a work does not apply in relation to:

(a) computer programs or any computer-generated work[1];
(b) any work made for the purpose of reporting current events[2];
(c) the publication in a newspaper, magazine or similar periodical, or an encyclopaedia, dictionary, yearbook or other collective work of reference, of a literary, dramatic, musical or artistic work made for the purposes of such publication or made available with the consent of the author for the purpose of such publication[3];
(d) works in which copyright originally vested in the author's employer as being produced in the course of employment or in the director's employer as being the person treated as author of the film, unless the author or director is identified at the time of the relevant act or has previously been identified in or on published copies of the work[4];
(e) works in which Crown or Parliamentary copyright subsists, or in which copyright originally vested in an international organisation, unless the author or director is identified at the time of the relevant act or has previously been identified in or on published copies of the work[5].

The right is not infringed by any act which will not infringe copyright by virtue of the provision[6] relating to anonymous or pseudonymous works[7], nor is it infringed by anything done for the purpose of avoiding the commission of an offence, or complying with the duty imposed by or under an enactment, or, in the case of the BBC, avoiding the inclusion of anything in a programme which offends good taste or decency or is likely to encourage or incite to crime or lead to disorder or be offensive to public feeling provided, where the author or director is identified or has previously been identified, that there is a sufficient disclaimer[8].

1 Copyright, Designs and Patents Act 1988, s 81 (1).
2 Ibid, s 81 (3).
3 Ibid, s 81 (4).
4 Ibid, s 82 (1) (a), (2). Where in such a case the right does apply, it is not infringed if there is a sufficient disclaimer: ibid, s 82 (2). For the meaning of 'sufficient disclaimer' see ibid, s 178.
5 Ibid, s 82 (1) (b), (c), (2). Where in such a case the right does apply, it is not infringed if there is a sufficient disclaimer: ibid s 82 (2).
6 Ie ibid, s 57 as amended by SI 1995/3297.
7 Ibid, s 81 (5).
8 Ibid, s 81 (6).

52. The right not to suffer false attribution of a work

A person has the right not to have a literary, dramatic, musical or artistic work falsely attributed to him or her as author, or a film falsely attributed to him or her as director[1]. The attribution may be express or implied[2], and the right is infringed by any person who issues to the public copies of the work on which there is a false attribution or exhibits in public an artistic work, or copy of an artistic work, in or on which there is a false attribution[3].

The right is also infringed by a person who, in the case of a literary, dramatic or musical work, performs the work in public, broadcasts it or includes it in a cable programme service as being the work of a person, or, in the case of a film, shows it in public, broadcasts it or includes it in a cable programme service as being directed by a person, knowing or having reason to believe that the attribution is false[4].

The right is infringed by the issue to the public or public display of material containing a false attribution in connection with any of the acts mentioned above[5], or by a person who in the course of a business possesses or deals[6] with a copy of a work in or on which there is a false attribution, or in the case of an artistic work, possesses or deals with the work itself when there is a false attribution in or on it, knowing or having reason to believe that there is such an attribution and that it is false[7]. In the case of an artistic work the right is also infringed by a person who in the course of a business deals with a work which has been altered after the author parted with possession of it as being the unaltered work of the author, or deals with a copy of such a work as being a copy of the unaltered work of the author, knowing or having reason to believe that this is not the case[8].

1 Copyright, Designs and Patents Act 1988, s 84 (1). This section also applies where a work is falsely represented as being an adaptation of a person's work, or a copy is falsely represented as being a copy made by the author: ibid s 84 (8). It re-enacts the Copyright Act 1956, s 43.
2 Copyright, Designs and Patents Act 1988, s 84 (1). See *Noah v Shuba* 1991 FSR 14.
3 Ibid, s 84 (2).
4 Ibid, s 84 (3).
5 Ibid, s 84 (4).
6 Ie selling or letting for hire, offering or exposing for sale or hire, exhibiting in public, or distributing: ibid, s 84 (7).
7 Ibid, s 84 (5).
8 Ibid, s 84 (6).

53. The right to privacy of certain photographs and films

Under the Copyright, Designs and Patents Act 1988 the person who commissioned the taking of a photograph or making of a film for private and domestic purposes is not necessarily the author. Nonetheless where copyright subsists in the resulting work, the person who commissioned the work has the right not to have copies of the work issued to the public, or the work exhibited or shown in public, or the work broadcast or included in a cable programme service; and any person who does or authorises the doing of any of those acts infringes that right[1].

The right is not infringed by acts which by virtue of certain statutory provisions would not infringe copyright in the work[2].

The right should not be confused with rights of privacy or publicity which may exist under foreign laws.

1 Copyright, Designs and Patents Act 1988, s 85 (1).
2 Ibid, s 85 (2). The statutory provisions are: s 31 (incidental inclusion), s 45 (Parliamentary and judicial proceedings), s 46 (Royal Commissions and statutory inquiries), s 50 (acts done under statutory authority), s 57 (anonymous or pseudonymous works).

54. Consent and waiver

It is not an infringement of any moral right to do any act to which the person entitled to the right has consented[1]. Any moral right may be waived by instrument in writing signed by the person giving up the right[2]. The waiver may relate to a specific work, to works of a specified description or to works generally, and may relate to existing or future works[3]. It may also be conditional or unconditional, and may be expressed to be revocable[4]. Unless a contrary intention is expressed, the waiver is presumed to extend to the copyright owner's licensees and successors in title[5].

Although certain moral rights (ie the right to be identified[6] and the right to object to derogatory treatment[7]) do not generally apply in respect of anything done by or with the copyright owner's authority where the work in question vested[8] in the author's or director's employer[9], it is nevertheless advisable to obtain an express waiver of all moral rights since the employer/employee relationship may on occasion be difficult to establish, and also because even in areas where moral rights are not conferred by the Act (such as in the case of sound recordings) it is possible that parallel moral rights may exist through (for example) a record producer's contribution to the melodic line of a musical work or a film director's contribution to the literary or dramatic work which comprises the screenplay.

1 Copyright, Designs and Patents Act 1988, s 87 (1).
2 Ibid, s 87 (2). Nothing in the Copyright, Designs and Patents Act 1988, Pt I, Ch IV (ss 77–89) is to be construed as excluding the operation of the general law of contract or estoppel in relation to an informal waiver or other transaction in relation to any moral right: ibid, s 87 (4).
3 Ibid, s 87 (3) (a).
4 Ibid, s 87 (3) (b).
5 Ibid, s 87 (3).
6 See the Copyright, Designs and Patents Act 1988, s 77 and section 47 ante.
7 See ibid, s 80 and section 50 ante.
8 Ie by virtue of ibid, ss 9 (2) (a) or 11 (2).
9 See ibid, ss 79 (3), 82 (2), and see further sections 49 and 51 ante.

55. Duration of moral rights and moral rights in revived copyright works

The right to be identified as author or director[1], the right to object to derogatory treatment of a work[2] and the right to privacy[3] of certain photographs and films continue to subsist for so long as copyright subsists in the work[4]. The right not to have a work falsely attributed[5] continues until 20 years after the death of the relevant person[6].

Moral rights are exercisable after 1 January 1996 by the author of a work or the director of a film in which revived copyright subsists[7]. Where the author or director died before 1 January 1996 the right to identification as author or director, the right to object to derogatory treatment of work or the right to privacy of certain photographs and films are exercisable after 1 January by the author's or director's personal representatives[8] and any infringement after 1 January 1996 of the right not to be falsely attributed is actionable by an author or director's personal representatives[9]. Any damages recovered by personal representatives in respect of an infringement after a person's death shall devolve as part of the estate as if the right of action had subsisted and been vested in the author or director immediately before his or her death[10].

Any waiver or assertion of moral rights which subsisted immediately before the expiry of copyright continues to have effect during the period of revived copyright[11].

The right to be identified as author of a work and the right to privacy in respect of certain photographs and films apply in relation to the whole or any substantial part of the work[12]. The right to object to derogatory treatment of work and false attribution apply in relation to the work or any part of the work[13].

1 See section 48 ante.
2 See section 50 ante.
3 See section 53 ante.
4 Copyright, Designs and Patents Act 1988, s 86 (1).
5 See section 52 ante.
6 Copyright, Designs and Patents Act 1988, s 86 (2).
7 Duration of Copyright and Rights in Performances Regulations 1995, reg 22(3).
8 Ibid, s 22(4)(a).
9 Ibid, s 22(4)(b).
10 Ibid, s 22(5).
11 Ibid, s 22(2).
12 Copyright, Designs and Patents Act 1988, s 89(1).
13 Ibid, s 89(2).

56. Transmission of moral rights

Moral rights are not assignable[1].

On the death of a person entitled to the right to identification of author or director[2], the right to object to derogatory treatment of a work[3] or the right to privacy[4], the right passes to such person as he or she may by testamentary disposition specifically direct[5]. If there is no such direction but the copyright in the work in question forms part of his or her estate, the right passes to the person to whom the copyright passes[6]. If or to the extent that the right does not pass in either of the above two ways, it is exercisable by the personal representatives[7]. Where copyright passes in part to one person and in part to another, any right which passes with the copyright is correspondingly divided[8].

Where, by virtue of the above provisions, a right becomes exercisable by more than one person:

it may, in the case of the right to identification of author or director be asserted by any of them[9];

it is, in the case of the right to object to derogatory treatment of work or the right to privacy of certain photographs and films, a right exercisable by each of them and is satisfied in relation to any of them if they consent to the treatment or act in question[10]; and

any waiver of the right[11] by one of them does not affect the rights of the others[12].

persons to whom moral rights pass are bound by any previous consents or waivers[13].

Any infringement after a person's death of the right not to suffer a false attribution[14] is actionable by his or her personal representatives[15]. Any damages recovered by personal representatives in respect of an infringement after a person's death devolve as part of the estate as if the right of action had subsisted and been vested in him or her immediately before his or her death[16].

1 Copyright, Designs and Patents Act 1988, s 94.
2 See section 47 ante.
3 See section 50 ante.
4 See section 53 ante.
5 Copyright, Designs and Patents Act 1988, s 95 (1) (a).
6 Ibid, s 95 (1) (b).
7 Ibid, s 95 (1) (c).
8 See ibid, s 95 (2).
9 Ibid, s 95 (3) (a).
10 Ibid, s 95 (3) (b).
11 Ie in accordance with ibid s 87: see section 54 ante.
12 Ibid, s 95 (3) (c).
13 Ibid, s 95 (4).
14 See section 52 ante.
15 Copyright, Designs and Patents Act 1988, s 95 (5).
16 Ibid, s 95 (6).

57. Transitional provisions for moral rights

With the exception of the right not to suffer false attribution[1], which was contained in the previous legislation[2], no act done before the commencement of the Copyright, Designs and Patents Act 1988[3] is actionable by virtue of any provision dealing with moral rights[4].

The right to be identified as author or director[5] and the right to object to derogatory treatment[6] do not apply in relation to a literary, dramatic, musical or artistic work the author of which died before 1 August 1989 or in relation to a film made before 1 August 1989[7]. Those rights, in relation to a literary, dramatic, musical or artistic work existing at the commencement date, do not apply, where copyright first vested in the author, to anything which by virtue of an assignment of copyright made or licence granted before commencement may be done without infringing copyright; and, where copyright first vested in a person other than the author, to anything done by or with the licence of the copyright owner[8]. In addition, those rights do not apply to anything done in relation to a record made in pursuance of the Copyright Act 1956, s 8[9] (now repealed).

The right to privacy[10] does not apply to photographs taken or films made before 1 August 1989[11].

1 See section 52 ante.
2 Ie in the Copyright Act 1956, s 43.
3 Ie 1 August 1989.
4 Copyright, Designs and Patents Act 1988, s 170, Sch 1, para 22 (1), (2).

5 See section 47 ante.
6 See section 51 ante.
7 Copyright, Designs and Patents Act 1988, Sch 1, para 23 (1), (2).
8 Ibid, Sch 1, para 23 (3).
9 Copyright, Designs and Patents Act 1988, Sch 1, para 23 (4) Section 8 of the Copyright Act 1956 provided a statutory licence to make sound recordings of musical works subject to the payment of royalty rate fixed at 6¼% by statute.
10 See section 83 ante.
11 Copyright, Designs and Patents Act 1988, Sch 1, para 24.

58. Remedies for infringement of moral rights

An infringement of a moral right is actionable as a breach of statutory duty owed to the person entitled to the right[1]. In proceedings brought by an author or director objecting to derogatory treatment of a work the court may, if it thinks it is an adequate remedy, grant an injunction on terms prohibiting the doing of any act unless a disclaimer is made, in such terms and in such manner as may be approved by the court, dissociating the author or director from the treatment of the work[2].

1 Copyright, Designs and Patents Act 1988, s 103(1).
2 Ibid, s 103(2).

H: Rights in performances

RIGHTS IN PERFORMANCES

59. Rights in performances generally

The Copyright and Related Rights Regulations 1996 introduced extensive new rights for performers by way of amendment to the 1988 Act.

The rights are referred to in the 1988 Act (as amended by the 1996 Regulations) as 'Performers' Property Rights'[1]. The former rights of performers and persons having recording rights created under the 1988 Act have been preserved and are now referred to as 'performers' non-property rights'[2] and 'recording rights'[3] respectively.

1 Copyright, Designs and Patents Act 1988, s 191A as amended by the Copyright and Related Rights Regulations 1996, reg 21.
2 Ibid, s 192A as amended.
3 Ibid, s 185–188 as amended.

60. Protection of rights in performances

A performer's consent is required to the exploitation of his or her performances[1] and the Copyright, Designs and Patents Act 1988 defines 'performance' as a dramatic or musical performance, a reading or recitation of a literary work, or a performance of a variety act or any similar presentation which is or so far as it is a live performance given by one or more individuals[2]. A person having contractual recording rights in relation to a performance may take action in respect of any unauthorised recording of such a performance[3].

'Recording' in relation to a performance, means a film or sound recording made directly from the live performance, made from a broadcast of or cable programme including the performance or made directly or indirectly from another recording of the performance[4]. Any act done before 1 January 1989 or in pursuance of arrangements made before that date is not to be regarded as infringing performers' rights or rights of persons having recording rights[5].

1 Copyright, Designs and Patents Act 1988, s 180(1).
2 Ibid, s 180(2).
3 Ibid, s 180(1).
4 Ibid, s 180(2).
5 Ibid, s 180(3).

61. Qualifying performance

A performance qualifies for protection if it is given by a qualifying individual or takes place in a qualifying country[1]. A qualifying individual is a citizen or subject, or a resident of, a qualifying country[2], and a qualifying country includes the United Kingdom, another member state of the EEC or any state in whose favour an Order in Council is made giving reciprocal protection under the Act, which will include countries which are parties to conventions relating to

43

performers' rights to which the United Kingdom is also a party (such as the Rome Convention for the Protection of Phonograms)[3].

A person who is a party to and has the benefit of an exclusive recording contract to which the performance is subject, or to whom the benefit of such a contract has been assigned, is granted rights provided that person is also a qualifying person[4].

1 Copyright, Designs and Patents Act 1988, s 181.
2 Ibid, s 206 (1).
3 Ibid, s 206 (1). The Performances (Reciprocal Protection) (Convention Countries) Order 1995, SI 1995/2990 designates countries which are party to the Rome Convention as enjoying reciprocal rights under the Copyright, Designs and Patents Act 1988, Pt II.
4 See ibid, ss 180 (1), 185 (2).

PERFORMERS' PROPERTY RIGHTS

62. Performers' property rights generally

The Copyright and Related Rights Regulations came into force on 1 December 1996 and confer on performers a reproduction right, a distribution right and a rental right and lending right. These are all classed as property rights.

The right of reproduction enables performers to authorise or prohibit the making of copies of a recording of the whole or any substantial part of a qualifying performance by a person other than for private and domestic use[1].

By the right of distribution a performer can authorise or prohibit the issue of copies to the public of the whole or any substantial part of the qualifying performance[2]. Issuing copies of a recording to the public includes the act of putting into circulation in the EEA copies not previously in circulation in the EEA by or with consent of the performer or putting into circulation outside the EEA copies not previously put into circulation in the EEA or elsewhere[3]. It does not include subsequent importation of such copies into the UK or another EEA state or any subsequent distribution, sale, hiring or loan of copies previously put into circulation[4].

The rental and lending right gives performers the exclusive right to authorise or prohibit the rental or lending to the public copies of the recording of the whole or any substantial part of a qualifying performance[5]. Rental is defined in the 1996 Regulations as making a copy of a recording available for use on terms that it will or may be returned for direct or indirect economic or commercial advantage[6] and lending means making a copy of a recording available for use, on terms that it will or may be returned otherwise than for direct or indirect economic or commercial advantage through an establishment which is accessible to the public[7].

1 Copyright, Designs and Patent Act 1988, s 182A as amended by the Copyright and Related Rights Regulations 1996.
2 Ibid, s 182B(1) as amended.
3 Ibid, s 182B(2) as amended.
4 Ibid, s 182B(3) as amended.
5 Ibid, s 182C(1) as amended.
6 Ibid, s 182C(2)(a) as amended.
7 Ibid, s 182C(2)(a) as amended.

63. Presumption of transfer

Where an agreement concerning film production is concluded between a performer and a film producer the performer shall be presumed, unless the agreement provides to the contrary, to have transferred to the film producer any rental right in relation to the film arising from the inclusion of a recording of the performance in the film[1]. This provision applies even if the transfer is not in writing and the right to equitable remuneration applies both where there is a presumed transfer and in the case of an actual transfer[2].

1 Copyright, Designs and Patents Act 1988, s 191F(1) as amended by the Copyright and Related Rights Regulations 1996.

2 Ibid, s 191F(2) as amended.

64. Equitable remuneration

Where a commercially published sound recording of the whole or any substantial part of a performance is played in public or is included in a broadcast or cable programme service[1] the performer is entitled to equitable remuneration from the owner of the sound recording. Similarly, where a performer has transferred his or her rental right concerning a sound recording or a film to the producer of the sound recording or film, the performer retains the right to equitable remuneration for the rental[2].

No right to equitable remuneration arises in respect of any rental of a sound recording or film before 1 April 1997 or in respect of any rental after that date of a sound recording or film made in pursuance of an agreement entered into before 1 July 1994 unless the author or performer or a successor in title has before 1 January 1997 notified the person by whom the remuneration would be payable that they intend to exercise that right[3].

Remuneration is not considered inequitable merely because it was paid by way of a single payment or at the time of the transfer of the rental right[4].

The right to equitable remuneration may not be assigned by the performer except to a collecting society for the purpose of enabling it to enforce the right on the performer's behalf[5]. An agreement is of no effect if it purports to exclude or restrict the right to equitable remuneration where the rental right is transferred or to prevent a person questioning the amount of equitable remuneration or to restrict the powers of the Copyright Tribunal[6].

The amount payable by way of equitable remuneration is as agreed by or on behalf of the persons by and to whom it is payable[7]. In default of agreement as to the amount payable by way of equitable remuneration the person by or to whom it is payable may apply to the Copyright Tribunal to determine the amount payable[8]. A person to or by whom equitable remuneration is payable may also apply to the Copyright Tribunal to vary any agreement as to the amount payable or to vary any previous determination of the Tribunal as to that amount[9].

1 Copyright, Designs and Patents Act 1988, s 182 D(I) as substituted by the Copyright and Related Rights Regulations 1996.
2 Ibid, s 191G(1) as substituted.
3 Copyright and Related Rights Regulations 1996, reg, 33.
4 Copyright, Designs and Patents Act 1988, s 191H(4) as amended by the Copyright and Related Rights Regulations 1996.
5 Ibid, s 182D(2), s 191 G (2), as amended.
6 Ibid, s 182D(7), s 191G(5) as amended.
7 Ibid, s 182D(3), s 191G(4) as amended.
8 Ibid, s 182D(4), s 191H(1) as amended.
9 Ibid, s 182D(5), s 191H(2) as amended.

65. Duration of performers' property rights

Performers' property rights subsist for a period of 50 years from the end of the calendar year in which the performance takes place or if during that period a recording of the performance is released 50 years from the end of the calendar year in which it is released[1].

1 Copyright, Designs and Patents Act 1988, s 191 as substituted by the Duration of Copyright and Rights in Performances Regulations 1995.

66. Transmission of performers' property rights

Performers' property rights are transmissible by assignment, by testamentary disposition or by operation of law[1].

An assignment of a performer's property rights is not effective unless it is in writing and signed by or on behalf of the assignor[2]. An exclusive licence must also be in writing and signed by or on behalf of the owner of a performer's property right[3]. A licence granted by the owner of a performer's property rights is binding on every successor in title to any interest in the rights, except a purchaser in good faith for valuable consideration without notice (actual or constructive) of the licence, or a person deriving title from such a purchaser[4].

An assignment or licence may be partial, that is limited so as to apply to one or more, but not all, of the things requiring the consent of the right owner, or to part, but not the whole, of the period for which the rights are to subsist[5]. Thus different persons may be entitled to different aspects of the performer's property rights in relation to a performance[6].

Where under a bequest (whether general or specific) a person is entitled to any material thing containing an original recording of a performance which was not published before the death of the testator, the bequest shall, unless a contrary indication is indicated, be construed as including any performer's rights in relation to the recording to which the testator was entitled immediately before his or her death[7].

1 Copyright, Designs and Patents Act 1988, s 191A(1) and s 191B(1) as amended by the Copyright and Related Rights Regulations 1996.
2 Ibid, s 191B(3) as amended.
3 Ibid, s 191D as amended.
4 Ibid, s 191B(4) as amended.
5 Ibid, s 191B(2) as amended.
6 Ibid, s 191A(3) as amended.
7 Ibid, s 191E as amended.

67. Infringement of performers' property rights

An infringement of a performer's property rights is actionable by the right owner[1]. In an action for infringement relief by way of damages, injunction and/or order for accounts is available to the performer as with the infringement of any other property right[2].

An exclusive licensee has the same rights and remedies in respect of matters occurring after the grant of the licence as if the licence had been an assignment[3]. Where an action for infringement of a performer's property rights relates to an action in respect of which the performer and the exclusive licensee have concurrent rights of action, the right's owner or exclusive licensee may not, without leave of the court, proceed with the action unless the other is joined as a plaintiff or added as defendant[4].

1 The Copyright, Designs and Patents Act 1988, s 191(I) as amended by the Copyright and Related Rights Regulations 1996.
2 Ibid, s 191I(2), as amended.
3 Ibid, s 191L(2), as amended.
4 Ibid, s 191M(1), as amended.

PERFORMERS' NON PROPERTY RIGHTS AND RECORDING RIGHTS

68. Performers' non property rights and recording rights generally

The non property rights of performers and the rights of persons having recording rights are the original rights, under the 1988 Act, to consent to the recording or live transmission of a performance, for the use of such recording and to the importing, possessing or dealing with the recording.

69. Infringement of performers' non property rights

A performer's non property rights are infringed by any person who without the performer's consent:

(a)   makes otherwise than for private and domestic use a recording of the whole or a substantial part of a qualifying performance directly from the live performance, or broadcasts live or includes live in a cable programme service the whole or any substantial part of a qualifying performance, or makes a recording of the whole or any substantial part of the qualifying performance directly from a broadcast of or cable programme including the live performance[1].

(b) shows or plays in public the whole or any substantial part of the qualifying performance, or broadcasts or includes in a cable programme service the whole or any substantial part of a qualifying performance by means of a recording which was and which that person knows or has reason to believe was made without the performer's consent[2].

(c) imports into the United Kingdom, other than for private and domestic use or in the course, of a business, possesses, sells or lets for hire offers or exposes for sale or hire or distributes a recording of a qualifying performance which is and which that person knows or has reason to believe is an illicit recording[3].

1 Copyright, Designs and Patents Act 1988, s 182, as substituted by the Copyright and Related Rights Regulations 1996.
2 Copyright, Designs and Patents Act 1988, s 183.
3 Ibid, s 184.

70. Infringement of recording rights

The rights of a person having recording rights are infringed by any person who without their consent or the consent of the performer:

(a) makes a recording[1] of the whole or any substantial part of the performance, otherwise than for private and domestic use[2];

(b) shows or plays in public, or broadcasts or includes in a cable programme service, the whole or any substantial part of a performance by means of a recording which was, and which that person knows or has reason to believe was, made without the appropriate consent[3];

(c) imports into the United Kingdom otherwise than for private and domestic use, or in the course of a business possesses, sells or lets for hire, offers or exposes for sale or hire, or distributes, a recording of a performance, which is and which that person knows or has reason to believe is, an illicit recording[4].

1 For the meaning of 'recording' see section 90 ante.
2 Copyright, Designs and Patents Act 1988, s 186(1).
3 Ibid, s 187 (1).
4 Ibid, s 188 (1).

71. Consent

The consent of a performer or a person having recording rights may be given in relation to a specific performance, a specified description of performances or performances generally, and may relate to past or future performances[1]. A person having recording rights in a performance is bound by any consent previously given by a person through whom they derive their rights under the exclusive recording contract or licence in question[2].

1 Copyright, Designs and Patents Act 1988 s 193(1) as substituted by the Copyright and Related Rights Regulations 1996. Where a performer's consent cannot be obtained, consent may be given by the Copyright Tribunal; see ibid, s 190.
2 Ibid, s 193 (2).

72. Remedies for infringement of performers' non property rights and of recording rights

Any infringement of the non property rights of a performer or a person having recording rights is actionable as a breach of statutory duty[1]. The court may also make an order for delivery up of illicit recordings[2] and there is a right of seizure of illicit recording[3].

Certain categories of infringement, including the making for sale or hire, importing or dealing in the course of business with an illicit recording, are subject to criminal sanctions[4].

1 Copyright, Designs and Patents Act 1988, s 194.
2 Ibid, s 195.
3 Ibid, s 196.
4 Ibid, s 198.

73. Transmission of performers' non property rights and recording rights

These rights are not assignable or transmissible[1]. However, on the death of a person entitled to performers' rights, the rights pass to such persons as he or she may by testamentary disposition specifically direct, and if, or to the extent, that there is no such direction the rights are exercisable by the personal representatives[2]. These provisions do not apply where the benefit of an exclusive recording contract has been assigned[3].

1 Copyright, Designs and Patents Act 1988, s 192A as amended by the Copyright and Related Rights Regulations 1996.
2 Copyright, Designs and Patents Act 1988, s 192A(1),(2) as amended.
3 Ibid, s 192B(2) as amended.

74. Duration of performers' non property rights

The rights of performers and persons having recording rights subsist for a period of 50 years from the end of the calendar year in which the performance takes place or if during that period a recording of the performance is released 50 years from the end of the calendar year in which it is released[1]. A recording is released when it is first published, played or shown in public, broadcast or included in a cable programme service[2]. Where a performer is not a national of an EEA state, the duration of the rights in the performance is that to which the performer is entitled in the country of which the performer is a national, provided that this period does not exceed 50 years[3].

Prior to 1 January 1996 performers' non-property rights subsisted for 50 years from the end of the calendar year in which the performance took place. Under the new provisions such rights may in some cases have been extended or, if they were protected in another EEA State on 1 July 1995, revived[4].

Extended performance rights are exercisable from 1 January 1996 by the person who was entitled to exercise those rights immediately before that date and revived performance rights are exercisable from 1 January 1996 in the case of rights which expired after the commencement of the Copyright, Designs and Patents Act 1988 by the person who was entitled to exercise those rights immediately before they expired and in the case of revived pre-1988 rights by the performer or the person who would have had recording rights or by their personal representatives[5].

No act done before 1 January 1996 shall be regarded as infringing revived performance rights in a performance[6]. It is not an infringement of revived performance rights to do anything after 1 January 1996 pursuant to arrangements made before 1 January 1995 or to issue to the public after 1 January 1996 a recording of a performance made before 1 July 1995[7].

It is not an infringement of revived performance rights in a performance to do anything after 1 January 1996 in relation to a sound recording or film made before 1 January 1996 or made in pursuance of arrangements made before that date which contains a recording of the performance if the recording of the performance was made before 1 July 1995 or pursuant to arrangements made before 1 July 1995[8].

It is not an infringement of revived performance rights in a performance to do anything after 1 January 1996 when the name and address of the person entitled to authorise the act cannot by reasonable enquiry be ascertained[9].

Where performance rights have been revived and a person wishes to exploit these rights, the consent of a performer shall be treated as having been given subject to the payment of a reasonable remuneration as may be agreed or determined in default of agreement by the Copyright Tribunal[10]. A person intending to use the revised performance rights must give reasonable notice of this intention stating when they intend to begin to do the acts concerned[11]. Once notice is given, consent is deemed to have been given[12] and therefore it is not possible to grant an exclusive license in respect of revived performance rights. If no notice is given, doing the act will infringe the performer's right[13].

1 Copyright, Designs and Patents Act 1988, s 191 as amended by the Duration of Copyright and Rights in Performances Regulations 1995.
2 Ibid, s 191(3), as amended.
3 Ibid, s 191(4), as amended.
4 Duration of Copyright and Rights in Performances Regulations 1995, reg 29.
5 Ibid, reg 31.
6 Ibid, reg 33(1).
7 Ibid, reg 33(2).
8 Ibid, reg 33(3).
9 Ibid, reg 33(4).
10 Ibid, reg 34 and reg 35.
11 Ibid, reg 34(2).
12 Ibid, reg 34(4).
13 Ibid, reg 34(3).

75. Permitted acts

Certain acts may be done in relation to a performance or recording notwithstanding the existence of performers' rights or recording rights; these include fair dealing for the purposes of criticism, review or news reporting, incidental inclusion and things done for instructional, educational purposes or parliamentary and judicial proceedings[1].

1 See the Copyright, Designs and Patents Act 1988, s 189, Sch 2.

I: The Copyright Tribunal and collective licensing

76. The Copyright Tribunal

The Copyright Tribunal was established as the Performing Right Tribunal under the Copyright Act 1956 and was renamed[1] and its jurisdiction extended by the Copyright, Designs and Patents Act 1988. The Act determines the constitution of the Tribunal and proceedings at hearings[2]. Rules as to procedure are set out by statutory instruments[3]. The purpose of the Tribunal is to hear and determine proceedings under the relevant sections of the Copyright, Designs and Patents Act 1988 relating to licensing schemes and bodies; sums payable for lending of certain works, for the use of revived copyright and revived performers' rights and for equitable remuneration; and the use as of right of sound recordings in broadcast of cable programme services. The Tribunal also has powers in reaction to television programme listings[4], and in relation to databases[5].

The Copyright Tribunal has the power to make an order in relation to the payment of the costs of parties to proceedings brought before it[6] and an appeal of a decision may be made to the High Court or Court of Session in Scotland on a point of law[7].

1 Copyright, Designs and Patents Act 1988, s 145(1).
2 Ibid, s 146–148.
3 SI 1989/1129
4 Broadcasting Act 1990, s 17.
5 Copyright and Rights in Databases Regulations 1997, regs 24 and 25.
6 Copyright Designs and Patents Act 1988, s 151.
7 Ibid, s 152.

77. Copyright and database right licensing

A 'licensing scheme' is defined by the Copyright, Designs and Patents Act 1988 as a scheme setting out the classes of case in which the operator of the scheme or the person on whose behalf the operator acts is willing to grant copyright licences and the terms on which these licences would be granted[1]. A 'licensing body' means a society or other organisation which has as its main object or one of its main objects the negotiation or granting of copyright licences as owner or prospective owner or as the agent of the owner[2].

References or applications may be made to the Copyright Tribunal in relation to the terms of a proposed licensing scheme[3] or, while a licensing scheme is in operation, in relation to a dispute between the operator of a scheme and a person claiming they require a licence of a type to which the scheme applies or an organisation claiming to represent such person[4] or in relation to the refusal to grant a licence or failure to do so within a reasonable time or the proposal for such a licence of terms which are unreasonable[5].

References or applications may also be made by a prospective licensee in respect of the terms on which a licensing body proposes to grant a licence[6], by a licensee for the continuation of a licence which is due to expire by effluxion of time or where notice has been given by the licensing body[7] and, within certain time limits, for review of orders made under certain applications[8]. The Act specifies the factors to be taken into account by the Copyright Tribunal when determining what is reasonable on a reference or application[9].

Such applications or referrals may be made with respect to:

(a) copying a work[10];
(b) rental or lending of copies of a work to the public[11];
(c) performing, showing or playing a work in public[12]; and
(d) broadcasting a work or including it in a cable programme service[13].

The Copyright, Designs and Patents Act 1988 contains provisions whch apply specifically to licences granted pursuant to licensing schemes or by licensing bodies in respect of the reprographic copying of published literary, dramatic or artistic works or the typographical arrangement of published editions[14]. In each such licence there is an implied undertaking by the operator of a licensing scheme or the licensing body to indemnify the licensee against any liability incurred by it by reason of it having infringed copyright by making or authorising the making of reprographic copy of a work in circumstances which are within the apparent scope of the licence[15]. Circumstances are within the apparent scope of the licence if it is not apparent from inspection of the licence and the work that it does not fall within the description of works to which the licence applies and if the licence does not expressly provide that it does not extend to copyright of the description infringed[16].

'Liability' includes liability to pay costs and the indemnity extends in relation to costs reasonably incurred by a licensee in connection with actual or contemplated proceedings against it for infringement of copyright as well as to sums which the licensee is liable to pay in respect of such infringement[17]. A scheme or licence in relation to reprographic copying of published literary, dramatic or artistic works or the typographical arrangement of published editions may contain reasonable provision with respect to the manner in which and time within which claims are to be made as well as provision enabling the operator of the licensing scheme or licensing body to take over the conduct of any proceedings affecting the amount of their liability to indemnify[18].

The Copyright, Designs and Patents Act 1988 contains a number of other provisions in relation to licensing schemes and licensing bodies, many of which relate to powers exercisable by the Secretary of State. The Secretary of State has power to extend licensing schemes and licences authorising the making of reprographic copies of published, literary, musical and artistic works or of typographical arrangements of published editions by or on behalf of educational establishments for the purpose of instruction[19]. The copyright owner in any work may apply to the Secretary of State for the variation or dishcarge of an order[20] or to the Copyright Tribunal to appeal against any order[21]. The Secretary of State may further enquire into the need for a new scheme or general licence for the making by educational establishments of reprographic copies of certain works and have the power to recommend the making of new provisions effected by means of Statutory Instrument[22].

The Broadcasting Act 1990[23] inserted into the Copyright, Designs and Patents Act 1988 provision for a statutory right to use sound recordings in broadcasts and cable programme services. The right arises in two specific instances. The first is where a licensing body refuses to grant or procure the grant to a proposed licensee of a licence whose terms allow unlimited needletime or such needletime as the proposed licensee has demanded, the payment terms of which are acceptable to the proposed licencee[24]. The second is where an existing licence limits the amount of needletime and a licensing body refuses to amend the licence to allow unlimited needletime or such amount as has been demanded by the licencee[25].

'Needletime' means the time in any period (whether determined as the number of hours in the period or a proportion of the period or otherwise) in which any recordings may be included in a broadcast or cable programme service[26]. Certain conditions are required to be complied with by a proposed or existing licencee who wishes to exercise the right. Notice must be given to the licensing body of the licencee's intention to exercise the right, requesting the licensing body to propose payment terms[27]. After receiving the proposal or after the expiry of a reasonable period, the licencee must give reasonable notice to the licensing body of the date on which the licensee proposes to begin exercising the right and the terms of payment in accordance with which the licensee intends to do so[28].

Where a proposed or existing licensee includes sound recordings in a broadcast or cable programme service and complies with any reasonable condition required by the relevant licensing body[29], provides it with such information as may reasonably be required in relation to the broadcast or cable service[30] and pays the licensing body or operator of the scheme[31] in accordance with its proposed payment terms[32] or the amount notified to it by the licensee[33] or the amount determined by any order of the Copyright Tribunal[34] the licensee or proposed licensee shall be in the same position as regards infringement of copyright as if it had at all material times been a holder of a licence granted by the owner of the copyright in question[35].

1 Copyright, Designs and Patents Act 1988, s 116(1).
2 Ibid, s 116(2).
3 Ibid, s 118.
4 Ibid, s 119.
5 Ibid, s 121.
6 Ibid, s 125.
7 Ibid, s 126.
8 Ibid, ss 120, 122, 127.
9 Ibid, ss 129–135. In *Working Mens Club and Institute Union v The Performing Right Society* [1992] RPC 227, the Copyright Tribunal held that it had a wide discretion and in this case compared a new tariff imposed by the Performing Right Society with an earlier one.
10 Copyright, Designs and Patents Act 1988, s 117(*a*), s 124(*a*) as substituted by the Copyright and Related Rights Regulations 1996.
11 Ibid, ss 117(b), 124(b).
12 Ibid, ss 117(c), 124(c).
13 Ibid, ss 117(d), 124(d).
14 Copyright, Designs and Patents Act 1988, s 136(1)(a).
15 Ibid, s 136(2).
16 Ibid, s 136(3).
17 Ibid, s 136(4).
18 Ibid, s 136(5).
19 Ibid, s 137.
20 Ibid, s 138.
21 Ibid, s 139.
22 Ibid, s 140.
23 This implemented both European Union Directive 89/552 on Television without Frontiers and certain recommendations of the Monopolies and Mergers Commission following an investigation of licensing practices of Phonographic Performance Limited. See section 80 post.
24 Copyright, Designs and Patents Act 1988, s 135A(2) as inserted by the Broadcasting Act 1990, s 175.
25 Ibid, s 135A(3).
26 Ibid, s 135A(5).
27 Ibid, s 135B(1)(a).
28 Ibid, s 135B(1)(b).
29 Ibid, s 135C(1)(a).
30 Ibid, s 135C(1)(b).
31 Ibid, s 135C(1)(c).
32 Ibid, s 135C(3)(a).
33 Ibid, s 135C(3)(b).
34 Ibid, s 135C(3).
35 Ibid, s 135C(1).

78. Licensing of performers' property rights

The Copyright and Related Rights Regulations 1996 introduced into the Copyright, Designs and Patents Act 1988 provisions giving the Copyright Tribunal jurisdiction over licensing schemes and licensing bodies granting licences in relation to performers' property rights.

A 'licensing scheme' is any scheme setting out the cases in which the operator of the scheme is prepared to grant a licence and the terms on which such licences will be granted[1]. A 'licensing body' means a society or other organisation which has as its main object the negotiating or granting of performers' property right licences whether as owner or prospective owner or agent of the owner of performers' property rights – provided that the objects include the granting of licences concerning the performance of more than one performer[2]. Performances recorded in a single recording or performances recorded in more than one recording where the performers are the same or the recordings are commissioned by a single firm, company or group of companies or their employees are not considered to be performances of more than one performer for the purposes of the legislation[3].

The Copyright Tribunal has jurisdiction in relation to references and applications with respect to licensing schemes operated by licensing bodies in relation to performers' property rights covering the performances of more than one performer so far as they relate to licences for copying and recording of the whole or any substantial part of a qualifying performance or renting or lending copies of the recording to the public[4]. References or applications may be made to the Copyright Tribunal in respect of existing licensing schemes or proposed licensing schemes[5] as well as in relation to any proposed licence or expiring licence[6]. The powers of the Copyright Tribunal in relation to performers' property licences are generally analogous to the powers of the Copyright Tribunal in relation to copyright licensing[7].

1 Copyright, Designs and Patents Act 1988, Sch 2A, para 1(1) as inserted by the Copyright and Related Rights Regulations 1996.
2 Ibid, para 1(2).
3 Ibid, para 1(4).
4 Ibid, para 2.
5 Ibid, paras 3, 4 amd 5.
6 Ibid, paras 10 and 11.
7 See s 77 ante.

79. Collecting societies generally

Collective licensing operates either by the copyright owner assigning their rights to the relevant society which is authorised to grant licences on their behalf and to enforce their rights against infringers, or the society acting as agent of its members for the purpose of granting licences and collecting revenue on their behalf. Some collecting societies offer blanket licence schemes to license certain rights subject to the payment of a fixed fee and the observance of certain terms. Such licence schemes are negotiated with main user organisations and their advantage to users is that no advance consent is needed[1].

Sums collected by collecting societies are divided among their members in accordance with their constitution. Accounting is generally effected on a twice-yearly basis.

1 See section 77 ante.

80. Performing Right Societies and Mechanical Collection Societies

The two largest performing and mechanical rights organisations in the United Kingdom are the Performing Right Society Limited ('PRS') and the Mechanical Copyright Protection Society Limited ('MCPS') now working together as the MCPS and PRS Alliance. Between them they have a membership of approximately 40,000 and an income in 1995 of more than £315 million[1]. The PRS consists of composers, authors and publishers of music and administers public performing rights, broadcasting rights, the right to include the work in a cable programme service and in the case of writers, film synchronisation rights[2]. The PRS does not usually grant licences to performers of copyright music but operates a number of blanket licence schemes with fixed tariffs settled by negotiation with music users associations or the Copyright Tribunal in which the licensee is the proprietor of the premises in which the public performance takes place. MCPS represents composers, authors and arrangers as well as music publishers and grants licences on behalf of members in respect of the recording of music for audio and video recordings, films, television, radio and cable programmes, and television and radio commercials[3]. It operates a number of licences and tariffs including those for videograms, films and television programmes and educational uses[4].

Both the PRS and Phonographic Performance Limited ('PPL') have recently been the subject of investigations and reports by the Monopolies and Mergers Commission. In 1988 the Monopolies and Mergers Commission concluded in relation to PPL that collective licensing bodies are the best available mechanism for licensing sound recordings and made 8 recommendations to restrain PPL from using their monopoly unfairly[5]. Eight years later the Monopolies and Mergers Commission reported on the work of the PRS and concluded that a monopoly situation did exist and that deficiencies existed within the structure of the PRS that operated against the interests of members and users. The report made 44 recommendations for changes within the PRS[6].

As at January 1998 the MCPS and the PRS have entered into a collaboration arrangement as the MCPS and PRS Alliance sharing resources and certain information while remaining independent. This reflects trends in continental Europe where GEMA in Germany, SIAE in Italy and SGAE in Spain all handle royalties for both performing and mechanical rights. In Holland the two separate organisations BUMA and STEMRA plan to merge.

The principal performing right organisations in the USA are the American Society of Composers, Authors and Publishers (ASCAP), the Broadcast Music Inc (BMI) and the Society of European Songwriters, Authors and Composers (SESAC). The Harry Fox Agency administers mechanical rights in the United States of America.

1 PRS and MCPS Annual Reports 1995.
2 See PRS Members' Handbook.
3 See MCPS Membership Pack.
4 Ibid.
5 MMC Report 'Collective Licensing' CM 530 1988.
6 MMC Report 'Performing Rights' CM 3147 1996.

81. Other collecting societies

There are a number of other collecting societies in the United Kingdom covering writers, artists, broadcasters and film and television producers. These include the Copyright Licensing Agency which issues licences to permit the copying of books, journals and periodicals by colleges, government departments, libraries and universities and it has recently introduced a rapid clearance system for issuing photocopying licences to business; the Designs and Artists Copyright Society Limited which licences the use of artistic work and the Education Recording Agency that licences the use of off-air recording of broadcasts and cable programmes to educational establishments. The Authors Licensing and Collecting Society licenses the exploitation of literary and dramatic works created by its members and Phonographic Performance Limited and Videogram Performance Limited authorise the public performance and broadcasting of records and videograms controlled by their members.

One of the most recently established collecting societies is ComPact Collections Limited which is a collective administration organisation for film and television producers and was established in 1996 to administer secondary or ancillary rights in particular the revenue arising from the exercise of cable re-transmission and private copying rights. ComPact is unique among collecting organisations in being a commercial collective administration organisation sponsored by the Producers Alliance for Cinema and Television (PACT) – the trade body representative of the industry whose interests ComPact serves.

82. International collecting societies

The Association de Gestion Internationale Collective des Ouvres Audio-visuelles (Association for the International Collective Management of Audio-visual Works, also known as AGICOA) is an international organisation of film producers and right-holders concerned with protecting their works against piracy and securing royalties from cable re-transmission of such audio-visual works. AGICOA has as members 14 major national producers' associations from 11 countries. It is a non-profit-making organisation which represents collectively the international community of producers and negotiates with cable distribution bodies in many countries, including Belgium, Holland, Luxembourg, Germany, Ireland, France, Sweden and Norway, and in certain other countries, including Austria, Denmark, Finland and Switzerland, claiming remuneration from proper public representative bodies on behalf of its members.

AGICOA co-operates with television broadcasters, local associations of film producers, national societies of composers, authors and artists in negotiating with cable distributors. It supplies cable distributors with the necessary rights for re-transmission of works and collects royalty income and distributes this income to film producers and rights-holders. AGICOA also maintains a computerised databank referred to as The International Register of Titles and Rights in Audio-Visual Works, which contains details of more than 100,000 films deposited by producers from countries all over the world and information relating to the various rights in these audio-visual works. The databank is maintained on a confidential basis and is not open to the public.

J: Copyright and European community law

83. European Community law and copyright

The primary source of law in the European Union is the European Union Treaty (formerly known as the Treaty of Rome and then the European Community Treaty) which was signed by the United Kingdom in 1972. The European Union is committed to achieving a single internal market within which there is free movement of goods and services. The laws of the European Union prevail over the national laws of member states which are required to conform their laws to European Union Directives, Regulations and Decisions.

There are a number of provisions in European Union law to ensure that the market between European Union member states is free from anti-competitive or restrictive practices or abuses, and the European Commission has issued various Directives relating to copyright and other rights. These Directives which bind each member state as to the stated objective but leave them free to choose the method by which the objective is achieved. Copyright law has been further shaped by Decisions of the European Court of Justice.

84. Copyright in Europe generally

Before the European Union Directive on harmonising the term of protection of copyright and certain related rights[1], the majority of states in the European Union had adopted the minimum term for the duration of copyright specified in the Berne Convention[2]. However there were a number of exceptions. Germany protected works of its nationals for 70 years from the death of the author and Spain for 60 years from the death of the author[3]. France granted a general term of 60 years from the death of the author but this was extended to 70 years from the death of the author for musical compositions with or without words. Three member states introduced extensions on the term of copyright to offset the effects of the two World Wars on the exploitation of authors' works. In Belgium the extension was ten years, in Italy the extension was eleven years and in France three separate extensions were provided, being six years in relation to World War I, eight years in relation to World War II and a further period of thirty years for the benefit of descendants of authors killed in action in World War II.

The Berne Convention provides a minimum term of protection of only 25 years for photographs and works of applied art[4]. In most member states works of applied art were protected for the same period as other works and photographs for 25 years. However, Germany, Spain and Italy provide a term of protection for photographs (considered to be artistic works[5]) equal to that of other artistic works.

Provisions for the protection of related rights also varied greatly between EU member states[6] and it was believed that the differences in terms of protection might give rise to barriers to the free movement of goods and services and distortions in competition between member states[7]. Harmonisation of the duration of copyright and related rights became fundamental to the creation of an internal market. Harmonisation could not have the effect of reducing the protection currently held by right holders in the European Union and was therefore established at 70 years after the death of the author for copyright works and 50 years for related rights from first publication, communication to the public, transmission or fixation[8].

1 See section 96 post. *Radio Telefis Eireann v EC Commission* [1991] 4 CMLR 586; *British Broadcasting Corporation v EC Commission* 1991 4 CMLR 669; *Independent Television Publications Ltd v EC Commission* 1991 4 CMLR 745. Cf *Volvo v Veng* 238/87 [1988]ECR 6211, [1989] 4 CMLR 122, ECJ (refusal to grant licences to potential competitors not an abuse of a dominant position in the absence of undesirable conduct such as unfair price maintenance).
2 See section 99 post.
3 Before 1987 the term of copyright in Spain was 80 years and works of authors who died before the Copyright Act 1987 (Spain) came into force continued to benefit from the longer term of protection.
4 This has been amended by the WIPO Copyright Treaty 1996. See section 102 post.
5 Certain member states had also enacted provisions covering matters such as posthumous works, collective works and works published in volumes or parts which were not dealt with in the Berne Convention.
6 See the Commission of the European Communities Proposal for a Council Directive Harmonising the Term of Protection of Copyright and Certain Related Rights COM(92) 33 final 1992.
7 See section 85 post.
8 See section 96 post.

85. Copyright and the internal market of the European Union

The free movement of goods and services, free unrestricted competition and the integration of a single market are key issues in the European Union and are protected by Articles 30–36, 59–66 and Articles 85 and 86, of the European Union Treaty[1]. While the European Union Treaty established a common market in Europe, it paid no specific attention to intellectual property rights. Copyright law remained of a national character and owners of copyright and other rights continued to be protected by the laws in individual European Union member states.

This led to a number of cases coming before the European Court of Justice where, either conflict had arisen between the exercise of intellectual property rights controlled by the owner or licensee and the free movement of goods manufactured by the owner or licensee in a neighbouring territory[2] or differing treatment of copyright in individual European Union member states had resulted in the fragmentation of the single market[3].

As a result the European Union has developed the doctrine of 'exhaustion' of rights to ensure the free movement of goods within the internal market[4] and has embarked upon a programme of harmonising copyright to protect rights, provide unrestricted competition and ensure free movement of goods and services within the single market[5].

Agreement was also reached in October 1991 between the European Union and the European Free Trade Association ('EFTA') to form a European Economic Area. The aim of the European Economic Area is to extend the European single market principles to EFTA countries and as a result the concept of the European Economic Area appears in United Kingdom copyright legislation of 1995 and 1996[6].

1 European Communities Act 1972.
2 See section 86 post.
3 See section 87 post.
4 See section 86 post.
5 See section 96 post.
6 See sections 9 to 14 ante.

86. Exhaustion of rights and parallel imports

Article 30 of the European Union Treaty provides that 'quantitative restrictions on imports and all measures having equivalent effect shall ... be prohibited between Member States'. Article 36 provides the circumstances when restrictions on imports, exports or goods in transit may be justified and includes for the protection of industrial or commercial property. Copyright and related rights fall within the ambit of Articles 30-36 as the European Court of Justice has taken the view that commercial exploitation of copyright raises the same issues as any other industrial or commercial property[1].

However, the European Court of Justice has decided that once goods have been put on the market in any European Union country by or with the consent of the copyright owner or licensor then any copyright restricting the distribution or circulation of those goods is 'exhausted' and intellectual property rights cannot be used to stop the article being re-sold elsewhere in the European Economic Area or prevent parallel importation. The copyright owner is free to choose the member state in which to put the work into circulation and cannot invoke their rights in another jurisdiction in the European Union to impede free movement of goods.

The European Court of Justice has stated that if the owner of intellectual property rights could rely on an exclusive right to exclude goods marketed elsewhere in the European Union this would legitimise the isolation of national markets[2]. Copyright does not permit right holders to claim the difference between the royalty payable in an importing country and that payable in an exporting country[3]. However, copyright holders can claim a higher royalty in a public performance of a recording within an importing state[4].

The doctrine of exhaustion of rights does have certain limitations. A distinction has been observed by the European Court of Justice between, on the one hand the treatment of literary and artistic works where copies are sold in the form of physical objects and on the other hand exclusive distribution rights in respect of film and broadcasting[5]. Rights are not exhausted if goods in which the copyright subsists have been put on the market outside the European Union with the consent of the right holder and are subsequently imported into the European Union[6].

If the release of goods in the market occurred without the consent of the right holder because the right has expired in the exporting state but not the importing state[7] or because the state concerned does not protect that particular right then the right is not exhausted[8].

1 *Musik-Vertrieb Membran v GEMA* [1981] 2 CMLR 44.
2 Ibid. See also *Deutsche Grammophon GmbH V Metro – SB Grossmärkte* [1971] ECR 487, [1971] CMLR 631.
3 *Musik-Vertrieb Membran v GEMA* [1981] 2 CMLR 44.
4 *Basset v Sacem* [1987] 3 CMLR 173.
5 *Coditel SA v Cine Vog Films* [1981] 2 CMLR 362.
6 *Polydor v Harlequin Record Shops* [1982] ECR 329, [1982] 1 CMLR 677.
7 *EMI Electrola GmbH v Patricia Im-und Export VGmbH* [1989] FFR 544, [1989] 2 CMLR 413.
8 *Warner Bros Inc v Christiansen* [1990] 3 CMLR 684.

87. Equal treatment of European Union nationals

In 1992, the European Court of Justice over-rode national law to prevent discrimination against a national of another member state of the European Union. Phil Collins had brought proceedings in Germany to prevent the distribution of an unauthorised recording of a live performance he gave in California. German law granted rights in such circumstances to German performers and to nationals of other European Union member states if the perform-ance took place in Germany. Accordingly Phil Collins was given no protection under German law.

The European Court of Justice ruled that this conflicted with the non-discrimination principle of Article 6 of the European Union Treaty and therefore German law could not refuse to grant relief to non-nationals[1]. This case had far reaching implications for the harmonisation of the duration of copyright in the European Union[2].

1 *Phil Collins v Imtrat H GmbH* [1993] 3 CMLR 773, [1994] FSR 166.
2 See section 11 ante.

88. Prevention, restriction or distortion of competition

European Union competition law affects both the licensing of works in which copyright subsists and the distribution of goods manufactured by or with the consent of a copyright owner or its licensee[1].

Article 85(1) of the European Union Treaty prohibits as incompatible with the common market all agreements between undertakings, decisions by associations of undertakings and concerted practices which may affect trade between member states and which have as their object or effect the prevention, restriction or distortion of competition. Examples of prohibited practices include but are not limited to:

(a)   directly or indirectly fixing purchase or selling prices or any other trading conditions;

(b)   limiting or controlling production markets, technical developments or investment;

(c)   sharing markets or sources of supply;

(d)   applying dissimilar conditions to equivalent transactions with other trading parties, thereby placing them at a competitive disadvantage;

(e)   making the conclusion of contracts subject to acceptance by other parties of supplementary obligations which, by their nature or according to commercial usage, have no connection with the subject of such contracts.

By virtue of Article 85(2) any agreements prohibited by the terms of Article 85(1) are automatically void.

There are three ways in which such an agreement may avoid breaching Article 85(1). The first is where the agreement is of minor importance, that is where the goods or services which are the subject of the agreement do not represent more than 5% of the total market for such goods or services and the aggregate annual turnover of the participating undertakings does not exceed 300 million ECU[2].

Second, it may be possible to claim individual exemption under Article 85(3) where the agreement or decision or practice contributes to improving the production or distribution of goods or contributes to promoting technical or economic progress or allows consumers a fair share of the resulting benefit; provided that the agreement decision or practice imposes only those restrictions which are indispensable to the attainment of these objectives and does not afford the possibility of eliminating competition in respect of a substantial part of the products in question.

Third, the European Commission has introduced certain 'block exemptions'. These include exclusive distribution agreements, exclusive purchasing agreements, parallel licence agreements and know-how agreements[3]. The Regulations identify the benefits that can result from the kind of agreement in question and list the criteria such agreements must meet. Any attempt to partition the common market by way of exclusive distributorship agreements will be contrary to Article 85(1)[4].

1   United Kingdom competition law is also relevant, ie the Restrictive Trade Practices Act 1976, the Competition Act 1980 and the Fair Trading Act 1973.

2   Notice of agreements of minor importance OJ 1986 C 231/2.

3   Regulations 1983/83 and 1984/84.

4   *Time-Limit SA v SABAM* [1979] 2 CMLR 578. Also *Valley Printing Company Ltd V BBC Bull Eur Com No 2* (1979) page 26.

89. Copyright and European Union competition law

The European Court of Justice has been required to consider whether the owner of copyright in a film was entitled to grant an exclusive licence to exhibit the film and whether that licence would infringe Article 85 (1)[1]. The Court stated that 'the mere fact that the owner of copyright in a film has granted to a sole licensee the exclusive rights to exhibit that film in the territory of a member state and, consequently, to prohibit during a specified period its showing by others, is not sufficient to justify the finding that such a contract must be regarded as the purpose, the means or the result of an agreement, decision or concerted practice prohibited by the Treaty'.

The Court decided that the characteristics of the film industry and the European Community market meant that a licence for exclusive exhibition is not in itself likely to prevent, restrict or distort competition. The Court did, however, recognise that 'although copyright in a film and the rights deriving from it, namely that of exhibiting the film, are not, therefore, as such, subject to the prohibitions contained in Article 85, the exercise of those rights may nonetheless come within the said prohibitions where there are economic or legal circumstances the effect of which is to restrict film distribution to an appreciable degree or to distort competition in the cinematograph market, regard being had to the specific characteristics of that market'[2]. It would appear that the provisions of Article 85 (1) might also apply if there was some unreasonable exploitation of the rights licensed[3].

In a case relating to patents the European Court of Justice concluded that an open licence would not fall foul of Article 85(1) but a licence giving the licensee an undertaking of absolute territorial protection from competition through parallel imports would[4].

Collective ownership or administration of intellectual property rights may in certain circumstances be anti-competitive. However, where collecting societies provide the least restrictive way of administering rights, by reason of the fact that an individual right holder would be unable to negotiate licences or monitor the use of copyright, then the vesting of rights in a collecting society will not infringe Article 85[5].

1 *Coditel SA v Cin J Vog Films* [1981] 2 CMLR 362.
2 Ibid.
3 See Green *Commercial Agreements and Competition Law; Practice and Procedure in the UK and the EEC* (1986) p 714 et seq; Bellamy and Child *The Common Market Law of Competition* (3rd Edn, 1987) p 386.
4 *Nungesser v EC Commission* [1982] ECR 2015, [1983] 1 CMLR 278.
5 *Ministère Public v Tournier and Verney* (1989) Times, 29 September.

90. Abuse of a dominant position

Article 86 of the European Union Treaty prohibits the abuse by one or more undertakings of a dominant position within the European Union or a substantial part of it that may affect trade between member states. Identifying the relevant market is of central importance to any proceedings brought under this article and an undertaking with a relatively small market share in the relevant market could be regarded as dominant if it holds key intellectual property or other rights. Examples of abuse prohibited under Article 86 include:

(a) imposition of unfair practices or trading conditions;
(b) limiting production, markets or technical developments to the prejudice of consumers;
(c) discriminating against different parties;
(d) including terms in contracts which are collateral to the subject.

As with cases brought under Article 85, the European Court of Justice has taken the view that the existence of exclusive property rights and the degree of monopoly conferred on the owner of such rights is not anti-competitive, but the manner in which these rights are exercised may distort competition and be an abuse of a dominant position. This position was repeated where copyright holders of television listings[1] refused to supply details of basic information on programmes to a new market entrant who wished to publish a weekly television guide. They were found to have exercised their right to reproduce protected work in ways contrary to Article 86, by preventing the emergence onto the market of a new product for which there was clearly a demand which was likely to compete with their own product[2].

All collecting societies may be in a dominant position in relation to the ownership and exploitation of copyright in the European Union and care must be taken to ensure there is no abuse of any such position contrary to Article 86 by, for example, refusing to issue licences or adopting discriminatory terms in licences[3].

1 *Radio Telefis Eireann (RTE) and Independent Television Publications (ITP) v Commission* 6 April 1995.
2 Ibid.
3 See section 79 ante.

K: European media-related Directives

91. Media-related Directives generally

The Commission of the European Union undertook a major review of copyright law in member states in 1988 with a view to tackling issues that have implications for the creation of an internal market. The Commission published a consultative document recommending six areas of legislation: piracy for commercial purposes; unauthorised reproduction of audio material in the home; introduction of provisions on distribution rights and rental rights; the legal protection of computer programs; databases and the role of the Community in multi-lateral and bilateral external relations[1]. Following consultations a further paper was issued setting out a working programme on copyright and neighbouring rights which emphasised that the protection of copyright must be strengthened and that the approach should be a comprehensive one. Since 1992 a number of Directives have been adopted in relation to copyright[2].

In 1995 the Commission of the European Communities published a further Green Paper entitled 'Copyright and Further Rights in the Information Society'[3]. The Commission looked at whether existing harmonisation of copyright is sufficient to protect the rights of copyright holders given the development of the new information infrastructure and the creation of new services and products which will enable digitally perfect reproduction and dissemination of protected works.

Areas where the Commission urged review are:

(a)   a right of reproduction to control copying in a digital environment;
(b)   the definition of communication to the public;
(c)   a right of digital transmission and dissemination;
(d)   a digital broadcasting right; and
(e)   whether present moral rights and their present lack of harmonisation are adequate in the new digital environment. The Green Paper further explores the rationalisation of the management of rights and new ways of identifying works through digitalisation. Substantial comments have been made on the Green Paper covering the need to look at the problem in a broader perspective both globally and economically; the role of basic human rights regarding privacy protection and freedom of expression; ownership of rights and the convergence of rights within a multimedia environment[4].

1 Commission of the European Communities Green Paper on Copyright and the Challenge of Technology Com (88) 172 final.
2 See sections 93 to 98 post.
3 Commission of the European Communities Green Paper on Copyright and Related Rights in the Information Society Com (95) 382 final.
4 Commission of the European Communities follow-up to the Green Paper on Copyright and Related Rights in the Information Society Com (96) 568 final.

92. Directive 89/552 on television without frontiers

The objective of this Directive is to eliminate the barriers which divide Europe, with a view to permitting and assuring the transition from national programme markets to a common programme production and distribution market. All member states are to abolish restrictions

60

relating to television broadcasting in cable operations which may impede the free movement of broadcasts within the European Union and distort competition[1].

All broadcasts are to comply with the law of the country from which they originate to ensure the free movement of broadcasts within the European Union without secondary control[2]. Member states are free to specify detailed criteria relating to language etc[3] and to lay down different conditions regarding the insertion of advertising in programmes[4].

Strict criteria are laid down in relation to advertising and sponsorship of the financing of television programmes and recommendations made for the inclusion of European works[5]. The Directive makes further provision for the broadcasting of cinematographic works and for measures to be taken in member states regarding the showing of programmes suitable for minors and providing a right to reply[6].

The provisions of the Directive have been implemented in the Broadcasting Act 1990 and the Copyright, Designs and Patents Act 1988[7].

1 Council Directive 89/552 EEC on the co-ordination of certain provisions laid down by law, regulation or administrative action in member states concerning the pursuit of television broadcasting authorities; Art 2.
2 Ibid.
3 Ibid, Art 8.
4 Ibid, Arts 10–21.
5 Ibid.
6 Ibid, Arts 22, 23.
7 Copyright, Designs and Patents Act 1988, as amended by the Broadcasting Act 1990, ss 135A to G. See aslo section 77 ante.

93. Directive 92/100 on rental rights

This Directive makes provision for a right for authors, performers, phonographic producers and film producers to authorise or prohibit the rental or lending of their work[1]. Rental and lending rights may be transferred or assigned or subject to the granting of a contractual licence and transfer is presumed in a contract between a performer and film producer.

Authors or performers are to receive equitable remuneration for their rental rights and this cannot be waived or transferred other than to a collecting society[2]. Provision is also made for equitable remuneration in relation to broadcasting and communication to the public of works of performers and other rights owners[3].

Member states are required to provide fixation rights for performers and broadcast organisations[4] and a reproduction right[5] and a distribution right for performers, phonographic producers, film producers and broadcasting organisations[6].

The Directive was implemented in the United Kingdom by the Copyright and Related Rights Regulations 1996 which came into effect on 1 December 1996.

1 Council Directive 92/100 EEC on rental rights and lending rights and on certain rights related to copyright in the field of intellectual property; Art 2.
2 Ibid, Art 4.
3 Ibid, Art 8(2).
4 Ibid, Art 6.
5 Ibid, Art 7.
6 Ibid, Art 9.

94. Directive 91/250 on computer programs

Introduced because computer programs were not clearly protected in all member states, the Directive provides that all computer programs are to be protected under copyright law as literary works[1]. 'Computer program' includes programs incorporated into hardware as well as software and preparatory design work. Protection does not extend to the ideas and principles which underlie any element of a computer program[2].

The Directive establishes precisely which restricted acts copyright owners are able to authorise or prohibit – including the rental of computer programs[3] – and certain types of activity which would normally amount to the infringement of copyright may be performed without authorisation, including loading and running programs, and the decompilation of programs to obtain information necessary to achieve interoperability with other programs[4].

The Directive was implemented in the United Kingdom by the Copyright (Computer Programs) Regulations 1992, SI 1992/3233 which came into effect on 1 January 1993.

1 Council Directive 91/250 EEC on the legal protection of computer programs, Art 1(1).
2 Ibid, Art 1(2).
3 Ibid, Art 4.
4 Ibid, Arts 5,6.

95. Directive 93/83 on satellite transmission and cable retransmission

Aimed at harmonising European Union law in relation to works which are the subject of cross-border satellite broadcasting and cable re-transmission, the Directive defines when the act of communication to the public by satellite takes place in relation to a programme. This is when the programme-carrying signals are introduced under the control or responsibility of the broadcasting organisation into an uninterrupted chain of communication leading to the satellite and down towards the earth[1]. The Directive also provides an exclusive right for authors to authorise communication to the public by satellite of copyright works[2]. This right may only be exercised through a collecting society.

The Directive was implemented in the UK by the Copyright and Related Rights Regulations 1996 which came into effect on 1 December 1996.

1 Council Directive 93/83 EEC on the coordination of certain rules concerning copyright and rights related to copyright applicable to satellite broadcasting and cable retransmission, Art 1(2)(b)
2 Ibid, Art 2.

96. Directive 93/98 on the term of protection of copyright

This Directive harmonised the term of copyright throughout the European Union at 70 years after the death of the author in the case of a film[1] and for related rights at 50 years from the event which starts the term (first publication, communication to the public, transmission or fixation[2]). The Directive applies to all works protected in at least one Member State at 1 July 1995[3].

Where a right holder is not a European Union national but qualifies for protection under an international copyright convention, the Directive provides that the term of protection is to be that granted in the country of origin of the work, provided it does not exceed the term in European Union States[4] as established by the Directive.

The Directive was implemented by the Duration of Copyright and Rights in Performances Regulations 1995 which came into effect on 1 January 1996.

1 Council Directive 93/98 EEC harmonising the term of protection of copyright and certain related rights, Arts 1, 2.
2 Ibid, Art 3.
3 Ibid, Art 10(2).
4 Ibid, Art 7(2).

97. Directive 96/9 on the legal protection of databases

This is the most recent media-related Directive to emanate from Europe and provides for the copyright protection of those databases which, by reason of the selection or arrangement of their contents, constitute their author's own intellectual creation[1]. A 'database' is a collection of independent works, data or other materials arranged in a systematic or methodical way and individually accessible by electronic or other means, and protection extends only to the creation of the database, not its content nor the computer program used in its construction or operation[2].

Copyright provides the author with the exclusive right to reproduce in whole or in part; to translate, adapt, arrange or alter the database; to distribute copies to the public; and to communicate display or perform to the public[3]. Any acts necessary by a lawful user for accessing the contents or using the database are not restricted by copyright[4].

The Directive further provides for a '*sui generis*' right – that is a right for the maker of the database where there has been substantial investment in the obtaining, verification or presentation of the contents to prevent extraction or reutilisation of the whole or a substantial part of it[5]. The term of protection for this '*sui generis*' right runs for 15 years from 1 January of the year following the date of completion of the making of the database or, if made available to the public during this time, 15 years from 1 January of the year following the date when the database was first made available[6].

The Directive was implemented by the Copyright and Rights in Databases Regulations 1997 which came into effect on 1 January 1998.

1 Council Directive 96/9/EC on the legal protection of databases, Art 3(1).
2 Ibid, Art 1.
3 Ibid, Art 5.
4 Ibid, Art 6(1).
5 Ibid, Art 7.
6 Ibid, Art 10.

L: International copyright law

98. International copyright conventions generally

The subsistence of copyright is governed by the laws of individual countries. Where a country is a signatory to an international copyright convention[1] (and most countries in the world are signatories to at least one such convention) the convention requires the country to apply certain minimum standards of copyright protection to works originating from other signatory countries. International copyright conventions determine the copyright protection not only of foreign works in the United Kingdom but also the protection of British works overseas. Together with legislation from the European Union[2] the conventions – most notably the Berne Convention for the Protection of Literary and Artistic Work and the Universal Copyright Convention – shape national and international legislation.

Copyright and the entertainment industries play an increasingly important role in world trade and two world organisations, the World Intellectual Property Organisation ('WIPO') and the World Trade Organisation ('WTO') have been specifically charged with developing and harmonising international copyright relations[3].

WIPO was established in 1967 as a specialist agency of the United Nations and is responsible both for the administration of the Berne Convention[4] and developing future policy. The WTO administers the trade-related aspects of the intellectual property rights agreement concluded during the Uruguay round of the negotiations in relation to the international General Agreement on Trades and Tariffs. It also assists in the administration of other international copyright conventions. In 1989 a Committee of Experts was appointed by the Assembly and Conference of Representatives of the Berne Union to examine amending the Berne Convention to take into account technological and other developments since 1971.

A conference was held in Geneva in December 1996 which settled the final form of the WIPO Copyright Treaty[5] and the WIPO Performances and Phonograms Treaty[6]. Each treaty is open for signature by any member state of WIPO and by the European Union, which for the first time will become a party to an international copyright convention in its own right. Each treaty will enter into force three months after 30 instruments of ratification or accession have been deposited with the Director General of WIPO.

1 See sections 99 to 102 post.
2 See sections 91 to 97 ante.
3 See sections 102 and 103 post.
4 See section 99 post.
5 See section 102 post.
6 See section 103 post.

99. Berne Convention for the Protection of Literary and Artistic Works 1886–1971

Originally signed on 9 November 1886, and most recently revised by the Paris Act of 1971[1], the Berne Convention is the principal international copyright convention. It lays down a minimum degree of copyright protection in all countries which are a party to it and establishes the principle of national treatment for works protected by copyright to avoid discrimination based on national origin.

64

Authors of works which are protected under the laws of one Berne Convention country enjoy in other foreign countries the rights which the laws of those other countries grant to their own nationals[2]. Conversely, foreign authors enjoy the same rights in any other Berne Convention country as that other country's own national authors[3]. The minimum term of protection specified by the Berne Convention is the life of the author plus 50 years[4]. It was left to individual countries to determine the term of protection for photographs provided it was at least 25 years[5]. Countries may grant a term of protection in excess of that provided by the Berne Convention.

Accession to the Berne Convention has retrospective effect so that works which are in the public domain in a country which is not a signatory to the Berne Convention will fall into copyright in that country when it accedes to the Berne Convention if they are still in copyright in their country of origin at the time of accession[6]. The Berne Convention requires its signatory states to provide for moral rights of authors[7] and further lays down that the exercise of rights under the Berne Convention is not subject to any registration formalities[8].

All member states of the European Union and European Free Trade Association are signatories to the Convention.

1 Membership of the Berne Convention as at January 1997 was 119 states.
2 Berne Convention for the Protection of Literary and Artistic Work, Art 5(1) although the term of protection must not be greater than that granted in the country of origin unless expressly provided for by legislation, Art 7(8).
3 Ibid, Art 5(3).
4 Ibid, Art 7(1).
5 See section 102 post.
6 Ibid, Art 18.
7 Ibid, Art 6 bis.
8 Ibid, Art 5(2).

100. Universal Copyright Convention 1952–1971 ('UCC')

The level of protection accorded to copyright works by the Berne Convention has always been relatively high and accordingly its membership has until recently been somewhat limited. Designed to bring the USA, (before it joined the Berne Convention in 1989), the former Union of Soviet Socialist Republics and other states into the international copyright community but without undermining the Berne Convention, the UCC provided for a lower minimum degree of protection[1]. As with the Berne Convention, each signatory state is required to accord to nationals of other signatory states the same level of copyright protection as for its own nationals[2].

The UCC does not provide for moral rights and, unlike the Berne Convention, it permits signatory states to make copyright protection conditional on the compliance with formalities under their own domestic law[3]. These formalities are deemed complied with for the initial period of copyright protection if a notice in the following form is affixed to all copies of copyright work from the time of their first publication:

© Copyright [name of author] [year of publication][4].

Where domestic law of a signatory state of the UCC provides that a subsequent period of copyright protection is dependent on renewal of copyright or some other procedure, these domestic formalities must be complied with to ensure protection[5]. Where a country is a signatory to both the Berne Convention and the UCC, the requirement in the UCC to observe domestic formalities may effectively be disregarded, because registration formalities are prohibited by the Berne Convention[6].

1 To safeguard the Berne Convention and ensure members would not renounce Berne in favour of the lower standards of the UCC, the UCC provided that works originating in a country that withdraws from Berne would not be protected under the UCC. The Universal Copyright Convention Art XVII. Membership of the Universal Copyright Convention comprised 95 States as at January 1997.
2 Ibid, Art II(1).
3 Ibid, Art III(1).
4 Ibid.
5 Ibid, Art III.
6 See note 8, section 99 ante.

101. International Convention for the Protection of Performers, Producers of Phonograms and Broadcasting Organisations 1961 ('Rome Convention')

The Rome Convention is also based on the principle of national treatment[1] and provides certain minimum standards of protection[2]. The term of protection is 20 years from the end of the year the fixation of a sound recording (or 'phonogram') was made or from the end of the year in which the performance or broadcast took place[3]. As with the UCC, copyright protection in contracting states depends on compliance with domestic formalities[4]. For published phonograms formalities are deemed to have been complied with if a notice consisting of

℗ [name of copyright owner] [year of publication]

is placed on all copies of the phonogram. If copies or their containers do not identify the producer or the producer's licensee then the notice must also include the name of the owner of the producer's rights[5].

Other international conventions include the Convention for the Protection of Producers of Phonograms against Unauthorised Duplication of their Phonograms, the Convention Relating to the Distribution of Programme Carrying Signals Transmitted by Satellite and the European Agreement on the Protection of Television Broadcasts. The most recent copyright treaties to be passed are the WIPO Copyright Treaty[6] and the WIPO Performances and Phonograms Treaty.[7]

1 International Convention for the Protection of Performers, Producers of Phonograms and Broadcasting Organisations, Arts 4–6. For information on national treatment see sections 99 and 100 ante.
2 Ibid, Art 7, 10, 12, 13.
3 Ibid, Art 14.
4 Ibid, Art 11.
5 Ibid.
6 See section 102 post.
7 See section 103 post.

102. WIPO[1] Copyright Treaty 1996

The objective of the Treaty is to supplement and update the international regime of protection for literary and artistic works in light of new economic, social, cultural and technological developments[2] and is based primarily on the Berne Convention but also on the Agreement on Trade-Related Aspects of Intellectual Property Rights Including Trade in Counterfeit Goods[3]. Its effect on international law is, in some cases, limited since the Copyright Treaty specifies a degree of protection already provided in many countries.

The Treaty states that copyright protection extends to expressions and not to ideas[4], procedures, methods of operation or mathematical concepts[5]. It clarifies the long-established proposition that computer programs are to be protected as literary works within the meaning of Article 2 of the Berne Convention[6] and compilations of data or other material which by reason of the selection or arrangement of their contents constitute intellectual creations are protected as such compilations whose protection is separate and distinct from any copyright which may subsist in the data or material contained in the compilation[7].

The Treaty requires states implementing it to provide that authors of literary and artistic works enjoy a right of distribution of their work through sale or other transfer of ownership[8] and the right to authorise any communication of their work to the public by wire or wireless means, including the making available to the public of their work in such a way that members of the public may access these works from a place and at a time individually chosen by them[9].

Under the Treaty authors of computer programs, cinematographic works and works embodied in phonograms enjoy a rental right, although this does not apply where the computer program is not the essential object of rental, and only applies in the case of cinematographic work where commercial rental has led to widespread copying of such work materially impairing the exclusive right of reproduction[10].

The Treaty requires states acceding to it to provide that the minimum term of protection of photographic works under the Berne Convention of 25 years[11] is extended to the life of the author plus 50 years[12].

1 See section 98 ante.
2 WIPO Copyright Treaty Preamble.
3 See section 98 ante.
4 This simple proposition is clarified in Laddie, Prescott and Vitoria *The Modern Law of Copyright and Designs* (Butterworths, 1995) pp 61–62 who argue that ideas, thoughts or information are undoubtedly protected under copyright law.
5 Ibid, Art 2.
6 Ibid, Art 4.
7 Ibid, Art 5.
8 Ibid, Art 6.
9 Ibid, Art 8.
10 Ibid, Art 7.
11 See section 3 ante.
12 WIPO Copyright Treaty, Art 9.

103. WIPO[1] Performances and Phonograms Treaty 1996

The objective of this Treaty is to maintain the protection of the rights of performers and producers of phonograms in as effective and uniform a way as possible and the treaty is designed to introduce new international rules and clarify the interpretation of existing rules in the light of new economic, social, cultural and technological developments[2]. As with the WIPO Copyright Treaty its effect on in international law is, in some cases, limited since the treaty specifies a degree of protection already provided in many countries.

The rights of performers and producers of phonograms will be extended in those countries that become signatories to the Treaty. Performers are defined as actors, singers, musicians, dancers and other persons who act, sing, deliver, declaim, play in, interpret or otherwise perform literary or artistic works or expressions of folklore[3]. Phonograms are fixations of the sounds of a performance or of other sounds or of a representation of sounds other than in the form of a fixation incorporated in a cinematographic or other audio-visual work[4].

The Treaty requires states acceding to it to provide that performers are accorded the right to be identified as performers of live performances or performances fixed in phonograms, except where omission is dictated by the manner of the use of the performance and the right to object to any distortion, mutilation or other modification of such performance that would be prejudicial to the performer's reputation[5].

States implementing the Treaty are required also to provide that performers will enjoy the economic right to authorise the broadcasting and communication to the public of unfixed performances and the fixation of their unfixed performances[6]. In relation to performances fixed in phonograms under the Treaty, performers are also to have the right to authorise their direct or indirect reproduction[7], their distribution to the public through sale or other transfer of ownership[8], the commercial rental[9] and the right to authorise the making available to the public of such performances by wire or wireless means in such a way that members of the public may access them from a place and at a time individually chosen by them[10].

Under the Treaty producers of phonograms are to be accorded reproduction rights[11], distribution rights[12], rental rights[13] and the right to authorise the making available to the public of their phonograms by wire or wireless means[14].

Both performers and producers of phonograms are to enjoy the right to a single equitable remuneration for the direct or indirect use of phonograms published for commercial purposes for broadcasting or for any communication to the public[15].

Protection under the Treaty is to be based on the principle of national treatment[16] and the term of protection to be granted to performers under the Treaty is a period of 50 years from the end of the year in which the performance was fixed in a phonogram[17] and for producers of phonograms protection is to last until the end of 50 years from the end of the year in which the phonogram was published or failing such publication within this time 50 years from the end of the year in which the fixation was made[18].

1 See section 2 ante.
2 WIPO Performances and Phonograms Treaty Preamble.
3 Ibid, Art 2 (a).
4 Ibid, Art 2 (b).
5 Ibid, Art 5.

6 Ibid, Art 6.
7 Ibid, Art 7.
8 Ibid, Art 8.
9 Ibid, Art 9.
10 Ibid, Art 10.
11 Ibid, Art 11.
12 Ibid, Art 12.
13 Ibid, Art 13.
14 Ibid, Art 14.
15 Ibid, Art 15 (1).
16 Ibid, Art 4.
17 Ibid, Art 17 (1).
18 Ibid, Art 17 (2).

104. Copyright in the United States of America generally

Pursuant to the provisions of the Berne Convention Implementation Act 1988 (USA), which came into force in the United States of America on 1 March 1989, the United States of America implemented certain obligations required pursuant to the Berne Convention, notably, removing the requirement to register copyright works pursuant to the Copyright Act 1976 (USA), and removing also the requirement that a copyright notice substantially in the form of that required under the Universal Copyright Convention should be displayed on all copies of the work from first publication in order to secure protection in the USA.

The Berne Convention Implementation Act does not, however, amend the period of copyright protection accorded under US law and expressly provides that US domestic law prevails over the Berne Convention and that no rights enjoyed pursuant to the Berne Convention are capable of being enforced in the USA. The Act does not make provision for moral rights[1], expressly excludes any retrospective effect of the implementation of the Berne Convention and prevents any work that is in the public domain in the United States of America from re-qualifying for copyright protection[2]. The United States of America has, however, recently introduced legislation that has the effect of making copyright protection retrospective if certain formalities are complied with[3].

The relevant legislation in the USA for the purposes of determining whether a work is eligible or not for copyright protection consists of the Copyright Act 1909 (USA) and the Copyright Act 1976 (USA) (which came into effect on 1 January 1978). Pursuant to the Act of 1909 an initial period of copyright protection of 28 years applied[4]. This initial period of protection was subject to the registration of the work in the United States Copyright Registry and the inclusion on all published copies of the work of a notice similar in form to that specified in the Universal Copyright Convention[5].

The initial period was capable of extension by a further 28 year period if a notice of renewal of copyright was filed in the US Copyright Registry prior to termination of the initial period[6]. The 56 year term created by the 28 year initial term and the renewal term was extended by a number of interim provisions in the 1960s which were enacted in the Copyright Act of 1976 thus providing for a further 19 year extension period which automatically applies to all works the copyright of which was renewed in the USA in the appropriate manner, giving a copyright protection period of 28 years plus 47 years (making 75 years in total).

The provisions of the Copyright Act of 1976 apply to works made or published after 1 January 1978 and provide for a term of copyright protection, in general, of the author's life and 50 years after his/her death, and, in respect of anonymous works and 'works made for hire'[7], of 75 years from the year of first publication or 100 years from the year of creation, whichever expires first[8].

1 Under the Visual Artists Representation Act 1990 (USA) limited moral rights are accorded visual artists.
2 Berne Convention Implementation Act 1988 (USA), s 12.
3 See section 105 post.
4 Copyright Act 1909 (USA), s 24.
5 Ibid, ss 10, 19.
6 Ibid, s 28.
7 See section 26 post.
8 Copyright Act 1976 (USA), s 302 (a), (c).

105. Restoration of copyright in the United States of America ('USA')

In December 1994, the USA passed its most widespread legislation in respect of copyright, implementing the GATT Agreement on Trade-Related Aspects of Intellectual Property Rights[1]. The most significant change introduced by the Uruguay Round Agreements Act 1994 is the restoration of copyright in works that have fallen into the 'public domain'[2] (ie they become unprotected by copyright).

Works would have fallen into the 'public domain' in the USA if they were not simultaneously published in the USA within 30 days of first publication, or they failed to contain a notice prescribed by Article III of the Universal Copyright Convention[3], or the copyright owners failed to effect timely renewal of copyright in the USA under the provisions of the 1909 Act[4].

As from 1 January 1996 copyright is restored to foreign copyright works in the public domain in the USA if they are original works, have at least one author or right holder from an eligible country, have not fallen into the public domain in the source country and were not published in the USA within 30 days of first publication in the eligible country. Restored copyright continues for the remainder of the term that would have been granted if the work had never entered the public domain[5]. The term is 75 years from the date of first publication[6].

The date of copyright restoration is automatic and requires no registration. However, to enforce the restored copyright against someone who has legally exploited the work while it was in the public domain (a 'Reliance Party') the copyright holder must either serve notice on the Reliance Party or file a Notice of Intent to Enforce a restored copyright ('NIE') in the federal register by 31 December 1997[7]. Once notified either actually or constructively, a Reliance Party is not permitted to make any more copies of a restored work or create derivative works and has a one year period in which to sell-off previously manufactured stock or to perform or display the work publicly[8].

Derivative works created before 8 December 1994, such as a remake of a European film, can continue to be exploited provided the Reliance Party pays reasonable compensation to the owner of the copyright in the underlying works. If the parties cannot agree compensation is to be set by the Federal Court[9].

Any person who before 1 January 1995 warranted or otherwise covenanted that a work or a performance did not infringe copyright in other works is not liable for any breaches of such warranty or promise arising as a result of the restoration of copyright[10].

1 Although the Agreement on Trade-Related Aspects of Intellectual Property Rights states that members are obliged to comply with the provisions of the Berne Convention, an exception has been inserted at the insistence of the USA that members are not obliged to confer moral rights on authors.
2 Other matters covered in the Act include repeal of deadline for expiry of protection of rental rights in computer programs, anti-bootlegging provisions and an infringement of copyright to fix the sounds or sounds and images of a live musical performance without the performer's permission.
3 See section 100 ante.
4 See section 104 ante.
5 17 USC S 104A(h)(6).
6 Ibid, s 104A(a).
7 Ibid, s 104A(d)(2). It is also necessary to register the copyright in works to recover attorneys' fees and statutory damages in an infringement action.
8 Ibid.
9 Ibid, s 104A(d)(3).
10 Ibid, s 104A(f).

106. Termination of grants of copyright in the USA

In the United States of America complex termination rights exist for any work which is not a 'work made for hire'. A 'work made for hire' is a work made by an employee in the course of his/her employment or a work specially ordered or commissioned for use as a contribution to a motion picture or audio visual (or other specified) work provided the parties sign an acknowledgment that it is a work made for hire[1].

Under US law, pre-1978 transfers or licences of rights may be terminated at any time during the period of 5 years beginning on the later of 56 years from the date on which copyright was first secured and 1 January 1978[2].

For any work written before 1 January 1978 the US term of copyright is an initial term of 28 years and (subject to the renewal of the copyright in the US Copyright Registry) a renewal term of 28 years. This 56 year term is automatically extended by a further term of 19 years. The termination provision applies only to the 19 year extension and is effected by written notice given at least 2 years and not more than 10 years in advance of the date chosen for termination, which can be any time within the 5 year period calculated from the later of the 56th year of the term of 1 January 1978[3]. Thus a copyright secured on 1 April 1950 might be terminated at any time within 5 years beginning from the later of the 56th year of the term or 1 January 1978. The later date is 1 April 2006, so the 5 year termination period would run from 1 April 2006 and end on 31 March 2011. The earliest date notice of termination could be given would be 1 April 1996 (10 years before 1 April 2006) and the latest date would be 31 March 2009 (2 years before 31 March 2011). Note that for post 1978 copyrights there is no need to be concerned with anniversaries, since dates of death are all extended to 31 December, but they are crucial in pre-1978 copyrights.

Pursuant to the Copyright Act 1976 (USA) an author can terminate a new grant within 5 years following the earlier of 35 years from publication or 40 years following the execution of the grant of rights, notwithstanding any agreement to the contrary[4].

The above termination provisions do not apply to any work which is a work made for hire[5].

1 See Copyright Act 1976 (USA), s 101 for definition of work made for hire.
2 Ibid, s 304(c)(4).
3 Ibid, s 304(c)(3).
4 Ibid, s 203(a)(3), (5).
5 Ibid, ss 203(a), 304(c).

107. Copyright in the rest of the world

Former Union of Soviet Socialist Republic ('USSR')

The USSR was not a signatory to the Berne Convention and did not accede to the Universal Copyright Convention until 1972. The result is that all literary, dramatic, musical or artistic works, films or sound recordings made before that time in the USSR would initially have been in the public domain in the United Kingdom unless at the time of first publication they satisfied the requirements then subsisting in relation to United Kingdom copyright protection. The copyright treaty position of each of the former Soviet Republics now needs to be considered separately in respect of works written or first published in such states prior to their succession from the Soviet Union. When the newly formed States accede to the Berne Convention it is likely that many works will fall into copyright in the United Kingdom. To date Estonia, Georgia, Latvia, Lithuania, the Republic of Moldova, the Russian Federation and the Ukraine have acceded to the Berne Convention.

Russia

Copyright legislation of the Russian Federation consists of the Law on Copyright and Neighbouring Rights adopted in July 1993 and the Law on Legal Protection of Computer Programs and Databases adopted in September 1992. Protection of most works is for the life of the author plus 50 years and the former law covers works created or performed before July 1993 in which copyright still subsists. Infringement occurring before 3 August 1993 is dealt with under former Soviet legislation.

Japan

The Copyright Act 1970 provides for copyright, moral rights and neighbouring rights in Japan. The duration of copyright protection for most works is the lifetime of the author plus 50 years. Foreign works are protected in Japan pursuant to the Berne Convention and the Universal

Copyright Convention. In accordance with Japan's international obligations, the Copyright Act (Japan) states that where the term of protection of a foreign work has expired in its country of origin before the expiration of its protection in Japan, that work is not entitled to a longer term of protection in Japan than the term applicable in the country of origin.

Pursuant to the Exceptional Provisions to the Copyrights of the Allied Powers and Allied Nationals Act (Japan) 1952, copyright works owned by Allied Powers and their nationals before World War II or acquired by them during World War II are entitled to an extension of the term of protection calculated from 7 December 1941 to the day before the date of the coming into effect of the Treaty of Peace with Japan. The extended period is calculated by number of days for each of the Allied Powers and ranges from 3,794 days for the United Kingdom and the United States of America to 4,413 days for Lebanon.

Since Japan adheres to the Berne Convention registration formalities are not a condition of the enjoyment of copyright protection. Nonetheless copyright registers exist covering registration of an author's real name, date of first publication or creation of a computer program, registration of copyright transactions and registration of neighbouring rights. Registration has legal implications, in particular a transfer of copyright in certain circumstances and use of copyright as security cannot be asserted against third parties unless it is registered.

China

The main sources of copyright law in China are the General Principles of Civil Law of the Peoples' Republic of China 1986 and the Copyright Act 1990. The Copyright Act provides for both economic rights – the right of economic exploitation, the right to authorise economic exploitation and the right to derive remuneration from economic exploitation – and personality rights. The term of protection for economic rights is the lifetime of the author plus 50 years and protection for personality rights is of unlimited duration. The Act covers both copyright works and rights related to copyright.

Article 2 of the Copyright Act of China provides for the protection of foreign works. Foreign works first published in China enjoy copyright protection in accordance with the Copyright Act and foreign works published outside China are entitled to protection under either bilateral treaties or international conventions[1]. On 1 July 1992 China acceded to both the Berne Convention and the Universal Copyright Convention and four months later acceded to the Geneva Convention for Protection of Producers of Phonograms against Unauthorised Duplication of their Phonograms. To implement certain provisions of the Conventions, the Chinese Government introduced the Implementation Rules of International Copyright Treaties in September 1992. It is important to note in relation to foreign works that where there are any differences in provisions of international treaties and the Copyright Act, the former prevail unless subject to any reservations made by the People's Republic of China.

1 See S M Stewart *International Copyrights and Neighbouring Rights* (Butterworths, 2nd edn Vol One 1989, Vol Two 1993).

M: Legal deposit laws

108. Legal deposit laws generally

Many countries have legislation requiring producers of publications to deposit their work in designated institutions in order to preserve and maintain their culture, heritage and social life for future generations and to provide free access and unrestricted use of this source of material for education and research purposes. Most countries require the deposit of all printed works produced within the country and many countries are revising legislation to extend requirements to cover non-print and electronic materials.

International initiatives to maintain copyright works include a recommendation adopted at the 37th session of the UNESCO General Conference in 1980 to safeguard and preserve moving images which has led to national initiatives in a number of countries for the legal deposit of moving images; a WIPO Treaty adopted in 1989 on the International Registration of Audio Visual Works and the establishment of the Federation Internationale des Archives du Film and international organisation based in Brussels.

109. Legal deposit laws in the United Kingdom

In the United Kingdom, the current statutory deposit scheme only covers printed publications. This scheme is provided by the sole unrepealed section of the 1911 Copyright Act[1] and imposes two obligations on the publisher of every book which is published in the United Kingdom. First the publisher is obliged to deliver, at the publisher's expense, within one month of publication a copy of the book to the British Library Board. Second the publisher has to deliver a further copy of the book to each of the remaining deposit libraries if they demand a copy[2]. A publisher is liable to a fine for failure to comply with these obligations.

The Theatres Act 1968 provides that where the public performance of a new play which is based on a written script is given in Great Britain, the person who presented the performance is required to deposit a copy of the script on which the play is based with the British Library Board within one month from the date of performance.

Currently the acts contained in the Copyright, Designs and Patents Act 1988 which permit libraries and archives to make and supply copies of material without infringing copyright only extend to literary, dramatic and musical works and typographical arrangements[3]. The copying etc of films is permitted only if it is not possible by reasonable inquiry to ascertain the identity of the principal director, the author of the screenplay, the author of the dialogue or the author of the music specially created for and used in the film died 70 years or more before the beginning of the calendar year in which the act is done[4]. Hence if urgent restoration work involving copying is needed to be carried out on films, it can only be undertaken in limited circumstances. The extent to which the country's cultural heritage is capable of being maintained is therefore restricted.

The 1988 Act makes specific provision for recordings of broadcasts or cable programmes to be made for the purpose of their being placed in an archive maintained by a designated body without infringing any copyright in the broadcast or cable programme or any work included in it[5]. A further provision in the Act provides that no copy so made will infringe any performer's right[6].

These provisions permit persons to record, off-air from broadcasts, recordings which are destined for the National Film and Television Archive, but they do not permit persons to make from audio-visual materials which they have in their possession recordings which are destined for deposit in the National Film and Television Archive.

The Broadcasting Act 1990 makes express provision[7] for the maintenance of a national television archive by a body nominated by the Independent Television Commission[8]. The nominated body is the British Film Institute, which is entitled to receive from the Independent Television Commission certain fees payable by Channel 3 and Channel 5 licensees in accordance with the provisions of the Broadcasting Act 1990. Although the British Film Institute has entered into contractual arrangements with the Channel Four Television Corporation and the British Broadcasting Corporation and BSkyB pursuant to which arrangements these broadcasters voluntarily contribute towards the maintenance of the National Film and Television Archive, there is currently no statutory obligation on the parties to do so.

In view of the increasing numbers of households serviced by cable and satellite broadcasting, and the proliferation of channels, the archive-recording of all broadcasting activities whether by satellite or cable is fast becoming a matter of concern. In February 1997 a consultation paper was published by the Department of National Heritage, the Scottish Office, the Welsh Office and the Department of Education Northern Ireland on 'Legal Deposit of Publications' The paper invites submissions on the existing system of legal deposit for print publication; options for its extension to electronic publications, sound recordings, film and video recordings and microform publications; the implications for intellectual property rights and permissible exceptions in respect of legally deposited material; and costs of an expanded legal deposit to publishers, repositories and with which the publications would be deposited and the taxpayer.

1 The Copyright Act 1911, s 15.
2 The deposit libraries are:
    The British Library
    The Bodleian Library, Oxford
    University Library, Cambridge
    The National Library of Scotland
    Library of Trinity College, Dublin
    National College of Wales.
3 See sections 36 to 42 ante.
4 Copyright, Designs and Patents Act 1988, s 66A.
5 Ibid, s 75.
6 Ibid, Sch 2, para 21.
7 Broadcasting Act 1990, s 185.
8 Copyright, Designs and Patents Act 1988, s 75. Currently the designated bodies are the British Film Institute, the British Library, the Music Performance Research Centre and the Scottish Film Council.

110. Legal deposit laws in the rest of the world

Since 1 January 1978 all works published in the United States of America with a copyright notice have been subject to the mandatory legal deposit requirement of the United States Copyright Act. When the USA acceded to the Berne Convention on 1 March 1989 the reference to the copyright notice was removed from the mandatory deposit provision. As a result of this change all copyright works which are published in the United States are subject to mandatory deposit whether published with or without a notice. Publication is defined as the distribution of copies of a work to the public by sale or other transfer of ownership or by rental release or lending. Categories of material subject to copyright include literary, musical and dramatic works; motion pictures; sound recordings; architectural work and CD Rom. The United States Copyright Office considers that all types of material are subject to mandatory deposit but lacks legal authority for collecting certain materials because 'publication' and 'transmission' are not closely defined for on-line publications. A recent report raises the need for revised legislation.

The material to be deposited in the United States Copyright Office in the case of a motion picture consists of one complete copy of the 'best edition' plus a separate description of its contents such as a continuity shooting script, press book or synopsis. Where two or more editions of a motion picture are published in the USA, the 'best edition' is the one preferred by the Library of Congress. Currently the Library accepts in descending order of preference:

(a) *Film* rather than another medium: preprint material by special arrangement, most widely distributed film gauge, 35 mm, 16 mm, 8 mm, special formats (such as 65 mm) only in exceptional cases, open reel rather than cartridge or cassette:

(b) *Videotape* most widely distributed tape gauge, 2-inch reel, 1-inch reel, ¾-inch cassette, ½-inch cassette (VHS rather than Beta);

(c) *Videodisk*

In the European Union, France's legal deposit law is the oldest in the world. Passed in 1537 and originally covering only the deposit of books by the printer, legislation has been successively revised to include phonographic and cinematographic works deposited by publishers and sound, audio-visual and multi-media documents. Most recent legislation that came into force on 1 January 1994[1] provides for the collection and preservation of documents, preparation and publication of national bibliographies and consultation of the documents under defined conditions, all material being deposited in the Bibliothèque Nationale de France and certain classes of material being held in other repositories. The material now covered includes printed, graphic, photographic, sound, audio-visual and multi-media documents, whatever the means of production, as soon as they are made accessible to the public by the publication of a physical carrier.

In Finland the Act and Statute on Legal Deposit Copies of 1980 covers printed products, sound and image recording, which are deposited with the National Library. A separate Act of 1984[2] covers motion pictures, films and videos, which are deposited in the Finnish Film Archive. Radio and television broadcasts and electronic publications are not currently covered. A working group has been set up by the Ministry of Education to prepare revised legislation.

In 1990 Norway introduced legislation[3] providing for the deposit of printed materials, sound recordings, films, videos and both static and dynamic electronic documents. The legislation has been framed in such a way that new electronic formats can be accommodated. the provisions allow the National Library to decide for itself as to what it will collect, which allows material to be acquired in a limited number of formats which can currently be handled leaving other types of material to be acquired when the National Library feels it has the technical capacity to process them.

1 Law No 92-546 of 20 June 1992 relating to Legal Deposit.
2 No 576 Act on the Archiving of Films 1984.
3 Statutes of the Norwegian Film Institute 1990.

PART 2

Copyright, Designs and Patents Act 1988

ARRANGEMENT OF SECTIONS

PART 1
COPYRIGHT

CHAPTER 1
SUBSISTENCE, OWNERSHIP AND DURATION OF COPYRIGHT

CHAPTER II
RIGHTS OF COPYRIGHT OWNER

CHAPTER III
ACTS PERMITTED IN RELATION TO COPYRIGHT WORKS

Copyright, Designs and Patents Act 1988

(1988 c 48)

An Act to restate the law of copyright, with amendments; to make fresh provision as to the rights of performers and others in performances; to confer a design right in original designs; to amend the Registered Designs Act 1949; to make provision with respect to patent agents and trade mark agents; to confer patents and designs jurisdiction on certain county courts; to amend the law of patents; to make provision with respect to devices designed to circumvent copy-protection of works in electronic form; to make fresh provision penalising the fraudulent reception of transmissions; to make the fraudulent application or use of a trade mark an offence; to make provision for the benefit of the Hospital for Sick Children, Great Ormond Street, London; to enable financial assistance to be given to certain international bodies; and for connected purposes

[15th November 1988]

BE IT ENACTED by the Queen's most Excellent Majesty, by and with the advice and consent of the Lords Spiritual and Temporal, and Commons, in this present Parliament assembled, and by the authority of the same, as follows–

PART I
COPYRIGHT

CHAPTER I
SUBSISTENCE, OWNERSHIP AND DURATION OF COPYRIGHT

Introductory

1 Copyright and copyright works

(1) Copyright is a property right which subsists in accordance with this Part in the following descriptions of work–

    (a) original literary, dramatic, musical or artistic works,
    (b) sound recordings, films, broadcasts or cable programmes, and
    (c) the typographical arrangement of published editions.

(2) In this Part 'copyright work' means a work of any of those descriptions in which copyright subsists.

(3) Copyright does not subsist in a work unless the requirements of this Part with respect to qualification for copyright protection are met (see section 153 and the provisions referred to there).

NOTE

Commencement order: SI 1989/816.

---

2 Rights subsisting in copyright works

(1) The owner of the copyright in a work of any description has the exclusive right to do the acts specified in Chapter II as the acts restricted by the copyright in a work of that description.

(2) In relation to certain descriptions of copyright work the following rights conferred by Chapter IV (moral rights) subsist in favour of the author, director or commissioner of the work, whether or not he is the owner of the copyright–

    (a) section 77 (right to be identified as author or director),
    (b) section 80 (right to object to derogatory treatment of work), and
    (c) section 85 (right to privacy of certain photographs and films).

NOTE
Commencement order: SI 1989/816.

Descriptions of work and related provisions

3 Literary, dramatic and musical works

(1) In this Part–

'literary work' means any work, other than a dramatic or musical work, which is written, spoken or sung, and accordingly includes–

(a) a table or compilation, [other than a database]
(b) a computer program[,
(c) preparatory design material for a computer program]; [and
(d) a database]

'dramatic work' includes a work of dance or mime; and
'musical work' means a work consisting of music, exclusive of any words or action intended to be sung, spoken or performed with the music.

(2) Copyright does not subsist in a literary, dramatic or musical work unless and until it is recorded, in writing or otherwise; and references in this Part to the time at which such a work is made are to the time at which it is so recorded.

(3) It is immaterial for the purposes of subsection (2) whether the work is recorded by or with the permission of the author; and where it is not recorded by the author, nothing in that subsection affects the question whether copyright subsists in the record as distinct from the work recorded.

NOTES
Commencement order: SI 1989/816.
Words in square brackets added by SI 1992/3233, reg 3 and SI 1997/3032, reg 5.

[3A Databases]

[(1) In this Part 'database' means a collection of independent works, data or other materials which–

(a) are arranged in a systematic or methodical way, and
(b) are individually accessible by electronic or other means.

(2) For the purpose of this Part a literary work consisting of a database is original if, and only if, by reason of the selection or arrangement of the contents of the database the database constitutes the author's own intellectual creation.]

NOTES
This section was inserted by the Copyright and Rights in Databases Regulations 1997, SI 1997/3032, reg 6. This section should be read in conjunction with regs 28, 29 and 30, contextualised in this Act at s 16 and Sch 1, para 12 respectively.
This section should also be read in conjunction with the following provisions of the Copyright and Rights in Databases Regulations 1997, SI 1997/3032 (commencement: 1 January 1998):

Copyright and Rights in Databases Regulations 1997, regs 12(1), 13(1), (2), (3) and 18

12 Interpretation
(1) In this Part–

'database' has the meaning given by section 3A(1) of the 1988 Act (as inserted by Regulation 6);
'extraction', in relation to any contents of a database, means the permanent or temporary transfer of those contents to another medium by any means or in any form;
'insubstantial', in relation to part of the contents of a database, shall be construed subject to Regulation 16(2);
'investment' includes any investment, whether of financial, human or technical resources;

'jointly', in relation to the making of a database, shall be construed in accordance with Regulation 14(6);

'lawful user', in relation to a database, means any person who (whether under a licence to do any of the acts restricted by any database right in the database or otherwise) has a right to use the database;

'maker', in relation to a database, shall be construed in accordance with Regulation 14;

're-utilisation', in relation to any contents of a database, means making those contents available to the public by any means;

'substantial', in relation to any investment, extraction or re-utilisation, means substantial in terms of quantity or quality or a combination of both.

13 Database right

(1) A property right ('database right') subsists, in accordance with this Part, in a database if there has been a substantial investment in obtaining, verifying or presenting the contents of the database.

(2) For the purposes of paragraph (1) it is immaterial whether or not the database or any of its contents is a copyright work, within the meaning of Part I of the 1988 Act.

(3) This Regulation has effect subject to Regulation 18.

18 Qualification for database right

(1) Database right does not subsist in a database unless, at the material time, its maker, or if it was made jointly, one or more of its makers, was–

- (a)   an individual who was a national of an EEA state or habitually resident within the EEA,
- (b)   a body which was incorporated under the law of an EEA state and which, at that time, satisfied one of the conditions in paragraph (2), or
- (c)   a partnership or other unincorporated body which was formed under the law of an EEA state and which, at that time, satisfied the condition in paragraph (2)(a).

(2) The conditions mentioned in paragraphs (1)(b) and (c) are–

- (a)   that the body has its central administration or principal place of business within the EEA, or
- (b)   that the body has its registered office within the EEA and the body's operations are linked on an ongoing basis with the economy of an EEA state.

(3) Paragraph (1) does not apply in any case falling within Regulation 14(4).

(4) In this Regulation–

- (a)   'EEA' and 'EEA state' have the meaning given by section 172A of the 1988 Act;
- (b)   'the material time' means the time when the database was made, or if the making extended over a period, a substantial part of that period.

4 Artistic works

(1) In this Part 'artistic work' means–

- (a)   a graphic work, photograph, sculpture or collage, irrespective of artistic quality,
- (b)   a work of architecture being a building or a model for a building, or
- (c)   a work of artistic craftsmanship.

(2) In this Part–

'building' includes any fixed structure, and a part of a building or fixed structure;

'graphic work' includes–

- (a)   any painting, drawing, diagram, map, chart or plan, and
- (b)   any engraving, etching, lithograph, woodcut or similar work;

'photograph' means a recording of light or other radiation on any medium on which an image is produced or from which an image may by any means be produced, and which is not part of a film;

'sculpture' includes a cast or model made for purposes of sculpture.

NOTE
Commencement order: SI 1989/816.

[5A] [Sound recordings]

[(1) In this Part 'sound recording' means–

- (a)   a recording of sounds, from which the sounds may be reproduced, or
- (b)   a recording of the whole or any part of a literary, dramatic or musical work, from which sounds reproducing the work or part may be produced,

regardless of the medium on which the recording is made or the method by which the sounds are reproduced or produced.

(2) Copyright does not subsist in a sound recording which is, or to the extent that it is, a copy taken from a previous sound recording.]

NOTE

This section was substituted with savings, together with s 5B for s 5 as originally enacted, by SI 1995 No 3297, reg 9(1); for savings see Part III thereof.

[5B] [Films]

[(1) In this Part 'film' means a recording on any medium from which a moving image may by any means be produced.

(2) The sound track accompanying a film shall be treated as part of the film for the purposes of this Part.

(3) Without prejudice to the generality of subsection (2), where that subsection applies–

(a) references in this Part to showing a film include playing the film sound track to accompany the film, and

(b) references to playing a sound recording do not include playing the film sound track to accompany the film.

(4) Copyright does not subsist in a film which is, or to the extent that it is, a copy taken from a previous film.

(5) Nothing in this section affects any copyright subsisting in a film sound track as a sound recording.]

NOTES

This section was substituted with savings, together with s 5A for s 5 as originally enacted, by SI 1995/3297, reg 9(1); for savings see Part III thereof.

This section should be read in conjunction with the following provisions of the Duration of Copyright and Rights in Performances Regulations 1995, SI 1995/3297 (commencement: 1 January 1996) and the Copyright and Related Rights Regulations 1996, SI 1996/2967 (commencement: 1 December 1996):

Duration of Copyright and Rights in Performances Regulations 1995, regs 13 and 26

Films not protected as such

13 In relation to a film in which copyright does not or did not subsist as such but which is or was protected–

(a) as an original dramatic work, or

(b) by virtue of the protection of the photographs forming part of the film,

references in the new provisions, and in this Part, to copyright in a film are to any copyright in the film as an original dramatic work or, as the case may be, in photographs forming part of the film.

26 Film sound tracks: application of new provisions

(1) The new provisions relating to the treatment of film sound tracks apply to existing sound tracks as from commencement.

(2) The owner of any copyright in a film has as from commencement corresponding rights as copyright owner in any existing sound track treated as part of the film; but without prejudice to any rights of the owner of the copyright in the sound track as a sound recording.

(3) Anything done before commencement under or in relation to the copyright in the sound recording continues to have effect and shall have effect, so far as concerns the sound track, in relation to the film as in relation to the sound recording.

(4) It is not an infringement of the copyright in the film (or of any moral right in the film) to do anything after commencement in pursuance of arrangements for the exploitation of the sound recording made before commencement.

Copyright and Related Rights Regulations 1996, regs 32 and 33

New rights: effect of pre-commencement film production agreement

32–(1) Sections 93A and 191F (presumption of transfer of rental right in case of production agreement) apply in relation to an agreement concluded before commencement.

As section 93A so applies, the restriction in subsection (3) of that section shall be omitted (exclusion of presumption in relation to screenplay, dialogue or music specifically created for the film).

(2) Sections 93B and 191G (right to equitable remuneration where rental right transferred) have effect accordingly, but subject to regulation 33 (right to equitable remuneration applicable to rental after 1st April 1997).

Right to equitable remuneration applicable to rental after 1st April 1997
33 No right to equitable remuneration under section 93B or 191G (right to equitable remuneration where rental right transferred) arises–

(a)   in respect of any rental of a sound recording or film before 1st April 1997, or

(b)   in respect of any rental after that date of a sound recording or film made in pursuance of an agreement entered into before 1st July 1994, unless the author or performer (or a successor in title of his) has before 1st January 1997 notified the person by whom the remuneration would be payable that he intends to exercise that right.

6 Broadcasts

(1) In this Part a 'broadcast' means a transmission by wireless telegraphy of visual images, sounds or other information which–

(a)   is capable of being lawfully received by members of the public, or

(b)   is transmitted for presentation to members of the public;

and references to broadcasting shall be construed accordingly.

(2) An encrypted transmission shall be regarded as capable of being lawfully received by members of the public only if decoding equipment has been made available to members of the public by or with the authority of the person making the transmission or the person providing the contents of the transmission.

(3) References in this Part to the person making a broadcast, broadcasting a work, or including a work in a broadcast are–

(a)   to the person transmitting the programme, if he has responsibility to any extent for its contents, and

(b)   to any person providing the programme who makes with the person transmitting it the arrangements necessary for its transmission;

and references in this Part to a programme, in the context of broadcasting, are to any item included in a broadcast.

[(4) For the purposes of this Part, the place from which a broadcast is made is the place where, under the control and responsibility of the person making the broadcast, the programme-carrying signals are introduced into an uninterrupted chain of communication (including, in the case of a satellite transmission, the chain leading to the satellite and down towards the earth).]

[(4A) Subsections (3) and (4) have effect subject to section 6A (safeguards in case of certain satellite broadcasts).]

(5) References in this Part to the reception of a broadcast include reception of a broadcast relayed by means of a telecommunications system.

(6) Copyright does not subsist in a broadcast which infringes, or to the extent that it infringes, the copyright in another broadcast or in a cable programme.

NOTES

Commencement order: SI 1989/816.

Para (4): substituted SI 1996/2967, reg 5.

Para (4A): added by SI 1996/2967, reg 6(1).

This section should be read in conjunction with the following provision of the Copyright and Related Rights Regulations 1996, SI 1996/2967 (commencement: 1 December 1996):

Copyright and Related Rights Regulations 1996, reg 28

Broadcasts

28 The provisions of–

regulation 5 (place where broadcast treated as made) and
regulation 6 (safeguards in relation to certain satellite broadcasts),

have effect in relation to broadcasts made after commencement.

[6A] [Safeguards in case of certain satellite broadcasts]
[(1) This section applies where the place from which a broadcast by way of satellite transmission is made is located in a country other than an EEA State and the law of that country fails to provide at least the following level of protection–

(a) exclusive rights in relation to broadcasting equivalent to those conferred by section 20 (infringement by broadcasting) on the authors of literary, dramatic, musical and artistic works, films and broadcasts;

(b) a right in relation to live broadcasting equivalent to that conferred on a performer by section 182(1)(b) (consent required for live broadcast of performance); and

(c) a right for authors of sound recordings and performers to share in a single equitable remuneration in respect of the broadcasting of sound recordings.

(2) Where the place from which the programme-carrying signals are transmitted to the satellite ('the uplink station') is located in an EEA State–

(a) that place shall be treated as the place from which the broadcast is made, and

(b) the person operating the uplink station shall be treated as the person making the broadcast.

(3) Where the uplink station is not located in an EEA State but a person who is established in an EEA State has commissioned the making of the broadcast–

(a) that person shall be treated as the person making the broadcast, and

(b) the place in which he has his principal establishment in the European Economic Area shall be treated as the place from which the broadcast is made.]

NOTES
Added by SI 1996/2967, reg 6(2).
This section should be read in conjunction with the following provision of the Copyright and Related Rights Regulations 1996, SI 1996/2967 (commencement: 1 December 1996):

Copyright and Related Rights Regulations 1996, reg 29

Satellite broadcasting: international co-production agreeements
29–(1) This regulation applies to an agreement concluded before 1st January 1995–

(a)   between two or more co-producers of a film, one of whom is a national of an EEA state, and

(b)   the provisions of which grant to the parties exclusive rights to exploit all communication to the public of the film in separate geographical areas.

(2) Where such an agreement giving such exclusive exploitation rights in relation to the United Kingdom does not expressly or by implication address satellite broadcasting from the United Kingdom, the person to whom those exclusive rights have been granted shall not make any such broadcast without the consent of any other party to the agreement whose language-related exploitation rights would be adversely affected by that broadcast.

7 Cable programmes
(1) In this Part–

'cable programme' means any item included in a cable programme service; and
'cable programme service' means a service which consists wholly or mainly in sending visual images, sounds or other information by means of a telecommunications system, otherwise than by wireless telegraphy, for reception–

(a) at two or more places (whether for simultaneous reception or at different times in response to requests by different users), or

(b) for presentation to members of the public,

and which is not, or so far as it is not, excepted by or under the following provisions of this section.

(2) The following are excepted from the definition of 'cable programme service'–

(a) a service or part of a service of which it is an essential feature that while visual images, sounds or other information are being conveyed by the person providing the service there will or may be sent from each place of reception, by means of the same system or (as the case may be) the same part of it, information (other than signals sent for the operation or control of the service) for reception by the person providing the service or other persons receiving it;

  (b) a service run for the purposes of a business where–

    (i) no person except the person carrying on the business is concerned in the control of the apparatus comprised in the system,

    (ii) the visual images, sounds or other information are conveyed by the system solely for purposes internal to the running of the business and not by way of rendering a service or providing amenities for others, and

    (iii) the system is not connected to any other telecommunications system;

  (c) a service run by a single individual where–

    (i) all the apparatus comprised in the system is under his control,

    (ii) the visual images, sounds or other information conveyed by the system are conveyed solely for domestic purposes of his, and

    (iii) the system is not connected to any other telecommunications system;

  (d) services where–

    (i) all the apparatus comprised in the system is situated in, or connects, premises which are in single occupation, and

    (ii) the system is not connected to any other telecommunications system,

other than services operated as part of the amenities provided for residents or inmates of premises run as a business;

  (e) services which are, or to the extent that they are, run for persons providing broadcasting or cable programme services or providing programmes for such services.

(3) The Secretary of State may by order amend subsection (2) so as to add or remove exceptions, subject to such transitional provision as appears to him to be appropriate.

(4) An order shall be made by statutory instrument; and no order shall be made unless a draft of it has been laid before and approved by resolution of each House of Parliament.

(5) References in this Part to the inclusion of a cable programme or work in a cable programme service are to its transmission as part of the service; and references to the person including it are to the person providing the service.

(6) Copyright does not subsist in a cable programme–

  (a) if it is included in a cable programme service by reception and immediate re-transmission of a broadcast, or

  (b) if it infringes, or to the extent that it infringes, the copyright in another cable programme or in a broadcast.

NOTE
Commencement order: SI 1989/816.

8 Published editions

(1) In this Part 'published edition', in the context of copyright in the typographical arrangement of a published edition, means a published edition of the whole or any part of one or more literary, dramatic or musical works.

(2) Copyright does not subsist in the typographical arrangement of a published edition if, or to the extent that, it reproduces the typographical arrangement of a previous edition.

NOTES
Commencement order: SI 1989/816.
This section should be read in conjunction with the following provision of the Copyright and Related Rights Regulations 1996, SI 1996/2967, (commencement: 1 December 1996):

Copyright and Related Rights Regulations 1996, reg 16

16 Publication right
(1) A person who after the expiry of copyright protection, publishes for the first time a previously unpublished work has, in accordance with the following provisions, a property right ('publication right') equivalent to copyright.

(2) For this purpose publication includes any communication to the public, in particular–

   (a)   the issue of copies to the public;
   (b)   making the work available by means of an electronic retrieval system;
   (c)   the rental or lending of copies of the work to the public;
   (d)   the performance, exhibition or showing of the work in public; or
   (e)   broadcasting the work or including it in a cable programme service.

(3) No account shall be taken for this purpose of any unauthorised act.
In relation to a time when there is no copyright in the work, an unauthorised act means an act done without the consent of the owner of the physical medium in which the work is embodied or on which it is recorded.
(4) A work qualifies for publication right protection only if–

   (a)   first publication is in the European Economic Area, and
   (b)   the publisher of the work is at the time of first publication a national of an EEA state.

Where two or more persons jointly publish the work, it is sufficient for the purposes of paragraph (b) if any of them is a national of an EEA state.
(5) No publication right arises from the publication of a work in which Crown copyright or Parliamentary copyright subsisted.
(6) Publication right expires at the end of the period of 25 years from the end of the calendar year in which the work was first published.
(7) In this regulation a 'work' means a literary, dramatic, musical or artistic work or a film.
(8) Expressions used in this regulation (other than 'publication') have the same meaning as in Part I.

Authorship and ownership of copyright

9 Authorship of work

(1) In this Part 'author', in relation to a work, means the person who creates it.
  (2) That person shall be taken to be–

  [(aa) in the case of a sound recording, the producer;
  (ab) in the case of a film, the producer and the principal director;]
  (b)   in the case of a broadcast, the person making the broadcast (see section 6(3)) or, in the case of a broadcast which relays another broadcast by reception and immediate re-transmission, the person making that other broadcast;
  (c)   in the case of a cable programme, the person providing the cable programme service in which the programme is included;
  (d)   in the case of the typographical arrangement of a published edition, the publisher.

(3) In the case of a literary, dramatic, musical or artistic work which is computer-generated, the author shall be taken to be the person by whom the arrangements necessary for the creation of the work are undertaken.
(4) For the purposes of this Part a work is of 'unknown authorship' if the identity of the author is unknown or, in the case of a work of joint authorship, if the identity of none of the authors is known.
(5) For the purposes of this Part the identity of an author shall be regarded as unknown if it is not possible for a person to ascertain his identity by reasonable inquiry; but if his identity is once known it shall not subsequently be regarded as unknown.

NOTES
Commencement order: SI 1989/816.
Sub-s (2): paras (aa), (ab) substituted, for para (a) as originally enacted, by SI 1996/2967, reg 18(1).
This section should be read in conjunction with the following provisions of the Copyright and Related Rights Regulations 1996, SI 1996/2967 (commencement: 1 December 1996) and the Copyright and Rights in Databases Regulations, SI 1997/3032 (commencement: 1 January 1998):

Copyright and Related Rights Regulations 1996, regs 19 and 36

Clarification of transitional provisions relating to pre-1989 photographs
19 Any question arising, in relation to photographs which were existing works within the meaning of Schedule 1, as to who is to be regarded as the author for the purposes of–

   (a)   regulations 15 and 16 of the Duration of Copyright and Rights in Performances Regulations 1995 (duration of copyright: application of new provisions subject to general saving), or

(b)   regulation 19(2)(b) of those regulations (ownership of revived copyright),

is to be determined in accordance with section 9 as in force on the commencement of those regulations (and not, by virtue of paragraph 10 of Schedule 1, in accordance with the law in force at the time when the work was made).

Authorship of films
36–(1) Regulation 18 (authorship of films) applies as from commencement in relation to films made on or after 1st July 1994.

(2) It is not an infringement of any right which the principal director has by virtue of these Regulations to do anything after commencement in pursuance of arrangements for the exploitation of the film made before 19th November 1992.

This does not affect any right of his to equitable remuneration under section 93B.

Copyright and Rights in Databases Regulations 1997, reg 14

14 The maker of a database
(1) Subject to paragraphs (2) to (4), the person who takes the initiative in obtaining, verifying or presenting the contents of a database and assumes the risk of investing in that obtaining, verification or presentation shall be regarded as the maker of, and as having made, the database.

(2) Where a database is made by an employee in the course of his employment, his employer shall be regarded as the maker of the database, subject to any agreement to the contrary.

(3) Subject to paragraph (4), where a database is made by Her Majesty or by an officer or servant of the Crown in the course of his duties, Her Majesty shall be regarded as the maker of the database.

(4) Where a database is made by or under the direction or control of the House of Commons or the House of Lords–

(a)   the House by whom, or under whose direction or control, the database is made shall be regarded as the maker of the database, and

(b)   if the database is made by or under the direction or control of both Houses, the two Houses shall be regarded as the joint makers of the database.

(5) For the purposes of this Part a database is made jointly if two or more persons acting together in collaboration take the initiative in obtaining, verifying or presenting the contents of the database and assume the risk of investing in that obtaining, verification or presentation.

(6) References in this Part to the maker of a database shall, except as otherwise provided, be construed, in relation to a database which is made jointly, as references to all the makers of the database.

---

10 Works of joint authorship
(1) In this Part a 'work of joint authorship' means a work produced by the collaboration of two or more authors in which the contribution of each author is not distinct from that of the other author or authors.

[(1A) A film shall be treated as a work of joint authorship unless the producer and the principal director are the same person.]

(2) A broadcast shall be treated as a work of joint authorship in any case where more than one person is to be taken as making the broadcast (see section 6(3)).

(3) References in this Part to the author of a work shall, except as otherwise provided, be construed in relation to a work of joint authorship as references to all the authors of the work.

NOTES
Commencement order: SI 1989/816.
Sub-s (1A): added by SI 1996/2967, reg 18(2).
See further, the Copyright and Related Rights Regulations 1996, SI 1996/2967, reg 36 which provides that the amendments made to this section by reg 18 thereof shall apply as from 1 December 1996 in relation to films made on or after 1 July 1994.

---

11 First ownership of copyright
(1) The author of a work is the first owner of any copyright in it, subject to the following provisions.

(2) Where a literary, dramatic, musical or artistic work[, or a film,] is made by an employee in the course of his employment, his employer is the first owner of any copyright in the work subject to any agreement to the contrary.

(3) This section does not apply to Crown copyright or Parliamentary copyright (see sections 163 and 165) or to copyright which subsists by virtue of section 168 (copyright of certain international organisations).

NOTES
Commencement order: SI 1989/816.
Sub-s (2): words in square brackets added by SI 1996/2967, reg 18(3).
See further, the Copyright and Related Rights Regulations 1996, SI 1996/2967, reg 36 which provides that the amendments made to this section by reg 18 thereof shall apply as from 1 December 1996 in relation to films made on or after 1 July 1994.
This section should be read in conjunction with the following provision of the Copyright and Rights in Databases Regulations 1997, SI 1997/3032 (commencement: 1 January 1998):

Copyright and Rights in Databases Regulations 1997, reg 15

15 First ownership of database right
The maker of a database is the first owner of database right in it.

Duration of copyright

[12] [Duration of copyright in literary, dramatic, musical or artistic works]
[(1) The following provisions have effect with respect to the duration of copyright in a literary, dramatic, musical or artistic work.

(2) Copyright expires at the end of the period of 70 years from the end of the calendar year in which the author dies, subject as follows.

(3) If the work is of unknown authorship, copyright expires–

    (a) at the end of the period of 70 years from the end of the calendar year in which the work was made, or

    (b) if during that period the work is made available to the public, at the end of the period of 70 years from the end of the calendar year in which it is first so made available,

subject as follows.

(4) Subsection (2) applies if the identity of the author becomes known before the end of the period specified in paragraph (a) or (b) of subsection (3).

(5) For the purposes of subsection (3) making available to the public includes–

    (a) in the case of a literary, dramatic or musical work–

        (i)   performance in public, or

        (ii) being broadcast or included in a cable programme service;

    (b) in the case of an artistic work–

        (i)   exhibition in public,

        (ii) a film including the work being shown in public, or

        (iii) being included in a broadcast or cable programme service;

but in determining generally for the purposes of that subsection whether a work has been made available to the public no account shall be taken of any unauthorised act.

(6) Where the country of origin of the work is not an EEA state and the author of the work is not a national of an EEA state, the duration of copyright is that to which the work is entitled in the country of origin, provided that does not exceed the period which would apply under subsections (2) to (5).

(7) If the work is computer-generated the above provisions do not apply and copyright expires at the end of the period of 50 years from the end of the calendar year in which the work was made.

(8) The provisions of this section are adapted as follows in relation to a work of joint authorship–

    (a) the reference in subsection (2) to the death of the author shall be construed–

        (i)   if the identity of all the authors is known, as a reference to the death of the last of them to die, and

        (ii) if the identity of one or more of the authors is known and the identity of one or more others is not, as a reference to the death of the last whose identity is known;

(b)   the reference in subsection (4) to the identity of the author becoming known shall be construed as a reference to the identity of any of the authors becoming known;

(c)   the reference in subsection (6) to the author not being a national of an EEA state shall be construed as a reference to none of the authors being a national of an EEA state.

(9) This section does not apply to Crown copyright or Parliamentary copyright (see sections 163 to 166) or to copyright which subsists by virtue of section 168 (copyright of certain international organisations).]

NOTE

This section was substituted with savings by SI 1995/3297, reg 5(1); for savings see Part III thereof.

This section should be read in conjunction with the following provisions of the Copyright and Rights in Databases Regulations, SI 1997/3032 (commencement: 1 January 1998):

Copyright and Rights in Databases Regulations 1997, regs 17, 29 and 30

17 Term of protection

(1) Database right in a database expires at the end of the period of fifteen years from the end of the calendar year in which the making of the database was completed.

(2) Where a database is made available to the public before the end of the period referred to in paragraph (1), database right in the database shall expire fifteen years from the end of the calendar year in which the database was first made available to the public.

(3) Any substantial change to the contents of a database, including a substantial change resulting from the accumulation of successive additions, deletions or alterations, which would result in the database being considered to be a substantial new investment shall qualify the database resulting from that investment for its own term of protection.

(4) This Regulation has effect subject to Regulation 30.

29 Saving for copyright in certain existing databases

(1) Where a database–

(a)   was created on or before 27th March 1996, and

(b)   is a copyright work immediately before commencement,

copyright shall continue to subsist in the database for the remainder of its copyright term.

(2) In this Regulation 'copyright term' means the period of the duration of copyright under section 12 of the 1988 Act (duration of copyright in literary, dramatic, musical or artistic works).

30 Database right: term applicable to certain existing databases

Where–

(a)   the making of a database was completed on or after 1st January 1983, and

(b)   on commencement, database right begins to subsist in the database,

database right shall subsist in the database for the period of fifteen years beginning with 1st January 1998.

[13A] [Duration of copyright in sound recordings]

[(1) The following provisions have effect with respect to the duration of copyright in a sound recording.

(2) Copyright expires–

(a)   at the end of the period of 50 years from the end of the calendar year in which it is made, or

(b)   if during that period it is released, 50 years from the end of the calendar year in which it is released;

subject as follows.

(3) For the purposes of subsection (2) a sound recording is 'released' when it is first published, played in public, broadcast or included in a cable programme service; but in determining whether a sound recording has been released no account shall be taken of any unauthorised act.

(4) Where the author of a sound recording is not a national of an EEA state, the duration of copyright is that to which the sound recording is entitled in the country of which the author is a national, provided that does not exceed the period which would apply under subsections (2) and (3).

(5) If or to the extent that the application of subsection (4) would be at variance with an international obligation to which the United Kingdom became subject prior to 29th October 1993, the duration of copyright shall be as specified in subsections (2) and (3).]

NOTES

This section was substituted with savings, together with s 13B for s 13 as originally enacted, by SI 1995/3297, reg 6(1); for savings see Part III thereof.

[13B] [Duration of copyright in films]
[(1) The following provisions have effect with respect to the duration of copyright in a film.

(2) Copyright expires at the end of the period of 70 years from the end of the calendar year in which the death occurs of the last to die of the following persons–

(a)   the principal director,
(b)   the author of the screenplay,
(c)   the author of the dialogue, or
(d)   the composer of music specially created for and used in the film;

subject as follows.

(3) If the identity of one or more of the persons referred to in subsection (2)(a) to (d) is known and the identity of one or more others is not, the reference in that subsection to the death of the last of them to die shall be construed as a reference to the death of the last whose identity is known.

(4) If the identity of the persons referred to in subsection (2)(a) to (d) is unknown, copyright expires at–

(a)   the end of the period of 70 years from the end of the calendar year in which the film was made, or
(b)   if during that period the film is made available to the public, at the end of the period of 70 years from the end of the calendar year in which it is first so made available.

(5) Subsections (2) and (3) apply if the identity of any of those persons becomes known before the end of the period specified in paragraph (a) or (b) of subsection (4).

(6) For the purposes of subsection (4) making available to the public includes–

(a)   showing in public, or
(b)   being broadcast or included in a cable programme service;

but in determining generally for the purposes of that subsection whether a film has been made available to the public no account shall be taken of any unauthorised act.

(7) Where the country of origin is not an EEA state and the author of the film is not a national of an EEA state, the duration of copyright is that to which the work is entitled in the country of origin, provided that does not exceed the period which would apply under subsections (2) to (6).

(8) In relation to a film of which there are joint authors, the reference in subsection (7) to the author not being a national of an EEA state shall be construed as a reference to none of the authors being a national of an EEA state.

(9) If in any case there is no person falling within paragraphs (a) to (d) of subsection (2), the above provisions do not apply and copyright expires at the end of the period of 50 years from the end of the calendar year in which the film was made.

(10) For the purposes of this section the identity of any of the persons referred to in subsection (2)(a) to (d) shall be regarded as unknown if it is not possible for a person to ascertain his identity by reasonable inquiry; but if the identity of any such person is once known it shall not subsequently be regarded as unknown.]

NOTES

This section was substituted with savings, together with s 13A for s 13 as originally enacted, by SI 1995/3297, reg 6(1); for savings see Part III thereof.
This section should be read in conjunction with the following provisions of the Duration of Copyright and Rights in Performances Regulations 1995, SI 1995/3297 (commencement: 1 December 1996):

Duration of Copyright and Rights in Performances Regulations 1995, regs 14–21, 23–25 and 36

Copyright: interpretation

14–(1) In the provisions of this Part relating to copyright–

(a)   'existing', in relation to a work, means made before commencement; and

(b)   'existing copyright work' means a work in which copyright subsisted immediately before commencement.

(2) For the purposes of those provisions a work of which the making extended over a period shall be taken to have been made when its making was completed.

(3) References in those provisions to 'moral rights' are to the rights conferred by Chapter IV of Part I of the 1988 Act.

Duration of copyright: general saving

15–(1) Copyright in an existing copyright work shall continue to subsist until the date on which it would have expired under the 1988 provisions if that date is later than the date on which copyright would expire under the new provisions.

(2) Where paragraph (1) has effect, section 57 of the 1988 Act (anonymous or pseudonymous works: acts permitted on assumptions as to expiry of copyright or death of author) applies as it applied immediately before commencement (that is, without the amendments made by Regulation 5(2)).

Duration of copyright: application of new provisions

16 The new provisions relating to duration of copyright apply–

(a)   to copyright works made after commencement;

(b)   to existing works which first qualify for copyright protection after commencement;

(c)   to existing copyright works, subject to Regulation 15 (general saving for any longer period applicable under 1988 provisions); and

(d)   to existing works in which copyright expired before 31st December 1995 but which were on 1st July 1995 protected in another EEA state under legislation relating to copyright or related rights.

Extended and revived copyright

17 In the following provisions of this Part–

'extended copyright' means any copyright which subsists by virtue of the new provisions after the date on which it would have expired under the 1988 provisions; and

'revived copyright' means any copyright which subsists by virtue of the new provisions after having expired under the 1988 provisions or any earlier enactment relating to copyright.

Ownership of extended copyright

18–(1) The person who is the owner of the copyright in a work immediately before commencement is as from commencement the owner of any extended copyright in the work, subject as follows.

(2) If he is entitled to copyright for a period less than the whole of the copyright period under the 1988 provisions, any extended copyright is part of the reversionary interest expectant on the termination of that period.

Ownership of revived copyright

19–(1) The person who was the owner of the copyright in a work immediately before it expired (the 'former copyright owner') is as from commencement the owner of any revived copyright in the work, subject as follows.

(2) If the former copyright owner has died before commencement, or in the case of a legal person has ceased to exist before commencement, the revived copyright shall vest–

(a)   in the case of a film, in the principal director of the film or his personal representatives, and

(b)   in any other case, in the author of the work or his personal representatives.

(3)   Where revived copyright vests in personal representatives by virtue of paragraph (2), it shall be held by them for the benefit of the person who would have been entitled to it had it been vested in the principal director or author immediately before his death and had devolved as part of his estate.

Prospective ownership of extended or revived copyright

20–(1) Where by an agreement made before commencement in relation to extended or revived copyright, and signed by or on behalf of the prospective owner of the copyright, the prospective owner purports to assign the extended or revived copyright (wholly or partially) to another person, then if, on commencement the assignee or another person claiming under him would be entitled as against all other persons to require the copyright to be vested in him, the copyright shall vest in the assignee or his successor in title by virtue of this paragraph.

(2) A licence granted by a prospective owner of extended or revived copyright is binding on every successor in title to his interest (or prospective interest) in the right, except a purchaser in good faith for valuable consideration and without notice (actual or constructive) of the licence or a person deriving title from such a purchaser; and references in Part I of the 1988 Act to doing anything with, or without, the licence of the copyright owner shall be construed accordingly.

(3) In paragraph (2) 'prospective owner' includes a person who is prospectively entitled to extended or revived copyright by virtue of such an agreement as is mentioned in paragraph (1).

Extended copyright: existing licences, agreement, &c

21–(1) Any copyright licence, any term or condition of an agreement relating to the exploitation of a copyright work, or any waiver or assertion of moral rights, which–

    (a)   subsists immediately before commencement in relation to an existing copyright work, and

    (b)   is not to expire before the end of the copyright period under the 1988 provisions,

shall continue to have effect during the period of any extended copyright, subject to any agreement to the contrary.

(2) Any copyright licence, or term or condition relating to the exploitation of a copyright work, imposed by order of the Copyright Tribunal which–

    (a)   subsists immediately before commencement in relation to an existing copyright work, and

    (b)   is not to expire before the end of the copyright period under the 1988 provisions,

shall continue to have effect during the period of any extended copyright, subject to any further order of the Tribunal.

Revived copyright: saving for acts of exploitation when work in public domain, &c

23–(1) No act done before commencement shall be regarded as infringing revived copyright in a work.

    (2)   It is not an infringement of revived copyright in a work–

    (a)   to do anything after commencement in pursuance of arrangements made before 1st January 1995 at a time when copyright did not subsist in the work, or

    (b)   to issue to the public after commencement copies of the work made before 1st July 1995 at a time when copyright did not subsist in the work.

(3) It is not an infringement of revived copyright in a work to do anything after commencement in relation to a literary, dramatic, musical or artistic work or a film made before commencement, or made in pursuance of arrangements made before commencement, which contains a copy of that work or is an adaptation of that work if–

    (a)   the copy or adaptation was made before 1st July 1995 at a time when copyright did not subsist in the work in which revived copyright subsists, or

    (b)   the copy or adaptation was made in pursuance of arrangements made before 1st July 1995 at a time when copyright did not subsist in the work in which revived copyright subsists.

(4) It is not an infringement of revived copyright in a work to do after commencement anything which is a restricted act in relation to the work if the act is done at a time when, or is done in pursuance of arrangements made at a time when, the name and address of a person entitled to authorise the act cannot by reasonable inquiry be ascertained.

(5) In this Regulation 'arrangements' means arrangements for the exploitation of the work in question.

(6) It is not an infringement of any moral right to do anything which by virtue of this Regulation is not an infringement of copyright.

Revived copyright: use as of right subject to reasonable royalty

24–(1) In the case of a work in which revived copyright subsists any acts restricted by the copyright shall be treated as licensed by the copyright owner, subject only to the payment of such reasonable royalty or other remuneration as may be agreed or determined in default of agreement by the Copyright Tribunal.

(2) A person intending to avail himself of the right conferred by this Regulation must give reasonable notice of his intention to the copyright owner, stating when he intends to begin to do the acts.

(3) If he does not give such notice, his acts shall not be treated as licensed.

(4) If he does give such notice, his acts shall be treated as licensed and a reasonable royalty or other remuneration shall be payable in respect of them despite the fact that its amount is not agreed or determined until later.

(5) This Regulation does not apply if or to the extent that a licence to do the acts could be granted by a licensing body (within the meaning of section 116(2) of the 1988 Act), whether or not under a licensing scheme.

(6) No royalty or other remuneration is payable by virtue of this Regulation in respect of anything for which a royalty or other remuneration is payable under Schedule 6 to the 1988 Act.

Revived copyright: application to Copyright Tribunal

25–(1) An application to settle the royalty or other remuneration payable in pursuance of Regulation 24 may be made to the Copyright Tribunal by the copyright owner or the person claiming to be treated as licensed by him.

(2) The Tribunal shall consider the matter and make such order as it may determine to be reasonable in the circumstances.

(3) Either party may subsequently apply to the Tribunal to vary the order, and the Tribunal shall consider the matter and make such order confirming or varying the original order as it may determine to be reasonable in the circumstances.

(4) An application under paragraph (3) shall not, except with the special leave of the Tribunal, be made within twelve months from the date of the original order or of the order on a previous application under that paragraph.

(5) An order under paragraph (3) has effect from the date on which it is made or such later date as may be specified by the Tribunal.

Construction of references to EEA states

36–(1) For the purpose of the new provisions relating to the term of copyright protection applicable to a work of which the country of origin is not an EEA state and of which the author is not a national of an EEA state–

(a) a work first published before 1st July 1995 shall be treated as published in an EEA state if it was on that date regarded under the law of the United Kingdom or another EEA state as having been published in that state;

(b) an unpublished film made before 1st July 1995 shall be treated as originating in an EEA state if it was on that date regarded under the law of the United Kingdom or another EEA state as a film whose maker had his headquarters in, or was domiciled or resident in, that state; and

(c) the author of a work made before 1st July 1995 shall be treated as an EEA national if he was on that date regarded under the law of the United Kingdom or another EEA state as a national of that state.

The references above to the law of another EEA state are to the law of that state having effect for the purposes of rights corresponding to those provided for in Part I of the 1988 Act.

(2) For the purposes of the new provisions relating to the term of protection applicable to a performance where the performer is not a national of an EEA state, the performer of a performance given before 1st July 1995 shall be treated as an EEA national if he was on that date regarded under the law of the United Kingdom or another EEA state as a national of that state.

The reference above to the law of another EEA state is to the law of that state having effect for the purposes of rights corresponding to those provided for in Part II of the 1988 Act.

(3) In this Regulation 'another EEA state' means an EEA state other than the United Kingdom.

[14] [Duration of copyright in broadcasts and cable programmes]

[(1) The following provisions have effect with respect to the duration of copyright in a broadcast or cable programme.

(2) Copyright in a broadcast or cable programme expires at the end of the period of 50 years from the end of the calendar year in which the broadcast was made or the programme was included in a cable programme service, subject as follows.

(3) Where the author of the broadcast or cable programme is not a national of an EEA state, the duration of copyright in the broadcast or cable programme is that to which it is entitled in the country of which the author is a national, provided that does not exceed the period which would apply under subsection (2).

(4) If or to the extent that the application of subsection (3) would be at variance with an international obligation to which the United Kingdom became subject prior to 29th October 1993, the duration of copyright shall be as specified in subsection (2).

(5) Copyright in a repeat broadcast or cable programme expires at the same time as the copyright in the original broadcast or cable programme; and accordingly no copyright arises in respect of a repeat broadcast or cable programme which is broadcast or included in a cable programme service after the expiry of the copyright in the original broadcast or cable programme.

(6) A repeat broadcast or cable programme means one which is a repeat either of a broadcast previously made or of a cable programme previously included in a cable programme service.]

NOTES
This section was substituted with savings by SI 1995/3297, reg 7(1); for savings see Part III thereof.

15 Duration of copyright in typographical arrangement of published editions

Copyright in the typographical arrangement of a published edition expires at the end of the period of 25 years from the end of the calendar year in which the edition was first published.

NOTES
Commencement order: SI 1989/816.

[15A] [Meaning of country of origin]

[(1) For the purposes of the provisions of this Part relating to the duration of copyright the country of origin of a work shall be determined as follows.

(2) If the work is first published in a Berne Convention country and is not simultaneously published elsewhere, the country of origin is that country.

(3) If the work is first published simultaneously in two or more countries only one of which is a Berne Convention country, the country of origin is that country.

(4) If the work is first published simultaneously in two or more countries of which two or more are Berne Convention countries, then–

    (a)   if any of those countries is an EEA state, the country of origin is that country; and
    (b)   if none of those countries is an EEA state, the country of origin is the Berne Convention country which grants the shorter or shortest period of copyright protection.

(5) If the work is unpublished or is first published in a country which is not a Berne Convention country (and is not simultaneously published in a Berne Convention country), the country of origin is–

    (a)   if the work is a film and the maker of the film has his headquarters in, or is domiciled or resident in a Berne Convention country, that country;
    (b)   if the work is–

        (i)   a work of architecture constructed in a Berne Convention country, or
        (ii) an artistic work incorporated in a building or other structure situated in a Berne Convention country,

        that country;

    (c)   in any other case, the country of which the author of the work is a national.

(6) In this section–

    (a)   a 'Berne Convention country' means a country which is a party to any Act of the International Convention for the Protection of Literary and Artistic Works signed at Berne on 9th September 1886; and
    (b)   references to simultaneous publication are to publication within 30 days of first publication.]

NOTES

This section was added with savings by SI 1995/3297, reg 8(1); for savings see Part III thereof.

CHAPTER II
RIGHTS OF COPYRIGHT OWNER

The acts restricted by copyright

16 The acts restricted by copyright in a work
(1) The owner of the copyright in a work has, in accordance with the following provisions of this Chapter, the exclusive right to do the following acts in the United Kingdom–

    (a)   to copy the work (see section 17);
    (b)   to issue copies of the work to the public (see section 18);
    [(ba)to rent or lend the work to the public (see section 18A);]
    (c)   to perform, show or play the work in public (see section 19);
    (d)   to broadcast the work or include it in a cable programme service (see section 20);
    (e)   to make an adaptation of the work or do any of the above in relation to an adaptation (see section 21);

and those acts are referred to in this Part as the 'acts restricted by the copyright'.

(2) Copyright in a work is infringed by a person who without the licence of the copyright owner does, or authorises another to do, any of the acts restricted by the copyright.

(3) References in this Part to the doing of an act restricted by the copyright in a work are to the doing of it–

    (a)   in relation to the work as a whole or any substantial part of it, and
    (b)   either directly or indirectly;

and it is immaterial whether any intervening acts themselves infringe copyright.

(4) This Chapter has effect subject to–

    (a)   the provisions of Chapter III (acts permitted in relation to copyright works), and

(b)   the provisions of Chapter VII (provisions with respect to copyright licensing).

NOTES

Commencement order: SI 1989/816.

Sub-s(1): words in square brackets added by SI 1996/2967, reg 10(1); for savings see part III thereof.

This section should be read in conjunction with the following provisions of the Duration of Copyright and Rights in Performances Regulations 1995, SI 1995/3297 (commencement: 1 January 1996) and the Copyright and Rights in Databases Regulations 1997, SI 1997/3032 (commencement: 1 January 1998):

Duration of Copyright and Rights in Performances Regulations 1995, regs 23, 31, 36

Revived copyright: saving for acts of exploitation when work in public domain, &c

23–(1) No act done before commencement shall be regarded as infringing revived copyright in a work.

(2) It is not an infringement of revived copyright in a work–

(a)   to do anything after commencement in pursuance of arrangements made before 1st January 1995 at a time when copyright did not subsist in the work, or

(b)   to issue to the public after commencement copies of the work made before 1st July 1995 at a time when copyright did not subsist in the work.

(3) It is not an infringement of revived copyright in a work to do anything after commencement in relation to a literary, dramatic, musical or artistic work or a film made before commencement, or made in pursuance of arrangements made before commencement, which contains a copy of that work or is an adaptation of that work if–

(a)   the copy or adaptation was made before 1st July 1995 at a time when copyright did not subsist in the work in which revived copyright subsists, or

(b)   the copy or adaptation was made in pursuance of arrangements made before 1st July 1995 at a time when copyright did not subsist in the work in which revived copyright subsists.

(4) It is not an infringement of revived copyright in a work to do after commencement anything which is a restricted act in relation to the work if the act is done at a time when, or is done in pursuance of arrangements made at a time when, the name and address of a person entitled to authorise the act cannot by reasonable inquiry be ascertained.

(5) In this Regulation 'arrangements' means arrangements for the exploitation of the work in question.

(6) It is not an infringement of any moral right to do anything which by virtue of this Regulation is not an infringement of copyright.

31 New rights: effect of pre-commencement authorisation of copying

Where before commencement–

(a)   the owner or prospective owner of copyright in a literary, dramatic, musical or artistic work has authorised a person to make a copy of the work, or

(b)   the owner or prospective owner of performers' rights in a performance has authorised a person to make a copy of a recording of the performance,

any new right in relation to that copy shall vest on commencement in the person so authorised, subject to any agreement to the contrary.

36 Authorship of films

(1) Regulation 18 (authorship of films) applies as from commencement in relation to films made on or after 1st July 1994.

(2) It is not an infringement of any right which the principal director has by virtue of these Regulations to do anything after commencement in pursuance of arrangements for the exploitation of the film made before 19th November 1992.

Copyright and Rights in Databases Regulations, regs 12(2)–(5), 16, 19, 23, 28

12–(2) The making of a copy of a database available for use, on terms that it will or may be returned, otherwise than for direct or indirect economic or commercial advantage, through an establishment which is accessible to the public shall not be taken for the purposes of this Part to constitute extraction or re-utilisation of the contents of the database.

(3) Where the making of a copy of a database available through an establishment which is accessible to the public gives rise to a payment the amount of which does not go beyond what is necessary to cover the costs of the establishment, there is no direct or indirect economic or commercial advantage for the purposes of paragraph (2).

(4) Paragraph (2) does not apply to the making of a copy of a database available for on-the-spot reference use.

(5) Where a copy of a database has been sold within the EEA by, or with the consent of, the owner of the database right in the database, the further sale within the EEA of that copy shall not be taken for the purposes of this Part to constitute extraction or re-utilisation of the contents of the database.

16 Acts infringing database right

(1) Subject to the provisions of this Part, a person infringes database right in a database if, without the consent of the owner of the right, he extracts or re-utilises all or a substantial part of the contents of the database.

(2) For the purposes of this Part, the repeated and systematic extraction or re-utilisation of insubstantial parts of the contents of a database may amount to the extraction or re-utilisation of a substantial part of those contents.

19 Avoidance of certain terms affecting lawful users

(1) A lawful user of a database which has been made available to the public in any manner shall be entitled to extract or re-utilise insubstantial parts of the contents of the database for any purpose.

(2) Where under an agreement a person has a right to use a database, or part of a database, which has been made available to the public in any manner, any term or condition in the agreement shall be void in so far as it purports to prevent that person from extracting or re-utilising insubstantial parts of the contents of the database, or of that part of the database, for any purpose.

23 Application of copyright provisions to database right

The following provisions of the 1988 Act—

sections 90 to 93 (dealing with rights in copyright works);
sections 96 to 98 (rights and remedies of copyright owner);
sections 101 and 102 (rights and remedies of exclusive licensee);

apply in relation to database right and databases in which that right subsists as they apply in relation to copyright and copyright works.

28 General savings

(1) Nothing in these Regulations affects any agreement made before commencement.

(2) No act done—

    (a) before commencement, or
    (b) after commencement, in pursuance of an agreement made before commencement,

shall be regarded as an infringement of database right in a database.

---

17 Infringement of copyright by copying

(1) The copying of the work is an act restricted by the copyright in every description of copyright work; and references in this Part to copying and copies shall be construed as follows.

(2) Copying in relation to a literary, dramatic, musical or artistic work means reproducing the work in any material form.
This includes storing the work in any medium by electronic means.

(3) In relation to an artistic work copying includes the making of a copy in three dimensions of a two-dimensional work and the making of a copy in two dimensions of a three-dimensional work.

(4) Copying in relation to a film, television broadcast or cable programme includes making a photograph of the whole or any substantial part of any image forming part of the film, broadcast or cable programme.

(5) Copying in relation to the typographical arrangement of a published edition means making a facsimile copy of the arrangement.

(6) Copying in relation to any description of work includes the making of copies which are transient or are incidental to some other use of the work.

NOTES

Commencement order: SI 1989/816.

---

18 Infringement by issue of copies to the public

(1) The issue to the public of copies of the work is an act restricted by the copyright in every description of copyright work.

[(2) References in this Part to the issue to the public of copies of a work are to—

    (a) the act of putting into circulation in the EEA copies not previously put into circulation in the EEA by or with the consent of the copyright owner, or
    (b) the act of putting into circulation outside the EEA copies not previously put into circulation in the EEA or elsewhere.

(3) References in this Part to the issue to the public of copies of a work do not include—

(a) any subsequent distribution, sale, hiring or loan of copies previously put into circula-
     tion (but see section 18A: infringement by rental or lending), or
(b) any subsequent importation of such copies into the United Kingdom or another EEA
     state,

except so far as paragraph (a) of subsection (2) applies to putting into circulation in the EEA
copies previously put into circulation outside the EEA.]

[(4) References in this Part to the issue of copies of a work include the issue of the
original.]

NOTES

Commencement order: SI 1989/816.
Sub-s (2): substituted by SI 1996/2967, reg 9(2).
Sub-s (3): added by SI 1992/3233, reg 4(2); substituted by SI 1996/2967, reg 9(2).
Sub-s (4): added by SI 1996/2967, reg 9(3).

[18A] [Infringement by rental or lending of work to the public]

[(1) The rental or lending of copies of the work to the public is an act restricted by the copyright
in–

(a) a literary, dramatic or musical work,
(b) an artistic work, other than–

  (i)   a work of architecture in the form of a building or a model for a building, or
  (ii) a work of applied art, or

(c) a film or a sound recording.

(2) In this Part, subject to the following provisions of this section–

(a) 'rental' means making a copy of the work available for use, on terms that it will or may
     be returned, for direct or indirect economic or commercial advantage, and
(b) 'lending' means making a copy of the work available for use, on terms that it will or
     may be returned, otherwise than for direct or indirect economic or commercial
     advantage, through an establishment which is accessible to the public.

(3) The expressions 'rental' and 'lending' do not include–

(a) making available for the purpose of public performance, playing or showing in public,
     broadcasting or inclusion in a cable programme service;
(b) making available for the purpose of exhibition in public; or
(c) making available for on-the-spot reference use.

(4) The expression 'lending' does not include making available between establishments
which are accessible to the public.

(5) Where lending by an establishment accessible to the public gives rise to a payment the
amount of which does not go beyond what is necessary to cover the operating costs of the
establishment, there is no direct or indirect economic or commercial advantage for the
purposes of this section.

(6) References in this Part to the rental or lending of copies of a work include the rental or
lending of the original.]

NOTES

Added by SI 1996/2967, reg 10(2).

This section should be read in conjunction with the following provision of the Copyright and Related Rights
Regulations 1996, SI 1996/2967 (commencement: 1 December 1996):

Copyright and Related Rights Regulations 1996, reg 34(1)

Savings for existing stocks

34–(1) Any new right in relation to a copyright work does not apply to a copy of the work acquired by a person before
commencement for the purpose of renting or lending it to the public.

19 Infringement by performance, showing or playing of work in public
(1) The performance of the work in public is an act restricted by the copyright in a literary, dramatic or musical work.

(2) In this Part 'performance', in relation to a work–

(a) includes delivery in the case of lectures, addresses, speeches and sermons, and
(b) in general, includes any mode of visual or acoustic presentation, including presentation by means of a sound recording, film, broadcast or cable programme of the work.

(3) The playing or showing of the work in public is an act restricted by the copyright in a sound recording, film, broadcast or cable programme.

(4) Where copyright in a work is infringed by its being performed, played or shown in public by means of apparatus for receiving visual images or sounds conveyed by electronic means, the person by whom the visual images or sounds are sent, and in the case of a performance the performers, shall not be regarded as responsible for the infringement.

NOTES
Commencement order: SI 1989/816.

20 Infringement by broadcasting or inclusion in a cable programme service
The broadcasting of the work or its inclusion in a cable programme service is an act restricted by the copyright in–

(a) a literary, dramatic, musical or artistic work,
(b) a sound recording or film, or
(c) a broadcast or cable programme.

NOTES
Commencement order: SI 1989/816.

21 Infringement by making adaptation or act done in relation to adaptation
(1) The making of an adaptation of the work is an act restricted by the copyright in a literary, dramatic or musical work.

For this purpose an adaptation is made when it is recorded, in writing or otherwise.

(2) The doing of any of the acts specified in sections 17 to 20, or subsection (1) above, in relation to an adaptation of the work is also an act restricted by the copyright in a literary, dramatic or musical work.

For this purpose it is immaterial whether the adaptation has been recorded, in writing or otherwise, at the time the act is done.

(3) In this Part 'adaptation'–

(a) in relation to a literary [work,] [other than a computer program, or a database, or in relation to a] or dramatic work, means–

(i) a translation of the work;
(ii) a version of a dramatic work in which it is converted into a non-dramatic work or, as the case may be, of a non-dramatic work in which it is converted into a dramatic work;
(iii) a version of the work in which the story or action is conveyed wholly or mainly by means of pictures in a form suitable for reproduction in a book, or in a newspaper, magazine or similar periodical;

[(ab) in relation to a computer program, means an arrangement or altered version of the program or a translation of it;]
[(ac) in relation to a database means an arrangement or altered version of the database or a translation of it;]
(b) in relation to a musical work, means an arrangement or transcription of the work.

(4) In relation to a computer program a 'translation' includes a version of the program in which it is converted into or out of a computer language or code or into a different computer language or code

(5) No inference shall be drawn from this section as to what does or does not amount to copying a work.

NOTES
Commencement order: SI 1989/816.
Sub-s (3): words in square brackets added by SI 1992/3233, reg 5(1), (2) and SI 1997/3032, reg 7.

Secondary infringement of copyright

22 Secondary infringement: importing infringing copy

The copyright in a work is infringed by a person who, without the licence of the copyright owner, imports into the United Kingdom, otherwise than for his private and domestic use, an article which is, and which he knows or has reason to believe is, an infringing copy of the work.

NOTE
Commencement order: SI 1989/816.

23 Secondary infringement: possessing or dealing with infringing copy

The copyright in a work is infringed by a person who, without the licence of the copyright owner–

(a)   possesses in the course of a business,
(b)   sells or lets for hire, or offers or exposes for sale or hire,
(c)   in the course of a business exhibits in public or distributes, or
(d)   distributes otherwise than in the course of a business to such an extent as to affect prejudicially the owner of the copyright,

an article which is, and which he knows or has reason to believe is, an infringing copy of the work.

NOTE
Commencement order: SI 1989/816.

24 Secondary infringement: providing means for making infringing copies

(1) Copyright in a work is infringed by a person who, without the licence of the copyright owner–

(a)   makes,
(b)   imports into the United Kingdom,
(c)   possesses in the course of a business, or
(d)   sells or lets for hire, or offers or exposes for sale or hire,

an article specifically designed or adapted for making copies of that work, knowing or having reason to believe that it is to be used to make infringing copies.

(2) Copyright in a work is infringed by a person who without the licence of the copyright owner transmits the work by means of a telecommunications system (otherwise than by broadcasting or inclusion in a cable programme service), knowing or having reason to believe that infringing copies of the work will be made by means of the reception of the transmission in the United Kingdom or elsewhere.

NOTE
Commencement order: SI 1989/816.

25 Secondary infringement: permitting use of premises for infringing performance

(1) Where the copyright in a literary, dramatic or musical work is infringed by a performance at a place of public entertainment, any person who gave permission for that place to be used for

the performance is also liable for the infringement unless when he gave permission he believed on reasonable grounds that the performance would not infringe copyright.

(2) In this section 'place of public entertainment' includes premises which are occupied mainly for other purposes but are from time to time made available for hire for the purposes of public entertainment.

NOTE
Commencement order: SI 1989/816.

---

26 Secondary infringement: provision of apparatus for infringing performance, &c

(1) Where copyright in a work is infringed by a public performance of the work, or by the playing or showing of the work in public, by means of apparatus for–

    (a) playing sound recordings,
    (b) showing films, or
    (c) receiving visual images or sounds conveyed by electronic means,

the following persons are also liable for the infringement.

(2) A person who supplied the apparatus, or any substantial part of it, is liable for the infringement if when he supplied the apparatus or part–

    (a) he knew or had reason to believe that the apparatus was likely to be so used as to infringe copyright, or
    (b) in the case of apparatus whose normal use involves a public performance, playing or showing, he did not believe on reasonable grounds that it would not be so used as to infringe copyright.

(3) An occupier of premises who gave permission for the apparatus to be brought onto the premises is liable for the infringement if when he gave permission he knew or had reason to believe that the apparatus was likely to be so used as to infringe copyright.

(4) A person who supplied a copy of a sound recording or film used to infringe copyright is liable for the infringement if when he supplied it he knew or had reason to believe that what he supplied, or a copy made directly or indirectly from it, was likely to be so used as to infringe copyright.

NOTE
Commencement order: SI 1989/816.

Infringing copies

27 Meaning of 'infringing copy'

(1) In this Part 'infringing copy', in relation to a copyright work, shall be construed in accordance with this section.

(2) An article is an infringing copy if its making constituted an infringement of the copyright in the work in question.

(3) An article is also an infringing copy if–

    (a) it has been or is proposed to be imported into the United Kingdom, and
    (b) its making in the United Kingdom would have constituted an infringement of the copyright in the work in question, or a breach of an exclusive licence agreement relating to that work.

(4) Where in any proceedings the question arises whether an article is an infringing copy and it is shown–

    (a) that the article is a copy of the work, and
    (b) that copyright subsists in the work or has subsisted at any time,

it shall be presumed until the contrary is proved that the article was made at a time when copyright subsisted in the work.

(5) Nothing in subsection (3) shall be construed as applying to an article which may lawfully be imported into the United Kingdom by virtue of any enforceable Community right within the meaning of section 2(1) of the European Communities Act 1972.

(6) In this Part 'infringing copy' includes a copy falling to be treated as an infringing copy by virtue of any of the following provisions–

> section 32(5) (copies made for purposes of instruction or examination),
> section 35(3) (recordings made by educational establishments for educational purposes),
> section 36(5) (reprographic copying by educational establishments for purposes of instruction),
> section 37(3)(b) (copies made by librarian or archivist in reliance on false declaration),
> section 56(2) (further copies, adaptations, &c of work in electronic form retained on transfer of principal copy),
> section 63(2) (copies made for purpose of advertising artistic work for sale),
> section 68(4) (copies made for purpose of broadcast or cable programme), or
> any provision of an order under section 141 (statutory licence for certain reprographic copying by educational establishments).

NOTE
Commencement order: SI 1989/816.

CHAPTER III
ACTS PERMITTED IN RELATION TO COPYRIGHT WORKS

Introductory

28 Introductory provisions
(1) The provisions of this Chapter specify acts which may be done in relation to copyright works notwithstanding the subsistence of copyright; they relate only to the question of infringement of copyright and do not affect any other right or obligation restricting the doing of any of the specified acts.

(2) Where it is provided by this Chapter that an act does not infringe copyright, or may be done without infringing copyright, and no particular description of copyright work is mentioned, the act in question does not infringe the copyright in a work of any description.

(3) No inference shall be drawn from the description of any act which may by virtue of this Chapter be done without infringing copyright as to the scope of the acts restricted by the copyright in any description of work.

(4) The provisions of this Chapter are to be construed independently of each other, so that the fact that an act does not fall within one provision does not mean that it is not covered by another provision.

NOTES
Commencement order: SI 1989/816.
See further, in relation to programme services: the Broadcasting Act 1990, s 176, Sch 17.

General

29 Research and private study
(1) Fair dealing with a literary [work other than a database, or a], dramatic, musical or artistic work for the purposes of research or private study does not infringe any copyright in the work or, in the case of a published edition, in the typographical arrangement.

[(1A) Fair dealing with a database for the purposes of research or private study does not infringe any copyright in the database provided that the source is indicated.]

(2) Fair dealing with the typographical arrangement of a published edition for the purposes mentioned in subsection (1) does not infringe any copyright in the arrangement.

(3) Copying by a person other than the researcher or student himself is not fair dealing if–

(a) in the case of a librarian, or a person acting on behalf of a librarian, he does anything which regulations under section 40 would not permit to be done under section 38 or 39 (articles or parts of published works: restriction on multiple copies of same material), or

(b) in any other case, the person doing the copying knows or has reason to believe that it will result in copies of substantially the same material being provided to more than one person at substantially the same time and for substantially the same purpose.

[(4) It is not fair dealing–

(a) to convert a computer program expressed in a low level language into a version expressed in a higher level language, or

(b) incidentally in the course of so converting the program, to copy it,

(these acts being permitted if done in accordance with section 50B (decompilation)).]

[(5) The doing of anything in relation to a database for the purposes of research for a commercial purpose is not fair dealing with the database.]

NOTES

Commencement order: SI 1989/816.

Sub-s (4): added by SI 1992/3233, reg 7.

See further, in relation to programme services: the Broadcasting Act 1990, s 176, Sch 17.

This section should be read in conjunction with Sch 1 of the Copyright and Rights in Databases Regulations 1997, SI 1997/3032. This is referred to at reg 20(2), contextualised in this Act at s 50D.

Words in square brackets and sub-s (1A) and (5) added by SI 1997/3032, reg 8.

This section should also be read in conjunction with the following provision of the Copyright and Rights in Databases Regulations 1997, SI 1997/3032 (commencement: 1 January 1998):

Copyright and Rights in Databases Regulations 1997, reg 20

20 Exceptions to database right

(1) Database right in a database which has been made available to the public in any manner is not infringed by fair dealing with a substantial part of its contents if–

(a) that part is extracted from the database by a person who is apart from this paragraph a lawful user of the database,

(b) it is extracted for the purpose of illustration for teaching or research and not for any commercial purpose, and

(c) the source is indicated.

(2) The provisions of Schedule 1 specify other acts which may be done in relation to a database notwithstanding the existence of database right.

30 Criticism, review and news reporting

(1) Fair dealing with a work for the purpose of criticism or review, of that or another work or of a performance of a work, does not infringe any copyright in the work provided that it is accompanied by a sufficient acknowledgement.

(2) Fair dealing with a work (other than a photograph) for the purpose of reporting current events does not infringe any copyright in the work provided that (subject to subsection (3)) it is accompanied by a sufficient acknowledgement.

(3) No acknowledgement is required in connection with the reporting of current events by means of a sound recording, film, broadcast or cable programme.

NOTES

Commencement order: SI 1989/816.

See further, in relation to programme services: the Broadcasting Act 1990, s 176, Sch 17.

This section should be read in conjunction with the Broadcasting Act 1996, s 137:

Broadcasting Act 1996, s 137

137 Avoidance of certain terms relating to use for purpose of news reporting of visual images from broadcast or cable programme

(1) Any provision in an agreement is void in so far as it purports to prohibit or restrict relevant dealing with a broadcast or cable programme in any circumstances where by virtue of section 30(2) of the Copyright, Designs and Patents Act 1988 (fair dealing for the purpose of reporting current events) copyright in the broadcast or cable programme is not infringed.

(2) In subsection (1)–

(a) 'relevant dealing', in relation to a broadcast or cable programme, means dealing by including visual images taken from it in another broadcast or cable programmme, and

(b) 'broadcast' and 'cable programme' have the same meaning as in Part I of the Copyright, Designs and Patents Act 1988.

31 Incidental inclusion of copyright material

(1) Copyright in a work is not infringed by its incidental inclusion in an artistic work, sound recording, film, broadcast or cable programme.

(2) Nor is the copyright infringed by the issue to the public of copies, or the playing, showing, broadcasting or inclusion in a cable programme service, of anything whose making was, by virtue of subsection (1), not an infringement of the copyright.

(3) A musical work, words spoken or sung with music, or so much of a sound recording, broadcast or cable programme as includes a musical work or such words, shall not be regarded as incidentally included in another work if it is deliberately included.

NOTES

Commencement order: SI 1989/816.

See further, in relation to programme services: the Broadcasting Act 1990, s 176, Sch 17.

Education

32 Things done for purposes of instruction or examination

(1) Copyright in a literary, dramatic, musical or artistic work is not infringed by its being copied in the course of instruction or of preparation for instruction, provided the copying–

(a) is done by a person giving or receiving instruction, and

(b) is not by means of a reprographic process.

(2) Copyright in a sound recording, film, broadcast or cable programme is not infringed by its being copied by making a film or film sound-track in the course of instruction, or of preparation for instruction, in the making of films or film sound-tracks, provided the copying is done by a person giving or receiving instruction.

(3) Copyright is not infringed by anything done for the purposes of an examination by way of setting the questions, communicating the questions to the candidates or answering the questions.

(4) Subsection (3) does not extend to the making of a reprographic copy of a musical work for use by an examination candidate in performing the work.

(5) Where a copy which would otherwise be an infringing copy is made in accordance with this section but is subsequently dealt with, it shall be treated as an infringing copy for the purpose of that dealing, and if that dealing infringes copyright for all subsequent purposes. For this purpose 'dealt with' means sold or let for hire or offered or exposed for sale or hire.

NOTES

Commencement order: SI 1989/816.

See further, in relation to programme services: the Broadcasting Act 1990, s 176, Sch 17.

33 Anthologies for educational use

(1) The inclusion of a short passage from a published literary or dramatic work in a collection which–

(a)   is intended for use in educational establishments and is so described in its title, and in any advertisements issued by or on behalf of the publisher, and

(b)   consists mainly of material in which no copyright subsists,

does not infringe the copyright in the work if the work itself is not intended for use in such establishments and the inclusion is accompanied by a sufficient acknowledgement.

(2) Subsection (1) does not authorise the inclusion of more than two excerpts from copyright works by the same author in collections published by the same publisher over any period of five years.

(3) In relation to any given passage the reference in subsection (2) to excerpts from works by the same author–

(a)   shall be taken to include excerpts from works by him in collaboration with another, and

(b)   if the passage in question is from such a work, shall be taken to include excerpts from works by any of the authors, whether alone or in collaboration with another.

(4) References in this section to the use of a work in an educational establishment are to any use for the educational purposes of such an establishment.

NOTES
Commencement order: SI 1989/816.
See further, in relation to programme services: the Broadcasting Act 1990, s 176, Sch 17.

34 Performing, playing or showing work in course of activities of educational establishment

(1) The performance of a literary, dramatic or musical work before an audience consisting of teachers and pupils at an educational establishment and other persons directly connected with the activities of the establishment–

(a)   by a teacher or pupil in the course of the activities of the establishment, or

(b)   at the establishment by any person for the purposes of instruction,

is not a public performance for the purposes of infringement of copyright.

(2) The playing or showing of a sound recording, film, broadcast or cable programme before such an audience at an educational establishment for the purposes of instruction is not a playing or showing of the work in public for the purposes of infringement of copyright.

(3) A person is not for this purpose directly connected with the activities of the educational establishment simply because he is the parent of a pupil at the establishment.

NOTES
Commencement order: SI 1989/816.
See further, in relation to programme services: the Broadcasting Act 1990, s 176, Sch 17.

35 Recording by educational establishments of broadcasts and cable programmes

(1) A recording of a broadcast or cable programme, or a copy of such a recording, may be made by or on behalf of an educational establishment for the educational purposes of that establishment without thereby infringing the copyright in the broadcast or cable programme, or in any work included in it.

(2) This section does not apply if or to the extent that there is a licensing scheme certified for the purposes of this section under section 143 providing for the grant of licences.

(3) Where a copy which would otherwise be an infringing copy is made in accordance with this section but is subsequently dealt with, it shall be treated as an infringing copy for the purposes of that dealing, and if that dealing infringes copyright for all subsequent purposes.

For this purpose 'dealt with' means sold or let for hire or offered or exposed for sale or hire.

NOTES
Commencement order: SI 1989/816.
See further: the Copyright (Application of Provisions Relating to Educational Establishments to Teachers) (No 2) Order 1989, SI 1989/1067, art 2.
See further, in relation to programme services: the Broadcasting Act 1990, s 176, Sch 17.

114   *Part 2*

36 Reprographic copying by educational establishments of passages from published works

(1) Reprographic copies of passages from published literary, dramatic or musical works may, to the extent permitted by this section, be made by or on behalf of an educational establishment for the purposes of instruction without infringing any copyright in the work, or in the typographical arrangement.

(2) Not more than one per cent of any work may be copied by or on behalf of an establishment by virtue of this section in any quarter, that is, in any period 1st January to 31st March, 1st April to 30th June, 1st July to 30th September or 1st October to 31st December.

(3) Copying is not authorised by this section if, or to the extent that, licences are available authorising the copying in question and the person making the copies knew or ought to have been aware of that fact.

(4) The terms of a licence granted to an educational establishment authorising the reprographic copying for the purposes of instruction of passages from published literary, dramatic or musical works are of no effect so far as they purport to restrict the proportion of a work which may be copied (whether on payment or free of charge) to less than that which would be permitted under this section.

(5) Where a copy which would otherwise be an infringing copy is made in accordance with this section but is subsequently dealt with, it shall be treated as an infringing copy for the purposes of that dealing, and if that dealing infringes copyright for all subsequent purposes.

For this purpose 'dealt with' means sold or let for hire or offered or exposed for sale or hire.

NOTES

Commencement order: SI 1989/816.
See further: the Copyright (Application of Provisions Relating to Educational Establishments to Teachers) (No 2) Order 1989, SI 1989/1067, art 2.
See further, in relation to programme services: the Broadcasting Act 1990, s 176, Sch 17.

[36A] [Lending of copies by educational establishments]
[Copyright in a work is not infringed by the lending of copies of the work by an educational establishment.]

NOTE

Added by SI 1996/2967, reg 11(1).

Libraries and archives

37 Libraries and archives: introductory
(1) In sections 38 to 43 (copying by librarians and archivists)–

(a) references in any provision to a prescribed library or archive are to a library or archive of a description prescribed for the purposes of that provision by regulations made by the Secretary of State; and
(b) references in any provision to the prescribed conditions are to the conditions so prescribed.

(2) The regulations may provide that, where a librarian or archivist is required to be satisfied as to any matter before making or supplying a copy of a work–

(a) he may rely on a signed declaration as to that matter by the person requesting the copy, unless he is aware that it is false in a material particular, and
(b) in such cases as may be prescribed, he shall not make or supply a copy in the absence of a signed declaration in such form as may be prescribed.

(3) Where a person requesting a copy makes a declaration which is false in a material particular and is supplied with a copy which would have been an infringing copy if made by him–

    (a)   he is liable for infringement of copyright as if he had made the copy himself, and

    (b)   the copy shall be treated as an infringing copy.

(4) The regulations may make different provision for different descriptions of libraries or archives and for different purposes.

(5) Regulations shall be made by statutory instrument which shall be subject to annulment in pursuance of a resolution of either House of Parliament.

(6) References in this section, and in sections 38 to 43, to the librarian or archivist include a person acting on his behalf.

NOTES
Commencement orders: SI 1989/816, SI 1989/955, SI 1989/1032.
See further, in relation to programme services: the Broadcasting Act 1990, s 176, Sch 17.

38 Copying by librarians: articles in periodicals
(1) The librarian of a prescribed library may, if the prescribed conditions are complied with, make and supply a copy of an article in a periodical without infringing any copyright in the text, in any illustrations accompanying the text or in the typographical arrangement.

(2) The prescribed conditions shall include the following–

    (a)   that copies are supplied only to persons satisfying the librarian that they require them for purposes of research or private study, and will not use them for any other purpose;

    (b)   that no person is furnished with more than one copy of the same article or with copies of more than one article contained in the same issue of a periodical; and

    (c)   that persons to whom copies are supplied are required to pay for them a sum not less than the cost (including a contribution to the general expenses of the library) attributable to their production.

NOTES
Commencement orders: SI 1989/816, SI 1989/955, SI 1989/1032.
See further, in relation to programme services: the Broadcasting Act 1990, s 176, Sch 17.

39 Copying by librarians: parts of published works
(1) The librarian of a prescribed library may, if the prescribed conditions are complied with, make and supply from a published edition a copy of part of a literary, dramatic or musical work (other than an article in a periodical) without infringing any copyright in the work, in any illustrations accompanying the work or in the typographical arrangement.

(2) The prescribed conditions shall include the following–

    (a)   that copies are supplied only to persons satisfying the librarian that they require them for purposes of research or private study, and will not use them for any other purpose;

    (b)   that no person is furnished with more than one copy of the same material or with a copy of more than a reasonable proportion of any work; and

    (c)   that person to whom copies are supplied are required to pay for them a sum not less than the cost (including a contribution to the general expenses of the library) attributable to their production.

NOTES
Commencement orders: SI 1989/816, SI 1989/955, SI 1989/1032.
See further, in relation to programme services: the Broadcasting Act 1990, s 176, Sch 17.

40 Restriction on production of multiple copies of the same material
(1) Regulations for the purposes of sections 38 and 39 (copying by librarian of article or part of published work) shall contain provision to the effect that a copy shall be supplied only to a

person satisfying the librarian that his requirement is not related to any similar requirement of another person.

(2) The regulations may provide–

(a) that requirements shall be regarded as similar if the requirements are for copies of substantially the same material at substantially the same time and for substantially the same purpose; and

(b) that requirements of persons shall be regarded as related if those persons receive instruction to which the material is relevant at the same time and place.

NOTES
Commencement orders: SI 1989/816, SI 1989/955, SI 1989/1032.
See further, in relation to programme services: the Broadcasting Act 1990, s 176, Sch 17.

[40A] [Lending of copies by libraries or archives]

[(1) Copyright in a work of any description is not infringed by the lending of a book by a public library if the book is within the public lending right scheme.

For this purpose–

(a) 'the public lending right scheme' means the scheme in force under section 1 of the Public Lending Right Act 1979, and

(b) a book is within the public lending right scheme if it is a book within the meaning of the provisions of the scheme relating to eligibility, whether or not it is in fact eligible.

(2) Copyright in a work is not infringed by the lending of copies of the work by a prescribed library or archive (other than a public library) which is not conducted for profit.]

NOTES
Added by SI 1996/2967, reg 11(2).
This section should be read in conjunction with the following provision of the Copyright and Related Rights Regulations 1996, SI 1996/2967 (commencement: 1 December 1996):

Copyright and Related Rights Regulations 1996, reg 35

Lending of copies by libraries or archives
35 Until the making of regulations under section 37 of the Copyright, Designs and Patents Act 1988 for the purposes of section 40A(2) of that Act (lending of copies by libraries or archives), the reference in section 40A(2) (and in paragraph 6B of Schedule 2) to a prescribed library or archive shall be construed as a reference to any library or archive in the United Kingdom prescribed by paragraphs 2 to 6 of Part A of Schedule 1 to the Copyright (Librarians and Archivists) (Copying of Copyright Material) Regulations 1989.

41 Copying by librarians: supply of copies to other libraries

(1) The librarian of a prescribed library may, if the prescribed conditions are complied with, make and supply to another prescribed library a copy of–

(a) an article in a periodical, or

(b) the whole or part of a published edition of a literary, dramatic or musical work,

without infringing any copyright in the text of the article or, as the case may be, in the work, in any illustrations accompanying it or in the typographical arrangement.

(2) Subsection (1)(b) does not apply if at the time the copy is made the librarian making it knows, or could by reasonable inquiry ascertain, the name and address of a person entitled to authorise the making of the copy.

NOTES
Commencement orders: SI 1989/816, SI 1989/955, SI 1989/1032.
See further, in relation to programme services: the Broadcasting Act 1990, s 176, Sch 17.

42 Copying by librarians or archivists: replacement copies of works

(1) The librarian or archivist of a prescribed library or archive may, if the prescribed conditions are complied with, make a copy from any item in the permanent collection of the library or archive–

(a)   in order to preserve or replace that item by placing the copy in its permanent collection in addition to or in place of it, or

(b)   in order to replace in the permanent collection of another prescribed library or archive an item which has been lost, destroyed or damaged,

without infringing the copyright in any literary, dramatic or musical work, in any illustrations accompanying such a work or, in the case of a published edition, in the typographical arrangement.

(2) The prescribed conditions shall include provision for restricting the making of copies to cases where it is not reasonably practicable to purchase a copy of the item in question to fulfil that purpose.

NOTES
Commencement orders: SI 1989/816, SI 1989/955, SI 1989/1032.
See further, in relation to programme services: the Broadcasting Act 1990, s 176, Sch 17.

43 Copying by librarians or archivists: certain unpublished works

(1) The librarian or archivist of a prescribed library or archive may, if the prescribed conditions are complied with, make and supply a copy of the whole or part of a literary, dramatic or musical work from a document in the library or archive without infringing any copyright in the work or any illustrations accompanying it.

(2) This section does not apply if–

(a)   the work had been published before the document was deposited in the library or archive, or

(b)   the copyright owner has prohibited copying of the work,
and at the time the copy is made the librarian or archivist making it is, or ought to be, aware of that fact.

(3) The prescribed conditions shall include the following–

(a)   that copies are supplied only to persons satisfying the librarian or archivist that they require them for purposes of research or private study and will not use them for any other purpose;

(b)   that no person is furnished with more than one copy of the same material; and

(c)   that persons to whom copies are supplied are required to pay for them a sum not less than the cost (including a contribution to the general expenses of the library or archive) attributable to their production.

NOTES
Commencement orders: SI 1989/816, SI 1989/955, SI 1989/1032.
See further, in relation to programme services: the Broadcasting Act 1990, s 176, Sch 17.

44 Copy of work required to be made as condition of export

If an article of cultural or historical importance or interest cannot lawfully be exported from the United Kingdom unless a copy of it is made and deposited in an appropriate library or archive, it is not an infringement of copyright to make that copy.

NOTES
Commencement order: SI 1989/816.
See further, in relation to programme services: the Broadcasting Act 1990, s 176, Sch 17.

Public administration

45 Parliamentary and judicial proceedings

(1) Copyright is not infringed by anything done for the purposes of parliamentary or judicial proceedings.

(2) Copyright is not infringed by anything done for the purposes of reporting such proceedings; but this shall not be construed as authorising the copying of a work which is itself a published report of the proceedings.

NOTES
Commencement order: SI 1989/816.
See further, in relation to programme services: the Broadcasting Act 1990, s 176, Sch 17.

46 Royal Commissions and statutory inquiries

(1) Copyright is not infringed by anything done for the purposes of the proceedings of a Royal Commission or statutory inquiry.

(2) Copyright is not infringed by anything done for the purpose of reporting any such proceedings held in public; but this shall not be construed as authorising the copying of a work which is itself a published report of the proceedings.

(3) Copyright in a work is not infringed by the issue to the public of copies of the report of a Royal Commission or statutory inquiry containing the work or material from it.

(4) In this section–

> 'Royal Commission' includes a Commission appointed for Northern Ireland by the Secretary of State in pursuance of the prerogative powers of Her Majesty delegated to him under section 7(2) of the Northern Ireland Constitution Act 1973; and
>
> 'statutory inquiry' means an inquiry held or investigation conducted in pursuance of a duty imposed or power conferred by or under an enactment.

NOTES
Commencement order: SI 1989/816.
See further, in relation to programme services: the Broadcasting Act 1990, s 176, Sch 17.

47 Material open to public inspection or on official register

(1) Where material is open to public inspection pursuant to a statutory requirement, or is on a statutory register, any copyright in the material as a literary work is not infringed by the copying of so much of the material as contains factual information of any description, by or with the authority of the appropriate person, for a purpose which does not involve the issuing of copies to the public.

(2) Where material is open to public inspection pursuant to a statutory requirement, copyright is not infringed by the copying or issuing to the public of copies of the material, by or with the authority of the appropriate person, for the purpose of enabling the material to be inspected at a more convenient time or place or otherwise facilitating the exercise of any right for the purpose of which the requirement is imposed.

(3) Where material which is open to public inspection pursuant to a statutory requirement, or which is on a statutory register, contains information about matters of general scientific, technical, commercial or economic interest, copyright is not infringed by the copying or issuing to the public of copies of the material, by or with the authority of the appropriate person, for the purpose of disseminating that information.

(4) The Secretary of State may by order provide that subsection (1), (2) or (3) shall, in such cases as may be specified in the order, apply only to copies marked in such manner as may be so specified.

(5) The Secretary of State may by order provide that subsections (1) to (3) apply, to such extent and with such modifications as may be specified in the order–

(a) to material made open to public inspection by–

    (i) an international organisation specified in the order, or

    (ii) a person so specified who has functions in the United Kingdom under an international agreement to which the United Kingdom is party, or

(b) to a register maintained by an international organisation specified in the order,

as they apply in relation to material open to public inspection pursuant to a statutory requirement or to a statutory register.

(6) In this section–

> 'appropriate person' means the person required to make the material open to public inspection or, as the case may be, the person maintaining the register;

'statutory register' means a register maintained in pursuance of a statutory requirement; and

'statutory requirement' means a requirement imposed by provision made by or under an enactment.

(7) An order under this section shall be made by statutory instrument which shall be subject to annulment in pursuance of a resolution of either House of Parliament.

NOTES
Commencement orders: SI 1989/816, SI 1989/955, SI 1989/1032.
Modified by the Copyright (Material Open to Public Inspection) (International Organisations) Order 1989, SI 1989/1098, arts 2, 3, the Copyright (Material Open to Public Inspection) (Marking of Copies of Maps) Order 1989, SI 1989/1099, art 2, and the Copyright (Material Open to Public Inspection) (Marking of Copies of Plans and Drawings) Order 1990, SI 1990/1427.
See further, in relation to programme services: the Broadcasting Act 1990, s 176, Sch 17.

48 Material communicated to the Crown in the course of public business

(1) This section applies where a literary, dramatic, musical or artistic work has in the course of public business been communicated to the Crown for any purpose, by or with the licence of the copyright owner and a document or other material thing recording or embodying the work is owned by or in the custody or control of the Crown.

(2) The Crown may, for the purpose for which the work was communicated to it, or any related purpose which could reasonably have been anticipated by the copyright owner, copy the work and issue copies of the work to the public without infringing any copyright in the work.

(3) The Crown may not copy a work, or issue copies of a work to the public, by virtue of this section if the work has previously been published otherwise than by virtue of this section.

(4) In subsection (1) 'public business' includes any activity carried on by the Crown.

(5) This section has effect subject to any agreement to the contrary between the Crown and the copyright owner.

[(6) In this section 'the Crown' includes a health service body, as defined in section 60(7) of the National Health Service and Community Care Act 1990, and a National Health Service trust established under Part I of that Act or the National Health Service (Scotland) Act 1978 [and also includes a health and social services body, as defined in Article 7(6) of the Health and Personal Social Services (Northern Ireland) Order 1991, and a Health and Social Services trust established under that Order]; and the reference in subsection (1) above to public business shall be construed accordingly.]

NOTES
Commencement order: SI 1989/816.
Sub-s (6): added by the National Health Service and Community Care Act 1990, s 60, Sch 8, Part I, para 3; words in square brackets therein added by SI 1991/194, art 7(2), Sch 2, Part I.
See further, in relation to programme services: the Broadcasting Act 1990, s 176, Sch 17.

49 Public records

Material which is comprised in public records within the meaning of the Public Records Act 1958, the Public Records (Scotland) Act 1937 or the Public Records Act (Northern Ireland) 1923 which are open to public inspection in pursuance of that Act, may be copied, and a copy may be supplied to any person, by or with the authority of any officer appointed under that Act, without infringement of copyright.

NOTES
Commencement order: SI 1989/816.
See further, in relation to programme services: the Broadcasting Act 1990, s 176, Sch 17.

50 Acts done under statutory authority

(1) Where the doing of a particular act is specifically authorised by an Act of Parliament, whenever passed, then, unless the Act provides otherwise, the doing of that act does not infringe copyright.

(2) Subsection (1) applies in relation to an enactment contained in Northern Ireland legislation as it applies in relation to an Act of Parliament.

(3) Nothing in this section shall be construed as excluding any defence of statutory authority otherwise available under or by virtue of any enactment.

NOTES

Commencement order: SI 1989/816.

See further, in relation to programme services: the Broadcasting Act 1990, s 176, Sch 17.

Computer programs: lawful users

[50A] [Back up copies]

[(1) It is not an infringement of copyright for a lawful user of a copy of a computer program to make any back up copy of it which it is necessary for him to have for the purposes of his lawful use.

(2) For the purposes of this section and sections 50B and 50C a person is a lawful user of a computer program if (whether under a licence to do any acts restricted by the copyright in the program or otherwise), he has a right to use the program.

(3) Where an act is permitted under this section, it is irrelevant whether or not there exists any term or condition in an agreement which purports to prohibit or restrict the act (such terms being, by virtue of section 296A, void).]

NOTES

This section was added by SI 1992/3233, reg 8.

[50B] [Decompilation]

[(1) It is not an infringement of copyright for a lawful user of a copy of a computer program expressed in a low level language–

  (a)   to convert it into a version expressed in a higher level language, or
  (b)   incidentally in the course of so converting the program, to copy it,

(that is, to 'decompile' it), provided that the conditions in subsection (2) are met.

(2) The conditions are that–

  (a)   it is necessary to decompile the program to obtain the information necessary to create an independent program which can be operated with the program decompiled or with another program ('the permitted objective'); and
  (b)   the information so obtained is not used for any purpose other than the permitted objective.

(3) In particular, the conditions in subsection (2) are not met if the lawful user–

  (a)   has readily available to him the information necessary to achieve the permitted objective;
  (b)   does not confine the decompiling to such acts as are necessary to achieve the permitted objective;
  (c)   supplies the information obtained by the decompiling to any person to whom it is not necessary to supply it in order to achieve the permitted objective; or
  (d)   uses the information to create a program which is substantially similar in its expression to the program decompiled or to do any act restricted by copyright.

(4) Where an act is permitted under this section, it is irrelevant whether or not there exists any term or condition in an agreement which purports to prohibit or restrict the act (such terms being, by virtue of section 296A, void).]

NOTE

This section was added by SI 1992/3233, reg 8.

[50C] [Other acts permitted to lawful users]
[(1) It is not an infringement of copyright for a lawful user of a copy of a computer program to copy or adapt it, provided that the copying or adapting–

    (a)   is necessary for his lawful use; and
    (b)   is not prohibited under any term or condition of an agreement regulating the circumstances in which his use is lawful.

    (2) It may, in particular, be necessary for the lawful use of a computer program to copy it or adapt it for the purpose of correcting errors in it.

    (3) This section does not apply to any copying or adapting permitted under section 50A or 50B.]

NOTE
    This section was added by SI 1992/3233, reg 8.

[50D] [Acts permitted in relation to databases]
[(1) It is not an infringement of copyright in a database for a person who has a right to use the database or any part of the database, (whether under a licence to do any of the acts restricted by the copyright in the database or otherwise) to do, in the exercise of that right, anything which is necessary for the purposes of access to and use of the contents of the database or of that part of the database.

    (2) Where an act which would otherwise infringe copyright in a database is permitted under this section, it is irrelevant whether or not there exists any term or condition in any agreement which purports to prohibit or restrict the act (such terms being, by virtue of section 296B, void).]

NOTE
    This section was added by SI 1997/3032, reg 9.
    Further permitted acts in relation to databases were introduced by reg 20 (s 29 and Sch 1).

Designs

51 Design documents and models
(1) It is not an infringement of any copyright in a design document or model recording or embodying a design for anything other than an artistic work or a typeface to make an article to the design or to copy an article made to the design.

    (2) Nor is it an infringement of the copyright to issue to the public, or include in a film, broadcast or cable programme service, anything the making of which was, by virtue of subsection (1), not an infringement of that copyright.

    (3) In this section–

      'design' means the design of any aspect of the shape or configuration (whether internal or external) of the whole or part of an article, other than surface decoration; and
      'design document' means any record of a design, whether in the form of a drawing, a written description, a photograph, data stored in a computer or otherwise.

NOTES
    Commencement order: SI 1989/816.
    See further, in relation to programme services: the Broadcasting Act 1990, s 176, Sch 17.

52 Effect of exploitation of design derived from artistic work
(1) This section applies where an artistic work has been exploited, by or with the licence of the copyright owner, by–

    (a)   making by an industrial process articles falling to be treated for the purposes of this Part as copies of the work, and
    (b)   marketing such articles, in the United Kingdom or elsewhere.

(2) After the end of the period of 25 years from the end of the calendar year in which such articles are first marketed, the work may be copied by making articles of any description, or doing anything for the purpose of making articles of any description, and anything may be done in relation to articles so made, without infringing copyright in the work.

(3) Where only part of an artistic work is exploited as mentioned in subsection (1), subsection (2) applies only in relation to that part.

(4) The Secretary of State may by order make provision–

(a)   as to the circumstances in which an article, or any description of article, is to be regarded for the purposes of this section as made by an industrial process;

(b)   excluding from the operation of this section such articles of a primarily literary or artistic character as he thinks fit.

(5) An order shall be made by statutory instrument which shall be subject to annulment in pursuance of a resolution of either House of Parliament.

(6) In this section–

(a)   references to articles do not include films; and

(b)   references to the marketing of an article are to its being sold or let for hire or offered or exposed for sale or hire.

NOTES

Commencement orders: SI 1989/816, SI 1989/955, SI 1989/1032.

See further, in relation to programme services: the Broadcasting Act 1990, s 176, Sch 17.

53   Things done in reliance on registration of design

(1) The copyright in an artistic work is not infringed by anything done–

(a)   in pursuance of an assignment or licence made or granted by a person registered under the Registered Designs Act 1949 as the proprietor of a corresponding design, and

(b)   in good faith in reliance on the registration and without notice of any proceedings for the cancellation of the registration or for rectifying the relevant entry in the register of designs;

and this is so notwithstanding that the person registered as the proprietor was not the proprietor of the design for the purposes of the 1949 Act.

(2) In subsection (1) a "corresponding design", in relation to an artistic work, means a design within the meaning of the 1949 Act which if applied to an article would produce something which would be treated for the purposes of this Part as a copy of the artistic work.

NOTES

Commencement order: SI 1989/816.

See further, in relation to programme services: the Broadcasting Act 1990, s 176, Sch 17.

Typefaces

54   Use of typeface in ordinary course of printing

(1) It is not an infringement of copyright in an artistic work consisting of the design of a typeface–

(a)   to use the typeface in the ordinary course of typing, composing text, typesetting or printing,

(b)   to possess an article for the purpose of such use, or

(c)   to do anything in relation to material produced by such use;

and this is so notwithstanding that an article is used which is an infringing copy of the work.

(2) However, the following provisions of this Part apply in relation to persons making, importing or dealing with articles specifically designed or adapted for producing material in a particular typeface, or possessing such articles for the purpose of dealing with them, as if the

production of material as mentioned in subsection (1) did infringe copyright in the artistic work consisting of the design of the typeface–

> section 24 (secondary infringement: making, importing, possessing or dealing with an article for making infringing copy),
> sections 99 and 100 (order for delivery up and right of seizure),
> section 107(2) (offence of making or possessing such an article), and
> section 108 (order for delivery up in criminal proceedings).

(3) The references in subsection (2) to "dealing with" an article are to selling, letting for hire, or offering or exposing for sale or hire, exhibiting in public, or distributing.

NOTES

Commencement order: SI 1989/816.
See further, in relation to programme services: the Broadcasting Act 1990, s 176, Sch 17.

---

55 Articles for producing material in particular typeface

(1) This section applies to the copyright in an artistic work consisting of the design of a typeface where articles specifically designed or adapted for producing material in that typeface have been marketed by or with the licence of the copyright owner.

(2) After the period of 25 years from the end of the calendar year in which the first such articles are marketed, the work may be copied by making further such articles, or doing anything for the purpose of making such articles, and anything may be done in relation to articles so made, without infringing copyright in the work.

(3) In subsection (1) 'marketed' means sold, let for hire or offered or exposed for sale or hire, in the United Kingdom or elsewhere.

NOTES

Commencement order: SI 1989/816.
See further, in relation to programme services: the Broadcasting Act 1990, s 176, Sch 17.

Works in electronic form

56 Transfers of copies of works in electronic form

(1) This section applies where a copy of a work in electronic form has been purchased on terms which, expressly or impliedly or by virtue of any rule of law, allow the purchaser to copy the work, or to adapt it or make copies of an adaptation, in connection with his use of it.

(2) If there are no express terms–

(a) prohibiting the transfer of the copy by the purchaser, imposing obligations which continue after a transfer, prohibiting the assignment of any licence or terminating any licence on a transfer, or
(b) providing for the terms on which a transferee may do the things which the purchaser was permitted to do,

anything which the purchaser was allowed to do may also be done without infringement of copyright by a transferee; but any copy, adaptation or copy of an adaptation made by the purchaser which is not also transferred shall be treated as an infringing copy for all purposes after the transfer.

(3) The same applies where the original purchased copy is no longer usable and what is transferred is a further copy used in its place.

(4) The above provisions also apply on a subsequent transfer, with the substitution for references in subsection (2) to the purchaser of references to the subsequent transferor.

NOTES

Commencement order: SI 1989/816.
See further, in relation to programme services: the Broadcasting Act 1990, s 176, Sch 17.

Miscellaneous: literary, dramatic, musical and artistic works

57 Anonymous or pseudonymous works: acts permitted on assumptions as to expiry of copyright or death of author

(1) Copyright in a literary, dramatic, musical or artistic work is not infringed by an act done at a time when, or in pursuance of arrangements made at a time when—

    (a)   it is not possible by reasonable inquiry to ascertain the identity of the author, and

    (b)   it is reasonable to assume—

        (i)   that copyright has expired, or

        (ii) that the author died [70 years] or more before the beginning of the calendar year in which the act is done or the arrangements are made.

(2) Subsection (1)(b)(ii) does not apply in relation to—

    (a)   a work in which Crown copyright subsists, or

    (b)   a work in which copyright originally vested in an international organisation by virtue of section 168 and in respect of which an Order under that section specifies a copyright period longer than 50 years [70 years].

(3) In relation to a work of joint authorship—

    (a)   the reference in subsection (1) to its being possible to ascertain the identity of the author shall be construed as a reference to its being possible to ascertain the identity of any of the authors, and

    (b)   the reference in subsection (1)(b)(ii) to the author having died shall be construed as a reference to all the authors having died.

NOTES

Commencement order: SI 1989/816.

Sub-ss (1), (2): words in square brackets substituted with savings by SI 1995/3297, reg 5(2); for savings see Part III thereof.

See further, in relation to programme services: the Broadcasting Act 1990, s 176, Sch 17.

58 Use of notes or recordings of spoken words in certain cases

(1) Where a record of spoken words is made, in writing or otherwise, for the purpose—

    (a)   of reporting current events, or

    (b)   of broadcasting or including in a cable programme service the whole or part of the work,

it is not an infringement of any copyright in the words as a literary work to use the record or material taken from it (or to copy the record, or any such material, and use the copy) for that purpose, provided the following conditions are met.

(2) The conditions are that—

    (a)   the record is a direct record of the spoken words and is not taken from a previous record or from a broadcast or cable programme;

    (b)   the making of the record was not prohibited by the speaker and, where copyright already subsisted in the work, did not infringe copyright;

    (c)   the use made of the record or material taken from it is not of a kind prohibited by or on behalf of the speaker or copyright owner before the record was made; and

    (d)   the use is by or with the authority of a person who is lawfully in possession of the record.

NOTES

Commencement order: SI 1989/816.

See further, in relation to programme services: the Broadcasting Act 1990, s 176, Sch 17.

59 Public reading or recitation

(1) The reading or recitation in public by one person of a reasonable extract from a published literary or dramatic work does not infringe any copyright in the work if it is accompanied by a sufficient acknowledgement.

(2) Copyright in a work is not infringed by the making of a sound recording, or the broadcasting or inclusion in a cable programme service, of a reading or recitation which by virtue of subsection (1) does not infringe copyright in the work, provided that the recording, broadcast or cable programme consists mainly of material in relation to which it is not necessary to rely on that subsection.

NOTES
Commencement order: SI 1989/816.
See further, in relation to programme services: the Broadcasting Act 1990, s 176, Sch 17.

60 Abstracts of scientific or technical articles

(1) Where an article on a scientific or technical subject is published in a periodical accompanied by an abstract indicating the contents of the article, it is not an infringement of copyright in the abstract, or in the article, to copy the abstract or issue copies of it to the public.

(2) This section does not apply if or to the extent that there is a licensing scheme certified for the purposes of this section under section 143 providing for the grant of licences.

NOTES
Commencement order: SI 1989/816.
See further, in relation to programme services: the Broadcasting Act 1990, s 176, Sch 17.

61 Recordings of folksongs

(1) A sound recording of a performance of a song may be made for the purpose of including it in an archive maintained by a designated body without infringing any copyright in the words as a literary work or in the accompanying musical work, provided the conditions in subsection (2) below are met.

(2) The conditions are that–

  (a) the words are unpublished and of unknown authorship at the time the recording is made,
  (b) the making of the recording does not infringe any other copyright, and
  (c) its making is not prohibited by any performer.

(3) Copies of a sound recording made in reliance on subsection (1) and included in an archive maintained by a designated body may, if the prescribed conditions are met, be made and supplied by the archivist without infringing copyright in the recording or the works included in it.

(4) The prescribed conditions shall include the following–

  (a) that copies are only supplied to persons satisfying the archivist that they require them for purposes of research or private study and will not use them for any other purpose, and
  (b) that no person is furnished with more than one copy of the same recording.

(5) In this section–

  (a) 'designated' means designated for the purposes of this section by order of the Secretary of State, who shall not designate a body unless satisfied that it is not established or conducted for profit,
  (b) 'prescribed' means prescribed for the purposes of this section by order of the Secretary of State, and
  (c) references to the archivist include a person acting on his behalf.

(6) An order under this section shall be made by statutory instrument which shall be subject to annulment in pursuance of a resolution of either House of Parliament.

NOTES
Commencement orders: SI 1989/816, SI 1989/955, SI 1989/1032.
See further, in relation to programme services: the Broadcasting Act 1990, s 176, Sch 17.

62 Representation of certain artistic works on public display
(1) This section applies to–

  (a) buildings, and
  (b) sculptures, models for buildings and works of artistic craftsmanship, if permanently situated in a public place or in premises open to the public.

  (2) The copyright in such a work is not infringed by–

  (a) making a graphic work representing it,
  (b) making a photograph or film of it, or
  (c) broadcasting or including in a cable programme service a visual image of it.

  (3) Nor is the copyright infringed by the issue to the public of copies, or the broadcasting or inclusion in a cable programme service, of anything whose making was, by virtue of this section, not an infringement of the copyright.

NOTES
Commencement order: SI 1989/816.
See further, in relation to programme services: the Broadcasting Act 1990, s 176, Sch 17.

63 Advertisement of sale of artistic work
(1) It is not an infringement of copyright in an artistic work to copy it, or to issue copies to the public, for the purpose of advertising the sale of the work.

  (2) Where a copy which would otherwise be an infringing copy is made in accordance with this section but is subsequently dealt with for any other purpose, it shall be treated as an infringing copy for the purposes of that dealing, and if that dealing infringes copyright for all subsequent purposes.

  For this purpose 'dealt with' means sold or let for hire, offered or exposed for sale or hire, exhibited in public or distributed.

NOTES
Commencement order: SI 1989/816.
See further, in relation to programme services: the Broadcasting Act 1990, s 176, Sch 17.

64 Making of subsequent works by same artist
Where the author of an artistic work is not the copyright owner, he does not infringe the copyright by copying the work in making another artistic work, provided he does not repeat or imitate the main design of the earlier work.

NOTES
Commencement order: SI 1989/816.
See further, in relation to programme services: the Broadcasting Act 1990, s 176, Sch 17.

65 Reconstruction of buildings
Anything done for the purposes of reconstructing a building does not infringe any copyright–

  (a) in the building, or
  (b) in any drawings or plans in accordance with which the building was, by or with the licence of the copyright owner, constructed.

NOTES
Commencement order: SI 1989/816.
See further, in relation to programme services: the Broadcasting Act 1990, s 176, Sch 17.

[Miscellaneous: lending of works and playing of sound recordings]

[66] [Lending to public of copies of certain works]
[(1) The Secretary of State may by order provide that in such cases as may be specified in the order the lending to the public of copies of literary, dramatic, musical or artistic works, sound

recordings or films shall be treated as licensed by the copyright owner subject only to the payment of such reasonable royalty or other payment as may be agreed or determined in default of agreement by the Copyright Tribunal.

(2) No such order shall apply if, or to the extent that, there is a licensing scheme certified for the purposes of this section under section 143 providing for the grant of licences.

(3) An order may make different provision for different cases and may specify cases by reference to any factor relating to the work, the copies lent, the lender or the circumstances of the lending.

(4) An order shall be made by statutory instrument; and no order shall be made unless a draft of it has been laid before and approved by a resolution of each House of Parliament.

(5) Nothing in this section affects any liability under section 23 (secondary infringement: possessing or dealing with infringing copy) in respect of the lending of infringing copies.]

NOTE
Substituted by SI 1996/2967, reg 11(3).

[Miscellaneous: films and sound recordings]

[66A] [Films: acts permitted on assumptions as to expiry of copyright, &c]
[(1) Copyright in a film is not infringed by an act done at a time when, or in pursuance of arrangements made at a time when–

(a)   it is not possible by reasonable inquiry to ascertain the identity of any of the persons referred to in section 13B(2)(a) to (d) (persons by reference to whose life the copyright period is ascertained), and

(b)   it is reasonable to assume–
    (i)   that copyright has expired, or
    (ii)   that the last to die of those persons died 70 years or more before the beginning of the calendar year in which the act is done or the arrangements are made.

(2) Subsection (1)(b)(ii) does not apply in relation to–

(a)   a film in which Crown copyright subsists, or

(b)   a film in which copyright originally vested in an international organisation by virtue of section 168 and in respect of which an Order under that section specifies a copyright period longer than 70 years.]

NOTES
This section was added with savings by SI 1995/3297, reg 6(2); for savings see Part III thereof.
This section should be read in conjunction with the following provision of the Copyright and Rights in Databases Regulations 1997, SI 1997/3032 (commencement: 1 January 1998):

Copyright and Rights in Databases Regulations 1997, reg 21

21 Acts permitted on assumption as to expiry of database right
(1) Database right in a database is not infringed by the extraction or re-utilisation of a substantial part of the contents of the database at a time when, or in pursuance of arrangements made at a time when–

(a)   it is not possible by reasonable inquiry to ascertain the identity of the maker, and
(b)   it is reasonable to assume that database right has expired.

(2) In the case of a database alleged to have been made jointly, paragraph (1) applies in relation to each person alleged to be one of the makers.

67 Playing of sound recordings for purposes of club, society, &c
(1) It is not an infringement of the copyright in a sound recording to play it as part of the activities of, or for the benefit of, a club, society or other organisation if the following conditions are met.

(2) The conditions are–

(a) that the organisation is not established or conducted for profit and its main objects are charitable or are otherwise concerned with the advancement of religion, education or social welfare, and

(b) that the proceeds of any charge for admission to the place where the recording is to be heard are applied solely for the purposes of the organisation.

NOTES
Commencement order: SI 1989/816.
See further, in relation to programme services: the Broadcasting Act 1990, s 176, Sch 17.

Miscellaneous: broadcasts and cable programmes

68 Incidental recording for purposes of broadcast or cable programme
(1) This section applies where by virtue of a licence or assignment of copyright a person is authorised to broadcast or include in a cable programme service–

(a) a literary, dramatic or musical work, or an adaptation of such a work,
(b) an artistic work, or
(c) a sound recording or film.

(2) He shall by virtue of this section be treated as licensed by the owner of the copyright in the work to do or authorise any of the following for the purposes of the broadcast or cable programme–

(a) in the case of a literary, dramatic or musical work, or an adaptation of such a work, to make a sound recording or film of the work or adaptation;
(b) in the case of an artistic work, to take a photograph or make a film of the work;
(c) in the case of a sound recording or film, to make a copy of it.

(3) That licence is subject to the condition that the recording, film, photograph or copy in question–

(a) shall not be used for any other purpose, and
(b) shall be destroyed within 28 days of being first used for broadcasting the work or, as the case may be, including it in a cable programme service.

(4) A recording, film, photograph or copy made in accordance with this section shall be treated as an infringing copy–

(a) for the purposes of any use in breach of the condition mentioned in subsection (3)(a), and
(b) for all purposes after that condition or the condition mentioned in subsection (3)(b) is broken.

NOTES
Commencement order: SI 1989/816.
See further, in relation to programme services: the Broadcasting Act 1990, s 176, Sch 17.

69 Recording for purposes of supervision and control of broadcasts and cable programmes
(1) Copyright is not infringed by the making or use by the British Broadcasting Corporation, for the purpose of maintaining supervision and control over programmes broadcast by them, of recordings of those programmes.
[(2) Copyright is not infringed by anything done in pursuance of–

(a) section 11(1), 95(1) or 167(1) of the Broadcasting Act 1990 or section 115(4) or (6), 116(5) or 117 of the Broadcasting Act 1996;
(b) a condition which, by virtue of section 11(2) or 95(2) of the Broadcasting Act 1990, is included in a licence granted under Part I or III of that Act or Part I or II of the Broadcasting Act 1996; or

(c) a direction given under section 109(2) of the Broadcasting Act 1990 (power of Radio Authority to require production of recordings etc).

(3) Copyright is not infringed by–

(a) the use by the Independent Television Commission or the Radio Authority, in connection with the performance of any of their functions under the Broadcasting Act 1990 or the Broadcasting Act 1996, of any recording, script or transcript which is provided to them under or by virtue of any provision of those Acts; or

(b) the use by the Broadcasting Standards Commission, in connection with any complaint made to them under the Broadcasting Act 1996, of any recording or transcript requested or required to be provided to them, and so provided, under section 115(4) or (6) or 116(5) of that Act.]

NOTES

Commencement order: SI 1989/816.
See further, in relation to programme services: the Broadcasting Act 1990, s 176, Sch 17.
Sub-ss (2), (3): substituted by the Broadcasting Act 1996, s 148(1), Sch 10, para 31.

70 Recording for purposes of time-shifting

The making for private and domestic use of a recording of a broadcast or cable programme solely for the purpose of enabling it to be viewed or listened to at a more convenient time does not infringe any copyright in the broadcast or cable programme or in any work included in it.

NOTES

Commencement order: SI 1989/816.
See further, in relation to programme services: the Broadcasting Act 1990, s 176, Sch 17.

71 Photographs of television broadcasts or cable programmes

The making for private and domestic use of a photograph of the whole or any part of an image forming part of a television broadcast or cable programme, or a copy of such a photograph, does not infringe any copyright in the broadcast or cable programme or in any film included in it.

NOTES

Commencement order: SI 1989/816.
See further, in relation to programme services: the Broadcasting Act 1990, s 176, Sch 17.

72 Free public showing or playing of broadcast or cable programme

(1) The showing or playing in public of a broadcast or cable programme to an audience who have not paid for admission to the place where the broadcast or programme is to be seen or heard does not infringe any copyright in–

(a) the broadcast or cable programme, or
(b) any sound recording or film included in it.

(2) The audience shall be treated as having paid for admission to a place–

(a) if they have paid for admission to a place of which that place forms part; or
(b) if goods or services are supplied at that place (or a place of which it forms part)–

(i) at prices which are substantially attributable to the facilities afforded for seeing or hearing the broadcast or programme, or
(ii) at prices exceeding those usually charged there and which are partly attributable to those facilities.

(3) The following shall not be regarded as having paid for admission to a place–

(a) persons admitted as residents or inmates of the place;
(b) persons admitted as members of a club or society where the payment is only for membership of the club or society and the provision of facilities for seeing or hearing

broadcasts or programmes is only incidental to the main purposes of the club or society.

(4) Where the making of the broadcast or inclusion of the programme in a cable programme service was an infringement of the copyright in a sound recording or film, the fact that it was heard or seen in public by the reception of the broadcast or programme shall be taken into account in assessing the damages for that infringement.

NOTES
Commencement order: SI 1989/816.
See further, in relation to programme services: the Broadcasting Act 1990, s 176, Sch 17.

[73] [Reception and re-transmission of broadcast in cable programme service]
[(1) This section applies where a broadcast made from a place in the United Kingdom is, by reception and immediate re-transmission, included in a cable programme service.

(2) The copyright in the broadcast is not infringed–

(a) if the inclusion is in pursuance of a relevant requirement, or
(b) if and to the extent that the broadcast is made for reception in the area in which the cable programme service is provided and forms part of a qualifying service.

(3) The copyright in any work included in the broadcast is not infringed if and to the extent that the broadcast is made for reception in the area in which the cable programme service is provided; but where the making of the broadcast was an infringement of the copyright in the work, the fact that the broadcast was re-transrnitted as a programme in a cable programme service shall be taken into account in assessing the damages for that infringement.

(4) Where–

(a) the inclusion is in pursuance of a relevant requirement, but
(b) to any extent, the area in which the cable programme service is provided ('the cable area') falls outside the area for reception in which the broadcast is made ('the broadcast area'),

the inclusion in the cable programme service (to the extent that it is provided for so much of the cable area as falls outside the broadcast area) of any work included in the broadcast shall, subject to subsection (5), be treated as licensed by the owner of the copyright in the work, subject only to the payment to him by the person making the broadcast of such reasonable royalty or other payment in respect of the inclusion of the broadcast in the cable programme service as may be agreed or determined in default of agreement by the Copyright Tribunal.

(5) Subsection (4) does not apply if, or to the extent that, the inclusion of the work in the cable programme service is (apart from that subsection) licensed by the owner of the copyright in the work.

(6) In this section 'qualifying service' means, subject to subsection (8), any of the following services–

(a) a regional or national Channel 3 service,
(b) Channel 4, Channel 5 and S4C,
(c) the teletext service referred to in section 49(2) of the Broadcasting Act 1990,
(d) the service referred to in section 57(1A)(a) of that Act (power of S4C to provide digital service), and
(e) the television broadcasting services and teletext service of the British Broadcasting Corporation;

and expressions used in this subsection have the same meaning as in Part I of the Broadcasting Act 1990.

(7) In this section 'relevant requirement' means a requirement imposed under–

(a) section 78A of the Broadcasting Act 1990 (inclusion of certain services in local delivery services provided by digital means), or
(b) paragraph 4 of Part III of Schedule 12 to that Act (inclusion of certain services in diffusion services originally licensed under the Cable and Broadcasting Act 1984).

(8) The Secretary of State may by order amend subsection (6) so as to add any service to, or remove any service from, the definition of 'qualifying service'.

(9) The Secretary of State may also by order–

(a) provide that in specified cases subsection (3) is to apply in relation to broadcasts of a specified description which are not made as mentioned in that subsection, or
(b) exclude the application of that subsection in relation to broadcasts of a specified description made as mentioned in that subsection.

(10) Where the Secretary of State exercises the power conferred by subsection (9)(b) in relation to broadcasts of any description, the order may also provide for subsection (4) to apply, subject to such modifications as may be specified in the order, in relation to broadcasts of that description.

(11) An order under this section may contain such transitional provision as appears to the Secretary of State to be appropriate.

(12) An order under this section shall be made by statutory instrument which shall be subject to annulment in pursuance of a resolution of either House of Parliament.]

NOTES
Commencement order: SI 1989/816.
Substituted, together with s 73A, for s 73 as originally enacted, by the Broadcasting Act 1996, s 138, Sch 9, para 1.
See further, in relation to programme services: the Broadcasting Act 1990, s 176, Sch 17.

[73A] [Royalty or other sum payable in pursuance of section 73(4)]
[(1) An application to settle the royalty or other sum payable in pursuance of subsection (4) of section 73 (reception and re-transmission of broadcast in cable programme service) may be made to the Copyright Tribunal by the copyright owner or the person making the broadcast.

(2) The Tribunal shall consider the matter and make such order as it may determine to be reasonable in the circumstances.

(3) Either party may subsequently apply to the Tribunal to vary the order, and the Tribunal shall consider the matter and make such order confirming or varying the original order as it may determine to be reasonable in the circumstances.

(4) An application under subsection (3) shall not, except with the special leave of the Tribunal, be made within twelve months from the date of the original order or of the order on a previous application under that subsection.

(5) An order under subsection (3) has effect from the date on which it is made or such later date as may be specified by the Tribunal.]

NOTE
Substituted, together with s 73, for s 73 as originally enacted, by the Broadcasting Act 1996, s 138, Sch 9, para 1.

74 Provision of sub-titled copies of broadcast or cable programme
(1) A designated body may, for the purpose of providing people who are deaf or hard of hearing, or physically or mentally handicapped in other ways, with copies which are sub-titled or otherwise modified for their special needs, make copies of television broadcasts or cable programmes and issue copies to the public, without infringing any copyright in the broadcasts or cable programmes or works included in them.

(2) A 'designated body' means a body designated for the purposes of this section by order of the Secretary of State, who shall not designate a body unless he is satisfied that it is not established or conducted for profit.

(3) An order under this section shall be made by statutory instrument which shall be subject to annulment in pursuance of a resolution of either House of Parliament.

(4) This section does not apply if, or to the extent that, there is a licensing scheme certified for the purposes of this section under section 143 providing for the grant of licences.

NOTES
Commencement orders: SI 1989/816, SI 1989/955, SI 1989/1032.
See further, in relation to programme services: the Broadcasting Act 1990, s 176, Sch 17.

75 Recording for archival purposes

(1) A recording of a broadcast or cable programme of a designated class, or a copy of such a recording, may be made for the purpose of being placed in an archive maintained by a designated body without thereby infringing any copyright in the broadcast or cable programme or in any work included in it.

(2) In subsection (1) 'designated' means designated for the purposes of this section by order of the Secretary of State, who shall not designate a body unless he is satisfied that it is not established or conducted for profit.

(3) An order under this section shall be made by statutory instrument which shall be subject to annulment in pursuance of a resolution of either House of Parliament.

NOTES
Commencement orders: SI 1989/816, SI 1989/955, SI 1989/1032.
See further, in relation to programme services: the Broadcasting Act 1990, s 176, Sch 17.

Adaptations

76 Adaptations

An act which by virtue of this Chapter may be done without infringing copyright in a literary, dramatic or musical work does not, where that work is an adaptation, infringe any copyright in the work from which the adaptation was made.

NOTES
Commencement order: SI 1989/816.
See further, in relation to programme services: the Broadcasting Act 1990, s 176, Sch 17.
This section should be read in conjunction with the following provision of the Copyright and Rights in Databases Regulations 1997, SI 1997/3032 (commencement: 1 January 1998):

Copyright and Rights in Databases Regulations 1997, Sch 1

Regulation 20(2)

SCHEDULE 1

EXCEPTIONS TO DATABASE RIGHT FOR PUBLIC ADMINISTRATION

Parliamentary and judicial proceedings

1 Database right in a database is not infringed by anything done for the purposes of parliamentary or judicial proceedings or for the purposes of reporting such proceedings.

Royal Commissions and statutory inquiries

2–(1) Database right in a database is not infringed by anything done for–

    (a)   the purposes of the proceedings of a Royal Commission or statutory inquiry, or
    (b)   the purpose of reporting any such proceedings held in public.

(2) Database right in a database is not infringed by the issue to the public of copies of the report of a Royal Commission or statutory inquiry containing the contents of the database.

(3) In this paragraph 'Royal Commission' and 'statutory inquiry' have the same meaning as in section 46 of the 1988 Act.

Material open to public inspection or on official register

3–(1) Where the contents of a database are open to public inspection pursuant to a statutory requirement, or are on a statutory register, database right in the database is not infringed by the extraction of all or a substantial part of the contents containing factual information of any description, by or with the authority of the appropriate person, for a purpose which does not involve re-utilisation of all or a substantial part of the contents.

(2) Where the contents of a database are open to public inspection pursuant to a statutory requirement, database right in the database is not infringed by the extraction or re-utilisation of all or a substantial part of the contents, by

or with the authority of the appropriate person, for the purpose of enabling the contents to be inspected at a more convenient time or place or otherwise facilitating the exercise of any right for the purpose of which the requirement is imposed.

(3) Where the contents of a database which is open to public inspection pursuant to a statutory requirement, or which is on a statutory register, contain information about matters of general scientific, technical, commercial or economic interest, database right in the database is not infringed by the extraction or re-utilisation of all or a substantial part of the contents, by or with the authority of the appropriate person, for the purpose of disseminating that information.

(4) In this paragraph–

'appropriate person' means the person required to make the contents of the database open to public inspection or, as the case may be, the person maintaining the register;

'statutory register' means a register maintained in pursuance of a statutory requirement; and

'statutory requirement' means a requirement imposed by provision made by or under an enactment.

Material communicated to the Crown in the course of public business

4–(1) This paragraph applies where the contents of a database have in the course of public business been communicated to the Crown for any purpose, by or with the licence of the owner of the database right and a document or other material thing recording or embodying the contents of the database is owned by or in the custody or control of the Crown.

(2) The Crown may, for the purpose for which the contents of the database were communicated to it, or any related purpose which could reasonably have been anticipated by the owner of the database right in the database, extract or re-utilise all or a substantial part of the contents without infringing database right in the database.

(3) The Crown may not re-utilise the contents of a database by virtue of this paragraph if the contents have previously been published otherwise than by virtue of this paragraph.

(4) In sub-paragraph (1) 'public business' includes any activity carried on by the Crown.

(5) This paragraph has effect subject to any agreement to the contrary between the Crown and the owner of the database right in the database.

Public records

5 The contents of a database which are comprised in public records within the meaning of the Public Records Act 1958, the Public Records (Scotland) Act 1937 or the Public Records Act (Northern Ireland) 1923 which are open to public inspection in pursuance of that Act, may be re-utilised by or with the authority of any officer appointed under that Act, without infringement of database right in the database.

Acts done under statutory authority

6–(1) Where the doing of a particular act is specifically authorised by an Act of Parliament, whenever passed, then, unless the Act provides otherwise, the doing of that act does not infringe database right in a database.

(2) Sub-paragraph (1) applies in relation to an enactment contained in Northern Ireland legislation as it applies in relation to an Act of Parliament.

(3) Nothing in this paragraph shall be construed as excluding any defence of statutory authority otherwise available under or by virtue of any enactment.

CHAPTER IV
MORAL RIGHTS

Right to be identified as author or director

77 Right to be identified as author or director

(1) The author of a copyright literary, dramatic, musical or artistic work, and the director of a copyright film, has the right to be identified as the author or director of the work in the circumstances mentioned in this section; but the right is not infringed unless it has been asserted in accordance with section 78.

(2) The author of a literary work (other than words intended to be sung or spoken with music) or a dramatic work has the right to be identified whenever–

(a) the work is published commercially, performed in public, broadcast or included in a cable programme service; or

(b) copies of a film or sound recording including the work are issued to the public;

and that right includes the right to be identified whenever any of those events occur in relation to an adaptation of the work as the author of the work from which the adaptation was made.

(3) The author of a musical work, or a literary work consisting of words intended to be sung or spoken with music, has the right to be identified whenever–

    (a) the work is published commercially;

    (b) copies of a sound recording of the work are issued to the public; or

    (c) a film of which the sound-track includes the work is shown in public or copies of such a film are issued to the public;

and that right includes the right to be identified whenever any of those events occur in relation to an adaptation of the work as the author of the work from which the adaptation was made.

(4) The author of an artistic work has the right to be identified whenever–

    (a) the work is published commercially or exhibited in public, or a visual image of it is broadcast or included in a cable programme service;

    (b) a film including a visual image of the work is shown in public or copies of such a film are issued to the public; or

    (c) in the case of a work of architecture in the form of a building or a model for a building, a sculpture or a work of artistic craftsmanship, copies of a graphic work representing it, or of a photograph of it, are issued to the public.

(5) The author of a work of architecture in the form of a building also has the right to be identified on the building as constructed or, where more than one building is constructed to the design, on the first to be constructed.

(6) The director of a film has the right to be identified whenever the film is shown in public, broadcast or included in a cable programme service or copies of the film are issued to the public.

(7) The right of the author or director under this section is–

    (a) in the case of commercial publication or the issue to the public of copies of a film or sound recording, to be identified in or on each copy or, if that is not appropriate, in some other manner likely to bring his identity to the notice of a person acquiring a copy,

    (b) in the case of identification on a building, to be identified by appropriate means visible to persons entering or approaching the building, and

    (c) in any other case, to be identified in a manner likely to bring his identity to the attention of a person seeing or hearing the performance, exhibition, showing, broadcast or cable programme in question;

and the identification must in each case be clear and reasonably prominent.

(8) If the author or director in asserting his right to be identified specifies a pseudonym, initials or some other particular form of identification, that form shall be used; otherwise any reasonable form of identification may be used.

(9) This section has effect subject to section 79 (exceptions to right).

NOTE

Commencement order: SI 1989/816.

---

78 Requirement that right be asserted

(1) A person does not infringe the right conferred by section 77 (right to be identified as author or director) by doing any of the acts mentioned in that section unless the right has been asserted in accordance with the following provisions so as to bind him in relation to that act.

(2) The right may be asserted generally, or in relation to any specified act or description of acts–

    (a) on an assignment of copyright in the work, by including in the instrument effecting the assignment a statement that the author or director asserts in relation to that work his right to be identified, or

    (b) by instrument in writing signed by the author or director.

(3) The right may also be asserted in relation to the public exhibition of an artistic work–

(a) by securing that when the author or other first owner of copyright parts with possession of the original, or of a copy made by him or under his direction or control, the author is identified on the original or copy, or on a frame, mount or other thing to which it is attached, or

(b) by including in a licence by which the author or other first owner of copyright authorises the making of copies of the work a statement signed by or on behalf of the person granting the licence that the author asserts his right to be identified in the event of the public exhibition of a copy made in pursuance of the licence.

(4) The persons bound by an assertion of the right under subsection (2) or (3) are–

(a) in the case of an assertion under subsection (2)(a), the assignee and anyone claiming through him, whether or not he has notice of the assertion;

(b) in the case of an assertion under subsection (2)(b), anyone to whose notice the assertion is brought;

(c) in the case of an assertion under subsection (3)(a), anyone into whose hands that original or copy comes, whether or not the identification is still present or visible;

(d) in the case of an assertion under subsection (3)(b), the licensee and anyone into whose hands a copy made in pursuance of the licence comes, whether or not he has notice of the assertion.

(5) In an action for infringement of the right the court shall, in considering remedies, take into account any delay in asserting the right.

NOTES
Commencement order: SI 1989/816.

79 Exceptions to right
(1) The right conferred by section 77 (right to be identified as author or director) is subject to the following exceptions.

(2) The right does not apply in relation to the following descriptions of work–

(a) a computer program;
(b) the design of a typeface;
(c) any computer-generated work.

(3) The right does not apply to anything done by or with the authority of the copyright owner where copyright in the work originally vested–

(a) in the author's employer by virtue of section 11(2) (works produced in course of employment), or
(b) in the director's employer by virtue of section 9(2)(a) (person to be treated as author of film).

(4) The right is not infringed by an act which by virtue of any of the following provisions would not infringe copyright in the work–

(a) section 30 (fair dealing for certain purposes), so far as it relates to the reporting of current events by means of a sound recording, film, broadcast or cable programme;
(b) section 31 (incidental inclusion of work in an artistic work, sound recording, film, broadcast or cable programme);
(c) section 32(3) (examination questions);
(d) section 45 (parliamentary and judicial proceedings);
(e) section 46(1) or (2) (Royal Commissions and statutory inquiries);
(f) section 51 (use of design documents and models);
(g) section 52 (effect of exploitation of design derived from artistic work);
(h) [section 57 or 66A (acts permitted on assumptions as to expiry of copyright, &c)].

(5) The right does not apply in relation to any work made for the purpose of reporting current events.

(6) The right does not apply in relation to the publication in–

(a) a newspaper, magazine or similar periodical, or

(b)   an encyclopaedia, dictionary, yearbook or other collective work of reference,

of a literary, dramatic, musical or artistic work made for the purposes of such publication or made available with the consent of the author for the purposes of such publication.

(7) The right does not apply in relation to–

(a)   a work in which Crown copyright or Parliamentary copyright subsists, or

(b)   a work in which copyright originally vested in an international organisation by virtue of section 168,

unless the author or director has previously been identified as such in or on published copies of the work.

NOTES

Commencement order: SI 1989/816.

Sub-s (4): words in square brackets substituted with savings by SI 1995/3297, reg 6(3); for savings see Part III thereof.

Right to object to derogatory treatment of work

80 Right to object to derogatory treatment of work

(1) The author of a copyright literary, dramatic, musical or artistic work, and the director of a copyright film, has the right in the circumstances mentioned in this section not to have his work subjected to derogatory treatment.

(2) For the purposes of this section–

(a)   'treatment' of a work means any addition to, deletion from or alteration to or adaptation of the work, other than–

(i)   a translation of a literary or dramatic work, or

(ii)   an arrangement or transcription of a musical work involving no more than a change of key or register; and

(b)   the treatment of a work is derogatory if it amounts to distortion or mutilation of the work or is otherwise prejudicial to the honour or reputation of the author or director;

and in the following provisions of this section references to a derogatory treatment of a work shall be construed accordingly.

(3) In the case of a literary, dramatic or musical work the right is infringed by a person who–

(a)   publishes commercially, performs in public, broadcasts or includes in a cable programme service a derogatory treatment of the work; or

(b)   issues to the public copies of a film or sound recording of, or including, a derogatory treatment of the work.

(4) In the case of an artistic work the right is infringed by a person who–

(a)   publishes commercially or exhibits in public a derogatory treatment of the work, or broadcasts or includes in a cable programme service a visual image of a derogatory treatment of the work,

(b)   shows in public a film including a visual image of a derogatory treatment of the work or issues to the public copies of such a film, or

(c)   in the case of–

(i)   a work of architecture in the form of a model for a building,

(ii)   a sculpture, or

(iii)   a work of artistic craftsmanship,

issues to the public copies of a graphic work representing, or of a photograph of, a derogatory treatment of the work.

(5) Subsection (4) does not apply to a work of architecture in the form of a building; but where the author of such a work is identified on the building and it is the subject of derogatory treatment he has the right to require the identification to be removed.

(6) In the case of a film, the right is infringed by a person who–

(a) shows in public, broadcasts or includes in a cable programme service a derogatory treatment of the film; or

(b) issues to the public copies of a derogatory treatment of the film.

(7) The right conferred by this section extends to the treatment of parts of a work resulting from a previous treatment by a person other than the author or director, if those parts are attributed to, or are likely to be regarded as the work of, the author or director.

(8) This section has effect subject to sections 81 and 82 (exceptions to and qualifications of right).

NOTE
Commencement order: SI 1989/816.

81 Exceptions to right

(1) The right conferred by section 80 (right to object to derogatory treatment of work) is subject to the following exceptions.

(2) The right does not apply to a computer program or to any computer-generated work.

(3) The right does not apply in relation to any work made for the purpose of reporting current events.

(4) The right does not apply in relation to the publication in–

(a) a newspaper, magazine or similar periodical, or

(b) an encyclopaedia, dictionary, yearbook or other collective work of reference,

of a literary, dramatic, musical or artistic work made for the purposes of such publication or made available with the consent of the author for the purposes of such publication.

Nor does the right apply in relation to any subsequent exploitation elsewhere of such a work without any modification of the published version.

(5) The right is not infringed by an act which by virtue of [section 57 or 66A (acts permitted on assumptions as to expiry of copyright, &c)] would not infringe copyright.

(6) The right is not infringed by anything done for the purpose of–

(a) avoiding the commission of an offence,

(b) complying with a duty imposed by or under an enactment, or

(c) in the case of the British Broadcasting Corporation, avoiding the inclusion in a programme broadcast by them of anything which offends against good taste or decency or which is likely to encourage or incite to crime or to lead to disorder or to be offensive to public feeling,

provided, where the author or director is identified at the time of the relevant act or has previously been identified in or on published copies of the work, that there is a sufficient disclaimer.

NOTES
Commencement order: SI 1989/816.
Sub-s (5): words in square brackets substituted with savings by SI 1995 No 3297, reg 6(3); for savings see Part III thereof.

82 Qualification of right in certain cases

(1) This section applies to–

(a) works in which copyright originally vested in the author's employer by virtue of section 11(2) (works produced in course of employment) or in the director's employer by virtue of section 9(2)(a) (person to be treated as author of film),

(b) works in which Crown copyright or Parliamentary copyright subsists, and

(c) works in which copyright originally vested in an international organisation by virtue of section 168.

(2) The right conferred by section 80 (right to object to derogatory treatment of work) does not apply to anything done in relation to such a work by or with the authority of the copyright owner unless the author or director–

(a)   is identified at the time of the relevant act, or

(b)   has previously been identified in or on published copies of the work;

and where in such a case the right does apply, it is not infringed if there is a sufficient disclaimer.

NOTE
Commencement order: SI 1989/816.

83 Infringement of right by possessing or dealing with infringing article
(1) The right conferred by section 80 (right to object to derogatory treatment of work) is also infringed by a person who–

(a)   possesses in the course of a business, or

(b)   sells or lets for hire, or offers or exposes for sale or hire, or

(c)   in the course of a business exhibits in public or distributes, or

(d)   distributes otherwise than in the course of a business so as to affect prejudicially the honour or reputation of the author or director,

an article which is, and which he knows or has reason to believe is, an infringing article.

(2) An 'infringing article' means a work or a copy of a work which–

(a)   has been subjected to derogatory treatment within the meaning of section 80, and

(b)   has been or is likely to be the subject of any of the acts mentioned in that section in circumstances infringing that right.

NOTE
Commencement order: SI 1989/816.

False attribution of work

84 False attribution of work
(1) A person has the right in the circumstances mentioned in this section–

(a)   not to have a literary, dramatic, musical or artistic work falsely attributed to him as author, and

(b)   not to have a film falsely attributed to him as director;

and in this section an 'attribution', in relation to such a work, means a statement (express or implied) as to who is the author or director.

(2) The right is infringed by a person who–

(a)   issues to the public copies of a work of any of those descriptions in or on which there is a false attribution, or

(b)   exhibits in public an artistic work, or a copy of an artistic work, in or on which there is a false attribution.

(3)The right is also infringed by a person who–

(a)   in the case of a literary, dramatic or musical work, performs the work in public, broadcasts it or includes it in a cable programme service as being the work of a person, or

(b)   in the case of a film, shows it in public, broadcasts it or includes it in a cable programme service as being directed by a person,

knowing or having reason to believe that the attribution is false.

(4) The right is also infringed by the issue to the public or public display of material containing a false attribution in connection with any of the acts mentioned in subsection (2) or (3).

(5) The right is also infringed by a person who in the course of a business–

(a)   possesses or deals with a copy of a work of any of the descriptions mentioned in subsection (1) in or on which there is a false attribution, or

(b) in the case of an artistic work, possesses or deals with the work itself when there is a false attribution in or on it,

knowing or having reason to believe that there is such an attribution and that it is false.

(6) In the case of an artistic work the right is also infringed by a person who in the course of a business–

(a) deals with a work which has been altered after the author parted with possession of it as being the unaltered work of the author, or

(b) deals with a copy of such a work as being a copy of the unaltered work of the author,

knowing or having reason to believe that that is not the case.

(7) References in this section to dealing are to selling or letting for hire, offering or exposing for sale or hire, exhibiting in public, or distributing.

(8) This section applies where, contrary to the fact–

(a) a literary, dramatic or musical work is falsely represented as being an adaptation of the work of a person, or

(b) a copy of an artistic work is falsely represented as being a copy made by the author of the artistic work,

as it applies where the work is falsely attributed to a person as author.

NOTE
Commencement order: SI 1989/816.

Right to privacy of certain photographs and films

85 Right to privacy of certain photographs and films

(1) A person who for private and domestic purposes commissions the taking of a photograph or the making of a film has, where copyright subsists in the resulting work, the right not to have–

(a) copies of the work issued to the public,
(b) the work exhibited or shown in public, or
(c) the work broadcast or included in a cable programme service;

and, except as mentioned in subsection (2), a person who does or authorises the doing of any of those acts infringes that right.

(2) The right is not infringed by an act which by virtue of any of the following provisions would not infringe copyright in the work–

(a) section 31 (incidental inclusion of work in an artistic work, film, broadcast or cable programme);
(b) section 45 (parliamentary and judicial proceedings);
(c) section 46 (Royal Commissions and statutory inquiries);
(d) section 50 (acts done under statutory authority);
(e) [section 57 or 66A (acts permitted on assumptions as to expiry of copyright, &c)].

NOTES
Commencement order: SI 1989/816.
Sub-s (2): words in square brackets substituted with savings by SI 1995/3297, reg 6(3); for savings see Part III thereof.

Supplementary

86 Duration of rights

(1) The rights conferred by section 77 (right to be identified as author or director), section 80 (right to object to derogatory treatment of work) and section 85 (right to privacy of certain photographs and films) continue to subsist so long as copyright subsists in the work.

(2) The right conferred by section 84 (false attribution) continues to subsist until 20 years after a person's death.

NOTES

Commencement order: SI 1989/816.

This section should be read in conjunction with the following provision of the the Duration of Copyright and Rights in Performances Regulations 1995, SI 1995/3297 (commencement: 1 January 1996):

Duration of Copyright and Rights in Performances Regulations 1995, reg 22

Revived copyright: exercise of moral rights

22–(1) The following provisions have effect with respect to the exercise of moral rights in relation to a work in which there is revived copyright.

(2) Any waiver or assertion of moral rights which subsisted immediately before the expiry of copyright shall continue to have effect during the period of revived copyright.

(3) Moral rights are exercisable after commencement by the author of a work or, as the case may be, the director of a film in which revived copyright subsists, as with any other copyright work.

(4) Where the author or director died before commencement–

(a) the rights conferred by–

section 77 (right to identification as author or director),
section 80 (right to object to derogatory treatment of work), or
section 85 (right to privacy of certain photographs and films),

are exercisable after commencement by his personal representatives, and

(b) any infringement after commencement of the right conferred by section 84 (false attribution) is actionable by his personal representatives.

(5) Any damages recovered by personal representatives by virtue of this Regulation in respect of an infringement after a person's death shall devolve as part of his estate as if the right of action had subsisted and been vested in him immediately before his death.

(6) Nothing in these Regulations shall be construed as causing a moral right to be exercisable if, or to the extent that, the right was excluded by virtue of paragraph 23 or 24 of Schedule 1 on the commencement of the 1988 Act or would have been so excluded if copyright had not previously expired.

87 Consent and waiver of rights

(1) It is not an infringement of any of the rights conferred by this Chapter to do any act to which the person entitled to the right has consented.

(2) Any of those rights may be waived by instrument in writing signed by the person giving up the right.

(3) A waiver–

(a) may relate to a specific work, to works of a specified description or to works generally, and may relate to existing or future works, and

(b) may be conditional or unconditional and may be expressed to be subject to revocation;

and if made in favour of the owner or prospective owner of the copyright in the work or works to which it relates, it shall be presumed to extend to his licensees and successors in title unless a contrary intention is expressed.

(4) Nothing in this Chapter shall be construed as excluding the operation of the general law of contract or estoppel in relation to an informal waiver or other transaction in relation to any of the rights mentioned in subsection (1).

NOTE

Commencement order: SI 1989/816.

88 Application of provisions to joint works

(1) The right conferred by section 77 (right to be identified as author or director) is, in the case of a work of joint authorship, a right of each joint author to be identified as a joint author and must be asserted in accordance with section 78 by each joint author in relation to himself.

(2) The right conferred by section 80 (right to object to derogatory treatment of work) is, in the case of a work of joint authorship, a right of each joint author and his right is satisfied if he consents to the treatment in question.

(3) A waiver under section 87 of those rights by one joint author does not affect the rights of the other joint authors.

(4) The right conferred by section 84 (false attribution) is infringed, in the circumstances mentioned in that section–

(a) by any false statement as to the authorship of a work of joint authorship, and

(b) by the false attribution of joint authorship in relation to a work of sole authorship;

and such a false attribution infringes the right of every person to whom authorship of any description is, whether rightly or wrongly, attributed.

(5) The above provisions also apply (with any necessary adaptations) in relation to a film which was, or is alleged to have been, jointly directed, as they apply to a work which is, or is alleged to be, a work of joint authorship.

A film is 'jointly directed' if it is made by the collaboration of two or more directors and the contribution of each director is not distinct from that of the other director or directors.

(6) The right conferred by section 85 (right to privacy of certain photographs and films) is, in the case of a work made in pursuance of a joint commission, a right of each person who commissioned the making of the work, so that–

(a) the right of each is satisfied if he consents to the act in question, and

(b) a waiver under section 87 by one of them does not affect the rights of the others.

NOTE
Commencement order: SI 1989/816.

---

89 Application of provisions to parts of works

(1) The rights conferred by section 77 (right to be identified as author or director) and section 85 (right to privacy of certain photographs and films) apply in relation to the whole or any substantial part of a work.

(2) The rights conferred by section 80 (right to object to derogatory treatment of work) and section 84 (false attribution) apply in relation to the whole or any part of a work.

NOTE
Commencement order: SI 1989/816.

CHAPTER V
DEALINGS WITH RIGHTS IN COPYRIGHT WORKS

Copyright

90 Assignment and licences

(1) Copyright is transmissible by assignment, by testamentary disposition or by operation of law, as personal or moveable property.

(2) An assignment or other transmission of copyright may be partial, that is, limited so as to apply–

(a) to one or more, but not all, of the things the copyright owner has the exclusive right to do;

(b) to part, but not the whole, of the period for which the copyright is to subsist.

(3) An assignment of copyright is not effective unless it is in writing signed by or on behalf of the assignor.

(4) A licence granted by a copyright owner is binding on every successor in title to his interest in the copyright, except a purchaser in good faith for valuable consideration and without notice (actual or constructive) of the licence or a person deriving title from such a purchaser; and references in this Part to doing anything with, or without, the licence of the copyright owner shall be construed accordingly.

NOTE

Commencement order: SI 1989/816.

This section applies in relation to the database right and databases as it applies in relation to copyright and copyright works. (Copyright and Rights in Databases Regulations 1997, SI 1997/3032, reg 23.)

91 Prospective ownership of copyright

(1) Where by an agreement made in relation to future copyright, and signed by or on behalf of the prospective owner of the copyright, the prospective owner purports to assign the future copyright (wholly or partially) to another person, then if, on the copyright coming into existence, the assignee or another person claiming under him would be entitled as against all other persons to require the copyright to be vested in him, the copyright shall vest in the assignee or his successor in title by virtue of this subsection.

(2) In this Part–

'future copyright' means copyright which will or may come into existence in respect of a future work or class of works or on the occurrence of a future event; and

'prospective owner' shall be construed accordingly, and includes a person who is prospectively entitled to copyright by virtue of such an agreement as is mentioned in subsection (1).

(3) A licence granted by a prospective owner of copyright is binding on every successor in title to his interest (or prospective interest) in the right, except a purchaser in good faith for valuable consideration and without notice (actual or constructive) of the licence or a person deriving title from such a purchaser; and references in this Part to doing anything with, or without, the licence of the copyright owner shall be construed accordingly.

NOTE

Commencement order: SI 1989/816.

This section applies in relation to the database right and databases as it applies in relation to copyright and copyright works. (Copyright and Rights in Databases Regulations 1997, SI 1997/3032, reg 23.)

This section should be read in conjunction with the following provisions of the Duration of Copyright and Rights in Performances Regulations 1995, SI 1995/3297 (commencement: 1 January 1996):

Duration of Copyright and Rights in Performances Regulations 1995, regs 19 and 20

Ownership of revived copyright

19–(1) The person who was the owner of the copyright in a work immediately before it expired (the 'former copyright owner') is as from commencement the owner of any revived copyright in the work, subject as follows.

(2) If the former copyright owner has died before commencement, or in the case of a legal person has ceased to exist before commencement, the revived copyright shall vest–

(a)   in the case of a film, in the principal director of the film or his personal representatives, and

(b)   in any other case, in the author of the work or his personal representatives.

(3) Where revived copyright vests in personal representatives by virtue of paragraph (2), it shall be held by them for the benefit of the person who would have been entitled to it had it been vested in the principal director or author immediately before his death and had devolved as part of his estate.

Prospective ownership of extended or revived copyright

20–(1) Where by an agreement made before commencement in relation to extended or revived copyright, and signed by or on behalf of the prospective owner of the copyright, the prospective owner purports to assign the extended or revived copyright (wholly or partially) to another person, then if, on commencement the assignee or another person claiming under him would be entitled as against all other persons to require the copyright to be vested in him, the copyright shall vest in the assignee or his successor in title by virtue of this paragraph.

(2) A licence granted by a prospective owner of extended or revived copyright is binding on every successor in title to his interest (or prospective interest) in the right, except a purchaser in good faith for valuable consideration and without notice (actual or constructive) of the licence or a person deriving title from such a purchaser; and references in Part I of the 1988 Act to doing anything with, or without, the licence of the copyright owner shall be construed accordingly.

(3) In paragraph (2) 'prospective owner' includes a person who is prospectively entitled to extended or revived copyright by virtue of such an agreement as is mentioned in paragraph (1).

92 Exclusive licences

(1) In this Part an 'exclusive licence' means a licence in writing signed by or on behalf of the copyright owner authorising the licensee to the exclusion of all other persons, including the

person granting the licence, to exercise a right which would otherwise be exercisable exclusively by the copyright owner.

(2) The licensee under an exclusive licence has the same rights against a successor in title who is bound by the licence as he has against the person granting the licence.

NOTE

Commencement order: SI 1989/816.

This section applies in relation to the database right and databases as it applies in relation to copyright and copyright works. (Copyright and Rights in Databases Regulations 1997, SI 1997/3032, reg 23.)

This section should be read in conjunction with the following provision of the the Duration of Copyright and Rights in Performances Regulations 1995, SI 1995/3297 (commencement: 1 January 1996):

Duration of Copyright and Rights in Performances Regulations 1995, reg 21

Extended copyright: existing licences, agreement, &c

21–(1) Any copyright licence, any term or condition of an agreement relating to the exploitation of a copyright work, or any waiver or assertion of moral rights, which–

    (a) subsists immediately before commencement in relation to an existing copyright work, and

    (b) is not to expire before the end of the copyright period under the 1988 provisions,

shall continue to have effect during the period of any extended copyright, subject to any agreement to the contrary.

(2) Any copyright licence, or term or condition relating to the exploitation of a copyright work, imposed by order of the Copyright Tribunal which–

    (a) subsists immediately before commencement in relation to an existing copyright work, and

    (b) is not to expire before the end of the copyright period under the 1988 provisions,

shall continue to have effect during the period of any extended copyright, subject to any further order of the Tribunal.

93 Copyright to pass under will with unpublished work

Where under a bequest (whether specific or general) a person is entitled, beneficially or otherwise, to–

    (a) an original document or other material thing recording or embodying a literary, dramatic, musical or artistic work which was not published before the death of the testator, or

    (b) an original material thing containing a sound recording or film which was not published before the death of the testator,

the bequest shall, unless a contrary intention is indicated in the testator's will or a codicil to it, be construed as including the copyright in the work in so far as the testator was the owner of the copyright immediately before his death.

NOTE

Commencement order: SI 1989/816.

This section applies in relation to the database right and databases as it applies in relation to copyright and copyright works. (Copyright and Rights in Databases Regulations 1997, SI 1997/3032, reg 23.)

[93A] [Presumption of transfer of rental right in case of film production agreement]

[(1) Where an agreement concerning film production is concluded between an author and a film producer, the author shall be presumed, unless the agreement provides to the contrary, to have transferred to the film producer any rental right in relation to the film arising by virtue of the inclusion of a copy of the author's work in the film.

(2) In this section 'author' means an author, or prospective author, of a literary, dramatic, musical or artistic work.

(3) Subsection (1) does not apply to any rental right in relation to the film arising by virtue of the inclusion in the film of the screenplay, the dialogue or music specifically created for and used in the film.

(4) Where this section applies, the absence of signature by or on behalf of the author does not exclude the operation of section 91(1) (effect of purported assignment of future copyright).

(5) The reference in subsection (1) to an agreement concluded between an author and a film producer includes any agreement having effect between those persons, whether made by them directly or through intermediaries.

(6) Section 93B (right to equitable remuneration on transfer of rental right) applies where there is a presumed transfer by virtue of this section as in the case of an actual transfer.]

NOTE

Added by SI 1996/2967, reg 12.

[Right to equitable remuneration where rental right transferred]

[93B] [Right to equitable remuneration where rental right transferred]
[(1) Where an author to whom this section applies has transferred his rental right concerning a sound recording or a film to the producer of the sound recording or film, he retains the right to equitable remuneration for the rental.

The authors to whom this section applies are–

(a)   the author of a literary, dramatic, musical or artistic work, and
(b)   the principal director of a film.

(2) The right to equitable remuneration under this section may not be assigned by the author except to a collecting society for the purpose of enabling it to enforce the right on his behalf.

The right is, however, transmissible by testamentary disposition or by operation of law as personal or moveable property; and it may be assigned or further transmitted by any person into whose hands it passes.

(3) Equitable remuneration under this section is payable by the person for the time being entitled to the rental right, that is, the person to whom the right was transferred or any successor in title of his.

(4) The amount payable by way of equitable remuneration is as agreed by or on behalf of the persons by and to whom it is payable, subject to section 93C (reference of amount to Copyright Tribunal).

(5) An agreement is of no effect in so far as it purports to exclude or restrict the right to equitable remuneration under this section.

(6) References in this section to the transfer of rental right by one person to another include any arrangement having that effect, whether made by them directly or through intermediaries.

(7) In this section a 'collecting society' means a society or other organisation which has as its main object, or one of its main objects, the exercise of the right to equitable remuneration under this section on behalf of more than one author.]

NOTES

Added by SI 1996/2967, reg 14(1).

This section should be read in conjunction with the following provisions of the Copyright and Related Rights Regulations, SI 1996/2967 (commencement: 1 December 1996):

Copyright and Related Rights Regulations 1996, regs 32 and 33

New rights: effect of pre-commencement film production agreement
32–(1) Sections 93A and 191F (presumption of transfer of rental right in case of production agreement) apply in relation to an agreement concluded before commencement.

As section 93A so applies, the restriction in subsection (3) of that section shall be omitted (exclusion of presumption in relation to screenplay, dialogue or music specifically created for the film).

(2) Sections 93B and 191G (right to equitable remuneration where rental right transferred) have effect accordingly, but subject to regulation 33 (right to equitable remuneration applicable to rental after 1st April 1997).

Right to equitable remuneration applicable to rental after 1st April 1997
33 No right to equitable remuneration under section 93B or 191G (right to equitable remuneration where rental right transferred) arises–

(a)   in respect of any rental of a sound recording or film before 1st April 1997, or

(b)   in respect of any rental after that date of a sound recording or film made in pursuance of an agreement entered into before 1st July 1994, unless the author or performer (or a successor in title of his) has before 1st January 1997 notified the person by whom the remuneration would be payable that he intends to exercise that right.

[93C] [Equitable remuneration: reference of amount to Copyright Tribunal]

[(1) In default of agreement as to the amount payable by way of equitable remuneration under section 93B, the person by or to whom it is payable may apply to the Copyright Tribunal to determine the amount payable.

(2) A person to or by whom equitable remuneration is payable under that section may also apply to the Copyright Tribunal–

(a)   to vary any agreement as to the amount payable, or

(b)   to vary any previous determination of the Tribunal as to that matter;

but except with the special leave of the Tribunal no such application may be made within twelve months from the date of a previous determination.

An order made on an application under this subsection has effect from the date on which it is made or such later date as may be specified by the Tribunal.

(3) On an application under this section the Tribunal shall consider the matter and make such order as to the method of calculating and paying equitable remuneration as it may determine to be reasonable in the circumstances, taking into account the importance of the contribution of the author to the film or sound recording.

(4) Remuneration shall not be considered inequitable merely because it was paid by way of a single payment or at the time of the transfer of the rental right.

(5) An agreement is of no effect in so far as it purports to prevent a person questioning the amount of equitable remuneration or to restrict the powers of the Copyright Tribunal under this section.]

NOTE

Added by SI 1996/2967, reg 14(1).

Moral rights

94 Moral rights not assignable

The rights conferred by Chapter IV (moral rights) are not assignable.

NOTE

Commencement order: SI 1989/816.

95 Transmission of moral rights on death

(1) On the death of a person entitled to the right conferred by section 77 (right to identification of author or director), section 80 (right to object to derogatory treatment of work) or section 85 (right to privacy of certain photographs and films)–

(a)   the right passes to such person as he may by testamentary disposition specifically direct,

(b)   if there is no such direction but the copyright in the work in question forms part of his estate, the right passes to the person to whom the copyright passes, and

(c)   if or to the extent that the right does not pass under paragraph (a) or (b) it is exercisable by his personal representatives.

(2) Where copyright forming part of a person's estate passes in part to one person and in part to another, as for example where a bequest is limited so as to apply–

(a)   to one or more, but not all, of the things the copyright owner has the exclusive right to do or authorise, or

(b)   to part, but not the whole, of the period for which the copyright is to subsist, any right which passes with the copyright by virtue of subsection (1) is correspondingly divided.

(3) Where by virtue of subsection (1)(a) or (b) a right becomes exercisable by more than one person–

(a)   it may, in the case of the right conferred by section 77 (right to identification of author or director), be asserted by any of them;

(b)   it is, in the case of the right conferred by section 80 (right to object to derogatory treatment of work) or section 85 (right to privacy of certain photographs and films), a right exercisable by each of them and is satisfied in relation to any of them if he consents to the treatment or act in question; and

(c)   any waiver of the right in accordance with section 87 by one of them does not affect the rights of the others.

(4) A consent or waiver previously given or made binds any person to whom a right passes by virtue of subsection (1).

(5) Any infringement after a person's death of the right conferred by section 84 (false attribution) is actionable by his personal representatives.

(6) Any damages recovered by personal representatives by virtue of this section in respect of an infringement after a person's death shall devolve as part of his estate as if the right of action had subsisted and been vested in him immediately before his death.

NOTE
Commencement order: SI 1989/816.

CHAPTER VI
REMEDIES FOR INFRINGEMENT

Rights and remedies of copyright owner

96 Infringement actionable by copyright owner

(1) An infringement of copyright is actionable by the copyright owner.

(2) In an action for infringement of copyright all such relief by way of damages, injunctions, accounts or otherwise is available to the plaintiff as is available in respect of the infringement of any other property right.

(3) This section has effect subject to the following provisions of this Chapter.

NOTE
Commencement order: SI 1989/816.
This section applies in relation to the database right and databases as it applies in relation to copyright and copyright works. (Copyright and Rights in Databases Regulations 1997, SI 1997/3032, reg 23.)

97 Provisions as to damages in infringement action

(1) Where in an action for infringement of copyright it is shown that at the time of the infringement the defendant did not know, and had no reason to believe, that copyright subsisted in the work to which the action relates, the plaintiff is not entitled to damages against him, but without prejudice to any other remedy.

(2) The court may in an action for infringement of copyright having regard to all the circumstances, and in particular to–

(a)   the flagrancy of the infringement, and

(b)   any benefit accruing to the defendant by reason of the infringement,

award such additional damages as the justice of the case may require.

NOTE
Commencement order: SI 1989/816.
This section applies in relation to the database right and databases as it applies in relation to copyright and copyright works. (Copyright and Rights in Databases Regulations 1997, SI 1997/3032, reg 23.)

98 Undertaking to take licence of right in infringement proceedings

(1) If in proceedings for infringement of copyright in respect of which a licence is available as of right under section 144 (powers exercisable in consequence of report of Monopolies and Mergers Commission) the defendant undertakes to take a licence on such terms as may be agreed or, in default of agreement, settled by the Copyright Tribunal under that section–

    (a) no injunction shall be granted against him,

    (b) no order for delivery up shall be made under section 99, and

    (c) the amount recoverable against him by way of damages or on an account of profits shall not exceed double the amount which would have been payable by him as licensee if such a licence on those terms had been granted before the earliest infringement.

(2) An undertaking may be given at any time before final order in the proceedings, without any admission of liability.

(3) Nothing in this section affects the remedies available in respect of an infringement committed before licences of right were available.

NOTE

Commencement order: SI 1989/816.

This section applies in relation to the database right and databases as it applies in relation to copyright and copyright works. (Copyright and Rights in Databases Regulations 1997, SI 1997/3032, reg 23.)

99 Order for delivery up

(1) Where a person–

    (a) has an infringing copy of a work in his possession, custody or control in the course of a business, or

    (b) has in his possession, custody or control an article specifically designed or adapted for making copies of a particular copyright work, knowing or having reason to believe that it has been or is to be used to make infringing copies,

the owner of the copyright in the work may apply to the court for an order that the infringing copy or article be delivered up to him or to such other person as the court may direct.

(2) An application shall not be made after the end of the period specified in section 113 (period after which remedy of delivery up not available); and no order shall be made unless the court also makes, or it appears to the court that there are grounds for making, an order under section 114 (order as to disposal of infringing copy or other article).

(3) A person to whom an infringing copy or other article is delivered up in pursuance of an order under this section shall, if an order under section 114 is not made, retain it pending the making of an order, or the decision not to make an order, under that section.

(4) Nothing in this section affects any other power of the court.

NOTES

Commencement order: SI 1989/816.

See further: the High Court and County Courts Jurisdiction Order 1991, SI 1991/724, arts 2(1)(n), 11, 12.

100 Right to seize infringing copies and other articles

(1) An infringing copy of a work which is found exposed or otherwise immediately available for sale or hire, and in respect of which the copyright owner would be entitled to apply for an order under section 99, may be seized and detained by him or a person authorised by him.

The right to seize and detain is exercisable subject to the following conditions and is subject to any decision of the court under section 114.

(2) Before anything is seized under this section notice of the time and place of the proposed seizure must be given to a local police station.

(3) A person may for the purpose of exercising the right conferred by this section enter premises to which the public have access but may not seize anything in the possession, custody or control of a person at a permanent or regular place of business of his, and may not use any force.

(4) At the time when anything is seized under this section there shall be left at the place where it was seized a notice in the prescribed form containing the prescribed particulars as to the

person by whom or on whose authority the seizure is made and the grounds on which it is made.

(5) In this section–

'premises' includes land, buildings, moveable structures, vehicles, vessels, aircraft and hovercraft; and

'prescribed' means prescribed by order of the Secretary of State.

(6) An order of the Secretary of State under this section shall be made by statutory instrument which shall be subject to annulment in pursuance of a resolution of either House of Parliament.

NOTE

Commencement orders: SI 1989/816, SI 1989/955, SI 1989/1032.

This section applies in relation to the database right and databases as it applies in relation to copyright and copyright works. (Copyright and Rights in Databases Regulations 1997, SI 1997/3032, reg 23.)

Rights and remedies of exclusive licensee

101 Rights and remedies of exclusive licensee

(1) An exclusive licensee has, except against the copyright owner, the same rights and remedies in respect of matters occurring after the grant of the licence as if the licence had been an assignment.

(2) His rights and remedies are concurrent with those of the copyright owner; and references in the relevant provisions of this Part to the copyright owner shall be construed accordingly.

(3) In an action brought by an exclusive licensee by virtue of this section a defendant may avail himself of any defence which would have been available to him if the action had been brought by the copyright owner.

NOTE

Commencement order: SI 1989/816.

102 Exercise of concurrent rights

(1) Where an action for infringement of copyright brought by the copyright owner or an exclusive licensee relates (wholly or partly) to an infringement in respect of which they have concurrent rights of action, the copyright owner or, as the case may be, the exclusive licensee may not, without the leave of the court, proceed with the action unless the other is either joined as a plaintiff or added as a defendant.

(2) A copyright owner or exclusive licensee who is added as a defendant in pursuance of subsection (1) is not liable for any costs in the action unless he takes part in the proceedings.

(3) The above provisions do not affect the granting of interlocutory relief on an application by a copyright owner or exclusive licensee alone.

(4) Where an action for infringement of copyright is brought which relates (wholly or partly) to an infringement in respect of which the copyright owner and an exclusive licensee have or had concurrent rights of action–

(a)   the court shall in assessing damages take into account–

(i)   the terms of the licence, and

(ii)   any pecuniary remedy already awarded or available to either of them in respect of the infringement;

(b)   no account of profits shall be directed if an award of damages has been made, or an account of profits has been directed, in favour of the other of them in respect of the infringement; and

(c)   the court shall if an account of profits is directed apportion the profits between them as the court considers just, subject to any agreement between them;

and these provisions apply whether or not the copyright owner and the exclusive licensee are both parties to the action.

(5) The copyright owner shall notify any exclusive licensee having concurrent rights before applying for an order under section 99 (order for delivery up) or exercising the right conferred by section 100 (right of seizure); and the court may on the application of the licensee make such order under section 99 or, as the case may be, prohibiting or permitting the exercise by the copyright owner of the right conferred by section 100, as it thinks fit having regard to the terms of the licence.

NOTES
Commencement order: SI 1989/816.
See further: the High Court and County Courts Jurisdiction Order 1991, SI 1991/724, arts 2(1)(n), 11, 12.
This section applies in relation to the database right and databases as it applies in relation to copyright and copyright works. (Copyright and Rights in Databases Regulations 1997, SI 1997/3032, reg 23.)

Remedies for infringement of moral rights

103 Remedies for infringement of moral rights

(1) An infringement of a right conferred by Chapter IV (moral rights) is actionable as a breach of statutory duty owed to the person entitled to the right.

(2) In proceedings for infringement of the right conferred by section 80 (right to object to derogatory treatment of work) the court may, if it thinks it is an adequate remedy in the circumstances, grant an injunction on terms prohibiting the doing of any act unless a disclaimer is made, in such terms and in such manner as may be approved by the court, dissociating the author or director from the treatment of the work.

NOTE
Commencement order: SI 1989/816.

Presumptions

104 Presumptions relevant to literary, dramatic, musical and artistic works

(1) The following presumptions apply in proceedings brought by virtue of this Chapter with respect to a literary, dramatic, musical or artistic work.

(2) Where a name purporting to be that of the author appeared on copies of the work as published or on the work when it was made, the person whose name appeared shall be presumed, until the contrary is proved–

(a) to be the author of the work;
(b) to have made it in circumstances not falling within section 11(2), 163, 165 or 168 (works produced in course of employment, Crown copyright, Parliamentary copyright or copyright of certain international organisations).

(3) In the case of a work alleged to be a work of joint authorship, subsection (2) applies in relation to each person alleged to be one of the authors.

(4) Where no name purporting to be that of the author appeared as mentioned in subsection (2) but–

(a) the work qualifies for copyright protection by virtue of section 155 (qualification by reference to country of first publication), and
(b) a name purporting to be that of the publisher appeared on copies of the work as first published,

the person whose name appeared shall be presumed, until the contrary is proved, to have been the owner of the copyright at the time of publication.

(5) If the author of the work is dead or the identity of the author cannot be ascertained by reasonable inquiry, it shall be presumed, in the absence of evidence to the contrary–

(a) that the work is an original work, and
(b) that the plaintiff's allegations as to what was the first publication of the work and as to the country of first publication are correct.

NOTE

Commencement order: SI 1989/816.

This section should be read in conjunction with the following provision of the Copyright and Rights in Databases Regulations 1997, SI 1997/3032 (commencement: 1 January 1998):

Copyright and Rights in Databases Regulations 1997, reg 22

22 Presumptions relevant to database right
(1) The following presumptions apply in proceedings brought by virtue of this Part of these Regulations with respect to a database.

(2) Where a name purporting to be that of the maker appeared on copies of the database as published, or on the database when it was made, the person whose name appeared shall be presumed, until the contrary is proved–

(a)   to be the maker of the database, and
(b)   to have made it in circumstances not falling within Regulation 14(2) to (4).

(3) Where copies of the database as published bear a label or a mark stating–

(a)   that a named person was the maker of the database, or
(b)   that the database was first published in a specified year,

the label or mark shall be admissible as evidence of the facts stated and shall be presumed to be correct until the contrary is proved.

(4) In the case of a database alleged to have been made jointly, paragraphs (2) and (3), so far as is applicable, apply in relation to each person alleged to be one of the makers.

105 Presumptions relevant to sound recordings and films

(1) In proceedings brought by virtue of this Chapter with respect to a sound recording, where copies of the recording as issued to the public bear a label or other mark stating–

(a)   that a named person was the owner of copyright in the recording at the date of issue of the copies, or
(b)   that the recording was first published in a specified year or in a specified country,

the label or mark shall be admissible as evidence of the facts stated and shall be presumed to be correct until the contrary is proved.

(2) In proceedings brought by virtue of this Chapter with respect to a film, where copies of the film as issued to the public bear a statement–

(a)   that a named person was the [director or producer] of the film,
[(aa) that a named person was the principal director, the author of the screenplay, the author of the dialogue or the composer of music specifically created for and used in the film,]
(b)   that a named person was the owner of copyright in the film at the date of issue of the copies, or
(c)   that the film was first published in a specified year or in a specified country,

the statement shall be admissible as evidence of the facts stated and shall be presumed to be correct until the contrary is proved.

(3) In proceedings brought by virtue of this Chapter with respect to a computer program, where copies of the program are issued to the public in electronic form bearing a statement–

(a)   that a named person was the owner of copyright in the program at the date of issue of the copies, or
(b)   that the program was first published in a specified country or that copies of it were first issued to the public in electronic form in a specified year,

the statement shall be admissible as evidence of the facts stated and shall be presumed to be correct until the contrary is proved.

(4) The above presumptions apply equally in proceedings relating to an infringement alleged to have occurred before the date on which the copies were issued to the public.

(5) In proceedings brought by virtue of this Chapter with respect to a film, where the film as shown in public, broadcast or included in a cable programme service bears a statement–

(a)   that a named person was the [director or producer] of the film, or [(aa) that a named person was the principal director of the film, the author of the screenplay, the author of the dialogue or the composer of music specifically created for and used in the film, or,]

(b) that a named person was the owner of copyright in the film immediately after it was made,

the statement shall be admissible as evidence of the facts stated and shall be presumed to be correct until the contrary is proved.

This presumption applies equally in proceedings relating to an infringement alleged to have occurred before the date on which the film was shown in public, broadcast or included in a cable programme service.

[(6) For the purposes of this section, a statement that a person was the director of a film shall be taken, unless a contrary indication appears, as meaning that he was the principal director of the film.]

NOTES
Commencement order: SI 1989/816.
Sub-s (2): in para (a) words in square brackets substituted, by SI 1996/2967, reg 18(4)(a); para (aa) added, by SI 1995/3297, reg 6(4).
Sub-s (5): in para (a) words in square brackets substituted, and para (aa) added, by SI 1996/2967, reg 18(4)(b).
Sub-s (6): added by SI 1996/2967, reg 18(4)(c).

106 Presumptions relevant to works subject to Crown copyright
In proceedings brought by virtue of this Chapter with respect to a literary, dramatic or musical work in which Crown copyright subsists, where there appears on printed copies of the work a statement of the year in which the work was first published commercially, that statement shall be admissible as evidence of the fact stated and shall be presumed to be correct in the absence of evidence to the contrary.

NOTE
Commencement order: SI 1989/816.

Offences

107 Criminal liability for making or dealing with infringing articles, &c
(1) A person commits an offence who, without the licence of the copyright owner–

(a) makes for sale or hire, or
(b) imports into the United Kingdom otherwise than for his private and domestic use, or
(c) possesses in the course of a business with a view to committing any act infringing the copyright, or
(d) in the course of a business–

　　(i)　sells or lets for hire, or
　　(ii)　offers or exposes for sale or hire, or
　　(iii)　exhibits in public, or
　　(iv)　distributes, or

(e) distributes otherwise than in the course of a business to such an extent as to affect prejudicially the owner of the copyright,

an article which is, and which he knows or has reason to believe is, an infringing copy of a copyright work.

(2) A person commits an offence who–

(a) makes an article specifically designed or adapted for making copies of a particular copyright work, or
(b) has such an article in his possession,

knowing or having reason to believe that it is to be used to make infringing copies for sale or hire or for use in the course of a business.

(3) Where copyright is infringed (otherwise than by reception of a broadcast or cable programme)–

(a) by the public performance of a literary, dramatic or musical work, or
(b) by the playing or showing in public of a sound recording or film,

any person who caused the work to be so performed, played or shown is guilty of an offence if he knew or had reason to believe that copyright would be infringed.

(4) A person guilty of an offence under subsection (1)(a), (b), (d)(iv) or (e) is liable–

(a) on summary conviction to imprisonment for a term not exceeding six months or a fine not exceeding the statutory maximum, or both;
(b) on conviction on indictment to a fine or imprisonment for a term not exceeding two years, or both.

(5) A person guilty of any other offence under this section is liable on summary conviction to imprisonment for a term not exceeding six months or a fine not exceeding level 5 on the standard scale, or both.

(6) Sections 104 to 106 (presumptions as to various matters connected with copyright) do not apply to proceedings for an offence under this section; but without prejudice to their application in proceedings for an order under section 108 below.

NOTE
Commencement order: SI 1989/816.

[107A] [Enforcement by local weights and measures authority]

[(1) It is the duty of every local weights and measures authority to enforce within their area the provisions of section 107.

(2) The following provisions of the Trade Descriptions Act 1968 apply in relation to the enforcement of that section by such an authority as in relation to the enforcement of that Act–

section 27 (power to make test purchases),
section 28 (power to enter premises and inspect and seize goods and documents),
section 29 (obstruction of authorised officers), and
section 33 (compensation for loss, &c of goods seized).

(3) Subsection (1) above does not apply in relation to the enforcement of section 107 in Northern Ireland, but it is the duty of the Department of Economic Development to enforce that section in Northern Ireland.

For that purpose the provisions of the Trade Descriptions Act 1968 specified in subsection (2) apply as if for the references to a local weights and measures authority and any officer of such an authority there were substituted references to that Department and any of its officers.

(4) Any enactment which authorises the disclosure of information for the purpose of facilitating the enforcement of the Trade Descriptions Act 1968 shall apply as if section 107 were contained in that Act and as if the functions of any person in relation to the enforcement of that section were functions under that Act.

(5) Nothing in this section shall be construed as authorising a local weights and measures authority to bring proceedings in Scotland for an offence.]

NOTE
This section is prospectively added by the Criminal Justice and Public Order Act 1994, s 165(2), as from a day to be appointed.

108 Order for delivery up in criminal proceedings

(1) The court before which proceedings are brought against a person for an offence under section 107 may, if satisfied that at the time of his arrest or charge–

(a) he had in his possession, custody or control in the course of a business an infringing copy of a copyright work, or
(b) he had in his possession, custody or control an article specifically designed or adapted for making copies of a particular copyright work, knowing or having reason to believe that it had been or was to be used to make infringing copies,

order that the infringing copy or article be delivered up to the copyright owner or to such other person as the court may direct.

(2) For this purpose a person shall be treated as charged with an offence–

    (a)   in England, Wales and Northern Ireland, when he is orally charged or is served with a summons or indictment;

    (b)   in Scotland, when he is cautioned, charged or served with a complaint or indictment.

(3) An order may be made by the court of its own motion or on the application of the prosecutor (or, in Scotland, the Lord Advocate or procurator-fiscal), and may be made whether or not the person is convicted of the offence, but shall not be made–

    (a)   after the end of the period specified in section 113 (period after which remedy of delivery up not available), or

    (b)   if it appears to the court unlikely that any order will be made under section 114 (order as to disposal of infringing copy or other article).

(4) An appeal lies from an order made under this section by a magistrates' court–

    (a)   in England and Wales, to the Crown Court, and

    (b)   in Northern Ireland, to the county court;

and in Scotland, where an order has been made under this section, the person from whose possession, custody or control the infringing copy or article has been removed may, without prejudice to any other form of appeal under any rule of law, appeal against that order in the same manner as against sentence.

(5) A person to whom an infringing copy or other article is delivered up in pursuance of an order under this section shall retain it pending the making of an order, or the decision not to make an order, under section 114.

(6) Nothing in this section affects the powers of the court under section 43 of the Powers of Criminal Courts Act 1973, [Part II of the Proceeds of Crime (Scotland) Act 1995] or <u>Article 7 of the Criminal Justice (Northern Ireland) Order 1980</u> [Article 11 of the Criminal Justice (Northern Ireland) Order 1994] (general provisions as to forfeiture in criminal proceedings).

NOTES

Commencement order: SI 1989/816.

Sub-s (6): words in square brackets substituted by the Criminal Procedure (Consequential Provisions) (Scotland) Act 1995, s 5, Sch 4, para 70(2); final words underlined prospectively repealed and subsequent words in square brackets prospectively substituted by the Criminal Justice (Northern Ireland) Order 1994, SI 1994/2795, art 26(1), Sch 2, para 13, as from a day to be appointed.

109 Search warrants

(1) Where a justice of the peace (in Scotland, a sheriff or justice of the peace) is satisfied by information on oath given by a constable (in Scotland, by evidence on oath) that there are reasonable grounds for believing–

    (a)   that an offence under section 107(1)(a), (b), (d)(iv) or (e) has been or is about to be committed in any premises, and

    (b)   that evidence that such an offence has been or is about to be committed is in those premises,

he may issue a warrant authorising a constable to enter and search the premises, using such reasonable force as is necessary.

(2) The power conferred by subsection (1) does not, in England and Wales, extend to authorising a search for material of the kinds mentioned in section 9(2) of the Police and Criminal Evidence Act 1984 (certain classes of personal or confidential material).

(3) A warrant under this section–

    (a)   may authorise persons to accompany any constable executing the warrant, and

    (b)   remains in force for 28 days from the date of its issue.

(4) In executing a warrant issued under this section a constable may seize an article if he reasonably believes that it is evidence that any offence under section 107(1) has been or is about to be committed.

(5) In this section 'premises' includes land, buildings, moveable structures, vehicles, vessels, aircraft and hovercraft.

NOTE

Commencement order: SI 1989/816.

110 Offence by body corporate: liability of officers

(1) Where an offence under section 107 committed by a body corporate is proved to have been committed with the consent or connivance of a director, manager, secretary or other similar officer of the body, or a person purporting to act in any such capacity, he as well as the body corporate is guilty of the offence and liable to be proceeded against and punished accordingly.

(2) In relation to a body corporate whose affairs are managed by its members 'director' means a member of the body corporate.

NOTE

Commencement order: SI 1989/816.

Provision for preventing importation of infringing copies

111 Infringing copies may be treated as prohibited goods

(1) The owner of the copyright in a published literary, dramatic or musical work may give notice in writing to the Commissioners of Customs and Excise–

    (a)   that he is the owner of the copyright in the work, and

    (b)   that he requests the Commissioners, for a period specified in the notice, to treat as prohibited goods printed copies of the work which are infringing copies.

(2) The period specified in a notice under subsection (1) shall not exceed five years and shall not extend beyond the period for which copyright is to subsist.

(3) The owner of the copyright in a sound recording or film may give notice in writing to the Commissioners of Customs and Excise–

    (a)   that he is the owner of the copyright in the work,

    (b)   that infringing copies of the work are expected to arrive in the United Kingdom at a time and a place specified in the notice, and

    (c)   that he requests the Commissioners to treat the copies as prohibited goods.

[(3A) The Commissioners may treat as prohibited goods only infringing copies of works which arrive in the United Kingdom–

    (a)   from outside the European Economic Area, or

    (b)   from within that Area but not having been entered for free circulation.

(3B) This section does not apply to goods entered, or expected to be entered, for free circulation, export, re-export or for a suspensive procedure in respect of which an application may be made under Article 3(1) of Council Regulation (EC) No 3295/94 laying down measures to prohibit the release for free circulation, export, re-export or entry for a suspensive procedure of counterfeit and pirated goods.]

(4) When a notice is in force under this section the importation of goods to which the notice relates, otherwise than by a person for his private and domestic use, [subject to subsections (3A) and (3B), is prohibited]; but a person is not by reason of the prohibition liable to any penalty other than forfeiture of the goods.

NOTES

Commencement order: SI 1989/816.

Sub-ss (3A), (3B): added by SI 1995/1445, reg 2(2).

Sub-s (4): words in square brackets substituted by SI 1995/1445, reg 2(3).

Council Regulation (EC) No 3295/94: OJ No L341, 30.12.94, p 8.

112 Power of Commissioners of Customs and Excise to make regulations
(1) The Commissioners of Customs and Excise may make regulations prescribing the form in which notice is to be given under section 111 and requiring a person giving notice–

   (a) to furnish the Commissioners with such evidence as may be specified in the regulations, either on giving notice or when the goods are imported, or at both those times, and

   (b) to comply with such other conditions as may be specified in the regulations.

(2) The regulations may, in particular, require a person giving such a notice–

   (a) to pay such fees in respect of the notice as may be specified by the regulations;

   (b) to give such security as may be so specified in respect of any liability or expense which the Commissioners may incur in consequence of the notice by reason of the detention of any article or anything done to an article detained;

   (c) to indemnify the Commissioners against any such liability or expense, whether security has been given or not.

(3) The regulations may make different provision as respects different classes of case to which they apply and may include such incidental and supplementary provisions as the Commissioners consider expedient.

(4) Regulations under this section shall be made by statutory instrument which shall be subject to annulment in pursuance of a resolution of either House of Parliament.

(5) Section 17 of the Customs and Excise Management Act 1979 (general provisions as to Commissioners' receipts) applies to fees paid in pursuance of regulations under this section as to receipts under the enactments relating to customs and excise.

NOTE
Commencement orders: SI 1989/816, SI 1989/955, SI 1989/1032.

Supplementary

113 Period after which remedy of delivery up not available
(1) An application for an order under section 99 (order for delivery up in civil proceedings) may not be made after the end of the period of six years from the date on which the infringing copy or article in question was made, subject to the following provisions.

(2) If during the whole or any part of that period the copyright owner–

   (a) is under a disability, or

   (b) is prevented by fraud or concealment from discovering the facts entitling him to apply for an order,

an application may be made at any time before the end of the period of six years from the date on which he ceased to be under a disability or, as the case may be, could with reasonable diligence have discovered those facts.

(3) In subsection (2) 'disability'–

   (a) in England and Wales, has the same meaning as in the Limitation Act 1980;

   (b) in Scotland, means legal disability within the meaning of the Prescription and Limitation (Scotland) Act 1973;

   (c) in Northern Ireland, has the same meaning as in the Statute of Limitations (Northern Ireland) 1958.

(4) An order under section 108 (order for delivery up in criminal proceedings) shall not, in any case, be made after the end of the period of six years from the date on which the infringing copy or article in question was made.

NOTE
Commencement order: SI 1989/816.

114 Order as to disposal of infringing copy or other article

(1) An application may be made to the court for an order that an infringing copy or other article delivered up in pursuance of an order under section 99 or 108, or seized and detained in pursuance of the right conferred by section 100, shall be–

(a) forfeited to the copyright owner, or

(b) destroyed or otherwise dealt with as the court may think fit,

or for a decision that no such order should be made.

(2) In considering what order (if any) should be made, the court shall consider whether other remedies available in an action for infringement of copyright would be adequate to compensate the copyright owner and to protect his interests.

(3) Provision shall be made by rules of court as to the service of notice on persons having an interest in the copy or other articles, and any such person is entitled–

(a) to appear in proceedings for an order under this section, whether or not he was served with notice, and

(b) to appeal against any order made, whether or not he appeared;

and an order shall not take effect until the end of the period within which notice of an appeal may be given or, if before the end of that period notice of appeal is duly given, until the final determination or abandonment of the proceedings on the appeal.

(4) Where there is more than one person interested in a copy or other article, the court shall make such order as it thinks just and may (in particular) direct that the article be sold, or otherwise dealt with, and the proceeds divided.

(5) If the court decides that no order should be made under this section, the person in whose possession, custody or control the copy or other article was before being delivered up or seized is entitled to its return.

(6) References in this section to a person having an interest in a copy or other article include any person in whose favour an order could be made in respect of it under this section or under section 204 or 231 of this Act or [section 19 of the Trade Marks Act 1994] (which make similar provision in relation to infringement of rights in performances, design right and trade marks).

NOTES

Commencement order: SI 1989/816.

Sub-s (6): words in square brackets substituted by the Trade Marks Act 1994, s 106(1), Sch 4, para 8(2).

See further: the High Court and County Courts Jurisdiction Order 1991, SI 1991/724, arts 2(1)(n), 11, 12.

115 Jurisdiction of county court and sheriff court

(1) In England, Wales and Northern Ireland a county court may entertain proceedings under–

section 99 (order for delivery up of infringing copy or other article),

section 102(5) (order as to exercise of rights by copyright owner where exclusive licensee has concurrent rights), or

section 114 (order as to disposal of infringing copy or other article),

[save that, in Northern Ireland, a county court may entertain such proceedings only] where the value of the infringing copies and other articles in question does not exceed the county court limit for actions in tort.

(2) In Scotland proceedings for an order under any of those provisions may be brought in the sheriff court.

(3) Nothing in this section shall be construed as affecting the jurisdiction of the High Court or, in Scotland, the Court of Session.

NOTES

Commencement order: SI 1989/816.

Sub-s (1): words in square brackets added by SI 1991/724, art 2(8), Schedule, Part I.

CHAPTER VII
COPYRIGHT LICENSING

Licensing schemes and licensing bodies

116 Licensing schemes and licensing bodies
(1) In this Part a 'licensing scheme' means a scheme setting out–

  (a) the classes of case in which the operator of the scheme, or the person on whose behalf he acts, is willing to grant copyright licences, and
  (b) the terms on which licences would be granted in those classes of case;

and for this purpose a 'scheme' includes anything in the nature of a scheme, whether described as a scheme or as a tariff or by any other name.

(2) In this Chapter a 'licensing body' means a society or other organisation which has as its main object, or one of its main objects, the negotiation or granting, either as owner or prospective owner of copyright or as agent for him, of copyright licences, and whose objects include the granting of licences covering works of more than one author.

(3) In this section 'copyright licences' means licences to do, or authorise the doing of, any of the acts restricted by copyright.

(4) References in this Chapter to licences or licensing schemes covering works of more than one author do not include licences or schemes covering only–

  (a) a single collective work or collective works of which the authors are the same, or
  (b) works made by, or by employees of or commissioned by, a single individual, firm, company or group of companies.

For this purpose a group of companies means a holding company and its subsidiaries, within the meaning of section 736 of the Companies Act 1985.

NOTE
Commencement order: SI 1989/816.

References and applications with respect to licensing schemes

[117] [Licensing schemes to which following sections apply]
[Sections 118 to 123 (references and applications with respect to licensing schemes) apply to licensing schemes which are operated by licensing bodies and cover works of more than one author, so far as they relate to licences for–

  (a) copying the work,
  (b) rental or lending of copies of the work to the public,
  (c) performing, showing or playing the work in public, or
  (d) broadcasting the work or including it in a cable programme service;

and references in those sections to a licensing scheme shall be construed accordingly.]

NOTES
Commencement order: SI 1989/816.
Substituted by SI 1996/2967, reg 15(2).
This section should be read in conjunction with Sch 2 of the Copyright and Rights in Databases Regulations 1997, SI 1997/3032, contextualised in this Act at Sch 2A.
This section should also be read in conjunction with the following provisions of the Copyright and Rights in Databases Regulations 1997, SI 1997/3032 (commencement: 1 January 1998):

Copyright and Rights in Databases Regulations 1997, regs 24 and 25

24 Licensing of database right
The provisions of Schedule 2 have effect with respect to the licensing of database right.

25 Database right: jurisdiction of Copyright Tribunal
(1) The Copyright Tribunal has jurisdiction under this Part to hear and determine proceedings under the following provisions of Schedule 2–

(a)   paragraph 3, 4 or 5 (reference of licensing scheme);
(b)   paragraph 6 or 7 (application with respect to licence under licensing scheme);
(c)   paragraph 10, 11 or 12 (reference or application with respect to licence by licensing body).

(2) The provisions of Chapter VIII of Part I of the 1988 Act (general provisions relating to the Copyright Tribunal) apply in relation to the Tribunal when exercising any jurisdiction under this Part.

(3) Provision shall be made by rules under section 150 of the 1988 Act prohibiting the Tribunal from entertaining a reference under paragraph 3, 4 or 5 of Schedule 2 (reference of licensing scheme) by a representative organisation unless the Tribunal is satisfied that the organisation is reasonably representative of the class of persons which it claims to represent.

118 Reference of proposed licensing scheme to tribunal

(1) The terms of a licensing scheme proposed to be operated by a licensing body may be referred to the Copyright Tribunal by an organisation claiming to be representative of persons claiming that they require licences in cases of a description to which the scheme would apply, either generally or in relation to any description of case.

(2) The Tribunal shall first decide whether to entertain the reference, and may decline to do so on the ground that the reference is premature.

(3) If the Tribunal decides to entertain the reference it shall consider the matter referred and make such order, either confirming or varying the proposed scheme, either generally or so far as it relates to cases of the description to which the reference relates, as the Tribunal may determine to be reasonable in the circumstances.

(4) The order may be made so as to be in force indefinitely or for such period as the Tribunal may determine.

NOTE
Commencement order: SI 1989/816.

119 Reference of licensing scheme to tribunal

(1) If while a licensing scheme is in operation a dispute arises between the operator of the scheme and–

(a)   a person claiming that he requires a licence in a case of a description to which the scheme applies, or
(b)   an organisation claiming to be representative of such persons,

that person or organisation may refer the scheme to the Copyright Tribunal in so far as it relates to cases of that description.

(2) A scheme which has been referred to the Tribunal under this section shall remain in operation until proceedings on the reference are concluded.

(3) The Tribunal shall consider the matter in dispute and make such order, either confirming or varying the scheme so far as it relates to cases of the description to which the reference relates, as the Tribunal may determine to be reasonable in the circumstances.

(4) The order may be made so as to be in force indefinitely or for such period as the Tribunal may determine.

NOTE
Commencement order: SI 1989/816.

120 Further reference of scheme to tribunal

(1) Where the Copyright Tribunal has on a previous reference of a licensing scheme under section 118 or 119, or under this section, made an order with respect to the scheme, then, while the order remains in force–

(a)   the operator of the scheme,
(b)   a person claiming that he requires a licence in a case of the description to which the order applies, or
(c)   an organisation claiming to be representative of such persons,

may refer the scheme again to the Tribunal so far as it relates to cases of that description.

(2) A licensing scheme shall not, except with the special leave of the Tribunal, be referred again to the Tribunal in respect of the same description of cases–

    (a)   within twelve months from the date of the order on the previous reference, or

    (b)   if the order was made so as to be in force for 15 months or less, until the last three months before the expiry of the order.

(3) A scheme which has been referred to the Tribunal under this section shall remain in operation until proceedings on the reference are concluded.

(4) The Tribunal shall consider the matter in dispute and make such order, either confirming, varying or further varying the scheme so far as it relates to cases of the description to which the reference relates, as the Tribunal may determine to be reasonable in the circumstances.

(5) The order may be made so as to be in force indefinitely or for such period as the Tribunal may determine.

NOTE

Commencement order: SI 1989/816.

121 Application for grant of licence in connection with licensing scheme

(1) A person who claims, in a case covered by a licensing scheme, that the operator of the scheme has refused to grant him or procure the grant to him of a licence in accordance with the scheme, or has failed to do so within a reasonable time after being asked, may apply to the Copyright Tribunal.

(2) A person who claims, in a case excluded from a licensing scheme, that the operator of the scheme either–

    (a)   has refused to grant him a licence or procure the grant to him of a licence, or has failed to do so within a reasonable time of being asked, and that in the circumstances it is unreasonable that a licence should not be granted, or

    (b)   proposes terms for a licence which are unreasonable,

may apply to the Copyright Tribunal.

(3) A case shall be regarded as excluded from a licensing scheme for the purposes of subsection (2) if–

    (a)   the scheme provides for the grant of licences subject to terms excepting matters from the licence and the case falls within such an exception, or

    (b)   the case is so similar to those in which licences are granted under the scheme that it is unreasonable that it should not be dealt with in the same way.

(4) If the Tribunal is satisfied that the claim is well-founded, it shall make an order declaring that, in respect of the matters specified in the order, the applicant is entitled to a licence on such terms as the Tribunal may determine to be applicable in accordance with the scheme or, as the case may be, to be reasonable in the circumstances.

(5) The order may be made so as to be in force indefinitely or for such period as the Tribunal may determine.

NOTE

Commencement order: SI 1989/816.

122 Application for review of order as to entitlement to licence

(1) Where the Copyright Tribunal has made an order under section 121 that a person is entitled to a licence under a licensing scheme, the operator of the scheme or the original applicant may apply to the Tribunal to review its order.

(2) An application shall not be made, except with the special leave of the Tribunal–

    (a)   within twelve months from the date of the order, or of the decision on a previous application under this section, or

    (b)   if the order was made so as to be in force for 15 months or less, or as a result of the decision on a previous application under this section is due to expire within 15 months of that decision, until the last three months before the expiry date.

(3) The Tribunal shall on an application for review confirm or vary its order as the Tribunal may determine to be reasonable having regard to the terms applicable in accordance with the licensing scheme or, as the case may be, the circumstances of the case.

NOTE
Commencement order: SI 1989/816.

123 Effect of order of tribunal as to licensing scheme

(1) A licensing scheme which has been confirmed or varied by the Copyright Tribunal–

    (a)   under section 118 (reference of terms of proposed scheme), or

    (b)   under section 119 or 120 (reference of existing scheme to Tribunal),

shall be in force or, as the case may be, remain in operation, so far as it relates to the description of case in respect of which the order was made, so long as the order remains in force.

(2) While the order is in force a person who in a case of a class to which the order applies–

    (a)   pays to the operator of the scheme any charges payable under the scheme in respect of a licence covering the case in question or, if the amount cannot be ascertained, gives an undertaking to the operator to pay them when ascertained, and

    (b)   complies with the other terms applicable to such a licence under the scheme,

shall be in the same position as regards infringement of copyright as if he had at all material times been the holder of a licence granted by the owner of the copyright in question in accordance with the scheme.

(3) The Tribunal may direct that the order, so far as it varies the amount of charges payable, has effect from a date before that on which it is made, but not earlier than the date on which the reference was made or, if later, on which the scheme came into operation.

If such a direction is made–

    (a)   any necessary repayments, or further payments, shall be made in respect of charges already paid, and

    (b)   the reference in subsection (2)(a) to the charges payable under the scheme shall be construed as a reference to the charges so payable by virtue of the order.

No such direction may be made where subsection (4) below applies.

(4) An order of the Tribunal under section 119 or 120 made with respect to a scheme which is certified for any purpose under section 143 has effect, so far as it varies the scheme by reducing the charges payable for licences, from the date on which the reference was made to the Tribunal.

(5) Where the Tribunal has made an order under section 121 (order as to entitlement to licence under licensing scheme) and the order remains in force, the person in whose favour the order is made shall if he–

    (a)   pays to the operator of the scheme any charges payable in accordance with the order or, if the amount cannot be ascertained, gives an undertaking to pay the charges when ascertained, and

    (b)   complies with the other terms specified in the order,

be in the same position as regards infringement of copyright as if he had at all material times been the holder of a licence granted by the owner of the copyright in question on the terms specified in the order.

NOTE
Commencement order: SI 1989/816.

References and applications with respect to licensing by licensing bodies

[124] [Licences to which following sections apply]

[Sections 125 to 128 (references and applications with respect to licensing by licensing bodies) apply to licences which are granted by a licensing body otherwise than in pursuance of a licensing scheme and cover works of more than one author, so far as they authorise–

(a) copying the work,

(b) rental or lending of copies of the work to the public,

(c) performing, showing or playing the work in public, or

(d) broadcasting the work or including it in a cable programme service;

and references in those sections to a licence shall be construed accordingly.]

NOTES
Commencement order: SI 1989/816.
Substituted by SI 1996/2967, reg 15(3).

125 Reference to tribunal of proposed licence

(1) The terms on which a licensing body proposes to grant a licence may be referred to the Copyright Tribunal by the prospective licensee.

(2) The Tribunal shall first decide whether to entertain the reference, and may decline to do so on the ground that the reference is premature.

(3) If the Tribunal decides to entertain the reference it shall consider the terms of the proposed licence and make such order, either confirming or varying the terms, as it may determine to be reasonable in the circumstances.

(4) The order may be made so as to be in force indefinitely or for such period as the Tribunal may determine.

NOTE
Commencement order: SI 1989/816.

126 Reference to tribunal of expiring licence

(1) A licensee under a licence which is due to expire, by effluxion of time or as a result of notice given by the licensing body, may apply to the Copyright Tribunal on the ground that it is unreasonable in the circumstances that the licence should cease to be in force.

(2) Such an application may not be made until the last three months before the licence is due to expire.

(3) A licence in respect of which a reference has been made to the Tribunal shall remain in operation until proceedings on the reference are concluded.

(4) If the Tribunal finds the application well-founded, it shall make an order declaring that the licensee shall continue to be entitled to the benefit of the licence on such terms as the Tribunal may determine to be reasonable in the circumstances.

(5) An order of the Tribunal under this section may be made so as to be in force indefinitely or for such period as the Tribunal may determine.

NOTE
Commencement order: SI 1989/816.

127 Application for review of order as to licence

(1) Where the Copyright Tribunal has made an order under section 125 or 126, the licensing body or the person entitled to the benefit of the order may apply to the Tribunal to review its order.

(2) An application shall not be made, except with the special leave of the Tribunal–

(a) within twelve months from the date of the order or of the decision on a previous application under this section, or

(b) if the order was made so as to be in force for 15 months or less, or as a result of the decision on a previous application under this section is due to expire within 15 months of that decision, until the last three months before the expiry date.

(3) The Tribunal shall on an application for review confirm or vary its order as the Tribunal may determine to be reasonable in the circumstances.

NOTE
Commencement order: SI 1989/816.

128 Effect of order of Tribunal as to licence

(1) Where the Copyright Tribunal has made an order under section 125 or 126 and the order remains in force, the person entitled to the benefit of the order shall if he–

 (a) pays to the licensing body any charges payable in accordance with the order or, if the amount cannot be ascertained, gives an undertaking to pay the charges when ascertained, and

 (b) complies with the other terms specified in the order,

be in the same position as regards infringement of copyright as if he had at all material times been the holder of a licence granted by the owner of the copyright in question on the terms specified in the order.

(2) The benefit of the order may be assigned–

 (a) in the case of an order under section 125, if assignment is not prohibited under the terms of the Tribunal's order; and

 (b) in the case of an order under section 126, if assignment was not prohibited under the terms of the original licence.

(3) The Tribunal may direct that an order under section 125 or 126, or an order under section 127 varying such an order, so far as it varies the amount of charges payable, has effect from a date before that on which it is made, but not earlier than the date on which the reference or application was made or, if later, on which the licence was granted or, as the case may be, was due to expire.

If such a direction is made–

 (a) any necessary repayments, or further payments, shall be made in respect of charges already paid, and

 (b) the reference in subsection (1)(a) to the charges payable in accordance with the order shall be construed, where the order is varied by a later order, as a reference to the charges so payable by virtue of the later order.

NOTE

Commencement order: SI 1989/816.

Factors to be taken into account in certain classes of case

129 General considerations: unreasonable discrimination

In determining what is reasonable on a reference or application under this Chapter relating to a licensing scheme or licence, the Copyright Tribunal shall have regard to–

 (a) the availability of other schemes, or the granting of other licences, to other persons in similar circumstances, and

 (b) the terms of those schemes or licences,

and shall exercise its powers so as to secure that there is no unreasonable discrimination between licensees, or prospective licensees, under the scheme or licence to which the reference or application relates and licensees under other schemes operated by, or other licences granted by, the same person.

NOTE

Commencement order: SI 1989/816.

---

130 Licences for reprographic copying

Where a reference or application is made to the Copyright Tribunal under this Chapter relating to the licensing of reprographic copying of published literary, dramatic, musical or artistic works, or the typographical arrangement of published editions, the Tribunal shall have regard to–

 (a) the extent to which published editions of the works in question are otherwise available,

(b)   the proportion of the work to be copied, and

(c)   the nature of the use to which the copies are likely to be put.

NOTE
Commencement order: SI 1989/816.

131 Licences for educational establishments in respect of works included in broadcasts or cable programmes

(1) This section applies to references or applications under this Chapter relating to licences for the recording by or on behalf of educational establishments of broadcasts or cable programmes which include copyright works, or the making of copies of such recordings, for educational purposes.

(2) The Copyright Tribunal shall, in considering what charges (if any) should be paid for a licence, have regard to the extent to which the owners of copyright in the works included in the broadcast or cable programme have already received, or are entitled to receive, payment in respect of their inclusion.

NOTE
Commencement order: SI 1989/816.

132 Licences to reflect conditions imposed by promoters of events

(1) This section applies to references or applications under this Chapter in respect of licences relating to sound recordings, films, broadcasts or cable programmes which include, or are to include, any entertainment or other event.

(2) The Copyright Tribunal shall have regard to any conditions imposed by the promoters of the entertainment or other event; and, in particular, the Tribunal shall not hold a refusal or failure to grant a licence to be unreasonable if it could not have been granted consistently with those conditions.

(3) Nothing in this section shall require the Tribunal to have regard to any such conditions in so far as they–

(a)   purport to regulate the charges to be imposed in respect of the grant of licences, or

(b)   relate to payments to be made to the promoters of any event in consideration of the grant of facilities for making the recording, film, broadcast or cable programme.

NOTES
Commencement order: SI 1989/816.

133 Licences to reflect payments in respect of underlying rights

[(1) In considering what charges should be paid for a licence–

(a)   on a reference or application under this Chapter relating to licences for the rental or lending of copies of a work, or

(b)   on an application under section 142 (royalty or other sum payable for lending of certain works),

the Copyright Tribunal shall take into account any reasonable payments which the owner of the copyright in the work is liable to make in consequence of the granting of the licence, or of the acts authorised by the licence, to owners of copyright in works included in that work.]

(2) On any reference or application under this Chapter relating to licensing in respect of the copyright in sound recordings, films, broadcasts or cable programmes, the Copyright Tribunal shall take into account, in considering what charges should be paid for a licence, any reasonable payments which the copyright owner is liable to make in consequence of the granting of the licence, or of the acts authorised by the licence, in respect of any performance included in the recording, film, broadcast or cable programme.

NOTES
Commencement order: SI 1989/816.
Sub-s (1): substituted by SI 1996/2967, reg 13(1).

134 Licences in respect of works included in re-transmissions

(1)[Subject to subsection (3A)] This section applies to references or applications under this Chapter relating to licences to include in a broadcast or cable programme service–

   (a)   literary, dramatic, musical or artistic works, or,
   (b)   sound recordings or films,

where one broadcast or cable programme ('the first transmission') is, by reception and immediate re-transmission, to be further broadcast or included in a cable programme service ('the further transmission').

(2) So far as the further transmission is to the same area as the first transmission, the Copyright Tribunal shall, in considering what charges (if any) should be paid for licences for either transmission, have regard to the extent to which the copyright owner has already received, or is entitled to receive, payment for the other transmission which adequately remunerates him in respect of transmissions to that area.

(3) So far as the further transmission is to an area outside that to which the first transmission was made, the Tribunal shall (except where subsection (4) applies) leave the further transmission out of account in considering what charges (if any) should be paid for licences for the first transmission.

[(3A) This section does not apply in relation to any application under section 73A (royalty or other sum payable in pursuance of section 73(4)).]

NOTES

Commencement order: SI 1989/816.
Sub-s (1): words in square brackets added by the Broadcasting Act 1996, s 138, Sch 9, para 2(2).
Sub-s (3A): added by the Broadcasting Act 1996, s 138, Sch 9, para 2(3).

---

135 Mention of specific matters not to exclude other relevant considerations

The mention in sections 129 to 134 of specific matters to which the Copyright Tribunal is to have regard in certain classes of case does not affect the Tribunal's general obligation in any case to have regard to all relevant considerations.

NOTE

Commencement order: SI 1989/816.
Sections 116 to 135 should be read in conjunction with the following provisions of the the Duration of Copyright and Rights in Performances Regulations 1995, SI 1995/3297 (commencement: 1 January 1996):

Duration of Copyright and Rights in Performances Regulations 1995, regs 24, 25, 34 and 35

Revived copyright: use as of right subject to reasonable royalty
24–(1) In the case of a work in which revived copyright subsists any acts restricted by the copyright shall be treated as licensed by the copyright owner, subject only to the payment of such reasonable royalty or other remuneration as may be agreed or determined in default of agreement by the Copyright Tribunal.

(2) A person intending to avail himself of the right conferred by this Regulation must give reasonable notice of his intention to the copyright owner, stating when he intends to begin to do the acts.

(3) If he does not give such notice, his acts shall not be treated as licensed.

(4) If he does give such notice, his acts shall be treated as licensed and a reasonable royalty or other remuneration shall be payable in respect of them despite the fact that its amount is not agreed or determined until later.

(5) This Regulation does not apply if or to the extent that a licence to do the acts could be granted by a licensing body (within the meaning of section 116(2) of the 1988 Act), whether or not under a licensing scheme.

(6) No royalty or other remuneration is payable by virtue of this Regulation in respect of anything for which a royalty or other remuneration is payable under Schedule 6 to the 1988 Act.

Revived copyright: application to Copyright Tribunal
25–(1) An application to settle the royalty or other remuneration payable in pursuance of Regulation 24 may be made to the Copyright Tribunal by the copyright owner or the person claiming to be treated as licensed by him.

(2) The Tribunal shall consider the matter and make such order as it may determine to be reasonable in the circumstances.

(3) Either party may subsequently apply to the Tribunal to vary the order, and the Tribunal shall consider the matter and make such order confirming or varying the original order as it may determine to be reasonable in the circumstances.

(4) An application under paragraph (3) shall not, except with the special leave of the Tribunal, be made within twelve months from the date of the original order or of the order on a previous application under that paragraph.

(5) An order under paragraph (3) has effect from the date on which it is made or such later date as may be specified by the Tribunal.

Revived performance rights: use as of right subject to reasonable remuneration
34–(1) In the case of a performance in which revived performance rights subsist any acts which require the consent of any person under Part II of the 1988 Act (the 'rights owner') shall be treated as having that consent, subject only to the payment of such reasonable remuneration as may be agreed or determined in default of agreement by the Copyright Tribunal.

(2) A person intending to avail himself of the right conferred by this Regulation must give reasonable notice of his intention to the rights owner, stating when he intends to begin to do the acts.

(3) If he does not give such notice, his acts shall not be treated as having consent.

(4) If he does give such notice, his acts shall be treated as having consent and reasonable remuneration shall be payable in respect of them despite the fact that its amount is not agreed or determined until later.

Revived performance rights: application to Copyright Tribunal
35–(1) An application to settle the remuneration payable in pursuance of Regulation 34 may be made to the Copyright Tribunal by the rights owner or the person claiming to be treated as having his consent.

(2) The Tribunal shall consider the matter and make such order as it may determine to be reasonable in the circumstances.

(3) Either party may subsequently apply to the Tribunal to vary the order, and the Tribunal shall consider the matter and make such order confirming or varying the original order as it may determine to be reasonable in the circumstances.

(4) An application under paragraph (3) shall not, except with the special leave of the Tribunal, be made within twelve months from the date of the original order or of the order on a previous application under that paragraph.

(5) An order under paragraph (3) has effect from the date on which it is made or such later date as may be specified by the Tribunal.

Use as of right of sound recordings in broadcasts and cable programme services

[135A] [Circumstances in which right available]
[(1) Section 135C applies to the inclusion in a broadcast or cable programme service of any sound recordings if–

   (a) a licence to include those recordings in the broadcast or cable programme service could be granted by a licensing body or such a body could procure the grant of a licence to do so,

   (b) the condition in subsection (2) or (3) applies, and

   (c) the person including those recordings in the broadcast or cable programme service has complied with section 135B.

(2) Where the person including the recordings in the broadcast or cable programme service does not hold a licence to do so, the condition is that the licensing body refuses to grant, or procure the grant of, such a licence, being a licence–

   (a) whose terms as to payment for including the recordings in the broadcast or cable programme service would be acceptable to him or comply with an order of the Copyright Tribunal under section 135D relating to such a licence or any scheme under which it would be granted, and

   (b) allowing unlimited needletime or such needletime as he has demanded.

(3) Where he holds a licence to include the recordings in the broadcast or cable programme service, the condition is that the terms of the licence limit needletime and the licensing body refuses to substitute or procure the substitution of terms allowing unlimited needletime or such needletime as he has demanded, or refuses to do so on terms that fall within subsection (2)(a).

(4) The references in subsection (2) to refusing to grant, or procure the grant of, a licence, and in subsection (3) to refusing to substitute or procure the substitution of terms, include failing to do so within a reasonable time of being asked.

(5) In the group of sections from this section to section 135G–

     'needletime' means the time in any period (whether determined as a number of hours in the period or a proportion of the period, or otherwise) in which any recordings may be included in a broadcast or cable programme service;

'sound recording' does not include a film sound track when accompanying a film.

(6) In sections 135B to 135G, 'terms of payment' means terms as to payment for including sound recordings in a broadcast or cable programme service.]

NOTE
This section was added by the Broadcasting Act 1990, s 175(1).

[135B] [Notice of intention to exercise right]

[(1) A person intending to avail himself of the right conferred by section 135C must–

(a) give notice to the licensing body of his intention to exercise the right, asking the body to propose terms of payment, and

(b) after receiving the proposal or the expiry of a reasonable period, give reasonable notice to the licensing body of the date on which he proposes to begin exercising that right, and the terms of payment in accordance with which he intends to do so.

(2) Where he has a licence to include the recordings in a broadcast or cable programme service, the date specified in a notice under subsection (1)(b) must not be sooner than the date of expiry of that licence except in a case falling within section 135A(3).

(3) Before the person intending to avail himself of the right begins to exercise it, he must–

(a) give reasonable notice to the Copyright Tribunal of his intention to exercise the right, and of the date on which he proposes to begin to do so, and

(b) apply to the Tribunal under section 135D to settle the terms of payment.]

NOTE
This section was added by the Broadcasting Act 1990, s 175(1).

[135C] [Conditions for exercise of right]

[(1) A person who, on or after the date specified in a notice under section 135B(1)(b), includes in a broadcast or cable programme service any sound recordings in circumstances in which this section applies, and who–

(a) complies with any reasonable condition, notice of which has been given to him by the licensing body, as to inclusion in the broadcasting or cable programme service of those recordings,

(b) provides that body with such information about their inclusion in the broadcast or cable programme service as it may reasonably require, and

(c) makes the payments to the licensing body that are required by this section,

shall be in the same position as regards infringement of copyright as if he had at all material times been the holder of a licence granted by the owner of the copyright in question.

(2) Payments are to be made at not less than quarterly intervals in arrears.

(3) The amount of any payment is that determined in accordance with any order of the Copyright Tribunal under section 135D or, if no such order has been made–

(a) in accordance with any proposal for terms of payment made by the licensing body pursuant to a request under section 135B, or

(b) where no proposal has been so made or the amount determined in accordance with the proposal so made is unreasonably high, in accordance with the terms of payment notified to the licensing body under section 135B(1)(b).

(4) Where this section applies to the inclusion in a broadcast or cable programme service of any sound recordings, it does so in place of any licence.]

NOTE
This section was added by the Broadcasting Act 1990, s 175(1).

[135D] [Applications to settle payments]

[(1) On an application to settle the terms of payment, the Copyright Tribunal shall consider the matter and make such order as it may determine to be reasonable in the circumstances.

(2) An order under subsection (1) has effect from the date the applicant begins to exercise the right conferred by section 135C and any necessary repayments, or further payments, shall be made in respect of amounts that have fallen due.]

NOTE
This section was added by the Broadcasting Act 1990, s 175(1).

[135E] [References etc about conditions, information and other terms]
[(1) A person exercising the right conferred by section 135C, or who has given notice to the Copyright Tribunal of his intention to do so, may refer to the Tribunal–

(a) any question whether any condition as to the inclusion in a broadcast or cable programme service of sound recordings, notice of which has been given to him by the licensing body in question, is a reasonable condition, or

(b) any question whether any information is information which the licensing body can reasonably require him to provide.

(2) On a reference under this section, the Tribunal shall consider the matter and make such order as it may determine to be reasonable in the circumstances.]

NOTE
This section was added by the Broadcasting Act 1990, s 175(1).

[135F] [Application for review of order]
[(1) A person exercising the right conferred by section 135C or the licensing body may apply to the Copyright Tribunal to review any order under section 135D or 135E.
   (2) An application shall not be made, except with the special leave of the Tribunal–

(a) within twelve months from the date of the order, or of the decision on a previous application under this section, or

(b) if the order was made so as to be in force for fifteen months or less, or as a result of a decision on a previous application is due to expire within fifteen months of that decision, until the last three months before the expiry date.

(3) On the application the Tribunal shall consider the matter and make such order confirming or varying the original order as it may determine to be reasonable in the circumstances.
   (4) An order under this section has effect from the date on which it is made or such later date as may be specified by the Tribunal.]

NOTE
This section was added by the Broadcasting Act 1990, s 175(1).

[135G] [Factors to be taken into account]
[(1) In determining what is reasonable on an application or reference under section 135D or 135E, or on reviewing any order under section 135F, the Copyright Tribunal shall–

(a) have regard to the terms of any orders which it has made in the case of persons in similar circumstances exercising the right conferred by section 135C, and

(b) exercise its powers so as to secure that there is no unreasonable discrimination between persons exercising that right against the same licensing body.

(2) In settling the terms of payment under section 135D, the Tribunal shall not be guided by any order it has made under any enactment other than that section.
   (3) Section 134 (factors to be taken into account: retransmissions) applies on an application or reference under sections 135D to 135F as it applies on an application or reference relating to a licence.]

NOTE
This section was added by the Broadcasting Act 1990, s 175(1).

[135H] [Power to amend sections 135A to 135G]
[(1) The Secretary of State may by order, subject to such transitional provision as appears to him to be appropriate, amend sections 135A to 135G so as–

(a) to include in any reference to sound recordings any works of a description specified in the order; or

(b) to exclude from any reference to a broadcast or cable programme service any broadcast or cable programme service of a description so specified.

(2) An order shall be made by statutory instrument; and no order shall be made unless a draft of it has been laid before and approved by resolution of each House of Parliament.]

NOTES
Added by the Broadcasting Act 1996, s 139(1).

Implied indemnity in schemes or licences for reprographic copying

136 Implied indemnity in certain schemes and licences for reprographic copying
(1) This section applies to–

(a) schemes for licensing reprographic copying of published literary, dramatic, musical or artistic works, or the typographical arrangement of published editions, and

(b) licences granted by licensing bodies for such copying,

where the scheme or licence does not specify the works to which it applies with such particularity as to enable licensees to determine whether a work falls within the scheme or licence by inspection of the scheme or licence and the work.
    (2) There is implied–

(a) in every scheme to which this section applies an undertaking by the operator of the scheme to indemnify a person granted a licence under the scheme, and

(b) in every licence to which this section applies an undertaking by the licensing body to indemnify the licensee,

against any liability incurred by him by reason of his having infringed copyright by making or authorising the making of reprographic copies of a work in circumstances within the apparent scope of his licence.
    (3) The circumstances of a case are within the apparent scope of a licence if–

(a) it is not apparent from inspection of the licence and the work that it does not fall within the description of works to which the licence applies; and

(b) the licence does not expressly provide that it does not extend to copyright of the description infringed.

(4) In this section 'liability' includes liability to pay costs; and this section applies in relation to costs reasonably incurred by a licensee in connection with actual or contemplated proceedings against him for infringement of copyright as it applies to sums which he is liable to pay in respect of such infringement.
    (5) A scheme or licence to which this section applies may contain reasonable provision–

(a) with respect to the manner in which, and time within which, claims under the undertaking implied by this section are to be made;

(b) enabling the operator of the scheme or, as the case may be, the licensing body to take over the conduct of any proceedings affecting the amount of his liability to indemnify.

NOTE
Commencement order: SI 1989/816.

Reprographic copying by educational establishments

137 Power to extend coverage of scheme or licence

(1) This section applies to–

    (a) a licensing scheme to which sections 118 to 123 apply (see section 117) and which is operated by a licensing body, or

    (b) a licence to which sections 125 to 128 apply (see section 124),

so far as it provides for the grant of licences, or is a licence, authorising the making by or on behalf of educational establishments for the purposes of instruction of reprographic copies of published literary, dramatic, musical or artistic works, or of the typographical arrangement of published editions.

(2) If it appears to the Secretary of State with respect to a scheme or licence to which this section applies that–

    (a) works of a description similar to those covered by the scheme or licence are unreasonably excluded from it, and

    (b) making them subject to the scheme or licence would not conflict with the normal exploitation of the works or unreasonably prejudice the legitimate interests of the copyright owners,

he may by order provide that the scheme or licence shall extend to those works.

(3) Where he proposes to make such an order, the Secretary of State shall give notice of the proposal to–

    (a) the copyright owners,

    (b) the licensing body in question, and

    (c) such persons or organisations representative of educational establishments, and such other persons or organisations, as the Secretary of State thinks fit.

(4) The notice shall inform those persons of their right to make written or oral representations to the Secretary of State about the proposal within six months from the date of the notice; and if any of them wishes to make oral representations, the Secretary of State shall appoint a person to hear the representations and report to him.

(5) In considering whether to make an order the Secretary of State shall take into account any representations made to him in accordance with subsection (4), and such other matters as appear to him to be relevant.

NOTES

    Commencement order: SI 1989/816.

    See further: the Copyright (Application of Provisions Relating to Educational Establishments to Teachers) (No 2) Order 1989, SI 1989/1067, art 2.

---

138 Variation or discharge of order extending scheme or licence

(1) The owner of the copyright in a work in respect of which an order is in force under section 137 may apply to the Secretary of State for the variation or discharge of the order, stating his reasons for making the application.

(2) The Secretary of State shall not entertain an application made within two years of the making of the original order, or of the making of an order on a previous application under this section, unless it appears to him that the circumstances are exceptional.

(3) On considering the reasons for the application the Secretary of State may confirm the order forthwith; if he does not do so, he shall give notice of the application to–

    (a) the licensing body in question, and

    (b) such persons or organisations representative of educational establishments, and such other persons or organisations, as he thinks fit.

(4) The notice shall inform those persons of their right to make written or oral representations to the Secretary of State about the application within the period of two months from the date of the notice; and if any of them wishes to make oral representations, the Secretary of State shall appoint a person to hear the representations and report to him.

(5) In considering the application the Secretary of State shall take into account the reasons for the application, any representations made to him in accordance with subsection (4), and such other matters as appear to him to be relevant.

(6) The Secretary of State may make such order as he thinks fit confirming or discharging the order (or, as the case may be, the order as previously varied), or varying (or further varying) it so as to exclude works from it.

NOTES

Commencement order: SI 1989/816.

See further: the Copyright (Application of Provisions Relating to Educational Establishments to Teachers) (No 2) Order 1989, SI 1989/1067, art 2.

139 Appeals against orders

(1) The owner of the copyright in a work which is the subject of an order under section 137 (order extending coverage of scheme or licence) may appeal to the Copyright Tribunal which may confirm or discharge the order, or vary it so as to exclude works from it, as it thinks fit having regard to the considerations mentioned in subsection (2) of that section.

(2) Where the Secretary of State has made an order under section 138 (order confirming, varying or discharging order extending coverage of scheme or licence)–

(a)   the person who applied for the order, or

(b)   any person or organisation representative of educational establishments who was given notice of the application for the order and made representations in accordance with subsection (4) of that section,

may appeal to the Tribunal which may confirm or discharge the order or make any other order which the Secretary of State might have made.

(3) An appeal under this section shall be brought within six weeks of the making of the order or such further period as the Tribunal may allow.

(4) An order under section 137 or 138 shall not come into effect until the end of the period of six weeks from the making of the order or, if an appeal is brought before the end of that period, until the appeal proceedings are disposed of or withdrawn.

(5) If an appeal is brought after the end of that period, any decision of the Tribunal on the appeal does not affect the validity of anything done in reliance on the order appealed against before that decision takes effect.

NOTES

Commencement order: SI 1989/816.

See further: the Copyright (Application of Provisions Relating to Educational Establishments to Teachers) (No 2) Order 1989, SI 1989/1067, art 2.

140 Inquiry whether new scheme or general licence required

(1) The Secretary of State may appoint a person to inquire into the question whether new provision is required (whether by way of a licensing scheme or general licence) to authorise the making by or on behalf of educational establishments for the purposes of instruction of reprographic copies of–

(a)   published literary, dramatic, musical or artistic works, or

(b)   the typographical arrangement of published editions,

of a description which appears to the Secretary of State not to be covered by an existing licensing scheme or general licence and not to fall within the power conferred by section 137 (power to extend existing schemes and licences to similar works).

(2) The procedure to be followed in relation to an inquiry shall be such as may be prescribed by regulations made by the Secretary of State.

(3) The regulations shall, in particular, provide for notice to be given to–

(a)   persons or organisations appearing to the Secretary of State to represent the owners of copyright in works of that description, and

(b)   persons or organisations appearing to the Secretary of State to represent educational establishments, and for the making of written or oral representations by such persons; but without prejudice to the giving of notice to, and the making of representations by, other persons and organisations.

(4) The person appointed to hold the inquiry shall not recommend the making of new provision unless he is satisfied–

  (a) that it would be of advantage to educational establishments to be authorised to make reprographic copies of the works in question, and

  (b) that making those works subject to a licensing scheme or general licence would not conflict with the normal exploitation of the works or unreasonably prejudice the legitimate interests of the copyright owners.

(5) If he does recommend the making of new provision he shall specify any terms, other than terms as to charges payable, on which authorisation under the new provision should be available.

(6) Regulations under this section shall be made by statutory instrument which shall be subject to annulment in pursuance of a resolution of either House of Parliament.

(7) In this section (and section 141) a 'general licence' means a licence granted by a licensing body which covers all works of the description to which it applies.

NOTES

Commencement order: SI 1989/816.

See further: the Copyright (Application of Provisions Relating to Educational Establishments to Teachers) (No 2) Order 1989, SI 1989/1067, art 2.

---

141 Statutory licence where recommendation not implemented

(1) The Secretary of State may, within one year of the making of a recommendation under section 140 by order provide that if, or to the extent that, provision has not been made in accordance with the recommendation, the making by or on behalf of an educational establishment, for the purposes of instruction, of reprographic copies of the works to which the recommendation relates shall be treated as licensed by the owners of the copyright in the works.

(2) For that purpose provision shall be regarded as having been made in accordance with the recommendation if–

  (a) a certified licensing scheme has been established under which a licence is available to the establishment in question, or

  (b) a general licence has been–

    (i) granted to or for the benefit of that establishment, or

    (ii) referred by or on behalf of that establishment to the Copyright Tribunal under section 125 (reference of terms of proposed licence), or

    (iii) offered to or for the benefit of that establishment and refused without such a reference,

and the terms of the scheme or licence accord with the recommendation.

(3) The order shall also provide that any existing licence authorising the making of such copies (not being a licence granted under a certified licensing scheme or a general licence) shall cease to have effect to the extent that it is more restricted or more onerous than the licence provided for by the order.

(4) The order shall provide for the licence to be free of royalty but, as respects other matters, subject to any terms specified in the recommendation and to such other terms as the Secretary of State may think fit.

(5) The order may provide that where a copy which would otherwise be an infringing copy is made in accordance with the licence provided by the order but is subsequently dealt with, it shall be treated as an infringing copy for the purposes of that dealing, and if that dealing infringes copyright for all subsequent purposes.

In this subsection 'dealt with' means sold or let for hire, offered or exposed for sale or hire, or exhibited in public.

(6) The order shall not come into force until at least six months after it is made.

(7) An order may be varied from time to time, but not so as to include works other than those to which the recommendation relates or remove any terms specified in the recommendation, and may be revoked.

(8) An order under this section shall be made by statutory instrument which shall be subject to annulment in pursuance of a resolution of either House of Parliament.

(9) In this section a 'certified licensing scheme' means a licensing scheme certified for the purposes of this section under section 143.

NOTES

Commencement order: SI 1989/816.
See further: the Copyright (Application of Provisions Relating to Educational Establishments to Teachers) (No 2) Order 1989, SI 1989/1067, art 2.

[Royalty or other sum payable for lending of certain works]

[142] [Royalty or other sum payable for lending of certain works]
[(1) An application to settle the royalty or other sum payable in pursuance of section 66 (lending of copies of certain copyright works) may be made to the Copyright Tribunal by the copyright owner or the person claiming to be treated as licensed by him.

(2) The Tribunal shall consider the matter and make such order as it may determine to be reasonable in the circumstances.

(3) Either party may subsequently apply to the Tribunal to vary the order, and the Tribunal shall consider the matter and make such order confirming or varying the original order as it may determine to be reasonable in the circumstances.

(4) An application under subsection (3) shall not, except with the special leave of the Tribunal, be made within twelve months from the date of the original order or of the order on a previous application under that subsection.

(5) An order under subsection (3) has effect from the date on which it is made or such later date as may be specified by the Tribunal.]

NOTES

Commencement order: SI 1989/816.
Substituted by SI 1996/2967, reg 13(2).

Certification of licensing schemes

143 Certification of licensing schemes
(1) A person operating or proposing to operate a licensing scheme may apply to the Secretary of State to certify the scheme for the purposes of–

   (a)   section 35 (educational recording of broadcasts or cable programmes),
   (b)   section 60 (abstracts of scientific or technical articles),
   [(c)   section 66 (lending to public of copies of certain works),
   (d)   section 74 (sub-titled copies of broadcasts or cable programmes for people who are deaf or hard of hearing), or
   (e)   section 141 (reprographic copying of published works by educational establishments).

(2) The Secretary of State shall by order made by statutory instrument certify the scheme if he is satisfied that it–

   (a)   enables the works to which it relates to be identified with sufficient certainty by persons likely to require licences, and
   (b)   sets out clearly the charges (if any) payable and the other terms on which licences will be granted.

(3) The scheme shall be scheduled to the order and the certification shall come into operation for the purposes of section 35, 60, 66, 74 or 141, as the case may be–

(a) on such date, not less than eight weeks after the order is made, as may be specified in the order, or

(b) if the scheme is the subject of a reference under section 118 (reference of proposed scheme), any later date on which the order of the Copyright Tribunal under that section comes into force or the reference is withdrawn.

(4) A variation of the scheme is not effective unless a corresponding amendment of the order is made; and the Secretary of State shall make such an amendment in the case of a variation ordered by the Copyright Tribunal on a reference under section 118, 119 or 120, and may do so in any other case if he thinks fit.

(5) The order shall be revoked if the scheme ceases to be operated and may be revoked if it appears to the Secretary of State that it is no longer being operated according to its terms.

NOTES
Commencement order: SI 1989/816.
Sub-s (1): para (c) substituted by SI 1996/2967, reg 11(4).

Powers exercisable in consequence of competition report

144 Powers exercisable in consequence of report of Monopolies and Mergers Commission

(1) Where the matters specified in a report of the Monopolies and Mergers Commission as being those which in the Commission's opinion operate, may be expected to operate or have operated against the public interest include–

(a) conditions in licences granted by the owner of copyright in a work restricting the use of the work by the licensee or the right of the copyright owner to grant other licences, or

(b) a refusal of a copyright owner to grant licences on reasonable terms,

the powers conferred by Part I of Schedule 8 to the Fair Trading Act 1973 (powers exercisable for purpose of remedying or preventing adverse effects specified in report of Commission) include power to cancel or modify those conditions and, instead or in addition, to provide that licences in respect of the copyright shall be available as of right.

(2) The references in sections 56(2) and 73(2) of that Act, and sections 10(2)(b) and 12(5) of the Competition Act 1980, to the powers specified in that Part of that Schedule shall be construed accordingly.

(3) A Minister shall only exercise the powers available by virtue of this section if he is satisfied that to do so does not contravene any Convention relating to copyright to which the United Kingdom is a party.

(4) The terms of a licence available by virtue of this section shall, in default of agreement, be settled by the Copyright Tribunal on an application by the person requiring the licence; and terms so settled shall authorise the licensee to do everything in respect of which a licence is so available.

(5) Where the terms of a licence are settled by the Tribunal, the licence has effect from the date on which the application to the Tribunal was made.

NOTE
Commencement order: SI 1989/816.

[Compulsory collective administration of certain rights]

[144A] [Collective exercise of certain rights in relation to cable re-transmission]

[(1) This section applies to the right of the owner of copyright in a literary, dramatic, musical or artistic work, sound recording or film to grant or refuse authorisation for cable re-transmission of a broadcast from another EEA member state in which the work is included.

That right is referred to below as 'cable re-transmission right'.

(2) Cable re-transmission right may be exercised against a cable operator only through a licensing body.

(3) Where a copyright owner has not transferred management of his cable re-transmission right to a licensing body, the licensing body which manages rights of the same category shall be deemed to be mandated to manage his right.

Where more than one licensing body manages rights of that category, he may choose which of them is deemed to be mandated to manage his right.

(4) A copyright owner to whom subsection (3) applies has the same rights and obligations resulting from any relevant agreement between the cable operator and the licensing body as have copyright owners who have transferred management of their cable re-transmission right to that licensing body.

(5) Any rights to which a copyright owner may be entitled by virtue of subsection (4) must be claimed within the period of three years beginning with the date of the cable re-transmission concerned.

(6) This section does not affect any rights exercisable by the maker of the broadcast, whether in relation to the broadcast or a work included in it.

(7) In this section–

'cable operator' means a person providing a cable programme service; and

'cable re-transmission' means the reception and immediate retransmission by way of a cable programme service of a broadcast.]

NOTE

Added by SI 1996/2967, reg 7.

CHAPTER VIII
THE COPYRIGHT TRIBUNAL

The Tribunal

145　The Copyright Tribunal

(1) The Tribunal established under section 23 of the Copyright Act 1956 is renamed the Copyright Tribunal.

(2) The Tribunal shall consist of a chairman and two deputy chairmen appointed by the Lord Chancellor, after consultation with the Lord Advocate, and not less than two or more than eight ordinary members appointed by the Secretary of State.

(3) A person is not eligible for appointment as chairman or deputy chairman [unless–

(a) he has a 7 year general qualification, within the meaning of section 71 of the Courts and Legal Services Act 1990;

(b) he is an advocate or solicitor in Scotland of at least 7 years' standing;

(c) he is a member of the Bar of Northern Ireland or solicitor of the Supreme Court of Northern Ireland of at least 7 years' standing; or

(d) he has held judicial office.]

NOTES

Commencement order: SI 1989/816.

Sub-s (3): words in square brackets substituted by the Courts and Legal Services Act 1990, s 71(2), Sch 10, para 73.

146　Membership of the Tribunal

(1) The members of the Copyright Tribunal shall hold and vacate office in accordance with their terms of appointment, subject to the following provisions.

(2) A member of the Tribunal may resign his office by notice in writing to the Secretary of State or, in the case of the chairman or a deputy chairman, to the Lord Chancellor.

(3) The Secretary of State or, in the case of the chairman or a deputy chairman, the Lord Chancellor may by notice in writing to the member concerned remove him from office if–

(a) he has become bankrupt or made an arrangement with his creditors or, in Scotland, his estate has been sequestrated or he has executed a trust deed for his creditors or entered into a composition contract, or

(b) he is incapacitated by physical or mental illness,

or if he is in the opinion of the Secretary of State or, as the case may be, the Lord Chancellor otherwise unable or unfit to perform his duties as member.

[(3A) A person who is the chairman or a deputy chairman of the Tribunal shall vacate his office on the day on which he attains the age of 70 years; but this subsection is subject to section 26(4) to (6) of the Judicial Pensions and Retirement Act 1993 (power to authorise continuance in office up to the age of 75 years).]

(4) If a member of the Tribunal is by reason of illness, absence or other reasonable cause for the time being unable to perform the duties of his office, either generally or in relation to particular proceedings, a person may be appointed to discharge his duties for a period not exceeding six months at one time or, as the case may be, in relation to those proceedings.

(5) The appointment shall be made–

(a) in the case of the chairman or deputy chairman, by the Lord Chancellor, who shall appoint a person who would be eligible for appointment to that office, and

(b) in the case of an ordinary member, by the Secretary of State;

and a person so appointed shall have during the period of his appointment, or in relation to the proceedings in question, the same powers as the person in whose place he is appointed.

(6) The Lord Chancellor shall consult the Lord Advocate before exercising his powers under this section.

NOTES

Commencement order: SI 1989/816.

Sub-s (3A): added by the Judicial Pensions and Retirement Act 1993, s 26, Sch 6, para 49.

---

147 Financial provisions

(1) There shall be paid to the members of the Copyright Tribunal such remuneration (whether by way of salaries or fees), and such allowances, as the Secretary of State with the approval of the Treasury may determine.

(2) The Secretary of State may appoint such staff for the Tribunal as, with the approval of the Treasury as to numbers and remuneration, he may determine.

(3) The remuneration and allowances of members of the Tribunal, the remuneration of any staff and such other expenses of the Tribunal as the Secretary of State with the approval of the Treasury may determine shall be paid out of money provided by Parliament.

NOTE

Commencement order: SI 1989/816.

---

148 Constitution for purposes of proceedings

(1) For the purposes of any proceedings the Copyright Tribunal shall consist of–

(a) a chairman, who shall be either the chairman or a deputy chairman of the Tribunal, and

(b) two or more ordinary members.

(2) If the members of the Tribunal dealing with any matter are not unanimous, the decision shall be taken by majority vote; and if, in such a case, the votes are equal the chairman shall have a further, casting vote.

(3) Where part of any proceedings before the Tribunal has been heard and one or more members of the Tribunal are unable to continue, the Tribunal shall remain duly constituted for the purpose of those proceedings so long as the number of members is not reduced to less than three.

(4) If the chairman is unable to continue, the chairman of the Tribunal shall–

(a) appoint one of the remaining members to act as chairman, and

(b) appoint a suitably qualified person to attend the proceedings and advise the members on any questions of law arising.

(5) A person is 'suitably qualified' for the purposes of subsection (4)(b) if he is, or is eligible for appointment as, a deputy chairman of the Tribunal.

NOTE

Commencement order: SI 1989/816.

Jurisdiction and procedure

149 Jurisdiction of the Tribunal

[The Copyright Tribunal has jurisdiction under this Part] to hear and determine proceedings under–

[(za) section 73 (determination of royalty or other remuneration to be paid with respect to re-transmission of broadcast including work);]

[(zb) section 93C (application to determine amount of equitable remuneration under section 93B);]

(a)   section 118, 119 or 120 (reference of licensing scheme);

(b)   section 121 or 122 (application with respect to entitlement to licence under licensing scheme);

(c)   section 125, 126 or 127 (reference or application with respect to licensing by licensing body);

[(cc) section 135D or 135E (application or reference with respect to use as of right of sound recordings in broadcasts or cable programme services);]

(d)   section 139 (appeal against order as to coverage of licensing scheme or licence);

(e)   section 142 (application to settle royalty or other sum payable for [lending of certain works]);

(f)   section 144(4) (application to settle terms of copyright licence available as of right);

NOTES

Commencement order: SI 1989/816.

First words in square brackets substituted by SI 1996/2967, reg 24(2)(a).

Para (za): added by the Broadcasting Act 1996, s 138, Sch 9, para 3.

Para (zb): added by SI 1996/2967, reg 14(2).

Para (cc): added by the Broadcasting Act 1990, s 175(2).

Para (e): words in square brackets substituted by SI 1996/2967, reg 13(3).

See further, in relation to programme services: the Broadcasting Act 1990, s 176, Sch 17.

---

150 General power to make rules

(1) The Lord Chancellor may, after consultation with the Lord Advocate, make rules for regulating proceedings before the Copyright Tribunal and, subject to the approval of the Treasury, as to the fees chargeable in respect of such proceedings.

[(2) The rules may apply in relation to the Tribunal, as respects proceedings in England and Wales or Northern Ireland, any of the provisions of Part I of the Arbitration Act 1996.]

(3) Provision shall be made by the rules–

(a)   prohibiting the Tribunal from entertaining a reference under section 118, 119, or 120 by a representative organisation unless the Tribunal is satisfied that the organisation is reasonably representative of the class of persons which it claims to represent;

(b)   specifying the parties to any proceedings and enabling the Tribunal to make a party to the proceedings any person or organisation satisfying the Tribunal that they have a substantial interest in the matter; and

(c)   requiring the Tribunal to give the parties to proceedings an opportunity to state their case, in writing or orally as the rules may provide.

(4) The rules may make provision for regulating or prescribing any matters incidental to or consequential upon any appeal from the Tribunal under section 152 (appeal to the court on point of law).

(5) Rules under this section shall be made by statutory instrument which shall be subject to annulment in pursuance of a resolution of either House of Parliament.

NOTES
Commencement orders: SI 1989/816, SI 1989/955, SI 1989/1032.
Sub-s (2): substituted with savings by the Arbitration Act 1996, s 107(1), Sch 3, para 50; for savings see SI 1996/3146.

151 Costs, proof of orders, &c

(1) The Copyright Tribunal may order that the costs of a party to proceedings before it shall be paid by such other party as the Tribunal may direct; and the Tribunal may tax or settle the amount of the costs, or direct in what manner they are to be taxed.

(2) A document purporting to be a copy of an order of the Tribunal and to be certified by the chairman to be a true copy shall, in any proceedings, be sufficient evidence of the order unless the contrary is proved.

(3) As respect proceedings in Scotland, the Tribunal has the like powers for securing the attendance of witnesses and the production of documents, and with regard to the examination of witnesses on oath, as an arbiter under a submission.

NOTE
Commencement order: SI 1989/816.

[151A] [Award of interest]

[(1) Any of the following, namely–

(a) a direction under section 123(3) so far as relating to a licence for broadcasting a work or including a work in a cable programme service;
(b) a direction under section 128(3) so far as so relating;
(c) an order under section 135D(1); and
(d) an order under section 135F confirming or varying an order under section 135D(1),

may award simple interest at such rate and for such period, beginning not earlier than the relevant date and ending not later than the date of the order, as the Copyright Tribunal thinks reasonable in the circumstances.

(2) In this section 'the relevant date' means–

(a) in relation to a direction under section 123(3), the date on which the reference was made;
(b) in relation to a direction under section 128(3), the date on which the reference or application was made;
(c) in relation to an order under section 135D(1), the date on which the first payment under section 135C(2) became due; and
(d) in relation to an order under section 135F, the date on which the application was made.]

NOTES
Added with savings by the Broadcasting Act 1996, s 139(2), (3).
This section shall be read in conjunction with the Broadcasting Act 1996, s 139(3). Commencement shall be on such day as the Secretary of State may by order made by statutory instrument apppoint:

139 Copyright licensing
(3) Subsection (2) does not apply in any case where the reference or application to the Copyright Tribunal was or is made before the commencement of this section.

Appeals

152 Appeal to the court on point of law

(1) An appeal lies on any point of law arising from a decision of the Copyright Tribunal to the High Court or, in the case of proceedings of the Tribunal in Scotland, to the Court of Session.

(2) Provision shall be made by rules under section 150 limiting the time within which an appeal may be brought.

(3) Provision may be made by rules under that section–

(a) for suspending, or authorising or requiring the Tribunal to suspend, the operation of orders of the Tribunal in cases where its decision is appealed against;

(b) for modifying in relation to an order of the Tribunal whose operation is suspended the operation of any provision of this Act as to the effect of the order;

(c) for the publication of notices or the taking of other steps for securing that persons affected by the suspension of an order of the Tribunal will be informed of its suspension.

NOTES
Commencement orders: SI 1989/816, SI 1989/955, SI 1989/1032.

CHAPTER IX
QUALIFICATION FOR AND EXTENT OF COPYRIGHT PROTECTION

Qualification for copyright protection

153 Qualification for copyright protection
(1) Copyright does not subsist in a work unless the qualification requirements of this Chapter are satisfied as regards–

(a) the author (see section 154), or

(b) the country in which the work was first published (see section 155), or

(c) in the case of a broadcast or cable programme, the country from which the broadcast was made or the cable programme was sent (see section 156).

(2) Subsection (1) does not apply in relation to Crown copyright or Parliamentary copyright (see sections 163 to 166) or to copyright subsisting by virtue of section 168 (copyright of certain international organisations).

(3) If the qualification requirements of this Chapter, or section 163, 165 or 168, are once satisfied in respect of a work, copyright does not cease to subsist by reason of any subsequent event.

NOTE
Commencement order: SI 1989/816.

154 Qualification by reference to author
(1) A work qualifies for copyright protection if the author was at the material time a qualifying person, that is–

(a) a British citizen, a British Dependent Territories citizen, a British National (Overseas), a British Overseas citizen, a British subject or a British protected person within the meaning of the British Nationality Act 1981, or

(b) an individual domiciled or resident in the United Kingdom or another country to which the relevant provisions of this Part extend, or

(c) a body incorporated under the law of a part of the United Kingdom or of another country to which the relevant provisions of this Part extend.

(2) Where, or so far as, provision is made by Order under section 159 (application of this Part to countries to which it does not extend), a work also qualifies for copyright protection if at the material time the author was a citizen or subject of, an individual domiciled or resident in, or a body incorporated under the law of, a country to which the Order relates.

(3) A work of joint authorship qualifies for copyright protection if at the material time any of the authors satisfies the requirements of subsection (1) or (2); but where a work qualifies for copyright protection only under this section, only those authors who satisfy those requirements shall be taken into account for the purposes of–

section 11(1) and (2) (first ownership of copyright; entitlement of author or author's employer),

[section 12 (duration of copyright), and section 9(4) (meaning of 'unknown authorship') so far as it applies for the purposes of section 12, and]

section 57 (anonymous or pseudonymous works: acts permitted on assumptions as to expiry of copyright or death of author).

(4) The material time in relation to a literary, dramatic, musical or artistic work is–

(a) in the case of an unpublished work, when the work was made or, if the making of the work extended over a period, a substantial part of that period;

(b) in the case of a published work, when the work was first published or, if the author had died before that time, immediately before his death.

(5) The material time in relation to other descriptions of work is as follows–

(a) in the case of a sound recording or film, when it was made;

(b) in the case of a broadcast, when the broadcast was made;

(c) in the case of a cable programme, when the programme was included in a cable programme service;

(d) in the case of the typographical arrangement of a published edition, when the edition was first published.

NOTES

Commencement order: SI 1989/816.

Sub-s (3): words underlined repealed with savings and subsequent words in square brackets substituted with savings by SI 1995/3297, reg 5(3); for savings see Part III thereof.

155 Qualification by reference to country of first publication

(1) A literary, dramatic, musical or artistic work, a sound recording or film, or the typographical arrangement of a published edition, qualifies for copyright protection if it is first published–

(a) in the United Kingdom, or

(b) in another country to which the relevant provisions of this Part extend.

(2) Where, or so far as, provision is made by Order under section 159 (application of this Part to countries to which it does not extend), such a work also qualifies for copyright protection if it is first published in a country to which the Order relates.

(3) For the purposes of this section, publication in one country shall not be regarded as other than the first publication by reason of simultaneous publication elsewhere; and for this purpose publication elsewhere within the previous 30 days shall be treated as simultaneous.

NOTE

Commencement order: SI 1989/816.

156 Qualification by reference to place of transmission

(1) A broadcast qualifies for copyright protection if it is made from, and a cable programme qualifies for copyright protection if it is sent from, a place in–

(a) the United Kingdom, or

(b) another country to which the relevant provisions of this Part extend.

(2) Where, or so far as, provision is made by Order under section 159 (application of this Part to countries to which it does not extend), a broadcast or cable programme also qualifies for copyright protection if it is made from or, as the case may be, sent from a place in a country to which the Order relates.

NOTE

Commencement order: SI 1989/816.

Extent and application of this Part

157 Countries to which this Part extends
(1) This Part extends to England and Wales, Scotland and Northern Ireland.

(2) Her Majesty may by Order in Council direct that this Part shall extend, subject to such exceptions and modifications as may be specified in the Order, to–

    (a) any of the Channel Islands,
    (b) the Isle of Man, or
    (c) any colony.

(3) That power includes power to extend, subject to such exceptions and modifications as may be specified in the Order, any Order in Council made under the following provisions of this Chapter.

(4) The legislature of a country to which this Part has been extended may modify or add to the provisions of this Part, in their operation as part of the law of that country, as the legislature may consider necessary to adapt the provisions to the circumstances of that country–

    (a) as regards procedure and remedies, or
    (b) as regards works qualifying for copyright protection by virtue of a connection with that country.

(5) Nothing in this section shall be construed as restricting the extent of paragraph 36 of Schedule 1 (transitional provisions: dependent territories where the Copyright Act 1956 or the Copyright Act 1911 remains in force) in relation to the law of a dependent territory to which this Part does not extend.

NOTE
  Commencement order: SI 1989/816.

---

158 Countries ceasing to be colonies
(1) The following provisions apply where a country to which this Part has been extended ceases to be a colony of the United Kingdom.

(2) As from the date on which it ceases to be a colony it shall cease to be regarded as a country to which this Part extends for the purposes of–

    (a) section 160(2)(a) (denial of copyright protection to citizens of countries not giving adequate protection to British works), and
    (b) sections 163 and 165 (Crown and Parliamentary copyright).

(3) But it shall continue to be treated as a country to which this Part extends for the purposes of sections 154 to 156 (qualification for copyright protection) until–

    (a) an Order in Council is made in respect of that country under section 159 (application of this Part to countries to which it does not extend), or
    (b) an Order in Council is made declaring that it shall cease to be so treated by reason of the fact that the provisions of this Part as part of the law of that country have been repealed or amended.

(4) A statutory instrument containing an Order in Council under subsection (3)(b) shall be subject to annulment in pursuance of a resolution of either House of Parliament.

NOTES
  Commencement order: SI 1989/816.

---

159 Application of this Part to countries to which it does not extend
(1) Her Majesty may by Order in Council make provision for applying in relation to a country to which this Part does not extend any of the provisions of this Part specified in the Order, so as to secure that those provisions–

(a) apply in relation to persons who are citizens or subjects of that country or are domiciled or resident there, as they apply to persons who are British citizens or are domiciled or resident in the United Kingdom, or

(b) apply in relation to bodies incorporated under the law of that country as they apply in relation to bodies incorporated under the law of a part of the United Kingdom, or

(c) apply in relation to works first published in that country as they apply in relation to works first published in the United Kingdom, or

(d) apply in relation to broadcasts made from or cable programmes sent from that country as they apply in relation to broadcasts made from or cable programmes sent from the United Kingdom.

(2) An Order may make provision for all or any of the matters mentioned in subsection (1) and may–

(a) apply any provisions of this Part subject to such exceptions and modifications as are specified in the Order; and

(b) direct that any provisions of this Part apply either generally or in relation to such classes of works, or other classes of case, as are specified in the Order.

(3) Except in the case of a Convention country or another member State of the European Economic Community, Her Majesty shall not make an Order in Council under this section in relation to a country unless satisfied that provision has been or will be made under the law of that country, in respect of the class of works to which the Order relates, giving adequate protection to the owners of copyright under this Part.

(4) In subsection (3) 'Convention country' means a country which is a party to a Convention relating to copyright to which the United Kingdom is also a party.

(5) A statutory instrument containing an Order in Council under this section shall be subject to annulment in pursuance of a resolution of either House of Parliament.

NOTE
Commencement orders: SI 1989/816, SI 1989/955, SI 1989/1032.

160 Denial of copyright protection to citizens of countries not giving adequate protection to British works

(1) If it appears to Her Majesty that the law of a country fails to give adequate protection to British works to which this section applies, or to one or more classes of such works, Her Majesty may make provision by Order in Council in accordance with this section restricting the rights conferred by this Part in relation to works of authors connected with that country.

(2) An Order in Council under this section shall designate the country concerned and provide that, for the purposes specified in the Order, works first published after a date specified in the Order shall not be treated as qualifying for copyright protection by virtue of such publication if at that time the authors are–

(a) citizens or subjects of that country (not domiciled or resident in the United Kingdom or another country to which the relevant provisions of this Part extend), or

(b) bodies incorporated under the law of that country;

and the Order may make such provision for all the purposes of this Part or for such purposes as are specified in the Order, and either generally or in relation to such class of cases as are specified in the Order, having regard to the nature and extent of that failure referred to in subsection (1).

(3) This section applies to literary, dramatic, musical and artistic works, sound recordings and films; and 'British works' means works of which the author was a qualifying person at the material time within the meaning of section 154.

(4) A statutory instrument containing an Order in Council under this section shall be subject to annulment in pursuance of a resolution of either House of Parliament.

NOTE
Commencement order: SI 1989/816.

Supplementary

161 Territorial waters and the continental shelf
(1) For the purposes of this Part the territorial waters of the United Kingdom shall be treated as part of the United Kingdom.

(2) This Part applies to things done in the United Kingdom sector of the continental shelf on a structure or vessel which is present there for purposes directly connected with the exploration of the sea bed or subsoil or the exploitation of their natural resources as it applies to things done in the United Kingdom.

(3) The United Kingdom sector of the continental shelf means the areas designated by order under section 1(7) of the Continental Shelf Act 1964.

NOTE

Commencement order: SI 1989/816.

162 British ships, aircraft and hovercraft
(1) This Part applies to things done on a British ship, aircraft or hovercraft as it applies to things done in the United Kingdom.

(2) In this section—

'British ship' means a ship which is a British ship for the purposes of the [Merchant Shipping Act 1995] otherwise than by virtue of registration in a country outside the United Kingdom; and

'British aircraft' and 'British hovercraft' mean an aircraft or hovercraft registered in the United Kingdom.

NOTES

Commencement order: SI 1989/816.

Sub-s (2): in definition 'British ship' words in square brackets substituted by the Merchant Shipping Act 1995, s 314(2), Sch 13, para 84(a).

CHAPTER X
MISCELLANEOUS AND GENERAL

Crown and Parliamentary copyright

163 Crown copyright
(1) Where a work is made by Her Majesty or by an officer or servant of the Crown in the course of his duties—

(a)   the work qualifies for copyright protection notwithstanding section 153(1) (ordinary requirement as to qualification for copyright protection), and
(b)   Her Majesty is the first owner of any copyright in the work.

(2) Copyright in such a work is referred to in this Part as 'Crown copyright', notwithstanding that it may be, or have been, assigned to another person.

(3) Crown copyright in a literary, dramatic, musical or artistic work continues to subsist—

(a)   until the end of the period of 125 years from the end of the calendar year in which the work was made, or
(b)   if the work is published commercially before the end of the period of 75 years from the end of the calendar year in which it was made, until the end of the period of 50 years from the end of the calendar year in which it was first so published.

(4) In the case of a work of joint authorship where one or more but not all of the authors are persons falling within subsection (1), this section applies only in relation to those authors and the copyright subsisting by virtue of their contribution to the work.

(5) Except as mentioned above, and subject to any express exclusion elsewhere in this Part, the provisions of this Part apply in relation to Crown copyright as to other copyright.

(6) This section does not apply to work if, or to the extent that, Parliamentary copyright subsists in the work (see sections 165 and 166).

NOTE
Commencement order: SI 1989/816.

164 Copyright in Acts and Measures

(1) Her Majesty is entitled to copyright in every Act of Parliament or Measure of the General Synod of the Church of England.

(2) The copyright subsists from Royal Assent until the end of the period of 50 years from the end of the calendar year in which Royal Assent was given.

(3) References in this Part to Crown copyright (except in section 163) include copyright under this section; and, except as mentioned above, the provisions of this Part apply in relation to copyright under this section as to other Crown copyright.

(4) No other copyright, or right in the nature of copyright, subsists in an Act or Measure.

NOTE
Commencement order: SI 1989/816.

165 Parliamentary copyright

(1) Where a work is made by or under the direction or control of the House of Commons or the House of Lords–

  (a) the work qualifies for copyright protection notwithstanding section 153(1) (ordinary requirement as to qualification for copyright protection), and

  (b) the House by whom, or under whose direction or control, the work is made is the first owner of any copyright in the work, and if the work is made by or under the direction or control of both Houses, the two Houses are joint first owners of copyright.

(2) Copyright in such a work is referred to in this Part as 'Parliamentary copyright', notwithstanding that it may be, or have been, assigned to another person.

(3) Parliamentary copyright in a literary, dramatic, musical or artistic work continues to subsist until the end of the period of 50 years from the end of the calendar year in which the work was made.

(4) For the purposes of this section, works made by or under the direction or control of the House of Commons or the House of Lords include–

  (a) any work made by an officer or employee of that House in the course of his duties, and

  (b) any sound recording, film, live broadcast or live cable programme of the proceedings of that House;

but a work shall not be regarded as made by or under the direction or control of either House by reason only of its being commissioned by or on behalf of that House.

(5) In the case of a work of joint authorship where one or more but not all of the authors are acting on behalf of, or under the direction or control of, the House of Commons or the House of Lords, this section applies only in relation to those authors and the copyright subsisting by virtue of their contribution to the work.

(6) Except as mentioned above, and subject to any express exclusion elsewhere in this Part, the provisions of this Part apply in relation to Parliamentary copyright as to other copyright.

(7) The provisions of this section also apply, subject to any exceptions or modifications specified by Order in Council, to works made by or under the direction or control of any other legislative body of a country to which this Part extends; and references in this Part to 'Parliamentary copyright' shall be construed accordingly.

(8) A statutory instrument containing an Order in Council under subsection (7) shall be subject to annulment in pursuance of a resolution of either House of Parliament.

NOTE
Commencement order: SI 1989/816.

166 Copyright in Parliamentary Bills

(1) Copyright in every Bill introduced into Parliament belongs, in accordance with the following provisions, to one or both of the Houses of Parliament.

(2) Copyright in a public Bill belongs in the first instance to the House into which the Bill is introduced, and after the Bill has been carried to the second House to both Houses jointly, and subsists from the time when the text of the Bill is handed in to the House in which it is introduced.

(3) Copyright in a private Bill belongs to both Houses jointly and subsists from the time when a copy of the Bill is first deposited in either House.

(4) Copyright in a personal Bill belongs in the first instance to the House of Lords, and after the Bill has been carried to the House of Commons to both Houses jointly, and subsists from the time when it is given a First Reading in the House of Lords.

(5) Copyright under this section ceases–

(a)   on Royal Assent, or

(b)   if the Bill does not receive Royal Assent, on the withdrawal or rejection of the Bill or the end of the Session:

Provided that, copyright in a Bill continues to subsist notwithstanding its rejection in any Session by the House of Lords if, by virtue of the Parliament Acts 1911 and 1949, it remains possible for it to be presented for Royal Assent in that Session.

(6) References in this Part to Parliamentary copyright (except in section 165) include copyright under this section; and, except as mentioned above, the provisions of this Part apply in relation to copyright under this section as to other Parliamentary copyright.

(7) No other copyright, or right in the nature of copyright, subsists in a Bill after copyright has once subsisted under this section; but without prejudice to the subsequent operation of this section in relation to a Bill which, not having passed in one Session, is reintroduced in a subsequent Session.

NOTE
Commencement order: SI 1989/816.

167 Houses of Parliament: supplementary provisions with respect to copyright

(1) For the purposes of holding, dealing with and enforcing copyright, and in connection with all legal proceedings relating to copyright, each House of Parliament shall be treated as having the legal capacities of a body corporate, which shall not be affected by a prorogation or dissolution.

(2) The functions of the House of Commons as owner of copyright shall be exercised by the Speaker on behalf of the House; and if so authorised by the Speaker, or in case of a vacancy in the office of Speaker, those functions may be discharged by the Chairman of Ways and Means or a Deputy Chairman.

(3) For this purpose a person who on the dissolution of Parliament was Speaker of the House of Commons, Chairman of Ways and Means or a Deputy Chairman may continue to act until the corresponding appointment is made in the next Session of Parliament.

(4) The functions of the House of Lords as owner of copyright shall be exercised by the Clerk of the Parliaments on behalf of the House; and if so authorised by him, or in case of a vacancy in the office of Clerk of the Parliaments, those functions may be discharged by the Clerk Assistant or the Reading Clerk.

(5) Legal proceedings relating to copyright–

(a)   shall be brought by or against the House of Commons in the name of 'The Speaker of the House of Commons'; and

(b)   shall be brought by or against the House of Lords in the name of 'The Clerk of the Parliaments'.

NOTE
Commencement order: SI 1989/816.

Other miscellaneous provisions

168 Copyright vesting in certain international organisations

(1) Where an original literary, dramatic, musical or artistic work–

(a)   is made by an officer or employee of, or is published by, an international organisation to which this section applies, and

(b)   does not qualify for copyright protection under section 154 (qualification by reference to author) or section 155 (qualification by reference to country of first publication),

copyright nevertheless subsists in the work by virtue of this section and the organisation is first owner of that copyright.

(2) The international organisations to which this section applies are those as to which Her Majesty has by Order in Council declared that it is expedient that this section should apply.

(3) Copyright of which an international organisation is first owner by virtue of this section continues to subsist until the end of the period of 50 years from the end of the calendar year in which the work was made or such longer period as may be specified by Her Majesty by Order in Council for the purpose of complying with the international obligations of the United Kingdom.

(4) An international organisation to which this section applies shall be deemed to have, and to have had at all material times, the legal capacities of a body corporate for the purpose of holding, dealing with and enforcing copyright and in connection with all legal proceedings relating to copyright.

(5) A statutory instrument containing an Order in Council under this section shall be subject to annulment in pursuance of a resolution of either House of Parliament.

NOTE
Commencement orders: SI 1989/816; SI 1989/955; SI 1989/1032.

169 Folklore, &c: anonymous unpublished works

(1) Where in the case of an unpublished literary, dramatic, musical or artistic work of unknown authorship there is evidence that the author (or, in the case of a joint work, any of the authors) was a qualifying individual by connection with a country outside the United Kingdom, it shall be presumed until the contrary is proved that he was such a qualifying individual and that copyright accordingly subsists in the work, subject to the provisions of this Part.

(2) If under the law of that country a body is appointed to protect and enforce copyright in such works, Her Majesty may by Order in Council designate that body for the purposes of this section.

(3) A body so designated shall be recognised in the United Kingdom as having authority to do in place of the copyright owner anything, other than assign copyright, which it is empowered to do under the law of that country; and it may, in particular, bring proceedings in its own name.

(4) A statutory instrument containing an Order in Council under this section shall be subject to annulment in pursuance of a resolution of either House of Parliament.

(5) In subsection (1) a 'qualifying individual' means an individual who at the material time (within the meaning of section 154) was a person whose works qualified under that section for copyright protection.

(6) This section does not apply if there has been an assignment of copyright in the work by the author of which notice has been given to the designated body; and nothing in this section affects the validity of an assignment of copyright made, or licence granted, by the author or a person lawfully claiming under him.

NOTE
Commencement order: SI 1989/816.

Transitional provisions and savings

170 Transitional provisions and savings

Schedule 1 contains transitional provisions and savings relating to works made, and acts or events occurring, before the commencement of this Part, and otherwise with respect to the operation of the provisions of this Part.

NOTE
Commencement order: SI 1989/816.

171 Rights and privileges under other enactments or the common law

(1) Nothing in this Part affects—

    (a) any right or privilege of any person under any enactment (except where the enactment is expressly repealed, amended or modified by this Act);

    (b) any right or privilege of the Crown subsisting otherwise than under an enactment;

    (c) any right or privilege of either House of Parliament;

    (d) the right of the Crown or any person deriving title from the Crown to sell, use or otherwise deal with articles forfeited under the laws relating to customs and excise;

    (e) the operation of any rule of equity relating to breaches of trust or confidence.

(2) Subject to those savings, no copyright or right in the nature of copyright shall subsist otherwise than by virtue of this Part or some other enactment in that behalf.

(3) Nothing in this Part affects any rule of law preventing or restricting the enforcement of copyright, on grounds of public interest or otherwise.

(4) Nothing in this Part affects any right of action or other remedy, whether civil or criminal, available otherwise than under this Part in respect of acts infringing any of the rights conferred by Chapter IV (moral rights).

(5) The savings in subsection (1) have effect subject to section 164(4) and section 166(7) (copyright in Acts, Measures and Bills: exclusion of other rights in the nature of copyright).

NOTE
Commencement order: SI 1989/816.

Interpretation

172 General provisions as to construction

(1) This Part restates and amends the law of copyright, that is, the provisions of the Copyright Act 1956, as amended.

(2) A provision of this Part which corresponds to a provision of the previous law shall not be construed as departing from the previous law merely because of a change of expression.

(3) Decisions under the previous law may be referred to for the purpose of establishing whether a provision of this Part departs from the previous law, or otherwise for establishing the true construction of this Part.

NOTES
Commencement order: SI 1989/816.
This section should be read in conjunction with the following provisions of the Duration of Copyright and Rights in Performances Regulations 1995, SI 1995/3297 (commencement: 1 January 1996) and the Copyright and Related Rights Regulations 1996, SI 1996/2967 (commencement: 1 December 1996):

Duration of Copyright and Rights in Peformances Regulations 1995, regs 12, 14 and 36(1) and (3)

Introductory
12–(1) References in this Part to 'commencement', without more, are to the date on which these Regulations come into force.

(2) In this Part–

'the 1988 Act' means the Copyright, Designs and Patents Act 1988;
'the 1988 provisions' means the provisions of that Act as they stood immediately before commencement (including the provisions of Schedule 1 to that Act continuing the effect of earlier enactments); and
'the new provisions' means the provisions of that Act as amended by these Regulations.

(3) Expressions used in this Part which are defined for the purposes of Part I or II of the 1988 Act, in particular references to the copyright owner, have the same meaning as in that Part.

Copyright: interpretation
14–(1) In the provisions of this Part relating to copyright–

(a) 'existing', in relation to a work, means made before commencement; and
(b) 'existing copyright work' means a work in which copyright subsisted immediately before commencement.

(2) For the purposes of those provisions a work of which the making extended over a period shall be taken to have been made when its making was completed.

(3) References in those provisions to 'moral rights' are to the rights conferred by Chapter IV of Part I of the 1988 Act.

Construction of references to EEA states
36–(1) For the purpose of the new provisions relating to the term of copyright protection applicable to a work of which the country of origin is not an EEA state and of which the author is not a national of an EEA state–

(a) a work first published before 1st July 1995 shall be treated as published in an EEA state if it was on that date regarded under the law of the United Kingdom or another EEA state as having been published in that state;
(b) an unpublished film made before 1st July 1995 shall be treated as originating in an EEA state if it was on that date regarded under the law of the United Kingdom or another EEA state as a film whose maker had his headquarters in, or was domiciled or resident in, that state; and
(c) the author of a work made before 1st July 1995 shall be treated as an EEA national if he was on that date regarded under the law of the United Kingdom or another EEA state as a national of that state.

The references above to the law of another EEA state are to the law of that state having effect for the purposes of rights corresponding to those provided for in Part I of the 1988 Act.

(3) In this Regulation 'another EEA state' means an EEA state other than the United Kingdom.

Copyright and Related Rights Regulations 1996, reg 25

Introductory
25–(1) In this Part–

'commencement' means the commencement of these Regulations; and
'existing', in relation to a work or performance, means made or given before commencement.

(2) For the purposes of this Part a work of which the making extended over a period shall be taken to have been made when its making was completed.

(3) In this Part a 'new right' means a right arising by virtue of these Regulations, in relation to a copyright work or a qualifying performance, to authorise or prohibit an act.

The expression does not include–

(a) a right corresponding to a right which existed immediately before commencement, or
(b) a right to remuneration arising by virtue of these Regulations.

(4) Expressions used in this Part have the same meaning in relation to copyright as they have in Part I of the Copyright, Designs and Patents Act 1988, and in relation to performances as in Part II of that Act.

[172A] [Meaning of EEA and related expressions]
[(1) In this Part–

'the EEA' means the European Economic Area;
'EEA national' means a national of an EEA state; and
'EEA state' means a state which is a contracting party to the EEA Agreement.]

[(2) References in this Part to a person being an EEA national shall be construed in relation to a body corporate as references to its being incorporated under the law of an EEA state.

(3) The 'EEA Agreement' means the Agreement on the European Economic Area signed at Oporto on 2nd May 1992, as adjusted by the Protocol signed at Brussels on 17th March 1993.]

173 Construction of references to copyright owner

(1) Where different persons are (whether in consequence of a partial assignment or otherwise) entitled to different aspects of copyright in a work, the copyright owner for any purpose of this Part is the person who is entitled to the aspect of copyright relevant for that purpose.

(2) Where copyright (or any aspect of copyright) is owned by more than one person jointly, references in this Part to the copyright owner are to all the owners, so that, in particular, any requirement of the licence of the copyright owner requires the licence of all of them.

174 Meaning of 'educational establishment' and related expressions

(1) The expression "educational establishment" in a provision of this Part means–

   (a) any school, and

   (b) any other description of educational establishment specified for the purposes of this Part, or that provision, by order of the Secretary of State.

(2) The Secretary of State may by order provide that the provisions of this Part relating to educational establishments shall apply, with such modifications and adaptations as may be specified in the order, in relation to teachers who are employed by a local education authority to give instruction elsewhere to pupils who are unable to attend an educational establishment.

(3) In subsection (1)(a) 'school'–

   (a) in relation to England and Wales, has the same meaning as in [the Education Act 1996];

   (b) in relation to Scotland, has the same meaning as in the Education (Scotland) Act 1962, except that it includes an approved school within the meaning of the Social Work (Scotland) Act 1968; and

   (c) in relation to Northern Ireland, has the same meaning as in the Education and Libraries (Northern Ireland) Order 1986.

(4) An order under subsection (1)(b) may specify a description of educational establishment by reference to the instruments from time to time in force under any enactment specified in the order.

(5) In relation to an educational establishment the expressions 'teacher' and 'pupil' in this Part include, respectively, any person who gives and any person who receives instruction.

(6) References in this Part to anything being done 'on behalf of' an educational establishment are to its being done for the purposes of that establishment by any person.

(7) An order under this section shall be made by statutory instrument which shall be subject to annulment in pursuance of a resolution of either House of Parliament.

175 Meaning of publication and commercial publication

(1) In this Part 'publication', in relation to a work–

   (a) means the issue of copies to the public, and

   (b) includes, in the case of a literary, dramatic, musical or artistic work, making it available to the public by means of an electronic retrieval system;

and related expressions shall be construed accordingly.

(2) In this Part 'commercial publication', in relation to a literary, dramatic, musical or artistic work means–

(a) issuing copies of the work to the public at a time when copies made in advance of the receipt of orders are generally available to the public, or

(b) making the work available to the public by means of an electronic retrieval system;

and related expressions shall be construed accordingly.

(3) In the case of a work of architecture in the form of a building, or an artistic work incorporated in a building, construction of the building shall be treated as equivalent to publication of the work.

(4) The following do not constitute publication for the purposes of this Part and references to commercial publication shall be construed accordingly–

(a) in the case of a literary, dramatic or musical work–

(i) the performance of the work, or

(ii) the broadcasting of the work or its inclusion in a cable programme service (otherwise than for the purposes of an electronic retrieval system);

(b) in the case of an artistic work–

(i) the exhibition of the work,

(ii) the issue to the public of copies of a graphic work representing, or of photographs of, a work of architecture in the form of a building or a model for a building, a sculpture or a work of artistic craftsmanship,

(iii) the issue to the public of copies of a film including the work, or

(iv) the broadcasting of the work or its inclusion in a cable programme service (otherwise than for the purposes of an electronic retrieval system);

(c) in the case of a sound recording or film–

(i) the work being played or shown in public, or

(ii) the broadcasting of the work or its inclusion in a cable programme service.

(5) References in this Part to publication or commercial publication do not include publication which is merely colourable and not intended to satisfy the reasonable requirements of the public.

(6) No account shall be taken for the purposes of this section of any unauthorised act.

NOTE
Commencement order: SI 1989/816.

176 Requirement of signature: application in relation to body corporate

(1) The requirement in the following provisions that an instrument be signed by or on behalf of a person is also satisfied in the case of a body corporate by the affixing of its seal–

section 78(3)(b) (assertion by licensor of right to identification of author in case of public exhibition of copy made in pursuance of the licence),

section 90(3) (assignment of copyright),

section 91(1) (assignment of future copyright),

section 92(1) (grant of exclusive licence).

(2) The requirement in the following provisions that an instrument be signed by a person is satisfied in the case of a body corporate by signature on behalf of the body or by the affixing of its seal–

section 78(2)(b) (assertion by instrument in writing of right to have author identified),

section 87(2) (waiver of moral rights).

NOTE
Commencement order: SI 1989/816.

177 Adaptation of expressions for Scotland
In the application of this Part to Scotland–

'account of profits' means accounting and payment of profits;
'accounts' means count, reckoning and payment;
'assignment' means assignation;
'costs' means expenses;
'defendant' means defender;
'delivery up' means delivery;
'estoppel' means personal bar;
'injunction' means interdict;
'interlocutory relief' means interim remedy; and
'plaintiff' means pursuer.

NOTE
Commencement order: SI 1989/816.

---

178 Minor definitions
In this Part–

'article', in the context of an article in a periodical, includes an item of any description;
'business' includes a trade or profession;
'collective work' means–

  (a) a work of joint authorship, or
  (b) a work in which there are distinct contributions by different authors or in which works or parts of works of different authors are incorporated;

'computer-generated', in relation to a work, means that the work is generated by computer in circumstances such that there is no human author of the work;
'country' includes any territory;
'the Crown' includes the Crown in right of Her Majesty's Government in Northern Ireland or in any country outside the United Kingdom to which this Part extends;
'electronic' means actuated by electric, magnetic, electro-magnetic, electro-chemical or electro-mechanical energy, and 'in electronic form' means in a form usable only by electronic means;
'employed', 'employee', 'employer' and 'employment' refer to employment under a contract of service or of apprenticeship;
'facsimile copy' includes a copy which is reduced or enlarged in scale;
'international organisation' means an organisation the members of which include one or more states;
'judicial proceedings' includes proceedings before any court, tribunal or person having authority to decide any matter affecting a person's legal rights or liabilities;
'parliamentary proceedings' includes proceedings of the Northern Ireland Assembly or of the European Parliament;
['producer', in relation to a sound recording or a film, means the person by whom the arrangements necessary for the making of the sound recording or film are undertaken;]
['public library' means a library administered by or on behalf of–

  (a) in England and Wales, a library authority within the meaning of the Public Libraries and Museums Act 1964;
  (b) in Scotland, a statutory library authority within the meaning of the Public Libraries (Scotland) Act 1955;
  (c) in Northern Ireland, an Education and Library Board within the meaning of the Education and Libraries (Northern Ireland) Order 1986;]

['rental right' means the right of a copyright owner to authorise or prohibit the rental of copies of the work (see section 18A);]
'reprographic copy' and 'reprographic copying' refer to copying by means of a reprographic process;
'reprographic process' means a process–

(a) for making facsimile copies, or

(b) involving the use of an appliance for making multiple copies,

and includes, in relation to a work held in electronic form, any copying by electronic means, but does not include the making of a film or sound recording;

'sufficient acknowledgement' means an acknowledgement identifying the work in question by its title or other description, and identifying the author unless–

(a) in the case of a published work, it is published anonymously;

(b) in the case of an unpublished work, it is not possible for a person to ascertain the identity of the author by reasonable inquiry;

'sufficient disclaimer', in relation to an act capable of infringing the right conferred by section 80 (right to object to derogatory treatment of work), means a clear and reasonably prominent indication–

(a) given at the time of the act, and

(b) if the author or director is then identified, appearing along with the identification,

that the work has been subjected to treatment to which the author or director has not consented;

'telecommunications system' means a system for conveying visual images, sounds or other information by electronic means;

'typeface' includes an ornamental motif used in printing;

'unauthorised', as regards anything done in relation to a work, means done otherwise than–

(a) by or with the licence of the copyright owner, or

(b) if copyright does not subsist in the work, by or with the licence of the author or, in a case where section 11(2) would have applied, the author's employer or, in either case, persons lawfully claiming under him, or

(c) in pursuance of section 48 (copying, &c of certain material by the Crown);

'wireless telegraphy' means the sending of electro-magnetic energy over paths not provided by a material substance constructed or arranged for that purpose[, but does not include the transmission of microwave energy between terrestrial fixed points];

'writing' includes any form of notation or code, whether by hand or otherwise and regardless of the method by which, or medium in or on which, it is recorded, and "written" shall be construed accordingly.

NOTES

Commencement order: SI 1989/816.

Definitions 'producer', 'public library' and 'rental right' added, definition 'rental' repealed, and in definition 'wireless telegraphy' words in square brackets added, by SI 1996/2967, regs 8, 10(3), 11(5), 18(5).

---

179 Index of defined expressions

The following Table shows provisions defining or otherwise explaining expressions used in this Part (other than provisions defining or explaining an expression used only in the same section)–

account of profits and accounts (in Scotland)	section 177
acts restricted by copyright	section 16(1)
adaptation	section 21(3)
archivist (in sections 37 to 43)	section 37(6)
article (in a periodical)	section 178
artistic work	section 4(1)
assignment (in Scotland)	section 177
author	sections 9 and 10(3)
broadcast (and related expressions)	section 6
building	section 4(2)
business	section 178
cable programme, cable programme service (and related expressions)	section 7

collective work	section 178
commencement (in Schedule 1)	paragraph 1(2) of that Schedule
commercial publication	section 175
computer-generated	section 178
copy and copying	section 17
copyright (generally)	section 1
copyright (in Schedule 1)	paragraph 2(2) of that Schedule
copyright owner	sections 101(2) and 173
Copyright Tribunal	section 145
copyright work	section 1(2)
costs (in Scotland)	section 177
country	section 178
[country of origin	section 15A]
the Crown	section 178
Crown copyright	sections 163(2) and 164(3)
[database	section 3A(1)]
defendant (in Scotland)	section 177
delivery up (in Scotland)	section 177
dramatic work	section 3(1)
educational establishment	section 174(1) to (4)
[[EEA,] EEA national and EEA state]	[section 172A]
electronic and electronic form	section 178
employed, employee, employer and employment	section 178
exclusive licence	section 92(1)
existing works (in Schedule 1)	paragraph 1(3) of that Schedule
facsimile copy	section 178
film	[section 5B]
future copyright	section 91(2)
general licence (in sections 140 and 141)	section 140(7)
graphic work	section 4(2)
infringing copy	section 27
injunction (in Scotland)	section 177
interlocutory relief (in Scotland)	section 177
international organisation	section 178
issue of copies to the public	[section 18]
joint authorship (work of)	sections 10(1) and (2)
judicial proceedings	section 178
[lawful user (in sections 50A to 50C)	section 50A(2)]
[lending	section 18A(2) to (6)]
librarian (in sections 37 to 43)	section 37(6)
licence (in sections 125 to 128)	section 124
licence of copyright owner	sections 90(4), 91(3) and 173
licensing body (in Chapter VII)	section 116(2)
licensing scheme (generally)	section 116(1)
licensing scheme (in sections 118 to 121)	section 117
literary work	section 3(1)
made (in relation to a literary, dramatic or musical work)	section 3(2)
musical work	section 3(1)
[needletime	section 135A]
the new copyright provisions (in Schedule 1)	paragraph 1(1) of that Schedule
the 1911 Act (in Schedule 1)	paragraph 1(1) of that Schedule
the 1956 Act (in Schedule 1)	paragraph 1(1) of that Schedule
on behalf of (in relation to an educational establishment)	section 174(5)
[original (in relation to a database)	section 3A(2)]

Parliamentary copyright	sections 165(2) and (7) and 166(6)
parliamentary proceeding	ssection 178
performance	section 19(2)
photograph	section 4(2)
plaintiff (in Scotland)	section 177
prescribed conditions (in sections 38 to 43)	section 37(1)(b)
prescribed library or archive (in sections 38 to 43)	section 37(1)(a)
[producer (in relation to a sound recording or film)	section 178]
programme (in the context of broadcasting)	section 6(3)
prospective owner (of copyright)	section 91(2)
[public library	section 178]
publication and related expressions	section 175
published edition (in the context of copyright in the typographical arrangement)	section 8
pupil	section 174(5)
rental	[section 18A(2) to (6)]
[rental right	section 178]
reprographic copies and reprographic copying	section 178
reprographic process	section 178
sculpture	section 4(2)
signed	section 176
sound recording	[sections 5A and 135A]
sufficient acknowledgement	section 178
sufficient disclaimer	section 178
teacher	section 174(5)
telecommunications system	section 178
[terms of payment	section 135A]
typeface	section 178
unauthorised (as regards things done in relation to a work)	section 178
unknown (in relation to the author of a work)	section 9(5)
unknown authorship (work of)	section 9(4)
wireless telegraphy	section 178
work (in Schedule 1)	paragraph 2(1) of that Schedule
work of more than one author (in Chapter VII)	section 116(4)
writing and written	section 178

NOTES

Commencement order: SI 1989/816.

Entry 'country of origin' added, and in entries 'film' and 'sound recording' words in square brackets substituted, by SI 1995/3297, regs 8(2), 9(5); entry beginning 'EEA,' added by SI 1995/3297, reg 11(2), word 'EEA,' added by SI 1996/2967, reg 9(6)(a); in entries 'issue of copies to the public' and 'rental' words in square brackets substituted, and entries 'lending', 'producer', 'public library' and 'rental right' added, by SI 1996/2967, regs 9(6)(b), 10(4), 11(6), 18(6); entry 'lawful user' added by SI 1992/3233, reg 9; entries 'needletime' and 'terms of payment' added by the Broadcasting Act 1990, s 175(3).

This section should be read in conjunction with the following provision of the Copyright and Rights in Databases Regulations 1997, SI 1997/3032 (commencement: 1 January 1998):

Copyright and Rights in Databases Regulations 1997, reg 12(1)

12 Interpretation
(1) In this Part–

'database' has the meaning given by section 3A(1) of the 1988 Act (as inserted by Regulation 6);

'extraction', in relation to any contents of a database, means the permanent or temporary transfer of those contents to another medium by any means or in any form;

'insubstantial', in relation to part of the contents of a database, shall be construed subject to Regulation 16(2);

'investment' includes any investment, whether of financial, human or technical resources;

'jointly', in relation to the making of a database, shall be construed in accordance with Regulation 14(6);

'lawful user', in relation to a database, means any person who (whether under a licence to do any of the acts restricted by any database right in the database or otherwise) has a right to use the database;

'maker', in relation to a database, shall be construed in accordance with Regulation 14;

're-utilisation', in relation to any contents of a database, means making those contents available to the public by any means;

'substantial', in relation to any investment, extraction or re-utilisation, means substantial in terms of quantity or quality or a combination of both.

PART II
RIGHTS IN PERFORMANCES

Introductory

180 Rights conferred on performers and persons having recording rights

(1) This Part confers rights–

(a) on a performer, by requiring his consent to the exploitation of his performances (see sections 181 to 184), and

(b) on a person having recording rights in relation to a performance, in relation to recordings made without his consent or that of the performer (see sections 185 to 188),

and creates offences in relation to dealing with or using illicit recordings and certain other related acts (see sections 198 and 201).

(2) In this Part–

'performance' means–

(a) a dramatic performance (which includes dance and mime),

(b) a musical performance,

(c) a reading or recitation of a literary work, or

(d) a performance of a variety act or any similar presentation,

which is, or so far as it is, a live performance given by one or more individuals; and

'recording', in relation to a performance, means a film or sound recording–

(a) made directly from the live performance,

(b) made from a broadcast of, or cable programme including, the performance, or

(c) made, directly or indirectly, from another recording of the performance.

(3) The rights conferred by this Part apply in relation to performances taking place before the commencement of this Part; but no act done before commencement, or in pursuance of arrangements made before commencement, shall be regarded as infringing those rights.

(4) The rights conferred by this Part are independent of–

(a) any copyright in, or moral rights relating to, any work performed or any film or sound recording of, or broadcast or cable programme including, the performance, and

(b) any other right or obligation arising otherwise than under this Part.

NOTES

Commencement order: SI 1989/816.

This section should be read in conjunction with the following provision of the Copyright and Related Rights Regulations 1996, SI 1996/2967 (commencement: 1 December 1996):

Copyright and Related Rights Regulations 1996, reg 31

New rights: effect of pre-commencement authorisation of copying

31–Where before commencement–

(a)   the owner or prospective owner of copyright in a literary, dramatic, musical or artistic work has authorised a person to make a copy of the work, or

(b)   the owner or prospective owner of performers' rights in a performance has authorised a person to make a copy of a recording of the performance,

any new right in relation to that copy shall vest on commencement in the person so authorised, subject to any agreement to the contrary.

Performers' rights

181 Qualifying performances

A performance is a qualifying performance for the purposes of the provisions of this Part relating to performers' rights if it is given by a qualifying individual (as defined in section 206) or takes place in a qualifying country (as so defined).

NOTE
Commencement order: SI 1989/816.

---

[182] [Consent required for recording, &c of live performance]

[(1) A performer's rights are infringed by a person who, without his consent–

(a)   makes a recording of the whole or any substantial part of a qualifying performance directly from the live performance,

(b)   broadcasts live, or includes live in a cable programme service, the whole or any substantial part of a qualifying performance,

(c)   makes a recording of the whole or any substantial part of a qualifying performance directly from a broadcast of, or cable programme including, the live performance.

(2) A performer's rights are not infringed by the making of any such recording by a person for his private and domestic use.

(3) In an action for infringement of a performer's rights brought by virtue of this section damages shall not be awarded against a defendant who shows that at the time of the infringement he believed on reasonable grounds that consent had been given.]

NOTES
Commencement order: SI 1989/816.
Substituted by SI 1996/2967, reg 20(1).

[182A] [Consent required for copying of recording]

[(1) A performer's rights are infringed by a person who, without his consent, makes, otherwise than for his private and domestic use, a copy of a recording of the whole or any substantial part of a qualifying performance.

(2) It is immaterial whether the copy is made directly or indirectly

(3) The right of a performer under this section to authorise or prohibit the making of such copies is referred to in this Part as 'reproduction right'.]

NOTE
Added by SI 1996/2967, reg 20(2).

[182B] [Consent required for issue of copies to the public]

[(1) A performer's rights are infringed by a person who, without his consent, issues to the public copies of a recording of the whole or any substantial part of a qualifying performance.

(2) References in this Part to the issue to the public of copies of a recording are to–

(a)   the act of putting into circulation in the EEA copies not previously put into circulation in the EEA by or with the consent of the performer, or

(b)   the act of putting into circulation outside the EEA copies not previously put into circulation in the EEA or elsewhere.

(3) References in this Part to the issue to the public of copies of a recording do not include–

    (a) any subsequent distribution, sale, hiring or loan of copies previously put into circulation (but see section 182C: consent required for rental or lending), or

    (b) any subsequent importation of such copies into the United Kingdom or another EEA state,

except so far as paragraph (a) of subsection (2) applies to putting into circulation in the EEA copies previously put into circulation outside the EEA.

(4) References in this Part to the issue of copies of a recording of a performance include the issue of the original recording of the live performance.

(5) The right of a performer under this section to authorise or prohibit the issue of copies to the public is referred to in this Part as 'distribution right'.]

NOTE

    Added by SI 1996/2967, reg 20(2).

[182C] [Consent required for rental or lending of copies to public]

[(1) A performer's rights are infringed by a person who, without his consent, rents or lends to the public copies of a recording of the whole or any substantial part of a qualifying performance.

(2) In this Part, subject to the following provisions of this section–

    (a) 'rental' means making a copy of a recording available for use, on terms that it will or may be returned, for direct or indirect economic or commercial advantage, and

    (b) 'lending' means making a copy of a recording available for use, on terms that it will or may be returned, otherwise than for direct or indirect economic or commercial advantage, through an establishment which is accessible to the public.

(3) The expressions 'rental' and 'lending' do not include–

    (a) making available for the purpose of public performance, playing or showing in public, broadcasting or inclusion in a cable programme service;

    (b) making available for the purpose of exhibition in public; or

    (c) making available for on-the-spot reference use.

(4) The expression 'lending' does not include making available between establishments which are accessible to the public.

(5) Where lending by an establishment accessible to the public gives rise to a payment the amount of which does not go beyond what is necessary to cover the operating costs of the establishment, there is no direct or indirect economic or commercial advantage for the purposes of this section.

(6) References in this Part to the rental or lending of copies of a recording of a performance include the rental or lending of the original recording of the live performance.

(7) In this Part–

    'rental right' means the right of a performer under this section to authorise or prohibit the rental of copies to the public, and

    'lending right' means the right of a performer under this section to authorise or prohibit the lending of copies to the public.]

NOTE

    Added by SI 1996/2967, reg 20(2).

[182D] [Right to equitable remuneration for exploitation of sound recording]

[(1) Where a commercially published sound recording of the whole or any substantial part of a qualifying performance–

    (a) is played in public, or

    (b) is included in a broadcast or cable programme service,

the performer is entitled to equitable remuneration from the owner of the copyright in the sound recording.

(2) The right to equitable remuneration under this section may not be assigned by the performer except to a collecting society for the purpose of enabling it to enforce the right on his behalf.

The right is, however, transmissible by testamentary disposition or by operation of law as personal or moveable property; and it may be assigned or further transmitted by any person into whose hands it passes.

(3) The amount payable by way of equitable remuneration is as agreed by or on behalf of the persons by and to whom it is payable, subject to the following provisions.

(4) In default of agreement as to the amount payable by way of equitable remuneration, the person by or to whom it is payable may apply to the Copyright Tribunal to determine the amount payable.

(5) A person to or by whom equitable remuneration is payable may also apply to the Copyright Tribunal–

    (a)   to vary any agreement as to the amount payable, or

    (b)   to vary any previous determination of the Tribunal as to that matter;

but except with the special leave of the Tribunal no such application may be made within twelve months from the date of a previous determination.

An order made on an application under this subsection has effect from the date on which it is made or such later date as may be specified by the Tribunal.

(6) On an application under this section the Tribunal shall consider the matter and make such order as to the method of calculating and paying equitable remuneration as it may determine to be reasonable in the circumstances, taking into account the importance of the contribution of the performer to the sound recording.

(7) An agreement is of no effect in so far as it purports–

    (a)   to exclude or restrict the right to equitable remuneration under this section, or

    (b)   to prevent a person questioning the amount of equitable remuneration or to restrict the powers of the Copyright Tribunal under this section.]

NOTE
Added by SI 1996/2967, reg 20(2).

183 Infringement of performer's rights by use of recording made without consent
A performer's rights are infringed by a person who, without his consent–

    (a)   shows or plays in public the whole or any substantial part of a qualifying performance, or

    (b)   broadcasts or includes in a cable programme service the whole or any substantial part of a qualifying performance,

by means of a recording which was, and which that person knows or has reason to believe was, made without the performer's consent.

NOTE
Commencement order: SI 1989/816.

184 Infringement of performer's rights by importing, possessing or dealing with illicit recording
(1) A performer's rights are infringed by a person who, without his consent–

    (a)   imports into the United Kingdom otherwise than for his private and domestic use, or

    (b)   in the course of a business possesses, sells or lets for hire, offers or exposes for sale or hire, or distributes,

a recording of a qualifying performance which is, and which that person knows or has reason to believe is, an illicit recording.

(2) Where in an action for infringement of a performer's rights brought by virtue of this section a defendant shows that the illicit recording was innocently acquired by him or a

predecessor in title of his, the only remedy available against him in respect of the infringement is damages not exceeding a reasonable payment in respect of the act complained of.

(3) In subsection (2) 'innocently acquired' means that the person acquiring the recording did not know and had no reason to believe that it was an illicit recording.

NOTE
Commencement order: SI 1989/816.

Rights of person having recording rights

185 Exclusive recording contracts and persons having recording rights

(1) In this Part an 'exclusive recording contract' means a contract between a performer and another person under which that person is entitled to the exclusion of all other persons (including the performer) to make recordings of one or more of his performances with a view to their commercial exploitation.

(2) References in this Part to a 'person having recording rights', in relation to a performance, are (subject to subsection (3)) to a person–

(a)   who is party to and has the benefit of an exclusive recording contract to which the performance is subject, or

(b)   to whom the benefit of such a contract has been assigned,

and who is a qualifying person.

(3) If a performance is subject to an exclusive recording contract but the person mentioned in subsection (2) is not a qualifying person, references in this Part to a 'person having recording rights' in relation to the performance are to any person–

(a)   who is licensed by such a person to make recordings of the performance with a view to their commercial exploitation, or

(b)   to whom the benefit of such a licence has been assigned,

and who is a qualifying person.

(4) In this section 'with a view to commercial exploitation' means with a view to the recordings being sold or let for hire, or shown or played in public.

NOTE
Commencement order: SI 1989/816.

186 Consent required for recording of performance subject to exclusive contract

(1) A person infringes the rights of a person having recording rights in relation to a performance who, without his consent or that of the performer, makes a recording of the whole or any substantial part of the performance, otherwise than for his private and domestic use.

(2) In an action for infringement of those rights brought by virtue of this section damages shall not be awarded against a defendant who shows that at the time of the infringement he believed on reasonable grounds that consent had been given.

NOTE
Commencement order: SI 1989/816.

187 Infringement of recording rights by use of recording made without consent

(1) A person infringes the rights of a person having recording rights in relation to a performance who, without his consent or, in the case of a qualifying performance, that of the performer–

(a)   shows or plays in public the whole or any substantial part of the performance, or

(b)   broadcasts or includes in a cable programme service the whole or any substantial part of the performance,

by means of a recording which was, and which that person knows or has reason to believe was, made without the appropriate consent.

(2) The reference in subsection (1) to 'the appropriate consent' is to the consent of–

(a) the performer, or
(b) the person who at the time the consent was given had recording rights in relation to the performance (or, if there was more than one such person, of all of them).

NOTE
Commencement order: SI 1989/816.

188 Infringement of recording rights by importing, possessing or dealing with illicit recording

(1) A person infringes the rights of a person having recording rights in relation to a performance who, without his consent or, in the case of a qualifying performance, that of the performer–

(a) imports into the United Kingdom otherwise than for his private and domestic use, or
(b) in the course of a business possesses, sells or lets for hire, offers or exposes for sale or hire, or distributes,

a recording of the performance which is, and which that person knows or has reason to believe is, an illicit recording.

(2) Where in an action for infringement of those rights brought by virtue of this section a defendant shows that the illicit recording was innocently acquired by him or a predecessor in title of his, the only remedy available against him in respect of the infringement is damages not exceeding a reasonable payment in respect of the act complained of.

(3) In subsection (2) 'innocently acquired' means that the person acquiring the recording did not know and had no reason to believe that it was an illicit recording.

NOTE
Commencement order: SI 1989/816.

Exceptions to rights conferred

189 Acts permitted notwithstanding rights conferred by this Part

The provisions of Schedule 2 specify acts which may be done notwithstanding the rights conferred by this Part, being acts which correspond broadly to certain of those specified in Chapter III of Part I (acts permitted notwithstanding copyright).

NOTE
Commencement order: SI 1989/816.

190 Power of tribunal to give consent on behalf of performer in certain cases

[(1) The Copyright Tribunal may, on the application of a person wishing to make a copy of a recording of a performance, give consent in a case where the identity or whereabouts of the person entitled to the reproduction right cannot be ascertained by reasonable inquiry.]

(2) Consent given by the Tribunal has effect as consent of [the person entitled to the reproduction right] for the purposes of–

(a) the provisions of this Part relating to performers' rights, and
(b) section 198(3)(a) (criminal liability: sufficient consent in relation to qualifying performances),

and may be given subject to any conditions specified in the Tribunal's order.

(3) The Tribunal shall not give consent under subsection (1)(a) except after the service or publication of such notices as may be required by rules made under section 150 (general procedural rules) or as the Tribunal may in any particular case direct.

(4) . . .

(5) In any case the Tribunal shall take into account the following factors–

(a)   whether the original recording was made with the performer's consent and is lawfully in the possession or control of the person proposing to make the further recording;

(b)   whether the making of the further recording is consistent with the obligations of the parties to the arrangements under which, or is otherwise consistent with the purposes for which, the original recording was made.

(6) Where the Tribunal gives consent under this section it shall, in default of agreement between the applicant and [the person entitled to the reproduction right], make such order as it thinks fit as to the payment to be made to [that person] in consideration of consent being given.

NOTES
Commencement order: SI 1989/816.
Sub-s (1): substituted by SI 1996/2967, reg 23(2).
Sub-ss (2), (6): words in square brackets substituted by SI 1996/2967, reg 23(3), (5).
Sub-s (4): repealed by SI 1996/2967, reg 23(4).

[Duration of rights]

[191]   [Duration of rights]
[(1) The following provisions have effect with respect to the duration of the rights conferred by this Part.

(2) The rights conferred by this Part in relation to a performance expire–

(a)   at the end of the period of 50 years from the end of the calendar year in which the performance takes place, or

(b)   if during that period a recording of the performance is released, 50 years from the end of the calendar year in which it is released,

subject as follows.

(3) For the purposes of subsection (2) a recording is 'released' when it is first published, played or shown in public, broadcast or included in a cable programme service; but in determining whether a recording has been released no account shall be taken of any unauthorised act.

(4) Where a performer is not a national of an EEA state, the duration of the rights conferred by this Part in relation to his performance is that to which the performance is entitled in the country of which he is a national, provided that does not exceed the period which would apply under subsections (2) and (3).

(5) If or to the extent that the application of subsection (4) would be at variance with an international obligation to which the United Kingdom became subject prior to 29th October 1993, the duration of the rights conferred by this Part shall be as specified in subsections (2) and (3).]

NOTES
Commencement order: SI 1989/816.
This section was substituted by SI 1995/3297, reg 10.
Cross-heading: words in square brackets substituted by SI 1996/2967, reg 21(5)(a).
This section should be read in conjunction with the following provisions of the Duration of Copyright and Rights in Performances Regulations 1995, SI 1995/3297 (commencement: 1 January 1996):

Duration of Copyright and Rights in Performances Regulations 1995, regs 27–35

Rights in performances: interpretation
27–(1) In the provisions of this Part relating to rights in performances–

(a)   'existing', in relation to a performance, means given before commencement; and

(b)   'existing protected performance' means a performance in relation to which rights under Part II of the 1988 Act (rights in performances) subsisted immediately before commencement.

(2) References in this Part to performers' rights are to the rights given by section 180(1)(a) of the 1988 Act and references to recording rights are to the rights given by section 180(1)(b) of that Act.

28 Duration of rights in performances: general saving:
Any rights under Part II of the 1988 Act in an existing protected performance shall continue to subsist until the date on which they would have expired under the 1988 provisions if that date is later than the date on which the rights would expire under the new provisions.

Duration of rights in performances: application of new provisions
29 The new provisions relating to the duration of rights under Part II of the 1988 Act apply–

(a)   to performances taking place after commencement;
(b)   to existing performances which first qualify for protection under Part II of the 1988 Act after commencement;
(c)   to existing protected performances, subject to Regulation 28 (general saving for any longer period applicable under 1988 provisions); and
(d)   to existing performances–

    (i)   in which rights under Part II of the 1988 Act expired after the commencement of that Part and before 31st December 1995, or
    (ii)   which were protected by earlier enactments relating to the protection of performers and in which rights under that Part did not arise by reason only that the performance was given at a date such that the rights would have ceased to subsist before the commencement of that Part,

but which were on 1st July 1995 protected in another EEA state under legislation relating to copyright or related rights.

Extended and revived performance rights
30 In the following provisions of this Part–

'extended performance rights' means rights under Part II of the 1988 Act which subsist by virtue of the new provisions after the date on which they would have expired under the 1988 provisions; and
'revived performance rights' means rights under Part II of the 1988 Act which subsist by virtue of the new provisions–

(a)   after having expired under the 1988 provisions, or
(b)   in relation to a performance which was protected by earlier enactments relating to the protection of performers and in which rights under that Part did not arise by reason only that the performance was given at a date such that the rights would have ceased to subsist before the commencement of that Part.

References in the following provisions of this Part to 'revived pre-1988 rights' are to revived performance rights within paragraph (b) of the above definition.

Entitlement to extended or revived performance rights
31–(1) Any extended performance rights are exercisable as from commencement by the person who was entitled to exercise those rights immediately before commencement, that is–

(a)   in the case of performers' rights, the performer or (if he has died) the person entitled by virtue of section 192(2) of the 1988 Act to exercise those rights;
(b)   in the case of recording rights, the person who was within the meaning of section 185 of the 1988 Act the person having those rights.

(2) Any revived performance rights are exercisable as from commencement–

(a)   in the case of rights which expired after the commencement of the 1988 Act, by the person who was entitled to exercise those rights immediately before they expired;
(b)   in the case of revived pre-1988 performers' rights, by the performer or his personal representatives;
(c)   in the case of revived pre-1988 recording rights, by the person who would have been the person having those rights immediately before the commencement of the 1988 Act or, if earlier, immediately before the death of the performer, applying the provisions of section 185 of that Act to the circumstances then obtaining.

(3) Any remuneration or damages received by a person's personal representatives by virtue of a right conferred on them by paragraph (1) or (2) shall devolve as part of that person's estate as if the right had subsisted and been vested in him immediately before his death.

Extended performance rights: existing consents, agreement, &c
32 Any consent, or any term or condition of an agreement, relating to the exploitation of an existing protected performance which–

(a)   subsists immediately before commencement, and
(b)   is not to expire before the end of the period for which rights under Part II of the 1988 Act subsist in relation to that performance,

shall continue to subsist during the period of any extended performance rights, subject to any agreement to the contrary.

Revived performance rights: saving for acts of exploitation when performance in public domain, &c
33–(1) No act done before commencement shall be regarded as infringing revived performance rights in a performance.

(2) It is not an infringement of revived performance rights in a performance–

(a)   to do anything after commencement in pursuance of arrangements made before 1st January 1995 at a time when the performance was not protected, or

(b)   to issue to the public after commencement a recording of a performance made before 1st July 1995 at a time when the performance was not protected.

(3) It is not an infringement of revived performance rights in a performance to do anything after commencement in relation to a sound recording or film made before commencement, or made in pursuance of arrangements made before commencement, which contains a recording of the performance if–

(a)   the recording of the performance was made before 1st July 1995 at a time when the performance was not protected, or

(b)   the recording of the performance was made in pursuance of arrangements made before 1st July 1995 at a time when the performance was not protected.

(4) It is not an infringement of revived performance rights in a performance to do after commencement anything at a time when, or in pursuance of arrangements made at a time when, the name and address of a person entitled to authorise the act cannot by reasonable inquiry be ascertained.

(5) In this Regulation 'arrangements' means arrangements for the exploitation of the performance in question.

(6)   References in this Regulation to a performance being protected are–

(a)   in relation to the period after the commencement of the 1988 Act, to rights under Part II of that Act subsisting in relation to the performance, and

(b)   in relation to earlier periods, to the consent of the performer being required under earlier enactments relating to the protection of performers.

Revived performance rights: use as of right subject to reasonable remuneration
34–(1) In the case of a performance in which revived performance rights subsist any acts which require the consent of any person under Part II of the 1988 Act (the 'rights owner') shall be treated as having that consent, subject only to the payment of such reasonable remuneration as may be agreed or determined in default of agreement by the Copyright Tribunal.

(2) A person intending to avail himself of the right conferred by this Regulation must give reasonable notice of his intention to the rights owner, stating when he intends to begin to do the acts.

(3) If he does not give such notice, his acts shall not be treated as having consent.

(4) If he does give such notice, his acts shall be treated as having consent and reasonable remuneration shall be payable in respect of them despite the fact that its amount is not agreed or determined until later.

Revived performance rights: application to Copyright Tribunal
35–(1) An application to settle the remuneration payable in pursuance of Regulation 34 may be made to the Copyright Tribunal by the rights owner or the person claiming to be treated as having his consent.

(2) The Tribunal shall consider the matter and make such order as it may determine to be reasonable in the circumstances.

(3) Either party may subsequently apply to the Tribunal to vary the order, and the Tribunal shall consider the matter and make such order confirming or varying the original order as it may determine to be reasonable in the circumstances.

(4) An application under paragraph (3) shall not, except with the special leave of the Tribunal, be made within twelve months from the date of the original order or of the order on a previous application under that paragraph.

(5)   An order under paragraph (3) has effect from the date on which it is made or such later date as may be specified by the Tribunal.

[Performers' property rights]

[191A] [Performers' property rights]
[(1) The following rights conferred by this Part on a performer–

reproduction right (section 182A),
distribution right (section 182B),
rental right and lending right (section 182C),

are property rights ('a performer's property rights').

(2) References in this Part to the consent of the performer shall be construed in relation to a performer's property rights as references to the consent of the rights owner.

(3) Where different persons are (whether in consequence of a partial assignment or otherwise) entitled to different aspects of a performer's property rights in relation to a performance, the rights owner for any purpose of this Part is the person who is entitled to the aspect of those rights relevant for that purpose.

(4) Where a performer's property rights (or any aspect of them) is owned by more than one person jointly, references in this Part to the rights owner are to all the owners, so that, in

particular, any requirement of the licence of the rights owner requires the licence of all of them.]

NOTES

Added by SI 1996/2967, reg 21(1).

This section should be read in conjunction with the following provision of the Copyright and Related Rights Regulations 1996, SI 1996/2967 (commencement: 1 December 1996):

Copyright and Related Rights Regulations 1996, reg 34(2)

Savings for existing stocks
34–(2) Any new right in relation to a qualifying performance does not apply to a copy of a recording of the performance acquired by a person before commencement for the purpose of renting or lending it to the public.

[191B] [Assignment and licences]

[(1) A performer's property rights are transmissible by assignment, by testamentary disposition or by operation of law, as personal or moveable property.

(2) An assignment or other transmission of a performer's property rights may be partial, that is, limited so as to apply–

(a)   to one or more, but not all, of the things requiring the consent of the rights owner;
(b)   to part, but not the whole, of the period for which the rights are to subsist.

(3) An assignment of a performer's property rights is not effective unless it is in writing signed by or on behalf of the assignor.

(4) A licence granted by the owner of a performer's property rights is binding on every successor in title to his interest in the rights, except a purchaser in good faith for valuable consideration and without notice (actual or constructive) of the licence or a person deriving title from such a purchaser; and references in this Part to doing anything with, or without, the licence of the rights owner shall be construed accordingly.]

NOTE

Added by SI 1996/2967, reg 21(1).

[191C] [Prospective ownership of a performer's property rights]

[(1) This section applies where by an agreement made in relation to a future recording of a performance, and signed by or on behalf of the performer, the performer purports to assign his performer's property rights (wholly or partially) to another person.

(2) If on the rights coming into existence the assignee or another person claiming under him would be entitled as against all other persons to require the rights to be vested in him, they shall vest in the assignee or his successor in title by virtue of this subsection.

(3) A licence granted by a prospective owner of a performer's property rights is binding on every successor in title to his interest (or prospective interest) in the rights, except a purchaser in good faith for valuable consideration and without notice (actual or constructive) of the licence or a person deriving title from such a purchaser.

References in this Part to doing anything with, or without, the licence of the rights owner shall be construed accordingly.

(4) In subsection (3) 'prospective owner' in relation to a performer's property rights means a person who is prospectively entitled to those rights by virtue of such an agreement as is mentioned in subsection (1).]

NOTE

Added by SI 1996/2967, reg 21(1).

[191D] [Exclusive licences]

[(1) In this Part an 'exclusive licence' means a licence in writing signed by or on behalf of the owner of a performer's property rights authorising the licensee to the exclusion of all other persons, including the person granting the licence, to do anything requiring the consent of the rights owner.

(2) The licensee under an exclusive licence has the same rights against a successor in title who is bound by the licence as he has against the person granting the licence.]

NOTE
Added by SI 1996/2967, reg 21(1).

[191E] [Performer's property right to pass under will with unpublished original recording]

[Where under a bequest (whether general or specific) a person is entitled beneficially or otherwise to any material thing containing an original recording of a performance which was not published before the death of the testator, the bequest shall, unless a contrary intention is indicated in the testator's will or a codicil to it, be construed as including any performer's rights in relation to the recording to which the testator was entitled immediately before his death.]

NOTE
Added by SI 1996/2967, reg 21(1).

[191F] [Presumption of transfer of rental right in case of film production agreement]

[(1) Where an agreement concerning film production is concluded between a performer and a film producer, the performer shall be presumed, unless the agreement provides to the contrary, to have transferred to the film producer any rental right in relation to the film arising from the inclusion of a recording of his performance in the film.

(2) Where the section applies, the absence of signature by or on behalf of the performer does not exclude the operation of section 191C (effect of purported assignment of future rights).

(3) The reference in subsection (1) to an agreement concluded between a performer and a film producer includes any agreement having effect between those persons, whether made by them directly or through intermediaries.

(4) Section 191G (right to equitable remuneration on transfer of rental right) applies where there is a presumed transfer by virtue of this section as in the case of an actual transfer.]

NOTE
Added by SI 1996/2967, reg 21(1).
See also the Copyright and Related Rights Regulations 1996, regs 32 and 33 set out after s 191G, post.

[191G] [Right to equitable remuneration where rental right transferred]

[(1) Where a performer has transferred his rental right concerning a sound recording or a film to the producer of the sound recording or film, he retains the right to equitable remuneration for the rental.

The reference above to the transfer of rental right by one person to another includes any arrangement having that effect, whether made by them directly or through intermediaries.

(2) The right to equitable remuneration under this section may not be assigned by the performer except to a collecting society for the purpose of enabling it to enforce the right on his behalf.

The right is, however, transmissible by testamentary disposition or by operation of law as personal or moveable property; and it may be assigned or further transmitted by any person into whose hands it passes.

(3) Equitable remuneration under this section is payable by the person for the time being entitled to the rental right, that is, the person to whom the right was transferred or any successor in title of his.

(4) The amount payable by way of equitable remuneration is as agreed by or on behalf of the persons by and to whom it is payable, subject to section 191H (reference of amount to Copyright Tribunal).

(5) An agreement is of no effect in so far as it purports to exclude or restrict the right to equitable remuneration under this section.

(6) In this section a 'collecting society' means a society or other organisation which has as its main object, or one of its main objects, the exercise of the right to equitable remuneration on behalf of more than one performer.]

NOTES

Added by SI 1996/2967, reg 21(1).

This section should be read in conjunction with the following provisions of the Copyright and Related Rights Regulations 1996, SI 1996/2967 (commencement: 1 December 1996):

Copyright and Related Rights Regulations 1996, regs 32 and 33

New rights: effect of pre-commencement film production agreement

32–(1) Sections 93A and 191F (presumption of transfer of rental right in case of production agreement) apply in relation to an agreement concluded before commencement.

As section 93A so applies, the restriction in subsection (3) of that section shall be omitted (exclusion of presumption in relation to screenplay, dialogue or music specifically created for the film).

(2) Sections 93B and 191G (right to equitable remuneration where rental right transferred) have effect accordingly, but subject to regulation 33 (right to equitable remuneration applicable to rental after 1st April 1997).

Right to equitable remuneration applicable to rental after 1st April 1997

33 No right to equitable remuneration under section 93B or 191G (right to equitable remuneration where rental right transferred) arises–

(a) in respect of any rental of a sound recording or film before 1st April 1997, or

(b) in respect of any rental after that date of a sound recording or film made in pursuance of an agreement entered into before 1st July 1994, unless the author or performer (or a successor in title of his) has before 1st January 1997 notified the person by whom the remuneration would be payable that he intends to exercise that right.

[191H] [Equitable remuneration: reference of amount to Copyright Tribunal]

[(1) In default of agreement as to the amount payable by way of equitable remuneration under section 191G, the person by or to whom it is payable may apply to the Copyright Tribunal to determine the amount payable.

(2) A person to or by whom equitable remuneration is payable may also apply to the Copyright Tribunal–

(a) to vary any agreement as to the amount payable, or

(b) to vary any previous determination of the Tribunal as to that matter;

but except with the special leave of the Tribunal no such application may be made within twelve months from the date of a previous determination.

An order made on an application under this subsection has effect from the date on which it is made or such later date as may be specified by the Tribunal.

(3) On an application under this section the Tribunal shall consider the matter and make such order as to the method of calculating and paying equitable remuneration as it may determine to be reasonable in the circumstances, taking into account the importance of the contribution of the performer to the film or sound recording.

(4) Remuneration shall not be considered inequitable merely because it was paid by way of a single payment or at the time of the transfer of the rental right.

(5) An agreement is of no effect in so far as it purports to prevent a person questioning the amount of equitable remuneration or to restrict the powers of the Copyright Tribunal under this section.]

NOTE

Added by SI 1996/2967, reg 21(1).

[191I] [Infringement actionable by rights owner]

[(1) An infringement of a performer's property rights is actionable by the rights owner.

(2) In an action for infringement of a performer's property rights all such relief by way of damages, injunctions, accounts or otherwise is available to the plaintiff as is available in respect of the infringement of any other property right.

(3) This section has effect subject to the following provisions of this Part.]

NOTE
Added by SI 1996/2967, reg 21(1).

[191J] [Provisions as to damages in infringement action]

[(1) Where in an action for infringement of a performer's property rights it is shown that at the time of the infringement the defendant did not know and had no reason to believe, that the rights subsisted in the recording to which the action relates, the plaintiff is not entitled to damages against him, but without prejudice to any other remedy.

(2) The court may in an action for infringement of a performer's property rights having regard to all the circumstances, and in particular to–

(a)   the flagrancy of the infringement, and
(b)   any benefit accruing to the defendant by reason of the infringement,

award such additional damages as the justice of the case may require.]

NOTE
Added by SI 1996/2967, reg 21(1).

[191K] [Undertaking to take licence of right in infringement proceedings]

[(1) If in proceedings for infringement of a performer's property rights in respect of which a licence is available as of right under paragraph 17 of Schedule 2A (powers exercisable in consequence of competition report) the defendant undertakes to take a licence on such terms as may be agreed or, in default of agreement, settled by the Copyright Tribunal under that paragraph–

(a)   no injunction shall be granted against him,
(b)   no order for delivery up shall be made under section 195, and
(c)   the amount recoverable against him by way of damages or on an account of profits shall not exceed double the amount which would have been payable by him as licensee if such a licence on those terms had been granted before the earliest infringement.

(2)   An undertaking may be given at any time before final order in the proceedings, without any admission of liability.

(3) Nothing in this section affects the remedies available in respect of an infringement committed before licences of right were available.]

NOTE
Added by SI 1996/2967, reg 21(1).

[191L] [Rights and remedies for exclusive licensee]

[(1) An exclusive licensee has, except against the owner of a performer's property rights, the same rights and remedies in respect of matters occurring after the grant of the licence as if the licence had been an assignment.

(2) His rights and remedies are concurrent with those of the rights owner; and references in the relevant provisions of this Part to the rights owner shall be construed accordingly.

(3) In an action brought by an exclusive licensee by virtue of this section a defendant may avail himself of any defence which would have been available to him if the action had been brought by the rights owner.]

NOTE
Added by SI 1996/2967, reg 21(1).

[191M] [Exercise of concurrent rights]

[(1) Where an action for infringement of a performer's property rights brought by the rights owner or an exclusive licensee relates (wholly or partly) to an infringement in respect of which they have concurrent rights of action, the rights owner or, as the case may be, the exclusive licensee may not, without the leave of the court, proceed with the action unless the other is either joined as plaintiff or added as a defendant.

(2) A rights owner or exclusive licensee who is added as a defendant in pursuance of subsection (1) is not liable for any costs in the action unless he takes part in the proceedings.

(3) The above provisions do not affect the granting of interlocutory relief on an application by the rights owner or exclusive licensee alone.

(4) Where an action for infringement of a performer's property rights is brought which relates (wholly or partly) to an infringement in respect of which the rights owner and an exclusive licensee have or had concurrent rights of action–

  (a) the court shall in assessing damages take into account–

     (i)   the terms of the licence, and
    (ii)   any pecuniary remedy already awarded or available to either of them in respect of the infringement;

  (b) no account of profits shall be directed if an award of damages has been made, or an account of profits has been directed, in favour of the other of them in respect of the infringement; and

  (c) the court shall if an account of profits is directed apportion the profits between them as the court considers just, subject to any agreement between them;

and these provisions apply whether or not the rights owner and the exclusive licensee are both parties to the action.

(5) The owner of a performer's property rights shall notify any exclusive licensee having concurrent rights before applying for an order under section 195 (order for delivery up) or exercising the right conferred by section 196 (right of seizure); and the court may on the application of the licensee make such order under section 195 or, as the case may be, prohibiting or permitting the exercise by the rights owner of the right conferred by section 196, as it thinks fit having regard to the terms of the licence.]

NOTES
Added by SI 1996/2967, reg 21(1).

[Non-property rights]

[192A] [Performers' non-property rights]
[(1) the rights conferred on a performer by–

> section 182 (consent required for recording, &c of live performance),
> section 183 (infringement of performer's rights by use of recording made without consent), and
> section 184 (infringement of performer's rights importing, possessing or dealing with illicit recording),

are not assignable or transmissible, except to the following extent.
  They are referred to in this Part as 'a performer's non-property rights'.
  (2) On the death of a person entitled to any such right–

  (a) the right passes to such person as he may by testamentary disposition specifically direct, and

  (b) if or to the extent that there is no such direction, the right is exercisable by his personal representatives.

(3) References in this Part to the performer, in the context of the person having any such right, shall be construed as references to the person for the time being entitled to exercise those rights.

(4) Where by virtue of subsection (2)(a) a right becomes exercisable by more than one person, it is exercisable by each of them independently of the other or others.

(5) Any damages recovered by personal representatives by virtue of this section in respect of an infringement after a person's death shall devolve as part of his estate as if the right of action had subsisted and been vested in him immediately before his death.]

NOTE

Substituted, together with s 192B, for s 192 as originally enacted, by SI 1996/2967, reg 21(2).

[192B] [Transmissibility of rights of person having recording rights]

[(1) The rights conferred by this Part on a person having recording rights are not assignable or transmissible.

(2) This does not affect section 185(2)(b) or (3)(b), so far as those provisions confer rights under this Part on a person to whom the benefit of a contract or licence is assigned.]

NOTES

Substituted, together with s 192A, for s 192 as originally enacted, by SI 1996/2967, reg 21(2).

This section should be read in conjunction with the following provision of the Copyright and Related Rights Regulations 1996, SI 1996/2967 (commencement: 1 December 1996):

Copyright and Related Rights Regulations 1996, reg 30

New rights: exercise of rights in relation to performances

30–(1) Any new right conferred by these Regulations in relation to a qualifying performance is exercisable as from commencement by the performer or (if he has died) by the person who immediately before commencement was entitled by virtue of section 192(2) to exercise the rights conferred on the performer by Part II in relation to that performance.

(2) Any remuneration or damages received by a person's personal representatives by virtue of a right conferred on them by paragraph (1) shall devolve as part of that person's estate as if the right had subsisted and been vested in him immediately before his death.

193 Consent

(1) Consent for the purposes of this Part [by a person having a performer's non-property rights, or by a person having recording rights,] may be given in relation to a specific performance, a specified description of performances or performances generally, and may relate to past or future performances.

(2) A person having recording rights in a performance is bound by any consent given by a person through whom he derives his rights under the exclusive recording contract or licence in question, in the same way as if the consent had been given by him.

(3) Where [a performer's non-property right] passes to another person, any consent binding on the person previously entitled binds the person to whom the right passes in the same way as if the consent had been given by him.

NOTES

Commencement order: SI 1989/816.

Cross-heading: words in square brackets substituted by virtue of SI 1996/2967, reg 21(2).

Sub-s (1): words in square brackets added by SI 1996/2967, reg 21(3)(a).

Sub-s (3): words in square brackets substituted by SI 1996/2967, reg 21(3)(b).

194 Infringement actionable as breach of statutory duty

An infringement of [–

(a) a performer's non-property rights, or

(b) any right conferred by this Part on a person having recording rights,] is actionable by the person entitled to the right as a breach of statutory duty.]

NOTES

Commencement order: SI 1989/816.

Cross-heading: words omitted repealed by SI 1996/2967, reg 21(5)(b).

Words in square brackets substituted by SI 1996/2967, reg 21(4).

[Delivery up or seizure of illicit recordings]

195 Order for delivery up

(1) Where a person has in his possession, custody or control in the course of a business an illicit recording of a performance, a person having performer's rights or recording rights in relation to the performance under this Part may apply to the court for an order that the recording be delivered up to him or to such other person as the court may direct.

(2) An application shall not be made after the end of the period specified in section 203; and no order shall be made unless the court also makes, or it appears to the court that there are grounds for making, an order under section 204 (order as to disposal of illicit recording).

(3) A person to whom a recording is delivered up in pursuance of an order under this section shall, if an order under section 204 is not made, retain it pending the making of an order, or the decision not to make an order, under that section.

(4) Nothing in this section affects any other power of the court.

NOTES
Commencement order: SI 1989/816.

Cross-heading: words in square brackets substituted by SI 1996/2967, reg 21(5)(c).

See further: the High Court and County Courts Jurisdiction Order 1991, SI 1991/724, arts 2(1)(*n*), 11, 12.

196 Right to seize illicit recordings

(1) An illicit recording of a performance which is found exposed or otherwise immediately available for sale or hire, and in respect of which a person would be entitled to apply for an order under section 195, may be seized and detained by him or a person authorised by him.

The right to seize and detain is exercisable subject to the following conditions and is subject to any decision of the court under section 204 (order as to disposal of illicit recording).

(2) Before anything is seized under this section notice of the time and place of the proposed seizure must be given to a local police station.

(3) A person may for the purpose of exercising the right conferred by this section enter premises to which the public have access but may not seize anything in the possession, custody or control of a person at a permanent or regular place of business of his and may not use any force.

(4) At the time when anything is seized under this section there shall be left at the place where it was seized a notice in the prescribed form containing the prescribed particulars as to the person by whom or on whose authority the seizure is made and the grounds on which it is made.

(5) In this section–

'premises' includes land, buildings, fixed or moveable structures, vehicles, vessels, aircraft and hovercraft; and

'prescribed' means prescribed by order of the Secretary of State.

(6) An order of the Secretary of State under this section shall be made by statutory instrument which shall be subject to annulment in pursuance of a resolution of either House of Parliament.

NOTE
Commencement orders: SI 1989/816, SI 1989/955, SI 1989/1032.

197 Meaning of 'illicit recording'

(1) In this Part 'illicit recording', in relation to a performance, shall be construed in accordance with this section.

(2) For the purposes of a performer's rights, a recording of the whole or any substantial part of a performance of his is an illicit recording if it is made, otherwise than for private purposes, without his consent.

(3) For the purposes of the rights of a person having recording rights, a recording of the whole or any substantial part of a performance subject to the exclusive recording contract is an illicit recording if it is made, otherwise than for private purposes, without his consent or that of the performer.

(4) For the purposes of sections 198 and 199 (offences and orders for delivery up in criminal proceedings), a recording is an illicit recording if it is an illicit recording for the purposes mentioned in subsection (2) or subsection (3).

(5) In this Part 'illicit recording' includes a recording falling to be treated as an illicit recording by virtue of any of the following provisions of Schedule 2–

> paragraph 4(3) (recordings made for purposes of instruction or examination),
> paragraph 6(2) (recordings made by educational establishments for educational purposes),
> paragraph 12(2) (recordings of performance in electronic form retained on transfer of principal recording), or
> paragraph 16(3) (recordings made for purposes of broadcast or cable programme),

but otherwise does not include a recording made in accordance with any of the provisions of that Schedule.

(6) It is immaterial for the purposes of this section where the recording was made.

NOTES

Commencement order: SI 1989/816.

Cross-heading: words in square brackets substituted by virtue of SI 1996/2967, reg 21(5)(c).

Offences

198 Criminal liability for making, dealing with or using illicit recordings

(1) A person commits an offence who without sufficient consent–

(a) makes for sale or hire, or

(b) imports into the United Kingdom otherwise than for his private and domestic use, or

(c) possesses in the course of a business with a view to committing any act infringing the rights conferred by this Part, or

(d) in the course of a business–

> (i) sells or lets for hire, or
> (ii) offers or exposes for sale or hire, or
> (iii) distributes,

a recording which is, and which he knows or has reason to believe is, an illicit recording.

(2) A person commits an offence who causes a recording of a performance made without sufficient consent to be–

(a) shown or played in public, or

(b) broadcast or included in a cable programme service,

thereby infringing any of the rights conferred by this Part, if he knows or has reason to believe that those rights are thereby infringed.

(3) In subsections (1) and (2) 'sufficient consent' means–

(a) in the case of a qualifying performance, the consent of the performer, and

(b) in the case of a non-qualifying performance subject to an exclusive recording contract–

> (i) for the purposes of subsection (1)(a) (making of recording), the consent of the performer or the person having recording rights, and
> (ii) for the purposes of subsection (1)(b), (c) and (d) and subsection (2) (dealing with or using recording), the consent of the person having recording rights.

The references in this subsection to the person having recording rights are to the person having those rights at the time the consent is given or, if there is more than one such person, to all of them.

(4) No offence is committed under subsection (1) or (2) by the commission of an act which by virtue of any provision of Schedule 2 may be done without infringing the rights conferred by this Part.

(5) A person guilty of an offence under subsection (1)(a), (b) or (d)(iii) is liable–

(a) on summary conviction to imprisonment for a term not exceeding six months or a fine not exceeding the statutory maximum, or both;

(b) on conviction on indictment to a fine or imprisonment for a term not exceeding two years, or both.

(6) A person guilty of any other offence under this section is liable on summary conviction to a fine not exceeding level 5 on the standard scale or imprisonment for a term not exceeding six months, or both.

NOTE
Commencement order: SI 1989/816.

[198A] [Enforcement by local weights and measures authority]

[(1) It is the duty of every local weights and measures authority to enforce within their area the provisions of section 198.

(2) The following provisions of the Trade Descriptions Act 1968 apply in relation to the enforcement of that section by such an authority as in relation to the enforcement of that Act–

section 27 (power to make test purchases),
section 28 (power to enter premises and inspect and seize goods and documents),
section 29 (obstruction of authorised officers), and
section 33 (compensation for loss, &c of goods seized).

(3) Subsection (1) above does not apply in relation to the enforcement of section 198 in Northern Ireland, but it is the duty of the Department of Economic Development to enforce that section in Northern Ireland.

For that purpose the provisions of the Trade Descriptions Act 1968 specified in subsection (2) apply as if for the references to a local weights and measures authority and any officer of such an authority there were substituted references to that Department and any of its officers.

(4) Any enactment which authorises the disclosure of information for the purpose of facilitating the enforcement of the Trade Descriptions Act 1968 shall apply as if section 198 were contained in that Act and as if the functions of any person in relation to the enforcement of that section were functions under that Act.

(5) Nothing in this section shall be construed as authorising a local weights and measures authority to bring proceedings in Scotland for an offence.]

NOTE
This section is prospectively added by the Criminal Justice and Public Order Act 1994, s 165(3), as from a day to be appointed.

199 Order for delivery up in criminal proceedings

(1) The court before which proceedings are brought against a person for an offence under section 198 may, if satisfied that at the time of his arrest or charge he had in his possession, custody or control in the course of a business an illicit recording of a performance, order that it be delivered up to a person having performers' rights or recording rights in relation to the performance or to such other person as the court may direct.

(2) For this purpose a person shall be treated as charged with an offence–

(a) in England, Wales and Northern Ireland, when he is orally charged or is served with a summons or indictment;

(b) in Scotland, when he is cautioned, charged or served with a complaint or indictment.

(3) An order may be made by the court of its own motion or on the application of the prosecutor (or, in Scotland, the Lord Advocate or procurator-fiscal), and may be made whether or not the person is convicted of the offence, but shall not be made–

(a) after the end of the period specified in section 203 (period after which remedy of delivery up not available), or

(b) if it appears to the court unlikely that any order will be made under section 204 (order as to disposal of illicit recording).

(4) An appeal lies from an order made under this section by a magistrates' court–

(a) in England and Wales, to the Crown Court, and

(b) in Northern Ireland, to the county court;

and in Scotland, where an order has been made under this section, the person from whose possession, custody or control the illicit recording has been removed may, without prejudice to any other form of appeal under any rule of law, appeal against that order in the same manner as against sentence.

(5) A person to whom an illicit recording is delivered up in pursuance of an order under this section shall retain it pending the making of an order, or the decision not to make an order, under section 204.

(6) Nothing in this section affects the powers of the court under section 43 of the Powers of Criminal Courts Act 1973, [Part II of the Proceeds of Crime (Scotland) Act 1995] or Article 7 of the Criminal Justice (Northern Ireland) Order 1980 [Article 11 of the Criminal Justice (Northern Ireland) Order 1994] (general provisions as to forfeiture in criminal proceedings).

NOTES

Commencement order: SI 1989/816.

Sub-s (6): words in square brackets substituted by the Criminal Procedure (Consequential Provisions) (Scotland) Act 1995, s 5, Sch 4, para 70(3); final words underlined prospectively repealed and subsequent words in square brackets prospectively substituted by the Criminal Justice (Northern Ireland) Order 1994, SI 1994/2795, art 26(1), Sch 2, para 14, as from a day to be appointed.

---

200 Search warrants

(1) Where a justice of the peace (in Scotland, a sheriff or justice of the peace) is satisfied by information on oath given by a constable (in Scotland, by evidence on oath) that there are reasonable grounds for believing–

(a) that an offence under section 198(1)(a), (b) or (d)(iii) (offences of making, importing or distributing illicit recordings) has been or is about to be committed in any premises, and

(b) that evidence that such an offence has been or is about to be committed is in those premises,

he may issue a warrant authorising a constable to enter and search the premises, using such reasonable force as is necessary.

(2) The power conferred by subsection (1) does not, in England and Wales, extend to authorising a search for material of the kinds mentioned in section 9(2) of the Police and Criminal Evidence Act 1984 (certain classes of personal or confidential material).

(3) A warrant under subsection (1)–

(a) may authorise persons to accompany any constable executing the warrant, and

(b) remains in force for 28 days from the date of its issue.

(4) In this section 'premises' includes land, buildings, fixed or moveable structures, vehicles, vessels, aircraft and hovercraft.

NOTE

Commencement order: SI 1989/816.

---

201 False representation of authority to give consent

(1) It is an offence for a person to represent falsely that he is authorised by any person to give consent for the purposes of this Part in relation to a performance, unless he believes on reasonable grounds that he is so authorised.

(2) A person guilty of an offence under this section is liable on summary conviction to imprisonment for a term not exceeding six months or a fine not exceeding level 5 on the standard scale or both.

NOTE
Commencement order: SI 1989/816.

202 Offence by body corporate: liability of officers

(1) Where an offence under this Part committed by a body corporate is proved to have been committed with the consent or connivance of a director, manager, secretary or other similar officer of the body, or a person purporting to act in any such capacity, he as well as the body corporate is guilty of the offence and liable to be proceeded against and punished accordingly.

(2) In relation to a body corporate whose affairs are managed by its members 'director' means a member of the body corporate.

NOTE
Commencement order: SI 1989/816.

Supplementary provisions with respect to delivery up and seizure

203 Period after which remedy of delivery up not available

(1) An application for an order under section 195 (order for delivery up in civil proceedings) may not be made after the end of the period of six years from the date on which the illicit recording in question was made, subject to the following provisions.

(2) If during the whole or any part of that period a person entitled to apply for an order—

  (a) is under a disability, or
  (b) is prevented by fraud or concealment from discovering the facts entitling him to apply,

an application may be made by him at any time before the end of the period of six years from the date on which he ceased to be under a disability or, as the case may be, could with reasonable diligence have discovered those facts.

(3) In subsection (2) 'disability'—

  (a) in England and Wales, has the same meaning as in the Limitation Act 1980;
  (b) in Scotland, means legal disability within the meaning of the Prescription and Limitations (Scotland) Act 1973;
  (c) in Northern Ireland, has the same meaning as in the Statute of Limitation (Northern Ireland) 1958.

(4) An order under section 199 (order for delivery up in criminal proceedings) shall not, in any case, be made after the end of the period of six years from the date on which the illicit recording in question was made.

NOTE
Commencement order: SI 1989/816.

204 Order as to disposal of illicit recording

(1) An application may be made to the court for an order that an illicit recording of a performance delivered up in pursuance of an order under section 195 or 199, or seized and detained in pursuance of the right conferred by section 196, shall be—

  (a) forfeited to such person having performer's rights or recording rights in relation to the performance as the court may direct, or
  (b) destroyed or otherwise dealt with as the court may think fit,

or for a decision that no such order should be made.

(2) In considering what order (if any) should be made, the court shall consider whether other remedies available in an action for infringement of the rights conferred by this Part would be adequate to compensate the person or persons entitled to the rights and to protect their interests.

(3) Provision shall be made by rules of court as to the service of notice on persons having an interest in the recording, and any such person is entitled–

(a)   to appear in proceedings for an order under this section, whether or not he was served with notice, and

(b)   to appeal against any order made, whether or not he appeared;

and an order shall not take effect until the end of the period within which notice of an appeal may be given or, if before the end of that period notice of appeal is duly given, until the final determination or abandonment of the proceedings on the appeal.

(4) Where there is more than one person interested in a recording, the court shall make such order as it thinks just and may (in particular) direct that the recording be sold, or otherwise dealt with, and the proceeds divided.

(5) If the court decides that no order should be made under this section, the person in whose possession, custody or control the recording was before being delivered up or seized is entitled to its return.

(6) References in this section to a person having an interest in a recording include any person in whose favour an order could be made in respect of the recording under this section or under section 114 or 231 of this Act or [section 19 of the Trade Marks Act 1994] (which make similar provision in relation to infringement of copyright, design right and trade marks).

NOTES

Commencement order: SI 1989/816.

Sub-s (6): words in square brackets substituted by the Trade Marks Act 1994, s 106(1), Sch 4, para 8(2).

See further: the High Court and County Courts Jurisdiction Order 1991, SI 1991/724, arts 2(1)(n), 11, 12.

205 Jurisdiction of county court and sheriff court

(1) In England, Wales and Northern Ireland a county court may entertain proceedings under–

section 195 (order for delivery up of illicit recording), or

section 204 (order as to disposal of illicit recording),

[save that, in Northern Ireland, a county court may entertain such proceedings only] where the value of the illicit recordings in question does not exceed the county court limit for actions in tort.

(2) In Scotland proceedings for an order under either of those provisions may be brought in the sheriff court.

(3) Nothing in this section shall be construed as affecting the jurisdiction of the High Court or, in Scotland, the Court of Session.

NOTES

Commencement order: SI 1989/816.

Sub-s (1): words in square brackets added by SI 1991/724, art 2(8), Schedule, Part I.

[Licensing of performers' property rights]

[205A] [Licensing of performers' property rights]

[The provisions of Schedule 2A have effect with respect to the licensing of performers' property rights.]

NOTE

Added by SI 1996/2967, reg 22(1).

[Jurisdiction of Copyright Tribunal]

[205B] [Jurisdiction of Copyright Tribunal]

[(1) The Copyright Tribunal has jurisdiction under this Part to hear and determine proceedings under–

(a)   section 182D (amount of equitable remuneration for exploitation of commercial sound recording);
(b)   section 190 (application to give consent on behalf of owner of reproduction right);
(c)   section 191H (amount of equitable remuneration on transfer of rental right);
[(cc) paragraph 19 of Schedule (determining of royalty or other remuneration to be paid with respect to re-transmission of broadcast including performance or recording);]
(d)   paragraph 3,4 or 5 of Schedule 2A (reference of licensing scheme);
(e)   paragraph 6 or 7 of that Schedule (application with respect to licence under licensing scheme);
(f)   paragraph 10, 11 or 12 of that Schedule (reference or application with respect to licensing by licensing body);
(g)   paragraph 15 of that Schedule (application to settle royalty for certain lending);
(h)   paragraph 17 of that Schedule (application to settle terms of licence available as of right).

(2) The provisions of Chapter VIII of Part I (general provisions relating to the Copyright Tribunal) apply in relation to the Tribunal when exercising any jurisdiction under this Part.

(3) Provision shall be made by rules under section 150 prohibiting the Tribunal from entertaining a reference under paragraph 3,4 or 5 of Schedule 2A (reference of licensing scheme) by a representative organisation unless the Tribunal is satisfied that the organisation is reasonably representative of the class of persons which it claims to represent.]

NOTE
Added by SI 1996/2967, reg 24(1) and sub-para (cc) added by the Broadcasting Act 1996, s 138, Sch 9, para 4.

Qualification for protection and extent

206 Qualifying countries, individuals and persons
(1) In this Part–

'qualifying country' means–

(a)   the United Kingdom,
(b)   another member State of the European Economic Community, or
(c)   to the extent that an Order under section 208 so provides, a country designated under that section as enjoying reciprocal protection;

'qualifying individual' means a citizen or subject of, or an individual resident in, a qualifying country; and
'qualifying person' means a qualifying individual or a body corporate or other body having legal personality which–

(a)   is formed under the law of a part of the United Kingdom or another qualifying country, and
(b)   has in any qualifying country a place of business at which substantial business activity is carried on.

(2) The reference in the definition of 'qualifying individual' to a person's being a citizen or subject of a qualifying country shall be construed–

(a)   in relation to the United Kingdom, as a reference to his being a British citizen, and
(b)   in relation to a colony of the United Kingdom, as a reference to his being a British Dependent Territories' citizen by connection with that colony.

(3) In determining for the purpose of the definition of "qualifying person" whether substantial business activity is carried on at a place of business in any country, no account shall be taken of dealings in goods which are at all material times outside that country.

NOTE
Commencement order: SI 1989/816.

207 Countries to which this Part extends
This Part extends to England and Wales, Scotland and Northern Ireland.

NOTE
Commencement order: SI 1989/816.

208 Countries enjoying reciprocal protection
(1) Her Majesty may by Order in Council designate as enjoying reciprocal protection under this Part–

(a) a Convention country, or
(b) a country as to which Her Majesty is satisfied that provision has been or will be made under its law giving adequate protection for British performances.

(2) A 'Convention country' means a country which is a party to a Convention relating to performers' rights to which the United Kingdom is also a party.

(3) A 'British performance' means a performance–

(a) given by an individual who is a British citizen or resident in the United Kingdom, or
(b) taking place in the United Kingdom.

(4) If the law of that country provides adequate protection only for certain descriptions of performance, an Order under subsection (1)(b) designating that country shall contain provision limiting to a corresponding extent the protection afforded by this Part in relation to performances connected with that country.

(5) The power conferred by subsection (1)(b) is exercisable in relation to any of the Channel Islands, the Isle of Man or any colony of the United Kingdom, as in relation to a foreign country.

(6) A statutory instrument containing an Order in Council under this section shall be subject to annulment in pursuance of a resolution of either House of Parliament.

NOTE
Commencement orders: SI 1989/816, SI 1989/955, SI 1989/1032.

209 Territorial waters and the continental shelf
(1) For the purposes of this Part the territorial waters of the United Kingdom shall be treated as part of the United Kingdom.

(2) This Part applies to things done in the United Kingdom sector of the continental shelf on a structure or vessel which is present there for purposes directly connected with the exploration of the sea bed or subsoil or the exploitation of their natural resources as it applies to things done in the United Kingdom.

(3) The United Kingdom sector of the continental shelf means the areas designated by order under section 1(7) of the Continental Shelf Act 1964.

NOTE
Commencement order: SI 1989/816.

210 British ships, aircraft and hovercraft
(1) This Part applies to things done on a British ship, aircraft or hovercraft as it applies to things done in the United Kingdom.

(2) In this section–

'British ship' means a ship which is a British ship for the purposes of the [Merchant Shipping Act 1995] otherwise than by virtue of registration in a country outside the United Kingdom; and

'British aircraft' and 'British hovercraft' mean an aircraft or hovercraft registered in the United Kingdom.

NOTES
Commencement order: SI 1989/816.
Sub-s (2): in definition "British ship" words in square brackets substituted by the Merchant Shipping Act 1995, s 314(2), Sch 13, para 84(b).

Interpretation

211 Expressions having same meaning as in copyright provisions
(1) The following expressions have the same meaning in this Part as in Part I (copyright)–

> broadcast,
> business,
> cable programme,
> cable programme service,
> country,
> defendant (in Scotland),
> delivery up (in Scotland),
> [EEA national,]
> film,
> literary work,
> published, and
> sound recording.

(2) The provisions of section 6(3) to (5), section 7(5) and 19(4) (supplementary provisions relating to broadcasting and cable programme services) apply for the purposes of this Part, and in relation to an infringement of the rights conferred by this Part, as they apply for the purposes of Part I and in relation to an infringement of copyright.

NOTES
Commencement order: SI 1989/816.
Sub-s (1): words in square brackets added with savings by SI 1995/3297, reg 11(3); for savings see Part III thereof.

212 Index of defined expressions
The following Table shows provisions defining or otherwise explaining expressions used in this Part (other than provisions defining or explaining an expression used only in the same section)–

broadcast (and related expressions)	section 211 (and section 6)
business	section 211(1) (and section 178)
cable programme, cable programme service (and related expressions)	section 211 (and section 7)
[consent of performer (in relation to performer's property rights)	section 191A(2)]
country	section 211(1) (and section 178)
defendant (in Scotland)	section 211(1) (and section 177)
delivery up (in Scotland)	section 211(1) (and section 177)
[distribution right	section 182B(5)]
[EEA national	section 211(1) (and section 172A)]
exclusive recording contract	section 185(1)
film	section 211(1) (and [section 5B])
illicit recording	section 197
[lending right	section 182C(7)]
literary work	section 211(1) (and section 3(1))
performance	section 180(2)
[performer's non-property rights	section 192A(1)]
[performer's property rights	section 191A(1)]
published	section 211(1) (and section 175)
qualifying country	section 206(1)

qualifying individual	section 206(1) and (2)
qualifying performance	section 181
qualifying person	section 206(1) and (3)
recording (of a performance)	section 180(2)
recording rights (person having)	section 185(2) and (3)
[rental right	section 182C(7)]
[reproduction right	section 182A(3)]
[rights owner (in relation to performer's property rights)	section 191A(3) and (4)]
sound recording	section 211(1) (and [section 5A])

NOTES

Commencement order: SI 1989/816.

Entries beginning 'consent of performer' and 'rights owner' and entries 'distribution right', 'lending right', 'performer's non-property rights', 'performer's property rights', 'rental right' and 'reproduction right' added by SI 1996/2967, regs 20(4), 21(6); entry 'EEA national' added, and in entries 'film' and 'sound recording' words in square brackets substituted, by SI 1995/3297, regs 9(6), 11(4).

This section should be read in conjunction with the following provision of the the Duration of Copyright and Rights in Performances Regulations 1995, SI 1995/3297 (commencement: 1 January 1996):

Duration of Copyright and Rights in Performances Regulations 1995, reg 36(2) and (3)

Construction of references to EEA states

36–(2) For the purposes of the new provisions relating to the term of protection applicable to a performance where the performer is not a national of an EEA state, the performer of a performance given before 1st July 1995 shall be treated as an EEA national if he was on that date regarded under the law of the United Kingdom or another EEA state as a national of that state.

The reference above to the law of another EEA state is to the law of that state having effect for the purposes of rights corresponding to those provided for in Part II of the 1988 Act.

(3) In this Regulation 'another EEA state' means an EEA state other than the United Kingdom.

PART III
DESIGN RIGHT

CHAPTER I
DESIGN RIGHT IN ORIGINAL DESIGNS

Introductory

213 Design right

(1) Design right is a property right which subsists in accordance with this Part in an original design.

(2) In this Part 'design' means the design of any aspect of the shape or configuration (whether internal or external) of the whole or part of an article.

(3) Design right does not subsist in–

(a)   a method or principle of construction,

(b)   features of shape or configuration of an article which–

(i)   enable the article to be connected to, or placed in, around or against, another article so that either article may perform its function, or

(ii)   are dependent upon the appearance of another article of which the article is intended by the designer to form an integral part, or

(c)   surface decoration.

(4) A design is not 'original' for the purposes of this Part if it is commonplace in the design field in question at the time of its creation.

(5) Design right subsists in a design only if the design qualifies for design right protection by reference to–

(a) the designer or the person by whom the design was commissioned or the designer employed (see sections 218 and 219), or

(b) the person by whom and country in which articles made to the design were first marketed (see section 220),

or in accordance with any Order under section 221 (power to make further provision with respect to qualification).

[(5A) Design right does not subsist in a design which consists of or contains a controlled representation within the meaning of the Olympic Symbol etc (Protection) Act 1995.]

(6) Design right does not subsist unless and until the design has been recorded in a design document or an article has been made to the design.

(7) Design right does not subsist in a design which was so recorded, or to which an article was made, before the commencement of this Part.

NOTES
Commencement order: SI 1989/816.
Sub-s (5A): added, in relation to designs created on or after 20 September 1995, by the Olympic Symbol etc (Protection) Act 1995, s 14.
Modified, in relation to semiconductor topographies by the Design Right (Semiconductor Topographies) Regulations 1989, SI 1989/1100.

214 The designer
(1) In this Part the 'designer', in relation to a design, means the person who creates it.

(2) In the case of a computer-generated design the person by whom the arrangements necessary for the creation of the design are undertaken shall be taken to be the designer.

NOTES
Commencement order: SI 1989/816.
Modified in relation to semiconductor topographies by the Design Right (Semiconductor Topographies) Regulations 1989, SI 1989/1100.

215 Ownership of design right
(1) The designer is the first owner of any design right in a design which is not created in pursuance of a commission or in the course of employment.

(2) Where a design is created in pursuance of a commission, the person commissioning the design is the first owner of any design right in it.

(3) Where, in a case not falling within subsection (2) a design is created by an employee in the course of his employment, his employer is the first owner of any design right in the design.

(4) If a design qualifies for design right protection by virtue of section 220 (qualification by reference to first marketing of articles made to the design), the above rules do not apply and the person by whom the articles in question are marketed is the first owner of the design right.

NOTES
Commencement order: SI 1989/816.
Modified in relation to semiconductor topographies by the Design Right (Semiconductor Topographies) Regulations 1989, SI 1989/1100.

216 Duration of design right
(1) Design right expires–

(a) fifteen years from the end of the calendar year in which the design was first recorded in a design document or an article was first made to the design, whichever first occurred, or

(b) if articles made to the design are made available for sale or hire within five years from the end of that calendar year, ten years from the end of the calendar year in which that first occurred.

(2) The reference in subsection (1) to articles being made available for sale or hire is to their being made so available anywhere in the world by or with the licence of the design right owner.

NOTES
Commencement order: SI 1989/816.
Modified in relation to semiconductor topographies by the Design Right (Semiconductor Topographies) Regulations 1989, SI 1989/1100.

Qualification for design right protection

217 Qualifying individuals and qualifying persons
(1) In this Part–

'qualifying individual' means a citizen or subject of, or an individual habitually resident in, a qualifying country; and

'qualifying person' means a qualifying individual or a body corporate or other body having legal personality which–

(a)   is formed under the law of a part of the United Kingdom or another qualifying country, and

(b)   has in any qualifying country a place of business at which substantial business activity is carried on.

(2) References in this Part to a qualifying person include the Crown and the government of any other qualifying country.

(3) In this section 'qualifying country' means–

(a)   the United Kingdom,

(b)   a country to which this Part extends by virtue of an Order under section 255,

(c)   another member State of the European Economic Community, or

(d)   to the extent that an Order under section 256 so provides, a country designated under that section as enjoying reciprocal protection.

(4) The reference in the definition of 'qualifying individual' to a person's being a citizen or subject of a qualifying country shall be construed–

(a)   in relation to the United Kingdom, as a reference to his being a British citizen, and

(b)   in relation to a colony of the United Kingdom, as a reference to his being a British Dependent Territories' citizen by connection with that colony.

(5) In determining for the purpose of the definition of "qualifying person" whether substantial business activity is carried on at a place of business in any country, no account shall be taken of dealings in goods which are at all material times outside that country.

NOTES
Commencement order: SI 1989/816.
Modified in relation to semiconductor topographies by the Design Right (Semiconductor Topographies) Regulations 1989, SI 1989/1100.

218 Qualification by reference to designer
(1) This section applies to a design which is not created in pursuance of a commission or in the course of employment.

(2) A design to which this section applies qualifies for design right protection if the designer is a qualifying individual or, in the case of a computer-generated design, a qualifying person.

(3) A joint design to which this section applies qualifies for design right protection if any of the designers is a qualifying individual or, as the case may be, a qualifying person.

(4) Where a joint design qualifies for design right protection under this section, only those designers who are qualifying individuals or qualifying persons are entitled to design right under section 215(1) (first ownership of design right: entitlement of designer).

NOTES
Commencement order: SI 1989/816.
Modified in relation to semiconductor topographies by the Design Right (Semiconductor Topographies) Regulations 1989, SI 1989/1100.

219 Qualification by reference to commissioner or employer

(1) A design qualifies for design right protection if it is created in pursuance of a commission from, or in the course of employment with, a qualifying person.

(2) In the case of a joint commission or joint employment a design qualifies for design right protection if any of the commissioners or employers is a qualifying person.

(3) Where a design which is jointly commissioned or created in the course of joint employment qualifies for design right protection under this section, only those commissioners or employers who are qualifying persons are entitled to design right under section 215(2) or (3) (first ownership of design right: entitlement of commissioner or employer).

NOTES
Commencement order: SI 1989/816.
Modified in relation to semiconductor topographies by the Design Right (Semiconductor Topographies) Regulations 1989, SI 1989/1100.

220 Qualification by reference to first marketing

(1) A design which does not qualify for design right protection under section 218 or 219 (qualification by reference to designer, commissioner or employer) qualifies for design right protection if the first marketing of articles made to the design–

   (a) is by a qualifying person who is exclusively authorised to put such articles on the market in the United Kingdom, and

   (b) takes place in the United Kingdom, another country to which this Part extends by virtue of an Order under section 255, or another member State of the European Economic Community.

(2) If the first marketing of articles made to the design is done jointly by two or more persons, the design qualifies for design right protection if any of those persons meets the requirements specified in subsection (1)(a).

(3) In such a case only the persons who meet those requirements are entitled to design right under section 215(4) (first ownership of design right: entitlement of first marketer of articles made to the design).

(4) In subsection (1)(a) 'exclusively authorised' refers–

   (a) to authorisation by the person who would have been first owner of design right as designer, commissioner of the design or employer of the designer if he had been a qualifying person, or by a person lawfully claiming under such a person, and

   (b) to exclusivity capable of being enforced by legal proceedings in the United Kingdom.

NOTES
Commencement order: SI 1989/816.
Modified in relation to semiconductor topographies by the Design Right (Semiconductor Topographies) Regulations 1989, SI 1989/1100.

221 Power to make further provision as to qualification

(1) Her Majesty may, with a view to fulfilling an international obligation of the United Kingdom, by Order in Council provide that a design qualifies for design right protection if such requirements as are specified in the Order are met.

(2) An Order may make different provision for different descriptions of design or article; and may make such consequential modifications of the operation of section 215 (ownership of design right) and sections 218 to 220 (other means of qualification) as appear to Her Majesty to be appropriate.

(3) A statutory instrument containing an Order in Council under this section shall be subject to annulment in pursuance of a resolution of either House of Parliament.

NOTES
Commencement order: SI 1989/816.
Modified in relation to semiconductor topographies by the Design Right (Semiconductor Topographies) Regulations 1989, SI 1989/1100.

Dealings with design right

222   Assignment and licences

(1) Design right is transmissible by assignment, by testamentary disposition or by operation of law, as personal or moveable property.

(2) An assignment or other transmission of design right may be partial, that is, limited so as to apply–

(a)   to one or more, but not all, of the things the design right owner has the exclusive right to do;

(b)   to part, but not the whole, of the period for which the right is to subsist.

(3) An assignment of design right is not effective unless it is in writing signed by or on behalf of the assignor.

(4) A licence granted by the owner of design right is binding on every successor in title to his interest in the right, except a purchaser in good faith for valuable consideration and without notice (actual or constructive) of the licence or a person deriving title from such a purchaser; and references in this Part to doing anything with, or without, the licence of the design right owner shall be construed accordingly.

NOTES
Commencement order: SI 1989/816.
Modified in relation to semiconductor topographies by the Design Right (Semiconductor Topographies) Regulations 1989, SI 1989/1100.

223   Prospective ownership of design right

(1) Where by an agreement made in relation to future design right, and signed by or on behalf of the prospective owner of the design right, the prospective owner purports to assign the future design right (wholly or partially) to another person, then if, on the right coming into existence, the assignee or another person claiming under him would be entitled as against all other persons to require the right to be vested in him, the right shall vest in him by virtue of this section.

(2) In this section–

'future design right' means design right which will or may come into existence in respect of a future design or class of designs or on the occurrence of a future event; and

'prospective owner' shall be construed accordingly, and includes a person who is prospectively entitled to design right by virtue of such an agreement as is mentioned in subsection (1).

(3) A licence granted by a prospective owner of design right is binding on every successor in title to his interest (or prospective interest) in the right, except a purchaser in good faith for valuable consideration and without notice (actual or constructive) of the licence or a person deriving title from such a purchaser; and references in this Part to doing anything with, or without, the licence of the design right owner shall be construed accordingly.

NOTES
Commencement order: SI 1989/816.
Modified in relation to semiconductor topographies by the Design Right (Semiconductor Topographies) Regulations 1989, SI 1989/1100.

224   Assignment of right in registered design presumed to carry with it design right

Where a design consisting of a design in which design right subsists is registered under the Registered Designs Act 1949 and the proprietor of the registered design is also the design right owner, an assignment of the right in the registered design shall be taken to be also an assignment of the design right, unless a contrary intention appears.

NOTES
Commencement order: SI 1989/816.
Modified in relation to semiconductor topographies by the Design Right (Semiconductor Topographies) Regulations 1989, SI 1989/1100.

225 Exclusive licences

(1) In this Part an 'exclusive licence' means a licence in writing signed by or on behalf of the design right owner authorising the licensee to the exclusion of all other persons, including the person granting the licence, to exercise a right which would otherwise be exercisable exclusively by the design right owner.

(2) The licensee under an exclusive licence has the same rights against any successor in title who is bound by the licence as he has against the person granting the licence.

NOTES
Commencement order: SI 1989/816.
Modified in relation to semiconductor topographies by the Design Right (Semiconductor Topographies) Regulations 1989, SI 1989/1100.

CHAPTER II
RIGHTS OF DESIGN RIGHT OWNER AND REMEDIES

Infringement of design right

226 Primary infringement of design right

(1) The owner of design right in a design has the exclusive right to reproduce the design for commercial purposes–

(a) by making articles to that design, or
(b) by making a design document recording the design for the purpose of enabling such articles to be made.

(2) Reproduction of a design by making articles to the design means copying the design so as to produce articles exactly or substantially to that design, and references in this Part to making articles to a design shall be construed accordingly.

(3) Design right is infringed by a person who without the licence of the design right owner does, or authorises another to do, anything which by virtue of this section is the exclusive right of the design right owner.

(4) For the purposes of this section reproduction may be direct or indirect, and it is immaterial whether any intervening acts themselves infringe the design right.

(5) This section has effect subject to the provisions of Chapter III (exceptions to rights of design right owner).

NOTES
Commencement order: SI 1989/816.
Modified in relation to semiconductor topographies by the Design Right (Semiconductor Topographies) Regulations 1989, SI 1989/1100.

227 Secondary infringement: importing or dealing with infringing article

(1) Design right is infringed by a person who, without the licence of the design right owner–

(a) imports into the United Kingdom for commercial purposes, or
(b) has in his possession for commercial purposes, or

(c)   sells, lets for hire, or offers or exposes for sale or hire, in the course of a business,

an article which is, and which he knows or has reason to believe is, an infringing article.

(2) This section has effect subject to the provisions of Chapter III (exceptions to rights of design right owner).

NOTES
Commencement order: SI 1989/816.
Modified in relation to semiconductor topographies by the Design Right (Semiconductor Topographies) Regulations 1989, SI 1989/1100.

228 Meaning of 'infringing article'
(1) In this Part 'infringing article', in relation to a design, shall be construed in accordance with this section.

(2) An article is an infringing article if its making to that design was an infringement of design right in the design.

(3) An article is also an infringing article if–

(a)   it has been or is proposed to be imported into the United Kingdom, and
(b)   its making to that design in the United Kingdom would have been an infringement of design right in the design or a breach of an exclusive licence agreement relating to the design.

(4) Where it is shown that an article is made to a design in which design right subsists or has subsisted at any time, it shall be presumed until the contrary is proved that the article was made at a time when design right subsisted.

(5) Nothing in subsection (3) shall be construed as applying to an article which may lawfully be imported into the United Kingdom by virtue of any enforceable Community right within the meaning of section 2(1) of the European Communities Act 1972.

(6) The expression 'infringing article' does not include a design document, notwithstanding that its making was or would have been an infringement of design right.

NOTES
Commencement order: SI 1989/816.
Modified in relation to semiconductor topographies by the Design Right (Semiconductor Topographies) Regulations 1989, SI 1989/1100.

Remedies for infringement

229 Rights and remedies of design right owner
(1) An infringement of design right is actionable by the design right owner.

(2) In an action for infringement of design right all such relief by way of damages, injunctions, accounts or otherwise is available to the plaintiff as is available in respect of the infringement of any other property right.

(3) The court may in an action for infringement of design right, having regard to all the circumstances and in particular to–

(a)   the flagrancy of the infringement, and
(b)   any benefit accruing to the defendant by reason of the infringement,

award such additional damages as the justice of the case may require.

(4) This section has effect subject to section 233 (innocent infringement).

NOTES
Commencement order: SI 1989/816.
Modified in relation to semiconductor topographies by the Design Right (Semiconductor Topographies) Regulations 1989, SI 1989/1100.

230 Order for delivery up
(1) Where a person–

(a) has in his possession, custody or control for commercial purposes an infringing article, or

(b) has in his possession, custody or control anything specifically designed or adapted for making articles to a particular design, knowing or having reason to believe that it has been or is to be used to make an infringing article,

the owner of the design right in the design in question may apply to the court for an order that the infringing article or other thing be delivered up to him or to such other person as the court may direct.

(2) An application shall not be made after the end of the period specified in the following provisions of this section; and no order shall be made unless the court also makes, or it appears to the court that there are grounds for making, an order under section 231 (order as to disposal of infringing article, &c).

(3) An application for an order under this section may not be made after the end of the period of six years from the date on which the article or thing in question was made, subject to subsection (4).

(4) If during the whole or any part of that period the design right owner–

(a) is under a disability, or

(b) is prevented by fraud or concealment from discovering the facts entitling him to apply for an order,

an application may be made at any time before the end of the period of six years from the date on which he ceased to be under a disability or, as the case may be, could with reasonable diligence have discovered those facts.

(5) In subsection (4) 'disability'–

(a) in England and Wales, has the same meaning as in the Limitation Act 1980;

(b) in Scotland, means legal disability within the meaning of the Prescription and Limitation (Scotland) Act 1973;

(c) in Northern Ireland, has the same meaning as in the Statute of Limitations (Northern Ireland) 1958.

(6) A person to whom an infringing article or other thing is delivered up in pursuance of an order under this section shall, if an order under section 231 is not made, retain it pending the making of an order, or the decision not to make an order, under that section.

(7) Nothing in this section affects any other power of the court.

NOTES
Commencement order: SI 1989/816.
Modified in relation to semiconductor topographies by the Design Right (Semiconductor Topographies) Regulations 1989, SI 1989/1100.
See further: the High Court and County Courts Jurisdiction Order 1991, SI 1991/724, arts 2(1)(n), 11, 12.

---

231 Order as to disposal of infringing articles, &c
(1) An application may be made to the court for an order that an infringing article or other thing delivered up in pursuance of an order under section 230 shall be–

(a) forfeited to the design right owner, or

(b) destroyed or otherwise dealt with as the court may think fit,

or for a decision that no such order should be made.

(2) In considering what order (if any) should be made, the court shall consider whether other remedies available in an action for infringement of design right would be adequate to compensate the design right owner and to protect his interests.

(3) Provision shall be made by rules of court as to the service of notice on persons having an interest in the article or other thing, and any such person is entitled–

(a) to appear in proceedings for an order under this section, whether or not he was served with notice, and

(b)   to appeal against any order made, whether or not he appeared;

and an order shall not take effect until the end of the period within which notice of an appeal may be given or, if before the end of that period notice of appeal is duly given, until the final determination or abandonment of the proceedings on the appeal.

(4) Where there is more than one person interested in an article or other thing, the court shall make such order as it thinks just and may (in particular) direct that the thing be sold, or otherwise dealt with, and the proceeds divided.

(5) If the court decides that no order should be made under this section, the person in whose possession, custody or control the article or other thing was before being delivered up or seized is entitled to its return.

(6) References in this section to a person having an interest in an article or other thing include any person in whose favour an order could be made in respect of it under this section or under section 114 or 204 of this Act or [section 19 of the Trade Marks Act 1994] (which make similar provision in relation to infringement of copyright, rights in performances and trade marks).

NOTES

Commencement order: SI 1989/816.
Sub-s (6): words in square brackets substituted by the Trade Marks Act 1994, s 106(1), Sch 4, para 8(2).
Modified in relation to semiconductor topographies by the Design Right (Semiconductor Topographies) Regulations 1989, SI 1989/1100.
See further: the High Court and County Courts Jurisdiction Order 1991, SI 1991/724, arts 2(1)(n), 11, 12.

232 Jurisdiction of county court and sheriff court
(1) In England, Wales and Northern Ireland a county court may entertain proceedings under–

section 230 (order for delivery up of infringing article, &c),

section 231 (order as to disposal of infringing article, &c), or

section 235(5) (application by exclusive licensee having concurrent rights),

[save that, in Northern Ireland, a county court may entertain such proceedings only] where the value of the infringing articles and other things in question does not exceed the county court limit for actions in tort.

(2) In Scotland proceedings for an order under any of those provisions may be brought in the sheriff court.

(3) Nothing in this section shall be construed as affecting the jurisdiction of the High Court or, in Scotland, the Court of Session.

NOTES

Commencement order: SI 1989/816.
Sub-s (1): words in square brackets added by SI 1991/724, art 2(8), Schedule, Part I.
Modified in relation to semiconductor topographies by the Design Right (Semiconductor Topographies) Regulations 1989, SI 1989/1100.

233 Innocent infringement
(1) Where in an action for infringement of design right brought by virtue of section 226 (primary infringement) it is shown that at the time of the infringement the defendant did not know, and had no reason to believe, that design right subsisted in the design to which the action relates, the plaintiff is not entitled to damages against him, but without prejudice to any other remedy.

(2) Where in an action for infringement of design right brought by virtue of section 227 (secondary infringement) a defendant shows that the infringing article was innocently acquired by him or a predecessor in title of his, the only remedy available against him in respect of the infringement is damages not exceeding a reasonable royalty in respect of the act complained of.

(3) In subsection (2) 'innocently acquired' means that the person acquiring the article did not know and had no reason to believe that it was an infringing article.

NOTES
Commencement order: SI 1989/816.
Modified in relation to semiconductor topographies by the Design Right (Semiconductor Topographies) Regulations 1989, SI 1989/1100.

234 Rights and remedies of exclusive licensee

(1) An exclusive licensee has, except against the design right owner, the same rights and remedies in respect of matters occurring after the grant of the licence as if the licence had been an assignment.

(2) His rights and remedies are concurrent with those of the design right owner; and references in the relevant provisions of this Part to the design right owner shall be construed accordingly.

(3) In an action brought by an exclusive licensee by virtue of this section a defendant may avail himself of any defence which would have been available to him if the action had been brought by the design right owner.

NOTES
Commencement order: SI 1989/816.
Modified in relation to semiconductor topographies by the Design Right (Semiconductor Topographies) Regulations 1989, SI 1989/1100.

235 Exercise of concurrent rights

(1) Where an action for infringement of design right brought by the design right owner or an exclusive licensee relates (wholly or partly) to an infringement in respect of which they have concurrent rights of action, the design right owner or, as the case may be, the exclusive licensee may not, without the leave of the court, proceed with the action unless the other is either joined as a plaintiff or added as a defendant.

(2) A design right owner or exclusive licensee who is added as a defendant in pursuance of subsection (1) is not liable for any costs in the action unless he takes part in the proceedings.

(3) The above provisions do not affect the granting of interlocutory relief on the application of the design right owner or an exclusive licensee.

(4) Where an action for infringement of design right is brought which relates (wholly or partly) to an infringement in respect of which the design right owner and an exclusive licensee have concurrent rights of action—

    (a)   the court shall, in assessing damages, take into account—

        (i)   the terms of the licence, and

        (ii) any pecuniary remedy already awarded or available to either of them in respect of the infringement;

    (b)   no account of profits shall be directed if an award of damages has been made, or an account of profits has been directed, in favour of the other of them in respect of the infringement; and

    (c)   the court shall if an account of profits is directed apportion the profits between them as the court considers just, subject to any agreement between them;

and these provisions apply whether or not the design right owner and the exclusive licensee are both parties to the action.

(5) The design right owner shall notify any exclusive licensee having concurrent rights before applying for an order under section 230 (order for delivery up of infringing article, &c); and the court may on the application of the licensee make such order under that section as it thinks fit having regard to the terms of the licence.

NOTES
Commencement order: SI 1989/816.
Modified in relation to semiconductor topographies by the Design Right (Semiconductor Topographies) Regulations 1989, SI 1989/1100.
See further: the High Court and County Courts Jurisdiction Order 1991, SI 1991/724, arts 2(1)(n), 11, 12.

CHAPTER III
EXCEPTIONS TO RIGHTS OF DESIGN RIGHT OWNERS

Infringement of copyright

236 Infringement of copyright

Where copyright subsists in a work which consists of or includes a design in which design right subsists, it is not an infringement of design right in the design to do anything which is an infringement of the copyright in that work.

NOTES
Commencement order: SI 1989/816.
Modified in relation to semiconductor topographies by the Design Right (Semiconductor Topographies) Regulations 1989, SI 1989/1100.

Availability of licences of right

237 Licences available in last five years of design right

(1) Any person is entitled as of right to a licence to do in the last five years of the design right term anything which would otherwise infringe the design right.

(2) The terms of the licence shall, in default of agreement, be settled by the comptroller.

(3) The Secretary of State may if it appears to him necessary in order to–

(a)   comply with an international obligation of the United Kingdom, or
(b)   secure or maintain reciprocal protection for British designs in other countries,

by order exclude from the operation of subsection (1) designs of a description specified in the order or designs applied to articles of a description so specified.

(4) An order shall be made by statutory instrument; and no order shall be made unless a draft of it has been laid before and approved by a resolution of each House of Parliament.

NOTES
Commencement order: SI 1989/974/816.
Modified in relation to semiconductor topographies by the Design Right (Semiconductor Topographies) Regulations 1989, SI 1989/1100.

238 Powers exercisable for protection of the public interest

(1) Where the matters specified in a report of the Monopolies and Mergers Commission as being those which in the Commission's opinion operate, may be expected to operate or have operated against the public interest include–

(a)   conditions in licences granted by a design right owner restricting the use of the design by the licensee or the right of the design right owner to grant other licences, or
(b)   a refusal of a design right owner to grant licences on reasonable terms,

the powers conferred by Part I of Schedule 8 to the Fair Trading Act 1973 (powers exercisable for purpose of remedying or preventing adverse effects specified in report of Commission) include power to cancel or modify those conditions and, instead or in addition, to provide that licences in respect of the design right shall be available as of right.

(2) The references in sections 56(2) and 73(2) of that Act, and sections 10(2)(b) and 12(5) of the Competition Act 1980, to the powers specified in that Part of that Schedule shall be construed accordingly.

(3) The terms of a licence available by virtue of this section shall, in default of agreement, be settled by the comptroller.

NOTES
Commencement order: SI 1989/816.
Modified in relation to semiconductor topographies by the Design Right (Semiconductor Topographies) Regulations 1989, SI 1989 No 1100.

239 Undertaking to take licence of right in infringement proceedings

(1) If in proceedings for infringement of design right in a design in respect of which a licence is available as of right under section 237 or 238 the defendant undertakes to take a licence on such terms as may be agreed or, in default of agreement, settled by the comptroller under that section–

(a)   no injunction shall be granted against him,

(b)   no order for delivery up shall be made under section 230, and

(c)   the amount recoverable against him by way of damages or on an account of profits shall not exceed double the amount which would have been payable by him as licensee if such a licence on those terms had been granted before the earliest infringement.

(2) An undertaking may be given at any time before final order in the proceedings, without any admission of liability.

(3) Nothing in this section affects the remedies available in respect of an infringement committed before licences of right were available.

NOTES

Commencement order: SI 1989/816.

Modified in relation to semiconductor topographies by the Design Right (Semiconductor Topographies) Regulations 1989, SI 1989/1100.

240 Crown use of designs

(1) A government department, or a person authorised in writing by a government department, may without the licence of the design right owner–

(a)   do anything for the purpose of supplying articles for the services of the Crown, or

(b)   dispose of articles no longer required for the services of the Crown;

and nothing done by virtue of this section infringes the design right.

(2) References in this Part to 'the services of the Crown' are to–

(a)   the defence of the realm,

(b)   foreign defence purposes, and

(c)   health service purposes.

(3) The reference to the supply of articles for "foreign defence purposes" is to their supply–

(a)   for the defence of a country outside the realm in pursuance of an agreement or arrangement to which the government of that country and Her Majesty's Government in the United Kingdom are parties; or

(b)   for use by armed forces operating in pursuance of a resolution of the United Nations or one of its organs.

(4) The reference to the supply of articles for "health service purposes" are to their supply for the purpose of providing–

(a)   pharmaceutical services,

(b)   general medical services, or

(c)   general dental services,

that is, services of those kinds under Part II of the National Health Service Act 1977, Part II of the National Health Service (Scotland) Act 1978 or the corresponding provisions of the law in force in Northern Ireland.

[(a)   pharmaceutical services, general medical services or general dental services under–

(i)   Part II of the National Health Service Act 1977,

(ii)   Part II of the National Health Service (Scotland) Act 1978, or

(iii)   the corresponding provisions of the law in force in Northern Ireland; or

(b)   personal medical services or personal dental services in accordance with arrangements made under–

(i)   section 28C of the 1977 Act,

    (ii)   section 17C of the 1978 Act, or

    (iii)   the corresponding provisions of the law in force in Northern Ireland.]

(5) In this Part–

    'Crown use', in relation to a design, means the doing of anything by virtue of this section which would otherwise be an infringement of design right in the design; and

    'the government department concerned', in relation to such use, means the government department by whom or on whose authority the act was done.

(6) The authority of a government department in respect of Crown use of a design may be given to a person either before or after the use and whether or not he is authorised, directly or indirectly, by the design right owner to do anything in relation to the design.

(7) A person acquiring anything sold in the exercise of powers conferred by this section, and any person claiming under him, may deal with it in the same manner as if the design right were held on behalf of the Crown.

NOTES

Commencement order: SI 1989/816.

Sub-s (4): words underlined prospectively repealed and subsequent words in square brackets prospectively substituted by the National Health Service (Primary Care) Act 1997, s 41(10), Sch 2, para 63, as from a day to be appointed.

Modified in relation to semiconductor topographies by the Design Right (Semiconductor Topographies) Regulations 1989, SI 1989/1100.

241 Settlement of terms for Crown use

(1) Where Crown use is made of a design, the government department concerned shall–

    (a)   notify the design right owner as soon as practicable, and

    (b)   give him such information as to the extent of the use as he may from time to time require,

unless it appears to the department that it would be contrary to the public interest to do so or the identity of the design right owner cannot be ascertained on reasonable inquiry.

(2) Crown use of a design shall be on such terms as, either before or after the use, are agreed between the government department concerned and the design right owner with the approval of the Treasury or, in default of agreement, are determined by the court.

In the application of this subsection to Northern Ireland the reference to the Treasury shall, where the government department referred to in that subsection is a Northern Ireland department, be construed as a reference to the Department of Finance and Personnel.

(3) Where the identity of the design right owner cannot be ascertained on reasonable inquiry, the government department concerned may apply to the court who may order that no royalty or other sum shall be payable in respect of Crown use of the design until the owner agrees terms with the department or refers the matter to the court for determination.

NOTES

Commencement order: SI 1989/816.

Modified in relation to semiconductor topographies by the Design Right (Semiconductor Topographies) Regulations 1989, SI 1989/1100.

242 Rights of third parties in case of Crown use

(1) The provisions of any licence, assignment or agreement made between the design right owner (or anyone deriving title from him or from whom he derives title) and any person other than a government department are of no effect in relation to Crown use of a design, or any act incidental to Crown use, so far as they–

    (a)   restrict or regulate anything done in relation to the design, or the use of any model, document or other information relating to it, or

    (b)   provide for the making of payments in respect of, or calculated by reference to such use;

and the copying or issuing to the public of copies of any such model or document in connection with the thing done, or any such use, shall be deemed not to be an infringement of any copyright in the model or document.

(2) Subsection (1) shall not be construed as authorising the disclosure of any such model, document or information in contravention of the licence, assignment or agreement.

(3) Where an exclusive licence is in force in respect of the design–

    (a) if the licence was granted for royalties–

        (i) any agreement between the design right owner and a government department under section 241 (settlement of terms for Crown use) requires the consent of the licensee, and

        (ii) the licensee is entitled to recover from the design right owner such part of the payment for Crown use as may be agreed between them or, in default of agreement, determined by the court;

    (b) if the licence was granted otherwise than for royalties–

        (i) section 241 applies in relation to anything done which but for section 240 (Crown use) and subsection (1) above would be an infringement of the rights of the licensee with the substitution for references to the design right owner of references to the licensee, and

        (ii) section 241 does not apply in relation to anything done by the licensee by virtue of an authority given under section 240.

(4) Where the design right has been assigned to the design right owner in consideration of royalties–

    (a) section 241 applies in relation to Crown use of the design as if the references to the design right owner included the assignor, and any payment for Crown use shall be divided between them in such proportion as may be agreed or, in default of agreement, determined by the court; and

    (b) section 241 applies in relation to any act incidental to Crown use as it applies in relation to Crown use of the design.

(5) Where any model, document or other information relating to a design is used in connection with Crown use of the design, or any act incidental to Crown use, section 241 applies to the use of the model, document or other information with the substitution for the references to the design right owner of references to the person entitled to the benefit of any provision of an agreement rendered inoperative by subsection (1) above.

(6) In this section–

    'act incidental to Crown use' means anything done for the services of the Crown to the order of a government department by the design right owner in respect of a design;

    'payment for Crown use' means such amount as is payable by the government department concerned by virtue of section 241; and

    'royalties' includes any benefit determined by reference to the use of the design.

NOTES

Commencement order: SI 1989/816.

Modified in relation to semiconductor topographies by the Design Right (Semiconductor Topographies) Regulations 1989, SI 1989/1100.

243 Crown use: compensation for loss of profit

(1) Where Crown use is made of a design, the government department concerned shall pay–

    (a) to the design right owner, or

    (b) if there is an exclusive licence in force in respect of the design, to the exclusive licensee,

compensation for any loss resulting from his not being awarded a contract to supply the articles made to the design.

(2) Compensation is payable only to the extent that such a contract could have been fulfilled from his existing manufacturing capacity; but is payable notwithstanding the existence of circumstances rendering him ineligible for the award of such a contract.

(3) In determining the loss, regard shall be had to the profit which would have been made on such a contract and to the extent to which any manufacturing capacity was under-used.

(4) No compensation is payable in respect of any failure to secure contracts for the supply of articles made to the design otherwise than for the services of the Crown.

(5) The amount payable shall, if not agreed between the design right owner or licensee and the government department concerned with the approval of the Treasury, be determined by the court on a reference under section 252; and it is in addition to any amount payable under section 241 or 242.

(6) In the application of this section to Northern Ireland, the reference in subsection (5) to the Treasury shall, where the government department concerned is a Northern Ireland department, be construed as a reference to the Department of Finance and Personnel.

NOTES

Commencement order: SI 1989/816.

Modified in relation to semiconductor topographies by the Design Right (Semiconductor Topographies) Regulations 1989, SI 1989/1100.

244 Special provision for Crown use during emergency

(1) During a period of emergency the powers exercisable in relation to a design by virtue of section 240 (Crown use) include power to do any act which would otherwise be an infringement of design right for any purpose which appears to the government department concerned necessary or expedient–

(a) for the efficient prosecution of any war in which Her Majesty may be engaged;
(b) for the maintenance of supplies and services essential to the life of the community;
(c) for securing a sufficiency of supplies and services essential to the well-being of the community;
(d) for promoting the productivity of industry, commerce and agriculture;
(e) for fostering and directing exports and reducing imports, or imports of any classes, from all or any countries and for redressing the balance of trade;
(f) generally for ensuring that the whole resources of the community are available for use, and are used, in a manner best calculated to serve the interests of the community; or
(g) for assisting the relief of suffering and the restoration and distribution of essential supplies and services in any country outside the United Kingdom which is in grave distress as the result of war.

(2) References in this Part to the services of the Crown include, as respects a period of emergency, those purposes; and references to 'Crown use' include any act which would apart from this section be an infringement of design right.

(3) In this section 'period of emergency' means a period beginning with such date as may be declared by Order in Council to be the beginning, and ending with such date as may be so declared to be the end, of a period of emergency for the purposes of this section.

(4) No Order in Council under this section shall be submitted to Her Majesty unless a draft of it has been laid before and approved by a resolution of each House of Parliament.

NOTES

Commencement order: SI 1989/816.

Modified in relation to semiconductor topographies by the Design Right (Semiconductor Topographies) Regulations 1989, SI 1989/1100.

General

245 Power to provide for further exceptions

(1) The Secretary of State may if it appears to him necessary in order to–

(a) comply with an international obligation of the United Kingdom, or
(b) secure or maintain reciprocal protection for British designs in other countries,

by order provide that acts of a description specified in the order do not infringe design right.

(2) An order may make different provision for different descriptions of design or article.

(3) An order shall be made by statutory instrument and no order shall be made unless a draft of it has been laid before and approved by a resolution of each House of Parliament.

NOTES

Commencement order: SI 1989/816.

Modified in relation to semiconductor topographies by the Design Right (Semiconductor Topographies) Regulations 1989, SI 1989/1100.

CHAPTER IV
JURISDICTION OF THE COMPTROLLER AND THE COURT

Jurisdiction of the comptroller

246 Jurisdiction to decide matters relating to design right

(1) A party to a dispute as to any of the following matters may refer the dispute to the comptroller for his decision–

  (a)   the subsistence of design right,
  (b)   the term of design right, or
  (c)   the identity of the person in whom design right first vested;

and the comptroller's decision on the reference is binding on the parties to the dispute.

(2) No other court or tribunal shall decide any such matter except–

  (a)   on a reference or appeal from the comptroller,
  (b)   in infringement or other proceedings in which the issue arises incidentally, or
  (c)   in proceedings brought with the agreement of the parties or the leave of the comptroller.

(3) The comptroller has jurisdiction to decide any incidental question of fact or law arising in the course of a reference under this section.

NOTES

Commencement order: SI 1989/816.

Modified in relation to semiconductor topographies by the Design Right (Semiconductor Topographies) Regulations 1989, SI 1989/1100.

247 Application to settle terms of licence of right

(1) A person requiring a licence which is available as of right by virtue of–

  (a)   section 237 (licences available in last five years of design right), or
  (b)   an order under section 238 (licences made available in the public interest),

may apply to the comptroller to settle the terms of the licence.

(2) No application for the settlement of the terms of a licence available by virtue of section 237 may be made earlier than one year before the earliest date on which the licence may take effect under that section.

(3) The terms of a licence settled by the comptroller shall authorise the licensee to do–

  (a)   in the case of licence available by virtue of section 237, everything which would be an infringement of the design right in the absence of a licence;
  (b)   in the case of a licence available by virtue of section 238, everything in respect of which a licence is so available.

(4) In settling the terms of a licence the comptroller shall have regard to such factors as may be prescribed by the Secretary of State by order made by statutory instrument.

(5) No such order shall be made unless a draft of it has been laid before and approved by a resolution of each House of Parliament.

(6) Where the terms of a licence are settled by the comptroller, the licence has effect–

(a) in the case of an application in respect of a licence available by virtue of section 237 made before the earliest date on which the licence may take effect under that section, from that date;

(b) in any other case, from the date on which the application to the comptroller was made.

NOTES

Commencement order: SI 1989/816.

Modified in relation to semiconductor topographies by the Design Right (Semiconductor Topographies) Regulations 1989, SI 1989/1100.

248 Settlement of terms where design right owner unknown

(1) This section applies where a person making an application under section 247 (settlement of terms of licence of right) is unable on reasonable inquiry to discover the identity of the design right owner.

(2) The comptroller may in settling the terms of the licence order that the licence shall be free of any obligation as to royalties or other payments.

(3) If such an order is made the design right owner may apply to the comptroller to vary the terms of the licence with effect from the date on which his application is made.

(4) If the terms of a licence are settled by the comptroller and it is subsequently established that a licence was not available as of right, the licensee shall not be liable in damages for, or for an account of profits in respect of, anything done before he was aware of any claim by the design right owner that a licence was not available.

NOTES

Commencement order: SI 1989/816.

Modified in relation to semiconductor topographies by the Design Right (Semiconductor Topographies) Regulations 1989, SI 1989/1100.

249 Appeals as to terms of licence of right

(1) An appeal lies from any decision of the comptroller under section 247 or 248 (settlement of terms of licence of right) to the Appeal Tribunal constituted under section 28 of the Registered Designs Act 1949.

(2) Section 28 of that Act applies to appeals from the comptroller under this section as it applies to appeals from the registrar under that Act; but rules made under that section may make different provision for appeals under this section.

NOTES

Commencement order: SI 1989/816.

Modified in relation to semiconductor topographies by the Design Right (Semiconductor Topographies) Regulations 1989, SI 1989/1100.

250 Rules

(1) The Secretary of State may make rules for regulating the procedure to be followed in connection with any proceeding before the comptroller under this Part.

(2) Rules may, in particular, make provision–

(a) prescribing forms;

(b) requiring fees to be paid;

(c) authorising the rectification of irregularities of procedure;

(d) regulating the mode of giving evidence and empowering the comptroller to compel the attendance of witnesses and the discovery of and production of documents;

(e) providing for the appointment of advisers to assist the comptroller in proceedings before him;

(f) prescribing time limits for doing anything required to be done (and providing for the alteration of any such limit); and

(g) empowering the comptroller to award costs and to direct how, to what party and from what parties, costs are to be paid.

(3) Rules prescribing fees require the consent of the Treasury.

(4) The remuneration of an adviser appointed to assist the comptroller shall be determined by the Secretary of State with the consent of the Treasury and shall be defrayed out of money provided by Parliament.

(5) Rules shall be made by statutory instrument which shall be subject to annulment in pursuance of a resolution of either House of Parliament.

NOTES
Commencement orders: SI 1989/816, SI 1989/955, SI 1989/1032.

Modified in relation to semiconductor topographies by the Design Right (Semiconductor Topographies) Regulations 1989, SI 1989/1100.

Jurisdiction of the court

251 References and appeals on design right matters
(1) In any proceedings before him under section 246 (reference of matter relating to design right), the comptroller may at any time order the whole proceedings or any question or issue (whether of fact or law) to be referred, on such terms as he may direct, to the High Court or, in Scotland, the Court of Session.

(2) The comptroller shall make such an order if the parties to the proceedings agree that he should do so.

(3) On a reference under this section the court may exercise any power available to the comptroller by virtue of this Part as respects the matter referred to it and, following its determination, may refer any matter back to the comptroller.

(4) An appeal lies from any decision of the comptroller in proceedings before him under section 246 (decisions on matters relating to design right) to the High Court or, in Scotland, the Court of Session.

NOTES
Commencement order: SI 1989/816.

Modified in relation to semiconductor topographies by the Design Right (Semiconductor Topographies) Regulations 1989, SI 1989/1100.

252 Reference of disputes relating to Crown use
(1) A dispute as to any matter which falls to be determined by the court in default of agreement under–

    (a)   section 241 (settlement of terms for Crown use),

    (b)   section 242 (rights of third parties in case of Crown use), or

    (c)   section 243 (Crown use: compensation for loss of profit),

may be referred to the court by any party to the dispute.

(2) In determining a dispute between a government department and any person as to the terms for Crown use of a design the court shall have regard to–

    (a)   any sums which that person or a person from whom he derives title has received or is entitled to receive, directly or indirectly, from any government department in respect of the design; and

    (b)   whether that person or a person from whom he derives title has in the court's opinion without reasonable cause failed to comply with a request of the department for the use of the design on reasonable terms.

(3) One of two or more joint owners of design right may, without the concurrence of the others, refer a dispute to the court under this section, but shall not do so unless the others are made parties; and none of those others is liable for any costs unless he takes part in the proceedings.

(4) Where the consent of an exclusive licensee is required by section 242(3)(*a*)(i) to the settlement by agreement of the terms for Crown use of a design, a determination by the court of the amount of any payment to be made for such use is of no effect unless the licensee has been notified of the reference and given an opportunity to be heard.

(5) On the reference of a dispute as to the amount recoverable as mentioned in section 242(3)(*a*)(ii) (right of exclusive licensee to recover part of amount payable to design right owner) the court shall determine what is just having regard to any expenditure incurred by the licensee–

- (a) in developing the design, or
- (b) in making payments to the design right owner in consideration of the licence (other than royalties or other payments determined by reference to the use of the design).

(6) In this section 'the court' means–

- (a) in England and Wales, the High Court or any patents county court having jurisdiction by virtue of an order under section 287 of this Act,
- (b) in Scotland, the Court of Session, and
- (c) in Northern Ireland, the High Court.

NOTES

Commencement order: SI 1989/816.

Modified in relation to semiconductor topographies by the Design Right (Semiconductor Topographies) Regulations 1989, SI 1989/1100.

CHAPTER V
MISCELLANEOUS AND GENERAL

Miscellaneous

253 Remedy for groundless threats of infringement proceedings

(1) Where a person threatens another person with proceedings for infringement of design right, a person aggrieved by the threats may bring an action against him claiming–

- (a) a declaration to the effect that the threats are unjustifiable;
- (b) an injunction against the continuance of the threats;
- (c) damages in respect of any loss which he has sustained by the threats.

(2) If the plaintiff proves that the threats were made and that he is a person aggrieved by them, he is entitled to the relief claimed unless the defendant shows that the acts in respect of which proceedings were threatened did constitute, or if done would have constituted, an infringement of the design right concerned.

(3) Proceedings may not be brought under this section in respect of a threat to bring proceedings for an infringement alleged to consist of making or importing anything.

(4) Mere notification that a design is protected by design right does not constitute a threat of proceedings for the purposes of this section.

NOTES

Commencement order: SI 1989/816.

Modified in relation to semiconductor topographies by the Design Right (Semiconductor Topographies) Regulations 1989, SI 1989/1100.

254 Licensee under licence of right not to claim connection with design right owner

(1) A person who has a licence in respect of a design by virtue of section 237 or 238 (licences of right) shall not, without the consent of the design right owner–

- (a) apply to goods which he is marketing, or proposes to market, in reliance on that licence a trade description indicating that he is the licensee of the design right owner, or
- (b) use any such trade description in an advertisement in relation to such goods.

(2) A contravention of subsection (1) is actionable by the design right owner.

(3) In this section 'trade description', the reference to applying a trade description to goods and 'advertisement' have the same meaning as in the Trade Descriptions Act 1968.

NOTES
Commencement order: SI 1989/816.
Modified in relation to semiconductor topographies by the Design Right (Semiconductor Topographies) Regulations 1989, SI 1989/1100.

Extent of operation of this Part

255 Countries to which this Part extends

(1) This Part extends to England and Wales, Scotland and Northern Ireland.

(2) Her Majesty may by Order in Council direct that this Part shall extend, subject to such exceptions and modifications as may be specified in the Order, to–

(a)   any of the Channel Islands,

(b)   the Isle of Man, or

(c)   any colony.

(3) That power includes power to extend, subject to such exceptions and modifications as may be specified in the Order, any Order in Council made under section 221 (further provision as to qualification for design right protection) or section 256 (countries enjoying reciprocal protection).

(4) The legislature of a country to which this Part has been extended may modify or add to the provisions of this Part, in their operation as part of the law of that country, as the legislature may consider necessary to adapt the provisions to the circumstances of that country; but not so as to deny design right protection in a case where it would otherwise exist.

(5) Where a country to which this Part extends ceases to be a colony of the United Kingdom, it shall continue to be treated as such a country for the purposes of this Part until–

(a)   an Order in Council is made under section 256 designating it as a country enjoying reciprocal protection, or

(b)   an Order in Council is made declaring that it shall cease to be so treated by reason of the fact that the provisions of this Part as part of the law of that country have been amended or repealed.

(6) A statutory instrument containing an Order in Council under subsection (5)(b) shall be subject to annulment in pursuance of a resolution of either House of Parliament.

NOTES
Commencement order: SI 1989/816.
Modified in relation to semiconductor topographies by the Design Right (Semiconductor Topographies) Regulations 1989, SI 1989/1100.

256 Countries enjoying reciprocal protection

(1) Her Majesty may, if it appears to Her that the law of a country provides adequate protection for British designs, by Order in Council designate that country as one enjoying reciprocal protection under this Part.

(2) If the law of a country provides adequate protection only for certain classes of British design, or only for designs applied to certain classes of article, any Order designating that country shall contain provision limiting, to a corresponding extent, the protection afforded by this Part in relation to designs connected with that country.

(3) An Order under this section shall be subject to annulment in pursuance of a resolution of either House of Parliament.

NOTES
Commencement orders: SI 1989/816, SI 1989/955, SI 1989/1032.
Modified in relation to semiconductor topographies by the Design Right (Semiconductor Topographies) Regulations 1989, SI 1989/1100.

257 Territorial waters and the continental shelf

(1) For the purposes of this Part the territorial waters of the United Kingdom shall be treated as part of the United Kingdom.

(2) This Part applies to things done in the United Kingdom sector of the continental shelf on a structure or vessel which is present there for purposes directly connected with the exploration of the sea bed or subsoil or the exploitation of their natural resources as it applies to things done in the United Kingdom.

(3) The United Kingdom sector of the continental shelf means the areas designated by order under section 1(7) of the Continental Shelf Act 1964.

NOTES
Commencement order: SI 1989/816.
Modified in relation to semiconductor topographies by the Design Right (Semiconductor Topographies) Regulations 1989, SI 1989/1100.

Interpretation

258 Construction of references to design right owner
(1) Where different persons are (whether in consequence of a partial assignment or otherwise) entitled to different aspects of design right in a work, the design right owner for any purpose of this Part is the person who is entitled to the right in the respect relevant for that purpose.

(2) Where design right (or any aspect of design right) is owned by more than one person jointly, references in this Part to the design right owner are to all the owners, so that, in particular, any requirement of the licence of the design right owner requires the licence of all of them.

NOTES
Commencement order: SI 1989/816.
Modified in relation to semiconductor topographies by the Design Right (Semiconductor Topographies) Regulations 1989, SI 1989/1100.

259 Joint designs
(1) In this Part a 'joint design' means a design produced by the collaboration of two or more designers in which the contribution of each is not distinct from that of the other or others.

(2) References in this Part to the designer of a design shall, except as otherwise provided, be construed in relation to a joint design as references to all the designers of the design.

NOTES
Commencement order: SI 1989/816.
Modified in relation to semiconductor topographies by the Design Right (Semiconductor Topographies) Regulations 1989, SI 1989/1100.

260 Application of provisions to articles in kit form
(1) The provisions of this Part apply in relation to a kit, that is, a complete or substantially complete set of components intended to be assembled into an article, as they apply in relation to the assembled article.

(2) Subsection (1) does not affect the question whether design right subsists in any aspect of the design of the components of a kit as opposed to the design of the assembled article.

NOTES
Commencement order: SI 1989/816.
Modified in relation to semiconductor topographies by the Design Right (Semiconductor Topographies) Regulations 1989, SI 1989/1100.

261 Requirement of signature: application in relation to body corporate
The requirement in the following provisions that an instrument be signed by or on behalf of a person is also satisfied in the case of a body corporate by the affixing of its seal–

   section 222(3) (assignment of design right),
   section 223(1) (assignment of future design right),
   section 225(1) (grant of exclusive licence).

NOTES
Commencement order: SI 1989/816.
Modified in relation to semiconductor topographies by the Design Right (Semiconductor Topographies) Regulations 1989, SI 1989/1100.

262 Adaptation of expressions in relation to Scotland

In the application of this Part to Scotland–

'account of profits' means accounting and payment of profits;
'accounts' means count, reckoning and payment;
'assignment' means assignation;
'costs' means expenses;
'defendant' means defender;
'delivery up' means delivery;
'injunction' means interdict;
'interlocutory relief' means interim remedy; and
'plaintiff' means pursuer.

NOTES
Commencement order: SI 1989/816.
Modified in relation to semiconductor topographies by the Design Right (Semiconductor Topographies) Regulations 1989, SI 1989/1100.

263 Minor definitions

(1) In this Part–

'British design' means a design which qualifies for design right protection by reason of a connection with the United Kingdom of the designer or the person by whom the design is commissioned or the designer is employed;
'business' includes a trade or profession;
'commission' means a commission for money or money's worth;
'the comptroller' means the Comptroller-General of Patents, Designs and Trade Marks;
'computer-generated', in relation to a design, means that the design is generated by computer in circumstances such that there is no human designer,
'country' includes any territory;
'the Crown' includes the Crown in right of Her Majesty's Government in Northern Ireland;
'design document' means any record of a design, whether in the form of a drawing, a written description, a photograph, data stored in a computer or otherwise;
'employee', 'employment' and 'employer' refer to employment under a contract of service or of apprenticeship;
'government department' includes a Northern Ireland department.

(2) References in this Part to 'marketing', in relation to an article, are to its being sold or let for hire, or offered or exposed for sale or hire, in the course of a business, and related expressions shall be construed accordingly; but no account shall be taken for the purposes of this Part of marketing which is merely colourable and not intended to satisfy the reasonable requirements of the public.

(3) References in this Part to an act being done in relation to an article for "commercial purposes" are to its being done with a view to the article in question being sold or hired in the course of a business.

NOTES
Commencement order: SI 1989/816.
Modified in relation to semiconductor topographies by the Design Right (Semiconductor Topographies) Regulations 1989, SI 1989/1100.

264 Index of defined expressions

The following Table shows provisions defining or otherwise explaining expressions used in this Part (other than provisions defining or explaining an expression used only in the same section)–

account of profits and accounts (in Scotland)	section 262
assignment (in Scotland)	section 262
British designs	section 263(1)
business	section 263(1)
commercial purposes	section 263(3)
commission	section 263(1)
the comptroller	section 263(1)
computer-generated	section 263(1)
costs (in Scotland)	section 262
country	section 263(1)
the Crown	section 263(1)
Crown use	sections 240(5) and 244(2)
defendant (in Scotland)	section 262
delivery up (in Scotland)	section 262
design	section 213(2)
design document	section 263(1)
designer	sections 214 and 259(2)
design right	section 213(1)
design right owner	sections 234(2) and 258
employee, employment and employer	section 263(1)
exclusive licence	section 225(1)
government department	section 263(1)
government department concerned (in relation to Crown use)	section 240(5)
infringing article	section 228
injunction (in Scotland)	section 262
interlocutory relief (in Scotland)	section 262
joint design	section 259(1)
licence (of the design right owner)	sections 222(4), 223(3) and 258
making articles to a design	section 226(2)
marketing (and related expressions)	section 263(2)
original	section 213(4)
plaintiff (in Scotland)	section 262
qualifying individual	section 217(1)
qualifying person	sections 217(1) and (2)
signed	section 261

NOTES

Commencement order: SI 1989/816.

Modified in relation to semiconductor topographies by the Design Right (Semiconductor Topographies) Regulations 1989, SI 1989/1100.

PART IV
REGISTERED DESIGNS

Amendments of the Registered Designs Act 1949

265 Registrable designs

(1) . . .

(2) The above amendment does not apply in relation to applications for registration made before the commencement of this Part; but the provisions of section 266 apply with respect to the right in certain designs registered in pursuance of such an application.

266 Provisions with respect to certain designs registered in pursuance of application made before commencement

(1) Where a design is registered under the Registered Designs Act 1949 in pursuance of an application made after 12th January 1988 and before the commencement of this Part which could not have been registered under section 1 of that Act as substituted by section 265 above–

   (a)   the right in the registered design expires ten years after the commencement of this Part, if it does not expire earlier in accordance with the 1949 Act, and

   (b)   any person is, after the commencement of this Part, entitled as of right to a licence to do anything which would otherwise infringe the right in the registered design.

(2) The terms of a licence available by virtue of this section shall, in default of agreement, be settled by the registrar on an application by the person requiring the licence; and the terms so settled shall authorise the licensee to do everything which would be an infringement of the right in the registered design in the absence of a licence.

(3) In settling the terms of a licence the registrar shall have regard to such factors as may be prescribed by the Secretary of State by order made by statutory instrument.

No such order shall be made unless a draft of it has been laid before and approved by a resolution of each House of Parliament.

(4) Where the terms of a licence are settled by the registrar, the licence has effect from the date on which the application to the registrar was made.

(5) Section 11B of the 1949 Act (undertaking to take licence of right in infringement proceedings), as inserted by section 270 below, applies where a licence is available as of right under this section, as it applies where a licence is available as of right under section 11A of that Act.

(6) Where a licence is available as of right under this section, a person to whom a licence was granted before the commencement of this Part may apply to the registrar for an order adjusting the terms of that licence.

(7) An appeal lies from any decision of the registrar under this section.

(8) This section shall be construed as one with the Registered Designs Act 1949.

267 Authorship and first ownership of designs

(1)–(3) . . .

(4) The amendments made by this section do not apply in relation to an application for registration made before the commencement of this Part.

268 Right given by registration of design

(1) . . .

(2) The above amendment does not apply in relation to a design registered in pursuance of an application made before the commencement of this Part.

269 Duration of right in registered design

(1) . . .

(2) The above amendment does not apply in relation to the right in a design registered in pursuance of an application made before the commencement of this Part.

NOTES

Commencement order: SI 1989/816.

Sub-s (1): substitutes the Registered Designs Act 1949, ss 8, 8A, 8B, for existing s 8.

270 Powers exercisable for protection of the public interest

. . .

NOTES

Commencement order: SI 1989/816.

This section adds the Registered Designs Act 1949, ss 11A, 11B.

271 Crown use: compensation for loss of profit

(1), (2) . . .

(3) The above amendments apply in relation to any Crown use of a registered design after the commencement of this section, even if the terms for such use were settled before commencement.

NOTES

Commencement order: SI 1989/816.

Sub-ss (1), (2): add the Registered Designs Act 1949, Sch 1, para 2A, and substitute Sch 1, para 3(1).

272 Minor and consequential amendments

The Registered Designs Act 1949 is further amended in accordance with Schedule 3 which contains minor amendments and amendments consequential upon the provisions of this Act.

NOTE

Commencement orders: SI 1989/816, SI 1990/1400.

Supplementary

273 Text of Registered Designs Act 1949 as amended

Schedule 4 contains the text of the Registered Designs Act 1949 as amended.

NOTE

Commencement order: SI 1990/1400.

PART V
PATENT AGENTS AND TRADE MARK AGENTS

Patent agents

274 Persons permitted to carry on business of a patent agent

(1) Any individual, partnership or body corporate may, subject to the following provisions of this Part, carry on the business of acting as agent for others for the purpose of–

(a)   applying for or obtaining patents, in the United Kingdom or elsewhere, or

(b)   conducting proceedings before the comptroller relating to applications for, or otherwise in connection with, patents.

(2) This does not affect any restriction under the European Patent Convention as to who may act on behalf of another for any purpose relating to European patents.

NOTES
Commencement order: SI 1990/1400.

275 The register of patent agents

(1) The Secretary of State may make rules requiring the keeping of a register of persons who act as agent for others for the purposes of applying for or obtaining patents; and in this Part a 'registered patent agent' means a person whose name is entered in the register kept under this section.

(2) The rules may contain such provision as the Secretary of State thinks fit regulating the registration of persons, and may in particular–

(a) require the payment of such fees as may be prescribed, and

(b) authorise in prescribed cases the erasure from the register of the name of any person registered in it, or the suspension of a person's registration.

(3) The rules may delegate the keeping of the register to another person, and may confer on that person–

(a) power to make regulations–

  (i) with respect to the payment of fees, in the cases and subject to the limits prescribed by rules, and

  (ii) with respect to any other matter which could be regulated by rules, and

(b) such other functions, including disciplinary functions, as may be prescribed by rules.

(4) Rules under this section shall be made by statutory instrument which shall be subject to annulment in pursuance of a resolution of either House of Parliament.

NOTE
Commencement order: SI 1990/1400.

276 Persons entitled to describe themselves as patent agents

(1) An individual who is not a registered patent agent shall not–

(a) carry on a business (otherwise than in partnership) under any name or other description which contains the words 'patent agent' or 'patent attorney'; or

(b) in the course of a business otherwise describe himself, or permit himself to be described, as a 'patent agent' or 'patent attorney'.

(2) A partnership shall not–

(a) carry on a business under any name or other description which contains the words 'patent agent' or 'patent attorney'; or

(b) in the course of a business otherwise describe itself, or permit itself to be described as, a firm of 'patent agents' or 'patent attorneys',

unless all the partners are registered patent agents or the partnership satisfies such conditions as may be prescribed for the purposes of this section.

(3) A body corporate shall not–

(a) carry on a business (otherwise than in partnership) under any name or other description which contains the words 'patent agent' or 'patent attorney'; or

(b) in the course of a business otherwise describe itself, or permit itself to be described as, a 'patent agent' or 'patent attorney',

unless all the directors of the body corporate are registered patent agents or the body satisfies such conditions as may be prescribed for the purposes of this section.

(4) Subsection (3) does not apply to a company which began to carry on business as a patent agent before 17th November 1917 if the name of a director or the manager of the company who

is a registered patent agent is mentioned as being so registered in all professional advertisements, circulars or letters issued by or with the company's consent on which its name appears.

(5) Where this section would be contravened by the use of the words 'patent agent' or 'patent attorney' in reference to an individual, partnership or body corporate, it is equally contravened by the use of other expressions in reference to that person, or his business or place of business, which are likely to be understood as indicating that he is entitled to be described as a 'patent agent' or 'patent attorney'.

(6) A person who contravenes this section commits an offence and is liable on summary conviction to a fine not exceeding level 5 on the standard scale; and proceedings for such an offence may be begun at any time within a year from the date of the offence.

(7) This section has effect subject to–

(a) section 277 (persons entitled to describe themselves as European patent attorneys, &c), and

(b) section 278(1) (use of term 'patent attorney' in reference to solicitors).

NOTES

Commencement order: SI 1990/1400.

Modification: any reference to solicitor(s) etc modified to include references to bodies recognised under the Administration of Justice Act 1985, s 9, by the Solicitors' Incorporated Practices Order 1991, SI 1991/2684, arts 4, 5, Sch 1.

277 Persons entitled to describe themselves as European patent attorneys, &c

(1) The term 'European patent attorney' or 'European patent agent' may be used in the following cases without any contravention of section 276.

(2) An individual who is on the European list may–

(a) carry on business under a name or other description which contains the words 'European patent attorney' or 'European patent agent', or

(b) otherwise describe himself, or permit himself to be described, as a 'European patent attorney' or 'European patent agent'.

(3) A partnership of which not less than the prescribed number or proportion of partners is on the European list may–

(a) carry on a business under a name or other description which contains the words 'European patent attorneys' or 'European patent agents', or

(b) otherwise describe itself, or permit itself to be described, as a firm which carries on the business of a 'European patent attorney' or 'European patent agent'.

(4) A body corporate of which not less than the prescribed number or proportion of directors is on the European list may–

(a) carry on a business under a name or other description which contains the words 'European patent attorney' or 'European patent agent', or

(b) otherwise describe itself, or permit itself to be described as, a company which carries on the business of a 'European patent attorney' or 'European patent agent'.

(5) Where the term 'European patent attorney' or 'European patent agent' may, in accordance with this section, be used in reference to an individual, partnership or body corporate, it is equally permissible to use other expressions in reference to that person, or to his business or place of business, which are likely to be understood as indicating that he is entitled to be described as a 'European patent attorney' or 'European patent agent.'

NOTES

Commencement order: SI 1990/1400.

278 Use of the term 'patent attorney': supplementary provisions

(1) The term 'patent attorney' may be used in reference to a solicitor, and a firm of solicitors may be described as a firm of 'patent attorneys', without any contravention of section 276.

(2) No offence is committed under the enactments restricting the use of certain expressions in reference to persons not qualified to act as solicitors–

- (a) by the use of the term 'patent attorney' in reference to a registered patent agent, or
- (b) by the use of the term 'European patent attorney' in reference to a person on the European list.

(3) The enactments referred to in subsection (2) are section 21 of the Solicitors Act 1974, section 31 of the Solicitors (Scotland) Act 1980 and Article 22 of the Solicitors (Northern Ireland) Order 1976.

NOTES
Commencement order: SI 1990/1400.
Modified by the Solicitors' Incorporated Practices Order 1991, SI 1991/2684, arts 4, 5, Sch 2.

279 Power to prescribe conditions, &c for mixed partnerships and bodies corporate

(1) The Secretary of State may make rules–

- (a) prescribing the conditions to be satisfied for the purposes of section 276 (persons entitled to describe themselves as patent agents) in relation to a partnership where not all the partners are qualified persons or a body corporate where not all the directors are qualified persons, and
- (b) imposing requirements to be complied with by such partnerships and bodies corporate.

(2) The rules may, in particular–

- (a) prescribe conditions as to the number or proportion of partners or directors who must be qualified persons;
- (b) impose requirements as to–
  - (i) the identification of qualified and unqualified persons in professional advertisements, circulars or letters issued by or with the consent of the partnership or body corporate and which relate to it or to its business; and
  - (ii) the manner in which a partnership or body corporate is to organise its affairs so as to secure that qualified persons exercise a sufficient degree of control over the activities of unqualified persons.

(3) Contravention of a requirement imposed by the rules is an offence for which a person is liable on summary conviction to a fine not exceeding level 5 on the standard scale.

(4) The Secretary of State may make rules prescribing for the purposes of section 277 the number or proportion of partners of a partnership or directors of a body corporate who must be qualified persons in order for the partnership or body to take advantage of that section.

(5) In this section 'qualified person'–

- (a) in subsections (1) and (2), means a person who is a registered patent agent, and
- (b) in subsection (4), means a person who is on the European list.

(6) Rules under this section shall be made by statutory instrument which shall be subject to annulment in pursuance of a resolution of either House of Parliament.

NOTES
Commencement order: SI 1990/1400.

280 Privilege for communications with patent agents

(1) This section applies to communications as to any matter relating to the protection of any invention, design, technical information, [or trade mark], or as to any matter involving passing off.

(2) Any such communication–

- (a) between a person and his patent agent, or
- (b) for the purpose of obtaining, or in response to a request for, information which a person is seeking for the purpose of instructing his patent agent,

is privileged from disclosure in legal proceedings in England, Wales or Northern Ireland in the same way as a communication between a person and his solicitor or, as the case may be, a communication for the purpose of obtaining, or in response to a request for, information which a person seeks for the purpose of instructing his solicitor.

(3) In subsection (2) 'patent agent' means–

    (a)   a registered patent agent or a person who is on the European list,

    (b)   a partnership entitled to describe itself as a firm of patent agents or as a firm carrying on the business of a European patent attorney, or

    (c)   a body corporate entitled to describe itself as a patent agent or as a company carrying on the business of a European patent attorney.

(4) It is hereby declared that in Scotland the rules of law which confer privilege from disclosure in legal proceedings in respect of communications extend to such communications as are mentioned in this section.

NOTES
Commencement order: SI 1990/1400.
Sub-s (1): words in square brackets substituted by the Trade Marks Act 1994, s 106(1), Sch 4, para 8(3).
Modification: references to trade marks or registered trade marks within the meaning of the Trade Marks Act 1938 shall, unless the context otherwise requires, be construed as references to trade marks or registered trade marks within the meaning of the Trade Marks Act 1994; see the Trade Marks Act 1994, Sch 4, para 1.

281 Power of comptroller to refuse to deal with certain agents

(1) This section applies to business under the Patents Act 1949, the Registered Designs Act 1949 or the Patents Act 1977.

(2) The Secretary of State may make rules authorising the comptroller to refuse to recognise as agent in respect of any business to which this section applies–

    (a)   a person who has been convicted of an offence under section 88 of the Patents Act 1949, section 114 of the Patents Act 1977 or section 276 of this Act;

    (b)   an individual whose name has been erased from and not restored to, or who is suspended from, the register of patent agents on the ground of misconduct;

    (c)   a person who is found by the Secretary of State to have been guilty of such conduct as would, in the case of an individual registered in the register of patent agents, render him liable to have his name erased from the register on the ground of misconduct;

    (d)   a partnership or body corporate of which one of the partners or directors is a person whom the comptroller could refuse to recognise under paragraph (a), (b) or (c) above.

(3) The rules may contain such incidental and supplementary provisions as appear to the Secretary of State to be appropriate and may, in particular, prescribe circumstances in which a person is or is not to be taken to have been guilty of misconduct.

(4) Rules made under this section shall be made by statutory instrument which shall be subject to annulment in pursuance of a resolution of either House of Parliament.

(5) The comptroller shall refuse to recognise as agent in respect of any business to which this section applies a person who neither resides nor has a place of business in the United Kingdom, the Isle of Man or another member State of the European Economic Community.

NOTES
Commencement order: SI 1990/1400.

282–284 (*Repealed, with savings, by the Trade Marks Act 1994, ss 105, 106(2), Sch 3, para 22(1), Sch 5.*)

Supplementary

285 Offences committed by partnerships and bodies corporate

(1) Proceedings for an offence under this Part alleged to have been committed by a partnership shall be brought in the name of the partnership and not in that of the partners; but without prejudice to any liability of theirs under subsection (4) below.

(2) The following provisions apply for the purposes of such proceedings as in relation to a body corporate–

    (a)   any rules of court relating to the service of documents;

    (b)   in England, Wales or Northern Ireland, Schedule 3 to the Magistrates' Courts Act 1980 or Schedule 4 to the Magistrates' Courts (Northern Ireland) Order 1981 (procedure on charge of offence).

(3) A fine imposed on a partnership on its conviction in such proceedings shall be paid out of the partnership assets.

(4) Where a partnership is guilty of an offence under this Part, every partner, other than a partner who is proved to have been ignorant of or to have attempted to prevent the commission of the offence, is also guilty of the offence and liable to be proceeded against and punished accordingly.

(5) Where an offence under this Part committed by a body corporate is proved to have been committed with the consent or connivance of a director, manager, secretary or other similar officer of the body, or a person purporting to act in any such capacity, he as well as the body corporate is guilty of the offence and liable to be proceeded against and punished accordingly.

NOTES
Commencement order: SI 1990/1400.

286 Interpretation
In this Part–

'the comptroller' means the Comptroller-General of Patents, Designs and Trade Marks;
'director', in relation to a body corporate whose affairs are managed by its members, means any member of the body corporate;
'the European list' means the list of professional representatives maintained by the European Patent Office in pursuance of the European Patent Convention;
'registered patent agent' has the meaning given by section 275(1);

NOTES
Commencement order: SI 1990/1400.
Definition omitted repealed by the Trade Marks Act 1994, s 106(2), Sch 5.

PART VI
PATENTS

Patents county courts

287 Patents county courts: special jurisdiction
(1) The Lord Chancellor may by order made by statutory instrument designate any county court as a patents county court and confer on it jurisdiction (its "special jurisdiction") to hear and determine such descriptions of proceedings–

    (a)   relating to patents or designs, or

    (b)   ancillary to, or arising out of the same subject matter as, proceedings relating to patents or designs,

as may be specified in the order.

(2) The special jurisdiction of a patents county court is exercisable throughout England and Wales, but rules of court may provide for a matter pending in one such court to be heard and determined in another or partly in that and partly in another.

(3) A patents county court may entertain proceedings within its special jurisdiction notwithstanding that no pecuniary remedy is sought.

248 *Part 2*

(4) An order under this section providing for the discontinuance of any of the special jurisdiction of a patents county court may make provision as to proceedings pending in the court when the order comes into operation.

(5) Nothing in this section shall be construed as affecting the ordinary jurisdiction of a county court.

NOTES
Commencement order: SI 1989/816.
This section does not extend to Scotland.

288 Financial limits in relation to proceedings within special jurisdiction of patents county court

(1) Her Majesty may by Order in Council provide for limits of amount or value in relation to any description of proceedings within the special jurisdiction of a patents county court.

(2) If a limit is imposed on the amount of a claim of any description and the plaintiff has a cause of action for more than that amount, he may abandon the excess; in which case a patents county court shall have jurisdiction to hear and determine the action, but the plaintiff may not recover more than that amount.

(3) Where the court has jurisdiction to hear and determine an action by virtue of subsection (2), the judgment of the court in the action is in full discharge of all demands in respect of the cause of action, and entry of the judgment shall be made accordingly.

(4) If the parties agree, by a memorandum signed by them or by their respective solicitors or other agents, that a patents county court shall have jurisdiction in any proceedings, that court shall have jurisdiction to hear and determine the proceedings notwithstanding any limit imposed under this section.

(5) No recommendation shall be made to Her Majesty to make an Order under this section unless a draft of the Order has been laid before and approved by a resolution of each House of Parliament.

NOTES
Commencement order: SI 1989/816.
Modification: any reference to solicitor(s) etc modified to include references to bodies recognised under the Administration of Justice Act 1985, s 9, by the Solicitors' Incorporated Practices Order 1991, SI 1991/2684, arts 4, 5, Sch 1.
This section does not extend to Scotland.

289 Transfer of proceedings between High Court and patents county court

(1) No order shall be made under section 41 of the County Courts Act 1984 (power of High Court to order proceedings to be transferred from the county court) in respect of proceedings within the special jurisdiction of a patents county court.

(2) In considering in relation to proceedings within the special jurisdiction of a patents county court whether an order should be made under section 40 or 42 of the County Courts Act 1984 (transfer of proceedings from or to the High Court), the court shall have regard to the financial position of the parties and may order the transfer of the proceedings to a patents county court or, as the case may be, refrain from ordering their transfer to the High Court notwithstanding that the proceedings are likely to raise an important question of fact or law.

NOTES
Commencement order: SI 1989/816.
This section does not extend to Scotland.

290 Limitation of costs where pecuniary claim could have been brought in patents county court

(1) Where an action is commenced in the High Court which could have been commenced in a patents county court and in which a claim for a pecuniary remedy is made, then, subject to the provisions of this section, if the plaintiff recovers less than the prescribed amount, he is not entitled to recover any more costs than those to which he would have been entitled if the action had been brought in the county court.

(2) For this purpose a plaintiff shall be treated as recovering the full amount recoverable in respect of his claim without regard to any deduction made in respect of matters not falling to be taken into account in determining whether the action could have been commenced in a patents county court.

(3) This section does not affect any question as to costs if it appears to the High Court that there was reasonable ground for supposing the amount recoverable in respect of the plaintiff's claim to be in excess of the prescribed amount.

(4) The High Court, if satisfied that there was sufficient reason for bringing the action in the High Court, may make an order allowing the costs or any part of the costs on the High Court scale or on such one of the county court scales as it may direct.

(5) This section does not apply to proceedings brought by the Crown.

(6) In this section 'the prescribed amount' means such amount as may be prescribed by Her Majesty for the purposes of this section by Order in Council.

(7) No recommendation shall be made to Her Majesty to make an Order under this section unless a draft of the Order has been laid before and approved by a resolution of each House of Parliament.

NOTES

Commencement order: SI 1989/816.
This section is prospectively repealed by the Courts and Legal Services Act 1990, s 125(7), Sch 20, as from a day to be appointed.
This section does not extend to Scotland.

291 Proceedings in patents county court

(1) Where a county court is designated a patents county court, the Lord Chancellor shall nominate a person entitled to sit as a judge of that court as the patents judge.

(2) County court rules shall make provision for securing that, so far as is practicable and appropriate–

(a) proceedings within the special jurisdiction of a patents county court are dealt with by the patents judge, and

(b) the judge, rather than a registrar or other officer of the court, deals with interlocutory matters in the proceedings.

(3) County court rules shall make provision empowering a patents county court in proceedings within its special jurisdiction, on or without the application of any party–

(a) to appoint scientific advisers or assessors to assist the court, or

(b) to order the Patent Office to inquire into and report on any question of fact or opinion.

(4) Where the court exercises either of those powers on the application of a party, the remuneration or fees payable to the Patent Office shall be at such rate as may be determined in accordance with county court rules and shall be costs of the proceedings unless otherwise ordered by the judge.

(5) Where the court exercises either of those powers of its own motion, the remuneration or fees payable to the Patent Office shall be at such rate as may be determined by the Lord Chancellor with the approval of the Treasury and shall be paid out of money provided by Parliament.

NOTES

Commencement order: SI 1989/816.
This section does not extend to Scotland.

292 Rights and duties of registered patent agents in relation to proceedings in patents county court

(1) A registered patent agent may do, in or in connection with proceedings in a patents county court which are within the special jurisdiction of that court, anything which a solicitor of the Supreme Court might do, other than prepare a deed.

(2) The Lord Chancellor may by regulations provide that the right conferred by subsection (1) shall be subject to such conditions and restrictions as appear to the Lord Chancellor to be necessary or expedient; and different provision may be made for different descriptions of proceedings.

(3) A patents county court has the same power to enforce an undertaking given by a registered patent agent acting in pursuance of this section as it has, by virtue of section 142 of the County Courts Act 1984, in relation to a solicitor.

(4) Nothing in section 143 of the County Courts Act 1984 (prohibition on persons other than solicitors receiving remuneration) applies to a registered patent agent acting in pursuance of this section.

(5) The provisions of county court rules prescribing scales of costs to be paid to solicitors apply in relation to registered patent agents acting in pursuance of this section.

(6) Regulations under this section shall be made by statutory instrument which shall be subject to annulment in pursuance of a resolution of either House of Parliament.

NOTES
Commencement order: SI 1989/816.
This section does not extend to Scotland.

Licences of right in respect of certain patents

293 Restriction of acts authorised by certain licences

NOTE
This section amends the Patents Act 1977, Sch 1, para 4, and adds Sch 1, para 4A.

294 When application may be made for settlement of terms of licence

NOTE
This section adds the Patents Act 1977, Sch 1, para 4B.

Patents: miscellaneous amendments

295 Patents: miscellaneous amendments
The Patents Act 1949 and the Patents Act 1977 are amended in accordance with Schedule 5.

NOTE
Commencement orders: SI 1989/816, SI 1990/1400, SI 1990/2168.

PART VII
MISCELLANEOUS AND GENERAL

Devices designed to circumvent copy-protection

296 Devices designed to circumvent copy-protection
(1) This section applies where copies of a copyright work are issued to the public, by or with the licence of the copyright owner, in an electronic form which is copy-protected.

(2) The person issuing the copies to the public has the same rights against a person who, knowing or having reason to believe that it will be used to make infringing copies—

  (a) makes, imports, sells or lets for hire, offers or exposes for sale or hire, or advertises for sale or hire, any device or means specifically designed or adapted to circumvent the form of copy-protection employed, or

  (b) publishes information intended to enable or assist persons to circumvent that form of copy-protection,

as a copyright owner has in respect of an infringement of copyright.

[(2A) Where the copies being issued to the public as mentioned in subsection (1) are copies of a computer program, subsection (2) applies as if for the words 'or advertises for sale or hire' there were substituted 'advertises for sale or hire or possesses in the course of a business'.]

(3) Further, he has the same rights under section 99 or 100 (delivery up or seizure of certain articles) in relation to any such device or means which a person has in his possession, custody or control with the intention that it should be used to make infringing copies of copyright works, as a copyright owner has in relation to an infringing copy.

(4) References in this section to copy-protection include any device or means intended to prevent or restrict copying of a work or to impair the quality of copies made.

(5) Expressions used in this section which are defined for the purposes of Part I of this Act (copyright) have the same meaning as in that Part.

(6) The following provisions apply in relation to proceedings under this section as in relation to proceedings under Part I (copyright)–

(a)   sections 104 to 106 of this Act (presumptions as to certain matters relating to copyright), and

(b)   section 72 of the Supreme Court Act 1981, section 15 of the Law Reform (Miscellaneous Provisions) (Scotland) Act 1985 and section 94A of the Judicature (Northern Ireland) Act 1978 (withdrawal of privilege against self-incrimination in certain proceedings relating to intellectual property);

and section 114 of this Act applies, with the necessary modifications, in relation to the disposal of anything delivered up or seized by virtue of subsection (3) above.

NOTES
Commencement order: SI 1989/816.
Sub-s (2A): added by SI 1992/3233, reg 10.

[Computer programs]

[296A]   [Avoidance of certain terms]
[(1) Where a person has the use of a computer program under an agreement, any term or condition in the agreement shall be void in so far as it purports to prohibit or restrict–

(a)   the making of any back up copy of the program which it is necessary for him to have for the purposes of the agreed use;

(b)   where the conditions in section 50B(2) are met, the decompiling of the program; or

(c)   the use of any device or means to observe, study or test the functioning of the program in order to understand the ideas and principles which underlie any element of the program.

(2) In this section, decompile, in relation to a computer program, has the same meaning as in section 50B.]

NOTE
Added by SI 1992/3233, reg 11.

[296B   Avoidance of certain terms relating to databases]
[Where under an agreement a person has a right to use a database or part of a database, any term or condition in the agreement shall be void in so far as it purports to prohibit or restrict the performance of any act which would but for section 50D infringe the copyright in the database.]

NOTE
Added by SI 1997/3032, reg 10.

Fraudulent reception of transmissions

297   Offence of fraudulently receiving programmes

(1) A person who dishonestly receives a programme included in a broadcasting or cable programme service provided from a place in the United Kingdom with intent to avoid payment of any charge applicable to the reception of the programme commits an offence and is liable on summary conviction to a fine not exceeding level 5 on the standard scale.

(2) Where an offence under this section committed by a body corporate is proved to have been committed with the consent or connivance of a director, manager, secretary or other similar officer of the body, or a person purporting to act in any such capacity, he as well as the body corporate is guilty of the offence and liable to be proceeded against and punished accordingly.

In relation to a body corporate whose affairs are managed by its members 'director' means a member of the body corporate.

NOTES
Commencement order: SI 1989/816.
See further: the Fraudulent Reception of Transmissions (Guernsey) Order 1989, SI 1989/2003, art 2.

[297A]   [Unauthorised decoders]

[(1) A person who makes, imports, sells or lets for hire, offers or exposes for sale or hire, or advertises for sale or hire, any unauthorised decoder shall be guilty of an offence and liable–

  (a)   on summary conviction, to a fine not exceeding the statutory maximum;
  (b)   on conviction on indictment, to imprisonment for a term not exceeding two years, or to a fine, or to both.]

(2) It is a defence to any prosecution for an offence under this section for the defendant to prove that he did not know, and had no reasonable ground for knowing, that the decoder was an unauthorised decoder.

(3) In this section–

'apparatus' includes any device, component or electronic data;
'decoder' means any apparatus which is designed or adapted to enable (whether on its own or with any other apparatus) an encrypted transmission to be decoded;
'transmission' means any programme included in a broadcasting or cable programme service which is provided from a place in the United Kingdom; and
'unauthorised', in relation to a decoder, means a decoder which will enable encrypted transmissions to be viewed in decoded form without payment of the fee (however imposed) which the person making the transmission, or on whose behalf it is made, charges for viewing those transmissions, or viewing any service of which they form part.]

NOTES
This section was added by the Broadcasting Act 1990, s 179(1).
Sub-s (1): substituted with savings by the Broadcasting Act 1996, s 140.

298   Rights and remedies in respect of apparatus, &c for unauthorised reception of transmissions

(1) A person who–

  (a)   makes charges for the reception of programmes included in a broadcasting or cable programme service provided from a place in the United Kingdom, or
  (b)   sends encrypted transmissions of any other description from a place in the United Kingdom,

is entitled to the following rights and remedies.

(2) He has the same rights and remedies against a person who–

  (a)   makes, imports or sells or lets for hire[, offers or exposes for sale or hire, or advertises for sale or hire,] any apparatus or device designed or adapted to enable or assist persons to receive the programmes or other transmissions when they are not entitled to do so, or

  (b) publishes any information which is calculated to enable or assist persons to receive the programmes or other transmissions when they are not entitled to do so,

as a copyright owner has in respect of an infringement of copyright.

(3) Further, he has the same rights under section 99 or 100 (delivery up or seizure of certain articles) in relation to any such apparatus or device as a copyright owner has in relation to an infringing copy.

(4) Section 72 of the Supreme Court Act 1981, section 15 of the Law Reform (Miscellaneous Provisions) (Scotland) Act 1985 and section 94A of the Judicature (Northern Ireland) Act 1978 (withdrawal of privilege against self-incrimination in certain proceedings relating to intellectual property) apply to proceedings under this section as to proceedings under Part I of this Act (copyright).

(5) In section 97(1) (innocent infringement of copyright) as it applies to proceedings for infringement of the rights conferred by this section, the reference to the defendant not knowing or having reason to believe that copyright subsisted in the work shall be construed as a reference to his not knowing or having reason to believe that his acts infringed the rights conferred by this section.

(6) Section 114 of this Act applies, with the necessary modifications, in relation to the disposal of anything delivered up or seized by virtue of subsection (3) above.

NOTES

    Commencement order: SI 1989/816.

    Sub-s (2): in para (a) words in square brackets added by the Broadcasting Act 1996, s 141.

    See further: the Fraudulent Reception of Transmissions (Guernsey) Order 1989, SI 1989/2003, art 2.

299 Supplementary provisions as to fraudulent reception

(1) Her Majesty may by Order in Council–

  (a) provide that section 297 applies in relation to programmes included in services provided from a country or territory outside the United Kingdom, and

  (b) provide that section 298 applies in relation to such programmes and to encrypted transmissions sent from such a country or territory.

(2) . . .

(3) A statutory instrument containing an Order in Council under subsection (1) shall be subject to annulment in pursuance of a resolution of either House of Parliament.

(4) Where sections 297 and 298 apply in relation to a broadcasting service or cable programme service, they also apply to any service run for the person providing that service, or a person providing programmes for that service, which consists wholly or mainly in the sending by means of a telecommunications system of sounds or visual images, or both.

(5) In sections 297 [, 297A] and 298, and this section, 'programme', 'broadcasting' and 'cable programme service', and related expressions, have the same meaning as in Part I (copyright).

NOTES

    Commencement order: SI 1989/816.

    Sub-s (2): repealed by the Broadcasting Act 1990, ss 179(2), 203(3), Sch 21.

    Sub-s (5): figure in square brackets added by the Broadcasting Act 1990, s 179(2).

300 *(Repealed by the Trade Marks Act 1994, s 106(2), Sch 5.)*

Provisions for the benefit of the Hospital for Sick Children

301 Provisions for the benefit of the Hospital for Sick Children

The provisions of Schedule 6 have effect for conferring on trustees for the benefit of the Hospital for Sick Children, Great Ormond Street, London, a right to a royalty in respect of the public performance, commercial publication, broadcasting or inclusion in a cable programme service of the play "Peter Pan" by Sir James Matthew Barrie, or of any adaptation of that work, notwithstanding that copyright in the work expired on 31st December 1987.

Financial assistance for certain international bodies

302 Financial assistance for certain international bodies

(1) The Secretary of State may give financial assistance, in the form of grants, loans or guarantees to–

(a) any international organisation having functions relating to trade marks or other intellectual property, or

(b) any Community institution or other body established under any of the Community Treaties having any such functions,

with a view to the establishment or maintenance by that organisation, institution or body of premises in the United Kingdom.

(2) Any expenditure of the Secretary of State under this section shall be defrayed out of money provided by Parliament; and any sums received by the Secretary of State in consequence of this section shall be paid into the Consolidated Fund.

NOTES

Commencement order: SI 1989/816.

Modification: references to trade marks or registered trade marks within the meaning of the Trade Marks Act 1938 shall, unless the context otherwise requires, be construed as references to trade marks or registered trade marks within the meaning of the Trade Marks Act 1994; see the Trade Marks Act 1994, Sch 4, para 1.

General

303 Consequential amendments and repeals

(1) The enactments specified in Schedule 7 are amended in accordance with that Schedule, the amendments being consequential on the provisions of this Act.

(2) The enactments specified in Schedule 8 are repealed to the extent specified.

NOTES

Commencement orders: SI 1989/816, SI 1990/1400, SI 1990/2168.

---

304 Extent

(1) Provision as to the extent of Part I (copyright), Part II (rights in performances) and Part III (design right) is to be found in sections 157, 207 and 255 respectively; the extent of the other provisions of this Act is as follows.

(2) Parts IV to VII extend to England and Wales, Scotland and Northern Ireland, except that–

(a) sections 287 to 292 (patents county courts) extend to England and Wales only,

(b) the proper law of the trust created by Schedule 6 (provisions for the benefit of the Hospital for Sick Children) is the law of England and Wales, and

(c) the amendments and repeals in Schedules 7 and 8 have the same extent as the enactments amended or repealed.

(3) The following provisions extend to the Isle of Man subject to any modifications contained in an Order made by Her Majesty in Council–

(a) sections 293 and 294 (patents: licences of right), and

(b) paragraphs 24 and 29 of Schedule 5 (patents: effect of filing international application for patent and power to extend time limits).

(4) Her Majesty may by Order in Council direct that the following provisions extend to the Isle of Man, with such exceptions and modifications as may be specified in the Order–

(a) Part IV (registered designs),

(b) Part V (patent agents),

(c) the provisions of Schedule 5 (patents: miscellaneous amendments) not mentioned in subsection (3) above,

(d) sections 297 to 299 (fraudulent reception of transmissions), and

(e) section 300 (fraudulent application or use of trade mark).

(5) Her Majesty may by Order in Council direct that sections 297 to 299 (fraudulent reception of transmissions) extend to any of the Channel Islands, with such exceptions and modifications as may be specified in the Order.

(6) Any power conferred by this Act to make provision by Order in Council for or in connection with the extent of provisions of this Act to a country outside the United Kingdom includes power to extend to that country, subject to any modifications specified in the Order, any provision of this Act which amends or repeals an enactment extending to that country.

NOTE
Commencement orders: SI 1989/816, SI 1989/1303.

305 Commencement

(1) The following provisions of this Act come into force on Royal Assent–

paragraphs 24 and 29 of Schedule 5 (patents: effect of filing international application for patent and power to extend time limits);

section 301 and Schedule 6 (provisions for the benefit of the Hospital for Sick Children).

(2) Sections 293 and 294 (licences of right) come into force at the end of the period of two months beginning with the passing of this Act.

(3) The other provisions of this Act come into force on such day as the Secretary of State may appoint by order made by statutory instrument, and different days may be appointed for different provisions and different purposes.

306 Short title

This Act may be cited as the Copyright, Designs and Patents Act 1988.

NOTE
Commencement order: SI 1989/816.

SCHEDULE 1
COPYRIGHT: TRANSITIONAL PROVISIONS AND SAVINGS

Section 170

Introductory

1.–(1) In this Schedule–

'the 1911 Act' means the Copyright Act 1911,

'the 1956 Act' means the Copyright Act 1956, and

'the new copyright provisions' means the provisions of this Act relating to copyright, that is, Part I (including this Schedule) and Schedules 3, 7 and 8 so far as they make amendments or repeals consequential on the provisions of Part I.

(2) References in this Schedule to 'commencement', without more, are to the date on which the new copyright provisions come into force.

(3) References in this Schedule to 'existing works' are to works made before commencement; and for this purpose a work of which the making extended over a period shall be taken to have been made when its making was completed.

2.–(1) In relation to the 1956 Act, references in this Schedule to a work include any work or other subject-matter within the meaning of that Act.

(2) In relation to the 1911 Act–

(a) references in this Schedule to copyright include the right conferred by section 24 of that Act in substitution for a right subsisting immediately before the commencement of that Act;

(b) references in this Schedule to copyright in a sound recording are to the copyright under that Act in records embodying the recording; and

(c) references in this Schedule to copyright in a film are to any copyright under that Act in the film (so far as it constituted a dramatic work for the purposes of that Act) or in photographs forming part of the film.

General principles: continuity of the law

3.–The new copyright provisions apply in relation to things existing at commencement as they apply in relation to things coming into existence after commencement, subject to any express provision to the contrary.

4.–(1) The provisions of this paragraph have effect for securing the continuity of the law so far as the new copyright provisions re-enact (with or without modification) earlier provisions.

(2) A reference in an enactment, instrument or other document to copyright, or to a work or other subject-matter in which copyright subsists, which apart from this Act would be construed as referring to copyright under the 1956 Act shall be construed, so far as may be required for continuing its effect, as being, or as the case may require, including, a reference to copyright under this Act or to works in which copyright subsists under this Act.

(3) Anything done (including subordinate legislation made), or having effect as done, under or for the purposes of a provision repealed by this Act has effect as if done under or for the purposes of the corresponding provision of the new copyright provisions.

(4) References (expressed or implied) in this Act or any other enactment, instrument or document to any of the new copyright provisions shall, so far as the context permits, be construed as including, in relation to times, circumstances and purposes before commencement, a reference to corresponding earlier provisions.

(5) A reference (express or implied) in an enactment, instrument or other document to a provision repealed by this Act shall be construed, so far as may be required for continuing its effect, as a reference to the corresponding provision of this Act.

(6) The provisions of this paragraph have effect subject to any specific transitional provision or saving and to any express amendment made by this Act.

Subsistence of copyright

5.–(1) Copyright subsists in an existing work after commencement only if copyright subsisted in it immediately before commencement.

(2) Sub-paragraph (1) does not prevent an existing work qualifying for copyright protection after commencement–

(a) under section 155 (qualification by virtue of first publication), or

(b) by virtue of an Order under section 159 (application of Part I to countries to which it does not extend).

6.–(1) Copyright shall not subsist by virtue of this Act in an artistic work made before 1st June 1957 which at the time when the work was made constituted a design capable of registration under the Registered Designs Act 1949 or under the enactments repealed by that Act, and was used, or intended to be used, as a model or pattern to be multiplied by an industrial process.

(2) For this purpose a design shall be deemed to be used as a model or pattern to be multiplied by any industrial process–

(a) when the design is reproduced or is intended to be reproduced on more than 50 single articles, unless all the articles in which the design is reproduced or is intended to be reproduced together form only a single set of articles as defined in section 44(1) of the Registered Designs Act 1949, or

(b) when the design is to be applied to–

  (i) printed paper hangings,
  (ii) carpets, floor cloths or oil cloths, manufactured or sold in lengths or pieces,
  (iii) textile piece goods, or textile goods manufactured or sold in lengths or pieces, or
  (iv) lace, not made by hand.

7.–(1) No copyright subsists in a film, as such, made before 1st June 1957.

(2) Where a film made before that date was an original dramatic work within the meaning of the 1911 Act, the new copyright provisions have effect in relation to the film as if it was an original dramatic work within the meaning of Part I.

(3) The new copyright provisions have effect in relation to photographs forming part of a film made before 1st June 1957 as they have effect in relation to photographs not forming part of a film.

8.–(1) A film sound-track to which section 13(9) of the 1956 Act applied before commencement (film to be taken to include sounds in associated sound-track) shall be treated for the purposes of the new copyright provisions not as part of the film, but as a sound recording.

(2) However–

(a) copyright subsists in the sound recording only if copyright subsisted in the film immediately before commencement, and it continues to subsist until copyright in the film expires;

(b) the author and first owner of copyright in the film shall be treated as having been author and first owner of the copyright in the sound recording; and

(c) anything done before commencement under or in relation to the copyright in the film continues to have effect in relation to the sound recording as in relation to the film.

9.–No copyright subsists in–

(a) a broadcast made before 1st June 1957, or

(b) a cable programme included in a cable programme service before 1st January 1985;

and any such broadcast or cable programme shall be disregarded for the purposes of section 14(5) (duration of copyright in repeats).

Authorship of work

10.–The question who was the author of an existing work shall be determined in accordance with the new copyright provisions for the purposes of the rights conferred by Chapter IV of Part I (moral rights), and for all other purposes shall be determined in accordance with the law in force at the time the work was made.

NOTE

This section should be read in conjunction with the following provision of the Copyright and Related Rights Regulations 1996, SI 1996/2967 (commencement: 1 December 1996):

Copyright and Related Rights Regulations 1996, reg 19

Clarification of transitional provisions relating to pre-1989 photographs
19 Any question arising, in relation to photographs which were existing works within the meaning of Schedule 1, as to who is to be regarded as the author for the purposes of–

(a) regulations 15 and 16 of the Duration of Copyright and Rights in Performances Regulations 1995 (duration of copyright: application of new provisions subject to general saving), or
(b) regulation 19(2)(b) of those regulations (ownership of revived copyright),

is to be determined in accordance with section 9 as in force on the commencement of those regulations (and not, by virtue of paragraph 10 of Schedule 1, in accordance with the law in force at the time when the work was made).

First ownership of copyright

11.–(1) The question who was first owner of copyright in an existing work shall be determined in accordance with the law in force at the time the work was made.

(2) Where before commencement a person commissioned the making of a work in circumstances falling within–

(a)   section 4(3) of the 1956 Act or paragraph (a) of the proviso to section 5(1) of the 1911 Act (photographs, portraits and engravings), or

(b)   the proviso to section 12(4) of the 1956 Act (sound recordings),

those provisions apply to determine first ownership of copyright in any work made in pursuance of the commission after commencement.

Duration of copyright in existing works

12.–(1) The following provisions have effect with respect to the duration of copyright in existing works.

The question which provision applies to a work shall be determined by reference to the facts immediately before commencement; and expressions used in this paragraph which were defined for the purposes of the 1956 Act have the same meaning as in that Act.

(2) Copyright in the following descriptions of work continues to subsist until the date on which it would have expired under the 1956 Act–

(a)   literary, dramatic or musical works in relation to which the period of 50 years mentioned in the proviso to section 2(3) of the 1956 Act (duration of copyright in works made available to the public after the death of the author) has begun to run;

(b)   engravings in relation to which the period of 50 years mentioned in the proviso to section 3(4) of the 1956 Act (duration of copyright in works published after the death of the author) has begun to run;

(c)   published photographs and photographs taken before 1st June 1957;

(d)   published sound recordings and sound recordings made before 1st June 1957;

(e)   published films and films falling within section 13(3)(a) of the 1956 Act (films registered under former enactments relating to registration of films).

(3) Copyright in anonymous or pseudonymous literary, dramatic, musical or artistic works (other than photographs) continues to subsist–

(a)   if the work is published, until the date on which it would have expired in accordance with the 1956 Act, and

(b)   if the work is unpublished, until the end of the period of 50 years from the end of the calendar year in which the new copyright provisions come into force or, if during that period the work is first made available to the public within the meaning of section 12(2) (duration of copyright in works of unknown authorship), the date on which copyright expires in accordance with that provision;

unless, in any case, the identity of the author becomes known before that date, in which case section 12(1) applies (general rule: life of the author plus 50 years).

(4) Copyright in the following descriptions of work continues to subsist until the end of the period of 50 years from the end of the calendar year in which the new copyright provisions come into force–

(a)   literary, dramatic and musical works of which the author has died and in relation to which none of the acts mentioned in paragraphs (a) to (e) of the proviso to section 2(3) of the 1956 Act has been done;

(b)   unpublished engravings of which the author has died;

(c)   unpublished photographs taken on or after 1st June 1957.

(5) Copyright in the following descriptions of work continues to subsist until the end of the period of 50 years from the end of the calendar year in which the new copyright provisions come into force–

(a)   unpublished sound recordings made on or after 1st June 1957;

(b)   films not falling within sub-paragraph (2)(e) above,

unless the recording or film is published before the end of that period in which case copyright in it shall continue until the end of the period of 50 years from the end of the calendar year in which the recording or film is published.

(6) Copyright in any other description of existing work continues to subsist until the date on which copyright in that description of work expires in accordance with sections 12 to 15 of this Act.

(7) The above provisions do not apply to works subject to Crown or Parliamentary copyright (see paragraphs 41 to 43 below).

NOTE

This section should be read in conjunction with the following provisions of the Copyright and Rights in Databases Regulations 1997, SI 1997/3032 (commencement: 1 January 1998):

Copyright and Rights in Databases Regulations 1997, regs 29 and 30

29 Saving for copyright in certain existing databases
(1) Where a database–

(a)   was created on or before 27th March 1996, and
(b)   is a copyright work immediately before commencement,

copyright shall continue to subsist in the database for the remainder of its copyright term.

(2) In this Regulation 'copyright term' means the period of the duration of copyright under section 12 of the 1988 Act (duration of copyright in literary, dramatic, musical or artistic works).

30 Database right: term applicable to certain existing databases
Where–

(a)   the making of a database was completed on or after 1st January 1983, and
(b)   on commencement, database right begins to subsist in the database,

database right shall subsist in the database for the period of fifteen years beginning with 1st January 1998.

Perpetual copyright under the Copyright Act 1775

13.–(1) The rights conferred on universities and colleges by the Copyright Act 1775 shall continue to subsist until the end of the period of 50 years from the end of the calendar year in which the new copyright provisions come into force and shall then expire.

(2) The provisions of the following Chapters of Part I–

Chapter III (acts permitted in relation to copyright works),
Chapter VI (remedies for infringement),
Chapter VII (provisions with respect to copyright licensing), and
Chapter VIII (the Copyright Tribunal),

apply in relation to those rights as they apply in relation to copyright under this Act.

Acts infringing copyright

14.–(1) The provisions of Chapters II and III of Part I as to the acts constituting an infringement of copyright apply only in relation to acts done after commencement; the provisions of the 1956 Act continue to apply in relation to acts done before commencement.

(2) So much of section 18(2) as extends the restricted act of issuing copies to the public to include the rental to the public of copies of sound recordings, films or computer programs does not apply in relation to a copy of a sound recording, film or computer program acquired by any person before commencement for the purpose of renting it to the public.

(3) For the purposes of section 27 (meaning of 'infringing copy') the question whether the making of an article constituted an infringement of copyright, or would have done if the article had been made in the United Kingdom, shall be determined–

(a)   in relation to an article made on or after 1st June 1957 and before commencement, by reference to the 1956 Act, and

(b)   in relation to an article made before 1st June 1957, by reference to the 1911 Act.

(4) For the purposes of the application of sections 31(2), 51(2) and 62(3) (subsequent exploitation of things whose making was, by virtue of an earlier provision of the section, not an infringement of copyright) to things made before commencement, it shall be assumed that the new copyright provisions were in force at all material times.

(5) Section 55 (articles for producing material in a particular typeface) applies where articles have been marketed as mentioned in subsection (1) before commencement with the substitution for the period mentioned in subsection (3) of the period of 25 years from the end of the calendar year in which the new copyright provisions come into force.

(6) Section 56 (transfer of copies, adaptations, &c of work in electronic form) does not apply in relation to a copy purchased before commencement.

(7) In section 65 (reconstruction of buildings) the reference to the owner of the copyright in the drawings or plans is, in relation to buildings constructed before commencement, to the person who at the time of the construction was the owner of the copyright in the drawings or plans under the 1956 Act, the 1911 Act or any enactment repealed by the 1911 Act.

NOTE

This section should be read in conjunction with the following provisions of the Copyright and Related Rights Regulations 1996, SI 1996/2967 (commencement: 1 December 1996):

Copyright and Related Rights Regulations 1996, regs 26, 27, 34(1) and 36

General rules
26–(1) Subject to anything in regulations 28 to 36 (special transitional provisions and savings), these regulations apply to copyright works made, and to performances given, before or after commencement.

(2) No act done before commencement shall be regarded as an infringement of any new right, or as giving rise to any right to remuneration arising by virtue of these Regulations.

Saving for certain existing agreements
27–(1) Except as otherwise expressly provided, nothing in these Regulations affects an agreement made before 19th November 1992.

(2) No act done in pursuance of any such agreement after commencement shall be regarded as an infringement of any new right.

Savings for existing stocks
34–(1) Any new right in relation to a copyright work does not apply to a copy of the work acquired by a person before commencement for the purpose of renting or lending it to the public.

Authorship of films
36–(1) Regulation 18 (authorship of films) applies as from commencement in relation to films made on or after 1st July 1994.

(2) It is not an infringement of any right which the principal director has by virtue of these Regulations to do anything after commencement in pursuance of arrangements for the exploitation of the film made before 19th November 1992.

This does not affect any right of his to equitable remuneration under section 93B.

15.–(1) Section 57 (anonymous or pseudonymous works: acts permitted on assumptions as to expiry of copyright or death of author) has effect in relation to existing works subject to the following provisions.

(2) Subsection (1)(b)(i) (assumption as to expiry of copyright) does not apply in relation to–

(a)   photographs, or
(b)   the rights mentioned in paragraph 13 above (rights conferred by the Copyright Act 1775).

(3) Subsection (1)(b)(ii) (assumption as to death of author) applies only–

(a)   where paragraph 12(3)(b) above applies (unpublished anonymous or pseudonymous works), after the end of the period of 50 years from the end of the calendar year in which the new copyright provisions come into force, or
(b)   where paragraph 12(6) above applies (cases in which the duration of copyright is the same under the new copyright provisions as under the previous law).

16.–The following provisions of section 7 of the 1956 Act continue to apply in relation to existing works–

   (a)   subsection (6) (copying of unpublished works from manuscript or copy in library, museum or other institution);

   (b)   subsection (7) (publication of work containing material to which subsection (6) applies), except paragraph (a) (duty to give notice of intended publication);

   (c)   subsection (8) (subsequent broadcasting, performance, &c of material published in accordance with subsection (7));

and subsection (9)(d) (illustrations) continues to apply for the purposes of those provisions.

17.–Where in the case of a dramatic or musical work made before 1st July 1912, the right conferred by the 1911 Act did not include the sole right to perform the work in public, the acts restricted by the copyright shall be treated as not including–

   (a)   performing the work in public,

   (b)   broadcasting the work or including it in a cable programme service, or

   (c)   doing any of the above in relation to an adaptation of the work;

and where the right conferred by the 1911 Act consisted only of the sole right to perform the work in public, the acts restricted by the copyright shall be treated as consisting only of those acts.

18.–Where a work made before 1st July 1912 consists of an essay, article or portion forming part of and first published in a review, magazine or other periodical or work of a like nature, the copyright is subject to any right of publishing the essay, article, or portion in a separate form to which the author was entitled at the commencement of the 1911 Act, or would if that Act had not been passed, have become entitled under section 18 of the Copyright Act 1842.

Designs

19.–(1) Section 51 (exclusion of copyright protection in relation to works recorded or embodied in design document or models) does not apply for ten years after commencement in relation to a design recorded or embodied in a design document or model before commencement.

   (2) During those ten years the following provisions of Part III (design right) apply to any relevant copyright as in relation to design right–

   (a)   sections 237 to 239 (availability of licences of right), and

   (b)   sections 247 and 248 (application to comptroller to settle terms of licence of right).

   (3) In section 237 as it applies by virtue of this paragraph, for the reference in subsection (1) to the last five years of the design right term there shall be substituted a reference to the last five years of the period of ten years referred to in sub-paragraph (1) above, or to so much of those last five years during which copyright subsists.

   (4) In section 239 as it applies by virtue of this paragraph, for the reference in subsection (1)(b) to section 230 there shall be substituted a reference to section 99.

   (5) Where a licence of right is available by virtue of this paragraph, a person to whom a licence was granted before commencement may apply to the comptroller for an order adjusting the terms of that licence.

   (6) The provisions of sections 249 and 250 (appeals and rules) apply in relation to proceedings brought under or by virtue of this paragraph as to proceedings under Part III.

   (7) A licence granted by virtue of this paragraph shall relate only to acts which would be permitted by section 51 if the design document or model had been made after commencement.

   (8) Section 100 (right to seize infringing copies, &c) does not apply during the period of ten years referred to in sub-paragraph (1) in relation to anything to which it would not apply if the design in question had been first recorded or embodied in a design document or model after commencement.

   (9) Nothing in this paragraph affects the operation of any rule of law preventing or restricting the enforcement of copyright in relation to a design.

20.–(1) Where section 10 of the 1956 Act (effect of industrial application of design corresponding to artistic work) applied in relation to an artistic work at any time before commencement, section 52(2) of this Act applies with the substitution for the period of 25 years mentioned there of the relevant period of 15 years as defined in section 10(3) of the 1956 Act.

(2) Except as provided in sub-paragraph (1), section 52 applies only where articles are marketed as mentioned in subsection (1)(b) after commencement.

Abolition of statutory recording licence

21.–Section 8 of the 1956 Act (statutory licence to copy records sold by retail) continues to apply where notice under subsection (1)(b) of that section was given before the repeal of that section by this Act, but only in respect of the making of records–

    (a)   within one year of the repeal coming into force, and

    (b)   up to the number stated in the notice as intended to be sold.

Moral rights

22.–(1) No act done before commencement is actionable by virtue of any provision of Chapter IV of Part I (moral rights).

(2) Section 43 of the 1956 Act (false attribution of authorship) continues to apply in relation to acts done before commencement.

23.–(1) The following provisions have effect with respect to the rights conferred by–

    (a)   section 77 (right to be identified as author or director), and

    (b)   section 80 (right to object to derogatory treatment of work).

(2) The rights do not apply–

    (a)   in relation to a literary, dramatic, musical and artistic work of which the author died before commencement; or

    (b)   in relation to a film made before commencement.

(3) The rights in relation to an existing literary, dramatic, musical or artistic work do not apply–

    (a)   where copyright first vested in the author, to anything which by virtue of an assignment of copyright made or licence granted before commencement may be done without infringing copyright;

    (b)   where copyright first vested in a person other than the author, to anything done by or with the licence of the copyright owner.

(4) The rights do not apply to anything done in relation to a record made in pursuance of section 8 of the 1956 Act (statutory recording licence).

24.–The right conferred by section 85 (right to privacy of certain photographs and films) does not apply to photographs taken or films made before commencement.

Assignments and licences

25.–(1) Any document made or event occurring before commencement which had any operation–

    (a)   affecting the ownership of the copyright in an existing work, or

    (b)   creating, transferring or terminating an interest, right or licence in respect of the copyright in an existing work,

has the corresponding operation in relation to copyright in the work under this Act.

(2) Expressions used in such a document shall be construed in accordance with their effect immediately before commencement.

26.–(1) Section 91(1) of this Act (assignment of future copyright: statutory vesting of legal interest on copyright coming into existence) does not apply in relation to an agreement made before 1st June 1957.

(2) The repeal by this Act of section 37(2) of the 1956 Act (assignment of future copyright: devolution of right where assignee dies before copyright comes into existence) does not affect the operation of that provision in relation to an agreement made before commencement.

27.-(1) Where the author of a literary, dramatic, musical or artistic work was the first owner of the copyright in it, no assignment of the copyright and no grant of any interest in it, made by him (otherwise than by will) after the passing of the 1911 Act and before 1st June 1957, shall be operative to vest in the assignee or grantee any rights with respect to the copyright in the work beyond the expiration of 25 years from the death of the author.

(2) The reversionary interest in the copyright expectant on the termination of that period may after commencement be assigned by the author during his life but in the absence of any assignment shall, on his death, devolve on his legal personal representatives as part of his estate.

(3) Nothing in this paragraph affects–

  (a) an assignment of the reversionary interest by a person to whom it has been assigned,
  (b) an assignment of the reversionary interest after the death of the author by his personal representatives or any person becoming entitled to it, or
  (c) any assignment of the copyright after the reversionary interest has fallen in.

(4) Nothing in this paragraph applies to the assignment of the copyright in a collective work or a licence to publish a work or part of a work as part of a collective work.

(5) In sub-paragraph (4) 'collective work' means–

  (a) any encyclopaedia, dictionary, yearbook, or similar work;
  (b) a newspaper, review, magazine, or similar periodical; and
  (c) any work written in distinct parts by different authors, or in which works or parts of works of different authors are incorporated.

28.-(1) This paragraph applies where copyright subsists in a literary, dramatic, musical or artistic work made before 1st July 1912 in relation to which the author, before the commencement of the 1911 Act, made such an assignment or grant as was mentioned in paragraph (a) of the proviso to section 24(1) of that Act (assignment or grant of copyright or performing right for full term of the right under the previous law).

(2) If before commencement any event has occurred or notice has been given which by virtue of paragraph 38 of Schedule 7 to the 1956 Act had any operation in relation to copyright in the work under that Act, the event or notice has the corresponding operation in relation to copyright under this Act.

(3) Any right which immediately before commencement would by virtue of paragraph 38(3) of that Schedule have been exercisable in relation to the work, or copyright in it, is exercisable in relation to the work or copyright in it under this Act.

(4) If in accordance with paragraph 38(4) of that Schedule copyright would, on a date after the commencement of the 1956 Act, have reverted to the author or his personal representatives and that date falls after the commencement of the new copyright provisions–

  (a) the copyright in the work shall revert to the author or his personal representatives, as the case may be, and
  (b) any interest of any other person in the copyright which subsists on that date by virtue of any document made before the commencement of the 1911 Act shall thereupon determine.

29.-Section 92(2) of this Act (rights of exclusive licensee against successors in title of person granting licence) does not apply in relation to an exclusive licence granted before commencement.

Bequests

30.-(1) Section 93 of this Act (copyright to pass under will with original document or other material thing embodying unpublished work)–

  (a) does not apply where the testator died before 1st June 1957, and
  (b) where the testator died on or after that date and before commencement, applies only in relation to an original document embodying a work.

(2) In the case of an author who died before 1st June 1957, the ownership after his death of a manuscript of his, where such ownership has been acquired under a testamentary disposition made by

him and the manuscript is of a work which has not been published or performed in public, is prima facie proof of the copyright being with the owner of the manuscript.

Remedies for infringement

31.–(1) Sections 96 and 97 of this Act (remedies for infringement) apply only in relation to an infringement of copyright committed after commencement; section 17 of the 1956 Act continues to apply in relation to infringements committed before commencement.

(2) Sections 99 and 100 of this Act (delivery up or seizure of infringing copies, &c) apply to infringing copies and other articles made before or after commencement; section 18 of the 1956 Act, and section 7 of the 1911 Act, (conversion damages, &c), do not apply after commencement except for the purposes of proceedings begun before commencement.

(3) Sections 101 to 102 of this Act (rights and remedies of exclusive licensee) apply where sections 96 to 100 of this Act apply; section 19 of the 1956 Act continues to apply where section 17 or 18 of that Act applies.

(4) Sections 104 to 106 of this Act (presumptions) apply only in proceedings brought by virtue of this Act; section 20 of the 1956 Act continues to apply in proceedings brought by virtue of that Act.

32.–Sections 101 and 102 of this Act (rights and remedies of exclusive licensee) do not apply to a licence granted before 1st June 1957.

33.–(1) The provisions of section 107 of this Act (criminal liability for making or dealing with infringing articles, &c) apply only in relation to acts done after commencement; section 21 of the 1956 Act (penalties and summary proceedings in respect of dealings which infringe copyright) continues to apply in relation to acts done before commencement.

(2) Section 109 of this Act (search warrants) applies in relation to offences committed before commencement in relation to which section 21A or 21B of the 1956 Act applied; sections 21A and 21B continue to apply in relation to warrants issued before commencement.

Copyright Tribunal: proceedings pending on commencement

34.–(1) The Lord Chancellor may, after consultation with the Lord Advocate, by rules make such provision as he considers necessary or expedient with respect to proceedings pending under Part IV of the 1956 Act immediately before commencement.

(2) Rules under this paragraph shall be made by statutory instrument which shall be subject to annulment in pursuance of a resolution of either House of Parliament.

Qualification for copyright protection

35.–Every work in which copyright subsisted under the 1956 Act immediately before commencement shall be deemed to satisfy the requirements of Part I of this Act as to qualification for copyright protection.

Dependent territories

36.–(1) The 1911 Act shall remain in force as part of the law of any dependent territory in which it was in force immediately before commencement until–

(a) the new copyright provisions come into force in that territory by virtue of an Order under section 157 of this Act (power to extend new copyright provisions), or

(b) in the case of any of the Channel Islands, the Act is repealed by Order under sub-paragraph (3) below.

(2) An Order in Council in force immediately before commencement which extends to any dependent territory any provisions of the 1956 Act shall remain in force as part of the law of that territory until–

(a) the new copyright provisions come into force in that territory by virtue of an Order under section 157 of this Act (power to extend new copyright provisions), or

(b) in the case of the Isle of Man, the Order is revoked by Order under sub-paragraph (3) below;

and while it remains in force such an Order may be varied under the provisions of the 1956 Act under which it was made.

(3) If it appears to Her Majesty that provision with respect to copyright has been made in the law of any of the Channel Islands or the Isle of Man otherwise than by extending the provisions of Part I of this Act, Her Majesty may by Order in Council repeal the 1911 Act as it has effect as part of the law of that territory or, as the case may be, revoke the Order extending the 1956 Act there.

(4) A dependent territory in which the 1911 or 1956 Act remains in force shall be treated, in the law of the countries to which Part I extends, as a country to which that Part extends; and those countries shall be treated in the law of such a territory as countries to which the 1911 Act or, as the case may be, the 1956 Act extends.

(5) If a country in which the 1911 or 1956 Act is in force ceases to be a colony of the United Kingdom, section 158 of this Act (consequences of country ceasing to be colony) applies with the substitution for the reference in subsection (3)(b) to the provisions of Part I of this Act of a reference to the provisions of the 1911 or 1956 Act, as the case may be.

(6) In this paragraph 'dependent territory' means any of the Channel Islands, the Isle of Man or any colony.

37.–(1) This paragraph applies to a country which immediately before commencement was not a dependent territory within the meaning of paragraph 36 above but–

(a) was a country to which the 1956 Act extended, or

(b) was treated as such a country by virtue of paragraph 39(2) of Schedule 7 to that Act (countries to which the 1911 Act extended or was treated as extending);

and Her Majesty may by Order in Council conclusively declare for the purposes of this paragraph whether a country was such a country or was so treated.

(2) A country to which this paragraph applies shall be treated as a country to which Part I extends for the purposes of sections 154 to 156 (qualification for copyright protection) until–

(a) an Order in Council is made in respect of that country under section 159 (application of Part I to countries to which it does not extend), or

(b) an Order in Council is made declaring that it shall cease to be so treated by reason of the fact that the provisions of the 1956 Act or, as the case may be, the 1911 Act, which extended there as part of the law of that country have been repealed or amended.

(3) A statutory instrument containing an Order in Council under this paragraph shall be subject to annulment in pursuance of a resolution of either House of Parliament.

Territorial waters and the continental shelf

38.–Section 161 of this Act (application of Part I to things done in territorial waters or the United Kingdom sector of the continental shelf) does not apply in relation to anything done before commencement.

British ships, aircraft and hovercraft

39.–Section 162 (British ships, aircraft and hovercraft) does not apply in relation to anything done before commencement.

Crown copyright

40.–(1) Section 163 of this Act (general provisions as to Crown copyright) applies to an existing work if–

(a) section 39 of the 1956 Act applied to the work immediately before commencement, and

(b)   the work is not one to which section 164, 165 or 166 applies (copyright in Acts, Measures and Bills and Parliamentary copyright: see paragraphs 42 and 43 below).

(2) Section 163(1)(b) (first ownership of copyright) has effect subject to any agreement entered into before commencement under section 39(6) of the 1956 Act.

41.–(1) The following provisions have effect with respect to the duration of copyright in existing works to which section 163 (Crown copyright) applies.

The question which provision applies to a work shall be determined by reference to the facts immediately before commencement; and expressions used in this paragraph which were defined for the purposes of the 1956 Act have the same meaning as in that Act.

(2) Copyright in the following descriptions of work continues to subsist until the date on which it would have expired in accordance with the 1956 Act–

(a)   published literary, dramatic or musical works;
(b)   artistic works other than engravings or photographs;
(c)   published engravings;
(d)   published photographs and photographs taken before 1st June 1957;
(e)   published sound recordings and sound recordings made before 1st June 1957;
(f)   published films and films falling within section 13(3)(a) of the 1956 Act (films registered under former enactments relating to registration of films).

(3) Copyright in unpublished literary, dramatic or musical works continues to subsist until–

(a)   the date on which copyright expires in accordance with section 163(3), or
(b)   the end of the period of 50 years from the end of the calendar year in which the new copyright provisions come into force,

whichever is the later.

(4) Copyright in the following descriptions of work continues to subsist until the end of the period of 50 years from the end of the calendar year in which the new copyright provisions come into force–

(a)   unpublished engravings;
(b)   unpublished photographs taken on or after 1st June 1957.

(5) Copyright in a film or sound recording not falling within sub-paragraph (2) above continues to subsist until the end of the period of 50 years from the end of the calendar year in which the new copyright provisions come into force, unless the film or recording is published before the end of that period, in which case copyright expires 50 years from the end of the calendar year in which it is published.

42.–(1) Section 164 (copyright in Acts and Measures) applies to existing Acts of Parliament and Measures of the General Synod of the Church of England.

(2) References in that section to Measures of the General Synod of the Church of England include Church Assembly Measures.

Parliamentary copyright

43.–(1) Section 165 of this Act (general provisions as to Parliamentary copyright) applies to existing unpublished literary, dramatic, musical or artistic works, but does not otherwise apply to existing works.

(2) Section 166 (copyright in Parliamentary Bills) does not apply–

(a)   to a public Bill which was introduced into Parliament and published before commencement,
(b)   to a private Bill of which a copy was deposited in either House before commencement, or
(c)   to a personal Bill which was given a First Reading in the House of Lords before commencement.

Copyright vesting in certain international organisations

44.–(1) Any work in which immediately before commencement copyright subsisted by virtue of section 33 of the 1956 Act shall be deemed to satisfy the requirements of section 168(1); but otherwise section 168 does not apply to works made or, as the case may be, published before commencement.

(2) Copyright in any such work which is unpublished continues to subsist until the date on which it would have expired in accordance with the 1956 Act, or the end of the period of 50 years from the end of the calendar year in which the new copyright provisions come into force, whichever is the earlier.

Meaning of 'publication'

45.–Section 175(3) (construction of building treated as equivalent to publication) applies only where the construction of the building began after commencement.

Meaning of 'unauthorised'

46.–For the purposes of the application of the definition in section 178 (minor definitions) of the expression 'unauthorised' in relation to things done before commencement–

(a) paragraph (a) applies in relation to things done before 1st June 1957 as if the reference to the licence of the copyright owner were a reference to his consent or acquiescence;

(b) paragraph (b) applies with the substitution for the words from 'or, in a case' to the end of the words 'or any person lawfully claiming under him'; and

(c) paragraph (c) shall be disregarded.

NOTES
Commencement orders: SI 1989/816, SI 1989/955, SI 1989/1032.
Para 9: words in square brackets substituted by SI 1995/3297, reg 7(2).
Modified in relation to semiconductor topographies by the Design Right (Semiconductor Topographies) Regulations 1989, SI 1989/1100.
See further, in relation to the authorship of pre-1989 photographs: the Copyright and Related Rights Regulations 1989, SI 1996/2967, reg 19.

SCHEDULE 2
RIGHTS IN PERFORMANCES: PERMITTED ACTS

Section 189

Introductory

1.–(1) The provisions of this Schedule specify acts which may be done in relation to a performance or recording notwithstanding the rights conferred by Part II; they relate only to the question of infringement of those rights and do not affect any other right or obligation restricting the doing of any of the specified acts.

(2) No inference shall be drawn from the description of any act which may by virtue of this Schedule be done without infringing the rights conferred by Part II as to the scope of those rights.

(3) The provisions of this Schedule are to be construed independently of each other, so that the fact that an act does not fall within one provision does not mean that it is not covered by another provision.

NOTE
This section should be read in conjunction with the following provisions of the Copyright and Related Rights Regulations 1996, SI 1996/2967 (commencement: 1 December 1996):

Copyright and Related Rights Regulations 1996, regs 26, 27, 31 and 34(2)

General rules
26–(1) Subject to anything in regulations 28 to 36 (special transitional provisions and savings), these regulations apply to copyright works made, and to performances given, before or after commencement.

(2) No act done before commencement shall be regarded as an infringement of any new right, or as giving rise to any right to remuneration arising by virtue of these Regulations.

Saving for certain existing agreements
27–(1) Except as otherwise expressly provided, nothing in these Regulations affects an agreement made before 19th November 1992.

(2) No act done in pursuance of any such agreement after commencement shall be regarded as an infringement of any new right.

New rights: effect of pre-commencement authorisation of copying
31–Where before commencement–

(a) the owner or prospective owner of copyright in a literary, dramatic, musical or artistic work has authorised a person to make a copy of the work, or

(b) the owner or prospective owner of performers' rights in a performance has authorised a person to make a copy of a recording of the performance,

any new right in relation to that copy shall vest on commencement in the person so authorised, subject to any agreement to the contrary.

Savings for existing stocks
34–(2) Any new right in relation to a qualifying performance does not apply to a copy of a recording of the performance acquired by a person before commencement for the purpose of renting or lending it to the public.

Criticism, reviews and news reporting

2.–(1) Fair dealing with a performance or recording–

(a) for the purpose of criticism or review, of that or another performance or recording, or of a work, or

(b) for the purpose of reporting current events,

does not infringe any of the rights conferred by Part II.

(2) Expressions used in this paragraph have the same meaning as in section 30.

Incidental inclusion of performance or recording

3.–(1) The rights conferred by Part II are not infringed by the incidental inclusion of a performance or recording in a sound recording, film, broadcast or cable programme.

(2) Nor are those rights infringed by anything done in relation to copies of, or the playing, showing, broadcasting or inclusion in a cable programme service of, anything whose making was, by virtue of sub-paragraph (1), not an infringement of those rights.

(3) A performance or recording so far as it consists of music, or words spoken or sung with music, shall not be regarded as incidentally included in a sound recording, broadcast or cable programme if it is deliberately included.

(4) Expressions used in this paragraph have the same meaning as in section 31.

Things done for purposes of instruction or examination

4.–(1) The rights conferred by Part II are not infringed by the copying of a recording of a performance in the course of instruction, or of preparation for instruction, in the making of films or film sound-tracks, provided the copying is done by a person giving or receiving instruction.

(2) The rights conferred by Part II are not infringed–

(a) by the copying of a recording of a performance for the purposes of setting or answering the questions in an examination, or

(b) by anything done for the purposes of an examination by way of communicating the questions to the candidates.

(3) Where a recording which would otherwise be an illicit recording is made in accordance with this paragraph but is subsequently dealt with, it shall be treated as an illicit recording for the purposes of that dealing, and if that dealing infringes any right conferred by Part II for all subsequent purposes.

For this purpose 'dealt with' means sold or let for hire, or offered or exposed for sale or hire.

(4) Expressions used in this paragraph have the same meaning as in section 32.

Playing or showing sound recording, film, broadcast or cable programme at educational establishment

5.–(1) The playing or showing of a sound recording, film, broadcast or cable programme at an educational establishment for the purposes of instruction before an audience consisting of teachers and pupils at the establishment and other persons directly connected with the activities of the establishment is not a playing or showing of a performance in public for the purposes of infringement of the rights conferred by Part II.

(2) A person is not for this purpose directly connected with the activities of the educational establishment simply because he is the parent of a pupil at the establishment.

(3) Expressions used in this paragraph have the same meaning as in section 34 and any provision made under section 174(2) with respect to the application of that section also applies for the purposes of this paragraph.

Recording of broadcasts and cable programmes by educational establishments

6.–(1) A recording of a broadcast or cable programme, or a copy of such a recording, may be made by or on behalf of an educational establishment for the educational purposes of that establishment without thereby infringing any of the rights conferred by Part II in relation to any performance or recording included in it.

(2) Where a recording which would otherwise be an illicit recording is made in accordance with this paragraph but is subsequently dealt with, it shall be treated as an illicit recording for the purposes of that dealing, and if that dealing infringes any right conferred by Part II for all subsequent purposes.

For this purpose 'dealt with' means sold or let for hire, or offered or exposed for sale or hire.

(3) Expressions used in this paragraph have the same meaning as in section 35 and any provision made under section 174(2) with respect to the application of that section also applies for the purposes of this paragraph.

[Lending of copies by educational establishments

6A.–(1) The rights conferred by Part II are not infringed by the lending of copies of a recording of a performance by an educational establishment.

(2) Expressions used in this paragraph have the same meaning as in section 36A; and any provision with respect to the application of that section made under section 174(2) (instruction given elsewhere than an educational establishment) applies also for the purposes of this paragraph.

Lending of copies by libraries or archives

6B.–(1) The rights conferred by Part II are not infringed by the lending of copies of a recording of a performance by a prescribed library or archive (other than a public library) which is not conducted for profit.

(2) Expressions used in this paragraph have the same meaning as in section 40A(2); and any provision under section 37 prescribing libraries or archives for the purposes of that section applies also for the purposes of this paragraph.]

Copy of work required to be made as condition of export

7.–(1) If an article of cultural or historical importance or interest cannot lawfully be exported from the United Kingdom unless a copy of it is made and deposited in an appropriate library or archive, it is not an infringement of any right conferred by Part II to make that copy.

(2) Expressions used in this paragraph have the same meaning as in section 44.

Parliamentary and judicial proceedings

8.–(1) The rights conferred by Part II are not infringed by anything done for the purposes of parliamentary or judicial proceedings or for the purpose of reporting such proceedings.

(2) Expressions used in this paragraph have the same meaning as in section 45.

Royal Commissions and statutory inquiries

9.–(1) The rights conferred by Part II are not infringed by anything done for the purposes of the proceedings of a Royal Commission or statutory inquiry or for the purpose of reporting any such proceedings held in public.

(2) Expressions used in this paragraph have the same meaning as in section 46.

Public records

10.–(1) Material which is comprised in public records within the meaning of the Public Records Act 1958, the Public Records (Scotland) Act 1937 or the Public Records Act (Northern Ireland) 1923 which are open to public inspection in pursuance of that Act, may be copied, and a copy may be supplied to any person, by or with the authority of any officer appointed under that Act, without infringing any right conferred by Part II.

(2) Expressions used in this paragraph have the same meaning as in section 49.

Acts done under statutory authority

11.–(1) Where the doing of a particular act is specifically authorised by an Act of Parliament, whenever passed, then, unless the Act provides otherwise, the doing of that act does not infringe the rights conferred by Part II.

(2) Sub-paragraph (1) applies in relation to an enactment contained in Northern Ireland legislation as it applies to an Act of Parliament.

(3) Nothing in this paragraph shall be construed as excluding any defence of statutory authority otherwise available under or by virtue of any enactment.

(4) Expressions used in this paragraph have the same meaning as in section 50.

Transfer of copies of works in electronic form

12.–(1) This paragraph applies where a recording of a performance in electronic form has been purchased on terms which, expressly or impliedly or by virtue of any rule of law, allow the purchaser to make further recordings in connection with his use of the recording.

(2) If there are no express terms–

(a) prohibiting the transfer of the recording by the purchaser, imposing obligations which continue after a transfer, prohibiting the assignment of any consent or terminating any consent on a transfer, or

(b) providing for the terms on which a transferee may do the things which the purchaser was permitted to do,

anything which the purchaser was allowed to do may also be done by a transferee without infringement of the rights conferred by this Part, but any recording made by the purchaser which is not also transferred shall be treated as an illicit recording for all purposes after the transfer.

(3) The same applies where the original purchased recording is no longer usable and what is transferred is a further copy used in its place.

(4) The above provisions also apply on a subsequent transfer, with the substitution for references in sub-paragraph (2) to the purchaser of references to the subsequent transferor.

(5) This paragraph does not apply in relation to a recording purchased before the commencement of Part II.

(6) Expressions used in this paragraph have the same meaning as in section 56.

Use of recordings of spoken works in certain cases

13.–(1) Where a recording of the reading or recitation of a literary work is made for the purpose–

(a) of reporting current events, or

(b) of broadcasting or including in a cable programme service the whole or part of the reading or recitation,

it is not an infringement of the rights conferred by Part II to use the recording (or to copy the recording and use the copy) for that purpose, provided the following conditions are met.

(2) The conditions are that–

(a) the recording is a direct recording of the reading or recitation and is not taken from a previous recording or from a broadcast or cable programme;

(b) the making of the recording was not prohibited by or on behalf of the person giving the reading or recitation;

(c) the use made of the recording is not of a kind prohibited by or on behalf of that person before the recording was made; and

(d) the use is by or with the authority of a person who is lawfully in possession of the recording.

(3) Expressions used in this paragraph have the same meaning as in section 58.

Recordings of folksongs

14.–(1) A recording of a performance of a song may be made for the purpose of including it in an archive maintained by a designated body without infringing any of the rights conferred by Part II, provided the conditions in sub-paragraph (2) below are met.

(2) The conditions are that–

(a) the words are unpublished and of unknown authorship at the time the recording is made,

(b) the making of the recording does not infringe any copyright, and

(c) its making is not prohibited by any performer.

(3) Copies of a recording made in reliance on sub-paragraph (1) and included in an archive maintained by a designated body may, if the prescribed conditions are met, be made and supplied by the archivist without infringing any of the rights conferred by Part II.

(4) In this paragraph–

'designated body' means a body designated for the purposes of section 61, and

'the prescribed conditions' means the conditions prescribed for the purposes of subsection (3) of that section;

and other expressions used in this paragraph have the same meaning as in that section.

[Lending of certain recordings

14A.–(1) The Secretary of State may by order provide that in such cases as may be specified in the order the lending to the public of copies of films or sound recordings shall be treated as licensed by the performer subject only to the payment of such reasonable royalty or other payment as may be agreed or determined in default of agreement by the Copyright Tribunal.

(2) No such order shall apply if, or to the extent that, there is a licensing scheme certified for the purposes of this paragraph under paragraph 16 of Schedule 2A providing for the grant of licences.

(3) An order may make different provision for different cases and may specify cases by reference to any factor relating to the work, the copies lent, the lender or the circumstances of the lending.

(4) An order shall be made by statutory instrument; and no order shall be made unless a draft of it has been laid before and approved by a resolution of each House of Parliament.

(5) Nothing in this section affects any liability under section 184(1)(b) (secondary infringement: possessing or dealing with illicit recording) in respect of the lending of illicit recordings.

(6) Expressions used in this paragraph have the same meaning as in section 66.]

Playing of sound recordings for purposes of club, society, &c

15.–(1) It is not an infringement of any right conferred by Part II to play a sound recording as part of the activities of, or for the benefit of, a club, society or other organisation if the following conditions are met.

(2) The conditions are–

(a)   that the organisation is not established or conducted for profit and its main objects are charitable or are otherwise concerned with the advancement of religion, education or social welfare, and

(b)   that the proceeds of any charge for admission to the place where the recording is to be heard are applied solely for the purposes of the organisation.

(3) Expressions used in this paragraph have the same meaning as in section 67.

Incidental recording for purposes of broadcast or cable programme

16.–(1) A person who proposes to broadcast a recording of a performance, or include a recording of a performance in a cable programme service, in circumstances not infringing the rights conferred by Part II shall be treated as having consent for the purposes of that Part for the making of a further recording for the purposes of the broadcast or cable programme.

(2) That consent is subject to the condition that the further recording–

(a)   shall not be used for any other purpose, and

(b)   shall be destroyed within 28 days of being first used for broadcasting the performance or including it in a cable programme service.

(3) A recording made in accordance with this paragraph shall be treated as an illicit recording–

(a)   for the purposes of any use in breach of the condition mentioned in sub-paragraph (2)(a), and

(b)   for all purposes after that condition or the condition mentioned in sub-paragraph (2)(b) is broken.

(4) Expressions used in this paragraph have the same meaning as in section 68.

Recordings for purposes of supervision and control of broadcasts and cable programmes

17.–(1) The rights conferred by Part II are not infringed by the making or use by the British Broadcasting Corporation, for the purpose of maintaining supervision and control over programmes broadcast by them, of recordings of those programmes.

[(2) The rights conferred by Part II are not infringed by anything done in pursuance of–

(a)   section 11(1), 95(1) or 167(1) of the Broadcasting Act 1990 or section 115(4) or (6), 116(5) or 117 of the Broadcasting Act 1996;

(b)   a condition which, by virtue of section 11(2) or 95(2) of the Broadcasting Act 1990, is included in a licence granted under Part I or III of that Act or Part I or II of the Broadcasting Act 1996; or

(c)   a direction given under section 109(2) of the Broadcasting Act 1990 (power of Radio Authority to require production of recordings etc).

(3) The rights conferred by Part II are not infringed by–

(a)   the use by the Independent Television Commission or the Radio Authority, in connection with the performance of any of their functions under the Broadcasting Act 1990 or the Broadcasting Act 1996, of any recording, script or transcript which is provided to them under or by virtue of any provision of those Acts; or

(b)   the use by the Broadcasting Standards Commission, in connection with any complaint made to them under the Broadcasting Act 1996, of any recording or transcript requested or required to be provided to them, and so provided, under section 115(4) or (6) or 116(5) of that Act.]

Free public showing or playing of broadcast or cable programme

18.–(1) The showing or playing in public of a broadcast or cable programme to an audience who have not paid for admission to the place where the broadcast or programme is to be seen or heard does not infringe any right conferred by Part II in relation to a performance or recording included in–

    (a)   the broadcast or cable programme, or

    (b)   any sound recording or film which is played or shown in public by reception of the broadcast or cable programme.

    (2) The audience shall be treated as having paid for admission to a place–

    (a)   if they have paid for admission to a place of which that place forms part; or

    (b)   if goods or services are supplied at that place (or a place of which it forms part)–

        (i)   at prices which are substantially attributable to the facilities afforded for seeing or hearing the broadcast or programme, or

        (ii)   at prices exceeding those usually charged there and which are partly attributable to those facilities.

    (3) The following shall not be regarded as having paid for admission to a place–

    (a)   persons admitted as residents or inmates of the place;

    (b)   persons admitted as members of a club or society where the payment is only for membership of the club or society and the provision of facilities for seeing or hearing broadcasts or programmes is only incidental to the main purposes of the club or society.

    (4) Where the making of the broadcast or inclusion of the programme in a cable programme service was an infringement of the rights conferred by Part II in relation to a performance or recording, the fact that it was heard or seen in public by the reception of the broadcast or programme shall be taken into account in assessing the damages for that infringement.

    (5) Expressions used in this paragraph have the same meaning as in section 72.

[Reception and re-transmission of broadcast in cable programme service

19.–(1) This paragraph applies where a broadcast made from a place in the United Kingdom is, by reception and immediate re-transmission, included in a cable programme service.

    (2) The rights conferred by Part II in relation to a performance or recording included in the broadcast are not infringed if and to the extent that the broadcast is made for reception in the area in which the cable programme service is provided; but where the making of the broadcast was an infringement of those rights, the fact that the broadcast was re-transmitted as a programme in a cable programme service shall be taken into account in assessing the damages for that infringement.

    (3) Where–

    (a)   the inclusion is in pursuance of a relevant requirement, but

    (b)   to any extent, the area in which the cable programme service is provided ('the cable area') falls outside the area for reception in which the broadcast is made ('the broadcast area'),

the inclusion in the cable programme service (to the extent that it is provided for so much of the cable area as falls outside the broadcast area) of any performance or recording included in the broadcast shall, subject to sub-paragraph (4), be treated as licensed by the owner of the rights conferred by Part II in relation to the performance or recording, subject only to the payment to him by the person making the broadcast of such reasonable royalty or other payment in respect of the inclusion of the broadcast in the cable programme service as may be agreed or determined in default of agreement by the Copyright Tribunal.

    (4) Sub-paragraph (3) does not apply if, or to the extent that, the inclusion of the work in the cable programme service is (apart from that sub-paragraph) licensed by the owner of the rights conferred by Part II in relation to the performance or recording.

    (5) The Secretary of State may by order–

(a) provide that in specified cases sub-paragraph (2) is to apply in relation to broadcasts of a specified description which are not made as mentioned in that sub-paragraph, or

(b) exclude the application of that sub-paragraph in relation to broadcasts of a specified description made as mentioned in that sub-paragraph.

(6) Where the Secretary of State exercises the power conferred by sub-paragraph (5)(b) in relation to broadcasts of any description, the order may also provide for sub-paragraph (3) to apply, subject to such modifications as may be specified in the order, in relation to broadcasts of that description.

(7) An order under this paragraph may contain such transitional provision as appears to the Secretary of State to be appropriate.

(8) An order under this paragraph shall be made by statutory instrument which shall be subject to annulment in pursuance of a resolution of either House of Parliament.

(9) Expressions used in this paragraph have the same meaning as in section 73.]

[**19A.**–(1) An application to settle the royalty or other sum payable in pursuance of sub-paragraph (3) of paragraph 19 may be made to the Copyright Tribunal by the owner of the rights conferred by Part II or the person making the broadcast.

(2) The Tribunal shall consider the matter and make such order as it may determine to be reasonable in the circumstances.

(3) Either party may subsequently apply to the Tribunal to vary the order, and the Tribunal shall consider the matter and make such order confirming or varying the original order as it may determine to be reasonable in the circumstances.

(4) An application under sub-paragraph (3) shall not, except with the special leave of the Tribunal, be made within twelve months from the date of the original order or of the order on a previous application under that sub-paragraph.

(5) An order under sub-paragraph (3) has effect from the date on which it is made or such later date as may be specified by the Tribunal.]

Provision of sub-titled copies of broadcast or cable programme

20.–(1) A designated body may, for the purpose of providing people who are deaf or hard of hearing, or physically or mentally handicapped in other ways, with copies which are sub-titled or otherwise modified for their special needs, make recordings of television broadcasts or cable programmes without infringing any right conferred by Part II in relation to a performance or recording included in the broadcast or cable programme.

(2) In this paragraph 'designated body' means a body designated for the purposes of section 74 and other expressions used in this paragraph have the same meaning as in that section.

Recording of broadcast or cable programme for archival purposes

21.–(1) A recording of a broadcast or cable programme of a designated class, or a copy of such a recording, may be made for the purpose of being placed in an archive maintained by a designated body without thereby infringing any right conferred by Part II in relation to a performance or recording included in the broadcast or cable programme.

(2) In this paragraph 'designated class' and 'designated body' means a class or body designated for the purposes of section 75 and other expressions used in this paragraph have the same meaning as in that section.

NOTES

Commencement order: SI 1989/816.

Paras 6A, 6B, 14A: added by SI 1996/2967, reg 20(3).

Para 17: sub-paras (2), (3) substituted, for sub-paras (2)–(4), as originally enacted, by the Broadcasting Act 1990, s 203(1), Sch 20, para 50(2), further substituted for certain purposes as from 1 October 1996, and prospectively substituted for remaining puposes as from a day to be appointed, by the Broadcasting Act 1996, s 148(1), Sch 10, para 32, for purposes see SI 1996/2120, art 4, Sch 1.

Para 19: substituted by the Broadcasting Act 1996, s 138, Sch 9, para 5.

Para 19A: added by the Broadcasting Act 1996, s 138, Sch 9, para 6.

SCHEDULE 2A
[LICENSING OF PERFORMER'S PROPERTY RIGHTS

Section 205A

[Licensing schemes and licensing bodies

1.–(1) In Part II a 'licensing scheme' means a scheme setting out–

    (a)   the classes of case in which the operator of the scheme, or the person on whose behalf he acts, is willing to grant performers' property right licences, and

    (b)   the terms on which licences would be granted in those classes of case;

and for this purpose a 'scheme' includes anything in the nature of a scheme, whether described as a scheme or as a tariff or by any other name.

(2) In Part II a 'licensing body' means a society or other organisation which has as its main object, or one of its main objects, the negotiating or granting, whether as owner or prospective owner of a performer's property rights or as agent for him, of performers' property right licences, and whose objects include the granting of licences covering the performances of more than one performer.

(3) In this paragraph 'performers' property right licences' means licences to do, or authorise the doing of, any of the things for which consent is required under section 182A, 182B or 182C.

(4) References in this Part to licences or licensing schemes covering the performances of more than one performer do not include licences or schemes covering only–

    (a)   performances recorded in a single recording,

    (b)   performances recorded in more than one recording where–

        (i)   the performers giving the performances are the same, or

        (ii)   the recordings are made by, or by employees of or commissioned by, a single individual, firm, company or group of companies.

For purpose a group of companies means a holding company and its subsidiaries within the meaning of section 736 of the Companies Act 1985.

References and applications with respect to licensing schemes

2.–Paragraphs 3 to 8 (references and applications with respect to licensing schemes) apply to licensing schemes operated by licensing bodies in relation to a performer's property rights which cover the performances of more than one performer, so far as they relate to licences for–

    (a)   copying a recording of the whole or any substantial part of a qualifying performance, or

    (b)   renting or lending copies of a recording to the public;

and in those paragraphs 'licensing scheme' means a licensing scheme of any of those descriptions.

Reference of proposed licensing scheme to tribunal

3.–(1) The terms of a licensing scheme proposed to be operated by a licensing body may be referred to the Copyright Tribunal by an organisation claiming to be representative of persons claiming that they require licences in cases of a description to which the scheme would apply, either generally or in relation to any description of case.

(2) The Tribunal shall first decide whether to entertain the reference, and may decline to do so on the ground that the reference is premature.

(3) If the Tribunal decides to entertain the reference it shall consider the matter referred and make such order, either confirming or varying the proposed scheme, either generally or so far as it relates to cases of the description to which the reference relates, as the Tribunal may determine to be reasonable in the circumstances.

(4) The order may be made so as to be in force indefinitely or for such period as the Tribunal may determine.

276   *Part 2*

Reference of licensing scheme to tribunal

4.–(1) If while a licensing scheme is in operation a dispute arises between the operator of the scheme and–

(a) a person claiming that he requires a licence in a case of a description to which the scheme applies, or

(b) an organisation claiming to be representative of such persons,

that person or organisation may refer the scheme to the Copyright Tribunal in so far as it relates to cases of that description.

(2) A scheme which has been referred to the Tribunal under this paragraph shall remain in operation until proceedings on the reference are concluded.

(3) The Tribunal shall consider the matter in dispute and make such order, either confirming or varying the scheme so far as it relates to cases of the description to which the reference relates, as the Tribunal may determine to be reasonable in the circumstances.

(4) The order may be made so as to be in force indefinitely or for such period as the Tribunal may determine.

Further reference of scheme to tribunal

5.–(1) Where the Copyright Tribunal has on a previous reference of a licensing scheme under paragraph 3 or 4, or under this paragraph, made an order with respect to the scheme, then, while the order remains in force–

(a) the operator of the scheme,

(b) a person claiming that he requires a licence in a case of the description to which the order applies, or

(c) an organisation claiming to be representative of such persons,

may refer the scheme again to the Tribunal so far as it relates to cases of that description.

(2) A licensing scheme shall not, except with the special leave of the Tribunal, be referred again to the Tribunal in respect of the same description of cases–

(a) within twelve months from the date of the order on the previous reference, or

(b) if the order was made so as to be in force for 15 months or less, until the last three months before the expiry of the order.

(3) A scheme which has been refereed to the Tribunal under this paragraph shall remain in operation until proceedings on the reference are concluded.

(4) The Tribunal shall consider the matter in dispute and make such order, either confirming, varying or further varying the scheme so far as it relates to cases of the description to which the reference relates, as the Tribunal may determine to be reasonable in the circumstances.

(5) The order may be made so as to be in force indefinitely or for such period as the Tribunal may determine.

Application for grant of licence in connection with licensing scheme

6.–(1) A person who claims, in a case covered by a licensing scheme, that the operator of the scheme has refused to grant him or procure the grant to him of a licence in accordance with the scheme, or has failed to do so within a reasonable time after being asked, may apply to the Copyright Tribunal.

(2) A person who claims, in a case excluded from a licensing scheme, that the operator of the scheme either–

(a) has refused to grant him a licence or procure the grant to him of a licence, or has failed to do so within a reasonable time of being asked, and that in the circumstances it is unreasonable that a licence should not be granted, or

(b) proposes terms for a licence which are unreasonable,

may apply to the Copyright Tribunal.

(3) A case shall be regarded as excluded from a licensing scheme for the purposes of sub-paragraph (2) if–

    (a)   the scheme provides for the grant of licences subject to terms excepting matters from the licence and the case falls within such an exception, or

    (b)   the case is so similar to those in which licences are granted under the scheme that it is unreasonable that it should not be dealt with in the same way.

(4) If the Tribunal is satisfied that the claim is well-founded, it shall make an order declaring that, in respect of the matters specified in the order, the applicant is entitled to a licence on such terms as the Tribunal may determine to be applicable in accordance with the scheme or, as the case may be, to be reasonable in the circumstances.

(5) The order may be made so as to be in force indefinitely or for such period as the Tribunal may determine.

Application for review of order as to entitlement to licence

7.–(1) Where the Copyright Tribunal has made an order under paragraph 6 that a person is entitled to a licence under a licensing scheme, the operator of the scheme or the original applicant may apply to the Tribunal to review its order.

(2) An application shall not be made, except with the special leave of the Tribunal–

    (a)   within twelve months from the date of the order, or of the decision on a previous application under this paragraph, or

    (b)   if the order was made so as to be in force for 15 months or less, or as a result of the decision on a previous application under this paragraph is due to expire within 15 months of that decision, until the last three months before the expiry date.

(3) The Tribunal shall on an application for review confirm or vary its order as the Tribunal may determine to be reasonable having regard to the terms applicable in accordance with the licensing scheme or, as the case may be, the circumstances of the case.

Effect of order of tribunal as to licensing scheme

8.–(1) A licensing scheme which has been confirmed or varied by the Copyright Tribunal–

    (a)   under paragraph 3 (reference of terms of proposed scheme), or

    (b)   under paragraph 4 or 5 (reference of existing scheme to Tribunal),

shall be in force or, as the case may be, remain in operation, so far as it relates to the description of case in respect of which the order was made, so long as the order remains in force.

(2) While the order is in force a person who in a case of a class to which the order applies–

    (a)   pays to the operator of the scheme any charges payable under the scheme in respect of a licence covering the case in question or, if the amount cannot be ascertained, gives an undertaking to the operator to pay them when ascertained, and

    (b)   complies with the other terms applicable to such a licence under the scheme,

shall be in the same position as regards infringement of performers' property rights as if he had at all material times been the holder of a licence granted by the rights owner in question in accordance with the scheme.

(3) The Tribunal may direct that the order, so far as it varies the amount of charges payable, has effect from a date before that on which it is made, but not earlier than the date on which the reference was made or, if later, on which the scheme came into operation.

If such a direction is made–

    (a)   any necessary repayments, or further payments, shall be made in respect of charges already paid, and

    (b)   the reference in sub-paragraph (2)(a) to the charges payable under the scheme shall be construed as a reference to the charges so payable by virtue of the order.

No such direction may be made where sub-paragraph (4) below applies.

(4) An order of the Tribunal under paragraph 4 or 5 made with respect to a scheme which is certified for any purpose under paragraph 16 has effect, so far as it varies the scheme by reducing the charges payable for licences, from the date on which the reference was made to the Tribunal.

(5) Where the Tribunal has made an order under paragraph 6 (order as to entitlement to licence under licensing scheme) and the order remains in force, the person in whose favour the order is made shall if he–

(a)   pays to the operator of the scheme any charges payable in accordance with the order or, if the amount cannot be ascertained, gives an undertaking to pay the charges when ascertained, and

(b)   complies with the other terms specified in the order,

be in the same position as regards infringement of performers' property rights as if he had at all material times been the holder of a licence granted by the rights owner in question on the terms specified in the order.

References and applications with respect to licensing by licensing bodies

9.–Paragraphs 10 to 13 (references and applications with respect to licensing by licensing bodies) apply to licences relating to a performer's property rights which cover the performance of more than one performer granted by a licensing body otherwise than in pursuance of a licensing scheme, so far as the licences authorise–

(a)   copying a recording of the whole or any substantial part of a qualifying performance, or

(b)   renting or lending copies of a recording to the public;

and references in those paragraphs to a licence shall be construed accordingly.

Reference to tribunal of proposed licence

10.–(1) The terms on which a licensing body proposes to grant a licence may be referred to the Copyright Tribunal by the prospective licensee.

(2) The Tribunal shall first decide whether to entertain the reference, and may decline to do so on the ground that the reference is premature.

(3) If the Tribunal decides to entertain the reference it shall consider the terms of the proposed licence and make such order, either confirming or varying the terms as it may determine to be reasonable in the circumstances.

(4) The order may be made so as to be in force indefinitely or for such period as the Tribunal may determine.

Reference to tribunal of expiring licence

11.–(1) A licensee under a licence which is due to expire, by effluxion of time or as a result of notice given by the licensing body, may apply to the Copyright Tribunal on the ground that it is unreasonable in the circumstances that the licence should cease to be in force.

(2) Such an application may not be made until the last three months before the licence is due to expire.

(3) A licence in respect of which a reference has been made to the Tribunal shall remain in operation until proceedings on the reference are concluded.

(4) If the Tribunal finds the application well-founded, it shall make an order declaring that the licensee shall continue to be entitled to the benefit of the licence on such terms as the Tribunal may determine to be reasonable in the circumstances.

(5) An order of the Tribunal under this paragraph may be made so as to be in force indefinitely or for such period as the Tribunal may determine.

Application for review of order as to licence

12.–(1) Where the Copyright Tribunal has made an order under paragraph 10 or 11, the licensing body or the person entitled to the benefit of the order may apply to the Tribunal to review its order.

(2) An application shall not be made, except with the special leave of the Tribunal–

(a)   within twelve months from the date of the order or of the decision on a previous application under this paragraph, or

(b)   if the order was made so as to be in force for 15 months or less, or as a result of the decision on a previous application under this paragraph is due to expire within 15 months of that decision, until the last three months before the expiry date.

(3) The Tribunal shall on an application for review confirm or vary its order as the Tribunal may determine to be reasonable in the circumstances.

Effect of order of tribunal as to licence

13.–(1) Where the Copyright Tribunal has made an order under paragraph 10 or 11 and the order remains in force, the person entitled to the benefit of the order shall if he–

(a)   pays to the licensing body any charges payable in accordance with the order or, if the amount cannot be ascertained, gives an undertaking to pay the charges when ascertained, and

(b)   complies with the other terms specified in the order,

be in the same position as regards infringement of performers' property rights as if he had at all material times been the holder of a licence granted by the rights owner in question on the terms specified in the order.

(2) The benefit of the order may be assigned–

(a)   in the case of an order under paragraph 10, if assignment is not prohibited under the terms of the Tribunal's order; and

(b)   in the case of an order under paragraph 11, if assignment was not prohibited under the terms of the original licence.

(3) The Tribunal may direct that an order under paragraph 10 or 11, or an order under paragraph 12 varying such an order, so far as it varies the amount of charges payable, has effect from a date before that on which it is made, but not earlier than the date on which the reference or application was made or, if later, on which the licence was granted or, as the case may be, was due to expire.

If such a direction is made–

(a)   any necessary repayments, or further payments, shall be made in respect of charges already paid, and

(b)   the reference in sub-paragraph (1)(a) to the charges payable in accordance with the order shall be construed, where the order is varied by a later order, as a reference to the charges so payable by virtue of the later order.

General considerations: unreasonable discrimination

14.–(1) In determining what is reasonable on a reference or application under this Schedule relating to a licensing scheme or licence, the Copyright Tribunal shall have regard to–

(a)   the availability of other schemes, or the granting of other licences, to other persons in similar circumstances, and

(b)   the terms of those schemes or licences,

and shall exercise its powers so as to secure that there is no unreasonable discrimination between licensees, or prospective licensees, under the scheme or licence to which the reference or application relates and licensees under other schemes operated by, or other licences granted by, the same person.

(2) This does not affect the Tribunal's general obligation in any case to have regard to all relevant circumstances.

Application to settle royalty or other sum payable for lending

15.–(1) An application to settle the royalty or other sum payable in pursuance of paragraph 14A of Schedule 2 (lending of certain recordings) may be made to the Copyright Tribunal by the owner of a performer's property rights or the person claiming to be treated as licensed by him.

(2) The Tribunal shall consider the matter and make such order as it may determine to be reasonable in the circumstances.

(3) Either party may subsequently apply to the Tribunal to vary the order, and the Tribunal shall consider the matter and make such order confirming or varying the original order as it may determine to be reasonable in the circumstances.

(4) An application under sub-paragraph (3) shall not, except with the special leave of the Tribunal, be made within twelve months from the date of the original order or of the order on a previous application under that sub-paragraph.

(5) An order under sub-paragraph (3) has effect from the date on which it is made or such later date as may be specified by the Tribunal.

Certification of licensing schemes

16.–(1) A person operating or proposing to operate a licensing scheme may apply to the Secretary of State to certify the scheme for the purposes of paragraph 14A of Schedule 2 (lending of certain recordings).

(2) The Secretary of State shall by order made by statutory instrument certify the scheme if he is satisfied that it–

(a)   enables the works to which it relates to be identified with sufficient certainty by persons likely to require licences, and

(b)   sets out clearly the charges (if any) payable and the other terms on which licences will be granted.

(3) The scheme shall be scheduled to the order and the certification shall come into operation for the purposes of paragraph 14A of Schedule 2–

(a)   on such date, not less than eight weeks after the order is made, as may be specified in the order, or

(b)   if the scheme is the subject of a reference under paragraph 3 (reference of proposed scheme), any later date on which the order of the Copyright Tribunal under that paragraph comes into force or the reference is withdrawn.

(4) A variation of the scheme is not effective unless a corresponding amendment of the order is made; and the Secretary of State shall make such an amendment in the case of a variation ordered by the Copyright Tribunal on a reference under paragraph 3, 4 or 5, and may do so in any other case if he thinks fit.

(5) The order shall be revoked if the scheme ceases to be operated and may be revoked if it appears to the Secretary of State that it is no longer being operated according to its terms.

Powers exercisable in consequence of competition report

17.–(1) Where the matters specified in a report of the Monopolies and Mergers Commission as being those which in the Commission's opinion operate, may be expected to operate or have operated against the public interest include–

(a)   conditions in licences granted by the owner of a performer's property rights restricting the use to which a recording may be put by the licensee or the right of the owner to grant other licences, or

(b)   a refusal of an owner of a performer's property rights to grant licences on reasonable terms,

the powers conferred by Part I of Schedule 8 to the Fair Trading Act 1973 (powers exercisable for purpose of remedying or preventing adverse effects specified in report of Commission) include power to cancel or modify those conditions and, instead or in addition, to provide that licences in respect of the performer's property rights shall be available as of right.

(2) The references in sections 56(2) and 73(2) of that Act, and sections 10(2)(b) and 12(5) of the Competition Act 1980, to the powers specified in that Part of the Schedule shall be construed accordingly.

(3) A Minister shall only exercise the powers available by virtue of this paragraph if he is satisfied that to do so does not contravene any Convention relating to performers' rights to which the United Kingdom is a party.

(4) The terms of a licence available by virtue of this paragraph shall, in default of agreement, be settled by the Copyright Tribunal on an application by the person requiring the licence; and terms so settled shall authorise the licensee to do everything in respect of which a licence is so available.

(5) Where the terms of a licence are settled by the Tribunal, the licence has effect from the date on which the application to the Tribunal was made.]

NOTE

Added by SI 1996/2967, reg 22(2).

Regulations 24 and 25 of the Copyright and Rights in Databases Regulations 1997, SI 1997/3032 which introduce Sch 2 are contextualised in this Act at s 117.

This section should be read in conjunction with the following provisions of the Copyright and Rights in Databases Regulations 1997, SI 1997/3032 (commencement: 1 January 1998):

Copyright and Rights in Databases Regulations 1997, Sch 2

Regulation 24

SCHEDULE 2
LICENSING OF DATABASE RIGHT

Licensing scheme and licensing bodies

1–(1) In this Schedule a 'licensing scheme' means a scheme setting out–

    (a)   the classes of case in which the operator of the scheme, or the person on whose behalf he acts, is willing to grant database right licences, and

    (b)   the terms on which licences would be granted in those classes of case;

and for this purpose a 'scheme' includes anything in the nature of a scheme, whether described as a scheme or as a tariff or by any other name.

(2) In this Schedule a 'licensing body' means a society or other organisation which has as its main object, or one of its main objects, the negotiating or granting, whether as owner or prospective owner of a database right or as agent for him, of database right licences, and whose objects include the granting of licences covering the databases of more than one maker.

(3) In this paragraph 'database right licences' means licences to do, or authorise the doing of, any of the things for which consent is required under Regulation 16.

2 Paragraphs 3 to 8 apply to licensing schemes which are operated by licensing bodies and cover databases of more than one maker so far as they relate to licences for extracting or re-utilising all or a substantial part of the contents of a database; and references in those paragraphs to a licensing scheme shall be construed accordingly.

Reference of proposed licensing scheme to tribunal

3–(1) The terms of a licensing scheme proposed to be operated by a licensing body may be referred to the Copyright Tribunal by an organisation claiming to be representative of persons claiming that they require licences in cases of a description to which the scheme would apply, either generally or in relation to any description of case.

(2) The Tribunal shall first decide whether to entertain the reference, and may decline to do so on the ground that the reference is premature.

(3) If the Tribunal decides to entertain the reference it shall consider the matter referred and make such order, either confirming or varying the proposed scheme, either generally or so far as it relates to cases of the description to which the reference relates, as the Tribunal may determine to be reasonable in the circumstances.

(4) The order may be made so as to be in force indefinitely or for such period as the Tribunal may determine.

Reference of licensing scheme to tribunal

4–(1) If while a licensing scheme is in operation a dispute arises between the operator of the scheme and–

    (a)   a person claiming that he requires a licence in a case of a description to which the scheme applies, or

    (b)   an organisation claiming to be representative of such persons,

that person or organisation may refer the scheme to the Copyright Tribunal in so far as it relates to cases of that description.

(2) A scheme which has been referred to the Tribunal under this paragraph shall remain in operation until proceedings on the reference are concluded.

(3) The Tribunal shall consider the matter in dispute and make such order, either confirming or varying the scheme so far as it relates to cases of the description to which the reference relates, as the Tribunal may determine to be reasonable in the circumstances.

(4) The order may be made so as to be in force indefinitely or for such period as the Tribunal may determine.

Further reference of scheme to tribunal

5–(1) Where the Copyright Tribunal has on a previous reference of a licensing scheme under paragraph 3 or 4, or under this paragraph, made an order with respect to the scheme, then, while the order remains in force–

    (a)   the operator of the scheme,

    (b)   a person claiming that he requires a licence in a case of the description to which the order applies, or

    (c)   an organisation claiming to be representative of such persons,

may refer the scheme again to the Tribunal so far as it relates to cases of that description.

(2) A licensing scheme shall not, except with the special leave of the Tribunal, be referred again to the Tribunal in respect of the same description of cases–

    (a)   within twelve months from the date of the order on the previous reference, or

    (b)   if the order was made so as to be in force for 15 months or less, until the last three months before the expiry of the order.

(3) A scheme which has been referred to the Tribunal under this section shall remain in operation until proceedings on the reference are concluded.

(4) The Tribunal shall consider the matter in dispute and make such order, either confirming, varying or further varying the scheme so far as it relates to cases of the description to which the reference relates, as the Tribunal may determine to be reasonable in the circumstances.

(5) The order may be made so as to be in force indefinitely or for such period as the Tribunal may determine.

Application for grant of licence in connection with licensing scheme

6–(1) A person who claims, in a case covered by a licensing scheme, that the operator of the scheme has refused to grant him or procure the grant to him of a licence in accordance with the scheme, or has failed to do so within a reasonable time after being asked, may apply to the Copyright Tribunal.

(2) A person who claims, in a case excluded from a licensing scheme, that the operator of the scheme either–

    (a)   has refused to grant him a licence or procure the grant to him of a licence, or has failed to do so within a reasonable time of being asked, and that in the circumstances it is unreasonable that a licence should not be granted, or

    (b)   proposes terms for a licence which are unreasonable,

may apply to the Copyright Tribunal.

(3) A case shall be regarded as excluded from a licensing scheme for the purposes of sub-paragraph (2) if–

    (a)   the scheme provides for the grant of licences subject to terms excepting matters from the licence and the case falls within such an exception, or

    (b)   the case is so similar to those in which licences are granted under the scheme that it is unreasonable that it should not be dealt with in the same way.

(4) If the Tribunal is satisfied that the claim is well-founded, it shall make an order declaring that, in respect of the matters specified in the order, the applicant is entitled to a licence on such terms as the Tribunal may determine to be applicable in accordance with the scheme or, as the case may be, to be reasonable in the circumstances.

(5) The order may be made so as to be in force indefinitely or for such period as the Tribunal may determine.

Application for review of order as to entitlement to licence

7–(1) Where the Copyright Tribunal has made an order under paragraph 6 that a person is entitled to a licence under a licensing scheme, the operator of the scheme or the original applicant may apply to the Tribunal to review its order.

(2) An application shall not be made, except with the special leave of the Tribunal–

    (a)   within twelve months from the date of the order, or of the decision on a previous application under this section, or

    (b)   if the order was made so as to be in force for 15 months or less, or as a result of the decision on a previous application under this section is due to expire within 15 months of that decision, until the last three months before the expiry date.

(3) The Tribunal shall on an application for review confirm or vary its order as the Tribunal may determine to be reasonable having regard to the terms applicable in accordance with the licensing scheme or, as the case may be, the circumstances of the case.

Effect of order of tribunal as to licensing scheme

8–(1) A licensing scheme which has been confirmed or varied by the Copyright Tribunal–

    (a)   under paragraph 3 (reference of terms of proposed scheme), or

    (b)   under paragraph 4 or 5 (reference of existing scheme to Tribunal),

shall be in force or, as the case may be, remain in operation, so far as it relates to the description of case in respect of which the order was made, so long as the order remains in force.

(2) While the order is in force a person who in a case of a class to which the order applies–

    (a)   pays to the operator of the scheme any charges payable under the scheme in respect of a licence covering the case in question or, if the amount cannot be ascertained, gives an undertaking to the operator to pay them when ascertained, and

(b)   complies with the other terms applicable to such a licence under the scheme,

shall be in the same position as regards infringement of database right as if he had at all material times been the holder of a licence granted by the owner of the database right in question in accordance with the scheme.

(3) The Tribunal may direct that the order, so far as it varies the amount of charges payable, has effect from a date before that on which it is made, but not earlier than the date on which the reference was made or, if later, on which the scheme came into operation.

If such a direction is made–

(a)   any necessary repayments, or further payments, shall be made in respect of charges already paid, and
(b)   the reference in sub-paragraph (2)(a) to the charges payable under the scheme shall be construed as a reference to the charges so payable by virtue of the order.

No such direction may be made where sub-paragraph (4) below applies.

(4) Where the Tribunal has made an order under paragraph 6 (order as to entitlement to licence under licensing scheme) and the order remains in force, the person in whose favour the order is made shall if he–

(a)   pays to the operator of the scheme any charges payable in accordance with the order or, if the amount cannot be ascertained, gives an undertaking to pay the charges when ascertained, and
(b)   complies with the other terms specified in the order,

be in the same position as regards infringement of database right as if he had at all material times been the holder of a licence granted by the owner of the database right in question on the terms specified in the order.

References and applications with respect to licences by licensing bodies

9 Paragraphs 10 to 13 (references and applications with respect to licensing by licensing bodies) apply to licences relating to database right which cover databases of more than one maker granted by a licensing body otherwise than in pursuance of a licensing scheme, so far as the licences authorise extracting or re-utilising all or a substantial part of the contents of a database; and references in those paragraphs to a licence shall be construed accordingly.

Reference to tribunal of proposed licence

10–(1) The terms on which a licensing body proposes to grant a licence may be referred to the Copyright Tribunal by the prospective licensee.

(2) The Tribunal shall first decide whether to entertain the reference, and may decline to do so on the ground that the reference is premature.

(3) If the Tribunal decides to entertain the reference it shall consider the terms of the proposed licence and make such order, either confirming or varying the terms, as it may determine to be reasonable in the circumstances.

(4) The order may be made so as to be in force indefinitely or for such period as the Tribunal may determine.

Reference to tribunal of expiring licence

11–(1) A licensee under a licence which is due to expire, by effluxion of time or as a result of notice given by the licensing body, may apply to the Copyright Tribunal on the ground that it is unreasonable in the circumstances that the licence should cease to be in force.

(2) Such an application may not be made until the last three months before the licence is due to expire.

(3) A licence in respect of which a reference has been made to the Tribunal shall remain in operation until proceedings on the reference are concluded.

(4) If the Tribunal finds the application well-founded, it shall make an order declaring that the licensee shall continue to be entitled to the benefit of the licence on such terms as the Tribunal may determine to be reasonable in the circumstances.

(5) An order of the Tribunal under this section may be made so as to be in force indefinitely or for such period as the Tribunal may determine.

Application for review of order as to licence

12–(1) Where the Copyright Tribunal has made an order under paragraph 10 or 11, the licensing body or the person entitled to the benefit of the order may apply to the Tribunal to review its order.

(2) An application shall not be made, except with the special leave of the Tribunal–

(a)   within twelve months from the date of the order or of the decision on a previous application under this paragraph, or
(b)   if the order was made so as to be in force for 15 months or less, or as a result of the decision on a previous application under this section is due to expire within 15 months of that decision, until the last three months before the expiry date.

(3) The Tribunal shall on an application for review confirm or vary its order as the Tribunal may determine to be reasonable in the circumstances.

Effect of order of tribunal as to licence

13–(1) Where the Copyright Tribunal has made an order under paragraph 10 or 11 and the order remains in force, the person entitled to the benefit of the order shall if he–

(a) pays to the licensing body any charges payable in accordance with the order or, if the amount cannot be ascertained, gives an undertaking to pay the charges when ascertained, and

(b) complies with the other terms specified in the order,

be in the same position as regards infringement of database right as if he had at all material times been the holder of a licence granted by the owner of the database right in question on the terms specified in the order.

(2) The benefit of the order may be assigned–

(a) in the case of an order under paragraph 10, if assignment is not prohibited under the terms of the Tribunal's order; and

(b) in the case of an order under paragraph 11, if assignment was not prohibited under the terms of the original licence.

(3) The Tribunal may direct that an order under paragraph 10 or 11, or an order under paragraph 12 varying such an order, so far as it varies the amount of charges payable, has effect from a date before that on which it is made, but not earlier than the date on which the reference or application was made or, if later, on which the licence was granted or, as the case may be, was due to expire.

If such a direction is made–

(a) any necessary repayments, or further payments, shall be made in respect of charges already paid, and

(b) the reference in sub-paragraph (1)(a) to the charges payable in accordance with the order shall be construed, where the order is varied by a later order, as a reference to the charges so payable by virtue of the later order.

General considerations: unreasonable discrimination

14 In determining what is reasonable on a reference or application under this Schedule relating to a licensing scheme or licence, the Copyright Tribunal shall have regard to–

(a) the availability of other schemes, or the granting of other licences, to other persons in similar circumstances, and

(b) the terms of those schemes or licences,

and shall exercise its powers so as to secure that there is no unreasonable discrimination between licensees, or prospective licensees, under the scheme or licence to which the reference or application relates and licensees under other schemes operated by, or other licences granted by, the same person.

Powers exercisable in consequence of competition report

15–(1) Where the matters specified in a report of the Monopolies and Mergers Commission as being those which in the Commission's opinion operate, may be expected to operate or have operated against the public interest include–

(a) conditions in licences granted by the owner of database right in a database restricting the use of the database by the licensee or the right of the owner of the database right to grant other licences, or

(b) a refusal of an owner of database right to grant licences on reasonable terms,

the powers conferred by Part I of Schedule 8 to the Fair Trading Act 1973 (powers exercisable for purpose of remedying or preventing adverse effects specified in report of Commission) include power to cancel or modify those conditions and, instead or in addition, to provide that licences in respect of the database right shall be available as of right.

(2) The references in sections 56(2) and 73(2) of that Act, and sections 10(2)(b) and 12(5) of the Competition Act 1980, to the powers specified in that Part of that Schedule shall be construed accordingly.

(3) The terms of a licence available by virtue of this paragraph shall, in default of agreement, be settled by the Copyright Tribunal on an application by the person requiring the licence; and terms so settled shall authorise the licensee to do everything in respect of which a licence is so available.

(4) Where the terms of a licence are settled by the Tribunal, the licence has effect from the date on which the application to the Tribunal was made.

(Sch 3 amends the Registered Designs Act 1949; Sch 4 sets out the text of the 1949 Act, as amended by this Act; Sch 5 amends the Patents Act 1977.)

SCHEDULE 6
PROVISIONS FOR THE BENEFIT OF THE HOSPITAL FOR SICK CHILDREN

Section 301

Interpretation

1.–(1) In this Schedule–

'the Hospital' means The Hospital for Sick Children, Great Ormond Street, London,
'the trustees' means the special trustees appointed for the Hospital under the National Health Service Act 1977; and
'the work' means the play 'Peter Pan' by Sir James Matthew Barrie.

(2) Expressions used in this Schedule which are defined for the purposes of Part I of this Act (copyright) have the same meaning as in that Part.

Entitlement to royalty

2.–(1) The trustees are entitled, subject to the following provisions of this Schedule, to a royalty in respect of any public performance, commercial publication, broadcasting or inclusion in a cable programme service of the whole or any substantial part of the work or an adaptation of it.

(2) Where the trustees are or would be entitled to a royalty, another form of remuneration may be agreed.

Exceptions

3.–No royalty is payable in respect of–

(a) anything which immediately before copyright in the work expired on 31st December 1987 could lawfully have been done without the licence, or further licence, of the trustees as copyright owners; or

(b) anything which if copyright still subsisted in the work could, by virtue of any provision of Chapter III of Part I of this Act (acts permitted notwithstanding copyright), be done without infringing copyright.

Saving

4.–No royalty is payable in respect of anything done in pursuance of arrangements made before the passing of this Act.

Procedure for determining amount payable

5.–(1) In default of agreement application may be made to the Copyright Tribunal which shall consider the matter and make such order regarding the royalty or other remuneration to be paid as it may determine to be reasonable in the circumstances.

(2) Application may subsequently be made to the Tribunal to vary its order, and the Tribunal shall consider the matter and make such order confirming or varying the original order as it may determine to be reasonable in the circumstances.

(3) An application for variation shall not, except with the special leave of the Tribunal, be made within twelve months from the date of the original order or of the order on a previous application for variation.

(4) A variation order has effect from the date on which it is made or such later date as may be specified by the Tribunal.

[(5) The provisions of Chapter VIII of Part I (general provisions relating to the Copyright Tribunal) apply in relation to the Tribunal when exercising any jurisdiction under this paragraph.]

Sums received to be held on trust

6.–The sums received by the trustees by virtue of this Schedule, after deduction of any relevant expenses, shall be held by them on trust for the purposes of the Hospital.

Right only for the benefit of the Hospital

7.–(1) The right of the trustees under this Schedule may not be assigned and shall cease if the trustees purport to assign or charge it.

(2) The right may not be the subject of an order under section 92 of the National Health Service Act 1977 (transfers of trust property by order of the Secretary of State) and shall cease if the Hospital ceases to have a separate identity or ceases to have purposes which include the care of sick children.

(3) Any power of Her Majesty, the court (within the meaning of [the Charities Act 1993]) or any other person to alter the trusts of a charity is not exercisable in relation to the trust created by this Schedule.

NOTES

Para 5: sub-para (5) added by SI 1996/2967, reg 24(3).
Para 7: in sub-para (3) words in square brackets substituted by the Charities Act 1993, s 98(1), Sch 6, para 30.

(Sch 7: insofar as unrepealed, contains consequential amendments and repeals.)

SCHEDULE 8
Repeals

Section 303(2)

Chapter	Short title	Extent of repeal
1939 c 107.	Patents, Designs, Copyright and Trade Marks (Emergency) Act 1939.	In section 10(1), the definition of 'copyright'.
1945 c 16.	Limitation (Enemies and War Prisoners) Act 1945.	In sections 2(1) and 4(a), the reference to section 10 of the Copyright Act 1911.
1949 c 88.	Registered Designs Act 1949.	In section 3(2), the words 'or original'. Section 5(5). In section 11(2), the words 'or original'. In section 14(3), the words 'or the Isle of Man'. Section 32. Section 33(2). Section 37(1). Section 38. In section 44(1), the definitions of 'copyright' and 'Journal'. In section 45, paragraphs (1) and (2). In section 46, paragraphs (1) and (2). Section 48(1). In Schedule 1, in paragraph 3(1), the words 'in such manner as may be prescribed by rules of court'. Schedule 2.
1956 c 74.	Copyright Act 1956.	The whole Act.
1957 c 6.	Ghana Independence Act 1957.	In Schedule 2, paragraph 12.
1957 c 60.	Federation of Malaya Independence Act 1957.	In Schedule 1, paragraphs 14 and 15.

1958 c 44.	Dramatic and Musical Performers' Protection Act 1958.	The whole Act.
1958 c 51.	Public Records Act 1958.	Section 11.
		Schedule 3.
1960 c 52.	Cyprus Independence Act 1960.	In the Schedule, paragraph 13.
1960 c 55.	Nigeria Independence Act 1960.	In Schedule 2, paragraphs 12 and 13.
1961 c 1.	Tanganyika Independence Act 1961.	In Schedule 2, paragraphs 13 and 14.
1961 c 16.	Sierra Leone Independence Act 1961.	In Schedule 3, paragraphs 13 and 14.
1961 c 25.	Patents and Designs (Renewals, Extensions and Fees) Act 1961.	The whole Act.
1962 c 40.	Jamaica Independence Act 1962.	In Schedule 2, paragraph 13.
1962 c 54.	Trinidad and Tobago Independence Act 1962.	In Schedule 2, paragraph 13.
1963 c 53.	Performers' Protection Act 1963.	The whole Act.
1964 c 46.	Malawi Independence Act 1964.	In Schedule 2, paragraph 13.
1964 c 65.	Zambia Independence Act 1964.	In Schedule 1, paragraph 9.
< ... >	< ... >	< ... >
1964 c 93.	Gambia Independence Act 1964.	In Schedule 2, paragraph 12.
1966 c 24.	Lesotho Independence Act 1966.	In the Schedule, paragraph 9.
1966 c 37.	Barbados Independence Act 1966.	In Schedule 2, paragraph 12.
1967 c 80.	Criminal Justice Act 1967.	In Parts I and IV of Schedule 3, the entries relating to the Registered Designs Act 1949.
1968 c 56.	Swaziland Independence Act 1968.	In the Schedule, paragraph 9.
1968 c 67.	Medicines Act 1968.	In section 92(2)(a), the words from 'or embodied' to 'film'.
		Section 98.
1968 c 68.	Design Copyright Act 1968.	The whole Act.
1971 c 4.	Copyright (Amendment) Act 1971.	The whole Act.
1971 c 23.	Courts Act 1971.	In Schedule 9, the entry relating to the Copyright Act 1956.
1971 c 62.	Tribunals and Inquiries Act 1971.	In Schedule 1, paragraph 24.
1972 c 32.	Performers' Protection Act 1972.	The whole Act.
1975 c 24.	House of Commons Disqualification Act 1975.	In Part II of Schedule 1, the entry relating to the Performing Right Tribunal.
1975 c 25.	Northern Ireland Assembly Disqualification Act 1975.	In Part II of Schedule 1, the entry relating to the Performing Right Tribunal.
1977 c 37.	Patents Act 1977.	Section 14(4) and (8).
		In section 28(3), paragraph (b) and the word 'and' preceding it.
		Section 28(5) to (9).
		Section 49(3).
		Section 72(3).
		Sections 84 and 85.
		Section 88.
		Section 104.
		In section 105, the words 'within the meaning of section 104 above'.
		Sections 114 and 115.
		Section 123(2)(k).
		In section 130(1), the definition of 'patent agent'.
		In section 130(7), the words '88(6) and (7),'.
		In Schedule 5, paragraphs 1 and 2, in paragraph 3 the words 'and 44(1)' and 'in each case', and paragraphs 7 and 8.

1979 c 2.	Customs and Excise Management Act 1979.	In Schedule 4, the entry relating to the Copyright Act 1956.
1980 c 21.	Competition Act 1980.	Section 14.
1981 c 68.	Broadcasting Act 1981.	Section 20(9)(a).
1982 c 35.	Copyright Act 1956 (Amendment) Act 1982.	The whole Act.
1983 c 42.	Copyright (Amendment) Act 1983.	The whole Act.
1984 c 46.	Cable and Broadcasting Act 1984.	Section 8(8).
		Section 16(4) and (5).
		Sections 22 to 24.
		Section 35(2) and (3).
		Sections 53 and 54.
		In section 56(2), the definition of 'the 1956 Act'.
		In Schedule 5, paragraphs 6, 7, 13 and 23.
1985 c 21.	Films Act 1985.	Section 7(2).
1985 c 41.	Copyright (Computer Software) Amendment Act 1985.	The whole Act.
1985 c 61.	Administration of Justice Act 1985.	Section 60.
1986 c 39.	Patents, Designs and Marks Act 1986.	In Schedule 2, paragraph 1(2)(a), in paragraph 1(2)(k) the words 'subsection (1)(j) of section 396 and' and in paragraph 1(2)(l) the words 'subsection (2)(i) of section 93'.
1988 c 1.	Income and Corporation Taxes Act 1988.	In Schedule 29, paragraph 5.

NOTES

Commencement orders: SI 1989/816, SI 1990/1400, SI 1990/2168.
Entry omitted repealed by the Statute Law (Repeals) Act 1993.

PART 3
Regulations and Directives

Destination tables

The tables below are for ease of reference and explain the destination within the Copyright, Designs and Patents Act of each individual regulation of the Duration of Copyright and Rights in Performances Regulations 1995, the Copyright and Related Rights Regulations 1996 and the Copyright and Rights in Databases Regulations 1997.

Where a regulation substitutes an earlier section of the Act, amends a section or is inserted directly into the Act as an additional section the place of substitution, insertion or amendment is given.

Where a regulation is to be read in conjunction with the Act but is not an amendment, insertion or substitution the regulation has been placed in its context within the Act and this context is given below.

Duration of Copyright and Rights in Performances Regulations 1995

Regulation	Destination
1	——
2	——
3	——
4	——
5 (1)	Substituted section 12
5 (2)	Amended section 57
5 (3)	Amended section 154
6 (1)	Substituted section 13
6 (2)	Inserted as section 66A
6 (3)	Amended sections 79 (4), 81(5), 85 (2)
6 (4)	Inserted as section 105 (2) (aa)
7 (1)	Substituted section 14
7 (2)	Amended Schedule 1 paragraph 9
8 (1)	Inserted as section 15A
8 (2)	Amended section 179
9 (1)	Substituted section 5
9 (2)	Amended section 80(6)
9 (3)	Amended section 117
9 (4)	Amended section 124
9 (5)	Amended section 179 (a)
9 (6)	Amended section 212
10	Substituted section 191
11 (1)	Inserted as section 172A
11 (2)	Amended section 179
11 (3)	Amended section 211(1)
11 (4)	Amended section 212
12	Contextualised after section 178
13	Contextualised after section 5B
14	Contextualised after sections 13B and 172
15	Contextualised after section 13B
16	Contextualised after section 13B
17	Contextualised after section 13B
18	Contextualised after section 13B and 91
19	Contextualised after sections 13B and 91
20	Contextualised after sections 13B and 91
21	Contextualised after sections 13B and 92
22	Contextualised after section 86
23	Contextualised after section 13B
24	Contextualised after sections 13B and 135
25	Contextualised after sections 13B and 135

27	Contextualised after section 191
28	Contextualised after section 191
29	Contextualised after section 191
30	Contextualised after section 191
31	Contextualised after section 191
32	Contextualised after section 191
33	Contextualised after section 191
34	Contextualised after sections 135 and 191
35	Contextualised after sections 135 and 191
36 (1)	Contextualised after sections 13B and 172
36 (2)	Contextualised after sections 13B and 212
36 (3)	Contextualised after sections 13B and 212

Copyright and Related Rights Regulations 1996

Regulation	Destination
1	——
2	——
3	——
4	——
5	Substituted section 6(4)
6 (1)	Inserted as section 6(4A)
6 (2)	Inserted as section 6A
7	Inserted as section 144A
8	Amended section 178
9 (1) (2) (3)	Amended section 18
9 (4)	Amended section 27
9 (5)	Substituted section 172A
9 (6)	Amended section 179
10 (1)	Inserted as section 18(ba)
10 (2)	Inserted as section 18A
10 (3)	Amended section 178
10 (4)	Amended section 179
11 (1)	Inserted as section 36A
11 (2)	Inserted as section 40A
11 (3)	Substituted section 66
11 (4)	Substituted section 143(1)(c)
11 (5)	Amended section 178
11 (6)	Amended section 179
11 (7)	——
12	Inserted as section 93A
13 (1)	Substituted section 133(1)
13 (2)	Substituted section 142
13 (3)	Amended section 149(e)
14 (1)	Inserted as sections 93B and 93C
14 (2)	Inserted as section 149(zb)
15 (1)	——
15 (2)	Substituted section 117
15 (3)	Substituted section 124
16	Contextualised after section 8
17	Contextualised after section 16
18 (1)	Amended section 9(2)
18 (2)	Inserted as section 10(1A)
18 (3)	Amended section 11
18 (4)	Amended section 105
18 (5)	Amended section 178
18 (6)	Amended section 179
19	Contextualised after section 9 and Schedule 1 paragraph 10
20 (1)	Substituted section 182
20 (2)	Inserted as sections 182A, 182B, 182C and 182D
20 (3)	Inserted as Schedule 2 paragraph 6A 6B and 14A

20 (4)	Amended section 212
21 (1)	Inserted as sections 191A, 191B, 191C, 191D, 191E, 191F, 191G, 191H, 191I, 191J, 191K, 191L and 191M
21 (2)	Substituted section 192
21 (3)	Amended section 193
21 (4)	Amended section 194
21 (5)	Amended headings from sections 191 to 195
21 (6)	Amended section 212
22 (1)	Inserted as section 205A
22 (2)	Inserted as Schedule 2A
23	Amended section 190
24 (1)	Inserted as section 205B
24 (2)	Amended section 149
24 (3)	Amended Schedule 6 paragraph 5
25	Contextualised after section 172
26	Contextualised after Schedule 1 paragraph 14 and Schedule 2 paragraph 1
27	Contextualised after Schedule 1 paragraph 14 and Schedule 2 paragraph 1
28	Contextualised after section 6
29	Contextualised after section 6A
30	Contextualised after section 192B
31	Contextualised after sections 16 and 180 and Schedule 1 paragraph 14 and Schedule 2 paragraph 1
32	Contextualised after sections 5B 93B and 191G
33	Contextualised after sections 5B 93B and 191G
34 (1)	Contextualised after section 18A and Schedule 1 paragraph 14
34 (2)	Contextualised after section 191A and Schedule 2 paragraph 1
35	Contextualised after section 40A
36	Contextualised after sections 9 and 16 and Schedule 1 paragraph 14

Copyright and Rights in Databases Regulations 1997

Regulation	Destination
1	———
2	———
3	———
4	———
5	Amended section 3(1)
6	Amended section 3A
7	Amended section 21
8	Amended section 29
9	Amended section 50D
10	Amended section 296B
11	Amended section 179
12(1)	Contextualised after section 3A and after section 179
12(2)	Contextualised after section 16
12(3)	Contextualised after section 16
12(4)	Contextualised after section 16
12(5)	Contextualised after section 16
13	Contextualised after section 3A
14	Contextualised after section 9
15	Contextualised after section 11
16	Contextualised after section 16
17	Contextualised after section 12
18	Contextualised after section 3A
19	Contextualised after section 16
20(1)	Contextualised after section 29
20(2)	Contextualised after section 76
21	Contextualised after section 66A
22	Contextualised after section 104

Duration of Copyright and Rights in Performances Regulations 1995

(SI 1995/3297)

Whereas a draft of the following Regulations has been approved by resolution of each House of Parliament:

Now, therefore, the Secretary of State, being a Minister designated for the purposes of section 2(2) of the European Communities Act 1972 in relation to measures relating to the protection of copyright and rights in performances, in exercise of powers conferred by section 2(2) and (4) of the said Act of 1972, hereby makes the following Regulations:–

NOTE
Made: 19 December 1995
Commencement: 1 January 1996

PART I
INTRODUCTORY PROVISIONS

1 Citation, commencement and extent
(1) These Regulations may be cited as the Duration of Copyright and Rights in Performances Regulations 1995.

(2) These Regulations come into force on 1st January 1996.

(3) These Regulations extend to the whole of the United Kingdom.

2 Interpretation
In these Regulations–

'EEA Agreement' means the Agreement on the European Economic Area signed at Oporto on 2nd May 1992, as adjusted by the Protocol signed at Brussels on 17th March 1993; and

'EEA state' means a state which is a contracting party to the EEA Agreement.

3 Implementation of Directive, &c
These Regulations make provision for the purpose of implementing–

(a) the main provisions of Council Directive No 93/98/EEC of 29th October 1993 harmonizing the term of protection of copyright and certain related rights; and

(b) certain obligations of the United Kingdom created by or arising under the EEA Agreement so far as relevant to the implementation of that Directive.

4 Scheme of the regulations
The Copyright, Designs and Patents Act 1988 is amended in accordance with the provisions of Part II of these Regulations, subject to the savings and transitional provisions in Part III of these Regulations.

PART II
AMENDMENTS OF THE COPYRIGHT, DESIGNS AND PATENTS ACT 1988

Copyright

5 Duration of copyright in literary, dramatic, musical or artistic works
(1) For section 12 (duration of copyright in literary, dramatic, musical or artistic works) substitute–

'12 Duration of copyright in literary, dramatic, musical or artistic works

(1) The following provisions have effect with respect to the duration of copyright in a literary, dramatic, musical or artistic work.

(2) Copyright expires at the end of the period of 70 years from the end of the calendar year in which the author dies, subject as follows.

(3) If the work is of unknown authorship, copyright expires–

(a) at the end of the period of 70 years from the end of the calendar year in which the work was made, or

(b) if during that period the work is made available to the public, at the end of the period of 70 years from the end of the calendar year in which it is first so made available,

subject as follows.

(4) Subsection (2) applies if the identity of the author becomes known before the end of the period specified in paragraph (a) or (b) of subsection (3).

(5) For the purposes of subsection (3) making available to the public includes–

(a) in the case of a literary, dramatic or musical work–

(i) performance in public, or

(ii) being broadcast or included in a cable programme service;

(b) in the case of an artistic work–

(i) exhibition in public,

(ii) a film including the work being shown in public, or

(iii) being included in a broadcast or cable programme service;

but in determining generally for the purposes of that subsection whether a work has been made available to the public no account shall be taken of any unauthorised act.

(6) Where the country of origin of the work is not an EEA state and the author of the work is not a national of an EEA state, the duration of copyright is that to which the work is entitled in the country of origin, provided that does not exceed the period which would apply under subsections (2) to (5).

(7) If the work is computer-generated the above provisions do not apply and copyright expires at the end of the period of 50 years from the end of the calendar year in which the work was made.

(8) The provisions of this section are adapted as follows in relation to a work of joint authorship–

(a) the reference in subsection (2) to the death of the author shall be construed–

(i) if the identity of all the authors is known, as a reference to the death of the last of them to die, and

(ii) if the identity of one or more of the authors is known and the identity of one or more others is not, as a reference to the death of the last whose identity is known;

(b) the reference in subsection (4) to the identity of the author becoming known shall be construed as a reference to the identity of any of the authors becoming known;

(c) the reference in subsection (6) to the author not being a national of an EEA state shall be construed as a reference to none of the authors being a national of an EEA state.

(9) This section does not apply to Crown copyright or Parliamentary copyright (see sections 163 to 166) or to copyright which subsists by virtue of section 168 (copyright of certain international organisations).'.

(2) In section 57 (anonymous or pseudonymous works: acts permitted on assumptions as to expiry of copyright or death of author), in subsection (1)(b)(ii) and subsection (2)(b) for '50 years' subsititute '70 years'.

(3) In section 154 (qualification for copyright preotection by reference to author), in subsection (3) for the paragraph referring to provisions of section 12 substitute–

'section 12 (duration of copyright), and section 9(4) (meaning of 'unknown authorship') so far as it applies for the purpose of section 12, and'.

6 Duration of copyright in sound recordings and films

(1) For section 13 (duration of copyright in sound recordings and films) substitute–

'13A Duration of copyright in sound recordings

(1) The following provisions have effect with respect to the duration of copyright in a sound recording.

(2) Copyright expires–

- (a)   at the end of the period of 50 years from the end of the calendar year in which it is made, or
- (b)   if during that period it is released, 50 years from the end of the calendar year in which it is released;

subject as follows.

(3) For the purposes of subsection (2) a sound recording is 'released' when it is first published, played in public, broadcast or included in a cable programme service; but in determining whether a sound recording has been released no account shall be taken of any unauthorised act.

(4) Where the author of a sound recording is not a national of an EEA state, the duration of copyright is that to which the sound recording is entitled in the country of which the author is a national, provided that does not exceed the period which would apply under subsections (2) and (3).

(5) If or to the extent that the application of subsection (4) would be at variance with an international obligation to which the United Kingdom became subject prior to 29th October 1993, the duration of copyright shall be as specified in subsections (2) and (3).]

13B Duration of copyright in films

(1) The following provisions have effect with respect to the duration of copyright in a film.

(2) Copyright expires at the end of the period of 70 years from the end of the calendar year in which the death occurs of the last to die of the following persons–

- (a)   the principal director,
- (b)   the author of the screenplay,
- (c)   the author of the dialogue, or
- (d)   the composer of music specially created for and used in the film;

subject as follows.

(3) If the identity of one or more of the persons referred to in subsection (2)(a) to (d) is known and the identity of one or more others is not, the reference in that subsection to the death of the last of them to die shall be construed as a reference to the death of the last whose identity is known.

(4) If the identity of the persons referred to in subsection (2)(a) to (d) is unknown, copyright expires at–

- (a)   the end of the period of 70 years from the end of the calendar year in which the film was made, or
- (b)   if during that period the film is made available to the public, at the end of the period of 70 years from the end of the calendar year in which it is first so made available.

(5) Subsections (2) and (3) apply if the identity of any of those persons becomes known before the end of the period specified in paragraph (a) or (b) of subsection (4).

(6) For the purposes of subsection (4) making available to the public includes–

- (a)   showing in public, or
- (b)   being broadcast or included in a cable programme service;

but in determining generally for the purposes of that subsection whether a film has been made available to the public no account shall be taken of any unauthorised act.

(7) Where the country of origin is not an EEA state and the author of the film is not a national of an EEA state, the duration of copyright is that to which the work is entitled in the country of origin, provided that does not exceed the period which would apply under subsections (2) to (6).

(8) In relation to a film of which there are joint authors, the reference in subsection (7) to the author not being a national of an EEA state shall be construed as a reference to none of the authors being a national of an EEA state.

(9) If in any case there is no person falling within paragraphs (a) to (d) of subsection (2), the above provisions do not apply and copyright expires at the end of the period of 50 years from the end of the calendar year in which the film was made.

(10) For the purposes of this section the identity of any of the persons referred to in subsection (2)(a) to (d) shall be regarded as unknown if it is not possible for a person to ascertain his identity by reasonable inquiry; but if the identity of any such person is once known it shall not subsequently be regarded as unknown.'.

(2) In Chapter III of Part I (acts permitted in relation to copyright works), after section 66 insert–

'Miscellaneous: films and sound recordings

66A Films: acts permitted on assumptions as to expiry of copyright, &c

(1) Copyright in a film is not infringed by an act done at a time when, or in pursuance of arrangements made at a time when–

(a) it is not possible by reasonable inquiry to ascertain the identity of any of the persons referred to in section 13B(2)(a) to (d) (persons by reference to whose life the copyright period is ascertained), and

(b) it is reasonable to assume–

(i) that copyright has expired, or

(ii) that the last to die of those persons died 70 years or more before the beginning of the calendar year in which the act is done or the arrangements are made.

(2) Subsection (1)(b)(ii) does not apply in relation to–

(a) a film in which Crown copyright subsists, or

(b) a film in which copyright originally vested in an international organisation by virtue of section 168 and in respect of which an Order under that section specifies a copyright period longer than 70 years.'

(3) In section 79(4), 81(5) and 85(2) (exceptions to moral rights: acts which would not infringe copyright) for 'section 57 (anonymous or pseudonymous works: acts permitted on assumptions as to expiry of copyright or death of author)' substitute 'section 57 or 66A (acts permitted on assumptions as to expiry of copyright, &c.)'

(4) In section 105(2) (presumptions relevant to filsm), after paragraph (a) insert–

'(aa) that a named person was the principal director, the author of the screenplay, the author of the dialogue or the composer of music specifically created for and used in the film,'.

7 Duration of copyright in broadcasts and cable programmes:

(1) For section 14 (duration of copyright in broadcasts and cable programmes) substitute–

'14 Duration of copyright in broadcasts and cable programmes

(1) The following provisions have effect with respect to the duration of copyright in a broadcast or cable programme.

(2) Copyright in a broadcast or cable programme expires at the end of the period of 50 years from the end of the calendar year in which the broadcast was made or the programme was included in a cable programme service, subject as follows.

(3) Where the author of the broadcast or cable programme is not a national of an EEA state, the duration of copyright in the broadcast or cable programme is that to which it is

entitled in the country of which the author is a national, provided that does not exceed the period which would apply under subsection (2).

(4) If or to the extent that the application of subsection (3) would be at variance with an international obligation to which the United Kingdom became subject prior to 29th October 1993, the duration of copyright shall be as specified in subsection (2).

(5) Copyright in a repeat broadcast or cable programme expires at the same time as the copyright in the original broadcast or cable programme; and accordingly no copyright arises in respect of a repeat broadcast or cable programme which is broadcast or included in a cable programme service after the expiry of the copyright in the original broadcast or cable programme.

(6) A repeat broadcast or cable programme means one which is a repeat either of a broadcast previously made or of a cable programme previously included in a cable programme service.'.

(2) In the closing words of paragraph 9 of Schedule 1 (repeats of pre-1957 broadcasts and pre-1985 cable programmes) for 'section 14(2)' substitute 'section 14(5)'.

8 Meaning of country of origin

(1) In Chapter I of Part I (subsistence, ownership and duration of copyright), after section 15 insert–

'15A Meaning of country of origin

(1) For the purposes of the provisions of this Part relating to the duration of copyright the country of origin of a work shall be determined as follows.

(2) If the work is first published in a Berne Convention country and is not simultaneously published elsewhere, the country of origin is that country.

(3) If the work is first published simultaneously in two or more countries only one of which is a Berne Convention country, the country of origin is that country.

(4) If the work is first published simultaneously in two or more countries of which two or more are Berne Convention countries, then–

(a) if any of those countries is an EEA state, the country of origin is that country; and

(b) if none of those countries is an EEA state, the country of origin is the Berne Convention country which grants the shorter or shortest period of copyright protection.

(5) If the work is unpublished or is first published in a country which is not a Berne Convention country (and is not simultaneously published in a Berne Convention country), the country of origin is–

(a) if the work is a film and the maker of the film has his headquarters in, or is domiciled or resident in a Berne Convention country, that country;

(b) if the work is–

(i) a work of architecture constructed in a Berne Convention country, or

(ii) an artistic work incorporated in a building or other structure situated in a Berne Convention country,

that country;

(c) in any other case, the country of which the author of the work is a national.

(6) In this section–

(a) a 'Berne Convention country' means a country which is a party to any Act of the International Convention for the Protection of Literary and Artistic Works signed at Berne on 9th September 1886; and

(b) references to simultaneous publication are to publication within 30 days of first publication.'

(2) In section 179 (index of defined expressions: Part I), at the appropriate place insert–

'country of origin   section 15A'.

9 Treatment of film sound tracks

(1) For section 5 (sound recordings and films) substitute–

'5A Sound recordings

(1) In this Part 'sound recording' means–

(a) a recording of sounds, from which the sounds may be reproduced, or

(b) a recording of the whole or any part of a literary, dramatic or musical work, from which sounds reproducing the work or part may be produced,

regardless of the medium on which the recording is made or the method by which the sounds are reproduced or produced.

(2) Copyright does not subsist in a sound recording which is, or to the extent that it is, a copy taken from a previous sound recording.]

5B Films

(1) In this Part 'film' means a recording on any medium from which a moving image may by any means be produced.

(2) The sound track accompanying a film shall be treated as part of the film for the purposes of this Part.

(3) Without prejudice to the generality of subsection (2), where that subsection applies–

(a) references in this Part to showing a film include playing the film sound track to accompany the film, and

(b) references to playing a sound recording do not include playing the film sound track to accompany the film.

(4) Copyright does not subsist in a film which is, or to the extent that it is, a copy taken from a previous film.

(5) Nothing in this section affects any copyright subsisting in a film sound track as a sound recording.'.

(2) In section 80(6) (derogatory treatment of film), omit the words following paragraph (b).

(3) In section 117 (licensing schemes to which ss 118 to 123 apply)–

(a) in paragraph (a) omit '(or film sound-tracks when accompanying a film)', and

(b) in paragraphy (b) omit '(other than film sound-track when accompanying a film)'.

(4) In section 124 (licneces to which ss 125 to 128 apply)–

(a) in paragraph (a) omit '(or film sound-tracks when accompanying a film)', and

(b) in paragraphy (b) omit '(other than film sound-track when accompanying a film)'.

(5) In section 179(a) (index of defined expressions: Part I)–

(a) in the entry relating to the expression 'film' for 'section 5' substitute 'section 5B'; and

(b) in the entry relating to the expression 'sound recording' for 'sections 5 and 135A' substitute 'section 5A and 135A'

In section 212 (index of defined expressions: Part II)–

(a) in the entry relating to the expression 'film' for 'section 5' substitute 'section 5B'; and

(b) in the entry relating to the expression 'sound recordings' for 'section 5' substitute 'section 5A'.

Rights in performances

10 Duration of rights in performances

In Part II (rights in performances), for section 191 (duration of rights) substitute–

'191 Duration of rights

(1) The following provisions have effect with respect to the duration of the rights conferred by this Part.

(2) The rights conferred by this Part in relation to a performance expire–

(a) at the end of the period of 50 years from the end of the calendar year in which the performance takes place, or

(b) if during that period a recording of the performance is released, 50 years from the end of the calendar year in which it is released,

subject as follows.

(3) For the purposes of subsection (2) a recording is 'released' when it is first published, played or shown in public, broadcast or included in a cable programme service; but in determining whether a recording has been released no account shall be taken of any unauthorised act.

(4) Where a performer is not a national of an EEA state, the duration of the rights conferred by this Part in relation to his performance is that to which the performance is entitled in the country of which he is a national, provided that does not exceed the period which would apply under subsections (2) and (3).

(5) If or to the extent that the application of subsection (4) would be at variance with an international obligation to which the United Kingdom became subject prior to 29th October 1993, the duration of the rights conferred by this Part shall be as specified in subsections (2) and (3).'.

Supplementary

11 Meaning of EEA national and EEA state

(1) In Chapter X of Part I (miscellaneous and general provisions), after section 172 insert–

'172A Meaning of EEA national and EEA state

(1) In this Part–

'EEA national' means a national of an EEA state; and
'EEA state' means a state which is a contracting party to the EEA Agreement.

(2) References in this Part to a person being an EEA national shall be construed in relation to a body corporate as references to its being incorporated under the law of an EEA state.

(3) The 'EEA Agreement' means the Agreement on the European Economic Area signed at Oporto on 2nd May 1992, as adjusted by the Protocol signed at Brussels on 17th March 1993.'

(2) In section 179 (index of defined expressions: Part I) at the appropriate place insert–

'EEA national and EEA state   sectiion 172A'.

(3) In section 211(1) (expresssions in Part II having same meaning as in Part I), at the appropriate place insert–

'EEA national,'.

(4) In section 212 (index of defined expressions: Part II), at the appropriate place insert–

'EEA national   section 211(1) (and section 172A)'.

PART III
SAVINGS AND TRANSITIONAL PROVISIONS

Introductory

12 Introductory

(1) References in this Part to 'commencement', without more, are to the date on which these Regulations come into force.

(2) In this Part–

'the 1988 Act' means the Copyright, Designs and Patents Act 1988;
'the 1988 provisions' means the provisions of that Act as they stood immediately before commencement (including the provisions of Schedule 1 to that Act continuing the effect of earlier enactments); and
'the new provisions' means the provisions of that Act as amended by these Regulations.

(3) Expressions used in this Part which are defined for the purposes of Part I or II of the 1988 Act, in particular references to the copyright owner, have the same meaning as in that Part.

13 Films not protected as such

In relation to a film in which copyright does not or did not subsist as such but which is or was protected–

(a)   as an original dramatic work, or
(b)   by virtue of the protection of the photographs forming part of the film,

references in the new provisions, and in this Part, to copyright in a film are to any copyright in the film as an original dramatic work or, as the case may be, in photographs forming part of the film.

Copyright

14 Copyright: interpretation

(1) In the provisions of this Part relating to copyright–

(a)   'existing', in relation to a work, means made before commencement; and
(b)   'existing copyright work' means a work in which copyright subsisted immediately before commencement.

(2) For the purposes of those provisions a work of which the making extended over a period shall be taken to have been made when its making was completed.

(3) References in those provisions to 'moral rights' are to the rights conferred by Chapter IV of Part I of the 1988 Act.

15 Duration of copyright: general saving

(1) Copyright in an existing copyright work shall continue to subsist until the date on which it would have expired under the 1988 provisions if that date is later than the date on which copyright would expire under the new provisions.

(2) Where paragraph (1) has effect, section 57 of the 1988 Act (anonymous or pseudonymous works: acts permitted on assumptions as to expiry of copyright or death of author) applies as it applied immediately before commencement (that is, without the amendments made by Regulation 5(2)).

16 Duration of copyright: application of new provisions

The new provisions relating to duration of copyright apply–

(a)   to copyright works made after commencement;
(b)   to existing works which first qualify for copyright protection after commencement;
(c)   to existing copyright works, subject to Regulation 15 (general saving for any longer period applicable under 1988 provisions); and
(d)   to existing works in which copyright expired before 31st December 1995 but which were on 1st July 1995 protected in another EEA state under legislation relating to copyright or related rights.

17 Extended and revived copyright

In the following provisions of this Part–

'extended copyright' means any copyright which subsists by virtue of the new provisions after the date on which it would have expired under the 1988 provisions; and 'revived copyright' means any copyright which subsists by virtue of the new provisions after having expired under the 1988 provisions or any earlier enactment relating to copyright.

18 Ownership of extended copyright

(1) The person who is the owner of the copyright in a work immediately before commencement is as from commencement the owner of any extended copyright in the work, subject as follows.

(2) If he is entitled to copyright for a period less than the whole of the copyright period under the 1988 provisions, any extended copyright is part of the reversionary interest expectant on the termination of that period.

19 Ownership of revived copyright

(1) The person who was the owner of the copyright in a work immediately before it expired (the 'former copyright owner') is as from commencement the owner of any revived copyright in the work, subject as follows.

(2) If the former copyright owner has died before commencement, or in the case of a legal person has ceased to exist before commencement, the revived copyright shall vest–

  (a) in the case of a film, in the principal director of the film or his personal representatives, and

  (b) in any other case, in the author of the work or his personal representatives.

(3) Where revived copyright vests in personal representatives by virtue of paragraph (2), it shall be held by them for the benefit of the person who would have been entitled to it had it been vested in the principal director or author immediately before his death and had devolved as part of his estate.

20 Prospective ownership of extended or revived copyright

(1) Where by an agreement made before commencement in relation to extended or revived copyright, and signed by or on behalf of the prospective owner of the copyright, the prospective owner purports to assign the extended or revived copyright (wholly or partially) to another person, then if, on commencement the assignee or another person claiming under him would be entitled as against all other persons to require the copyright to be vested in him, the copyright shall vest in the assignee or his successor in title by virtue of this paragraph.

(2) A licence granted by a prospective owner of extended or revived copyright is binding on every successor in title to his interest (or prospective interest) in the right, except a purchaser in good faith for valuable consideration and without notice (actual or constructive) of the licence or a person deriving title from such a purchaser; and references in Part I of the 1988 Act to doing anything with, or without, the licence of the copyright owner shall be construed accordingly.

(3) In paragraph (2) 'prospective owner' includes a person who is prospectively entitled to extended or revived copyright by virtue of such an agreement as is mentioned in paragraph (1).

21 Extended copyright: existing licences, agreement, &c

(1) Any copyright licence, any term or condition of an agreement relating to the exploitation of a copyright work, or any waiver or assertion of moral rights, which–

  (a) subsists immediately before commencement in relation to an existing copyright work, and

  (b) is not to expire before the end of the copyright period under the 1988 provisions,

shall continue to have effect during the period of any extended copyright, subject to any agreement to the contrary.

(2) Any copyright licence, or term or condition relating to the exploitation of a copyright work, imposed by order of the Copyright Tribunal which–

  (a) subsists immediately before commencement in relation to an existing copyright work, and

  (b) is not to expire before the end of the copyright period under the 1988 provisions,

shall continue to have effect during the period of any extended copyright, subject to any further order of the Tribunal.

22 Revived copyright: exercise of moral rights
(1) The following provisions have effect with respect to the exercise of moral rights in relation to a work in which there is revived copyright.

(2) Any waiver or assertion of moral rights which subsisted immediately before the expiry of copyright shall continue to have effect during the period of revived copyright.

(3) Moral rights are exercisable after commencement by the author of a work or, as the case may be, the director of a film in which revived copyright subsists, as with any other copyright work.

(4) Where the author or director died before commencement–

   (a)   the rights conferred by–

       section 77 (right to identification as author or director),
       section 80 (right to object to derogatory treatment of work), or
       section 85 (right to privacy of certain photographs and films),

   are exercisable after commencement by his personal representatives, and

   (b)   any infringement after commencement of the right conferred by section 84 (false attribution) is actionable by his personal representatives.

(5) Any damages recovered by personal representatives by virtue of this Regulation in respect of an infringement after a person's death shall devolve as part of his estate as if the right of action had subsisted and been vested in him immediately before his death.

(6) Nothing in these Regulations shall be construed as causing a moral right to be exercisable if, or to the extent that, the right was excluded by virtue of paragraph 23 or 24 of Schedule 1 on the commencement of the 1988 Act or would have been so excluded if copyright had not previously expired.

23 Revived copyright: saving for acts of exploitation when work in public domain, &c
(1) No act done before commencement shall be regarded as infringing revived copyright in a work.

(2) It is not an infringement of revived copyright in a work–

   (a)   to do anything after commencement in pursuance of arrangements made before 1st January 1995 at a time when copyright did not subsist in the work, or
   (b)   to issue to the public after commencement copies of the work made before 1st July 1995 at a time when copyright did not subsist in the work.

(3) It is not an infringement of revived copyright in a work to do anything after commencement in relation to a literary, dramatic, musical or artistic work or a film made before commencement, or made in pursuance of arrangements made before commencement, which contains a copy of that work or is an adaptation of that work if–

   (a)   the copy or adaptation was made before 1st July 1995 at a time when copyright did not subsist in the work in which revived copyright subsists, or
   (b)   the copy or adaptation was made in pursuance of arrangements made before 1st July 1995 at a time when copyright did not subsist in the work in which revived copyright subsists.

(4) It is not an infringement of revived copyright in a work to do after commencement anything which is a restricted act in relation to the work if the act is done at a time when, or is done in pursuance of arrangements made at a time when, the name and address of a person entitled to authorise the act cannot by reasonable inquiry be ascertained.

(5) In this Regulation 'arrangements' means arrangements for the exploitation of the work in question.

(6) It is not an infringement of any moral right to do anything which by virtue of this Regulation is not an infringement of copyright.

24 Revived copyright: use as of right subject to reasonable royalty
(1) In the case of a work in which revived copyright subsists any acts restricted by the copyright shall be treated as licensed by the copyright owner, subject only to the payment of such

reasonable royalty or other remuneration as may be agreed or determined in default of agreement by the Copyright Tribunal.

(2) A person intending to avail himself of the right conferred by this Regulation must give reasonable notice of his intention to the copyright owner, stating when he intends to begin to do the acts.

(3) If he does not give such notice, his acts shall not be treated as licensed.

(4) If he does give such notice, his acts shall be treated as licensed and a reasonable royalty or other remuneration shall be payable in respect of them despite the fact that its amount is not agreed or determined until later.

(5) This Regulation does not apply if or to the extent that a licence to do the acts could be granted by a licensing body (within the meaning of section 116(2) of the 1988 Act), whether or not under a licensing scheme.

(6) No royalty or other remuneration is payable by virtue of this Regulation in respect of anything for which a royalty or other remuneration is payable under Schedule 6 to the 1988 Act.

25 Revived copyright: application to Copyright Tribunal

(1) An application to settle the royalty or other remuneration payable in pursuance of Regulation 24 may be made to the Copyright Tribunal by the copyright owner or the person claiming to be treated as licensed by him.

(2) The Tribunal shall consider the matter and make such order as it may determine to be reasonable in the circumstances.

(3) Either party may subsequently apply to the Tribunal to vary the order, and the Tribunal shall consider the matter and make such order confirming or varying the original order as it may determine to be reasonable in the circumstances.

(4) An application under paragraph (3) shall not, except with the special leave of the Tribunal, be made within twelve months from the date of the original order or of the order on a previous application under that paragraph.

(5) An order under paragraph (3) has effect from the date on which it is made or such later date as may be specified by the Tribunal.

26 Film sound tracks: application of new provisions

(1) The new provisions relating to the treatment of film sound tracks apply to existing sound tracks as from commencement.

(2) The owner of any copyright in a film has as from commencement corresponding rights as copyright owner in any existing sound track treated as part of the film; but without prejudice to any rights of the owner of the copyright in the sound track as a sound recording.

(3) Anything done before commencement under or in relation to the copyright in the sound recording continues to have effect and shall have effect, so far as concerns the sound track, in relation to the film as in relation to the sound recording.

(4) It is not an infringement of the copyright in the film (or of any moral right in the film) to do anything after commencement in pursuance of arrangements for the exploitation of the sound recording made before commencement.

Rights in performances

27 Rights in performances: interpretation

(1) In the provisions of this Part relating to rights in performances–

(a) 'existing', in relation to a performance, means given before commencement; and
(b) 'existing protected performance' means a performance in relation to which rights under Part II of the 1988 Act (rights in performances) subsisted immediately before commencement.

(2) References in this Part to performers' rights are to the rights given by section 180(1)(a) of the 1988 Act and references to recording rights are to the rights given by section 180(1)(b) of that Act.

28 Duration of rights in performances: general saving
Any rights under Part II of the 1988 Act in an existing protected performance shall continue to subsist until the date on which they would have expired under the 1988 provisions if that date is later than the date on which the rights would expire under the new provisions.

29 Duration of rights in performances: application of new provisions
The new provisions relating to the duration of rights under Part II of the 1988 Act apply–

(a) to performances taking place after commencement;
(b) to existing performances which first qualify for protection under Part II of the 1988 Act after commencement;
(c) to existing protected performances, subject to Regulation 28 (general saving for any longer period applicable under 1988 provisions); and
(d) to existing performances–

    (i)   in which rights under Part II of the 1988 Act expired after the commencement of that Part and before 31st December 1995, or
    (ii) which were protected by earlier enactments relating to the protection of performers and in which rights under that Part did not arise by reason only that the performance was given at a date such that the rights would have ceased to subsist before the commencement of that Part,

but which were on 1st July 1995 protected in another EEA state under legislation relating to copyright or related rights.

30 Extended and revived performance rights
In the following provisions of this Part–

'extended performance rights' means rights under Part II of the 1988 Act which subsist by virtue of the new provisions after the date on which they would have expired under the 1988 provisions; and

'revived performance rights' means rights under Part II of the 1988 Act which subsist by virtue of the new provisions–

(a) after having expired under the 1988 provisions, or
(b) in relation to a performance which was protected by earlier enactments relating to the protection of performers and in which rights under that Part did not arise by reason only that the performance was given at a date such that the rights would have ceased to subsist before the commencement of that Part.

References in the following provisions of this Part to 'revived pre-1988 rights' are to revived performance rights within paragraph (b) of the above definition.

31 Entitlement to extended or revived performance rights
(1) Any extended performance rights are exercisable as from commencement by the person who was entitled to exercise those rights immediately before commencement, that is–

(a) in the case of performers' rights, the performer or (if he has died) the person entitled by virtue of section 192(2) of the 1988 Act to exercise those rights;
(b) in the case of recording rights, the person who was within the meaning of section 185 of the 1988 Act the person having those rights.

(2) Any revived performance rights are exercisable as from commencement–

(a) in the case of rights which expired after the commencement of the 1988 Act, by the person who was entitled to exercise those rights immediately before they expired;
(b) in the case of revived pre-1988 performers' rights, by the performer or his personal representatives;
(c) in the case of revived pre-1988 recording rights, by the person who would have been the person having those rights immediately before the commencement of the 1988 Act or, if earlier, immediately before the death of the performer, applying the provisions of section 185 of that Act to the circumstances then obtaining.

(3) Any remuneration or damages received by a person's personal representatives by virtue of a right conferred on them by paragraph (1) or (2) shall devolve as part of that person's estate as if the right had subsisted and been vested in him immediately before his death.

32 Extended performance rights: existing consents, agreement, &c
Any consent, or any term or condition of an agreement, relating to the exploitation of an existing protected performance which–

  (a)   subsists immediately before commencement, and
  (b)   is not to expire before the end of the period for which rights under Part II of the 1988 Act subsist in relation to that performance,

shall continue to subsist during the period of any extended performance rights, subject to any agreement to the contrary.

33 Revived performance rights: saving for acts of exploitation when performance in public domain, &c
(1) No act done before commencement shall be regarded as infringing revived performance rights in a performance.
   (2) It is not an infringement of revived performance rights in a performance–

  (a)   to do anything after commencement in pursuance of arrangements made before 1st January 1995 at a time when the performance was not protected, or
  (b)   to issue to the public after commencement a recording of a performance made before 1st July 1995 at a time when the performance was not protected.

   (3) It is not an infringement of revived performance rights in a performance to do anything after commencement in relation to a sound recording or film made before commencement, or made in pursuance of arrangements made before commencement, which contains a recording of the performance if–

  (a)   the recording of the performance was made before 1st July 1995 at a time when the performance was not protected, or
  (b)   the recording of the performance was made in pursuance of arrangements made before 1st July 1995 at a time when the performance was not protected.

   (4) It is not an infringement of revived performance rights in a performance to do after commencement anything at a time when, or in pursuance of arrangements made at a time when, the name and address of a person entitled to authorise the act cannot by reasonable inquiry be ascertained.
   (5) In this Regulation 'arrangements' means arrangements for the exploitation of the performance in question.
   (6) References in this Regulation to a performance being protected are–

  (a)   in relation to the period after the commencement of the 1988 Act, to rights under Part II of that Act subsisting in relation to the performance, and
  (b)   in relation to earlier periods, to the consent of the performer being required under earlier enactments relating to the protection of performers.

34 Revived performance rights: use as of right subject to reasonable remuneration
(1) In the case of a performance in which revived performance rights subsist any acts which require the consent of any person under Part II of the 1988 Act (the 'rights owner') shall be treated as having that consent, subject only to the payment of such reasonable remuneration as may be agreed or determined in default of agreement by the Copyright Tribunal.
   (2) A person intending to avail himself of the right conferred by this Regulation must give reasonable notice of his intention to the rights owner, stating when he intends to begin to do the acts.
   (3) If he does not give such notice, his acts shall not be treated as having consent.
   (4) If he does give such notice, his acts shall be treated as having consent and reasonable remuneration shall be payable in respect of them despite the fact that its amount is not agreed or determined until later.

35 Revived performance rights: application to Copyright Tribunal
(1) An application to settle the remuneration payable in pursuance of Regulation 34 may be made to the Copyright Tribunal by the rights owner or the person claiming to be treated as having his consent.

(2) The Tribunal shall consider the matter and make such order as it may determine to be reasonable in the circumstances.

(3) Either party may subsequently apply to the Tribunal to vary the order, and the Tribunal shall consider the matter and make such order confirming or varying the original order as it may determine to be reasonable in the circumstances.

(4) An application under paragraph (3) shall not, except with the special leave of the Tribunal, be made within twelve months from the date of the original order or of the order on a previous application under that paragraph.

(5) An order under paragraph (3) has effect from the date on which it is made or such later date as may be specified by the Tribunal.

Supplementary

36 Construction of references to EEA states
(1) For the purpose of the new provisions relating to the term of copyright protection applicable to a work of which the country of origin is not an EEA state and of which the author is not a national of an EEA state–

(a) a work first published before 1st July 1995 shall be treated as published in an EEA state if it was on that date regarded under the law of the United Kingdom or another EEA state as having been published in that state;

(b) an unpublished film made before 1st July 1995 shall be treated as originating in an EEA state if it was on that date regarded under the law of the United Kingdom or another EEA state as a film whose maker had his headquarters in, or was domiciled or resident in, that state; and

(c) the author of a work made before 1st July 1995 shall be treated as an EEA national if he was on that date regarded under the law of the United Kingdom or another EEA state as a national of that state.

The references above to the law of another EEA state are to the law of that state having effect for the purposes of rights corresponding to those provided for in Part I of the 1988 Act.

(2) For the purposes of the new provisions relating to the term of protection applicable to a performance where the performer is not a national of an EEA state, the performer of a performance given before 1st July 1995 shall be treated as an EEA national if he was on that date regarded under the law of the United Kingdom or another EEA state as a national of that state.

The reference above to the law of another EEA state is to the law of that state having effect for the purposes of rights corresponding to those provided for in Part II of the 1988 Act.

(3) In this Regulation 'another EEA state' means an EEA state other than the United Kingdom.

Copyright and Related Rights Regulations 1996

(SI 1996/2967)

Whereas a draft of the following Regulations has been approved by resolution of each House of Parliament:

Now, therefore, the Secretary of State, being a Minister designated for the purposes of section 2(2) of the European Communities Act 1972 in relation to measures relating to the protection of copyright and rights in performances, in exercise of powers conferred by section 2(2) and (4) of the said Act of 1972, hereby makes the following Regulations:

NOTE
Made: 26 November 1996
Commencement: 1 December 1996

PART I
INTRODUCTORY PROVISIONS

1 Citation, commencement and extent
(1) These Regulations may be cited as the Copyright and Related Rights Regulations 1996.

(2) These Regulations come into force on 1st December 1996.

(3) These Regulations extend to the whole of the United Kingdom.

2 Interpretation
In these Regulations–

'EEA Agreement' means the Agreement on the European Economic Area signed at Oporto on 2nd May 1992, as adjusted by the Protocol signed at Brussels on 17th March 1993; and

'EEA state' means a state which is a contracting party to the EEA Agreement.

3 Implementation of Directives, &c
These Regulations make provision for the purpose of implementing–

(a) Council Directive No 92/100/EEC of 19 November 1992 on rental right and lending right and on certain rights related to copyright in the field of intellectual property;

(b) Council Directive No 93/83/EEC of 27 September 1993 on the coordination of certain rules concerning copyright and rights related to copyright applicable to satellite broadcasting and cable retransmission;

(c) the provisions of Council Directive No 93/98/EEC of 29 October 1993 harmonizing the term of protection of copyright and certain related rights, so far as not implemented by the Duration of Copyright and Rights in Performances Regulations 1995; and

(d) certain obligations of the United Kingdom created by or arising under the EEA Agreement so far as relevant to the implementation of those Directives.

4 Scheme of the regulations
The Copyright, Designs, and Patents Act 1988 is amended in accordance with the provisions of Part II of these Regulations, subject to the savings and transitional provisions in Part III of these Regulations.

PART II
AMENDMENTS OF THE COPYRIGHT, DESIGNS AND PATENTS ACT 1988

Satellite broadcasts and cable re-transmission

5 Place where broadcast treated as made
For section 6(4) (broadcasts: place where regarded as made) substitute–

'(4) For the purposes of this Part, the place from which a broadcast is made is the place where, under the control and responsibility of the person making the broadcast, the programme-carrying signals are introduced into an uninterrupted chain of communication (including, in the case of a satellite transmission, the chain leading to the tellite and down towards the earth).'.

6 Safeguards in relation to certain satellite broadcasts

(1) In section 6 (broadcasts), after subsection (4) insert–

'(4A) Subsections (3) and (4) have effect subject to section 6A (safeguards in case of certain satellite broadcasts).'

(2) After that section insert–

'6A Safeguards in case of certain satellite broadcasts

(1) This section applies where the place from which a broadcast by way of satellite transmission is made is located in a country other than an EEA State and the law of that country fails to provide at least the following level of protection–

    (a)   exclusive rights in relation to broadcasting equivalent to those conferred by section 20 (infringement by broadcasting) on the authors of literary, dramatic, musical and artistic works, films and broadcasts;

    (b)   a right in relation to live broadcasting equivalent to that conferred on a performer by section 182(1)(b) (consent required for live broadcast of performance); and

    (c)   a right for authors of sound recordings and performers to share in a single equitable remuneration in respect of the broadcasting of sound recordings.

(2) Where the place from which the programme-carrying signals are transmitted to the satellite ('the uplink station') is located in an EEA State–

    (a)   that place shall be treated as the place from which the broadcast is made, and

    (b)   the person operating the uplink station shall be treated as the person making the broadcast.

(3) Where the uplink station is not located in an EEA State but a person who is established in an EEA State has commissioned the making of the broadcast–

    (a)   that person shall be treated as the person making the broadcast, and

    (b)   the place in which he has his principal establishment in the European Economic Area shall be treated as the place from which the broadcast is made.'.

7 Exercise of rights in relation to cable re-transmission

In Chapter VII of Part I (provisions as to copyright licensing), after section 144 insert–

'Compulsory collective administration of certain rights

144A Collective exercise of certain rights in relation to cable re-transmission

(1) This section applies to the right of the owner of copyright in a literary, dramatic, musical or artistic work, sound recording or film to grant or refuse authorisation or cable re-transmission of a broadcast from another EEA member state in which the work is included.

That right is referred to below as 'cable re-transmission right'.

(2) Cable re-transmission right may be exercised against a cable operator only through a licensing body.

(3) Where a copyright owner has not transferred management of his cable re-transmission right to a licensing body, the licensing body which manages rights of the same category shall be deemed to be mandated to manage his right.

Where more than one licensing body manages rights of that category, he may choose which of them is deemed to be mandated to manage his right.

(4) A copyright owner to whom subsection (3) applies has the same rights and obligations resulting from any relevant agreement between the cable operator and the licensing body as have copyright owners who have transferred management of their cable re-transmission right to that licensing body.

(5) Any rights to which a copyright owner may be entitled by virtue of subsection (4) must be claimed within the period of three years beginning with the date of the cable re-transmission concerned.

(6) This section does not affect any rights exercisable by the maker of the broadcast, whether in relation to the broadcast or a work included in it.

(7) In this section–

'cable operator' means a person providing a cable programme service; and
'cable re-transmission' means the reception and immediate retransmission by way of a cable programme service of a broadcast.'.

8 Meaning of wireless telegraphy

In section 178 (minor definitions), in the definition of 'wireless telegraphy' at the end insert ', but does not include the transmission of microwave energy between terrestrial fixed points'.

Distribution right

9 Issue of copies of work to the public: extension of right

(1) Section 18 (infringement of copyright by issue of copies of work to public) is amended as follows.

(2) For subsections (2) and (3) (meaning of issue of copies to the public) substitute–

'(2) References in this Part to the issue to the public of copies of a work are to–

(a) the act of putting into circulation in the EEA copies not previously put into circulation in the EEA by or with the consent of the copyright owner, or
(b) the act of putting into circulation outside the EEA copies not previously put into circulation in the EEA or elsewhere.

(3) References in this Part to the issue to the public of copies of a work do not include–

(a) any subsequent distribution, sale, hiring or loan of copies previously put into circulation (but see section 18A: infringement by rental or lending), or
(b) any subsequent importation of such copies into the United Kingdom or another EEA state,

except so far as paragraph (a) of subsection (2) applies to putting into circulation in the EEA copies previously put into circulation outside the EEA.'.

(3) After subsection (3) add–

'(4) References in this Part to the issue of copies of a work include the issue of the original.'.

(4) In consequence of the above amendments, in section 27 (meaning of 'infringing copy') omit subsection (3A) and the words 'Subject to subsection (3A),' in subsection (3).

(5) In section 172A (meaning of EEA national and EEA state), for the sidenote and subsection (1) substitute–

'172A Meaning of EEA and related expressions

(1) In this Part–

'the EEA' means the European Economic Area;
'EEA national' means a national of an EEA state; and
'EEA state' means a state which is a contracting party to the EEA Agreement.'.

(6) In section 179 (index of defined expressions)–

(a) in the first column of the entry relating to the expressions 'EEA national' and 'EEA state', at the beginning insert 'EEA,', and
(b) in the second column of the entry relating to the expression 'issue of copies to the public' for 'section 18(2)' substitute 'section 18'.

Rental and lending right

10 Rental or lending of copyright work

(1) In section 16 (the acts restricted by copyright in a work), in subsection (1), after paragraph (b) insert–

'(ba) to rent or lend the work to the public (see section 18A);'.

(2) After section 18 (infringement of copyright by issue of copies of work), insert–

'18A Infringement by rental or lending of work to the public

(1) The rental or lending of copies of the work to the public is an act restricted by the copyright in–

(a)   a literary, dramatic or musical work,

(b)   an artistic work, other than–

    (i)   a work of architecture in the form of a building or a model for a building, or

    (ii)   a work of applied art, or

(c)   a film or a sound recording.

(2) In this Part, subject to the following provisions of this section–

(a)   'rental' means making a copy of the work available for use, on terms that it will or may be returned, for direct or indirect economic or commercial advantage, and

(b)   'lending' means making a copy of the work available for use, on terms that it will or may be returned, otherwise than for direct or indirect economic or commercial advantage, through an establishment which is accessible to the public.

(3) The expressions 'rental' and 'lending' do not include–

(a)   making available for the purpose of public performance, playing or showing in public, broadcasting or inclusion in a cable programme service;

(b)   making available for the purpose of exhibition in public; or

(c)   making available for on-the-spot reference use.

(4) The expression 'lending' does not include making available between establishments which are accessible to the public.

(5) Where lending by an establishment accessible to the public gives rise to a payment the amount of which does not go beyond what is necessary to cover the operating costs of the establishment, there is no direct or indirect economic or commercial advantage for the purposes of this section.

(6) References in this Part to the rental or lending of copies of a work include the rental or lending of the original.'.

(3) In section 178 (minor definitions), at the appropriate place insert–

'"rental right" means the right of a copyright owner to authorise or prohibit the rental of copies of the work (see section 18A);';

and omit the definition of 'rental'.

(4) In section 179 (index of defined expressions), in the entry relating to the expression 'rental' for 'section 178' substitute 'section 18A(2) to (6)'; and at the appropriate places insert–

'lending   section 18A(2) to (6)'
'rental right   section 178'.

11 Permitted lending of copyright works

(1) In Chapter III of Part I (acts permitted in relation to copyright works), in the sections relating to education, after section 36 insert–

'36A Lending of copies by educational establishments

Copyright in a work is not infringed by the lending of copies of the work by an educational establishment.'.

(2) In the same Chapter, in the sections relating to libraries and archives, after section 40 insert–

'40A Lending of copies by libraries or archives

(1) Copyright in a work of any description is not infringed by the lending of a book by a public library if the book is within the public lending right scheme.

For this purpose–

(a) 'the public lending right scheme' means the scheme in force under section 1 of the Public Lending Right Act 1979, and

(b) a book is within the public lending right scheme if it is a book within the meaning of the provisions of the scheme relating to eligibility, whether or not it is in fact eligible.

(2) Copyright in a work is not infringed by the lending of copies of the work by a prescribed library or archive (other than a public library) which is not conducted for profit.'

(3) In the same Chapter for section 66 (rental of sound recordings, films and computer programs), and the heading preceding it, substitute–

'Miscellaneous: lending of works and playing of sound recordings

66 Lending to public of copies of certain works

(1) The Secretary of State may by order provide that in such cases as may be specified in the order the lending to the public of copies of literary, dramatic, musical or artistic works, sound recordings or films shall be treated as licensed by the copyright owner subject only to the payment of such reasonable royalty or other payment as may be agreed or determined in default of agreement by the Copyright Tribunal.

(2) No such order shall apply if, or to the extent that, there is a licensing scheme certified for the purposes of this section under section 143 providing for the grant of licences.

(3) An order may make different provision for different cases and may specify cases by reference to any factor relating to the work, the copies lent, the lender or the circumstances of the lending.

(4) An order shall be made by statutory instrument; and no order shall be made unless a draft of it has been laid before and approved by a resolution of each House of Parliament.

(5) Nothing in this section affects any liability under section 23 (secondary infringement: possessing or dealing with infringing copy) in respect of the lending of infringing copies.'.

(4) In section 143(1) (certification of licensing schemes: relevant provisions), for paragraph (c) substitute–

'(c) section 66 (lending to public of copies of certain works),'.

(5) In section 178 (minor definitions), insert at the appropriate place–

' "public library" means a library administered by or on behalf of–

(a) in England and Wales, a library authority within the meaning of the Public Libraries and Museums Act 1964;

(b) in Scotland, a statutory library authority within the meaning of the Public Libraries (Scotland) Act 1955;

(c) in Northern Ireland, an Education and Library Board within the meaning of the Education and Libraries (Northern Ireland) Order 1986;'.

(6) In section 179 (index of defined expressions), at the appropriate place insert–

'public library   section 178'

(7) The following provisions (which relate to lending by public libraries) are repealed–

section 4(2) of the Public Libraries (Scotland) Act 1955,

section 8(6) of the Public Libraries and Museums Act 1964,
Article 77(3) of the Education and Libraries (Northern Ireland) Order 1986,
paragraphs 6, 8 and 34 of Schedule 7 to the Copyright, Designs and Patents Act 1988
(which insert the above provisions).

12 Presumption of transfer of rental right in case of film production agreement

In Chapter V of Part I (dealings with rights in copyright works), after section 93 insert–

'93A Presumption of transfer of rental right in case of film production agreement

(1) Where an agreement concerning film production is concluded between an author and a film producer, the author shall be presumed, unless the agreement provides to the contrary, to have transferred to the film producer any rental right in relation to the film arising by virtue of the inclusion of a copy of the author's work in the film.

(2) In this section 'author' means an author, or prospective author, of a literary, dramatic, musical or artistic work.

(3) Subsection (1) does not apply to any rental right in relation to the film arising by virtue of the inclusion in the film of the screenplay, the dialogue or music specifically created for and used in the film.

(4) Where this section applies, the absence of signature by or on behalf of the author does not exclude the operation of section 91(1) (effect of purported assignment of future copyright).

(5) The reference in subsection (1) to an agreement concluded between an author and a film producer includes any agreement having effect between those persons, whether made by them directly or through intermediaries.

(6) Section 93B (right to equitable remuneration on transfer of rental right) applies where there is a presumed transfer by virtue of this section as in the case of an actual transfer.'.

13 Rental and lending: applications to Copyright Tribunal

(1) In section 133 (licences to reflect payments in respect of underlying rights), for subsection (1) (considerations relevant to rental of certain works) substitute–

'(1) In considering what charges should be paid for a licence–

(a)   on a reference or application under this Chapter relating to licences for the rental or lending of copies of a work, or

(b)   on an application under section 142 (royalty or other sum payable for lending of certain works),

the Copyright Tribunal shall take into account any reasonable payments which the owner of the copyright in the work is liable to make in consequence of the granting of the licence, or of the acts authorised by the licence, to owners of copyright in works included in that work.'.

(2) For section 142 (royalty or other sum payable for rental of sound recording, film or computer program), and the heading preceding it, substitute–

'Royalty or other sum payable for lending of certain works

142 Royalty or other sum payable for lending of certain works

(1) An application to settle the royalty or other sum payable in pursuance of section 66 (lending of copies of certain copyright works) may be made to the Copyright Tribunal by the copyright owner or the person claiming to be treated as licensed by him.

(2) The Tribunal shall consider the matter and make such order as it may determine to be reasonable in the circumstances.

(3) Either party may subsequently apply to the Tribunal to vary the order, and the Tribunal shall consider the matter and make such order confirming or varying the original order as it may determine to be reasonable in the circumstances.

(4) An application under subsection (3) shall not, except with the special leave of the Tribunal, be made within twelve months from the date of the original order or of the order on a previous application under that subsection.

(5) An order under subsection (3) has effect from the date on which it is made or such later date as may be specified by the Tribunal.'.

(3) In section 149 (jurisdiction of the Copyright Tribunal), in paragraph (e) for 'rental of sound recording, film or computer program' substitute 'lending of certain works'.

14 Right to equitable remuneration where rental right transferred
(1) In Chapter V of Part I (dealings with rights in copyright works), after section 93A (inserted by regulation 12) insert–

'Right to equitable remuneration where rental right transferred

93B Right to equitable remuneration where rental right transferred
(1) Where an author to whom this section applies has transferred his rental right concerning a sound recording or a film to the producer of the sound recording film, he retains the right to equitable remuneration for the rental.

The authors to whom this section applies are–

   (a) the author of a literary, dramatic, musical or artistic work, and

   (b) the principal director of a film.

(2) The right to equitable remuneration under this section may not be assigned by the author except to a collecting society for the purpose of enabling it to enforce the right on his behalf.

The right is, however, transmissible by testamentary disposition or by operation of law as personal or moveable property; and it may be assigned or further transmitted by any person into whose hands it passes.

(3) Equitable remuneration under this section is payable by the person for the time being entitled to the rental right, that is, the person to whom the right was transferred or any successor in title of his.

(4) The amount payable by way of equitable remuneration is as agreed by or on behalf of the persons by and to whom it is payable, subject to section 93C (reference of amount to Copyright Tribunal).

(5) An agreement is of no effect in so far as it purports to exclude or restrict the right to equitable remuneration under this section.

(6) References in this section to the transfer of rental right by one person to another include any arrangement having that effect, whether made by them directly or through intermediaries.

(7) In this section a 'collecting society' means a society or other organisation which has as its main object, or one of its main objects, the exercise of the right to equitable remuneration under this section on behalf of more than one author.

93C Equitable remuneration: reference of amount to Copyright Tribunal
(1) In default of agreement as to the amount payable by way of equitable remuneration under section 93B, the person by or to whom it is payable may apply to the Copyright Tribunal to determine the amount payable.

(2) A person to or by whom equitable remuneration is payable under that section may also apply to the Copyright Tribunal–

   (a) to vary any agreement as to the amount payable, or

   (b) to vary any previous determination of the Tribunal as to that matter;

but except with the special leave of the Tribunal no such application may be made within twelve months from the date of a previous determination.

An order made on an application under this subsection has effect from the date on which it is made or such later date as may be specified by the Tribunal.

(3) On an application under this section the Tribunal shall consider the matter and make such order as to the method of calculating and paying equitable remuneration as it may determine to be reasonable in the circumstances, taking into account the importance of the contribution of the author to the film or sound recording.

(4) Remuneration shall not be considered inequitable merely because it was paid by way of a single payment or at the time of the transfer of the rental right.

(5) An agreement is of no effect in so far as it purports to prevent a person questioning the amount of equitable remuneration or to restrict the powers of the Copyright Tribunal under this section.'.

(2) In section 149 (jurisdiction of the Copyright Tribunal), before paragraph (a) insert–

'(zb) section 93C (application to determine amount of equitable remuneration under section 93 B);'.

15 Consequential modification of provisions relating to licensing
(1) Chapter VII of Part I (copyright licensing) is amended as follows.
(2) For section 117 (licensing schemes about which references and applications may be made) substitute–

'117 Licensing schemes to which the following sections apply
Sections 118 to 123 (references and applications with respect to licensing schemes) apply to licensing schemes which are operated by licensing bodies and cover works of more than one author, so far as they relate to licences for–

(a) copying the work,
(b) rental or lending of copies of the work to the public,
(c) performing, showing or playing the work in public, or
(d) broadcasting the work or including it in a cable programme service;

and references in those sections to a licensing scheme shall be construed accordingly.'.

(3) For section 124 (licences about which references and applications may be made) substitute–

'124 Licences to which following sections apply
Sections 125 to 128 (references and applications with respect to licensing by licensing bodies) apply to licences which are granted by a licensing body otherwise than in pursuance of a licensing scheme and cover works of more than one author, so far as they authorise–

(a) copying the work,
(b) rental or lending of copies of the work to the public,
(c) performing, showing or playing the work in public, or
(d) broadcasting the work or including it in a cable programme service;

and references in those sections to a licence shall be construed accordingly.'.

Publication right

16 Publication right
(1) A person who after the expiry of copyright protection, publishes for the first time a previously unpublished work has, in accordance with the following provisions, a property right ('publication right') equivalent to copyright.
(2) For this purpose publication includes any communication to the public, in particular–

(a) the issue of copies to the public;
(b) making the work available by means of an electronic retrieval system;
(c) the rental or lending of copies of the work to the public;
(d) the performance, exhibition or showing of the work in public; or
(e) broadcasting the work or including it in a cable programme service.

(3) No account shall be taken for this purpose of any unauthorised act.
In relation to a time when there is no copyright in the work, an unauthorised act means an act done without the consent of the owner of the physical medium in which the work is embodied or on which it is recorded.
(4) A work qualifies for publication right protection only if–

(a) first publication is in the European Economic Area, and

(b)   the publisher of the work is at the time of first publication a national of an EEA state.

Where two or more persons jointly publish the work, it is sufficient for the purposes of paragraph (b) if any of them is a national of an EEA state.

(5) No publication right arises from the publication of a work in which Crown copyright or Parliamentary copyright subsisted.

(6) Publication right expires at the end of the period of 25 years from the end of the calendar year in which the work was first published.

(7) In this regulation a 'work' means a literary, dramatic, musical or artistic work or a film.

(8) Expressions used in this regulation (other than 'publication') have the same meaning as in Part I.

17 Application of copyright provisions to publication right

(1) The substantive provisions of Part I relating to copyright (but not moral rights in copyright works), that is, the relevant provisions of–

Chapter II (rights of copyright owner),
Chapter III (acts permitted in relation to copyright works),
Chapter V (dealings with rights in copyright works),
Chapter VI (remedies for infringement), and
Chapter VII (copyright licensing),

apply in relation to publication right as in relation to copyright, subject to the following exceptions and modifications.

(2) The following provisions do not apply–

(a)   in Chapter III (acts permitted in relation to copyright works), sections 57, 64, 66A and 67;

(b)   in Chapter VI (remedies for infringement), sections 104 to 106;

(c)   in Chapter VII (copyright licensing), section 116(4).

(3) The following provisions have effect with the modifications indicated–

(a)   in section 107(4) and (5) (offences of making or dealing in infringing articles, &c), the maximum punishment on summary conviction is imprisonment for a term not exceeding three months or a fine not exceeding level 5 on the standard scale, or both;

(b)   in sections 116(2), 117 and 124 for 'works of more than one author' substitute 'works of more than one publisher'.

(4) The other relevant provisions of Part I, that is–

in Chapter 1, provisions defining expressions used generally in Part I,
Chapter VIII (the Copyright Tribunal),
in Chapter IX–

section 161 (territorial waters and the continental shelf), and
section 162 (British ships, aircraft and hovercraft), and

in Chapter X–

section 171(1) and (3) (savings for other rules of law, &c), and
sections 172 to 179 (general interpretation provisions),

apply, with any necessary adaptations, for the purposes of supplementing the substantive provisions of that Part as applied by this regulation.

(5) Except where the context otherwise requires, any other enactment relating to copyright (whether passed or made before or after these regulations) applies in relation to publication right as in relation to copyright.

In this paragraph 'enactment' includes an enactment contained in subordinate legislation within the meaning of the Interpretation Act 1978.

Authorship of films and certain photographs

18 Authorship of films

(1) In section 9(2) (person to be taken to be author of work), for paragraph (a) (sound recordings and films) substitute–

'(aa) in the case of a sound recording, the producer;
(ab) in the case of a film, the producer and the principal director;'.

(2) In section 10 (works of joint authorship), after subsection (1) insert–

'(1A) A film shall be treated as a work of joint authorship unless the producer and the principal director are the same person.'.

(3) In section 11 (first ownership of copyright), in subsection (2) (work made by employee in course of employment) after 'literary, dramatic, musical or artistic work' insert ', or a film,'.

(4) In section 105 (presumptions relevant to sound recordings and films)–

(a)   in subsections (2)(a) and (5)(a) for 'author or director' substitute 'director or producer',

(b)   in subsection (5), after paragraph (a) insert–

'(aa) that a named person was the principal director of the film, the author of the screenplay, the author of the dialogue or the composer of music specifically created for and used in the film, or,'.

and

(c)   after subsection (5) add–

'(6) For the purposes of this section, a statement that a person was the director of a film shall be taken, unless a contrary indication appears, as meaning that he was the principal director of the film.'

(5) In section 178 (minor definitions), at the appropriate place insert–

'"producer", in relation to a sound recording or a film, means the person by whom the arrangements necessary for the making of the sound recording or film are undertaken;'.

(6) In section 179 (index of defined expressions), at the appropriate place insert–

'"producer" (in relation to a sound recording or film) section 178'.

19 Clarification of transitional provisions relating to pre-1989 photographs
Any question arising, in relation to photographs which were existing works within the meaning of Schedule 1, as to who is to be regarded as the author for the purposes of–

(a)   regulations 15 and 16 of the Duration of Copyright and Rights in Performances Regulations 1995 (duration of copyright: application of new provisions subject to general saving), or

(b)   regulation 19(2)(b) of those regulations (ownership of revived copyright),

is to be determined in accordance with section 9 as in force on the commencement of those regulations (and not, by virtue of paragraph 10 of Schedule 1, in accordance with the law in force at the time when the work was made).

Performers' rights

20 Extension of performers' right

(1) For section 182 (performers' rights: consent required for recording or live transmission of performance) substitute–

'**182 Consent required for recording, &c of live performance**
(1) A performer's rights are infringed by a person who, without his consent–

(a)   makes a recording of the whole or any substantial part of a qualifying performance directly from the live performance,

(b) broadcasts live, or includes live in a cable programme service, the whole or any substantial part of a qualifying performance,

(c) makes a recording of the whole or any substantial part of a qualifying performance directly from a broadcast of, or cable programme including, the live performance.

(2) A performer's rights are not infringed by the making of any such recording by a person for his private and domestic use.

(3) In an action for infringement of a performer's rights brought by virtue of this section damages shall not be awarded against a defendant who shows that at the time of the infringement he believed on reasonable grounds that consent had been given.'.

(2) After that section insert–

'182A Consent required for copying of recording

(1) A performer's rights are infringed by a person who, without his consent, makes, otherwise than for his private and domestic use, a copy of a recording of the whole or any substantial part of a qualifying performance.

(2) It is immaterial whether the copy is made directly or indirectly.

(3) The right of a performer under this section to authorise or prohibit the making of such copies is referred to in this Part as "reproduction right".'

182B Consent required for issue of copies to public

(1) A performer's rights are infringed by a person who, without his consent, issues to the public copies of a recording of the whole or any substantial part of a qualifying performance.

(2) References in this Part to the issue to the public of copies of a recording are to–

(a) the act of putting into circulation in the EEA copies not previously put into circulation in the EEA by or with the consent of the performer, or

(b) the act of putting into circulation outside the EEA copies not previously put into circulation in the EEA or elsewhere.

(3) References in this Part to the issue to the public of copies of a recording do not include–

(a) any subsequent distribution, sale, hiring or loan of copies previously put into circulation (but see section 182C: consent required for rental or lending), or

(b) any subsequent importation of such copies into the United Kingdom or another EEA state,

except so far as paragraph (a) of subsection (2) applies to putting into circulation in the EEA copies previously put into circulation outside the EEA.

(4) References in this Part to the issue of copies of a recording of a performance include the issue of the original recording of the live performance.

(5) The right of a performer under this section to authorise or prohibit the issue of copies to the public is referred to in this Part as "distribution right".

182C Consent required for rental or lending of copies to public

(1) A performer's rights are infringed by a person who, without his consent, rents or lends to the public copies of a recording of the whole or any substantial part of a qualifying performance.

(2) In this Part, subject to the following provisions of this section–

(a) 'rental' means making a copy of a recording available for use, on terms that it will or may be returned, for direct or indirect economic or commercial advantage, and

(b) 'lending' means making a copy of a recording available for use, on terms that it will or may be returned, otherwise than for direct or indirect economic or commercial advantage, through an establishment which is accessible to the public.

(3) The expressions 'rental' and 'lending' do not include–

(a)   making available for the purpose of public performance, playing or showing in public, broadcasting or inclusion in a cable programme service;

(b)   making available for the purpose of exhibition in public; or

(c)   making available for on-the-spot reference use.

(4) The expression 'lending' does not include making available between establishments which are accessible to the public.

(5) Where lending by an establishment accessible to the public gives rise to a payment the amount of which does not go beyond what is necessary to cover the operating costs of the establishment, there is no direct or indirect economic or commercial advantage for the purposes of this section.

(6) References in this Part to the rental or lending of copies of a recording of a performance include the rental or lending of the original recording of the live performance.

(7) In this Part–

'rental right' means the right of a performer under this section to authorise or prohibit the rental of copies to the public, and

'lending right' means the right of a performer under this section to authorise or prohibit the lending of copies to the public.

182D   Right to equitable remuneration for exploitation of sound recording

(1) Where a commercially published sound recording of the whole or any substantial part of a qualifying performance–

(a)   is played in public, or

(b)   is included in a broadcast or cable programme service,

the performer is entitled to equitable remuneration from the owner of the copyright in the sound recording.

(2) The right to equitable remuneration under this section may not be assigned by the performer except to a collecting society for the purpose of enabling it to enforce the right on his behalf.

The right is, however, transmissible by testamentary disposition or by operation of law as personal or moveable property; and it may be assigned or further transmitted by any person into whose hands it passes.

(3) The amount payable by way of equitable remuneration is as agreed by or on behalf of the persons by and to whom it is payable, subject to the following provisions.

(4) In default of agreement as to the amount payable by way of equitable remuneration, the person by or to whom it is payable may apply to the Copyright Tribunal to determine the amount payable.

(5) A person to or by whom equitable remuneration is payable may also apply to the Copyright Tribunal–

(a)   to vary any agreement as to the amount payable, or

(b)   to vary any previous determination of the Tribunal as to that matter;

but except with the special leave of the Tribunal no such application may be made within twelve months from the date of a previous determination.

An order made on an application under this subsection has effect from the date on which it is made or such later date as may be specified by the Tribunal.

(6) On an application under this section the Tribunal shall consider the matter and make such order as to the method of calculating and paying equitable remuneration as it may determine to be reasonable in the circumstances, taking into account the importance of the contribution of the performer to the sound recording.

(7) An agreement is of no effect in so far as it purports–

(a)   to exclude or restrict the right to equitable remuneration under this section, or

(b)   to prevent a person questioning the amount of equitable remuneration or to restrict the powers of the Copyright Tribunal under this section.'.

(3) In Schedule 2 (rights in performances: permitted acts), after paragraph 6 insert–

'Lending of copies by educational establishments

6A–(1) The rights conferred by Part II are not infringed by the lending of copies of a recording of a performance by an educational establishment.

(2) Expressions used in this paragraph have the same meaning as in section 36A; and any provision with respect to the application of that section made under section 174(2) (instruction given elsewhere than an educational establishment) applies also for the purposes of this paragraph.

Lending of copies by libraries or archives

6B–(1) The rights conferred by Part II are not infringed by the lending of copies of a recording of a performance by a prescribed library or archive (other than a public library) which is not conducted for profit.

(2) Expressions used in this paragraph have the same meaning as in section 40A(2); and any provision under section 37 prescribing libraries or archives for the purposes of that section applies also for the purposes of this paragraph.'';

and after paragraph 14 insert–

'Lending of certain recordings

14A–(1) The Secretary of State may by order provide that in such cases as may be specified in the order the lending to the public of copies of films or sound recordings shall be treated as licensed by the performer subject only to the payment of such reasonable royalty or other payment as may be agreed or determined in default of agreement by the Copyright Tribunal.

(2) No such order shall apply if, or to the extent that, there is a licensing scheme certified for the purposes of this paragraph under paragraph 16 of Schedule 2A providing for the grant of licences.

(3) An order may make different provision for different cases and may specify cases by reference to any factor relating to the work, the copies lent, the lender or the circumstances of the lending.

(4) An order shall be made by statutory instrument; and no order shall be made unless a draft of it has been laid before and approved by a resolution of each House of Parliament.

(5) Nothing in this section affects any liability under section 184(1)(b) (secondary infringement: possessing or dealing with illicit recording) in respect of the lending of illicit recordings.

(6) Expressions used in this paragraph have the same meaning as in section 66.'.

(4) In section 212 (index of defined expressions: Part II), at the appropriate places insert–

'distribution right   section 182B(5)'
'lending right   section 182C(7)'
'rental right   section 182C(7)'
'reproduction right   section 182A(3)'

21 Performers' property rights
(1) After section 191 insert–

'Performers' property rights

191A Performers' property rights
(1) The following rights conferred by this Part on a performer–

   reproduction right (section 182A),
   distribution right (section 182B),
   rental right and lending right (section 182C),

are property rights ("a performer's property rights" ').

(2) References in this Part to the consent of the performer shall be construed in relation to a performer's property rights as references to the consent of the rights owner.

(3) Where different persons are (whether in consequence of a partial assignment or otherwise) entitled to different aspects of a performer's property rights in relation to a performance, the rights owner for any purpose of this Part is the person who is entitled to the aspect of those rights relevant for that purpose.

(4) Where a performer's property rights (or any aspect of them) is owned by more than one person jointly, references in this Part to the rights owner are to all the owners, so that, in particular, any requirement of the licence of the rights owner requires the licence of all of them.

191B Assignment and licences

(1) A performer's property rights are transmissible by assignment, by testamentary disposition or by operation of law, as personal or moveable property.

(2) An assignment or other transmission of a performer's property rights may be partial, that is, limited so as to apply–

(a)   to one or more, but not all, of the things requiring the consent of the rights owner;
(b)   to part, but not the whole, of the period for which the rights are to subsist.

(3) An assignment of a performer's property rights is not effective unless it is in writing signed by or on behalf of the assignor.

(4) A licence granted by the owner of a performer's property rights is binding on every successor in title to his interest in the rights, except a purchaser in good faith for valuable consideration and without notice (actual or constructive) of the licence or a person deriving title from such a purchaser; and references in this Part to doing anything with, or without, the licence of the rights owner shall be construed accordingly.

191C Prospective ownership of a performer's property rights

(1) This section applies where by an agreement made in relation to a future recording of a performance, and signed by or on behalf of the performer, the performer purports to assign his performer's property rights (wholly or partially) to another person.

(2) If on the rights coming into existence the assignee or another person claiming under him would be entitled as against all other persons to require the rights to be vested in him, they shall vest in the assignee or his successor in title by virtue of this subsection.

(3) A licence granted by a prospective owner of a performer's property rights is binding on every successor in title to his interest (or prospective interest) in the rights, except a purchaser in good faith for valuable consideration and without notice (actual or constructive) of the licence or a person deriving title from such a purchaser.

References in this Part to doing anything with, or without, the licence of the rights owner shall be construed accordingly.

(4) In subsection (3) 'prospective owner' in relation to a performer's property rights means a person who is prospectively entitled to those rights by virtue of such an agreement as is mentioned in subsection (1).

191D Exclusive licences

(1) In this Part an "exclusive licence" means a licence in writing signed by or on behalf of the owner of a performer's property rights authorising the licensee to the exclusion of all other persons, including the person granting the licence, to do anything requiring the consent of the rights owner.

(2) The licensee under an exclusive licence has the same rights against a successor in title who is bound by the licence as he has against the person granting the licence.

191E Performer's property right to pass under will with unpublished original recording

Where under a bequest (whether general or specific) a person is entitled beneficially or otherwise to any material thing containing an original recording of a performance which was not published before the death of the testator, the bequest shall, unless a contrary intention is indicated in the testator's will or a codicil to it, be construed as including any performer's rights in relation to the recording to which the testator was entitled immediately before his death.

191F Presumption of transfer of rental right in case of film production agreement

(1) Where an agreement concerning film production is concluded between a performer and a film producer, the performer shall be presumed, unless the agreement provides to the contrary, to have transferred to the film producer any rental right in relation to the film arising from the inclusion of a recording of his performance in the film.

(2) Where the section applies, the absence of signature by or on behalf of the performer does not exclude the operation of section 191C (effect of purported assignment of future rights).

(3) The reference in subsection (1) to an agreement concluded between a performer and a film producer includes any agreement having effect between those persons, whether made by them directly or through intermediaries.

(4) Section 191G (right to equitable remuneration on transfer of rental right) applies where there is a presumed transfer by virtue of this section as in the case of an actual transfer.

191G Right to equitable remuneration where rental right transferred

(1) Where a performer has transferred his rental right concerning a sound recording or a film to the producer of the sound recording or film, he retains the right to equitable remuneration for the rental.

The reference above to the transfer of rental right by one person to another includes any arrangement having that effect, whether made by them directly or through intermediaries.

(2) The right to equitable remuneration under this section may not be assigned by the performer except to a collecting society for the purpose of enabling it to enforce the right on his behalf.

The right is, however, transmissible by testamentary disposition or by operation of law as personal or moveable property; and it may be assigned or further transmitted by any person into whose hands it passes.

(3) Equitable remuneration under this section is payable by the person for the time being entitled to the rental right, that is, the person to whom the right was transferred or any successor in title of his.

(4) The amount payable by way of equitable remuneration is as agreed by or on behalf of the persons by and to whom it is payable, subject to section 191H (reference of amount to Copyright Tribunal).

(5) An agreement is of no effect in so far as it purports to exclude or restrict the right to equitable remuneration under this section.

(6) In this section a 'collecting society' means a society or other organisation which has as its main object, or one of its main objects, the exercise of the right to equitable remuneration on behalf of more than one performer.

191H Equitable remuneration: reference of amount to Copyright Tribunal

(1) In default of agreement as to the amount payable by way of equitable remuneration under section 191G, the person by or to whom it is payable may apply to the Copyright Tribunal to determine the amount payable.

(2) A person to or by whom equitable remuneration is payable may also apply to the Copyright Tribunal–

(a) to vary any agreement as to the amount payable, or
(b) to vary any previous determination of the Tribunal as to that matter;

but except with the special leave of the Tribunal no such application may be made within twelve months from the date of a previous determination.

An order made on an application under this subsection has effect from the date on which it is made or such later date as may be specified by the Tribunal.

(3) On an application under this section the Tribunal shall consider the matter and make such order as to the method of calculating and paying equitable remuneration as it

may determine to be reasonable in the circumstances, taking into account the importance of the contribution of the performer to the film or sound recording.

(4) Remuneration shall not be considered inequitable merely because it was paid by way of a single payment or at the time of the transfer of the rental right.

(5) An agreement is of no effect in so far as it purports to prevent a person questioning the amount of equitable remuneration or to restrict the powers of the Copyright Tribunal under this section.

191I Infringement actionable by rights owner

(1) An infringement of a performer's property rights is actionable by the rights owner.

(2) In an action for infringement of a performer's property rights all such relief by way of damages, injunctions, accounts or otherwise is available to the plaintiff as is available in respect of the infringement of any other property right.

(3) This section has effect subject to the following provisions of this Part.

191J Provisions as to damages in infringement action

(1) Where in an action for infringement of a performer's property rights it is shown that at the time of the infringement the defendant did not know, and had no reason to believe, that the rights subsisted in the recording to which the action relates, the plaintiff is not entitled to damages against him, but without prejudice to any other remedy.

(2) The court may in an action for infringement of a performer's property rights having regard to all the circumstances, and in particular to–

(a) the flagrancy of the infringement, and

(b) any benefit accruing to the defendant by reason of the infringement,

award such additional damages as the justice of the case may require.

191K Undertaking to take licence of right in infringement proceedings

(1) If in proceedings for infringement of a performer's property rights in respect of which a licence is available as of right under paragraph 17 of Schedule 2A (powers exercisable in consequence of competition report) the defendant undertakes to take a licence on such terms as may be agreed or, in default of agreement, settled by the Copyright Tribunal under that paragraph–

(a) no injunction shall be granted against him,

(b) no order for delivery up shall be made under section 195, and

(c) the amount recoverable against him by way of damages or on an account of profits shall not exceed double the amount which would have been payable by him as licensee if such a licence on those terms had been granted before the earliest infringement.

(2) An undertaking may be given at any time before final order in the proceedings, without any admission of liability.

(3) Nothing in this section affects the remedies available in respect of an infringement committed before licences of right were available.

191L Rights and remedies for exclusive licensee

(1) An exclusive licensee has, except against the owner of a performer's property rights, the same rights and remedies in respect of matters occurring after the grant of the licence as if the licence had been an assignment.

(2) His rights and remedies are concurrent with those of the rights owner; and references in the relevant provisions of this Part to the rights owner shall be construed accordingly.

(3) In an action brought by an exclusive licensee by virtue of this section a defendant may avail himself of any defence which would have been available to him if the action had been brought by the rights owner.

191M Exercise of concurrent rights

(1) Where an action for infringement of a performer's property rights brought by the rights owner or an exclusive licensee relates (wholly or partly) to an infringement in respect of

which they have concurrent rights of action, the rights owner or, as the case may be, the exclusive licensee may not, without the leave of the court, proceed with the action unless the other is either joined as plaintiff or added as a defendant.

(2) A rights owner or exclusive licensee who is added as a defendant in pursuance of subsection (1) is not liable for any costs in the action unless he takes part in the proceedings.

(3) The above provisions do not affect the granting of interlocutory relief on an application by the rights owner or exclusive licensee alone.

(4) Where an action for infringement of a performer's property rights is brought which relates (wholly or partly) to an infringement in respect of which the rights owner and an exclusive licensee have or had concurrent rights of action–

- (a) the court shall in assessing damages take into account–

  - (i) the terms of the licence, and
  - (ii) any pecuniary remedy already awarded or available to either of them in respect of the infringement;

- (b) no account of profits shall be directed if an award of damages has been made, or an account of profits has been directed, in favour of the other of them in respect of the infringement; and

- (c) the court shall if an account of profits is directed apportion the profits between them as the court considers just, subject to any agreement between them;

and these provisions apply whether or not the rights owner and the exclusive licensee are both parties to the action.

(5) The owner of a performer's property rights shall notify any exclusive licensee having concurrent rights before applying for an order under section 195 (order for delivery up) or exercising the right conferred by section 196 (right of seizure); and the court may on the application of the licensee make such order under section 195 or, as the case may be, prohibiting or permitting the exercise by the rights owner of the right conferred by section 196, as it thinks fit having regard to the terms of the licence.'.

(2) For section 192 (transmission of rights) substitute–

'Non-property rights

192A Performers' non-property rights

(1) the rights conferred on a performer by–

  section 182 (consent required for recording, &c of live performance),
  section 183 (infringement of performer's rights by use of recording made without consent), and
  section 184 (infringement of performer's rights importing, possessing or dealing with illicit recording),

  are not assignable or transmissible, except to the following extent.

They are referred to in this Part as 'a performer's non-property rights'.

(2) On the death of a person entitled to any such right–

- (a) the right passes to such person as he may by testamentary disposition specifically direct, and
- (b) if or to the extent that there is no such direction, the right is exercisable by his personal representatives.

(3) References in this Part to the performer, in the context of the person having any such right, shall be construed as references to the person for the time being entitled to exercise those rights.

(4) Where by virtue of subsection (2)(a) a right becomes exercisable by more than one person, it is exercisable by each of them independently of the other or others.

(5) Any damages recovered by personal representatives by virtue of this section in respect of an infringement after a person's death shall devolve as part of his estate as if the right of action had subsisted and been vested in him immediately before his death.

192B   Transmissibility of rights of person having recording rights
(1) The rights conferred by this Part on a person having recording rights are not assignable or transmissible.

(2) This does not affect section 185(2)(b) or (3)(b), so far as those provisions confer rights under this Part on a person to whom the benefit of a contract or licence is assigned.'.

(3) In section 193 (consent)–

(a)   in subsection (1), after 'Consent for the purposes of this Part' insert 'by a person having a performer's non-property rights, or by a person having recording rights,'; and

(b)   in subsection (3), for 'a right conferred by this Part' substitute 'a performer's non-property right'.

(4) In section 194 (infringement actionable as breach of statutory duty), for 'any of the rights conferred by this Part' substitute '–

(a)   a performer's non-property rights, or
(b)   any right conferred by this Part on a person having recording rights,'.

(5) The headings in Part II falsified by the above amendments are amended as follows–

(a)   for the heading before section 191 substitute–

'Duration of rights';

(b)   omit the heading before section 194;
(c)   before section 195 insert the heading–

'Delivery up or seizure of illicit recordings'.

(6) In section 212 (index of defined expressions: Part II), at the appropriate places insert–

'consent of performer (in relation to performer's property rights)	section 191A(2)'
'performer's non-property rights	section 192A(1)'
'performer's property rights	section 191A(1)'
'rights owner (in relation to performer's property rights)	section 191A(3) and (4)'

Performers' rights

22   Licensing of performers' property rights
(1) In Part II (performers' rights), after section 205 insert–

'Licensing of performers' property rights

205A   Licensing of performers' property rights
The provisions of Schedule 2A have effect with respect to the licensing of performers' property rights.'.

(2) After Schedule 2 insert–

'SCHEDULE 2A
LICENSING OF PERFORMERS' PROPERTY RIGHTS

Licensing schemes and licensing bodies

1–(1) In Part II a 'licensing scheme' means a scheme setting out–

(a) the classes of case in which the operator of the scheme, or the person on whose behalf he acts, is willing to grant performers' property right licences, and

(b) the terms on which licences would be granted in those classes of case;

and for this purpose a 'scheme' includes anything in the nature of a scheme, whether described as a scheme or as a tariff or by any other name.

(2) In Part II a 'licensing body' means a society or other organisation which has as its main object, or one of its main objects, the negotiating or granting, whether as owner or prospective owner of a performer's property rights or as agent for him, of performers' property right licences, and whose objects include the granting of licences covering the performances of more than one performer.

(3) In this paragraph 'performers' property right licences' means licences to do, or authorise the doing of, any of the things for which consent is required under section 182A, 182B or 182C.

(4) References in this Part to licences or licensing schemes covering the performances of more than one performer do not include licences or schemes covering only–

(a) performances recorded in a single recording,

(b) performances recorded in more than one recording where–

    (i) the performers giving the performances are the same, or

    (ii) the recordings are made by, or by employees of or commissioned by, a single individual, firm, company or group of companies.

For purpose a group of companies means a holding company and its subsidiaries within the meaning of section 736 of the Companies Act 1985.

References and applications with respect to licensing schemes

2 Paragraphs 3 to 8 (references and applications with respect to licensing schemes) apply to licensing schemes operated by licensing bodies in relation to a performer's property rights which cover the performances of more than one performer, so far as they relate to licences for–

(a) copying a recording of the whole or any substantial part of a qualifying performance, or

(b) renting or lending copies of a recording to the public;

and in those paragraphs 'licensing scheme' means a licensing scheme of any of those descriptions.

Reference of proposed licensing scheme to tribunal

3–(1) The terms of a licensing scheme proposed to be operated by a licensing body may be referred to the Copyright Tribunal by an organisation claiming to be representative of persons claiming that they require licences in cases of a description to which the scheme would apply, either generally or in relation to any description of case.

(2) The Tribunal shall first decide whether to entertain the reference, and may decline to do so on the ground that the reference is premature.

(3) If the Tribunal decides to entertain the reference it shall consider the matter referred and make such order, either confirming or varying the proposed scheme, either generally or so far as it relates to cases of the description to which the reference relates, as the Tribunal may determine to be reasonable in the circumstances.

(4) The order may be made so as to be in force indefinitely or for such period as the Tribunal may determine.

Reference of licensing scheme to tribunal

4–(1) If while a licensing scheme is in operation a dispute arises between the operator of the scheme and–

(a) a person claiming that he requires a licence in a case of a description to which the scheme applies, or

(b)   an organisation claiming to be representative of such persons,

that person or organisation may refer the scheme to the Copyright Tribunal in so far as it relates to cases of that description.

(2) A scheme which has been referred to the Tribunal under this paragraph shall remain in operation until proceedings on the reference are concluded.

(3) The Tribunal shall consider the matter in dispute and make such order, either confirming or varying the scheme so far as it relates to cases of the description to which the reference relates, as the Tribunal may determine to be reasonable in the circumstances.

(4) The order may be made so as to be in force indefinitely or for such period as the Tribunal may determine.

Further reference of scheme to tribunal

5–(1) Where the Copyright Tribunal has on a previous reference of a licensing scheme under paragraph 3 or 4, or under this paragraph, made an order with respect to the scheme, then, while the order remains in force–

(a)   the operator of the scheme,

(b)   a person claiming that he requires a licence in a case of the description to which the order applies, or

(c)   an organisation claiming to be representative of such persons,

may refer the scheme again to the Tribunal so far as it relates to cases of that description.

(2) A licensing scheme shall not, except with the special leave of the Tribunal, be referred again to the Tribunal in respect of the same description of cases–

(a)   within twelve months from the date of the order on the previous reference, or

(b)   if the order was made so as to be in force for 15 months or less, until the last three months before the expiry of the order.

(3) A scheme which has been referred to the Tribunal under this paragraph shall remain in operation until proceedings on the reference are concluded.

(4) The Tribunal shall consider the matter in dispute and make such order, either confirming, varying or further varying the scheme so far as it relates to cases of the description to which the reference relates, as the Tribunal may determine to be reasonable in the circumstances.

(5) The order may be made so as to be in force indefinitely or for such period as the Tribunal may determine.

Application for grant of licence in connection with licensing scheme

6–(1) A person who claims, in a case covered by a licensing scheme, that the operator of the scheme has refused to grant him or procure the grant to him of a licence in accordance with the scheme, or has failed to do so within a reasonable time after being asked, may apply to the Copyright Tribunal.

(2) A person who claims, in a case excluded from a licensing scheme, that the operator of the scheme either–

(a)   has refused to grant him a licence or procure the grant to him of a licence, or has failed to do so within a reasonable time of being asked, and that in the circumstances it is unreasonable that a licence should not be granted, or

(b)   proposes terms for a licence which are unreasonable,

may apply to the Copyright Tribunal.

(3) A case shall be regarded as excluded from a licensing scheme for the purposes of sub-paragraph (2) if–

(a)   the scheme provides for the grant of licences subject to terms excepting matters from the licence and the case falls within such an exception, or

(b)   the case is so similar to those in which licences are granted under the scheme that it is unreasonable that it should not be dealt with in the same way.

(4) If the Tribunal is satisfied that the claim is well-founded, it shall make an order declaring that, in respect of the matters specified in the order, the applicant is entitled to a licence on such terms as

the Tribunal may determine to be applicable in accordance with the scheme or, as the case may be, to be reasonable in the circumstances.

(5) The order may be made so as to be in force indefinitely or for such period as the Tribunal may determine.

Application for review of order as to entitlement to licence

7–(1) Where the Copyright Tribunal has made an order under paragraph 6 that a person is entitled to a licence under a licensing scheme, the operator of the scheme or the original applicant may apply to the Tribunal to review its order.

(2) An application shall not be made, except with the special leave of the Tribunal–

(a) within twelve months from the date of the order, or of the decision on a previous application under this paragraph, or

(b) if the order was made so as to be in force for 15 months or less, or as a result of the decision on a previous application under this paragraph is due to expire within 15 months of that decision, until the last three months before the expiry date.

(3) The Tribunal shall on an application for review confirm or vary its order as the Tribunal may determine to be reasonable having regard to the terms applicable in accordance with the licensing scheme or, as the case may be, the circumstances of the case.

Effect of order of tribunal as to licensing scheme

8–(1) A licensing scheme which has been confirmed or varied by the Copyright Tribunal–

(a) under paragraph 3 (reference of terms of proposed scheme), or

(b) under paragraph 4 or 5 (reference of existing scheme to Tribunal),

shall be in force or, as the case may be, remain in operation, so far as it relates to the description of case in respect of which the order was made, so long as the order remains in force.

(2) While the order is in force a person who in a case of a class to which the order applies–

(a) pays to the operator of the scheme any charges payable under the scheme in respect of a licence covering the case in question or, if the amount cannot be ascertained, gives an undertaking to the operator to pay them when ascertained, and

(b) complies with the other terms applicable to such a licence under the scheme,

shall be in the same position as regards infringement of performers' property rights as if he had at all material times been the holder of a licence granted by the rights owner in question in accordance with the scheme.

(3) The Tribunal may direct that the order, so far as it varies the amount of charges payable, has effect from a date before that on which it is made, but not earlier than the date on which the reference was made or, if later, on which the scheme came into operation.

If such a direction is made–

(a) any necessary repayments, or further payments, shall be made in respect of charges already paid, and

(b) the reference in sub-paragraph (2)(*a*) to the charges payable under the scheme shall be construed as a reference to the charges so payable by virtue of the order.

No such direction may be made where sub paragraph (4) below applies.

(4) An order of the Tribunal under paragraph 4 or 5 made with respect to a scheme which is certified for any purpose under paragraph 16 has effect, so far as it varies the scheme by reducing the charges payable for licences, from the date on which the reference was made to the Tribunal.

(5) Where the Tribunal has made an order under paragraph 6 (order as to entitlement to licence under licensing scheme) and the order remains in force, the person in whose favour the order is made shall if he–

(a) pays to the operator of the scheme any charges payable in accordance with the order or, if the amount cannot be ascertained, gives an undertaking to pay the charges when ascertained, and

(b) complies with the other terms specified in the order;

be in the same position as regards infringement of performers' property rights as if he had at all material times been the holder of a licence granted by the rights owner in question on the terms specified in the order.

References and applications with respect to licensing by licensing bodies

9 Paragraphs 10 to 13 (references and applications with respect to licensing by licensing bodies) apply to licences relating to a performer's property rights which cover the performance of more than one performer granted by a licensing body otherwise than in pursuance of a licensing scheme, so far as the licences authorise–

(a)   copying a recording of the whole or any substantial part of a qualifying performance, or

(b)   renting or lending copies of a recording to the public;

and references in those paragraphs to a licence shall be construed accordingly.

Reference to tribunal of proposed licence

10–(1) The terms on which a licensing body proposes to grant a licence may be referred to the Copyright Tribunal by the prospective licensee.

(2) The Tribunal shall first decide whether to entertain the reference, and may decline to do so on the ground that the reference is premature.

(3) If the Tribunal decides to entertain the reference it shall consider the terms of the proposed licence and make such order, either confirming or varying the terms as it may determine to be reasonable in the circumstances.

(4) The order may be made so as to be in force indefinitely or for such period as the Tribunal may determine.

Reference to tribunal of expiring licence

11–(1) A licensee under a licence which is due to expire, by effluxion of time or as a result of notice given by the licensing body, may apply to the Copyright Tribunal on the ground that it is unreasonable in the circumstances that the licence should cease to be in force.

(2) Such an application may not be made until the last three months before the licence is due to expire.

(3) A licence in respect of which a reference has been made to the Tribunal shall remain in operation until proceedings on the reference are concluded.

(4) If the Tribunal finds the application well-founded, it shall make an order declaring that the licensee shall continue to be entitled to the benefit of the licence on such terms as the Tribunal may determine to be reasonable in the circumstances.

(5) An order of the Tribunal under this paragraph may be made so as to be in force indefinitely or for such period as the Tribunal may determine.

Application for review of order as to licence

12–(1) Where the Copyright Tribunal has made an order under paragraph 10 or 11, the licensing body or the person entitled to the benefit of the order may apply to the Tribunal to review its order.

(2) An application shall not be made, except with the special leave of the Tribunal–

(a)   within twelve months from the date of the order or of the decision on a previous application under this paragraph, or

(b)   if the order was made so as to be in force for 15 months or less, or as a result of the decision on a previous application under this paragraph is due to expire within 15 months of that decision, until the last three months before the expiry date.

(3) The Tribunal shall on an application for review confirm or vary its order as the Tribunal may determine to be reasonable in the circumstances.

Effect of order of tribunal as to licence

13–(1) Where the Copyright Tribunal has made an order under paragraph 10 or 11 and the order remains in force, the person entitled to the benefit of the order shall if he–

(a)   pays to the licensing body any charges payable in accordance with the order or, if the amount cannot be ascertained, gives an undertaking to pay the charges when ascertained, and

(b)   complies with the other terms specified in the order,

be in the same position as regards infringement of performers' property rights as if he had at all material times been the holder of a licence granted by the rights owner in question on the terms specified in the order.

(2) The benefit of the order may be assigned–

(a)   in the case of an order under paragraph 10, if assignment is not prohibited under the terms of the Tribunal's order; and

(b)   in the case of an order under paragraph 11, if assignment was not prohibited under the terms of the original licence.

(3) The Tribunal may direct that an order under paragraph 10 or 11, or an order under paragraph 12 varying such an order, so far as it varies the amount of charges payable, has effect from a date before that on which it is made, but not earlier than the date on which the reference or application was made or, if later, on which the licence was granted or, as the case may be, was due to expire.

If such a direction is made–

(a)   any necessary repayments, or further payments, shall be made in respect of charges already paid, and

(b)   the reference in sub-paragraph (1)(*a*) to the charges payable in accordance with the order shall be construed, where the order is varied by a later order, as a reference to the charges so payable by virtue of the later order.

General considerations: unreasonable discrimination

14–(1) In determining what is reasonable on a reference or application under this Schedule relating to a licensing scheme or licence, the Copyright Tribunal shall have regard to–

(a)   the availability of other schemes, or the granting of other licences, to other persons in similar circumstances, and

(b)   the terms of those schemes or licences,

and shall exercise its powers so as to secure that there is no unreasonable discrimination between licensees, or prospective licensees, under the scheme or licence to which the reference or application relates and licensees under other schemes operated by, or other licences granted by, the same person.

(2) This does not affect the Tribunal's general obligation in any case to have regard to all relevant circumstances.

Application to settle royalty or other sum payable for lending

15–(1) An application to settle the royalty or other sum payable in pursuance of paragraph 14A of Schedule 2 (lending of certain recordings) may be made to the Copyright Tribunal by the owner of a performer's property rights or the person claiming to be treated as licensed by him.

(2) The Tribunal shall consider the matter and make such order as it may determine to be reasonable in the circumstances.

(3) Either party may subsequently apply to the Tribunal to vary the order, and the Tribunal shall consider the matter and make such order confirming or varying the original order as it may determine to be reasonable in the circumstances.

(4) An application under sub-paragraph (3) shall not, except with the special leave of the Tribunal, be made within twelve months from the date of the original order or of the order on a previous application under that sub-paragraph.

(5) An order under sub-paragraph (3) has effect from the date on which it is made or such later date as may be specified by the Tribunal

Certification of licensing schemes

16–(1) A person operating or proposing to operate a licensing scheme may apply to the Secretary of State to certify the scheme for the purposes of paragraph 14A of Schedule 2 (lending of certain recordings).

(2) The Secretary of State shall by order made by statutory instrument certify the scheme if he is satisfied that it–

(a) enables the works to which it relates to be identified with sufficient certainty by persons likely to require licences, and

(b) sets out clearly the charges (if any) payable and the other terms on which licences will be granted.

(3) The scheme shall be scheduled to the order and the certification shall come into operation for the purposes of paragraph 14A of Schedule 2–

(a) on such date, not less than eight weeks after the order is made, as may be specified in the order, or

(b) if the scheme is the subject of a reference under paragraph 3 (reference of proposed scheme), any later date on which the order of the Copyright Tribunal under that paragraph comes into force or the reference is withdrawn.

(4) A variation of the scheme is not effective unless a corresponding amendment of the order is made; and the Secretary of State shall make such an amendment in the case of a variation ordered by the Copyright Tribunal on a reference under paragraph 3, 4 or 5, and may do so in any other case if he thinks fit.

(5) The order shall be revoked if the scheme ceases to be operated and may be revoked if it appears to the Secretary of State that it is no longer being operated according to its terms.

Powers exercisable in consequence of competition report

17–(1) Where the matters specified in a report of the Monopolies and Mergers Commission as being those which in the Commission's opinion operate, may be expected to operate or have operated against the public interest include–

(a) conditions in licences granted by the owner of a performer's property rights restricting the use to which a recording may be put by the licensee or the right of the owner to grant other licences, or

(b) a refusal of an owner of a performer's property rights to grant licences on reasonable terms,

the powers conferred by Part I of Schedule 8 to the Fair Trading Act 1973 (powers exercisable for purpose of remedying or preventing adverse effects specified in report of Commission) include power to cancel or modify those conditions and, instead or in addition, to provide that licences in respect of the performer's property rights shall be available as of right.

(2) The references in sections 56(2) and 73(2) of that Act, and sections 10(2)(*b*) and 12(5) of the Competition Act 1980, to the powers specified in that Part of that Schedule shall be construed accordingly.

(3) A Minister shall only exercise the powers available by virtue of this paragraph if he is satisfied that to do so does not contravene any Convention relating to performers' rights to which the United Kingdom is a party.

(4) The terms of a licence available by virtue of this paragraph shall, in default of agreement, be settled by the Copyright Tribunal on an application by the person requiring the licence; and terms so settled shall authorise the licensee to do everything in respect of which a licence is so available.

(5) Where the terms of a licence are settled by the Tribunal, the licence has effect from the date on which the application to the Tribunal was made.'.

23 Performers' rights: power of Copyright Tribunal to give consent

(1) Section 190 (power of tribunal to give consent on behalf of performer in certain cases) is amended as follows.

(2) For subsection (1) substitute—

'(1) The Copyright Tribunal may, on the application of a person wishing to make a copy of a recording of a performance, give consent in a case where the identity or whereabouts of the person entitled to the reproduction right cannot be ascertained by reasonable inquiry.'.

(3) In subsection (2) for 'the performer' substitute 'the person entitled to the reproduction right'.

(4) Omit subsection (4).

(5) In subsection (6)—

    (a) for 'the performer' in the first place where it occurs substitute 'the person entitled to the reproduction right', and

    (b) for 'the performer' in the second place where it occurs substitute 'that person'.

24 Performers' rights: jurisdiction of Copyright Tribunal

(1) After section 205A (inserted by regulation 22(1)) insert—

'Jurisdiction of Copyright Tribunal

205B Jurisdiction of Copyright Tribunal

(1) The Copyright Tribunal has jurisdiction under this Part to hear and determine proceedings under—

    (a) section 182D (amount of equitable remuneration for exploitation of commercial sound recording);

    (b) section 190 (application to give consent on behalf of owner of reproduction right);

    (c) section 191H (amount of equitable remuneration on transfer of rental right);

    (d) paragraph 3, 4 or 5 of Schedule 2A (reference of licensing scheme);

    (e) paragraph 6 or 7 of that Schedule (application with respect to licence under licensing scheme);

    (f) paragraph 10, 11 or 12 of that Schedule (reference or application with respect to licensing by licensing body);

    (g) paragraph 15 of that Schedule (application to settle royalty for certain lending);

    (h) paragraph 17 of that Schedule (application to settle terms of licence available as of right).

(2) The provisions of Chapter VIII of Part I (general provisions relating to the Copyright Tribunal) apply in relation to the Tribunal when exercising any jurisdiction under this Part.

(3) Provision shall be made by rules under section 150 prohibiting the Tribunal from entertaining a reference under paragraph 3, 4 or 5 of Schedule 2A (reference of licensing scheme) by a representative organisation unless the Tribunal is satisfied that the organisation is reasonably representative of the class of persons which it claims to represent.'.

(2) In section 149 (jurisdiction of the Tribunal)—

    (a) in the opening words for 'The function of the Copyright Tribunal is' substitute 'The Copyright Tribunal has jurisdiction under this Part';

    (b) omit paragraphs (*g*) and (*h*).

(3) In paragraph 5 of Schedule 6 (determination by Tribunal of royalty or other remuneration to be paid), after sub-paragraph (4) add—

'(5) The provisions of Chapter VIII of Part I (general provisions relating to the Copyright Tribunal) apply in relation to the Tribunal when exercising any jurisdiction under this paragraph.'.

PART III
TRANSITIONAL PROVISIONS AND SAVINGS

General provisions

25 Introductory

(1) In this Part–

'commencement' means the commencement of these Regulations; and

'existing', in relation to a work or performance, means made or given before commencement.

(2) For the purposes of this Part a work of which the making extended over a period shall be taken to have been made when its making was completed.

(3) In this Part a 'new right' means a right arising by virtue of these Regulations, in relation to a copyright work or a qualifying performance, to authorise or prohibit an act.

The expression does not include–

(a) a right corresponding to a right which existed immediately before commencement, or

(b) a right to remuneration arising by virtue of these Regulations.

(4) Expressions used in this Part have the same meaning in relation to copyright as they have in Part I of the Copyright, Designs and Patents Act 1988, and in relation to performances as in Part II of that Act.

26 General rules

(1) Subject to anything in regulations 28 to 36 (special transitional provisions and savings), these regulations apply to copyright works made, and to performances given, before or after commencement.

(2) No act done before commencement shall be regarded as an infringement of any new right, or as giving rise to any right to remuneration arising by virtue of these Regulations.

27 Saving for certain existing agreements

(1) Except as otherwise expressly provided, nothing in these Regulations affects an agreement made before 19th November 1992.

(2) No act done in pursuance of any such agreement after commencement shall be regarded as an infringement of any new right.

Special provisions

28 Broadcasts

The provisions of–

regulation 5 (place where broadcast treated as made) and
regulation 6 (safeguards in relation to certain satellite broadcasts),

have effect in relation to broadcasts made after commencement.

29 Satellite broadcasting: international co-production agreements

(1) This regulation applies to an agreement concluded before 1st January 1995–

(a) between two or more co-producers of a film, one of whom is a national of an EEA state, and

(b) the provisions of which grant to the parties exclusive rights to exploit all communication to the public of the film in separate geographical areas.

(2) Where such an agreement giving such exclusive exploitation rights in relation to the United Kingdom does not expressly or by implication address satellite broadcasting from the United Kingdom, the person to whom those exclusive rights have been granted shall not make any such broadcast without the consent of any other party to the agreement whose language-related exploitation rights would be adversely affected by that broadcast.

30 New rights: exercise of rights in relation to performances

(1) Any new right conferred by these Regulations in relation to a qualifying performance is exercisable as from commencement by the performer or (if he has died) by the person who immediately before commencement was entitled by virtue of section 192(2) to exercise the rights conferred on the performer by Part II in relation to that performance.

(2) Any remuneration or damages received by a person's personal representatives by virtue of a right conferred on them by paragraph (1) shall devolve as part of that person's estate as if the right had subsisted and been vested in him immediately before his death.

31 New rights: effect of pre-commencement authorisation of copying
Where before commencement–

   (a)   the owner or prospective owner of copyright in a literary, dramatic, musical or artistic work has authorised a person to make a copy of the work, or

   (b)   the owner or prospective owner of performers' rights in a performance has authorised a person to make a copy of a recording of the performance,

any new right in relation to that copy shall vest on commencement in the person so authorised, subject to any agreement to the contrary.

32 New rights: effect of pre-commencement film production agreement
(1) Sections 93A and 191F (presumption of transfer of rental right in case of production agreement) apply in relation to an agreement concluded before commencement.

As section 93A so applies, the restriction in subsection (3) of that section shall be omitted (exclusion of presumption in relation to screenplay, dialogue or music specifically created for the film).

(2) Sections 93B and 191G (right to equitable remuneration where rental right transferred) have effect accordingly, but subject to regulation 33 (right to equitable remuneration applicable to rental after 1st April 1997).

33 Right to equitable remuneration applicable to rental after 1st April 1997
No right to equitable remuneration under section 93B or 191G (right to equitable remuneration where rental right transferred) arises–

   (a)   in respect of any rental of a sound recording or film before 1st April 1997, or

   (b)   in respect of any rental after that date of a sound recording or film made in pursuance of an agreement entered into before 1st July 1994, unless the author or performer (or a successor in title of his) has before 1st January 1997 notified the person by whom the remuneration would be payable that he intends to exercise that right.

34 Savings for existing stocks
(1) Any new right in relation to a copyright work does not apply to a copy of the work acquired by a person before commencement for the purpose of renting or lending it to the public.

(2) Any new right in relation to a qualifying performance does not apply to a copy of a recording of the performance acquired by a person before commencement for the purpose of renting or lending it to the public .

35 Lending of copies by libraries or archives
Until the making of regulations under section 37 of the Copyright, Designs and Patents Act 1988 for the purposes of section 40A(2) of that Act (lending of copies by libraries or archives), the reference in section 40A(2) (and in paragraph 6B of Schedule 2) to a prescribed library or archive shall be construed as a reference to any library or archive in the United Kingdom prescribed by paragraphs 2 to 6 of Part A of Schedule 1 to the Copyright (Librarians and Archivists) (Copying of Copyright Material) Regulations 1989.

36 Authorship of films
(1) Regulation 18 (authorship of films) applies as from commencement in relation to films made on or after 1st July 1994.

(2) It is not an infringement of any right which the principal director has by virtue of these Regulations to do anything after commencement in pursuance of arrangements for the exploitation of the film made before 19th November 1992.

This does not affect any right of his to equitable remuneration under section 93B.

Copyright and Rights in Databases Regulations 1997

(SI 1997/3032)

Whereas a draft of the following Regulations has been approved by a resolution of each House of Parliament:

Now, therefore, the Secretary of State, being a Minister designated for the purposes of section 2(2) of the European Communities Act 1972 in relation to measures relating to copyright and measures relating to the prevention of unauthorised extraction of the contents of a database and of unauthorised re-utilisation of those contents, in exercise of the powers conferred by section 2(2) and (4) of that Act, hereby makes the following Regulations–

NOTE

Made: 18 December 1997
Commencement: 1 January 1998

PART I
INTRODUCTORY PROVISIONS

1 Citation, commencement and extent
(1) These Regulations may be cited as the Copyright and Rights in Databases Regulations 1997.

(2) These Regulations come into force on 1st January 1998.

(3) These Regulations extend to the whole of the United Kingdom.

2 Implementation of Directive
(1) These Regulations make provision for the purpose of implementing–

(a) Council Directive No 96/9/EC of 11 March 1996 on the legal protection of databases, and

(b) certain obligations of the United Kingdom created by or arising under the EEA Agreement so far as relating to the implementation of that Directive.

(2) In this Regulation 'the EEA Agreement' means the Agreement on the European Economic Area signed at Oporto on 2nd May 1992, as adjusted by the Protocol signed at Brussels on 17th March 1993.

3 Interpretation
In these Regulations 'the 1988 Act' means the Copyright, Designs and Patents Act 1988.

4 Scheme of the Regulations
(1) The 1988 Act is amended in accordance with the provisions of Part II of these Regulations, subject to the savings and transitional provisions in Part IV of these Regulations.

(2) Part III of these Regulations has effect subject to those savings and transitional provisions.

PART II
AMENDMENT OF THE COPYRIGHT, DESIGNS AND PATENTS ACT 1988

5 Copyright in databases
In section 3(1), in the definition of 'literary work'–

(a) in paragraph (a) after 'compilation' insert 'other than a database';

(b) at the end of paragraph (b) leave out 'and';

(c) at the end of paragraph (c) insert

'and

(d)   a database;'.

6 Meaning of 'database'
After section 3 insert–

3A Databases
(1) In this Part 'database' means a collection of independent works, data or other materials which–

(a)   are arranged in a systematic or methodical way, and

(b)   are individually accessible by electronic or other means.

(2) For the purposes of this Part a literary work consisting of a database is original if, and only if, by reason of the selection or arrangement of the contents of the database the database constitutes the author's own intellectual creation.'.

7 Meaning of 'adaptation' in relation to database
In section 21 (infringement by making adaptation or act done in relation to adaptation), in subsection (3)–

(a)   in paragraph (a), for 'other than a computer program or' substitute 'other than a computer program or a database, or in relation to a', and

(b)   after paragraph (ab) insert–

(ac) in relation to a database, means an arrangement or altered version of the database or a translation of it;'.

8 Research
(1) In section 29 (research and private study), in subsection (1), after 'literary' insert 'work, other than a database, or a'.

(2) After subsection (1) of that section insert–

'(1A) Fair dealing with a database for the purposes of research or private study does not infringe any copyright in the database provided that the source is indicated.'.

(3) After subsection (4) of that section insert–

'(5) The doing of anything in relation to a database for the purposes of research for a commercial purpose is not fair dealing with the database.'.

9 Permitted acts in relation to databases
After section 50C insert–

'Databases: permitted acts

50D Acts permitted in relation to databases
(1) It is not an infringement of copyright in a database for a person who has a right to use the database or any part of the database, (whether under a licence to do any of the acts restricted by the copyright in the database or otherwise) to do, in the exercise of that right, anything which is necessary for the purposes of access to and use of the contents of the database or of that part of the database.

(2) Where an act which would otherwise infringe copyright in a database is permitted under this section, it is irrelevant whether or not there exists any term or condition in any agreement which purports to prohibit or restrict the act (such terms being, by virtue of section 296B, void).'.

10 Avoidance of certain terms
After section 296A insert–

'Databases

296B Avoidance of certain terms relating to databases
Where under an agreement a person has a right to use a database or part of a database, any term or condition in the agreement shall be void in so far as it purports to prohibit or restrict the performance of any act which would but for section 50D infringe the copyright in the database.'.

11 Defined expressions
In section 179 (index of defined expressions), in the appropriate place in alphabetical order insert–

database	section 3A(1)'
'original (in relation to a database)	section 3A(2)'.

PART III
DATABASE RIGHT

12 Interpretation
(1) In this Part–
   'database' has the meaning given by section 3A(1) of the 1988 Act (as inserted by Regulation 6);
   'extraction', in relation to any contents of a database, means the permanent or temporary transfer of those contents to another medium by any means or in any form;
   'insubstantial', in relation to part of the contents of a database, shall be construed subject to Regulation 16(2);
   'investment' includes any investment, whether of financial, human or technical resources;
   'jointly', in relation to the making of a database, shall be construed in accordance with Regulation 14(6);
   'lawful user', in relation to a database, means any person who (whether under a licence to do any of the acts restricted by any database right in the database or otherwise) has a right to use the database;
   'maker', in relation to a database, shall be construed in accordance with Regulation 14;
   're-utilisation', in relation to any contents of a database, means making those contents available to the public by any means;
   'substantial', in relation to any investment, extraction or re-utilisation, means substantial in terms of quantity or quality or a combination of both.

(2) The making of a copy of a database available for use, on terms that it will or may be returned, otherwise than for direct or indirect economic or commercial advantage, through an establishment which is accessible to the public shall not be taken for the purposes of this Part to constitute extraction or re-utilisation of the contents of the database.

(3) Where the making of a copy of a database available through an establishment which is accessible to the public gives rise to a payment the amount of which does not go beyond what is necessary to cover the costs of the establishment, there is no direct or indirect economic or commercial advantage for the purposes of paragraph (2).

(4) Paragraph (2) does not apply to the making of a copy of a database available for on-the-spot reference use.

(5) Where a copy of a database has been sold within the EEA by, or with the consent of, the owner of the database right in the database, the further sale within the EEA of that copy shall not be taken for the purposes of this Part to constitute extraction or re-utilisation of the contents of the database.

13 Database right
(1) A property right ('database right') subsists, in accordance with this Part, in a database if there has been a substantial investment in obtaining, verifying or presenting the contents of the database.

(2) For the purposes of paragraph (1) it is immaterial whether or not the database or any of its contents is a copyright work, within the meaning of Part I of the 1988 Act.

(3) This Regulation has effect subject to Regulation 18.

14 The maker of a database

(1) Subject to paragraphs (2) to (4), the person who takes the initiative in obtaining, verifying or presenting the contents of a database and assumes the risk of investing in that obtaining, verification or presentation shall be regarded as the maker of, and as having made, the database.

(2) Where a database is made by an employee in the course of his employment, his employer shall be regarded as the maker of the database, subject to any agreement to the contrary.

(3) Subject to paragraph (4), where a database is made by Her Majesty or by an officer or servant of the Crown in the course of his duties, Her Majesty shall be regarded as the maker of the database.

(4) Where a database is made by or under the direction or control of the House of Commons or the House of Lords–

    (a) the House by whom, or under whose direction or control, the database is made shall be regarded as the maker of the database, and

    (b) if the database is made by or under the direction or control of both Houses, the two Houses shall be regarded as the joint makers of the database.

(5) For the purposes of this Part a database is made jointly if two or more persons acting together in collaboration take the initiative in obtaining, verifying or presenting the contents of the database and assume the risk of investing in that obtaining, verification or presentation.

(6) References in this Part to the maker of a database shall, except as otherwise provided, be construed, in relation to a database which is made jointly, as references to all the makers of the database.

15 First ownership of database right

The maker of a database is the first owner of database right in it.

16 Acts infringing database right

(1) Subject to the provisions of this Part, a person infringes database right in a database if, without the consent of the owner of the right, he extracts or re-utilises all or a substantial part of the contents of the database.

(2) For the purposes of this Part, the repeated and systematic extraction or re-utilisation of insubstantial parts of the contents of a database may amount to the extraction or re-utilisation of a substantial part of those contents.

17 Term of protection

(1) Database right in a database expires at the end of the period of fifteen years from the end of the calendar year in which the making of the database was completed.

(2) Where a database is made available to the public before the end of the period referred to in paragraph (1), database right in the database shall expire fifteen years from the end of the calendar year in which the database was first made available to the public.

(3) Any substantial change to the contents of a database, including a substantial change resulting from the accumulation of successive additions, deletions or alterations, which would result in the database being considered to be a substantial new investment shall qualify the database resulting from that investment for its own term of protection.

(4) This Regulation has effect subject to Regulation 30.

18 Qualification for database right

(1) Database right does not subsist in a database unless, at the material time, its maker, or if it was made jointly, one or more of its makers, was–

    (a) an individual who was a national of an EEA state or habitually resident within the EEA,

    (b) a body which was incorporated under the law of an EEA state and which, at that time, satisfied one of the conditions in paragraph (2), or

(c)   a partnership or other unincorporated body which was formed under the law of an EEA state and which, at that time, satisfied the condition in paragraph (2)(a).

(2) The conditions mentioned in paragraphs (1)(b) and (c) are–

(a)   that the body has its central administration or principal place of business within the EEA, or

(b)   that the body has its registered office within the EEA and the body's operations are linked on an ongoing basis with the economy of an EEA state.

(3) Paragraph (1) does not apply in any case falling within Regulation 14(4).

(4) In this Regulation–

(a)   'EEA' and 'EEA state' have the meaning given by section 172A of the 1988 Act;

(b)   'the material time' means the time when the database was made, or if the making extended over a period, a substantial part of that period.

19   Avoidance of certain terms affecting lawful users

(1) A lawful user of a database which has been made available to the public in any manner shall be entitled to extract or re-utilise insubstantial parts of the contents of the database for any purpose.

(2) Where under an agreement a person has a right to use a database, or part of a database, which has been made available to the public in any manner, any term or condition in the agreement shall be void in so far as it purports to prevent that person from extracting or re-utilising insubstantial parts of the contents of the database, or of that part of the database, for any purpose.

20   Exceptions to database right

(1) Database right in a database which has been made available to the public in any manner is not infringed by fair dealing with a substantial part of its contents if–

(a)   that part is extracted from the database by a person who is apart from this paragraph a lawful user of the database,

(b)   it is extracted for the purpose of illustration for teaching or research and not for any commercial purpose, and

(c)   the source is indicated.

(2) The provisions of Schedule 1 specify other acts which may be done in relation to a database notwithstanding the existence of database right.

21   Acts permitted on assumption as to expiry of database right

(1) Database right in a database is not infringed by the extraction or re-utilisation of a substantial part of the contents of the database at a time when, or in pursuance of arrangements made at a time when–

(a)   it is not possible by reasonable inquiry to ascertain the identity of the maker, and

(b)   it is reasonable to assume that database right has expired.

(2) In the case of a database alleged to have been made jointly, paragraph (1) applies in relation to each person alleged to be one of the makers.

22   Presumptions relevant to database right

(1) The following presumptions apply in proceedings brought by virtue of this Part of these Regulations with respect to a database.

(2) Where a name purporting to be that of the maker appeared on copies of the database as published, or on the database when it was made, the person whose name appeared shall be presumed, until the contrary is proved–

(a)   to be the maker of the database, and

(b)   to have made it in circumstances not falling within Regulation 14(2) to (4).

(3) Where copies of the database as published bear a label or a mark stating–

(a)   that a named person was the maker of the database, or

(b)   that the database was first published in a specified year,

the label or mark shall be admissible as evidence of the facts stated and shall be presumed to be correct until the contrary is proved.

(4) In the case of a database alleged to have been made jointly, paragraphs (2) and (3), so far as is applicable, apply in relation to each person alleged to be one of the makers.

23   Application of copyright provisions to database right
The following provisions of the 1988 Act–

sections 90 to 93 (dealing with rights in copyright works);
sections 96 to 98 (rights and remedies of copyright owner);
sections 101 and 102 (rights and remedies of exclusive licensee);

apply in relation to database right and databases in which that right subsists as they apply in relation to copyright and copyright works.

24   Licensing of database right
The provisions of Schedule 2 have effect with respect to the licensing of database right.

25   Database right: jurisdiction of Copyright Tribunal
(1) The Copyright Tribunal has jurisdiction under this Part to hear and determine proceedings under the following provisions of Schedule 2–

(a)   paragraph 3, 4 or 5 (reference of licensing scheme);
(b)   paragraph 6 or 7 (application with respect to licence under licensing scheme);
(c)   paragraph 10, 11 or 12 (reference or application with respect to licence by licensing body).

(2) The provisions of Chapter VIII of Part I of the 1988 Act (general provisions relating to the Copyright Tribunal) apply in relation to the Tribunal when exercising any jurisdiction under this Part.

(3) Provision shall be made by rules under section 150 of the 1988 Act prohibiting the Tribunal from entertaining a reference under paragraph 3, 4 or 5 of Schedule 2 (reference of licensing scheme) by a representative organisation unless the Tribunal is satisfied that the organisation is reasonably representative of the class of persons which it claims to represent.

PART IV
SAVINGS AND TRANSITIONAL PROVISIONS

26   Introductory
(1) In this Part 'commencement' means the commencement of these Regulations.

(2) Expressions used in this Part which are defined for the purposes of Part I of the 1988 Act have the same meaning as in that Part.

27   General rule
Subject to Regulations 28 and 29, these Regulations apply to databases made before or after commencement.

28   General savings
(1) Nothing in these Regulations affects any agreement made before commencement.

(2) No act done–

(a)   before commencement, or
(b)   after commencement, in pursuance of an agreement made before commencement,

shall be regarded as an infringement of database right in a database.

29   Saving for copyright in certain existing databases
(1) Where a database–

(a)   was created on or before 27th March 1996, and

(b)   is a copyright work immediately before commencement,

copyright shall continue to subsist in the database for the remainder of its copyright term.

(2) In this Regulation 'copyright term' means the period of the duration of copyright under section 12 of the 1988 Act (duration of copyright in literary, dramatic, musical or artistic works).

30 Database right: term applicable to certain existing databases

Where–

(a)   the making of a database was completed on or after 1st January 1983, and

(b)   on commencement, database right begins to subsist in the database,

database right shall subsist in the database for the period of fifteen years beginning with 1st January 1998.

Regulation 20(2)

SCHEDULE 1

EXCEPTIONS TO DATABASE RIGHT FOR PUBLIC ADMINISTRATION

Parliamentary and judicial proceedings

1 Database right in a database is not infringed by anything done for the purposes of parliamentary or judicial proceedings or for the purposes of reporting such proceedings.

Royal Commissions and statutory inquiries

2–(1) Database right in a database is not infringed by anything done for–

(a)   the purposes of the proceedings of a Royal Commission or statutory inquiry, or

(b)   the purpose of reporting any such proceedings held in public.

(2) Database right in a database is not infringed by the issue to the public of copies of the report of a Royal Commission or statutory inquiry containing the contents of the database.

(3) In this paragraph 'Royal Commission' and 'statutory inquiry' have the same meaning as in section 46 of the 1988 Act.

Material open to public inspection or on official register

3–(1) Where the contents of a database are open to public inspection pursuant to a statutory requirement, or are on a statutory register, database right in the database is not infringed by the extraction of all or a substantial part of the contents containing factual information of any description, by or with the authority of the appropriate person, for a purpose which does not involve re-utilisation of all or a substantial part of the contents.

(2) Where the contents of a database are open to public inspection pursuant to a statutory requirement, database right in the database is not infringed by the extraction or re-utilisation of all or a substantial part of the contents, by or with the authority of the appropriate person, for the purpose of enabling the contents to be inspected at a more convenient time or place or otherwise facilitating the exercise of any right for the purpose of which the requirement is imposed.

(3) Where the contents of a database which is open to public inspection pursuant to a statutory requirement, or which is on a statutory register, contain information about matters of general scientific, technical, commercial or economic interest, database right in the database is not infringed by the extraction or re-utilisation of all or a substantial part of the contents, by or with the authority of the appropriate person, for the purpose of disseminating that information.

(4) In this paragraph–

'appropriate person' means the person required to make the contents of the database open to public inspection or, as the case may be, the person maintaining the register;

'statutory register' means a register maintained in pursuance of a statutory requirement; and

'statutory requirement' means a requirement imposed by provision made by or under an enactment.

Material communicated to the Crown in the course of public business

4–(1) This paragraph applies where the contents of a database have in the course of public business been communicated to the Crown for any purpose, by or with the licence of the owner of the database right and a document or other material thing recording or embodying the contents of the database is owned by or in the custody or control of the Crown.

(2) The Crown may, for the purpose for which the contents of the database were communicated to it, or any related purpose which could reasonably have been anticipated by the owner of the database right in the database, extract or re-utilise all or a substantial part of the contents without infringing database right in the database.

(3) The Crown may not re-utilise the contents of a database by virtue of this paragraph if the contents have previously been published otherwise than by virtue of this paragraph.

(4) In sub-paragraph (1) 'public business' includes any activity carried on by the Crown.

(5) This paragraph has effect subject to any agreement to the contrary between the Crown and the owner of the database right in the database.

Public records

5 The contents of a database which are comprised in public records within the meaning of the Public Records Act 1958, the Public Records (Scotland) Act 1937 or the Public Records Act (Northern Ireland) 1923 which are open to public inspection in pursuance of that Act, may be re-utilised by or with the authority of any officer appointed under that Act, without infringement of database right in the database.

Acts done under statutory authority

6–(1) Where the doing of a particular act is specifically authorised by an Act of Parliament, whenever passed, then, unless the Act provides otherwise, the doing of that act does not infringe database right in a database.

(2) Sub-paragraph (1) applies in relation to an enactment contained in Northern Ireland legislation as it applies in relation to an Act of Parliament.

(3) Nothing in this paragraph shall be construed as excluding any defence of statutory authority otherwise available under or by virtue of any enactment.

Regulation 24

SCHEDULE 2

LICENSING OF DATABASE RIGHT

Licensing scheme and licensing bodies

1–(1) In this Schedule a 'licensing scheme' means a scheme setting out–

    (a)   the classes of case in which the operator of the scheme, or the person on whose behalf he acts, is willing to grant database right licences, and

    (b)   the terms on which licences would be granted in those classes of case;

and for this purpose a 'scheme' includes anything in the nature of a scheme, whether described as a scheme or as a tariff or by any other name.

(2) In this Schedule a 'licensing body' means a society or other organisation which has as its main object, or one of its main objects, the negotiating or granting, whether as owner or prospective owner of a database right or as agent for him, of database right licences, and whose objects include the granting of licences covering the databases of more than one maker.

(3) In this paragraph 'database right licences' means licences to do, or authorise the doing of, any of the things for which consent is required under Regulation 16.

2 Paragraphs 3 to 8 apply to licensing schemes which are operated by licensing bodies and cover databases of more than one maker so far as they relate to licences for extracting or re-utilising all or a substantial part of the contents of a database; and references in those paragraphs to a licensing scheme shall be construed accordingly.

Reference of proposed licensing scheme to tribunal

3–(1) The terms of a licensing scheme proposed to be operated by a licensing body may be referred to the Copyright Tribunal by an organisation claiming to be representative of persons claiming that they require licences in cases of a description to which the scheme would apply, either generally or in relation to any description of case.

(2) The Tribunal shall first decide whether to entertain the reference, and may decline to do so on the ground that the reference is premature.

(3) If the Tribunal decides to entertain the reference it shall consider the matter referred and make such order, either confirming or varying the proposed scheme, either generally or so far as it relates to cases of the description to which the reference relates, as the Tribunal may determine to be reasonable in the circumstances.

(4) The order may be made so as to be in force indefinitely or for such period as the Tribunal may determine.

Reference of licensing scheme to tribunal

4–(1) If while a licensing scheme is in operation a dispute arises between the operator of the scheme and–

    (a)   a person claiming that he requires a licence in a case of a description to which the scheme applies, or

    (b)   an organisation claiming to be representative of such persons,

that person or organisation may refer the scheme to the Copyright Tribunal in so far as it relates to cases of that description.

(2) A scheme which has been referred to the Tribunal under this paragraph shall remain in operation until proceedings on the reference are concluded.

(3) The Tribunal shall consider the matter in dispute and make such order, either confirming or varying the scheme so far as it relates to cases of the description to which the reference relates, as the Tribunal may determine to be reasonable in the circumstances.

(4) The order may be made so as to be in force indefinitely or for such period as the Tribunal may determine.

Further reference of scheme to tribunal

5–(1) Where the Copyright Tribunal has on a previous reference of a licensing scheme under paragraph 3 or 4, or under this paragraph, made an order with respect to the scheme, then, while the order remains in force–

    (a)   the operator of the scheme,

    (b)   a person claiming that he requires a licence in a case of the description to which the order applies, or

    (c)   an organisation claiming to be representative of such persons,

may refer the scheme again to the Tribunal so far as it relates to cases of that description.

(2) A licensing scheme shall not, except with the special leave of the Tribunal, be referred again to the Tribunal in respect of the same description of cases–

    (a)   within twelve months from the date of the order on the previous reference, or

    (b)   if the order was made so as to be in force for 15 months or less, until the last three months before the expiry of the order.

(3) A scheme which has been referred to the Tribunal under this section shall remain in operation until proceedings on the reference are concluded.

(4) The Tribunal shall consider the matter in dispute and make such order, either confirming, varying or further varying the scheme so far as it relates to cases of the description to which the reference relates, as the Tribunal may determine to be reasonable in the circumstances.

(5) The order may be made so as to be in force indefinitely or for such period as the Tribunal may determine.

Application for grant of licence in connection with licensing scheme

6–(1) A person who claims, in a case covered by a licensing scheme, that the operator of the scheme has refused to grant him or procure the grant to him of a licence in accordance with the scheme, or has failed to do so within a reasonable time after being asked, may apply to the Copyright Tribunal.

(2) A person who claims, in a case excluded from a licensing scheme, that the operator of the scheme either–

(a) has refused to grant him a licence or procure the grant to him of a licence, or has failed to do so within a reasonable time of being asked, and that in the circumstances it is unreasonable that a licence should not be granted, or

(b) proposes terms for a licence which are unreasonable,

may apply to the Copyright Tribunal.

(3) A case shall be regarded as excluded from a licensing scheme for the purposes of sub-paragraph (2) if–

(a) the scheme provides for the grant of licences subject to terms excepting matters from the licence and the case falls within such an exception, or

(b) the case is so similar to those in which licences are granted under the scheme that it is unreasonable that it should not be dealt with in the same way.

(4) If the Tribunal is satisfied that the claim is well-founded, it shall make an order declaring that, in respect of the matters specified in the order, the applicant is entitled to a licence on such terms as the Tribunal may determine to be applicable in accordance with the scheme or, as the case may be, to be reasonable in the circumstances.

(5) The order may be made so as to be in force indefinitely or for such period as the Tribunal may determine.

Application for review of order as to entitlement to licence

7–(1) Where the Copyright Tribunal has made an order under paragraph 6 that a person is entitled to a licence under a licensing scheme, the operator of the scheme or the original applicant may apply to the Tribunal to review its order.

(2) An application shall not be made, except with the special leave of the Tribunal–

(a) within twelve months from the date of the order, or of the decision on a previous application under this section, or

(b) if the order was made so as to be in force for 15 months or less, or as a result of the decision on a previous application under this section is due to expire within 15 months of that decision, until the last three months before the expiry date.

(3) The Tribunal shall on an application for review confirm or vary its order as the Tribunal may determine to be reasonable having regard to the terms applicable in accordance with the licensing scheme or, as the case may be, the circumstances of the case.

Effect of order of tribunal as to licensing scheme

8–(1) A licensing scheme which has been confirmed or varied by the Copyright Tribunal–

(a) under paragraph 3 (reference of terms of proposed scheme), or

(b) under paragraph 4 or 5 (reference of existing scheme to Tribunal),

shall be in force or, as the case may be, remain in operation, so far as it relates to the description of case in respect of which the order was made, so long as the order remains in force.

(2) While the order is in force a person who in a case of a class to which the order applies–

(a) pays to the operator of the scheme any charges payable under the scheme in respect of a licence covering the case in question or, if the amount cannot be ascertained, gives an undertaking to the operator to pay them when ascertained, and

(b) complies with the other terms applicable to such a licence under the scheme,

shall be in the same position as regards infringement of database right as if he had at all material times been the holder of a licence granted by the owner of the database right in question in accordance with the scheme.

(3) The Tribunal may direct that the order, so far as it varies the amount of charges payable, has effect from a date before that on which it is made, but not earlier than the date on which the reference was made or, if later, on which the scheme came into operation.

If such a direction is made–

(a) any necessary repayments, or further payments, shall be made in respect of charges already paid, and

(b)   the reference in sub-paragraph (2)(a) to the charges payable under the scheme shall be construed as a reference to the charges so payable by virtue of the order.

No such direction may be made where sub-paragraph (4) below applies.

(4) Where the Tribunal has made an order under paragraph 6 (order as to entitlement to licence under licensing scheme) and the order remains in force, the person in whose favour the order is made shall if he–

(a)   pays to the operator of the scheme any charges payable in accordance with the order or, if the amount cannot be ascertained, gives an undertaking to pay the charges when ascertained, and

(b)   complies with the other terms specified in the order,

be in the same position as regards infringement of database right as if he had at all material times been the holder of a licence granted by the owner of the database right in question on the terms specified in the order.

References and applications with respect to licences by licensing bodies

9 Paragraphs 10 to 13 (references and applications with respect to licensing by licensing bodies) apply to licences relating to database right which cover databases of more than one maker granted by a licensing body otherwise than in pursuance of a licensing scheme, so far as the licences authorise extracting or re-utilising all or a substantial part of the contents of a database; and references in those paragraphs to a licence shall be construed accordingly.

Reference to tribunal of proposed licence

10–(1) The terms on which a licensing body proposes to grant a licence may be referred to the Copyright Tribunal by the prospective licensee.

(2) The Tribunal shall first decide whether to entertain the reference, and may decline to do so on the ground that the reference is premature.

(3) If the Tribunal decides to entertain the reference it shall consider the terms of the proposed licence and make such order, either confirming or varying the terms, as it may determine to be reasonable in the circumstances.

(4) The order may be made so as to be in force indefinitely or for such period as the Tribunal may determine.

Reference to tribunal of expiring licence

11–(1) A licensee under a licence which is due to expire, by effluxion of time or as a result of notice given by the licensing body, may apply to the Copyright Tribunal on the ground that it is unreasonable in the circumstances that the licence should cease to be in force.

(2) Such an application may not be made until the last three months before the licence is due to expire.

(3) A licence in respect of which a reference has been made to the Tribunal shall remain in operation until proceedings on the reference are concluded.

(4) If the Tribunal finds the application well-founded, it shall make an order declaring that the licensee shall continue to be entitled to the benefit of the licence on such terms as the Tribunal may determine to be reasonable in the circumstances.

(5) An order of the Tribunal under this section may be made so as to be in force indefinitely or for such period as the Tribunal may determine.

Application for review of order as to licence

12–(1) Where the Copyright Tribunal has made an order under paragraph 10 or 11, the licensing body or the person entitled to the benefit of the order may apply to the Tribunal to review its order.

(2) An application shall not be made, except with the special leave of the Tribunal–

(a)   within twelve months from the date of the order or of the decision on a previous application under this paragraph, or

(b)   if the order was made so as to be in force for 15 months or less, or as a result of the decision on a previous application under this section is due to expire within 15 months of that decision, until the last three months before the expiry date.

(3) The Tribunal shall on an application for review confirm or vary its order as the Tribunal may determine to be reasonable in the circumstances.

Effect of order of tribunal as to licence

13–(1) Where the Copyright Tribunal has made an order under paragraph 10 or 11 and the order remains in force, the person entitled to the benefit of the order shall if he–

    (a)   pays to the licensing body any charges payable in accordance with the order or, if the amount cannot be ascertained, gives an undertaking to pay the charges when ascertained, and

    (b)   complies with the other terms specified in the order,

be in the same position as regards infringement of database right as if he had at all material times been the holder of a licence granted by the owner of the database right in question on the terms specified in the order.

    (2) The benefit of the order may be assigned–

    (a)   in the case of an order under paragraph 10, if assignment is not prohibited under the terms of the Tribunal's order; and

    (b)   in the case of an order under paragraph 11, if assignment was not prohibited under the terms of the original licence.

    (3) The Tribunal may direct that an order under paragraph 10 or 11, or an order under paragraph 12 varying such an order, so far as it varies the amount of charges payable, has effect from a date before that on which it is made, but not earlier than the date on which the reference or application was made or, if later, on which the licence was granted or, as the case may be, was due to expire.

    If such a direction is made–

    (a)   any necessary repayments, or further payments, shall be made in respect of charges already paid, and

    (b)   the reference in sub-paragraph (1)(a) to the charges payable in accordance with the order shall be construed, where the order is varied by a later order, as a reference to the charges so payable by virtue of the later order.

General considerations: unreasonable discrimination

14 In determining what is reasonable on a reference or application under this Schedule relating to a licensing scheme or licence, the Copyright Tribunal shall have regard to–

    (a)   the availability of other schemes, or the granting of other licences, to other persons in similar circumstances, and

    (b)   the terms of those schemes or licences,

and shall exercise its powers so as to secure that there is no unreasonable discrimination between licensees, or prospective licensees, under the scheme or licence to which the reference or application relates and licensees under other schemes operated by, or other licences granted by, the same person.

Powers exercisable in consequence of competition report

15–(1) Where the matters specified in a report of the Monopolies and Mergers Commission as being those which in the Commission's opinion operate, may be expected to operate or have operated against the public interest include–

    (a)   conditions in licences granted by the owner of database right in a database restricting the use of the database by the licensee or the right of the owner of the database right to grant other licences, or

    (b)   a refusal of an owner of database right to grant licences on reasonable terms,

the powers conferred by Part I of Schedule 8 to the Fair Trading Act 1973 (powers exercisable for purpose of remedying or preventing adverse effects specified in report of Commission) include power to cancel or modify those conditions and, instead or in addition, to provide that licences in respect of the database right shall be available as of right.

    (2) The references in sections 56(2) and 73(2) of that Act, and sections 10(2)(b) and 12(5) of the Competition Act 1980, to the powers specified in that Part of that Schedule shall be construed accordingly.

(3) The terms of a licence available by virtue of this paragraph shall, in default of agreement, be settled by the Copyright Tribunal on an application by the person requiring the licence; and terms so settled shall authorise the licensee to do everything in respect of which a licence is so available.

(4) Where the terms of a licence are settled by the Tribunal, the licence has effect from the date on which the application to the Tribunal was made.

EXPLANATORY NOTE

(This note is not part of the Regulations)

These Regulations implement the provisions of Council Directive No 96/9/EC of 11 March 1996 (OJ No L77, 27.3.96, page 20) on the legal protection of databases ('the Directive'). The Regulations come into force on 1st January 1998.

The Directive harmonises the laws of member states relating to the protection of copyright in databases and also introduces a new *sui generis* right to prevent extraction and re-utilisation of the contents of a database ('database right').

The Copyright, Designs and Patents Act 1988 ('the Act') makes no specific provision for databases. The Act currently makes provision for protection of copyright in compilations. A database may fall to be considered as a type of compilation. The Directive requires that a database be defined and that copyright protection should only be accorded to a database which by virtue of the selection or arrangement of the contents constitutes the author's own intellectual creation.

In relation to copyright in databases, Part II of the Regulations (Regulations 5–11) amend and modify Part I of the Act in order to properly align its provisions with those of the Directive for those matters where the Act makes no specific provision or makes different provision. In particular, the Regulations–

(a)   modify the definition of literary work in section 3 by including database, as defined in the Directive (regulations 5 and 6);

(b)   introduce new section 3A defining the meaning of 'original' in relation to databases so that a database is only accorded copyright protection where the conditions of that section are satisfied (regulation 6);

(c)   make provision for adaptation and translation in relation to a database at section 21 (regulation 7);

(d)   amend section 29 so as to remove research for a commercial purpose from the general application of the fair dealing provision in relation to a database (regulation 8);

(e)   introduce new section 50D containing specific exceptions to the exclusive rights of the copyright owner which permit any person having a right to use a database to do any acts that are necessary for access to and use of the contents of the database without infringing copyright (regulation 9);

(f)   introduce new section 296B which renders void any term in an agreement which seeks to prohibit or restrict the doing of any act permitted under section 50D (regulation 10).

In relation to database right, the Directive provides a right for the maker of a database in which there has been a substantial investment in the obtaining, verification or presentation of the contents of the database to prevent extraction and/or re-utilisation of the whole or a substantial part of the contents of the database. Database right is to apply irrespective of the eligibility of the database for protection by copyright and without prejudice to rights existing in the contents of the database.

Part III of the Regulations (Regulations 12–25) provide for database right and in particular–

(a)   make provision for the interpretation of certain terms, in particular database, extraction, insubstantial, investment, jointly, lawful user, maker, re-utilisation and substantial; and exclude public lending from database right (regulation 12);

(b)   create a new property right, 'database right' for a database in respect of which there has been a substantial investment (regulation 13);

(c)   provide that the maker of a database is the person who takes the initiative and risk of investing in obtaining, verifying or presenting the contents and that the maker is the first owner of database right (regulations 14 and 15);

(d)   provide for the acts infringing database right (regulation 16);

(e)   provide that the duration of the term of protection of database right is to be 15 years from the end of the calendar year in which the making of the database was completed and that substantial changes give rise to a further term of protection (regulation 17);

(f) provide that database right does not subsist in a database unless when the database was made, or if the making extended over a period, a substantial part of that period, its maker or one of its makers meets the qualifying conditions for database right to subsist (regulation 18);

(g) provide that lawful users are entitled to extract or re-utilise insubstantial parts of a database and render void any term or condition in an agreement which seeks to prohibit or restrict such extraction or re-utilisation (regulations 19 and 20);

(h) provide specific exceptions to database right for a lawful user and other acts which may be done in relation to a database (regulation 20 and Schedule 1);

(i) provide for acts permitted on assumption as to expiry of database right and certain presumptions relevant to database right (regulations 21 and 22);

(j) apply in relation to database right certain provisions of Part I of the Act as they apply to copyright in particular dealing with the rights in copyright works, rights and remedies of rights owners and exclusive licensees (regulation 23);

(k) provide for licensing of database right and extension of the jurisdiction of the Copyright Tribunal to hear and determine proceedings relating to the licensing of database right (regulations 24 and 25 and Schedule 2).

These Regulations apply to databases made before and after the 1st January 1998. However, there is a general saving in relation to agreements made before commencement; in particular acts done in pursuance of such agreements whether before or after commencement are not regarded as infringing database right (regulations 27 and 28). In relation to a database which was created on or before 27th March 1996 (the date of publication of the Directive) and which is a copyright work immediately before commencement, copyright will continue to subsist in such a database for the remainder of the term of copyright (regulation 29). In relation to a database which was completed on or after 1st January 1983 in which database right subsists at 1st January 1998, such a database qualifies for a term of protection of 15 years from 1st January 1998 (regulation 30).

A Compliance Cost Assessment is available, copies of which have been placed in the libraries of both Houses of Parliament. Copies of the assessment are available to the public from the Copyright Directorate of The Patent Office, 25 Southampton Buildings, London WC2A 1AY.

Directives

COUNCIL DIRECTIVE

of 19 November 1992

on rental right and lending right and on certain rights related to copyright in the field of intellectual property

(92/100/EEC)

THE COUNCIL OF THE EUROPEAN COMMUNITIES,

Having regard to the Treaty establishing the European Economic Community, and in particular Articles 57(2), 66 and 100a thereof,

Having regard to the proposal from the Commission,

In cooperation with the European Parliament,

Having regard to the opinion of the Economic and Social Committee,

Whereas differences exist in the legal protection provided by the laws and practices of the Member States for copyright works and subject matter of related rights protection as regards rental and lending; whereas such differences are sources of barriers to trade and distortions of competition which impede the achievement and proper functioning of the internal market;

Whereas such differences in legal protection could well become greater as Member States adopt new and different legislation or as national case-law interpreting such legislation develops differently;

Whereas such differences should therefore be eliminated in accordance with the objective of introducing an area without internal frontiers as set out in Article 8a of the Treaty so as to institute, pursuant to Article 3(f) of the Treaty, a system ensuring that competition in the common market is not distorted;

Whereas rental and lending of copyright works and the subject matter of related rights protection is playing an increasingly important role in particular for authors, performers and producers of phonograms and films; whereas piracy is becoming an increasing threat;

Whereas the adequate protection of copyright works and subject matter of related rights protection by rental and lending rights as well as the protection of the subject matter of related rights protection by the fixation right, reproduction right, distribution right, right to broadcast and communication to the public can accordingly be considered as being of fundamental importance for the Community's economic and cultural development;

Whereas copyright and related rights protection must adapt to new economic developments such as new forms of exploitation;

Whereas the creative and artistic work of authors and performers necessitates an adequate income as a basis for further creative and artistic work, and the investments required particularly for the production of phonograms and films are especially high and risky; whereas the possibility for securing that income and recouping that investment can only effectively be guaranteed through adequate legal protection of the rightholders concerned;

Whereas these creative, artistic and entrepreneurial activities are, to a large extent, activities of self-employed persons; whereas the pursuit of such activities must be made easier by providing a harmonized legal protection within the Community;

Whereas, to the extent that these activities principally constitute services, their provision must equally be facilitated by the establishment in the Community of a harmonized legal framework;

Whereas the legislation of the Member States should be approximated in such a way so as not to conflict with the international conventions on which many Member States' copyright and related rights laws are based;

Whereas the Community's legal framework on the rental right and lending right and on certain rights related to copyright can be limited to establishing that Member States provide rights with respect to rental and lending for certain groups of rightholders and further to establishing the rights of fixation, reproduction, distribution, broadcasting and communication to the public for certain groups of rightholders in the field of related rights protection;

Whereas it is necessary to define the concepts of rental and lending for the purposes of this Directive;

Whereas it is desirable, with a view to clarity, to exclude from rental and lending within the meaning of this Directive certain forms of making available, as for instance making available phonograms or films (cinematographic or audiovisual works or moving images, whether or not accompanied by sound) for the purpose of public performance or broadcasting, making available for the purpose of exhibition, or making available for on-the-spot reference use; whereas lending within the meaning of this Directive does not include making available between establishments which are accessible to the public;

Whereas, where lending by an establishment accessible to the public gives rise to a payment the amount of which does not go beyond what is necessary to cover the operating costs of the establishment, there is no direct or indirect economic or commercial advantage within the meaning of this Directive;

Whereas it is necessary to introduce arrangements ensuring that an unwaivable equitable remuneration is obtained by authors and performers who must retain the possibility to entrust the administration of this right to collecting societies representing them;

Whereas the equitable remuneration may be paid on the basis of one or several payments at any time on or after the conclusion of the contract;

Whereas the equitable remuneration must take account of the importance of the contribution of the authors and performers concerned to the phonogram or film;

Whereas it is also necessary to protect the rights at least of authors as regards public lending by providing for specific arrangements; whereas, however, any measures based on Article 5 of this Directive have to comply with Community law, in particular with Article 7 of the Treaty;

Whereas the provisions of Chapter II do not prevent Member States from extending the presumption set out in Article 2(5) to the exclusive rights included in that chapter; whereas furthermore the provisions of Chapter II do not prevent Member States from providing for a rebuttable presumption of the authorization of exploitation in respect of the exclusive rights of performers provided for in those articles, in so far as such presumption is compatible with the International Convention for the Protection of Performers, Producers of Phonograms and Broadcasting Organizations (hereinafter referred to as the Rome Convention);

Whereas Member States may provide for more far-reaching protection for owners of rights related to copyright than that required by Article 8 of this Directive;

Whereas the harmonized rental and lending rights and the harmonized protection in the field of rights related to copyright should not be exercised in a way which constitutes a disguised restriction on trade between Member States or in a way which is contrary to the rule of media exploitation chronology, as recognized in the Judgment handed down in *Société Cinéthèque v FNCF*,

HAS ADOPTED THIS DIRECTIVE:

CHAPTER I

RENTAL AND LENDING RIGHT

Article 1

Object of harmonization

1. In accordance with the provisions of this Chapter, Member States shall provide, subject to Article 5, a right to authorize or prohibit the rental and lending of originals and copies of copyright works, and other subject matter as set out in Article 2(1).

2. For the purposes of this Directive, 'rental' means making available for use, for a limited period of time and for direct or indirect economic or commercial advantage.

3. For the purposes of this Directive, 'lending' means making available for use, for a limited period of time and not for direct or indirect economic or commercial advantage, when it is made through establishments which are accessible to the public.

4. The rights referred to in paragraph 1 shall not be exhausted by any sale or other act of distribution of originals and copies of copyright works and other subject matter as set out in Article 2(1).

Article 2

Rightholders and subject matter of rental and lending right

1. The exclusive right to authorize or prohibit rental and lending shall belong:

- — to the author in respect of the original and copies of his work,
- — to the performer in respect of fixations of his performance,
- — to the phonogram producer in respect of his phonograms, and
- — to the producer of the first fixation of a film in respect of the original and copies of his film. For the purposes of this Directive, the term 'film' shall designate a cinematographic or audiovisual work or moving images, whether or not accompanied by sound.

2. For the purposes of this Directive the principal director of a cinematographic or audiovisual work shall be considered as its author or one of its authors. Member States may provide for others to be considered as its co-authors.

3. This Directive does not cover rental and lending rights in relation to buildings and to works of applied art.

4. The rights referred to in paragraph 1 may be transferred, assigned or subject to the granting of contractual licences.

5. Without prejudice to paragraph 7, when a contract concerning film production is concluded, individually or collectively, by performers with a film producer, the performer covered by this contract shall be presumed, subject to contractual clauses to the contrary, to have transferred his rental right, subject to Article 4.

6. Member States may provide for a similar presumption as set out in paragraph 5 with respect to authors.

7. Member States may provide that the signing of a contract concluded between a performer and a film producer concerning the production of a film has the effect of authorizing rental, provided that such contract provides for an equitable remuneration within the meaning of Article 4. Member States may also provide that this paragraph shall apply *mutatis mutandis* to the rights included in Chapter II.

Article 3

Rental of computer programs

This Directive shall be without prejudice to Article 4(c) of Council Directive 91/250/EEC of 14 May 1991 on the legal protection of computer programs.

Article 4

Unwaivable right to equitable remuneration

1. Where an author or performer has transferred or assigned his rental right concerning a phonogram or an original or copy of a film to a phonogram or film producer, that author or performer shall retain the right to obtain an equitable remuneration for the rental.

2. The right to obtain an equitable remuneration for rental cannot be waived by authors or performers.

3. The administration of this right to obtain an equitable remuneration may be entrusted to collecting societies representing authors or performers.

4. Member States may regulate whether and to what extent administration by collecting societies of the right to obtain an equitable remuneration may be imposed, as well as the question from whom this remuneration may be claimed or collected.

Article 5

Derogation from the exclusive public lending right

1. Member States may derogate from the exclusive right provided for in Article 1 in respect of public lending, provided that at least authors obtain a remuneration for such lending. Member

States shall be free to determine this remuneration taking account of their cultural promotion objectives.

2. When Member States do not apply the exclusive lending right provided for in Article 1 as regards phonograms, films and computer programs, they shall introduce, at least for authors, a remuneration.

3. Member States may exempt certain categories of establishments from the payment of the remuneration referred to in paragraphs 1 and 2.

4. The Commission, in cooperation with the Member States, shall draw up before 1 July 1997 a report on public lending in the Community. It shall forward this report to the European Parliament and to the Council.

CHAPTER II

RIGHTS RELATED TO COPYRIGHT

Article 6

Fixation right

1. Member States shall provide for performers the exclusive right to authorize or prohibit the fixation of their performances.

2. Member States shall provide for broadcasting organizations the exclusive right to authorize or prohibit the fixation of their broadcasts, whether these broadcasts are transmitted by wire or over the air, including by cable or satellite.

3. A cable distributor shall not have the right provided for in paragraph 2 where it merely retransmits by cable the broadcasts of broadcasting organizations.

Article 7

Reproduction right

1. Member States shall provide the exclusive right to authorize or prohibit the direct or indirect reproduction:

— for performers, of fixations of their performances,
— for phonogram producers, of their phonograms,
— for producers of the first fixations of films, in respect of the original and copies of their films, and
— for broadcasting organizations, of fixations of their broadcasts, as set out in Article 6(2).

2. The reproduction right referred to in paragraph 1 may be transferred, assigned or subject to the granting of contractual licences.

Article 8

Broadcasting and communication to the public

1. Member States shall provide for performers the exclusive right to authorize or prohibit the broadcasting by wireless means and the communication to the public of their performances, except where the performance is itself already a broadcast performance or is made from a fixation.

2. Member States shall provide a right in order to ensure that a single equitable remuneration is paid by the user, if a phonogram published for commercial purposes, or a reproduction of such phonogram, is used for broadcasting by wireless means or for any communication to the public, and to ensure that this remuneration is shared between the relevant performers and phonogram producers. Member States may, in the absence of agreement between the performers and phonogram producers, lay down the conditions as to the sharing of this remuneration between them.

3. Member States shall provide for broadcasting organizations the exclusive right to authorize or prohibit the rebroadcasting of their broadcasts by wireless means, as well as the communication to the public of their broadcasts if such communication is made in places accessible to the public against payment of an entrance fee.

354   *Part 3*

Article 9

Distribution right

1. Member States shall provide:

— for performers, in respect of fixations of their performances,
— for phonogram producers, in respect of their phonograms,
— for producers of the first fixations of films, in respect of the original and copies of their films,
— for broadcasting organizations, in respect of fixations of their broadcast as set out in Article 6(2),

the exclusive right to make available these objects, including copies thereof, to the public by sale or otherwise, hereafter referred to as the 'distribution right'.

2. The distribution right shall not be exhausted within the Community in respect of an object as referred to in paragraph 1, except where the first sale in the Community of that object is made by the rightholder or with his consent.

3. The distribution right shall be without prejudice to the specific provisions of Chapter I, in particular Article 1(4).

4. The distribution right may be transferred, assigned or subject to the granting of contractual licences.

Article 10

Limitations to rights

1. Member States may provide for limitations to the rights referred to in Chapter II in respect of:

(a) private use;
(b) use of short excerpts in connection with the reporting of current events;
(c) ephemeral fixation by a broadcasting organization by means of its own facilities and for its own broadcasts;
(d) use solely for the purposes of teaching or scientific research.

2. Irrespective of paragraph 1, any Member State may provide for the same kinds of limitations with regard to the protection of performers, producers of phonograms, broadcasting organizations and of producers of the first fixations of films, as it provides for in connection with the protection of copyright in literary and artistic works. However, compulsory licences may be provided for only to the extent to which they are compatible with the Rome Convention.

3. Paragraph 1(a) shall be without prejudice to any existing or future legislation on remuneration for reproduction for private use.

CHAPTER III

DURATION

Article 11

Duration of authors' rights

Without prejudice to further harmonization, the authors' rights referred to in this Directive shall not expire before the end of the term provided by the Berne Convention for the Protection of Literary and Artistic Works.

Article 12

Duration of related rights

Without prejudice to further harmonization, the rights referred to in this Directive of performers, phonogram producers and broadcasting organizations shall not expire before the end of the respective terms provided by the Rome Convention. The rights referred to in this Directive for producers of the first fixations of films shall not expire before the end of a period of 20 years computed from the end of the year in which the fixation was made.

NOTE
Articles 11 and 12 are repealed by 93/98/EEC.

CHAPTER IV

COMMON PROVISIONS

Article 13

Application in time

1. This Directive shall apply in respect of all copyright works, performances, phonograms, broadcasts and first fixations of films referred to in this Directive which are, on 1 July 1994, still protected by the legislation of the Member States in the field of copyright and related rights or meet the criteria for protection under the provisions of this Directive on that date.
2. This Directive shall apply without prejudice to any acts of exploitation performed before 1 July 1994.
3. Member States may provide that the rightholders are deemed to have given their authorization to the rental or lending of an object referred to in Article 2 (1) which is proven to have been made available to third parties for this purpose or to have been acquired before 1 July 1994. However, in particular where such an object is a digital recording, Member States may provide that rightholders shall have a right to obtain an adequate remuneration for the rental or lending of that object.
4. Member States need not apply the provisions of Article 2(2) to cinematographic or audiovisual works created before 1 July 1994.
5. Member States may determine the date as from which the Article 2(2) shall apply, provided that that date is no later than 1 July 1997.
6. This Directive shall, without prejudice to paragraph 3 and subject to paragraphs 8 and 9, not affect any contracts concluded before the date of its adoption.
7. Member States may provide, subject to the provisions of paragraphs 8 and 9, that when rightholders who acquire new rights under the national provisions adopted in implementation of this Directive have, before 1 July 1994, given their consent for exploitation, they shall be presumed to have transferred the new exclusive rights.
8. Member States may determine the date as from which the unwaivable right to an equitable remuneration referred to in Article 4 exists, provided that that date is no later than 1 July 1997.
9. For contracts concluded before 1 July 1994, the unwaivable right to an equitable remuneration provided for in Article 4 shall apply only where authors or performers or those representing them have submitted a request to that effect before 1 January 1997. In the absence of agreement between rightholders concerning the level of remuneration, Member States may fix the level of equitable remuneration.

Article 14

Relation between copyright and related rights

Protection of copyright-related rights under this Directive shall leave intact and shall in no way affect the protection of copyright.

Article 15

Final provisions

1. Member States shall bring into force the laws, regulations and administrative provisions necessary to comply with this Directive not later than 1 July 1994. They shall forthwith inform the Commission thereof.

When Member States adopt these measures, they shall contain a reference to this Directive or shall be accompanied by such reference at the time of their official publication. The methods of making such a reference shall be laid down by the Member States.
2. Member States shall communicate to the Commission the main provisions of domestic law which they adopt in the field covered by this Directive.

Article 16

This Directive is addressed to the Member States.

Done at Brussels, 19 November 1992.

COUNCIL DIRECTIVE

of 27 September 1993

on the coordination of certain rules concerning copyright and rights related to copyright applicable to satellite broadcasting and cable retransmission

(93/83/EEC)

THE COUNCIL OF THE EUROPEAN COMMUNITIES,

Having regard to the Treaty establishing the European Economic Community, and in particular Articles 57(2) and 66 thereof,

Having regard to the proposal from the Commission,

In cooperation with the European Parliament,

Having regard to the opinion of the Economic and Social Committee,

(1) Whereas the objectives of the Community as laid down in the Treaty include establishing an ever closer union among the peoples of Europe, fostering closer relations between the States belonging to the Community and ensuring the economic and social progress of the Community countries by common action to eliminate the barriers which divide Europe;

(2) Whereas, to that end, the Treaty provides for the establishment of a common market and an area without internal frontiers; whereas measures to achieve this include the abolition of obstacles to the free movement of services and the institution of a system ensuring that competition in the common market is not distorted; whereas, to that end, the Council may adopt directives for the coordination of the provisions laid down by law, regulation or administrative action in Member States concerning the taking up and pursuit of activities as self-employed persons;

(3) Whereas broadcasts transmitted across frontiers within the Community, in particular by satellite and cable, are one of the most important ways of pursuing these Community objectives, which are at the same time political, economic, social, cultural and legal;

(4) Whereas the Council has already adopted Directive 89/552/EEC of 3 October 1989 on the coordination of certain provisions laid down by law, regulation or administrative action in Member States concerning the pursuit of television broadcasting activities, which makes provision for the promotion of the distribution and production of European television programmes and for advertising and sponsorship, the protection of minors and the right of reply;

(5) Whereas, however, the achievement of these objectives in respect of cross-border satellite broadcasting and the cable retransmission of programmes from other Member States is currently still obstructed by a series of differences between national rules of copyright and some degree of legal uncertainty; whereas this means that holders of rights are exposed to the threat of seeing their works exploited without payment of remuneration or that the individual holders of exclusive rights in various Member States block the exploitation of their rights; whereas the legal uncertainty in particular constitutes a direct obstacle in the free circulation of programmes within the Community;

(6) Whereas a distinction is currently drawn for copyright purposes between communication to the public by direct satellite and communication to the public by communications satellite; whereas, since individual reception is possible and affordable nowadays with both types of satellite, there is no longer any justification for this differing legal treatment;

(7) Whereas the free broadcasting of programmes is further impeded by the current legal uncertainty over whether broadcastsing by a satellite whose signals can be received directly affects the rights in the country of transmission only or in all countries of reception together; whereas, since communications satellites and direct satellites are treated alike for copyright purposes, this legal uncertainty now affects almost all programmes broadcast in the Community by satellite;

(8) Whereas, furthermore, legal certainty, which is a prerequisite for the free movement of broadcasts within the Community, is missing where programmes transmitted across frontiers are fed into and retransmitted through cable networks;

(9) Whereas the development of the acquisition of rights on a contractual basis by authorization is already making a vigorous contribution to the creation of the desired European audiovisual area; whereas the continuation of such contractual agreements should be ensured and their smooth application in practice should be promoted wherever possible;

(10) Whereas at present cable operators in particular cannot be sure that they have actually acquired all the programme rights covered by such an agreement;

(11) Whereas, lastly, parties in different Member States are not all similarly bound by obligations which prevent them from refusing without valid reason to negotiate on the acquisition of the rights necessary for cable distribution or allowing such negotiations to fail;

(12) Whereas the legal framework for the creation of a single audiovisual area laid down in Directive 89/552/EEC must, therefore, be supplemented with reference to copyright;

(13) Whereas, therefore, an end should be put to the differences of treatment of the transmission of programmes by communications satellite which exist in the Member States, so that the vital distinction throughout the Community becomes whether works and other protected subject matter are communicated to the public; whereas this will also ensure equal treatment of the suppliers of cross-border broadcasts, regardless of whether they use a direct broadcasting satellite or a communications satellite;

(14) Whereas the legal uncertainty regarding the rights to be acquired which impedes cross-border satellite broadcasting should be overcome by defining the notion of communication to the public by satellite at a Community level; whereas this definition should at the same time specify where the act of communication takes place; whereas such a definition is necessary to avoid the cumulative application of several national laws to one single act of broadcasting; whereas communication to the public by satellite occurs only when, and in the Member State where, the programme-carrying signals are introduced under the control and responsibility of the broadcasting organization into an uninterrupted chain of communication leading to the satellite and down towards the earth; whereas normal technical procedures relating to the programme-carrying signals should not be considered as interruptions to the chain of broadcasting;

(15) Whereas the acquisition on a contractual basis of exclusive broadcasting rights should comply with any legislation on copyright and rights related to copyright in the Member State in which communication to the public by satellite occurs;

(16) Whereas the principle of contractual freedom on which this Directive is based will make it possible to continue limiting the exploitation of these rights, especially as far as certain technical means of transmission or certain language versions are concerned;

(17) Whereas, in ariving at the amount of the payment to be made for the rights acquired, the parties should take account of all aspects of the broadcast, such as the actual audience, the potential audience and the language version;

(18) Whereas the application of the country-of-origin principle contained in this Directive could pose a problem with regard to existing contracts; whereas this Directive should provide for a period of five years for existing contracts to be adapted, where necessary, in the light of the Directive; whereas the said country-of-origin principle should not, therefore, apply to existing contracts which expire before 1 January 2000; whereas if by that date parties still have an interest in the contract, the same parties should be entitled to renegotiate the conditions of the contract;

(19) Whereas existing international co-production agreements must be interpreted in the light of the economic purpose and scope envisaged by the parties upon signature; whereas in the past international co-production agreements have often not expressly and specifically addressed communication to the public by satellite within the meaning of this Directive a particular form of exploitation; whereas the underlying philosophy of many existing international co-production agreements is that the rights in the co-production are exercised separately and independently by each co-producer, by dividing the exploitation rights between them along territorial lines; whereas, as a general rule, in the situation where a communication to the public by satellite authorized by one co-producer would prejudice the value of the exploitation rights of another co-producer, the interpretation of such an existing agreement

would normally suggest that the latter co-producer would have to give his consent to the authorization, by the former co-producer, of the communication to the public by satellite; whereas the language exclusivity of the latter co-producer will be prejudiced where the language version or versions of the communication to the public, including where the version is dubbed or subtitled, coincide(s) with the language or the languages widely understood in the territory allotted by the agreement to the latter co-producer; whereas the notion of exclusivity should be understood in a wider sense where the communication to the public by satellite concerns a work which consists merely of images and contains no dialogue or subtitles; whereas a clear rule is necessary in cases where the international co-production agreement does not expressly regulate the division of rights in the specific case of communication to the public by satellite within the meaning of this Directive;

(20) Whereas communications to the public by satellite from non-member countries will under certain conditions be deemed to occur within a Member State of the Community;

(21) Whereas it is necessary to ensure that protection for authors, performers, producers of phonograms and broadcasting organizations is accorded in all Member States and that this protection is not subject to a statutory licence system; whereas only in this way is it possible to ensure that any difference in the level of protection within the common market will not create distortions of competition;

(22) Whereas the advent of new technologies is likely to have an impact on both the quality and the quantity of the exploitation of works and other subject matter;

(23) Whereas in the light of these developments the level of protection granted pursuant to this Directive to all rightholders in the areas covered by this Directive should remain under consideration;

(24) Whereas the harmonization of legislation envisaged in this Directive entails the harmonization of the provisions ensuring a high level of protection of authors, performers, phonogram producers and broadcasting organizations; whereas this harmonization should not allow a broadcasting organization to take advantage of differences in levels of protection by relocating activities, to the detriment of audiovisual productions;

(25) Wheres the protection provided for rights related to copyright should be aligned on that contained in Council Directive 92/100/EEC of 19 November 1992 on rental right and lending right and on certain rights related to copyright in the field of intellectual property for the purposes of communication to the public by satellite; whereas, in particular, this will ensure that performers and phonogram producers are guaranteed an appropriate remuneration for the communication to the public by satellite of their performances or phonograms;

(26) Whereas the provisions of Article 4 do not prevent Member States from extending the presumption set out in Article 2(5) of Directive 92/100/EEC to the exclusive rights referred to in Article 4; whereas, furthermore, the provisions of Article 4 do not prevent Member States from providing for a rebuttable presumption of the authoriztion of exploitation in respect of the exclusive rights of performers referred to in that Article, in so far as such presumption is compatible with the International Convention for the Protection of Performers, Producers of Phonograms and Broadcasting Organizations;

(27) Whereas the cable retransmission of programmes from other Member States is an act subject to copyright and, as the case may be, rights related to copyright; whereas the cable operator must, therefore, obtain the authorization from every holder of rights in each part of the programme retransmitted; whereas, pursuant to this Directive, the authorizations should be granted contractually unless a temporary exception is provided for in the case of existing legal licence schemes;

(28) Whereas, in order to ensure that the smooth operation of contractual arrangements is not called into question by the intervention of outsiders holding rights in individual parts of the programme, provision should be made, through the obligation to have recourse to a collecting society, for the exclusive collective exercise of the authorization right to the extent that this is required by the special features of cable retransmission; whereas the authorization right as such remains intact and only the exercise of this right is regulated to some extent, so that the right to authorize a cable retransmission can still be assigned; whereas this Directive does not affect the exercise of moral rights;

(29) Whereas the exemption provided for in Article 10 should not limit the choice of holders of rights to transfer their rights to a collecting society and thereby have a direct share in the

remuneration paid by the cable distributor for cable retransmission;

(30) Whereas contractual arrangements regarding the authorization of cable retransmission should be promoted by additional measures; whereas a party seeking the conclusion of a general contract should, for its part, be obliged to submit collective proposals for an agreement; whereas, furthermore, any party shall be entitled, at any moment, to call upon the assistance of impartial mediators whose task is to assist negotiations and who may submit proposals; whereas any such proposals and any opposition thereto should be served on the parties concerned in accordance with the applicable rules concerning the service of legal documents, in particular as set out in existing international conventions; whereas, finally, it is necessary to ensure that the negotiations are not blocked without valid justification or that individual holders are not prevented without valid justification from taking part in the negotiations; whereas none of these measures for the promotion of the acquisition of rights calls into question the contractual nature of the acquisition of cable retransmission rights;

(31) Whereas for a transitional period Member States should be allowed to retain existing bodies with jurisdiction in their territory over cases where the right to retransmit a programme by cable to the public has been unreasonably refused or offered on unreasonable terms by a broadcasting organization; whereas it is understood that the right of parties concerned to be heard by the body should be guaranteed and that the existence of the body should not prevent the parties concerned from having normal access to the courts;

(32) Whereas, however, Community rules are not needed to deal with all of those matters, the effects of which perhaps with some commercially insignificant exceptions, are felt only inside the borders of a single Member State;

(33) Whereas minimum rules should be laid down in order to establish and guarantee free and uninterrupted cross-border broadcasting by satellite and simultaneous, unaltered cable retransmission of programmes broadcast from other Member States, on an essentially contractual basis;

(34) Whereas this Directive should not prejudice further harmonization in the field of copyright and rights related to copyright and the collective administration of such rights; whereas the possibility for Member States to regulate the activities of collecting societies should not prejudice the freedom of contractual negotiation of the rights provided for in this Directive, on the understanding that such negotiation takes place within the framework of general or specific national rules with regard to competition law or the prevention of abuse of monopolies;

(35) Whereas it should, therefore, be for the Member States to supplement the general provisions needed to achieve the objectives of this Directive by taking legislative and administrative measures in their domestic law, provided that these do not run counter to the objectives of this Directive and are compatible with Community law;

(36) Whereas this Directive does not affect the applicability of the competition rules in Articles 85 and 86 of the Treaty,

HAS ADOPTED THIS DIRECTIVE:

CHAPTER I

DEFINITIONS

Article 1

Definitions

1. For the purpose of this Directive, 'satellite' means any satellite operating on frequency bands which, under telecommunications law, are reserved for the broadcast of signals for reception by the public or which are reserved for closed, point-to-point communication. In the latter case, however, the circumstances in which individual reception of the signals takes place must be comparable to those which apply in the first case.

2. (a) For the purpose of this Directive, 'communication to the public by satellite' means the act of introducing, under the control and responsibility of the broadcasting organization, the programme-carrying signals intended for reception by the public into an uninterrupted chain of communication leading to the satellite and down towards the earth.

(b) The act of communication to the public by satellite occurs solely in the Member State where, under the control and responsibility of the broadcasting organization, the programme-carrying signals are introduced into an uninterrupted chain of communication leading to the satellite and down towards the earth.

(c) If the programme-carrying signals are encrypted, then there is communication to the public by satellite on condition that the means for decrypting the broadcast are provided to the public by the broadcasting organization or with its consent.

(d) Where an act of communication to the public by satellite occurs in a non-Community State which does not provide the level of protection provided for under Chapter II,

   (i) if the programme-carrying signals are transmitted to the satellite from an uplink situation situated in a Member State, that act of communication to the public by satellite shall be deemed to have occurred in that Member State and the rights provided for under Chapter II shall be exercisable against the person operating the uplink station; or

   (ii) if there is no use of an uplink station situated in a Member State but a broadcasting organization established in a Member State has commissioned the act of communication to the public by satellite, that act shall be deemed to have occured in the Member State in which the broadcasting organization has its principal establishment in the Community and the rights provided for under Chapter II shall be exercisable against the broadcasting organization.

3. For the purposes of this Directive, 'cable retransmission' means the simultaneous, unaltered and unabridged retransmission by a cable or microwave system for reception by the public of an initial transmission from another Member State, by wire or over the air, including that by satellite, of television or radio programmes intended for reception by the public.

4. For the purposes of this Directive 'collecting society' means any organization which manages or administers copyright or rights related to copyright as its sole purpose or as one of its main purposes.

5. For the purposes of this Directive, the principal director of a cinematographic or audiovisual work shall be considered as its author or one of its authors. Member States may provide for others to be considered as its co-authors.

CHAPTER II

BROADCASTING OF PROGRAMMES BY SATELLITE

Article 2

Broadcasting right

Member States shall provide an exclusive right for the author to authorize the communication to the public by satellite of copyright works, subject to the provisions set out in this chapter.

Article 3

Acquisition of broadcasting rights

1. Member States shall ensure that the authorization referred to in Article 2 may be acquired only by agreement.

2. A Member State may provide that a collective agreement between a collecting society and a broadcasting organization concerning a given category of works may be extended to right-holders of the same category who are not represented by the collecting society, provided that:

— the communication to the public by satellite simulcasts a terrestrial broadcast by the same broadcaster, and

— the unrepresented rightholder shall, at any time, have the possibility of excluding the extension of the collective agreement to his works and of exercising his rights either individually or collectively.

3. Paragraph 2 shall not apply to cinematographic works, including works created by a process analogous to cinematography.

4. Where the law of a Member State provides for the extension of a collective agreement in accordance with the provisions of paragraph 2, that Member States shall inform the Commission which broadcasting organizations are entitled to avail themselves of that law. The Commission shall publish this information in the *Official Journal of the European Communities* (C series).

Article 4

Rights of performers, phonogram producers and broadcasting organizations

1. For the purposes of communication to the public by satellite, the rights of performers, phonogram producers and broadcasting organizations shall be protected in accordance with the provisions of Articles 6, 7, 8 and 10 of Directive 92/100/EEC.

2. For the purposes of paragraph 1, 'broadcasting by wireless means' in Directive 92/100/EEC shall be understood as including communication to the public by satellite.

3. With regard to the exercise of the rights referred to in paragraph 1, Articles 2 (7) and 12 of Directive 92/100/EEC shall apply.

Article 5

Relation between copyright and related rights

Protection of copyright-related rights under this Directive shall leave intact and shall in no way affect the protection of copyright.

Article 6

Minimum protection

1. Member States may provide for more far-reaching protection for holders of rights related to copyright than that required by Article 8 of Directive 92/100/EEC.

2. In applying paragraph 1 Member States shall observe the definitions contained in Article 1(1) and (2).

Article 7

Transitional provisions

1. With regard to the application in time of the rights referred to in Article 4(1) of this Directive, Article 13(1), (2), (6) and (7) of Directive 92/100/EEC shall apply. Article 13(4) and (5) of Directive 92/100/EEC shall apply *mutatis mutandis*.

2. Agreements concerning the exploitation of works and other protected subject matter which are in force on the date mentioned in Article 14(1) shall be subject to the provisions of Articles 1(2), 2 and 3 as from 1 January 2000 if they expire after that date.

3. When an international co-production agreement concluded before the date mentioned in Article 14 (1) between a co-producer from a Member State and one or more co-producers from other Member States or third countries expressly provides for a system of division of exploitation rights between the co-producers by geographical areas for all means of communication to the public, without distinguishing the arrangement applicable to communication to the public by satellite from the provisions applicable to the other means of communication, and where communication to the public by satellite of the co-production would prejudice the exclusivity, in particular the language exclusivity, of one of the co-producers or his assignees in a given territory, the authorization by one of the co-producers or his assignees for a communication to the public by satellite shall require the prior consent of the holder of that exclusivity, whether co-producer or assignee.

CHAPTER III

CABLE RETRANSMISSION

Article 8

Cable retransmission right

1. Member States shall ensure that when programmes from other Member States are retransmitted by cable in their territory the applicable copyright and related rights are observed and that such retransmission takes place on the basis of individual or collective contractual agreements between copyright owners, holders of related rights and cable operators.

2. Notwithstanding paragraph 1, Member States may retain until 31 December 1997 such statutory licence systems which are in operation or expressly provided for by national law on 31 July 1991.

Article 9

Exercise of the cable retransmission right

1. Member States shall ensure that the right of copyright owners and holders or related rights to grant or refuse authorization to a cable operator for a cable retransmission may be exercised only through a collecting society.

2. Where a rightholder has not transferred the management of his rights to a collecting society, the collecting society which manages rights of the same category shall be deemed to be mandated to manage his rights. Where more than one collecting society manages rights of that category, the rightholder shall be free to choose which of those collecting societies is deemed to be mandated to manage his rights. A rightholder referred to in this paragraph shall have the same rights and obligations resulting from the agreement between the cable operator and the collecting society which is deemed to be mandated to manage his rights as the rightholders who have mandated that collecting society and he shall be able to claim those rights within a period, to be fixed by the Member State concerned, which shall not be shorter than three years from the date of the cable retransmission which includes his work or other protected subject matter.

3. A Member State may provide that, when a right-holder authorizes the initial transmission within its territory of a work or other protected subject matter, he shall be deemed to have agreed not to exercise his cable retransmission rights on an individual basis but to exercise them in accordance with the provisions of this Directive.

Article 10

Exercise of the cable retransmission right by broadcasting organizations

Member States shall ensure that Article 9 does not apply to the rights exercised by a broadcasting organization in respect of its own transmission, irrespective of whether the rights concerned are its own or have been transferred to it by other copyright owners and/or holders of related rights.

Article 11

Mediators

1. Where no agreement is concluded regarding authorization of the cable retransmission of a broadcast. Member States shall ensure that either party may call upon the assistance of one or more mediators.

2. The task of the mediators shall be to provide assistance with negotiation. They may also submit proposals to the parties.

3. It shall be assumed that all the parties accept a proposal as referred to in paragraph 2 if none of them expresses its opposition within a period of three months. Notice of the proposal and of any opposition thereto shall be served on the parties concerned in accordance with the applicable rules concerning the service of legal documents.

4. The mediators shall be so selected that their independence and impartiality and beyond reasonable doubt.

Article 12

Prevention of the abuse of negotiating positions

1. Member States shall ensure by means of civil or administrative law, as appropriate, that the parties enter and conduct negotiations regarding authorization for cable retransmission in good faith and do not prevent or hinder negotiation without valid justification.

2. A Member State which, on the date mentioned in Article 14(1), has a body with jurisdiction in its territory over cases where the right to retransmit a programme by cable to the public in that Member State has been unreasonably refused or offered on unreasonable terms by a broadcasting organization may retain that body.

3. Paragraph 2 shall apply for a transitional period of eight years from the date mentioned in Article 14(1).

CHAPTER IV

GENERAL PROVISIONS

Article 13

Collective administration of rights

This Directive shall be without prejudice to the regulation of the activities of collecting societies by the Member States.

Article 14

Final provisions

1. Member States shall bring into force the laws, regulations and administrative provisions necessary to comply with this Directive before 1 January 1995. They shall immediately inform the Commission thereof.

When Member States adopt these measures, the latter shall contain a reference to this Directive or shall be accompanied by such reference at the time of their official publication. The methods of making such a reference shall be laid down by the Member States.

2. Member States shall communicate to the Commission the provisions of national law which they adopt in the field covered by this Directive.

3. Not later than 1 January 2000, the Commission shall submit to the European Parliament, the Council and the Economic and Social Committee a report on the application of this Directive and, if necessary, make further proposals to adapt it to developments in the audio and audiovisual sector.

Article 15

This Directive is addressed to the Member States.

Done at Brussels, 27 September 1993.

COUNCIL DIRECTIVE

of 29 October 1993

harmonizing the term of protection of copyright and certain related rights

(93/98/EEC)

THE COUNCIL OF THE EUROPEAN COMMUNITIES,

Having regard to the Treaty establishing the European Economic Community, and in particular Articles 57(2), 66 and 100a thereof,

Having regard to the proposal from the Commission,

In cooperation with the European Parliament,

Having regard to the opinion of the Economic and Social Committee,

(1) Whereas the Berne Convention for the Protection of Literary and Artistic Works and the International Convention for the protection of performers, producers of phonograms and broadcasting organizations (Rome Convention) lay down only minimum terms of protection of the rights they refer to, leaving the Contracting States free to grant longer terms; whereas certain Member States have exercised this entitlement; whereas in addition certain Member States have not become party to the Rome Convention;

(2) Whereas there are consequently differences between the national laws governing the terms of protection of copyright and related rights, which are liable to impede the free movement of goods and freedom to provide services, and to distort competition in the common market; whereas therefore with a view to the smooth operation of the internal market, the laws

of the Member States should be harmonized so as to make terms of protection identical throughout the Community;

(3) Whereas harmonization must cover not only the terms of protection as such, but also certain implementing arrangements such as the date from which each term of protection is calculated;

(4) Whereas the provisions of this Directive do not affect the application by the Member States of the provisions of Article 14a (2) (b), (c) and (d) and (3) of the Berne Convention;

(5) Whereas the minimum term of protection laid down by the Berne Convention, namely the life of the author and 50 years after his death, was intended to provide protection for the author and the first two generations of his descendants; whereas the average lifespan in the Community has grown longer, to the point where this term is no longer sufficient to cover two generations;

(6) Whereas certain Member States have granted a term longer than 50 years after the death of the author in order to offset the effects of the world wars on the exploitation of authors' works;

(7) Whereas for the protection of related rights certain Member States have introduced a term of 50 years after lawful publication or lawful communication to the public;

(8) Whereas under the Community position adopted for the Uruguay Round negotiations under the General Agreement on Tariffs and Trade (GATT) the term of protection for producers of phonograms should be 50 years after first publication;

(9) Whereas due regard for established rights is one of the general principles of law protected by the Community legal order; whereas, therefore, a harmonization of the terms of protection of copyright and related rights cannot have the effect of reducing the protection currently enjoyed by rightholders in the Community; whereas in order to keep the effects of transitional measures to a minimum and to allow the internal market to operate in practice, the harmonization of the term of protection should take place on a long term basis;

(10) Whereas in its communication of 17 January 1991 'Follow-up to the Green Paper – Working programme of the Commission in the field of copyright and neighbouring rights' the Commission stresses the need to harmonize copyright and neighbouring rights at a high level of protection since these rights are fundamental to intellectual creation and stresses that their protection ensures the maintenance and development of creativity in the interest of authors, cultural industries, consumers and society as a whole;

(11) Whereas in order to establish a high level of protection which at the same time meets the requirements of the internal market and the need to establish a legal environment conducive to the harmonious development of literary and artistic creation in the Community, the term of protection for copyright should be harmonized at 70 years after the death of the author or 70 years after the work is lawfully made available to the public, and for related rights at 50 years after the event which sets the term running;

(12) Whereas collections are protected according to Article 2(5) of the Berne Convention when, by reason of the selection and arrangement of their content, they constitute intellectual creations; whereas those works are protected as such, without prejudice to the copyright in each of the works forming part of such collections, whereas in consequence specific terms of protection may apply to works included in collections;

(13) Whereas in all cases where one or more physical persons are identified as authors the term of protection should be calculated after their death; whereas the question of authorship in the whole or a part of a work is a question of fact which the national courts may have to decide;

(14) Whereas terms of protection should be calculated from the first day of January of the year following the relevant event, as they are in the Berne and Rome Conventions;

(15) Whereas Article 1 of Council Directive 91/250/EEC of 14 May 1991 on the legal protection of computer programs provides that Member States are to protect computer programs, by copyright, as literary works within the meaning of the Berne Convention; whereas this Directive harmonizes the term of protection of literary works in the Community; whereas Article 8 of Directive 91/250/EEC, which merely makes provisional arrangements governing the term of protection of computer programs, should accordingly be repealed;

(16) Whereas Articles 11 and 12 of Council Directive 92/100/EEC of 19 November 1992 on rental right and lending right and on certain rights related to copyright in the field of

intellectual property make provision for minimum terms of protection only, subject to any further harmonization; whereas this Directive provides such further harmonization; whereas these Articles should accordingly be repealed;

(17) Whereas the protection of photographs in the Member States is the subject of varying regimes; whereas in order to achieve a sufficient harmonization of the term of protection of photographic works, in particular of those which, due to their artistic or professional character, are of importance within the internal market, it is necessary to define the level of originality required in this Directive; whereas a photographic work within the meaning of the Berne Convention is to be considered original if it is the author's own intellectual creation reflecting his personality, no other criteria such as merit or purpose being taken into account; whereas the protection of other photographs should be left to national law;

(18) Whereas, in order to avoid differences in the term of protection as regards related rights it is necessary to provide the same starting point for the calculation of the term throughout the Community; whereas the performance, fixation, transmission, lawful publication, and lawful communication to the public, that is to say the means of making a subject of a related right perceptible in all appropriate ways to persons in general, should be taken into account for the calculation of the term of protection regardless of the country where this performance, fixation, transmission, lawful publication, or lawful communication to the public takes place;

(19) Whereas the rights of broadcasting organizations in their broadcasts, whether these broadcasts are transmitted by wire or over the air, including by cable or satellite, should not be perpetual; whereas it is therefore necessary to have the term of protection running from the first transmission of a particular broadcast only; whereas this provision is understood to avoid a new term running in cases where a broadcast is identical to a previous one;

(20) Whereas the Member States should remain free to maintain or introduce other rights related to copyright in particular in relation to the protection of critical and scientific publications; whereas, in order to ensure transparency at Community level, it is however necessary for Member States which introduce new related rights to notify the Commission;

(21) Whereas it is useful to make clear that the harmonization brought about by this Directive does not apply to moral rights;

(22) Whereas, for works whose country of origin within the meaning of the Berne Convention is a third country and whose author is not a Community national, comparison of terms of protection should be applied, provided that the term accorded in the Community does not exceed the term laid down in this Directive;

(23) Whereas where a rightholder who is not a Community national qualifies for protection under an international agreement the term of protection of related rights should be the same as that laid down in this Directive, except that it should not exceed that fixed in the country of which the rightholder is a national;

(24) Whereas comparison of terms should not result in Member States being brought into conflict with their international obligations;

(25) Whereas, for the smooth functioning of the internal market this Directive should be applied as from 1 July 1995;

(26) Whereas Member States should remain free to adopt provisions on the interpretation, adaptation and further execution of contracts on the exploitation of protected works and other subject matter which were concluded before the extension of the term of protection resulting from this Directive;

(27) Whereas respect of acquired rights and legitimate expectations is part of the Community legal order; whereas Member States may provide in particular that in certain circumstances the copyright and related rights which are revived pursuant to this Directive may not give rise to payments by persons who undertook in good faith the exploitation of the works at the time when such works lay within the public domain,

HAS ADOPTED THIS DIRECTIVE:

Article 1

Duration of authors' rights

1. The rights of an author of a literary or artistic work within the meaning of Article 2 of the Berne Convention shall run for the life of the author and for 70 years after his death, irrespective of the date when the work is lawfully made available to the public.

2. In the case of a work of joint authorship the term referred to in paragraph 1 shall be calculated from the death of the last surviving author.

3. In the case of anonymous or pseudonymous works, the term of protection shall run for seventy years after the work is lawfully made available to the public. However, when the pseudonym adopted by the author leaves no doubt as to his identity, or if the author discloses his identity during the period referred to in the first sentence, the term of protection applicable shall be that laid down in paragraph 1.

4. Where a Member State provides for particular provisions on copyright in respect of collective works or for a legal person to be designated as the rightholder, the term of protection shall be calculated according to the provisions of paragraph 3, except if the natural persons who have created the work as such are identified as such in the versions of the work which are made available to the public. This paragraph is without prejudice to the rights of identified authors whose identifiable contributions are included in such works, to which contributions paragraph 1 or 2 shall apply.

5. Where a work is published in volumes, parts, instalments, issues or episodes and the term of protection runs from the time when the work was lawfully made available to the public, the term of protection shall run for each such item separately.

6. In the case of works for which the term of protection is not calculated from the death of the author or authors and which have not been lawfully made available to the public within seventy years from their creation, the protection shall terminate.

Article 2

Cinematographic or audiovisual works

1. The principal director of a cinematographic or audiovisual work shall be considered as its author or one of its authors. Member States shall be free to designate other co-authors.

2. The term of protection of cinematographic or audiovisual works shall expire 70 years after the death of the last of the following persons to survive, whether or not these persons are designated as co-authors: the principal director, the author of the screenplay, the author of the dialogue and the composer of music specifically created for use in the cinematographic or audiovisual work.

Article 3

Duration of related rights

1. The rights of performers shall expire 50 years after the date of the performance. However, if a fixation of the performance is lawfully published or lawfully communicated to the public within this period, the rights shall expire 50 years from the date of the first such publication or the first such communication to the public, whichever is the earlier.

2. The rights of producers of phonograms shall expire 50 years after the fixation is made. However, if the phonogram is lawfully published or lawfully communicated to the public during this period, the rights shall expire 50 years from the date of the first such publication or the first such communication to the public, whichever is the earlier.

3. The rights of producers of the first fixation of a film shall expire 50 years after the fixation is made. However, if the film is lawfully published or lawfully communicated to the public during this period, the rights shall expire 50 years from the date of the first such publication or the first such communication to the public, whichever is the earlier. The term 'film' shall designate a cinematographic or audiovisual work or moving images, whether or not accompanied by sound.

4. The rights of broadcasting organizations shall expire 50 years after the first transmission of a broadcast, whether this broadcast is transmitted by wire or over the air, including by cable or satellite.

Article 4

Protection of previously unpublished works

Any person who, after the expiry of copyright protection, for the first time lawfully publishes or lawfully communicates to the public a previously unpublished work, shall benefit from a protection equivalent to the economic rights of the author. The term of protection of such rights shall be 25 years from the time when the work was first lawfully published or lawfully communicated to the public.

Article 5

Critical and scientific publications

Member States may protect critical and scientific publications of works which have come into the public domain. The maximum term of protection of such rights shall be 30 years from the time when the publication was first lawfully published.

Article 6

Protection of photographs

Photographs which are original in the sense that they are the author's own intellectual creation shall be protected in accordance with Article 1. No other criteria shall be applied to determine their eligibility for protection. Member States may provide for the protection of other photographs.

Article 7

Protection vis-à-vis third countries

1. Where the country of origin of a work, within the meaning of the Berne Convention, is a third country, and the author of the work is not a Community national, the term of protection granted by the Member States shall expire on the date of expiry of the protection granted in the country of origin of the work, but may not exceed the term laid down in Article 1.

2. The terms of protection laid down in Article 3 shall also apply in the case of rightholders who are not Community nationals, provided Member States grant them protection. However, without prejudice to the international obligations of the Member States, the term of protection granted by Member States shall expire no later than the date of expiry of the protection granted in the country of which the rightholder is a national and may not exceed the term laid down in Article 3.

3. Member States which, at the date of adoption of this Directive, in particular pursuant to their international obligations, granted a longer term of protection than that which would result from the provisions, referred to in paragraphs 1 and 2 may maintain this protection until the conclusion of international agreements on the term of protection by copyright or related rights.

Article 8

Calculation of terms

The terms laid down in this Directive are calculated from the first day of January of the year following the event which gives rise to them.

Article 9

Moral rights

This Directive shall be without prejudice to the provisions of the Member States regulating moral rights.

Article 10

Application in time

1. Where a term of protection, which is longer than the corresponding term provided for by this Directive, is already running in a Member State on the date referred to in Article 13(1), this Directive shall not have the effect of shortening that term of protection in that Member State.

2. The terms of protection provided for in this Directive shall apply to all works and subject matter which are protected in at least one Member State, on the date referred to in Article

13(1), pursuant to national provisions on copyright or related rights or which meet the criteria for protection under Directive 92/100/EEC.

3. This Directive shall be without prejudice to any acts of exploitation performed before the date referred to in Article 13(1). Member States shall adopt the necessary provisions to protect in particular acquired rights of third parties.

4. Member States need not apply the provisions of Article 2(1) to cinematographic or audiovisual works created before 1 July 1994.

5. Member States may determine the date as from which Article 2(1) shall apply, provided that date is no later than 1 July 1997.

Article 11

Technical adaptation

1. Article 8 of Directive 91/250/EEC is hereby repealed.

2. Articles 11 and 12 of Directive 92/100/EEC are hereby repealed.

Article 12

Notification procedure

Member States shall immediately notify the Commission of any governmental plan to grant new related rights, including the basic reasons for their introduction and the term of protection envisaged.

Article 13

General provisions

1. Member States shall bring into force the laws, regulations and administrative provisions necessary to comply with Articles 1 to 11 of this Directive before 1 July 1995.

When Member States adopt these provisions, they shall contain a reference to this Directive or shall be accompanied by such reference at the time of their official publication. The methods of making such a reference shall be laid down by the Member States.

Member States shall communicate to the Commission the texts of the provisions of national law which they adopt in the field governed by this Directive.

2. Member States shall apply Article 12 from the date of notification of this Directive.

Article 14

This Directive is addressed to the Member States.

Done at Brussels, 29 October 1993.

COUNCIL DIRECTIVE

of 11 March 1996

on the legal protection of databases

(96/9/EC)

THE EUROPEAN PARLIAMENT AND THE COUNCIL OF THE EUROPEAN UNION,

Having regard to the Treaty establishing the European Community, and in particular Article 57, 66 and 100a thereof,

Having regard to the proposal from the Commission,

Having regard to the opinion of the Economic and Social Committee,

Acting in accordance with the procedure laid down in Article 189b of the Treaty,

(1) Whereas databases are at present not sufficiently protected in all Member States by existing legislation; whereas such protection, where it exists, has different attributes;

(2) Whereas such differences in the legal protection of databases offered by the legislation of the Member States have direct negative effects on the functioning of the internal market as regards databases and in particular on the freedom of natural and legal persons to provide on-line database goods and services on the basis of harmonised legal arrangements throughout the Community; whereas such differences could well become more pronounced as Member States introduce new legislation in this field, which is now taking on an increasingly international dimension;

(3) Whereas existing differences distorting the functioning of the internal market need to be removed and new ones prevented from arising, while differences not adversely affecting the functioning of the internal market or the development of an information market within the Community need not be removed or prevented from arising;

(4) Whereas copyright protection for databases exists in varying forms in the Member States according to legislation or case-law, and whereas, if differences in legislation in the scope and conditions of protection remain between the Member States, such unharmonized intellectual property rights can have the effect of preventing the free movement of goods or services within the Community

(5) Whereas copyright remains an appropriate form of exclusive right for authors who have created databases;

(6) Whereas, nevertheless, in the absence of a harmonised system of unfair-competition legislation or of case-law, other measures are required in addition to prevent the unauthorised extraction and/or re-utilisation of the contents of a database;

(7) Whereas the making of databases requires the investment of considerable human, technical and financial resources while such databases can be copied or accessed at a fraction of the cost needed to design them independently;

(8) Whereas the unauthorised extraction and/or re-utilisation of the contents of a database constitute acts which can have serious economic and technical consequences;

(9) Whereas databases are a vital tool in the development of an information market within the Community; whereas this tool will also be of use in many other fields;

(10) Whereas the exponential growth, in the Community and worldwide, in the amount of information generated and processed annually in all sectors of commerce and industry calls for investment in all the Member States in advanced information processing systems

(11) Whereas there is at present a very great imbalance in the level of investment in the database sector both as between the Member States and between the Community and the world's largest database-producing third countries;

(12) Whereas such an investment in modern information storage and processing systems will not take place within the Community unless a stable and uniform legal protection regime is introduced for the protection of the rights of makers of databases;

(13) Whereas this Directive protects collections, sometimes called 'compilations', of works, data or other materials which are arranged, stored and accessed by means which include electronic, electromagnetic or electro-optical processes or analogous processes

(14) Whereas protection under this Directive should be extended to cover non-electronic databases;

(15) Whereas the criteria used to determine whether a database should be protected by copyright should be defined to the fact that the selection or the arrangement of the contents of the database is the author's own intellectual creation; whereas such protection should cover the structure of the database;

(16) Whereas no criterion other than originality in the sense of the author's intellectual creation should be applied to determine the eligibility of the database for copyright protection, and in particular no aesthetic or qualitative criteria should be applied;

(17) Whereas the term 'database' should be understood to include literary, artistic, musical or other collections of works or collections of other material such as texts, sound, images, numbers, facts, and data; whereas it should cover collections of independent works, data or other materials which are systematically or methodically arranged and can be individually accessed; whereas this means that a recording or an audiovisual, cinematographic, literary or musical work as such does not fall within the scope of this Directive;

(18) Whereas this Directive is without prejudice to the freedom of authors to decide whether, or in what manner, they will allow their works to be included in a database, in

particular whether or not the authorisation given is exclusive; whereas the protection of databases by the sui generis right is without prejudice to existing rights over their contents, and whereas in particular where an author or the holder of a related right permits some of his works or subject matter to be included in a database pursuant to a non-exclusive agreement, a third party may make use of those works or subject matter subject to the required consent of the author or of the holder of the related right without the sui generis right of the maker of the database being invoked to prevent him doing so, on condition that those works or subject matter are neither extracted from the database nor re-utilised on the basis thereof

(19) Whereas, as a rule, the compilation of several recordings of musical performances on a CD does not come within the scope of this Directive, both because, as a compilation, it does not meet the conditions for copyright protection and because it does not represent a substantial enough investment to be eligible under the sui generis right;

(20) Whereas protection under this Directive may also apply to the materials necessary for the operation or consultation of certain databases such as thesaurus and indexation systems

(21) Whereas the protection provided for in this Directive relates to databases in which works, data or other materials have been arranged systematically or methodically; whereas it is not necessary for those materials to have been physically stored in an organised manner

(22) Whereas electronic databases within the meaning of this Directive may also include devices such as CD-ROM and CD-i;

(23) Whereas the term 'database' should not be taken to extend to computer programs used in the making or operation of a database, which are protected by Council Directive 91/250/EEC of 14 May 1991 on the legal protection of computer programs

(24) Whereas the rental and lending of databases in the field of copyright and related rights are governed exclusively by Council Directive 92/100/EEC of 19 November 1992 on rental right and lending right and on certain rights related to copyright in the field of intellectual property;

(25) Whereas the term of copyright is already governed by Council Directive 93/98/EEC of 29 October 1993 harmonising the term of protection of copyright and certain related rights;

(26) Whereas works protected by copyright and subject matter protected by related rights, which are incorporated into a database, remain nevertheless protected by the respective exclusive rights and may not be incorporated into, or extracted from, the database without the permission of the rightholder or his successors in title;

(27) Whereas copyright in such works and related rights in subject matter thus incorporated into a database are in no way affected by the existence of a separate right in the selection or arrangement of these works and subject matter in a database;

(28) Whereas the moral rights of the natural person who created the database belong to the author and should be exercised according to the legislation of the Member States and the provisions of the Berne Convention for the Protection of Literary and Artistic Works; whereas such moral rights remain outside the scope of this Directive;

(29) Whereas the arrangements applicable to databases created by employees are left to the discretion of the Member States; whereas, therefore nothing in this Directive prevents Member States from stipulating in their legislation that where a database is created by an employee in the execution of his duties or following the instructions given by his employer, the employer exclusively shall be entitled to exercise all economic rights in the database so created, unless otherwise provided by contract;

(30) Whereas the author's exclusive rights should include the right to determine the way in which his work is exploited and by whom, and in particular to control the distribution of his work to unauthorised persons;

(31) Whereas the copyright protection of databases includes making databases available by means other than the distribution of copies

(32) Whereas Member States are required to ensure that their national provisions are at least materially equivalent in the case of such acts subject to restrictions as are provided for by this Directive;

(33) Whereas the question of exhaustion of the right of distribution does not arise in the case of on-line databases, which come within the field of provision of services; whereas this also applies with regard to a material copy of such a database made by the user of such a service with the consent of the rightholder; whereas, unlike CD-ROM or CD-i, where the intellectual

property is incorporated in a material medium, namely an item of goods, every on-line service is in fact an act which will have to be subject to authorisation where the copyright so provides;

(34) Whereas, nevertheless, once the rightholder has chosen to make available a copy of the database to a user, whether by an on-line service or by other means of distribution, that lawful user must be able to access and use the database for the purposes and in the way set out in the agreement with the rightholder, even if such access and use necessitate performance of otherwise restricted acts;

(35) Whereas a list should be drawn up of exceptions to restricted acts, taking into account the fact that copyright as covered by this Directive applies only to the selection or arrangements of the contents of a database; whereas Member States should be given the option of providing for such exceptions in certain cases; whereas, however, this option should be exercised in accordance with the Berne Convention and to the extent that the exceptions relate to the structure of the database; whereas a distinction should be drawn between exceptions for private use and exceptions for reproduction for private purposes, which concerns provisions under national legislation of some Member States on levies on blank media or recording equipment;

(36) Whereas the term 'scientific research' within the meaning of this Directive covers both the natural sciences and the human sciences;

(37) Whereas Article 10 (1) of the Berne Convention is not affected by this Directive;

(38) Whereas the increasing use of digital recording technology exposes the database maker to the risk that the contents of his database may be copied and rearranged electronically, without his authorisation, to produce a database of identical content which, however, does not infringe any copyright in the arrangement of his database;

(39) Whereas, in addition to aiming to protect the copyright in the original selection or arrangement of the contents of a database, this Directive seeks to safeguard the position of makers of databases against misappropriation of the results of the financial and professional investment made in obtaining and collection the contents by protecting the whole or sub-stantial parts of a database against certain acts by a user or competitor;

(40) Whereas the object of this sui generis right is to ensure protection of any investment in obtaining, verifying or presenting the contents of a database for the limited duration of the right; whereas such investment may consist in the deployment of financial resources and/or the expending of time, effort and energy;

(41) Whereas the objective of the sui generis right is to give the maker of a database the option of preventing the unauthorised extraction and/or re-utilisation of all or a substantial part of the contents of that database; whereas the maker of a database is the person who takes the initiative and the risk of investing; whereas this excludes subcontractors in particular from the definition of maker;

(42) Whereas the special right to prevent unauthorised extraction and/or re-utilisation relates to acts by the user which go beyond his legitimate rights and thereby harm the investment; whereas the right to prohibit extraction and/or re-utilisation of all or a substantial part of the contents relates not only to the manufacture of a parasitical competing product but also to any user who, through his acts, causes significant detriment, evaluated qualitatively or quantitatively, to the investment;

(43) Whereas, in the case of on-line transmission, the right to prohibit re-utilisation is not exhausted either as regards the database or as regards a material copy of the database or of part thereof made by the addressee of the transmission with the consent of the rightholder;

(44) Whereas, when on-screen display of the contents of a database necessitates the permanent or temporary transfer of all or a substantial part of such contents to another medium, that act should be subject to authorisation by the rightholder;

(45) Whereas the right to prevent unauthorised extraction and/or re-utilisation does not in any way constitute an extension of copyright protection to mere facts or data;

(46) Whereas the existence of a right to prevent the unauthorised extraction and/or re-utilisation of the whole or a substantial part of works, data or materials from a database should not give rise to the creation of a new right in the works, data or materials themselves;

(47) Whereas, in the interests of competition between suppliers of information products and services, protection by the sui generis right must not be afforded in such a way as to facilitate

abuses of a dominant position, in particular as regards the creation and distribution of new products and services which have an intellectual, documentary, technical, economic or commercial added value; whereas, therefore, the provisions of this Directive are without prejudice to the application of Community or national competition rules;

(48) Whereas the objective of this Directive, which is to afford an appropriate and uniform level of protection of databases as a means to secure the remuneration of the maker of the database, is different from the aim of Directive 95/46/EC of the European Parliament and of the Council of 24 October 1995 on the protection of individuals with regard to the processing of personal data and on the free movement of such data, which is to guarantee free circulation of personal data on the basis of harmonised rules designed to protect fundamental rights, notably the right to privacy which is recognised in Article 8 of the European Convention for the Protection of Human Rights and Fundamental Freedoms; whereas the provisions of this Directive are without prejudice to data protection legislation;

(49) Whereas, notwithstanding the right to prevent extraction and/or re-utilisation of all or a substantial part of a database, it should be laid down that the maker of a database or rightholder may not prevent a lawful user of the database from extracting and re-utilising insubstantial parts; whereas, however, that user may not unreasonably prejudice either the legitimate interests of the holder of the sui generis right or the holder of copyright or a related right in respect of the works or subject matter contained in the database;

(50) Whereas the Member States should be given the option of providing for exceptions to the right to prevent the unauthorised extraction and/or re-utilisation of a substantial part of the contents of a database in the case of extraction for private purposes, for the purposes of illustration for teaching or scientific research, or where extraction and/or re-utilisation are/is carried out in the interests of public security or for the purposes of an administrative or judicial procedure; whereas such operations must not prejudice the exclusive rights of the maker to exploit the database and their purpose must not be commercial;

(51) Whereas the Member States, where they avail themselves of the option to permit a lawful user of a database to extract a substantial part of the contents for the purposes of illustration for teaching or scientific research, may limit that permission to certain categories of teaching or scientific research institution;

(52) Whereas those Member States which have specific rules providing for a right comparable to the sui generis right provided for in this Directive should be permitted to retain, as far as the new right is concerned, the exceptions traditionally specified by such rules;

(53) Whereas the burden of proof regarding the date of completion of the making of a database lies with the maker of the database;

(54) Whereas the burden of proof that the criteria exist for concluding that a substantial modification of the contents of a database is to be regarded as a substantial new investment lies with the maker of the database resulting from such investment;

(55) Whereas a substantial new investment involving a new term of protection may include a substantial verification of the contents of the database;

(56) Whereas the right to prevent unauthorised extraction and/or re-utilisation in respect of a database should apply to databases whose makers are nationals or habitual residents of third countries or to those produced by legal persons not established in a Member State, within the meaning of the Treaty, only if such third countries offer comparable protection to databases produced by nationals of a Member State or persons who have their habitual residence in the territory of the Community;

(57) Whereas, in addition to remedies provided under the legislation of the Member States for infringements of copyright or other rights, Member States should provide for appropriate remedies against unauthorised extraction and/or re-utilisation of the contents of a database;

(58) Whereas, in addition to the protection given under this Directive to the structure of the database by copyright, and to its contents against unauthorised extraction and/or re-utilisation under the sui generis right, other legal provisions in the Member States relevant to the supply of database goods and services continue to apply;

(59) Whereas this Directive is without prejudice to the application to databases composed of audiovisual works of any rules recognised by a Member State's legislation concerning the broadcasting of audiovisual programmes;

(60) Whereas some Member States currently protect under copyright arrangements databases which do not meet the criteria for eligibility for copyright protection laid down in this

Directive; whereas, even if the databases concerned are eligible for protection under the right laid down in this Directive to prevent unauthorised extraction and/or re-utilisation of their contents, the term of protection under that right is considerably shorter than that which they enjoy under the national arrangements currently in force; whereas harmonisation of the criteria for determining whether a database is to be protected by copyright may not have the effect of reducing the term of protection currently enjoyed by the rightholders concerned; whereas a derogation should be laid down to that effect; whereas the effects of such derogation must be confined to the territories of the Member States concerned;

HAVE ADOPTED THIS DIRECTIVE:

CHAPTER I

Article 1

Scope

1. This Directive concerns the legal protection of databases in any form.
2. For the purposes of this Directive, 'database' shall mean a collection of independent works, data or other materials arranged in a systematic or methodical way and individually accessible by electronic or other means.
3. Protection under this Directive shall not apply to computer programs used in the making or operation of databases accessible by electronic means.

Article 2

Limitations on the scope

This Directive shall apply without prejudice to Community provisions relating to:

    (a)   the legal protection of computer programs;
    (b)   rental right, lending right and certain rights related to copyright in the field of intellectual property;
    (c)   the term of protection of copyright and certain related rights.

CHAPTER II

COPYRIGHT

Article 3

Object of protection

1. In accordance with this Directive, databases which, by reason of the selection or arrangement of their contents, constitute the author's own intellectual creation shall be protected as such by copyright. No other criteria shall be applied to determine their eligibility for that protection.
2. The copyright protection of databases provided for by this Directive shall not extend to their contents and shall be without prejudice to any rights subsisting in those contents themselves.

Article 4

Database authorship

1. The author of a database shall be the natural person or group of natural persons who created the base or, where the legislation of the Member States so permits, the legal person designated as the rightholder by that legislation.
2. Where collective works are recognised by the legislation of a Member State, the economic rights shall be owned by the person holding the copyright.
3. In respect of a database created by a group of natural persons jointly, the exclusive rights shall be owned jointly.

Article 5

Restricted acts

In respect of the expression of the database which is protectable by copyright, the author of a database shall have the exclusive right to carry out or to authorise:

(a)   temporary or permanent reproduction by any means and in any form, in whole or in part;

(b)   translation, adaptation, arrangement and any other alteration;

(c)   any form of distribution to the public of the database or of copies thereof. The first sale in the Community of a copy of the database by the rightholder or with his consent shall exhaust the right to control resale of that copy within the Community;

(d)   any communication, display or performance to the public;

(e)   any reproduction, distribution, communication, display or performance to the public of the results of the acts referred to in (b).

Article 6

Exceptions to restricted acts

1. The performance by the lawful user of a database or of a copy thereof of any of the acts listed in Article 5 which is necessary for the purposes of access to the contents of the databases and normal use of the contents by the lawful user shall not require the authorisation of the author of the database. Where the lawful user is authorised to use only part of the database, this provision shall apply only to that part.

2. Member States shall have the option of providing for limitations on the rights set out in Article 5 in the following cases

(a)   in the case of reproduction for private purposes of a non-electronic database;

(b)   where there is use for the sole purpose of illustration for teaching or scientific research, as long as the source is indicated and to the extent justified by the non-commercial purpose to be achieved;

(c)   where there is use for the purposes of public security of for the purposes of an administrative or judicial procedure;

(d)   where other exceptions to copyright which are traditionally authorised under national law are involved, without prejudice to points (a), (b) and (c).

3. In accordance with the Berne Convention for the protection of Literary and Artistic Works, this Article may not be interpreted in such a way as to allow its application to be used in a manner which unreasonably prejudices the rightholder's legitimate interests or conflicts with normal exploitation of the database.

CHAPTER III

SUI GENERIS RIGHT

Article 7

Object of protection

1. Member States shall provide for a right for the maker of a database which shows that there has been qualitatively and/or quantitatively a substantial investment in either the obtaining, verification or presentation of the contents to prevent extraction and/or re-utilisation of the whole or of a substantial part, evaluated qualitatively and/or quantitatively, of the contents of that database.

2. For the purposes of this Chapter:

(a)   'extraction' shall mean the permanent or temporary transfer of all or a substantial part of the contents of a database to another medium by any means or in any form;

(b)   're-utilisation' shall mean any form of making available to the public all or a substantial part of the contents of a database by the distribution of copies, by renting, by on-line or other forms of transmission. The first sale of a copy of a database within the Community by the rightholder or with his consent shall exhaust the right to control resale of that copy within the Community;

Public lending is not an act of extraction or re-utilisation.

3. The right referred to in paragraph 1 may be transferred, assigned or granted under contractual licence.

4. The right provided for in paragraph 1 shall apply irrespective of the eligibility of that database for protection by copyright or by other rights. Moreover, it shall apply irrespective of eligibility of the contents of that database for protection by copyright or by other rights. Protection of databases under the right provided for in paragraph 1 shall be without prejudice to rights existing in respect of their contents.

5. The repeated and systematic extraction and/or re-utilisation of insubstantial parts of the contents of the database implying acts which conflict with a normal exploitation of that database or which unreasonably prejudice the legitimate interests of the maker of the database shall not be permitted.

Article 8

Rights and obligations of lawful users

1. The maker of a database which is made available to the public in whatever manner may not prevent a lawful user of the database from extracting and/or re-utilising insubstantial parts of its contents, evaluated qualitatively and/or quantitatively, for any purposes whatsoever. Where the lawful user is authorised to extract and/or re-utilise only part of the database, this paragraph shall apply only to that part.

2. A lawful user of a database which is made available to the public in whatever manner may not perform acts which conflict with normal exploitation of the database or unreasonably prejudice the legitimate interests of the maker of the database.

3. A lawful user of a database which is made available to the public in any manner may not cause prejudice to the holder of a copyright or related right in respect of the works or subject matter contained in the database.

Article 9

Exceptions to the sui generis right

Member States may stipulate that lawful users of a database which is made available to the public in whatever manner may, without the authorisation of its maker, extract or re-utilise a substantial part of its contents:

    (a)   in the case of extraction for private purposes of the contents of a non-electronic database;

    (b)   in the case of extraction for the purposes of illustration for teaching or scientific research, as long as the source is indicated and to the extent justified by the non-commercial purpose to be achieved;

    (c)   in the case of extraction and/or re-utilisation for the purposes of public security or an administrative or judicial procedure.

Article 10

Term of protection

1. The right provided for in Article 7 shall run from the date of completion of the making of the database. It shall expire fifteen years from the first of January of the year following the date of completion.

2. In the case of a database which is made available to the public in whatever manner before expiry of the period provided for in paragraph 1, the term of protection by that right shall expire fifteen years from the first of January of the year following the date when the database was first made available to the public.

3. Any substantial change, evaluated qualitatively or quantitatively, to the contents of a database, including any substantial change resulting from the accumulation of successive additions, deletions or alterations, which would result in the database being considered to be a substantial new investment, evaluated qualitatively or quantitatively, shall qualify the database resulting from that investment for its own term of protection.

Article 11

Beneficiaries of protection under the sui generis right

1. The right provided for in Article 7 shall apply to database whose makers or rightholders are nationals of a Member State or who have their habitual residence in the territory of the Community.

2. Paragraph 1 shall also apply to companies and firms formed in accordance with the law of a Member State and having their registered office, central administration or principal place of business within the Community; however, where such a company or firm has only its registered office in the territory of the Community, its operations must be genuinely linked on an ongoing basis with the economy of a Member State.

3. Agreements extending the right provided for in Article 7 to databases made in third countries and falling outside the provisions of paragraphs 1 and 2 shall be concluded by the Council acting on a proposal from the Commission. The term of any protection extended to databases by virtue of that procedure shall not exceed that available pursuant to Article 10.

CHAPTER IV

COMMON PROVISIONS

Article 12

Remedies

Member States shall provide appropriate remedies in respect of infringements of the rights provided for in this Directive.

Article 13

Continued application of other legal provisions

This Directive shall be without prejudice to provisions concerning in particular copyright, rights related to copyright or any other rights or obligations subsisting in the data, works or other materials incorporated into a database, patent rights, trade marks, design rights, the protection of national treasures, laws on restrictive practices and unfair competition, trade secrets, security, confidentiality, data protection and privacy, access to public documents, and the law of contract.

Article 14

Application over time

1. Protection pursuant to this Directive as regards copyright shall also be available in respect of databases created prior to the date referred to Article 16 (1) which on that date fulfil the requirements laid down in this Directive as regards copyright protection of databases.

2. Notwithstanding paragraph 1, where a database protected under copyright arrangements in a Member State on the date of publication of this Directive does not fulfil the eligibility criteria for copyright protection laid down in Article 3 (1), this Directive shall not result in any curtailing in that Member State of the remaining term of protection afforded under those arrangements.

3. Protection pursuant to the provisions of this Directive as regards the right provided for in Article 7 shall also be available in respect of databases the making of which was completed not more than fifteen years prior to the date referred to in Article 16 (1) and which on that date fulfil the requirements laid down in Article 7.

4. The protection provided for in paragraphs 1 and 3 shall be without prejudice to any acts concluded and rights acquired before the date referred to in those paragraphs.

5. In the case of a database the making of which was completed not more than fifteen years prior to the date referred to in Article 16 (1), the term of protection by the right provided for in Article 7 shall expire fifteen years from the first of January following that date.

Article 15

Binding nature of certain provisions

Any contractual provision contrary to Articles 6 (1) and 8 shall be null and void.

Article 16

Final provisions

1. Member States shall bring into force the laws, regulations and administrative provisions necessary to comply with this Directive before 1 January 1998. When Member States adopt these provisions, they shall contain a reference to this Directive or shall be accompanied by such reference on the occasion of their official publication. The methods of making such reference shall be laid down by Member States.

2. Member States shall communicate to the Commission the text of the provisions of domestic law which they adopt in the field governed by this Directive.

3. Not later than at the end of the third year after the date referred to in paragraph 1, and every three years thereafter, the Commission shall submit to the European Parliament, the Council and the Economic and Social Committee a report on the application of this Directive, in which, inter alia, on the basis of specific information supplied by the Member States, it shall examine in particular the application of the sui generis right, including Articles 8 and 9, and shall verify especially whether the application of this right has led to abuse of a dominant position or other interference with free competition which would justify appropriate measures being taken, including the establishment of non-voluntary licensing arrangements. Where necessary, it shall submit proposals for adjustment of this Directive in line with developments in the area of databases.

Article 17

This Directive is addressed to the Member States.

Done at Strasbourg, 11 March 1996.

Index